SURVEY
OF
SOCIAL
SCIENCE

SURVEY
OF
SOCIAL
SCIENCE

SOCIOLOGY SERIES

Volume 4
1387-1844

Political Action Committees and Special Interest Groups—
Social Stratification: Analysis and Overview

Edited by
FRANK N. MAGILL

Consulting Editor
HÉCTOR L. DELGADO
UNIVERSITY OF ARIZONA

SALEM PRESS

Pasadena, California   Englewood Cliffs, New Jersey

Library of Congress Cataloging-in-Publication Data
Survey of social science. Sociology series / [edited by]
Frank N. Magill; consulting editor, Héctor L. Delgado.
    v. cm.
    Includes bibliographical references and index.
    1. Sociology—Encyclopedias.   I. Magill, Frank
Northen, 1907-   . II. Delgado, Héctor L., 1949-   .
HM17.S86   1994   94-31770
301'.03—dc20   CIP
ISBN 0-89356-739-6 (set)
ISBN 0-89356-743-4 (volume 4)

CONTENTS

SOCIOLOGY

SURVEY
OF
SOCIAL
SCIENCE

POLITICAL ACTION COMMITTEES AND SPECIAL INTEREST GROUPS

Type of sociology: Major social institutions
Field of study: Politics and the state

Political action committees (PACs) and special interest groups are groups organized around a particular political candidate or issue of social, political, or economic concern. PACs are usually defined as the fundraising arms of political candidates or special interest groups.

Principal terms

LOBBYIST: an individual who works for an interest group and whose main job is to further the agenda of that interest group by persuading legislators and administration officials to support policies and take actions that favor the group's goals

POLITICAL ACTION COMMITTEE (PAC): a political organization whose purpose is to further the goals of a particular special interest group or political candidate, primarily through fundraising

PUBLIC INTEREST GROUP: in theory, a group that seeks a collective good that does not exclusively benefit the members of the organization

SINGLE-ISSUE GROUP: a group marked by zealous commitment to a single issue or cause such as opposition to abortion or gun control; such groups usually depend solely on membership contributions to further their political agenda

SPECIAL INTEREST GROUP: a group, usually organized around a particular set of social, political, or economic issues, that tries to influence public policy; often used in a derogatory sense to describe a group dedicated to narrow-minded or self-serving interests

Overview

An interest group is any group organized around a common set of interests that tries to influence governmental policy. The group may have a relatively narrow set of interests, as is the case with single-issue groups, or it may have more broad-based concerns, as is the case with some special interest or public interest groups. Some interest groups may offer select benefits to their members. The American Association of Retired Persons (AARP), for example, offers its members numerous services ranging from insurance, to banking, to retirement planning. Other interest groups, such as those considered public interest groups, often seek legislative changes that will not individually benefit the membership but will instead benefit society as a whole. Whether an interest group is considered a single-issue group, a special interest group, or a public interest group, however, is primarily determined by one's point of view.

Single-issue and special interest groups are usually those organizations with which one does not agree, and public interest groups are those with which one agrees. Ultimately, all interest groups are special interest groups. Regardless of their label, however, what many interest groups have in common is a connection to one or more political action committees (PACs).

A PAC's main purpose is to raise money from businesses, individuals, unions, and other organizations and to contribute these funds to political candidates. PACs are often formed to get a particular candidate elected. PACs are also formed, however, to act as the fundraising arms of special interest groups that want to contribute not simply to one political candidate but to a number of candidates whom the interest groups believe will support their agendas.

PACs are also a way for individuals to assert more influence over election campaigns than they would normally have. This is because under current law an individual may only contribute $1,000 to a candidate's campaign. Theoretically, however, this same individual may give up to $5,000 to a single PAC. This PAC, as long as it has been registered for six months, has more than fifty contributors, and has contributed to five or more campaigns, can also give $5,000 to candidate "A," $15,000 to candidate "A's" national party, and $5,000 to any other PAC—which could then also funnel that $5,000 to candidate "A." Theoretically, then, it is possible for one person to contribute indirectly, through a PAC, up to $11,000. Political clout through PAC contributions is increased because wealthy individuals can also have their family members and their employees (by offering them incentives) contribute the same amount of money. It is possible, therefore, for one individual to contribute indirectly hundreds of thousands of dollars to a single candidate, although this much is usually reserved for presidential hopefuls. Large contributions can pay off handsomely for the contributor. Grateful winning presidents usually offer diplomatic positions, such as ambassadorships, to their biggest political supporters.

There are basically four types of PACs: labor PACs, corporate and business PACs, industry-wide PACs, and ideological PACs. Each of the four types of PACs has different purposes for its fundraising efforts.

Labor PACs are the fundraising arms of labor unions. Their purpose is to raise money to finance the campaigns of political candidates who demonstrate commitment to the labor union's specific causes. Although labor PACs raise and spend less money than do business and corporate PACs, they remain a powerful collective force in election campaigns because virtually all of their money is spent on Democrats.

Corporate PACs are the fundraising arms of particular corporations. Their purpose is to finance the campaigns of candidates who will further the business interests of the corporations they represent. Corporate and business PACs, unlike labor PACs, which support only candidates who exhibit a commitment to the group's cause, tend to contribute to various candidates across the political spectrum in order to "hedge their bets" and pick a winner every time. The only exception is that since incumbents usually have a better chance of winning elections than challengers do, corporate PACs tend to contribute more heavily to incumbent candidates. Critics of PACs argue that the disproportionate contributions of corporate and business PACs to incumbents explains why it is so difficult for challengers to win elections.

Corporations wield power not only because they can form their own PACs but also because they can contribute to trade association PACs that support their business interests. Corporate PACs are also influential because they tend to spend more than other PACs do. In 1986, for example, they outspent labor's $31 million by $18 million.

Trade association PACs, or industry-wide PACs, such as the National Association of Manufacturers (NAM), usually represent the somewhat diverse interests of a loose coalition of businesses and corporations. They are often repositories for funds contributed by individual corporations which are earmarked for campaigns that support the generalized business interests of the various corporations.

Ideological PACs, like labor PACs, also raise money to finance the campaigns of political candidates who demonstrate commitment to the group's specific cause or causes. These causes, however, are driven by a larger set of ideological beliefs. Examples of ideological PACs are the Right to Life Coalition, the National Rifle Association (NRA), and the National Conservative Political Action Committee (NCPAC). Ideological PACs spend most of their money on presidential campaigns and tend to be more directly involved in developing, grooming, and supporting candidates committed to their causes than either labor or corporate PACs.

Some ideological PACs are single-issue groups that can wield considerable power simply on the basis of their intense commitment to that one issue. The Right to Life Coalition, for example, is opposed to all abortions and any public funding for them. The NRA is opposed to all handgun registration and all gun control. In both cases, these groups' commitment to a single issue allows them to mobilize extensive membership support, which makes them very visible on Capitol Hill. As a result, regardless of any other legislation a congressperson supports, if he or she is in favor of gun control or abortion rights, he or she can expect intense negative political pressure from the NRA or the Right to Life Coalition. Because of the perceived power of ideological PACs, particularly those that are single-issue groups, they are often a source of concern for legislators and the objects of criticism of those who favor limiting the political power of PACs.

Applications

There are various strategies that special interest groups use to further their goals, such as organizing mass media campaigns; soliciting funds and membership through direct mail campaigns; lobbying local, state, and national representatives; and raising money, through PACs, for political candidates' campaigns.

Some special interest groups, such as the National Conservative Political Action Committee, use the mass media to further their interests. This group, for example, received media prominence because of its claims that it defeated numerous liberal Democratic candidates by means of widespread negative advertising campaigns that it ran against these candidates in the 1986 and 1988 elections. Greenpeace, an environmental activist group, is an example of a special interest group that also uses the mass media to gain attention for its political agenda. Rather than purchasing media time to air its positions, however, Greenpeace prefers to stage events, such as dramatic protests against environmentally unfriendly corporations, designed to gain media and public attention. This is done in the hopes that such negative attention will force these companies to change their policies.

Other special interest groups shy away from mass media attention to further their goals and instead prefer direct mail campaigns to gain support for their cause. Groups such as the National Rifle Association (NRA), for example, use direct mail campaigns both to raise large sums of money to support the election bids of anti-gun control legislators and to maintain a strong membership in their association.

Other special interest groups focus primarily on lobbying to further their goals. Lobbyists perform a number of tasks, from testifying at congressional hearings and contacting government officials directly to writing legislation and mounting grassroots campaigns. Perhaps the most important job of lobbyists, however, is to provide lawmakers with technical and political information about pending legislation. Because they must vote on a large number of issues each year, congresspeople have come to rely on lobbyists to keep them supplied with technical information about bills and the political positions of various constituents. Although this information is extremely helpful to congresspeople, it must be remembered that a lobbyists's job is to further the agenda of a special interest group by influencing legislators who have the power to pass legislation. The NRA, for example, until the 1993 passage of the Brady Bill, which requires a five-day waiting period for the purchase of a handgun, had been a powerful force in blocking gun control legislation, in part because of the effectiveness of its lobbying efforts on Capitol Hill.

Other special interest groups focus primarily on fundraising, through PACs, to finance the election campaigns of political candidates who are sympathetic to the group's particular interests. PAC money can both influence election results and ensure access to elected officials.

PAC money particularly influences election results for challengers. Although money rarely guarantees that an incumbent will be defeated or elected, PAC influence can certainly make the difference in a close race. In 1985, for example, the NRA claimed to have been successful in winning seats for 95 percent of the candidates it supported.

The influence of PAC money in political campaigns has also increased along with the mounting expenses of running campaigns. This is, in part, a result of the extended time periods over which campaigns are now run. For example, the preprimary period in election campaigns is currently more important and more expensive than the primary campaign itself. It is even more costly, in some cases, than the general election campaign. As a result, the battle for larger amounts of money early in the preprimary campaign has made PAC money a significant source of revenue.

PAC money also buys access to legislators, either directly or indirectly, through access to the elected official's staff members. The power of PAC money should not be underestimated; as Thomas R. Dye and Harmon Zeigler (1989) point out, "Washington politicians *believe* PACs are more powerful than they are, and in a city in which image and reality are scrambled beyond recognition, a reputation for power is just about as good as the real thing."

Context

Attitudes toward interest groups vary widely. For example James Madison, one of the framers of American government, believed that interest groups were a dangerous but unavoidable manifestation of democracy. He believed that interest groups invited the formation of factions that might wield undue influence over government. To avoid the dominance of certain groups, he helped to create a system of federal and state checks and balances. Despite Madison's fears, however, the First Amendment guarantees citizens' right to form and belong to interest groups as well as to use them "to petition the government for a redress of grievances" (Dye and Zeigler, 1989).

Contemporary political scientists, by contrast, often argue that interest groups, rather than being a necessary evil, serve an important function in a healthy democracy. Interest groups, some claim, offer a channel through which the individual can meaningfully relate to the larger political system. In this sense, interest groups are the moderately powerful link between the relatively powerless individual and the extremely powerful policy making elites.

The contemporary public's view of interest groups, however, is somewhat different from that of either Madison or the political scientists. By the mid-1980's, many Americans began to believe that interest groups had become too powerful. When asked in a 1984 survey which groups they believed had either too much or too little power, however, the majority believed that labor groups had too much power, whereas senior citizens' and farmers' groups had too little. In other words, despite their generic condemnation of interest group influence, the majority of the public favored those interest groups that might benefit them personally.

Although interest groups have existed as long as the United States has been a functioning democracy, PACs are a relatively recent phenomenon, dating from the mid-1970's. The passage of the Federal Election Campaign Act in 1974 made possible the formation of PACs. The first PACs created were by organized labor. Forming a PAC allowed organized labor to maneuver around a prohibition against using union dues to finance elections. With the advent of the Federal Election Campaign Act, labor could instead raise money directly to support politicians whose election platforms favored its interests.

There has been tremendous growth in PACs since the passage of the 1974 Election Reform Act. According to Dye and Zeigler, "as political parties have declined in their ability to organize and finance campaigns, interest groups have moved in rapidly to fill the gap." By the end of 1974, there were approximately 600 registered PACs. More than a decade later, there were more than 4,000. By 1988, there were 386 labor PACs, more than 1,000 ideological PACs, and more than 1,700 corporate or industry-wide PACs. PACs have also gained a steadily increasing influence on congressional leaders. In 1978, only sixty-three representatives received half or more of their campaign money from PACs. Eight years later that number had jumped to 194, according to Dye and Zeigler.

The increasing influence of PAC money on Congress has been accompanied by a growing public sentiment, from the mid-1980's on, that PACs and special interest groups were becoming too powerful and were disproportionately affecting election outcomes and public policy decisions. This sentiment was often driven by the realization that a significant percentage of Americans were not represented by special interest groups and that the working class was less likely than the managerial and professional classes were to have membership in special interest groups. Many people believed that this amounted to unequal access to both legislators and political power.

Bibliography

Dye, Thomas R., and Harmon Zeigler. *American Politics in the Media Age*. 3d ed. Pacific Grove, Calif.: Brooks/Cole, 1989. This book has a chapter on interest group politics which explores the rise and influence of PACs, the role of interest groups in public policy, and the increasing influence of Hollywood and the Washington lobbyists on election results and governmental decision making. This highly readable chapter provides a complete primer on understanding PACs and their relationship to special interest groups.

Freedman, Leonard. *Power and Politics in America*. 6th ed. Pacific Grove, Calif.: Brooks/Cole, 1991. This book has a chapter entitled "Interest Groups and the Public Interest" in which the author reviews the "range of interest groups in America, the purposes they serve, and the methods they use to influence political decisions." The author also examines "five rival interpretations of how well the interest groups system is working and the extent to which it represents a balance between contending forces." Guiding the chapter is the central question "What is the public interest?"

Hrebenar, Ronald, and Ruth Scott. *Interest Group Politics in America*. Englewood Cliffs, N.J.: Prentice-Hall, 1982. Although this volume is somewhat dated, the authors provide an exhaustive and in-depth look at the rise of interest groups in America, their various roles and functioning, and the implications of their influence in government.

Ippolito, Dennis, and Thomas Walker. *Political Parties, Interest Groups, and Public Policy*. Englewood Cliffs, N.J.: Prentice-Hall, 1980. A detailed analysis of the interactions among party politics, interest groups, and public policy in America.

Paletz, David, and Robert Entman. *Media Power Politics*. New York: Free Press, 1981. The authors devote a chapter to the discussion of interest groups. Writing from a neo-Marxist perspective, they explore the differences in goals, media treatment, and effects of marginal interest groups, business interest groups/lobbies, and public interest groups such as Common Cause. Not surprisingly, the authors argue that "media coverage of interest groups helps to preserve the basic distribution of power in America by the way it presents organized demands for change."

Susan Mackey-Kallis

Cross-References

Democracy and Democratic Governments, 483; Inequalities in Political Power, 972; Party Politics in the United States, 1343; Political Influence by Religious Groups, 1394; Political Machines and Bosses, 1400; Political Socialization, 1407; Political Sociology, 1414.

POLITICAL INFLUENCE BY RELIGIOUS GROUPS

Type of sociology: Major social institutions
Fields of study: Religion; Sources of social change

Political influence by religious groups refers to the ways in which communities of people sharing specific religious beliefs and/or observances affect governments. This topic concerns the organized public activities of established religions rather than the endeavors of individual adherents or the private endeavors, such as prayers and meditations, of groups.

Principal terms
CULT: a religion regarded as spurious or unorthodox by society at large
ESTABLISHED RELIGION: a system of religious beliefs and ritual that has many adherents and is historically grounded in a particular society
FUNDAMENTALISM: a religious movement that stresses strict and literal obedience to a set of basic beliefs
HUMANISM: a doctrine or attitude that rejects the supernatural and stresses a way of life that is based on human interests or values
LIBERATION THEOLOGY: a religious movement that interprets human existence in terms of the experience of oppression
MORAL MAJORITY: a conservative evangelical movement that espouses a pro-life, pro-traditional family, and pro-America political agenda
SOCIAL GOSPEL MOVEMENT: a religious movement that seeks to bring the social order into conformity with liberal Protestant Christian principles
WORLD COUNCIL OF CHURCHES: an ecumenical organization composed of representatives of many established denominations that often makes statements concerning international affairs
ZIONISM: an international movement dedicated to the support of modern Israel

Overview

The relationship between religion and government is not clear in American society. Whereas political liberals in the United States tend to claim that America originated as a secular state, many political conservatives contend that America originated as a Christian nation. In support of their view, liberals point out that the Federalist Papers, the U.S. Constitution, and the Declaration of Independence contain no or very few references to God or to the Bible; that James Madison and Thomas Jefferson generally did not quote from the Bible in their writings; and that the Founding Fathers emphasized natural law rather than divine law when affirming people's rights. Conservatives counter that John Jay, one of the authors of the Federalist Papers, was a conservative

Christian and that the term "natural law" as used by early Americans was borrowed from *Blackstone's Commentaries*, where it referred to divine law; that the Mayflower Compact of 1620, the Fundamental Orders of Connecticut of 1638-1639, the Congressional Thanksgiving Day Proclamations of 1780 and 1782, and other theological statements are important to the American heritage; and that one cannot discount the significance of theologically conservative schools such as Harvard and Yale in providing leaders for early America.

In the United States, religious groups have most often exerted political influence through the ballot box. Paul J. Kleppner has shown, for example, to what extent religion influenced the vote of German and Irish immigrants in Pittsburgh in 1860: "German-American and Irish-American Protestants were more likely to vote for Lincoln than were their fellow countrymen of the Roman Catholic faith. . . . The polarization of the vote cannot be explained in terms of ethnic responses, but in terms of differences in religious attitudes within each group."

The two national elections in U.S. history that most raised questions concerning the possibility that a religious group would influence a candidate if elected, and the propriety of that influence, were the presidental elections of 1928 and 1960. In 1928, the Democratic governor of New York, Alfred E. Smith, was soundly defeated by the Republican candidate, Herbert Hoover. Many observers claimed that the reason for Hoover's landslide victory was that Smith was a Roman Catholic. In 1960, John F. Kennedy, the Democratic candidate, became the first Roman Catholic to be elected president of the United States. The razor-thin margin of victory was gained only after Kennedy affirmed the separation of church and state in a speech to the Houston Ministerial Association.

One of the periods in U.S. history when religious groups most often tried to exert political influence occurred at the end of the nineteenth century. In the late 1800's, the extraordinary growth of cities, large-scale, brutal labor conflicts, and the obvious extremes of wealth and poverty caused liberal Christians to react against the individualistic gospel of personal salvation affirmed by orthodox and fundamentalist groups. Many socially conscious Christians came to believe that through political democracy, people could help God build an ideal society in which brothers and sisters would live together in cooperation, love, and justice. Although most proponents of the Social Gospel were Protestants, members of the Commission on the Church and Social Service and liberal Roman Catholics also participated. A well-known example was Father Edward McGlynn, rector of St. Stephen's, one of the most important Roman Catholic parishes of New York, who was president of the Anti-Poverty Society and who became a spokesperson for the United Labor Party, which supported the mayoral campaign of Henry George in 1886.

The Social Gospel era polarized religious attitudes toward social problems in the United States. For example, while many liberal Christians supported Prohibition, many other Christians did not. In fact, conservative Protestants in general were against any further meddling in the social order. Revivalists such as Billy Sunday preached a message laced with anti-Red, anti-labor, and anti-foreign sentiments. Fundamentalists in particular opposed the Social Gospel because of its associations with evolution, liberalism, and modernism.

Whereas conservative Christians in the United States have continued to emphasize biblical literalism, traditional family values, and patriotism, some evangelicals have organized themselves politically in order to further their agenda. Two spokespersons for the new Christian Right are Jerry Falwell, the Baptist organizer of the Moral Majority, and Pat Robertson, the Assembly of God leader who is the head of the Christian Broadcasting Network and the host of the "700 Club." Both preachers established national political organizations to support a religious, conservative social agenda.

Meanwhile, political influence by liberal religious groups has also continued since the Social Gospel era. The most noteworthy example is the efforts of the Southern Christian Leadership Conference and Martin Luther King, Jr., in the 1960's on behalf of desegregation in America. Jesse Jackson's presidential primary campaigns of 1984 and 1988 also reasserted the religious metaphors about social justice and encouraged African American church linkages with politics. Because religious groups often see the world as their parish, African American theologians from the United States in the 1980's joined other liberation theologians in calling for U.S. sanctions against South Africa's policy of apartheid.

Finally, as American religions attempt to influence foreign policy, non-American or international religious groups attempt to influence the decisions made by the United States government. Thus, for example, the World Council of Churches has issued pronouncements concerning world peace, racism, refugees, human rights violations, and other issues. Its pronouncements have often been leftist in orientation, and during the 1970's and 1980's, the WCC was accused of being controlled by Marxist sympathizers. As another example, the Roman Catholic Vatican Council II, which ended in 1964, attempted to open a dialogue about the morality of nuclear deterrence.

Applications

Considering the diversity of religious activity in the United States, it is no surprise to find myriad channels through which religions affect American culture and government. In fact, religious groups have organized and cooperated either for or against almost all issues that are important to American society. It may be useful at this point to look at two different types of political involvement: the attempt by conservative Christians to influence the American elections of 1980 and the attempt by American Jews to influence Israel's policy on drafting women into military service.

During the 1970's, conservative Christians more and more came to believe that feminism, homosexuality, and abortion were eminent threats to family values and thus to the American way of life. In presidential elections held in the 1960's, Baptists had voted predominantly Republican, and in the 1972 election, evangelicals voted more than four to five in favor of Richard Nixon. In 1976, the Southern Baptist minister and televangelist Jerry Falwell formed the National Christian Action Coalition and began to organize rallies around the nation that he hoped would influence the political future of the United States. By 1979, the NCAC had evolved into the Moral Majority, an openly political organization working toward a "pro-life, pro-traditional family, pro-moral" America.

The centerpiece of the Moral Majority's strategy for the 1980 presidential election was to galvanize and mobilize the support of conservative, anti-abortion Christians behind the candidacy of Ronald Reagan. Tactics included capitalizing on fundamentalist opposition to the Equal Rights Amendment by stressing the connection between the ERA and abortion; wooing disaffected Democrats by attacking the dangers of secular humanism through such television specials as "America, You're Too Young to Die," which was shown on prime time on more than two hundred television stations; and unifying the Republican party by building alliances with like-minded, conservative Christian leaders from other denominations, mainly the Assemblies of God and the Roman Catholic church.

The Moral Majority and other conservative religious political organizations such as the Religious Roundtable, Christian Voice, and the National Right to Life Committee joined in an uneasy coalition with political right wingers and single-issue pro-lifers in what came to be called the New Right. The result of the 1980 elections was to split off enough of the traditional Democratic voters from labor unions, blue-collar workers, ethnic groups, Southerners, and Roman Catholics to provide the GOP with a landslide victory. At the state level, Republicans gained four governorships and 220 state legislative posts; at the national level, Republicans gained the presidency and forty-five congressional seats. In all, pro-life votes in Congress increased by thirty to thirty-five.

A different type of example of a religious group's influence on government concerns the National Service Law for Women, which the Knesset, Israel's governing institution, passed in August of 1953. Under the provisions of a 1949 act, women who, for religious reasons, objected to military service were exempted from service. The new law provided that most women who were released from military service for religious reasons were to serve for two years in a National Labor Service, working in hospitals, immigrant camps, or similar situations.

Even though the law further exempted any women whose lifestyles did not allow them to leave home before marriage, many non-Zionists opposed it. Many Jews believed that the law would lead to false religious declarations. Among the opposition were some powerful groups in the United States, including the Union of Orthodox Rabbis and Agudath Israel of America. At the time that the bill came before the Knesset, demonstrators threatened to cut back on Diaspora funding, threatening to undermine the United Jewish Appeal and the sales of State of Israel Bonds.

In February of 1954, after the law had been passed, there was a large demonstration outside the Israeli Consulate in New York protesting what was called "religious persecution" in Israel. Some violence was associated with the demonstration, and leaflets were passed out asking that telegrams be sent to Congress demanding that the United States halt aid to Israel.

Moshe Sharett, who had assumed office as the prime minister of Israel in January of 1954, directed the Minister of Labor to act generously in exempting those women from national service who requested an exemption on the grounds of conscience or family lifestyle. By April of that year, word had been passed to orthodox Jewish circles in the United States that the law would not be enforced. Although there were many factors leading to the decision not to enforce the National Service Law for Women, certainly the fear of continued demonstrations and efforts to curb funding to Israel by American Jews influenced Israeli policy.

Context

In the Western world, Judaism, Islam, and, for most of its history, Christianity have assumed the propriety of religious influence on government. Muslims in particular have not accepted a separation between the secular and the sacred.

In Christian thought, the nature of the relationship between church and state has been the subject of discussion since at least the time of Saint Augustine, an early churchman who lived in Roman north Africa at the beginning of the fifth century. In *The City of God* (413-426), Augustine argued that Alaric's sack of Rome in 410 was occasioned by divine providence. Basic to his argument were the claims that there can be no city without justice and that the perfect city would be the spiritual city of all who practice the justice of Christ, its head.

Although the mix of religion and government is worrisome to many people in modern American society, few would claim that the so-called separation of church and state in the United States intended that religion and politics have nothing to do with each other. As the sociologist Robert N. Bellah has noted, the Constitution protects the free exercise of religion at the same time that it prohibits a religious establishment. "It is religious freedom or free exercise which is the controlling idea. Prohibition of the establishment of a particular religion is required because it would be an infringement on religious freedom" (1981).

Bibliography

Dunn, Charles W., ed. *American Political Theology: Historical Perspective and Theoretical Analysis*. New York: Praeger, 1984. Dunn's book is a collection of important primary sources related to the impact of theology on American politics. The work, which concludes with the author's theory of American political theology, includes an essay by the author that explores the theological dimensions of presidential leadership.

Fairclough, Adam. *To Redeem the Soul of America: The Southern Christian Leadership Conference and Martin Luther King, Jr.* Athens: University of Georgia Press, 1987. This study traces the history of the SCLC from its origins through the Abernathy years. It includes a helpful chronology of important events covering the years 1953 to 1968 as well as extensive notes and an index of important terms.

Liebman, Charles S. *Pressure Without Sanctions: The Influence of World Jewry on Israeli Policy*. Rutherford, N.J.: Fairleigh Dickinson University Press, 1977. This book explores the relationship of Diaspora Jews to Israeli policy. Especially interesting are several case studies examining the possible influence of American Jews. The work contains comprehensive notes, a bibliography, and an index of important terms.

Liebman, Robert C., and Robert Wuthnow. *The New Christian Right: Mobilization and Legitimation.* Hawthorne, N.Y.: Aldine, 1983. This collection of essays, edited by two sociologists, explores the ideology, organizations, constituency, cultural environment, and mobilization of the new Christian right. The book includes a bibliography.

Robbins, Thomas, and Dick Anthony. *In Gods We Trust: New Patterns of Religious Pluralism in America.* New Brunswick, N.J.: Transaction Books, 1981. In this collection of papers, the authors deal with the many cultural and political influences of new religious groups in America. Topics include the decline of familism and the undermining of dominant cultural value-orientations, and special attention is devoted to current controversies regarding religious innovation. The book includes a bibliography.

Schmidt, Jean Miller. *Souls or the Social Order: The Two-Party System in American Protestantism.* New York: Carlson, 1991. This volume is part of the excellent series of Chicago Studies in the History of American Religion, edited by Jerald C. Brauer and Martin Marty. The author traces the context, development, and tensions engendered by the Social Gospel in American Protestantism. The book includes notes, a bibliography, and an index of important terms.

Shriver, Peggy L. *The Bible Vote: Religion and the New Right.* New York: Pilgrim, 1981. In this study, an Assistant General Secretary of the National Council of Churches of Christ in the U.S.A. analyzes the goals and the political program of the new religious right in America. The author also examines the origins and the leading groups of the movement.

James M. Dawsey

Cross-References

Civil Religion and Politics, 259; Inequalities in Political Power, 972; Party Politics in the United States, 1343; Political Action Committees and Special Interest Groups, 1387; The Separation of Church and State, 1714; Social Movements, 1826; The Sociology of Religion, 1952; Values and Value Systems, 2143.

POLITICAL MACHINES AND BOSSES

Type of sociology: Major social institutions
Field of study: Politics and the state

The term "political machine" has been most typically used to describe the local party organizations that were thought to dominate politics in United States cities during the late nineteenth century and early twentieth century. The "boss" was the political machine's controlling head. Both terms carried negative, even pejorative, connotations. Only since the 1920's have students analyzed more dispassionately the role, functions, and significance of the political machine and boss.

Principal terms

BOSS: the controlling head of a hierarchically structured party organization popularly known as a political machine

BROKER POLITICS: a form of politics in which party leaders act to balance and accommodate conflicting interests in such a way as to build a winning coalition

ENTITLEMENT: a government benefit receipt which is determined by formalized criteria that allow minimal administrative discretion

FUNCTIONALISM: as formulated by Talcott Parsons and Robert K. Merton, an approach to sociological analysis that rests upon a complex of interlocking premises—all forms of human activity and all human institutions are interrelated and thus constitute a social system; all such activities and institutions perform a definite function in that system; and every social system has universally constant needs (or "functional prerequisites") that must be fulfilled if the society is to continue as a going concern

MACHINE: when used in a social context, a hierarchically structured organization that defines and pursues goals with sufficient regularity to resemble a mechanical device

MUCKRAKER: the name applied by president Theodore Roosevelt to journalists who exposed political and business misdeeds during the early years of the twentieth century; the term "muckraking" has become synonymous with the exposure of wrongdoing for the purpose of stimulating reform

PARTICIPANT-OBSERVER METHOD: a research technique first applied in anthropology but extended to sociology and political science at the University of Chicago in the 1920's whereby the student of an institution or group lives among the people being studied

PATRONAGE: the benefits—offices, contracts, and the like—with which political leaders reward their followers to ensure their future loyalty

POLITICAL MACHINE: a party organization made of professional
politicians whose primary goal is to win and maintain power;
although political machines have existed at different levels of
government, in many places, and at many times, historically the
heyday of the political machine and the boss has been identified with
the late nineteenth- and early twentieth-century U.S. city.

Overview

"Such words as 'boss' and 'machine' now imply evil," former president Theodore
Roosevelt observed in his autobiography, "but both the implication the words carry
and the definition of the words themselves are somewhat vague. A leader is necessary;
but his opponents always call him a boss. An organization is necessary; but the men
in opposition always call it a machine."

In the broad sense of organizations devoted to the acquisition and maintenance of
political power, political machines have existed at all times and in all places where
voting has been involved. John M. Allswang has provided probably the most satisfac-
tory neutral definition: "a system hierarchical in structure, highly responsive to
immediate needs of the electorate, strongly focussed on political control as an end in
itself, and generally very partisan."

Historians sometimes point to Aaron Burr (1756-1836) as the first American
political boss, but the professional politician emerged as a distinctive type in the United
States during the Jacksonian era (1828-1836), when the necessity of mobilizing the
large number of newly enfranchised voters put a premium upon efficient party
organization. From the start, publications such as *Niles' Weekly Register* attacked the
new breed of party leaders as "persons who have little, if any, regard for the welfare
of the republic, unless as immediately connected with, or dependent on, their own
private pursuits."

The bitter struggle against the political organization headed by William Marcy
Tweed that had come to dominate New York City politics in the 1860's was pivotal in
fixing the negative, even pejorative, image that became attached to the terms "political
machine" and "boss." The picture of the "Tweed Ring" which was popularized by its
opponents—and presented in strikingly graphic form in the cartoons of Thomas Nast
in *Harper's Weekly* —was of vulgar, cynically selfish, and corrupt men who cared only
for their own material gain. To the extent that there was any interest in the sources of
the Ring's support, the explanation drew upon nativist and anti-Roman Catholic
stereotypes to blame the city's large number of immigrants for lacking the higher moral
sensitivity of native-stock Protestants.

This approach to the political machine was confirmed for the educated lay public
by the English observer James Bryce in his widely read and applauded account of
American government, politics, and society *The American Commonwealth* (1888).
Bryce believed that the central fact of American political life was the existence of
full-time professional party managers. These he called "the machine." The machine
was motivated by narrow self-interest: "desire for office, and for office as a means of

gain." Bryce was perceptive about some of the factors responsible for the role played in American politics by the party organization: the frequency of elections, the large number of offices to be voted for, the lack of major ideological divisions, and the preoccupation of most Americans (especially the "best men") with business. Although it existed at all levels of American government, the machine was most powerful in the rapidly growing cities. Bryce placed the major blame on the "ignorant masses"— "largely Irish and Germans, together with Poles and Russians, Bohemians, negroes, Frenchmen, Italians, and such native Americans as have fallen from their first estate into drink or penury."

Similar perceptions of the political machine and the political boss were entrenched in the emerging academic discipline of political science by Moisei I. Ostrogorski's monumental *Democracy and the Organization of Political Parties*, which was published in 1902 with a preface by Bryce. Ostrogorski had a firmer grasp than Bryce had of the structure of the machine. Emphasizing the key role of patronage in machine politics, Ostrogorski described the machine in essential feudal terms as a hierarchical ladder of lesser and greater lords, each with his own set of vassals and dependents—or, as he put the matter, "each Machine being in reality composed of a number of smaller and smaller Machines which form so many microcosms within it." That hierarchical structure culminated in the boss: "the extraordinary powers" exercised by the machine "centre eventually in a single man—the boss." The boss in turn had risen to the top by "natural selection." Like Bryce, Ostrogorski saw the boss as the personification of the machine's cynical quest for power and gain. He put more emphasis than Bryce had on the role of favor-seeking businessmen in financing the machine, but he similarly placed the major responsibility for the corruption of municipal politics on the "lower orders."

Applications

The Bryce-Ostrogorski picture found a receptive audience among most middle-class Americans of the time, given their cultural biases and penchant for Victorian moral absolutes. The image of corrupt and boss-dominated municipal politics was reinforced during the early years of the twentieth century by the sensationalized exposures of a group of journalists whom president Theodore Roosevelt labeled muckrakers. The most famous, and in many ways the most sophisticated, of the group was Lincoln Steffens. In a series of articles written for *McClure's Magazine* in 1902 and 1903, which were collected in book form as *The Shame of the Cities* (1904), Steffens brought the problem of city misgovernment to the forefront of public consciousness. Steffens was less inclined than his contemporaries were to blame the immigrant masses for the cities' troubles; he was aware that the machine attracted their support by providing assistance to those in need. He found the respectable middle class at least as culpable because of its indifference to politics; he even attacked the privilege-seeking "big business man" as "the chief source of corruption." He retained an optimistic faith, however, that exposure of the evils that he found would spur the average citizen—"the people"—to recapture city government from the "boodlers."

The muckrakers were the catalyst for a countrywide movement during the Progressive era for the reform of municipal government. The movement's primary thrust was the adoption of institutional changes aimed at reducing the power of the boss and the machine. Reformers sought to remedy the diffusion of power resulting from a large number of elective offices by centralizing authority and thereby responsibility. Larger cities typically adopted the so-called strong-mayor plan; smaller ones experimented with the commission or city manager form. Nonpartisan elections were supposed to eliminate the distorting influence of national partisan loyalties. In many instances, reformers attempted to weaken the influence of neighborhood-based lower-middle and working class politicians by substituting citywide elections for ward elections to the city council. The direct primary was intended to break the grip of the machine over nominations. The initiative, referendum, and recall were used to allow the voters to override representatives who had betrayed their trust. The more radical of the reformers—Tom Johnson in Cleveland was the leading example—fought to eliminate the corrupting influence of privilege-seeking businessmen through public ownership of transit facilities and utilities.

A few perceptive analysts recognized that the loyalty given the machine by the urban lower class was the result of the welfare-like assistance that the boss and his lieutenants supplied, but the welfare-state alternative to the political machine made no more than limited progress until the New Deal was instituted in the 1930's. In the short run, astute local politicians exploited the new programs from Washington for the relief of the unemployed and distressed to build their own machines. In the long run, however, the transformation of federal government assistance programs into so-called entitlements for which eligibility was determined by formalized criteria allowing minimal administrative discretion took away the political machine's most powerful tool for cementing loyalty.

Probably the most important factor in undermining the traditional machine was the loss of its constituency as the immigrant generation passed from the scene. The immigrants' children and grandchildren were more secure, more fully acculturated, more physically and socially mobile—and thus less in need of the services that the boss had provided than their parents and grandparents had been. By the post-World War II era, the old-style political machine had fallen apart except in a handful of special cases—the most striking exception being Chicago under Mayor Richard J. Daley (1955-1976).

Context

Paradoxically, the decline of the political machine was accompanied by a more realistic understanding, and a more positive appreciation, of its role. The lead in a more systematic and less judgmental study of urban politics was taken by University of Chicago political scientists Charles E. Merriam (*Chicago: A More Intimate View of Urban Politics*, 1929) and Harold F. Gosnell (*Negro Politicians: The Rise of Negro Politics in Chicago*, 1935, and *Machine Politics: Chicago Model*, 1937). The major contribution of the so-called Chicago school was its emphasis on who voted for the machine and why. Asking why in turn directed attention to the services that the machine provided for its constituents. This approach was further developed in J. T. Salter's *Boss Rule: Portraits in City Politics* (1935). A pioneer in applying the participant-observer method to the study of politics, Salter studied the workings of the Philadelphia Republican machine by living in one of its strongholds. Pinpointing the "division" (precinct) leader as the key man in the machine, Salter saw as central his "service function"—primarily, his role as an "intermediary between the citizen and the state." Accordingly, the machine was most powerful in the areas of the city where that intermediary function was most needed—those with the "most unemployment, most conflict with the law, most difficulty in paying rent . . . and these areas are more often than not districts in which a preponderant number of foreign-born and colored people live."

These insights were placed in a larger conceptual framework by the sociologist Robert K. Merton in his *Social Theory and Social Structure* (1949; rev. ed. 1957). Merton was not primarily interested in urban politics as such; his goal was to discern and explain the behavioral patterns underlying all forms of social action. Developing a mode of analysis that became known as "functionalism," Merton concluded that the machine was successful because it served functions that were "at the time not adequately fulfilled by other existing patterns and structures." He emphasized three such functions. The first was the machine's indispensable coordinating role given the diffusion of authority and separation of powers characterizing the American governmental system. The second was the way that the boss reconciled and accommodated conflicting group interests by means of informal mechanisms when the formal machinery of government lacked the capacity to do so. The third was how the machine provided not simply immediate assistance but longer-term social mobility for the hordes of newcomers flocking to the nation's cities.

Urban historians have since gone even further in challenging the accuracy of the Bryce-Ostrogorski picture. Although not denying the waste and corruption that existed, the newer scholarship has underlined the remarkable achievements of late nineteenth century American city government in dealing with the needs and problems resulting from rapid population growth. "By century's close," Jon C. Teaford argues in his *The Unheralded Triumph: City Government in America, 1870-1900* (1984), "American city dwellers enjoyed, on the average, as high a standard of public services as any urban residents in the world." At the same time, the more recent scholarship calls into question the image of the all-powerful boss. Factionalism and localism, rather than centralized control, characterized late nineteenth century urban politics. The few citywide machines that were successful were fragile, makeshift coalitions. "In fact," Teaford concludes, "the term *machine*, with its connotations of impersonal efficiency and effortless, automatic production seems ill-suited to the tentative network of alliances linking party leaders in the city. . . . Likewise, the word *boss* seems misleading when applied to the party leaders who bartered and bargained to ensure some semblance of order. . . . 'Broker' better describes the role of the major party leaders than does the pejorative 'dictator.'"

Bibliography

Allswang, John M. *Bosses, Machines, and Urban Voters: An American Symbiosis.* Port Washington, N.Y.: Kennikat Press, 1977. The first chapter is an invaluable survey of the changing image/perceptions of the political machine and boss in the popular and scholarly literature. There follow case studies of bosses William M. Tweed and Charles Murphy in New York City and "Big Bill" Thompson, Anton Cermak, and Richard J. Daley in Chicago. A revised edition—Baltimore: The Johns Hopkins University Press, 1986—surveys developments in Chicago since the first edition.

Gosnell, Harold F. *Machine Politics: Chicago Model.* Chicago: University of Chicago Press, 1937. This classic example of the Chicago school of urban politics still warrants reading. As Cornell University political scientist Theodore J. Lowi wrote in his foreword to the 1968 reissue of the work by the University of Chicago Press, Gosnell's "book goes further than any other single work to capture what political behavior was like under machine conditions."

O'Connor, Edwin. *The Last Hurrah.* Boston: Little, Brown, 1956. A fictionalized biography of the colorful, big-city, Irish-American boss "Frank Skeffington," loosely based on the life and career of Boston's James M. Curley. O'Connor paints a nostalgic, romanticized portrait of the machine politician as warm-hearted and caring. This book did much to popularize what became the most generally accepted explanations for the decline of the old-style machine: the New Deal's nationalization of the social welfare functions that the boss had once performed, and the coming of age of the children and grandchildren of the immigrant generation, who no longer required the services that the boss had formerly provided.

Riordon, William L. *Plunkitt of Tammany Hall.* New York: McClure, Phillips, 1905. These informal reflections by George Washington Plunkitt, a district leader in New York City's Tammany Hall, recorded by newspaperman Riordon, give a rare view of the political machine from within. Plunkitt is illuminating about the prerequisites for political success and the services performed by the machine which won voter loyalty. The book was reprinted by Alfred A. Knopf in 1948; a paperback edition was published by E. P. Dutton in 1963.

Steffens, Lincoln. *The Autobiography of Lincoln Steffens.* New York: Harcourt, Brace, 1931. Steffen's *The Shame of the Cities* (1904) was probably the most influential of the muckrakers' exposures of municipal corruption during the Progressive era. In the *Autobiography*, Steffens recalls in graphic detail his writing of the work, gives vivid portraits of the many colorful personalities he encountered, and reflects on his findings in the light of his later experience. Not simply a fascinating story, but a work of literary artistry.

Teaford, Jon C. *The Unheralded Triumph: City Government in America, 1870-1900.* Baltimore: The Johns Hopkins University Press, 1984. An important revisionist study that successfully challenges what has long passed for accepted wisdom about late nineteenth century American urban government and politics. Teaford not only shows the impressive achievements in improved municipal services and facilities but also rebuts the legend of city domination by all-powerful bosses.

Zink, Harold. *City Bosses in the United States: A Study of Twenty Municipal Bosses.* Durham, N.C.: Duke University Press, 1930. This work consists primarily of brief case studies of the lives and careers of twenty late nineteenth and early twentieth century municipal bosses. The first seven chapters attempt to draw from this data generalizations about their common characteristics. The most important ones that Zink found were "better than average personal morality" (at least in family life and drinking); a capacity and willingness for hard work; and a reputation for loyalty to friends and reliability in keeping promises.

John Braeman

Cross-References

Democracy and Democratic Governments, 483; Inequalities in Political Power, 972; Political Action Committees and Special Interest Groups, 1387; Political Influence by Religious Groups, 1394; Political Socialization, 1407; Political Sociology, 1414; Power: The Pluralistic Model, 1484; The Power Elite, 1491; The State: Functionalist versus Conflict Perspectives, 1972; White-Collar and Corporate Crime, 2179.

POLITICAL SOCIALIZATION

Type of sociology: Major social institutions
Field of study: Politics and the state

Political socialization refers to the process by which the institutions of society—the family, peers, the church, the schools, and the mass media—influence the extent to which members participate in the governance of society, especially through voting. A primary concern is how individuals learn knowledge, attitudes, values, and behaviors appropriate to participation in a democratic society.

> *Principal terms*
> AGENDA-SETTING: the tendency of the mass media to influence what issues the public believes are important by covering certain issues more often than others
> KNOWLEDGE GAP HYPOTHESIS: the proposition that better-educated individuals tend to acquire information at a faster rate than less-educated individuals so that the gap in knowledge between these groups increases
> NEGATIVE ADVERTISING: in a political campaign, the strategy of promoting one's preferred position or candidate by criticizing the opposing position or candidate
> POLITICAL APATHY: the attitude that political participation does not make much difference and that politicians are all alike
> PUBLIC OPINION: the public's expression of its preferences on issues of public interest or policy
> SPIRAL OF SILENCE HYPOTHESIS: the proposition that public opinion is influenced by what people perceive to be the majority opinion in that they increase their silence if in the minority

Overview

Socialization is the process of teaching members of society the cognitions, attitudes, and behaviors they need to maintain the society. Political socialization is concerned with how individuals acquire political cognitions, attitudes, and behaviors. The purpose of political socialization in a democracy is to develop citizens who are politically knowledgeable and who actively participate in the decision-making process. This participation primarily involves taking part in the election process.

Political cognitions refer to beliefs about the political system and knowledge of its institutions, officials, and practices. They include awareness of how the system operates, awareness of issues of public concerns, and awareness of particular leaders of the society. Political attitudes are the positive or negative feelings one has toward the political system. These include attitudes toward public officials, political issues, and the political process itself. They also include attitudes toward whether the individual's involvement in the process makes a difference. Political behaviors concern how active the individual is in the process—the extent to which the individual participates. Political behaviors include membership in political organizations, activity in social movements and political campaigns, and voting.

The general assumption of socialization has been that the individual is a tabula rasa, or a blank sheet on which society prints its beliefs, attitudes, and behaviors. It is now recognized that individuals do have innate differences that affect them, such as intelligence and motivation. Nevertheless, the emphasis in the study of political socialization continues to be on how external institutions such as the family, peers, the church, and the mass media influence the individual. Political socialization primarily involves the study of certain agents of influence and change on the individual as he or she learns to participate in the governance of society. The participating citizen in a democracy is seen as someone who has a high level of knowledge about the political process, current issues of public concern, and public officials and candidates for office and their stands on significant issues, and who actively supports those in agreement with his or her own positions.

Although political socialization is a life-long process, the emphasis has been on how children and adolescents acquire the relevant skills and values of citizenship. Herbert H. Hyman, a political scientist at Columbia University, wrote *Political Socialization* in 1959. He pointed out that there is a certain regularity to adult political life in terms of level of activity and support of a particular party. This implies a developmental or learning process stemming primarily from the family, wherein political orientations are taught. This book provided the focus of early research on political socialization and led to hundreds of studies being conducted on the topic during the following decades.

Hyman's work followed the voting studies conducted during the 1940's by Paul Lazersfeld, Bernard Berelson, Hazel Gaudet, and William McPhee, sociologists at Columbia University. They found that 75 percent of the vote could be described as hereditary: Voters tended to vote for the same party that their parents did. Influences that changed their opinions often came from interpersonal sources. These sources of influence are called public opinion leaders.

The importance of the family in political socialization inspired the work of Steven Chaffee and Jack McLeod, mass media researchers at the University of Wisconsin. They developed a model of family communication patterns. These patterns categorize the orientations families use in gathering information and relating to people. Some families are more oriented toward issues than others are. Some families are more oriented toward maintaining positive relationships among people. These differing orientations can affect how much people are likely to use the mass media for political information.

Research found that the political socialization process begins with vague emotional identification with political attitudes and authority figures such as the president of the United States. In late childhood, a more sophisticated understanding of the process begins. Knowledge of political issues and institutions develops in adolescence, and there is less identification with individual personalities. Some distrust and cynicism also begin to develop. The process of relying more on the mass media for political information also tends to begin in adolescence.

Since the mid-1970's, research has focused increasingly on the role of the mass media (television, radio, newspapers, and magazines), although the family is still considered the primary force in socializing the child to politics. Research topics include mass media impact on issues considered important, attitudes toward the political system, political knowledge, and political behaviors. The influence of the mass media in these areas is believed to be substantial, but it is not always found to be positive. People seem to learn the relative importance of certain issues from the mass media. They also may develop negative attitudes toward politics from the tendency of the mass media to emphasize negative political news. While people can gain important political information from the mass media, this will only be true of people who actually use the media. Those who do not use them know less about politics and become more dependent on others for political views. It has been argued that this may lead to a society of information haves and have-nots, with severe consequences for democratic societies. Political activity and voting can also be affected if people develop a sense of distrust of the political process because of the media's emphasis on negative coverage.

Applications

One of the research applications that has generated considerable interest is the concept of agenda-setting. Communication research through the 1960's found little evidence for a mass affect on the audience by the major media. Media were found to be agents of reinforcement rather than change. People seemed to select the particular information that supported their already determined attitudes. A group of researchers at the University of North Carolina, however, established a research program beginning with the 1968 presidential election and continuing with the 1972 election in which they found support for what they called the agenda-setting hypothesis.

In 1977 Donald L. Shaw and Maxwell E. McCombs published *The Emergence of American Political Issues: The Agenda-Setting Function of the Press*. The authors, and several of their colleagues, such as David Weaver of the University of Indiana, reported the results of a panel of potential voters who reported what issues were most important to them in the election. At the same time, content analyses were performed on the news shows of the three major networks and on the local newspaper in June and October of the election year. They found that while the media did not significantly change attitudes (the finding of previous voting studies as well), the issues that people said were important were the issues that the media had covered most frequently. The media may not be effective in changing attitudes, but they do seem effective in influencing what people think about. Research on this topic since then has been considerable, and findings have been generally supportive. There is also some support for the finding that newspapers are more effective than television in setting the public agenda.

The media, then, seem to have a certain amount of influence on what issues are deemed important by the public. Public opinion on these issues, however, still seems to be most affected by personal influence. Elisabeth Noelle-Neumann, in her influential work *The Spiral of Silence: Public Opinion, Our Social Skin* (1984), argues that the media can have indirect influence on public opinion change. She argues that people have a fear of social isolation. They are more willing to express their views if they feel that others hold similar views. If people believe that their views have less support, they are more likely to be silent. Hence, majority opinion might be perceived as stronger than it actually is. The media may serve to inhibit rather than increase public discussion. Noelle-Neumann contends that public opinion as reflected by the media serves to build a consensus that binds people together. The negative aspect of this is that the silent minority is less likely to be heard.

Another area in which the media may have a negative impact is the area of political knowledge. The media are a major source of political information, especially among adolescents. Television seems to be the most important medium for acquiring information among the young and those new to the society. Newspapers are more important to adults. Philip Tichenor and his colleagues at the University of Minnesota have proposed that better educated individuals acquire political information at a faster rate than those less educated, possibly leading to an increasing knowledge gap between these groups. Other researchers find that interest in a particular issue is an important consideration in people's acquisition of information: If interest in an issue is high, the knowledge gap may decrease.

The relationship between media use and political behavior is less strong. Some studies find that media use leads to increased political activity, whereas others find no relationship. Some studies have found that use of a specific medium (television) may decrease activity. James D. Wright, a sociologist at the University of Massachusetts, argues that there are two factors that lead to political alienation: feelings of powerlessness and feelings of distrust. Since the 1950's, feelings of alienation and political apathy have increased. More people are developing the feeling that they cannot affect the political system, and fewer people say they trust politicians.

During this same period, Roper public opinion surveys have found an increasing reliance on television as the primary source of news. Studies have found television news to emphasize "bad" or "negative" news. Problems with the government structure, leaders, the economy, public safety, roads and cars—every facet of American society—are analyzed and criticized. (Many studies have found that the dominant category of television news is crime.) Mass communication researchers such as Garrett O'Keefe and Erwin Atwood have provided evidence that the media are also negative in their coverage of political candidates. Moreover, candidates themselves have increased the use of negative advertising. All these factors support the development of political apathy. The result is that fewer people register to vote and fewer registered voters actually do vote.

Context

The valued citizen in a society, especially in a democracy, is someone who knows about politics and how the system works. It is someone who is familiar with the philosophical differences among political parties and who is familiar with party positions on significant issues. It is someone who is knowledgeable about candidates for office and what they stand for. Valued citizens also attend to political news and evaluate facts to determine their own positions on significant issues. The valued citizen is someone who has developed a sense of trust in the democratic process and who has developed a sense of competence about his or her own ability to influence that process. Finally, the valued citizen in a democracy is someone who participates actively in the process, supporting those officials and candidates who share his or her vision of a better society and world. It is extremely important to know the extent to which society is successful in developing such citizens.

The early view of political socialization was of a process moving from a basic orientation, learned in the family, to more complex attitudes and behaviors in adult life. Peers were presented as having the strongest influence on voting behaviors through interpersonal communication, while the mass media were presented as having only limited influence. The primary agents of socialization were the family and peers. The mass media were seen as having a much less significant role.

Research since the 1960's has increasingly found that the mass media do play a significant role in the political socialization process. Early research on the role of the mass media in political behavior looked primarily at effects on voting decisions. The presumption was that the media could have a powerful effect on attitudes and, as a result, on behaviors. Analysis of the effects of propaganda done in the 1930's supported this view. More careful empirical investigation of voting behavior in the 1940's, however, presented a different picture. The media were found to have a much more limited effect than had been suspected.

Research has placed increasing emphasis on knowledge as a key variable. Since the 1960's, the media have been found to have a significant effect in this area. Participants in the political process do gain knowledge of political issues and personalities from the mass media, and knowledge affects attitudes toward the political process. One possible detrimental effect of the knowledge gained from the media comes from the agenda-setting aspect of the mass media's presentation of political issues. If people's own views are not being emphasized or reported by the media, they may believe (whether rightly or wrongly) that they are in the minority. They may therefore be less inclined to discuss their opinions on issues, thus leading to the increasing spiral of silence hypothesized by Noelle-Neumann. Moreover, the less educated may be at an increasing disadvantage regarding politics as political information becomes more plentiful and complex. Yet the importance of an enlightened citizenry has been argued since the days of Plato, and regardless of the problems involved, the mass media will continue to play a significant role in political socialization.

Bibliography

Dionne, E. J., Jr. *Why Americans Hate Politics.* New York: Simon & Schuster, 1991.
The thesis of this book is that the two political parties' concern for separate ide-

ologies has led to a divisive debate between them and a series of false choices with which the general public cannot identify. Hence, the public cannot develop political consensus. Very readable but lacks conceptual grounding in political theory.

Hyman, Herbert H. *Political Socialization*. New York: Free Press, 1959. This watershed work, the classic work taking a conceptual and empirical approach, significantly increased the study of political socialization. Terms are defined, and the relative roles of the family, age, small groups, and psychological and geographical mobility are analyzed. The mass media are not yet portrayed as a major factor.

Johnson-Cartee, Karen S., and Gary A. Copeland. *Negative Political Advertising: Coming of Age*. Hillsdale, N.J.: Lawrence Erlbaum, 1991. An excellent work detailing the historical context of negative advertisements, containing a comprehensive summary of prior research and an analysis of more than one thousand television ads. The authors suggest that such ads can help voters interpret issues but can have negative effects on politicians themselves.

Lavrakas, Paul J., and Jack Holley, eds. *Polling and Presidential Election Coverage*. Newbury Park, Calif.: Sage Publications, 1991. This volume of case studies and critical essays argues that while there is no evidence that exit poll results decrease voter turnout, the emphasis of news polls on who is ahead in the election (the "horse-race") detracts from issues and casts trailing candidates in a light that they have difficulty overcoming.

Lemert, James B., et al. *News Verdicts, the Debates, and Presidential Campaigns*. New York: Praeger, 1991. This comprehensive analysis of the Bush-Dukakis debates finds that debates tend to reinforce prior voter convictions rather than instigate dramatic change. Post-debate media analysis, however, does seem to bring about some voter change.

Noelle-Neumann, Elisabeth. *The Spiral of Silence: Public Opinion, Our Social Skin*. Chicago: University of Chicago Press, 1984. The original work presenting the thesis that public opinion is learned within a context of conformity. The author draws upon the work of Alexis de Tocqueville, John Locke, Jean-Jacques Rousseau, and the more recent empirical work of Solomon Asch.

Renshon, Stanley Allen, ed. *Handbook of Political Socialization: Theory and Research*. New York: Free Press, 1977. This is an excellent work containing articles on the role of family, peers, the schools, and the mass media in the political socialization process. Outcomes of the process in terms of the learning of morals, values, and political participation are also presented. Index and bibliography.

Swanson, David L., and Dan Nimmo, eds. *New Directions in Political Communication: A Resource Book*. Newbury Park, Calif.: Sage Publications, 1990. Mass communication is stressed as a primary factor affecting political socialization. The emphasis moves away from voting studies to the study of political language learning, critical theory, decision-making processes, and cultural research. An excellent source for outlooks current in the 1980's. Index and select bibliography.

Roger D. Haney

Cross-References

Authoritarian and Totalitarian Governments, 153; Democracy and Democratic Governments, 483; Political Action Committees and Special Interest Groups, 1387; Political Influence by Religious Groups, 1394; Political Machines and Bosses, 1400; School Socialization, 1693; Socialization: The Family, 1880; Socialization: The Mass Media, 1887; Socialization: Religion, 1894.

POLITICAL SOCIOLOGY

Type of sociology: Major social institutions
Field of study: Politics and the state

Political sociology is a subfield in the disciplines of political science and sociology which is primarily concerned with the social basis of power. Four competing perspectives—Marxist, neo-Marxist, pluralist, and elitist—have dominated the field since World War II.

Principal terms

ELITISTS: theorists who believe that in all societies, including industrial democracies, a small group (not the masses) rules

INSTRUMENTALISTS: those who believe that the state is an instrument in the hands of the ruling class

MARXISTS: followers of Marx and Engels, who believe that a capitalist state is an instrument for maintaining bourgeois domination of the working class

PLURALISTS: theorists who believe in multiple competing elites and a dispersion of power in a democracy

STRUCTURAL NEO-MARXISTS: theorists who believe in the relative autonomy of the capitalist state

Overview

Political sociology as a field of study overlaps the disciplines of political science and sociology. Political sociology has developed in its present form since World War II. It is primarily concerned with an understanding of the social basis of power and authority. Sociologist Marvin E. Olsen has defined political sociology as "the study of power relations between the political and social systems in nation-states that result in the creation and operation of sociopolitical organization."

Both sociologists—Talcott Parsons, Reinhard Bendix, Ralf Dahrendorf, C. Wright Mills, Seymour Martin Lipset, and G. William Domhoff, for example—and political scientists—such as Robert Dahl, Ralph Miliband, and Kenneth Prewitt—have contributed to the theoretical and empirical studies of political sociology. The writings of Karl Marx and Max Weber have substantially influenced the scholarship in this field. The followers of Marx and Weber take radically different views of a sociology of politics; the debate among political sociologists has often taken the form of a dialogue between and among the Marxists and the Weberians. Eclectic scholars, on the other hand, use the insights, concepts, and methodologies derived from the writings of both Marx and Weber in a selective and nondogmatic manner in order to clarify the dynamics of power and authority relationships in modern societies.

The question of where power resides and how it should be studied is at the core of the disagreement among the proponents of different approaches. In the vast literature on political sociology, four distinct approaches to power and authority can be identified: the Marxist, the pluralist, the power elite, and the neo-Marxist. The Marxists take what has been called an "instrumentalist" view of political power. For Marx and Friedrich Engels, the state, which they considered to be in the realm of superstructure determined by the economic substructure of society, is an instrument in the hands of the ruling class, which dominates the state to further its own interest. In a capitalist society, according to Marx and Engels, the state acts as a "committee for managing the common affairs of the whole bourgeoisie."

According to Marx, class conflict is derived from economic factors or social relations generated by the mode of production. The capitalists' control of the means of production gives them direct (or strong indirect) control of the state. Marx, Engels, and later orthodox Marxists thus analyze the various ways in which the modern state is an instrument of class rule and is used for exploitation of the proletariat, or wage worker, by capital and for the maintenance of the political domination of the bourgeoisie.

Mainstream American political sociology is critical of a class-based theory of politics and generally rejects Marxist instrumentalism because it provides an economic determinist view of social stratification. By contrast, the pluralists—who take their intellectual inspiration from Weber's concepts of authority and rationality—have argued that modern societies consist of a variety of interest groups and that the government acts essentially as a broker to facilitate compromise among them. Power, in this view, is conceived to be widely dispersed among government officials, private individuals, organized interest groups, associations, and a variety of organizations; no one group holds all the power.

A commonly used pluralist definition of power is that of Robert Dahl: "[Person] A has power over [person] B to the extent that he can get B to do something that B would not otherwise do." In *Modern Political Analysis* (1984), Dahl suggests that power means getting others to comply "by creating the prospect of severe sanctions against noncompliance." Defined thus, power is a relational, rather than an abstract, concept: It exists in an interaction, not in a static state. Three types of power have been identified: authority, coercion, and manipulation. While authority is the exercise of legitimate power because it entails the voluntary submission of B to A's directives, coercion is accompanied by sanctions in the form of either rewards or punishments. Manipulation, on the other hand, is the use of power by A over B when A does not have legitimate power or authority over B and when B is unaware of A's intention.

In *The Theory of Social and Economic Organization* (1947), Weber distinguishes three ideal types of legitimacy upon which a power relationship may rest: "traditional," "legal-rational," and "charismatic" authority. Traditional authority rests on "an established belief in the sanctity of immemorial traditions," such as the authority of a king or tribal chief. Rational authority, by contrast, rests "on a belief in the 'legality' of patterns of normative rules," which means that the superior is "himself subject to an impersonal order, and orients his actions to it in his own dispositions and commands." An example is the exercise of authority in modern bureaucratic capitalist states in the

West. Charismatic authority is mixed and transitional, and it rests on "devotion to the specific and exceptional sanctity, heroism or exemplary character of an individual person" and on "the normative patterns or order revealed or ordained by him." Authority of this kind has been exercised by such diverse religious and political leaders as Jesus Christ, Mahatma Gandhi, and Adolf Hitler.

Two divergent responses to the pluralist approach came in the 1960's and 1970's: the elitist and the neo-Marxist approaches. Elite theorists reject the pluralist notion that power in industrial democracies is dispersed among a number of competing groups. At the same time, they deny the Marxist claim that political power is a function of class location. Inspired by the works of C. Wright Mills and Italian political sociologists Vilfredo Pareto and Gaetano Mosca, the elite theorists believe that in all societies, including industrial democracies, only a minority—the elites—makes the major decisions and governs the masses. Unlike Marx's ruling class, elite membership changes over time. Social mobility allows non-elites to become elites through assimilation and cooperation; these elites share a consensus regarding certain basic values of the society and rules of the game, especially of the political system. Thus the elite theory posits that, in modern democracy, power is exercised by the elites over the masses.

The focus of a dominant neo-Marxist view is on political power and the imperative of capital accumulation and class conflict in capitalist societies. It is critical of instrumentalism as an adequate approach to a Marxist analysis of state and politics, because instrumentalism does not offer a coherent account of the distinctive properties and limits of state power. Nicos Poulantzas, Louis Althusser, Ernesto Laclau, and Claude Offe are among the leading structural neo-Marxists who reject economism and class reductionism. They agree with the position taken by structuralist writers such as Antonio Gramsci that state functions are determined by the structure of society, including its ideological and political practices, rather than by individuals in positions of state power.

In his most influential book, *Political Power and Social Classes* (1973), Poulantzas defines the state in terms of its necessary and objective function in the reproduction of social cohesion through its political and ideological apparatuses. He extends the concept of the "relative autonomy" of the capitalist state beyond any specific capitalists or the capitalist class and views the state as a crystallization of complex social relations. By doing this, Poulantzas "brought the state [which had been ignored in the pluralist literature] back in" to the center of political sociology in the 1970's. In *Class, Crisis, and the State* (1978), Erik Olin Wright examines the relationship between class and state and suggests ways to test the Marxist conception of class and state empirically.

Applications

The insights gained from the various theories, approaches, and concepts of political sociology have been applied by scholars in their empirical studies to locate the social basis of power and authority in industrial and industrializing societies. Since World

War II, significant research has been done to analyze power in American society using pluralist and elitist perspectives.

Robert Dahl's *Who Governs? Democracy and Power in an American City* (1961) is the most important empirical study in the pluralist tradition and is one of the most widely cited books in the social sciences. In his study of community power structure in New Haven, Connecticut, Dahl employs decisional analysis and concentrates on analyzing power. He studies party nominations to public office, urban redevelopment, and public education and identifies the changing patterns of leadership and the politics of influence in New Haven. Dahl's findings refute the thesis of Floyd Hunter in *Community Power Structure: A Study of Decision Makers* (1953), in which Hunter found that local politics in Atlanta, Georgia, was largely controlled, directly or indirectly, by dominant economic interests. It also argues against the thesis of C. Wright Mills in *The Power Elite* (1956) that the United States is run by a combination of "the high military, the corporation executives, and the political directorate."

Through the use of sophisticated social science methodology combining middle-range empiricism with broad-range theory, Dahl showed that political power, which was once concentrated in a few hands, is widely dispersed among competing groups in New Haven. Based on the findings of the New Haven study, Dahl generalized that political power is widely dispersed among competing interest groups in a plural democracy. Following Dahl's classic study, pluralism emerged as the dominant approach in the field of political sociology in the 1960's, and scholars have since employed it to study power in the United States and other industrial democracies.

Dahl's thesis and the pluralist approach have, however, been challenged on empirical and theoretical grounds, notably by critics employing the elitist perspective such as G. William Domhoff, Thomas Dye, G. Lowell Field, John Higley, Kenneth Prewitt, and Alan Stone. Domhoff, a pioneer in research on the American ruling class who has advanced an analysis of American society based on the insights of power structure theory, has provided the most sustained critique of the pluralist view that power is lodged in a variety of interest groups and in the people as a whole through party politics and elections. Grounding his analysis in Mills's concept of the power elite and E. Digby Baltzell's American business aristocracy, Domhoff in *Who Rules America?* (1967) rejects Dahl's pluralist thesis and demonstrates that a small, socially identifiable group—a national upper class or power elite, whose members have well-established ways of training and perpetuating new members—is the governing class in the United States.

Domhoff elaborates his power-structure thesis in other studies. In *The Powers That Be* (1979), he shows that the upper class in the United States, a tiny segment of the population (0.5 percent), controls more than 25 percent of the country's private wealth and annual income. The economic power of the upper class, he argues, allows this class to subordinate the other social classes and dominate the government. Through contingency, reputational, and positional analysis, Domhoff demonstrates that the upper class is a cohesive ruling class in America. In *The Power Elite and the State* (1990), he elaborates his power structure thesis by applying Michael Mann's theory of social power to an analysis of several major policy initiatives at the national level in the twentieth century United States.

Thomas R. Dye's study *Who's Running America? Institutional Leadership in the United States* (1976) uses biographical data of more than five thousand members of government and business elites to demonstrate that power in the United States is concentrated in the hands of a small number of government and business elites. He shows that there is a corporate interlocking among a number of firms and a "revolving door" between governmental and business elites. Dye concludes that power is "concentrated in large institutions—corporations, banks, utilities, insurance companies, broadcasting networks, the White House, Congress and the Washington bureaucracy, the military establishment, the prestigious law firms, the foundations, and the universities."

The 1980's and early 1990's witnessed an effort by a few scholars, notably John Higley, Michael Burton, and G. Lowell Field, to develop a new elite framework for political analysis by synthesizing elements of elite and class theories. The new elite framework has been applied to the study of political stability and the emergence of democracy in the West. In "The Elite Variable in Democratic Transitions and Breakdowns," in *American Sociological Review* 54 (February, 1989), Higley and Burton analyze the relationships between types of national elites, elite transformations, and political stability in the Western nation-states since 1500. Their study shows that "a consensually unified national elite," as in Sweden, Britain, or the United States, "produces a stable regime that may evolve into modern democracy."

Context

The changing sociopolitical conditions in developed and developing societies since World War II have provided the context within which political sociologists have sought to answer important questions related to the central thrust of the field—the relationship between power and politics. Much of their scholarly attention has been focused on the study of the conditions that facilitate democracy. The Fascist and Nazi challenge to liberal democracy in the 1930's and 1940's and the communist challenge both before and after World War II gave impetus to a number of studies on democracy. In his classic study *Political Man: The Social Bases of Power* (1960), Seymour Lipset identified conditions that make democracy work in any society: an open class system, economic wealth, an egalitarian value system, a capitalist economy, literacy, and high participation in voluntary associations. A year later, Dahl offered the pluralist view of American democracy in his famous study of New Haven.

The political sociologists who were influenced by the radical antiestablishment movement of the 1960's, however, challenged the prevailing dominant pluralist approach. They applied Mills's power elite framework to the study of society and politics, which resulted in an intense debate between the pluralists and elitists in the 1960's. A new debate started in the 1970's when the neo-Marxists responded to the pluralist, elitist, and instrumental Marxist frameworks. The contribution of the structural neo-Marxists, who are inspired by the class analysis of Marx as interpreted by

Althusser, Gramsci, and other structuralists, and who use the nation-state as a unit of analysis, has mostly been at an abstract theoretical level. In particular, they have interpreted the role of the capitalist state and its relationship to the capitalist class.

The neo-Marxist perspective was advanced at a time (the late 1960's and early 1970's) when the world was undergoing major changes. A détente was reached with the Soviet Union, a new diplomatic opening with China occurred, and the United States withdrew from Vietnam. The Watergate scandal focused attention on abuses of governmental power. Social scientists were searching for new frameworks to explain these changes. The 1970's witnessed a rich, lively, and often polemical debate between the neo-Marxists and the Marxists on the one hand and the elitists on the other. In a number of empirical studies, the neo-Marxists sought to verify their theory, especially the "relative autonomy of state." Their approach lost much of its appeal in the wake of the "Reagan Revolution" in the early 1980's, whereas scholarly interest in the elitist framework continued in the 1980's. Domhoff, Dye, and others refuted the pluralist perspective by producing new evidence in support of the thesis they had put forth in earlier studies. No such effort was made on behalf of the pluralist perspective. The elitist perspective was further enriched in the 1980's and early 1990's by the contributions of scholars who, by advancing an elite conflict theory and a new elite paradigm, sought to reestablish the classical elite theory.

In the 1980's, scholarly attention also went to the study of democracy, especially the breakdown of democratic regimes and the transitions from authoritarian to democratic governments. Through empirical studies on Mediterranean and Latin American states, political sociologists made an effort to discern a pattern and to identify the social, political, and economic conditions that allowed less industrialized and developing nations to become democratic. The collapse of communism in Eastern Europe and the former Soviet Union, accompanied by a global resurgence of democracy, provided further impetus to studies on democracy. Political sociologists in the early 1990's gave attention to the question of whether the democratic expansion of the 1980's and early 1990's will be stabilized, consolidated, and sustained in the environments of the new democratic states.

Bibliography

Dahl, Robert. *Who Governs? Democracy and Power in an American City.* New Haven, Conn.: Yale University Press, 1961. Examines the changing patterns of leadership and the distribution of political resources in New Haven, Connecticut.

Dahrendorf, Ralf. *Class and Class Conflict in Industrial Society.* Stanford, Calif.: Stanford University Press, 1959. The author provides a critique of various theories of class and class conflict and offers his own theory of the "coercion of social structure."

Domhoff, G. William. *Who Rules America?* Englewood Cliffs, N.J.: Prentice-Hall, 1967. Using the perspective of the elite theory, especially that of E. Digby Baltzell, C. Wright Mills, and Paul Sweezy, Domhoff argues that a small, socially identifiable group—a national upper class or power elite—is the governing class in America.

Dye, Thomas R. *Who's Running America? Institutional Leadership in the United States*. Englewood Cliffs, N.J.: Prentice-Hall, 1976. Through the use of biographical data of five thousand members, Dye applies power structure theory to his analysis of the elites who, he holds, rule the United States.

Field, G. Lowell, and John Higley. *Elitism*. Boston: Routledge & Kegan Paul, 1980. The authors provide a detailed survey of the literature on elite theory and restate the elitist paradigm by focusing on elite unity and disunity.

Miliband, Ralph. *The State in Capitalist Society: An Analysis of the Western System of Power*. London: Weidenfeld & Nicolson, 1969. The leading British Marxist explains how class inequalities may be transformed into power differences within modern capitalist societies. His "instrumentalist" view came under serious criticism by structuralists such as Nicos Poulantzas.

Mills, C. Wright. *The Power Elite*. New York: Oxford University Press, 1956. In this highly influential and controversial book, which initiated extensive discussion of power and the American social structure, Mills argues that the United States is run by a combination of "the high military, the corporation executives, and the political directorate."

Poulantzas, Nicos. *Political Power and Social Classes*. Translated by Timothy O'Hagan. London: NLB and Sheed and Ward, 1973. Deeply influenced by neo-Marxist structuralists such as Antonio Gramsci and Louis Althusser, Poulantzas presents a structural view of the state and classes. The most influential political sociology book of the early 1970's.

Prewitt, Kenneth, and Alan Stone. *The Ruling Elites: Elite Theory, Power, and American Democracy*. New York: Harper & Row, 1973. The authors provide an excellent review of the various perspectives on elite theory and systematically test the propositions of the "power elite" versus pluralist theory using the data on American elites.

Sunil K. Sahu

Cross-References

Democracy and Democratic Governments, 483; Inequalities in Political Power, 972; Legitimacy and Authority, 1055; Party Politics in the United States, 1343; Political Socialization, 1407; Power: The Pluralistic Model, 1484; The State: Functionalist versus Conflict Perspectives, 1972; Traditional, Charismatic, and Rational-Legal Authority, 2064.

POPULATION GROWTH AND POPULATION CONTROL

Type of sociology: Population studies or demography
Field of study: Sociological perspectives and principles

World population has experienced extraordinary growth over the past 250 years, particularly since World War II. With little prospect for slowing population growth through changing mortality and migration, contemporary population control is primarily implemented by reducing birth and fertility rates.

Principal terms
> BIRTH CONTROL: deliberate control over the number and spacing of births; also referred to as fertility control, family planning, and planned parenthood
> EUGENICS: theories about improving the qualities of the human race that are often controversially linked to racism, ethnocentrism, and genocide
> FAMILY PLANNING PROGRAMS: organized social efforts to support the goal of small families; to provide knowledge, information, and means of birth control; and to encourage people to participate in birth control
> FECUNDITY: the capacity of women to produce births
> FERTILITY: the childbearing performance, rather than physiological capability, of an individual, a couple, a group, or a population
> GROWTH RATE: the change (increase or decrease) in population during a period divided by the average population during that period
> POPULATION CONTROL: refers to control over the size, growth, distribution, and characteristics of populations; most often used with respect to population growth
> POPULATION GROWTH: denotes increase, stability, or decrease in population size at successive dates
> POPULATION MOMENTUM: a situation in which a large cohort of women born at a time of high fertility will themselves produce large numbers of children, even if each woman has a relatively small number of children

Overview

For more than 1 million years, the world's human population, which was held in check by high death rates, grew very slowly, at a rate of scarcely above zero. At the time of the earliest formation of agricultural settlements, approximately 8,000 B.C.E., world population was estimated to be between 8 and 10 million. Even with the emergence of agrarian societies, world population grew slowly, reaching 300 million in 1 C.E. In the mid-1600's, world population totaled approximately 500 million. Since the advent of the Industrial Revolution, in approximately 1750, world population has increased extraordinarily, passing the 1 billion mark in 1800. The second billion was added by 1930, which took about 130 years, and the third billion was added in only thirty years, by 1960. World population reached 4 billion by 1974, only fourteen years later, and 5 billion in 1987, just thirteen years later. World population reached 5.5 billion in 1992 and is projected by the United Nations to reach 8.5 billion in 2025. While world population reached only 0.5 billion after more than one million years' evolution, 5 billion more people were added in 340 years after 1650. Very rapid population growth first occurred in Western countries during the late nineteenth century and the early twentieth century. The so-called population explosion, however, generally refers to the unprecedented population growth that occurred in developing countries after World War II.

Population growth is determined by three geographic processes: fertility (births), mortality (deaths), and migration. Population growth is simply natural increase, or the difference between births and deaths, if migration is not a factor. Historically, death rates have declined earlier than birth rates, causing population to grow at an acceler-ated rate. Death rates in developing countries declined dramatically after World War II, while birth rates remained high, resulting in the contemporary population explosion.

The consequences of rapid population growth are complex and have been debated for centuries. In a positive light, some scholars believe that rapid population growth does not impede economic growth and development, and that moderate population growth can even stimulate consumption and encourage technological innovation. Many scholars believe, however, that rapid population growth in many developing countries has diverted scarce resources away from long-term investments in develop-ment toward emergency relief efforts. Moreover, rapid population growth has contrib-uted to global problems such as the depletion of nonrenewable resources, including fossil fuels, minerals, and agricultural land; degradation of the environment, including global warming, acid rain, and pollution; and urban crowding, resulting in dire social and health conditions. Most national governments wish to slow population growth to a level that would permit adequate capital investment, provision of food, public facilities, education, employment opportunities, and environmentally sustainable development.

Population control refers to efforts intended to affect growth, size, distribution, migration, and characteristics of populations. In this article, the discussion is restricted to control of population growth and size. Population control can act directly through governmental interventions, such as adjusting laws and policies for age of marriage, abortion, migration, and family planning. Policies can also act indirectly through socioeconomic incentives and disincentives to promote desired levels of reproduction. Both direct governmental interventions and indirect incentives and disincentives can be either pronatal or antinatal. Although some countries that are experiencing low or negative population growth are attempting to encourage population growth, antinatal population control is the dominant goal for most developing countries.

To have an impact, population control must affect at least one of three demographic processes: birth, death, or migration. Clearly, increasing death rates for the purpose of slowing population growth is unacceptable. Some demographers argue that high infant death rates contribute to high birth rates in developing countries. Families wishing to assure having a sufficient number of children may have too many out of fear that some will die at early ages. If infant death rates are lowered, these demographers argue, families will elect to have fewer children, resulting in lower overall population growth. Migration can be important to population change in a specific region or a country, but it is not a factor in determining world population size. Large-scale emigration to the "new continents" acted as a significant population safety-valve in European history. With the current international migration restrictions, migration is no longer feasible on levels sufficient to lessen population pressure for rapidly growing countries. With little prospect for slowing growth through changing mortality and migration, population control is primarily implemented by reducing birth and fertility rates.

American demographer John Bongaarts indicated in 1978 that there are some intermediate or proximate variables through which social factors (cultural patterns and norms, education, economic status, and so forth) influence fertility. According to Bongaarts, the four most important intermediate variables are proportion of women married, contraceptive use, use of abortion, and duration of breast feeding. The first proximate determinant, proportion married, is usually shaped by the average age at marriage, the proportion of women who never marry, and divorce and separation rates. In most societies, marriage increases women's likelihood of becoming pregnant. Thus, policies designed to delay age of marriage can act to reduce population growth.

The remaining three proximate determinants are related to birth control. Birth control can be achieved by applying a variety of means that can interrupt the process of conception or gestation and avert births. Traditional contraceptive methods include prolonged breast feeding, which reduces female ovulation, male withdrawal during intercourse (coitus interruptus), and the rhythm method, or periodic abstinence timed to avoid intercourse when females are most likely to become pregnant. Modern contraceptive methods include sterilization, pills, injections and skin implants, intra-uterine devices (IUDs), diaphragms, and condoms. Surgical and, more recently, chemical abortion techniques have also been widely used as means of birth control. Birth control within marriage has a profound impact on population growth. Without extensive use of birth control within marriage, sustained low levels of population growth are not likely to be achieved.

Applications

Application of population control usually refers to governmental interventions that attempt to control population growth through altering individual reproduction behavior. After World War II, concern about mushrooming population growth in the developing countries stimulated innovation and international diffusion of family planning programs. Understanding how family planning programs affect reproductive behavior will help analysts understand the practice of population control in the developing countries. Some policy analysts argue that the widespread practice of birth control only comes about with sufficient socioeconomic development, as was the pattern among many industrialized nations. American demographer John Knodel's studies of European historical fertility decline suggest, however, that the idea of family limitation can spread from place to place. Once the possibility of controlling births is realized, increased practice of family limitation can occur under a wide variety of social and economic conditions. Therefore, the diffusion of norms for family planning has been an essential component of family planning programs in developing countries.

Family planning programs are defined by American demographers William Petersen and Renee Petersen, in *Dictionary of Demography: Terms, Concepts, and Institutions* (1986), as "government-administered efforts to provide birth-control information and means, and to induce members of a target population to use them." This definition indicates three functions of family planning programs: education, service provision, and motivation. The most common activity of family planning programs is to educate people about family planning. Mass-media communication and education programs, including print, television, radio, songs, dramas, and films on family planning, have been produced in hundreds of languages and are used through-out the world. Large-scale educational campaigns, as well as regular interpersonal communications, have been organized to encourage a positive social climate for family planning, advocate the norms of the small family, and spread awareness of the possibility of realizing desired family size.

A second common activity of family planning programs is the provision of contra-ceptives and family planning services. According to surveys conducted in eighty-five developing countries in the late 1970's and early 1980's, from 50 percent to 90 percent of married women of childbearing age wanted either to limit or to space births, yet many of those women did not use contraceptives and lacked knowledge of or access to effective, modern contraceptives. This indicated a substantial unmet need for birth control. Government family planning programs in most developing countries, often with support from nongovernmental agencies, provide a full range of modern contra-ceptives, as well as services, free of charge or at substantially subsidized prices. Services include pregnancy testing, information on infertility, instruction in contra-ceptive use, and, in some cases, sterilization and other surgical procedures.

The third common activity of family planning programs is provision of incentives and disincentives for controlling reproduction. When traditional norms encourage large families and discourage open discussion of sexual matters, couples may lack motivation to have a small family, and those who do not want more children may be ambivalent about using contraceptives. Some family planning programs provide economic and social incentives and disincentives to encourage family limitation. Incentives include subsidized family planning services, compensation for time and effort taken to undergo surgical sterilization, insertion of contraceptive implants and intrauterine devices, and, in a few cases, induced abortion. Disincentives are usually aimed at increasing the cost of child rearing by assessing fees for child-related services—such as day care, health care, and education—for larger families. Incentives and disincentives are incorporated in tax, pension, medical, housing, and child education programs in some developing countries, thus linking family planning with other forms of social and economic support.

Since the onset of the international family planning movement in the 1960's, the prevalence of contraceptive use in developing countries increased from 9 percent in the early 1960's to approximately 45 percent in the late 1980's. According to the Demographic and Health Survey (DHS) and Family Planning Survey (FPS), the average total number of times that women in developing countries gave birth in their lifetimes declined from about six in the 1960's to approximately four in the early 1990's. Although it is difficult to estimate the exact contribution of family planning programs to fertility decline in developing countries, it is clear that family planning programs have helped to reduce fertility and control population growth.

Governmental interventions may also encourage increases in fertility and population growth. In contrast to developing countries, Eastern European countries have taken measures to stimulate population growth since the mid-1960's. Governmental measures used to encourage higher fertility have included limiting the availability and distribution of modern contraceptives, imposing restrictions on abortion services, and providing incentives for larger family size. Tax reductions, housing and food subsidies, and income supplements can act as incentives for increasing family size.

Context

Both pro- and antinatalist government policies can be dated back to the fourteenth and fifteenth centuries in Europe. Historically, government interventions were likely to encourage fertility, and they focused on influencing marriage age and prevalence of marriage. Birth control was generally practiced in resistance to official and religious authorities before the twentieth century.

Social promotion of birth control first emerged in the grass roots birth control movement in England in the late nineteenth century. The movement later spread to other European countries and the United States. Although this birth control movement was basically social-reform-related—supporting women's health, sexual equality, family welfare, and eugenics—population control through birth control was a significant concern. This movement widely disseminated the concept of birth control and information about contraceptive technology to the public, and significantly contributed to fertility decline and the slower growth of Western populations in the late nineteenth century and early twentieth century.

India's government implemented the first large-scale modern family planning programs in 1951 and 1952, which were intended to slow population growth through reducing fertility. Various Asian countries followed suit in the late 1950's, and family planning became an international social movement in the 1960's and 1970's. Since then, family planning programs have been widely established in the developing countries with the assistance of the United Nations and other international organizations. By 1989, a majority of developing countries, accounting for 82 percent of the developing world's population, had adopted family planning programs.

Current knowledge suggests that family planning programs have supported fertility decline in developing countries since the 1970's. The practice of family planning in developing countries for more than two decades has provided evidence that the process of human population growth can be changed by means of organized social efforts. To a certain extent, fertility change and population growth are no longer spontaneous processes; instead, they are a matter of choice. The world is still a long way from ending the population explosion, however, even with recent fertility declines. Because of population momentum resulting from the large proportion of young people in developing countries, world population will continue to grow for decades. World population grew at a rate of about 1.7 percent in 1992. The world population will double in forty-one years if this growth rate does not decline. Because the world population is overwhelmingly large, the absolute increase in population size is large in spite of diminishing fertility rates. The annual increase in world population was approximately 73 million in the 1970's, 85 million in the 1980's, and 93 million in 1992, the equivalent of adding the population of Mexico to the world every year.

World population is likely to stabilize eventually. The sooner this stability is reached, the smaller the overall size is likely to be and the more likely it is that the planet will stay within sustainable limits. Population control will continue to be a long-run strategy, and family planning programs will continue to play an important role in slowing world population growth.

Bibliography

Donaldson, Peter, and Amy Ong Tsui. *The International Family Planning Movement.* Washington, D.C.: Population Reference Bureau, 1990. This bulletin summarizes the development of the international birth control movement from the early 1900's to the present. It is very helpful in terms of understanding the history of the birth control movement and features of modern family planning programs.

Ehrlich, Paul R., and Anne H. Ehrlich. *The Population Explosion.* New York: Simon & Schuster, 1990. In his book *The Population Bomb* (1968), Paul Ehrlich warned of impending disaster if the population explosion was not brought under control. Now, Ehrlich and Ehrlich think that the population bomb has detonated. The book argues that unprecedented overpopulation causes global problems in both developing and developed countries.

Phillips, James F., and John A. Ross. *Family Planning Programmes and Fertility.* Oxford, England: Clarendon Press, 1992. This book is a collection of current studies of fertility and family planning. It includes an overview of the role of family planning programs, the relations between supply and demand for family planning, and the limits of family planning effectiveness.

Puri, Sunetra. *Family Planning in Five Countries.* London: International Planned Parenthood Federation, 1989. This document is a rich reference on family planning programs throughout the world.

Scientific American. *The Human Population.* San Francisco: W. H. Freeman, 1974. Despite its age, this book remains an excellent introduction to the basic causes and consequences of population growth.

Weeks, John R. *Population: An Introduction to Concepts and Issues.* 4th ed. Belmont, Calif.: Wadsworth, 1989. This is an excellent introductory text on population studies for audiences with different academic disciplines. Discusses basic concepts of population growth and population related socioeconomic issues.

World Bank. *World Development Report, 1984.* New York: Oxford University Press, 1984. This report, edited by American demographer Nancy Birdsall, is devoted to issues of population growth and family planning. It is a rich source of statistics and case studies from developing countries.

Jichuan Wang
James H. Fisher
Jiajian Chen

Cross-References

Demographic Transition Theory of Population Growth, 499; Demography, 506; Fertility, Mortality, and the Crude Birthrate, 761; Infant Mortality, 978; Life Expectancy, 1087; Malthusian Theory of Population Growth, 1113; Population Size and Human Ecology, 1428; Population Structure: Age and Sex Ratios, 1434; Zero Population Growth, 2215.

POPULATION SIZE AND HUMAN ECOLOGY

Type of sociology: Population studies or demography

Population size refers to the number of individuals in a given area; it is dependent first on the population's growth rate and ultimately on the carrying capacity of the ecosystem. Human ecology is concerned with these issues as they relate to the earth's growing human population.

Principal terms
BIRTHRATE: the number of individuals born in a defined period per 1,000 individuals; this is the per capita birthrate
CARRYING CAPACITY: the population density of a given species that can be sustained indefinitely in an ecosystem
DEATH RATE: the number of individuals dying in a defined period per 1,000 individuals; this is the per capita death rate
DEMOGRAPHY: the study of population statistics, including birthrates and death rates
DENSITY-DEPENDENT FACTORS: factors that regulate population size that depend on the size of the population, such as crowding and food supply
DENSITY-INDEPENDENT FACTORS: factors that regulate population size that are independent of the size of the population, such as volcanic eruptions
ECOSYSTEM: an interacting community of organisms and their nonliving environment
LOGISTIC GROWTH: a pattern of population growth in which a population starts growing slowly, increases rapidly, and then levels off
POPULATION: a group of individuals of given species in a defined geographic region

Overview

To understand population size, researchers need to apply basic ecological principles to the study of human populations. "Ecology" comes from the Greek words *oikos* ("house") and *logos* ("to study"). Ecology, then, is the study of the interrelationship of organisms and their environment, their "house." One aspect of ecology is population ecology, which is concerned with measuring changes in population size over time. This area is becoming increasingly important as human populations expand and have greater impacts on the ability of ecosystems to support such large populations.

A population is a group of individuals of the same species living in a given geographic area. All populations, from the smallest bacteria to elephants, show certain characteristics. The first characteristic that scientists can measure is population size, or the number of individuals. For small populations, it is easy to count all the individuals. As populations get larger, sociologists and ecologists resort to sampling a population in a given area to determine population density (*N* stands for population density, the number of individuals per area).

Populations show another characteristic, which is change. A population increases with every birth and decreases with every death. (To simplify the model here, immigration and emigration, which can also affect population density, will be ignored.) Thus, the change of population over time will be the number of births minus the number of deaths. A population grows if the number of births is greater than the number of deaths and decreases if the deaths exceed births.

Population experts are usually concerned with changes in population size, and they use birthrates and death rates instead of actual numbers. For example, if there are 34 births per 1,000 individuals per year, the birthrate would be 0.034 per year. If there were 12 deaths per 1,000 individuals per year, then the death rate would be 0.012 per year. Population ecologists use "r" as the birthrate minus the death rate, or the growth rate of a population. In this example, it would be 34 minus 12, or 22. This would give a growth rate of r = 0.022 per year.

One feature of r is that r can be used to calculate the doubling time of a population, or how long it will take in years for a population to increase to twice its size. The doubling time is a function of r, not of the population size. The equation for calculating doubling time is

$$\text{doubling time} = \frac{\ln 2}{r}$$

where the ln (natural logarithm) 2 = 0.693. For example, a population growing at 3 percent per year (r = 0.03) would have a doubling time of approximately twenty-three years. If a population had 1,000 individuals, in twenty-three years it would have 2,000 individuals. If the population density was ten million, then after twenty-three years the population would have twenty million individuals.

The maximum possible growth rate for a population is noted as r_{max}. This can occur only under conditions of unlimited food supply, space, and other important resources. A population under these conditions is said to be undergoing exponential growth. The effects of unchecked exponential growth are surprising, even mind-boggling. To understand this, one may consider a bacterium that can reproduce by fission every twenty minutes. After twenty minutes, there would be two bacteria; after forty minutes, there would be four. If this process were to continue unabated for only a day and a half, there would be a foot-deep layer of these bacteria covering the earth. Any organism, if its numbers could continue to grow exponentially, would cover the earth.

Most populations can maintain exponential growth only for short periods. As the population density increases, resources become limited and population growth slows. Eventually, population density reaches a maximum size because of the limitation of resources. This maximum population size is called the carrying capacity of the environment. The population density will oscillate but will stabilize around the level of the carrying capacity.

The carrying capacity of an ecosystem depends on a number of factors, including both physical and biotic factors. Physical factors include temperature, water availability, salinity, sunlight, and pH (a measure of acidity). Other physical factors include natural disasters such as volcanoes, fires, and earthquakes. Physical factors usually affect the same percentage of a population regardless of population density. These factors are considered to be density-independent and will keep a population below the carrying capacity of the environment.

Biotic factors are the result of the interactions of populations of different species in the same ecosystem. A variety of species in the same environment are looking for food, space, water, light, and other resources. There is competition among members of the same species for food, water, and space, but there may also be competition between different species for similar food resources. Other biotic factors that can affect population density are predators and parasites. As the population density increases, limitation of key resources affects population growth rates and slows them for all species. This is called density-dependent regulation. Biotic factors often hold population density below the carrying capacity of the environment.

Applications

Population size does not increase and then reach a steady state at the carrying capacity. Populations usually show cycles with marked fluctuations. A good example of this phenomenon is the type of fluctuation caused by predator-prey relationships, such as that of the snowshoe hare and the Canadian lynx. The snowshoe hare population fluctuates in ten-year cycles. As the hare population fluctuates, so does the lynx population. The lynx population shows a slight lag in its population cycle; it is still increasing and reaching its maximum population as the snowshoe hare population begins to decrease. It is thought that the increase in the hare population overexploits the vegetation and reduces the carrying capacity of the ecosystem. Additionally, the increase in the lynx population decreases the snowshoe hare population.

Human factors can have a marked influence on plant and animal populations. In 1906, for example, approximately 4,000 mule deer lived on the Kaibab Plateau in Arizona. In 1906, President Theodore Roosevelt declared the plateau a "wildlife refuge." Humans then started a systematic removal of predators such as wolves, coyotes, and mountain lions from the Kaibab Plateau. These predators had kept the mule deer population in check. After twenty years, the wolves were completely eliminated, and the other predators greatly reduced in number. The deer population exploded, and damage to vegetation occurred from overgrazing. Even trees that mule deer usually ignored were browsed as high as the deer could reach. By 1924, the mule deer population was estimated to be between 50,000 and 100,000. During the next two winters, about 60 percent of the deer starved to death. The deer had overshot the carrying capacity of the environment. The population has now stabilized at a much lower density (10,000), the new carrying capacity of the environment. The carrying capacity of the plateau could have been higher except for the extensive environmental damage that occurred because of overbrowsing by the mule deer.

In the future, the greatest impact of the human population will be caused by the sheer numbers of humans populating the earth. The human population stood at 5 million about ten thousand years ago. At that time, humans generally existed as hunter-gatherer tribespeople. Then a transition to agricultural society occurred, and humans began producing more food. The advancement of agriculture enabled the human population to grow steadily but slowly for the next nine thousand years. It is estimated that by the year 1650, the human population was 500 million people. With the advent of the Industrial Revolution, the human population grew more rapidly and by 1900 it stood at about 1.6 billion. Other advances, such as better nutrition, public sanitation, and small medical advances, helped to lower the death rate and extend the human lifespan. The twentieth century saw major agricultural advances, which have increased the food supply, as well as major medical breakthroughs such as antibiotics and vaccines. These factors allowed the human population to grow to 5.6 billion by 1990 and allow it to increase by 80 million per year.

It took the human population until the year 1850 to reach the first billion people, but it took only eighty years to reach the second billion. It then took only forty-five years for the population to double again. Thus, the growth rate of the human population has been increasing over time. In the early 1990's, the growth rate stood at 1.8 percent ($r = 0.018$), which gives the doubling time of approximately forty years.

By the 1960's, the growth rate was slowing slightly. This was attributable to a decrease in the growth rate in the more developed countries, such as those in North America and Europe. The less developed countries, however, found primarily in Asia and Africa, still have growth rates of nearly 3 percent, which translate into a doubling time of twenty-three years. Other countries, such as China, have imposed limits (China's is one child per couple) to slow the growth rate. It will take many years for such efforts to slow worldwide population growth. In the early 1990's, the world's population was projected to reach 6.3 billion by the year 2000. A further projection predicts that by the year 2110 the human population will be close to ten billion.

The carrying capacity of the entire earth is unknown. Like any other population studied, humans have constraints such as food resources that must be obtained. The green revolution of the 1960's increased food production by using high-yield grain varieties, and it allowed the human population to continue increasing. This intensive agriculture relies heavily on fossil fuels, however, which are nonrenewable. Alternative energy sources may be required for continued growth of the human population. Other technological advances may allow humans to increase the carrying capacity of the earth, but the extent to which this will happen cannot be predicted.

Context

The first influential essay on population growth was Thomas Malthus' *An Essay on the Principle of Population*, published in 1798. Malthus considered the rate of population growth and the rate at which the food supply could grow. He stated that populations, when left unchecked, would increase with exponential growth but that the food supply would only grow arithmetically. He believed that with further growth, the human population would exceed the ability of the agriculture system to feed it. Thus, Malthus concluded, famine would play a major role in keeping populations in check.

The predictions that Malthus made turned out to be erroneous. He failed to foresee the profound effects of the Industrial Revolution. The invention of the steam engine, utilization of coal for energy, and increased mechanization of farming all enabled food production to be increased. Famines did occur, but emigration to other countries reduced the effect of famine in Europe in the nineteenth century. Further mechanization occurred with the advent of the internal combustion engine, which allowed farmers to increase farm production in marginal lands. One such area was the Great Plains of the United States. Before settlers arrived, the Great Plains was a large area with perennial native grasses holding the soil. Then farmers began to plant crops in place of the native grasses. The Great Plains area is normally dry and windy and occasionally has long periods of drought. One such drought occurred between 1926 and 1934. Hot, dry winds raised thick clouds of dust that darkened the sky. The region was nicknamed the Dust Bowl. This was an early warning of man's environmental impact and the hazards of increasing food production.

The next warning was a book called *The Population Bomb*, written in 1968 by Paul Ehrlich. Ehrlich warned of the population explosion that was occurring. It was noted in 1967 that many people worldwide had inadequate diets, for example. People equalling approximately 20 percent of the earth's population were undernourished in that they did not have a sufficient intake of calories to be healthy. People totalling about 60 percent of the world's population were malnourished in that they lacked essential proteins and vitamins in their diets. All this was occurring during what was supposedly the green revolution of the 1960's.

Twenty years later, Ehrlich estimated that more than 200 million people have died of famine since the 1960's, most of them being children. In addition, another 1.8 billion people were added to the earth's human population. This population growth has had an undeniable impact on the environment. Tropical forests are being burned in order to put the land to agricultural use. This process is releasing carbon dioxide into the air and contributing to global warming. Other impacts include the depletion of the ozone layer (which protects the earth from ultraviolet light), air and water pollution, and acid rain. Human population growth must be slowed in the future. Whether the slowing will be voluntary or will be caused by environmental forces is unknown.

Bibliography

Campbell, Neil A. *Biology*. 3d ed. Redwood City, Calif.: Benjamin/Cummings, 1993. An introductory college textbook geared to the biology major but easily understood by the high school student. Chapters 46 through 49, on ecology, cover the basic aspects such as population growth, community ecology, and ecosystems. References are given at the end of the chapter for further reading. Helpful tables and diagrams.

Ehrlich, Paul R. *The Population Bomb*. New York: Ballantine, 1968. Ehrlich's short paperback book caused something of a sensation when it was published. It gives the reader some historical context on the population problem as it was seen in the late 1960's.

Ehrlich, Paul R., and Anne Ehrlich. *The Population Explosion*. New York: Simon & Schuster, 1990. A follow-up book to *The Population Bomb*. It not only talks about the population problem but also relates it to the environmental changes that are occurring on the planet.

Malthus, Thomas R. *An Essay on the Principle of Population*. Edited by Philip Appleman. New York: W. W. Norton, 1976. A book that contains the original 1798 essay by Thomas Malthus along with critical essays. It also contains contemporary opinions on Malthus' work. Not easy to read, but it provides historical context regarding human population problems and how they have been perceived at different times.

Mix, Michael C., Paul Farber, and Keith King. *Biology: The Network of Life*. New York: HarperCollins, 1992. An easy-to-read biology text for nonmajors. Chapters 5 through 9 give a basic introduction to ecology. Chapter 10 relates this work to human populations. Includes effective diagrams and tables.

ReVelle, Penelope, and Charles ReVelle. *The Global Environment: Securing a Sustainable Future*. Boston: Jones and Bartlett, 1992. An environmental science textbook discussing the major environmental problems being faced. Chapters 5 and 6 discuss human population issues. Easy to read and includes a considerable amount of information.

Lonnie J. Guralnick

Cross-References

Demographic Factors and Social Change, 492; Demographic Transition Theory of Population Growth, 499; Demography, 506; Malthusian Theory of Population Growth, 1113; Population Growth and Population Control, 1421; Population Structure: Age and Sex Ratios, 1434; Zero Population Growth, 2215.

POPULATION STRUCTURE: AGE AND SEX RATIOS

Type of sociology: Population studies or demography

Any human population consists of people of various ages and of both sexes. The percentages of people of different ages as well as the ratio of males to females in a population help determine how quickly the population will grow and therefore the effect it will have on the earth's resources.

Principal terms

AGE STRUCTURE: the number of individuals of various ages that compose a population

COHORT: a group of individuals of the same age; a cohort can be tracked through time to determine its past, present, and future impact on society

LESS DEVELOPED COUNTRY (LDC): a country with a low level of industrialization and a low standard of living

MORE DEVELOPED COUNTRY (MDC): a country that is highly industrialized and has a high standard of living

PER CAPITA GROWTH RATE: the number of births minus the number of deaths divided by 1,000 per year; it is usually designated "r"

POSTREPRODUCTIVE AGE GROUP: individuals past the age of reproduction who therefore cannot increase the population size

PREREPRODUCTIVE AGE GROUP: individuals before the age of reproduction; they have the potential to increase the population size

REPRODUCTIVE AGE GROUP: individuals who are currently adding to the population

Overview

A population is a group of organisms of one species residing in a well-defined geographic area. Populations have many well-defined characteristics, such as births, deaths, immigration, and emigration. These parameters can be used to characterize the growth of a population. The sum of the births and immigrations shows how much the population is increasing; dividing this number per 1,000 individuals gives the rate of per capita increase. The sum of the deaths and emigrations shows how much the population is decreasing; dividing this per 1,000 individuals gives the rate of per capita decrease. Subtracting deaths and emigrations from births plus immigrations gives the growth rate (called "r") of the population. Dividing this by 1,000 gives the per capita growth rate. If "r" is positive, then the population is growing; if "r" is negative, then the population is declining. At zero, the population is stable. This condition is called zero population growth (ZPG).

When one studies a population, one discovers that the individuals of the population are of many different ages. The population composition can be considered either young or old, depending on the relative numbers of young and old individuals. This gives the population what is called an age distribution or age structure. The reproductive ability and the mortality of the individuals is related to their ages. Thus, the population growth rate is a function of the age structure of the population. A population with a large number of young individuals who are either prereproductive or at reproductive age usually has a fairly large growth rate because it has a low mortality rate. Populations with a large number of individuals of postreproductive age are generally declining because they have a high mortality rate. Populations with an even distribution show a stable population density, with replacement equaling mortality.

To determine the shape of an age structure, a researcher groups individuals into different age categories of approximately five- to ten-year periods called cohorts. Then the population is grouped into sexes, and the numbers of males and females are counted. These groupings result in an illustration that typically looks like a stacked bar graph. A relatively simple age structure consists of dividing the population into three age categories: prereproductive (zero to fourteen years), reproductive (fifteen to forty-four years), and postreproductive (forty-five to eighty and older). A rapidly expanding population has a broad base of young individuals and tapers to a point (as a pyramid does). A stable population has relatively flat edges, giving an even proportion of all age groups. A declining population has a narrow base, with increasing numbers of individuals in the older age categories.

Another important parameter in the composition of a population is the relative number of males and females, or the population's sex composition. Age-sex factors have significant ramifications for the population growth rate and its pattern. The exact ratio of males to females changes over time because of the differential mortality displayed by males and females. Males at all ages, however, show a higher mortality rate than females do. Males show a 12 percent higher mortality rate in utero. Because more males are conceived than females, there are still more male children born than female children despite this higher mortality rate. Approximately 106 males are born for every 100 females. Even in the first week of life, more males than females die. Male children are also more likely to die of sudden infant death syndrome (SIDS).

At age twenty, the sex ratio has declined and reached 100 males for every 100 females. This is attributable to the difference in mortality between the sexes being the greatest in young adults: The death rate for males in the fifteen to twenty-four age bracket is three times greater than that for females. Among the leading causes of death are human immunodeficiency virus (HIV) infection, suicide, and homicide. The sex ratio continues to change at ages above the fifteen to twenty-four age group. After the 100 to 100 ratio at age twenty, since male mortality remains higher, the female percentage of the population increases. Above age fifty, males statistically have about twice as great a chance as females to die. By age eighty-five, there are 62 males for every 100 females.

Another factor affecting the sex ratio is migration. In the United States, males and females are equally likely to migrate. In Latin American countries, on the other hand, women are more likely than men to migrate to the city to find jobs, often as domestic workers. These migration patterns may cause a bulge in the age structure of a population.

Applications

The sociological implications of age and sex structure can be illustrated by using the United States as an example. In the year 1900, the United States population showed a well-proportioned pyramid shape with a broad base tapering to a point for all age groups. By 1940, the base of the pyramid had become smaller because of declining birthrates in the 1920's and 1930's. Therefore, there were fewer persons in the prereproductive ages than in the reproductive ages. What saved the base from being reduced even farther was the decline in the mortality of infants, which fell by 50 percent. There were also more individuals in the postreproductive periods: The average life expectancy had increased by fifteen years because of advances in the medical field.

The 1958 pyramid again showed the broad base observed in 1900, reflecting the famous post-World War II "baby boom" generation. The birthrate increased dramatically in 1946, and the high rate lasted until the early 1960's. This cohort is now moving through the age pyramid. By 1985, the baby boomers were in the twenty- and thirty-year-old age category. The baby boom was followed by a "baby bust" period. Interestingly, while the baby boomers have had fewer children, the birthrate nevertheless began rising after the baby bust cohort because of the sheer numbers of the baby boomers. Following the baby bust cohort, an increase in the base of the pyramid occurred.

The sociological impact of the baby boom generation was, is, and will be enormous. Adequate education facilities had to be built and expanded. Large numbers of baby boomers, especially women, entered the workforce, and jobs had to be created to employ them. These women in turn delayed having their children until later in life, which accounted for a small baby boom in the 1990's. In addition, the increase in births during the baby boom period produced what Joseph A. McFalls describes as "a marriage squeeze," which occurred in the 1970's and 1980's because more women than men had been born during the baby boom. This fact, along with the mortality gap, has created many changes in the American family, including more single women, higher rates of out-of-wedlock births, an older age of marriage, increasing divorce, and rising female employment and earnings.

The impact of the baby boom group will be felt as this cohort ages. Between the years 2006 and 2015, the oldest members of the baby boom generation will turn sixty. This group subsequently will cause the over-sixty-five age group to increase from 32 million to 60 million, with a disproportionately larger number of females than males by the year 2035. This phenomenon will put a tremendous strain on the health field. As the elderly proportion of the population increases, so does the proportion of chronically ill people. A majority tend to be women with chronic ailments such as osteoporosis and Alzheimer's disease. Since women statistically live longer than men, many will be widows, a fact which may affect their incomes, living arrangements, and many other social interactions.

The Social Security system will be placed under strain as the older population increases. Because of continuing advances in medical technology, the baby boom cohort will live longer than previous generations and will therefore be collecting Social Security payments for a longer period. In addition, there will be a smaller labor force putting money into the system. In 1940, children outnumbered the over-sixty-five group by four to one. In the year 2035, that ratio will have declined to one to one (some predict it will decline even more).

The United States has a typical age structure for what is often called a "more developed country" (MDC). These countries also include Russia and most European countries, which have an annual growth rate of about 0.6 percent (a net increase of 6 individuals per 1,000). The MDCs, therefore, have an age structure with relatively flat edges and approximately equal proportions of individuals in each age class.

The "less developed countries," or LDCs, of Latin America, Africa, and Asia show an average annual growth rate of 2.1 percent. Kenya is an extreme example, with an annual growth rate of almost 3.5 percent. The LDCs collectively show an age structure with a very broad base and a rapidly expanding population. In other words, they have a large number of individuals in the prereproductive and reproductive age classes. This phenomenon has occurred because modernization, including medical technology, has allowed the mortality rate to decrease and has increased life expectancies. Programs have been initiated to educate and inform people about contraception and slow the birthrate. Yet even if these programs were sufficiently successful to reduce the population growth rate to the replacement level (zero population growth), the population would continue to grow for a time under the pressure of the increasing numbers reaching reproductive age.

The sex ratios of various populations can be strongly influenced by migration patterns. In the early 1900's, males outnumbered females by twenty-seven to one among Chinese immigrants to the United States. A more recent example is the unbalanced sex ratio of the population of the United Arab Emirates (UAR), which came about because of the immigration of Asians and others to work in the oil fields. Most of the migrants were males who either had no families or did not bring them with them.

Context

Beginning in the late seventeenth century, rapid increases in population size occurred in Europe because of the Industrial Revolution. In 1798, Thomas Malthus published *An Essay on the Principle of Population*, in which he predicted that the population growth would soon outstrip food production and famine would keep populations under control.

One societal impact of the Industrial Revolution was to move labor from the farms into the city and factory jobs. This in turn raised the standard of living and fueled population growth. In addition, mechanization of the farm enabled food production to keep up with population growth. By the 1900's, medical advances had significantly reduced the mortality rate; coupled with a stable birthrate, this further increased population growth.

The impact of the combination of industrialization and population growth in the MDCs can be observed in their utilization of food, space, and energy resources. A small percentage of the population of a more developed country is able to produce enough food for the country's population. Therefore, more people are encouraged to leave rural areas and migrate to the cities, exacerbating crowding, pollution, and poverty.

The majority of the world's population is found in the less developed countries. Significant rapid population growth often has political and social implications. China, for example, instituted a policy of allowing a family to have only one child. This policy has affected the population's sex ratio, because there is a cultural preference for sons. The sex ratio has increased to 111 males born for every 100 females. This may be attributable to the fact that many families conceal the birth of daughters as long as possible so they can try to produce a son. The so-called green revolution has increased the world's food supply, but the mechanization that transformed food production in the MDCs has not occurred in the LDCs. Farmers in the LDCs, therefore, still need children to help with the farm labor. This need has kept the birthrates high and the base of the pyramid very broad. Children are also seen as a form of social security to help one in one's old age.

Another problem faced by the populations of LDCs is a lack of resources to fuel industrialization. Wood fuel is a scarce commodity in some areas, and it is being used faster than it can be replaced. In Brazil, the tropical rainforest is being burned to produce agricultural land. This has the effect of releasing carbon dioxide and contributing to the greenhouse effect. Other environmental effects will be felt as the LDCs become more industrialized. The major problem will continue to be population growth. Solutions to the interwoven problems of population growth and industrialization must be found in long-term planning that fosters environmentally sound technology.

Bibliography

Ehrlich, Paul R., and Anne Ehrlich. *The Population Explosion*. New York: Simon & Schuster, 1990. A follow-up book to *The Population Bomb*, published by Ehrlich in 1968. It not only talks about the population problem but also relates the problem to the environmental changes that are occurring on the planet. Easy to read.

Heer, David M. *Society and Population*. 2d ed. Englewood Cliffs, N.J.: Prentice-Hall, 1975. A short paperback book that is easy to read. It includes sections on population processes and discusses their impact on society. It takes an international approach.

McFalls, Joseph A., Jr. *Population: A Lively Introduction*. Washington, D.C.: Population Reference Bureau, 1991. A short paperback with plentiful facts and figures. Includes good diagrams of age structures. Discusses age and sex as well as other parameters and their effect on populations.

Miller, G. Tyler, Jr. *Environmental Science*. 3d ed. Belmont, Calif.: Wadsworth, 1991. An easily read yet provocative textbook which relates environmental problems to population problems and their impacts on society. Good pictures and diagrams. Chapters 1 and 2 discuss populations and cultural changes. Chapter 6 discusses human population dynamics.

Mix, Michael C., Paul Farber, and Keith King. *Biology: The Network of Life*. New York: HarperCollins, 1992. An easy-to-read biology text for nonmajors. Chapters 5 through 9 give a basic introduction to ecology. Chapter 10 relates this work to human populations. Informative diagrams and tables.

ReVelle, Penelope, and Charles ReVelle. *The Global Environment: Securing a Sustainable Future*. Boston: Jones and Bartlett, 1992. An environmental science textbook that discusses major environmental problems. Chapters 5 and 6 discuss human population issues. Easy to read and presents a considerable amount of information.

Volpe, E. Peter. *Biology and Human Concerns*. 4th ed. Dubuque: Iowa: Wm. C. Brown, 1993. An interesting biology book that is very easy to read and contains good pictures and diagrams. Part 5 discusses ecology and the environment. Chapters 42 and 43 discuss population dynamics; chapter 48 covers the human impact on the environment.

Weeks, John R. *Population*. 4th ed. Belmont, Calif.: Wadsworth, 1989. A good introductory textbook on population and its sociological implications. More in-depth than Heer's book. Chapter 8 on age and sex structure gives a good analysis of the impact of both on populations.

Lonnie J. Guralnick

Cross-References

PORNOGRAPHY

Type of sociology: Deviance and social control
Field of study: Forms of deviance

Pornography is generally considered to be written, visual, or spoken material that shows or describes sexual acts or the genitals and is intended to be arousing to the viewer. Legal controversies focus on what is defined as "obscene," implying a societal judgment that the material is offensive. Whether pornography has harmful effects has been the subject of both philosophical debate and scientific research.

Principal terms

CHILD PORNOGRAPHY: pornographic material that depicts children in sexual ways

EROTICA: a morally neutral term to describe any literature or art that has a sexual theme

PERPETRATOR: a person who carries out an act, specifically a violent act

PORNOGRAPHY: written and visual materials of a sexual nature that are used for sexual arousal

PRURIENT: sexually immoral or lewd

Overview

Businesspeople and entrepreneurs seeking to make money have always focused on the needs of other human beings. This is true when it comes to people's sexual needs and desires as much as it is true in any other area. People have a biological drive to engage in sexual activities and are fascinated with many aspects of sexuality. A multimillion-dollar industry has evolved that supplies pornographic material which enables some people to experience sexual pleasure and release.

Definitions of what is considered pornographic must be viewed within the context of a society's views on sexuality in general. The sexual and erotic imagery that is commonplace in the media today would have seemed jarring, even appalling, to many people in the 1940's, let alone people in nineteenth century Victorian England, where even piano legs were often covered with cloth to make them seem more modest. Sex pervades the media today to the extent that people who do not seek suggestive or sexual images often have difficulty avoiding them. It is almost impossible to look at a popular magazine or watch an evening of television without seeing references to sex or advertisements that use sexual messages to sell products. Particularly since the 1960's, advertisers have used nudity and the suggestion of intercourse to sell everything from tires to perfume in the hope that consumers will identify with the sexually attractive people in their ads and will believe that using the advertised product will make them just as desirable.

Defining and labeling pornography is difficult because there is no true societal consensus on what types of sexually oriented material are acceptable and what types are unacceptable. (Two major exceptions are the broad objections to the depiction of children in sexual situations and to violence and cruelty being linked to explicit sexual depictions.) Opinions vary among subgroups in society and from individual to individual. What one person views as pornography may be seen by another as a literary classic or as harmless entertainment. Therefore, the federal government has, since the late 1950's, tried to minimize its involvement in "legislating morality."

The words "erotic," "pornographic," and "obscene" are sometimes used to distinguish among different types of sexual materials for legal purposes. "Erotica" comes from the Greek word for sexual love. It refers to sexual materials that are not thought to be demeaning or degrading. The term "pornography," on the other hand, comes from the Greek for prostitution and refers to materials that are demeaning or degrading.

Some see the terms erotic and pornographic as being essentially interchangeable and instead draw a distinction between soft-core and hard-core pornography. With reference to visual materials, soft-core erotica or pornography ranges from nude and suggestive photographs to depictions of sexual acts that are suggestive rather than explicit. Hard-core pornography, on the other hand, is defined as sexual material that is explicit in the depiction of the genitals and sexual activities.

In American law, the term "obscenity" is used for materials that are deemed sexually offensive and immoral to the extent that they can be held to be illegal. (In its original use, the term referred to anything that should be kept from sight; it was not applied exclusively to sexual matters.) Under this concept, something can be considered erotic or pornographic but not obscene, and therefore can be legal. The First Amendment to the Constitution, providing freedom of speech and of the press, is often cited in the defense of allowing sexually explicit materials to be available. Material is protected by the First Amendment unless it is deemed obscene.

The first American law concerning sexual materials was the Comstock Act, passed in 1873. It made the mailing of any material considered obscene to be a felony. Even information on birth control was at one time not allowed to be sent through the mail; conception, after all, involves sex. The 1973 Supreme Court case *Miller v. State of California*, however, significantly changed the interpretation of the law by instituting a narrow definition of what could be considered obscene. To be obscene, material must be devoid of any "serious literary, artistic, political, or scientific value" and must be "patently offensive." Moreover, it must be found that the average person, applying "contemporary community standards," would say that the work, overall, appeals to the prurient interest. This last item introduced the idea that different "communities" may have differing standards on what material is prurient and offensive, thereby making the definition of what constitutes obscenity even more difficult.

Pornography in the United States may be said to have entered a new era in the early 1980's, and the change was attributable to technology. The rapid proliferation of videocassette recorders (VCRs) enabled people to buy or rent sexually explicit videos and view them in the privacy of their own homes. Previously, in order to watch sexually explicit films, people had to either go to theaters that specialized in such films, go to adult book stores or arcades, or buy 8 millimeter films. The home market for pornographic videos expanded rapidly and dramatically. It was estimated in the early 1990's that X-rated videotapes accounted for about one-sixth of the stock of video stores and for perhaps nearly two-fifths of video rentals. Surveys suggested that about one-third of adult males and one-fifth of adult females had seen an X-rated video within the previous year. In addition, the expansion of cable television systems provided a market for sexually explicit films, although when broadcast via cable the most explicit scenes are sometimes cut or electronically masked. These two markets for film and video pornography created a large industry and because it was clear that even many "suburban housewives" were watching these materials, made it nearly impossible for it to be deemed legally obscene.

Nevertheless, over the years there have been many attempts by citizens' groups, local governments, and school boards to ban some sexually explicit materials. They are usually opposed by others who argue that such bans violate the First Amendment. The problem is always where the line should be drawn. Music is also subject to regulation under the law; in 1990, an album by rap group 2 Live Crew was ruled obscene by a federal court.

The United States is one of the few countries in the world that guarantees freedom of speech to its citizens. Many people are offended by some of the sexually explicit material available, but regulating what people are allowed to read, hear, or watch is always a controversial issue. Banning certain material, it has frequently been argued, could have serious repercussions for the right to free speech in general.

Applications

President Lyndon B. Johnson formed the U.S. Commission on Obscenity and Pornography in the late 1960's; it consisted primarily of scientists. The commission's 1971 report confirmed that men and women are sexually aroused by pornography and erotica and concluded that general behavior was not affected by it in negative ways. Moreover, the report referenced a study in Denmark showing that an increase in the availability of pornography because of legalization resulted in a decreased number of sex crimes.

Studies conducted in Canada and England either supported the commission's findings or produced primarily inconclusive results. It was in the early to mid-1980's that evidence began to surface suggesting that, in fact, some men are negatively affected by pornography. A 1984 study found that some men were likely to be aggressive and have negative views of women after viewing violent pornography, especially violent materials that showed women having a positive reaction to being raped.

As a result of studies conducted in the 1980's, President Ronald Reagan formed the United States Attorney General's Commission on Obscenity and Pornography, also known as the Meese Commission. The Meese Commission drew very different conclusions than had the earlier commission. It claimed in 1985 to have found a causal connection between exposure to sexual materials and sexual behavior. The commission made about a hundred recommendations to try to prevent the distribution of erotic materials.

There were many criticisms of the Meese Commission's work, however; even some commission members were critical of the published report, saying that while they found pornography objectionable and offensive to women, the panel's report was flawed and prepared too hurriedly. First, the commission funded no original work. Second, some of its legal recommendations did not follow from its data. Social scientists proceeded to point out that what the research showed was not that exposure to aggressive or violent pornography affects sexual behavior in itself but that it affects aggressive behavior. It appears that although the viewing of aggression often leads to aggressive behavior, it is not the viewing of sexual behavior that leads to aggressive behavior. It may actually be that pornography helps some viewers or readers lose sexual energy that might otherwise lead to sexual crimes. In other words, those who are going to victimize will most likely do so regardless of their use of pornographic materials.

More recent research has shown what happens when adults watch or read violent pornographic materials. Viewing sex and violence combined tends to increase males' acceptance of aggression toward females. In these materials, people who perpetrate violence are rarely shown in a negative light and are rarely shown being punished. Evidence suggests that society should be most concerned about the harmful effects of exposure to violent images that portray the myth that women enjoy, or in some way benefit from, rape or other forms of sexual violence.

Child pornography is probably the most destructive form of pornography available. Authorities estimate that thousands of children under the age of eighteen become involved in child pornography each year. Many of them have run away from home; many also become prostitutes. Children who get pulled into this business suffer extreme emotional damage. Psychologists report that children involved in sexual acts and nude modeling often become withdrawn, anxious, depressed, guilty, and distrustful of adults in general. As adults they often find themselves incapable of having normal intimate relationships.

Lawmakers have criminalized child pornography, creating strict laws against all forms of it. For example, in 1982 the United States Supreme Court unanimously ruled that publishers and distributors of child pornography could be prosecuted for child abuse; prosecutors do not have to prove that the material was obscene. Similarly, the Child Protection and Obscenity Act of 1988 provides stiff penalties for those who produce, distribute or sell child pornography.

Because children are incapable of giving informed consent when it comes to sex, perpetrators can be charged under child abuse laws, avoiding arguments about First Amendment rights. Many believe that child abuse is the more appropriate charge, claiming that depictions of either nude or clothed children are not necessarily obscene but that forcing children to participate in pornography is. Child pornography is presently the only type of sexually explicit material that is legally banned in the United States.

Context

Throughout history, sex has had a place in literature, art, and mythology. The ancient Greeks described fertility rites in explicit language, while the Romans told wild stories of sexual adventures. During the Victorian Age of the nineteenth century, societal forces vigorously attempted to decrease the amount of erotic writing available to the public. They were never completely successful; pornography was even sold on the streets of London. Eroticism became more prevalent in English literature in the twentieth century. Novels such as D. H. Lawrence's *Lady Chatterly's Lover* (1928) and James Joyce's *Ulysses* (1922) were highly controversial in the United States. *Ulysses* was banned until 1933, when U.S. District Judge John M. Woolsey finally declared it to be acceptable because of the author's attempt to devise a new literary method. Since the 1960's in American society, there have only been local efforts to censor erotic literature.

Magazines were the most widely available purveyors of visual pornography until the 1980's. In 1933 *Esquire: The Magazine for Men* was the first magazine to discuss sex in such a way as to make the topic acceptable, at least to some. *Playboy* magazine was introduced in 1953 and, with the exception of *National Geographic*, was the first widely distributed magazine to show photographs of bare breasts and buttocks. Balancing its photographs with articles on men's issues and respected fiction, *Playboy* reached a peak of more than seven million readers in the early 1970's. By 1987 this figure had fallen to around 3.4 million. Other sexually oriented magazines followed, including *Playgirl* for female readers. In 1970 *Penthouse* was the first widely distributed magazine to show models' pubic hair. Pubic hair is now commonly shown, but before the time of *Penthouse*, it was hidden with clothing or removed from photographs via special techniques such as air brushing.

The degree of censorship in the motion picture industry has varied through the years. It was present but not especially strong in film's earlier years, but it became quite restrictive with the mandatory institution of the Hays Code in 1934. The code was put into practice because outcries against indecency in film caused the federal government to pressure Hollywood into regulating its production. Prime among the forces pushing for regulation was the Catholic church's Legion of Decency. Rules proliferated under the Hays Code; it prohibited long or overly passionate kisses. If a couple was shown in bed together, one person's foot was supposed to be touching the floor. The Hays Code remained more or less in effect through the 1960's; then, in 1968, the G, PG, R, and X rating system was put into effect. A 1967 Swedish film entitled *I Am Curious (Yellow)* became a cause célèbre when it was seized by U.S. Customs agents on its way into the country; it later became the first X-rated film to show in regular (as opposed to adult) theaters. The film was actually quite mild compared with later X-rated films. The 1968 rating system was designed to protect potential viewers. Surprisingly, however, rape scenes are far more common in R-rated and PG-rated films than in X-rated ones. In fact, most X-rated films show mutually consensual sex rather than forced sex or sexual violence.

Bibliography

Burstyn, Varda, ed. *Women Against Censorship*. Vancouver, Canada: Douglas & McIntyre, 1985. From a unique viewpoint, the contributors argue that women have nothing to gain by advocating censorship and are unanimous in the view that censorship will be used against women who seek permanent changes in the status quo in that censorship will perpetuate the conditions that promote violence against women. Positive solutions and suggestions for change are provided.

Donnerstein, Edward, Daniel Linz, and Steven Penrod. *The Question of Pornography*. New York: Free Press, 1987. A comprehensive summary is given of the scientific research on the effects of sexually explicit images as they influence the behavior of people. Research by the Commission on Obscenity and Pornography is included, in addition to laboratory studies on the effects of pornography on antisocial attitudes, to determine whether it is the sexual explicitness of the material or messages about violence that are harmful. Contemporary legal and regulatory issues are discussed.

Kappeler, Susanne. *The Pornography of Representation*. Minneapolis: University of Minnesota Press, 1986. According to the author, pornography needs to be examined from the perspective of how the material is represented, as opposed to focusing on the content per se. She presents examples from art, literature, and the cinema.

Stoller, Robert J. *Porn: Myths for the Twentieth Century*. New Haven, Conn.: Yale University Press, 1991. Written by a psychoanalyst, the book contains case studies of people who create and produce pornography. The author examines the origin and dynamics of erotic excitement.

Zillmann, Dolf, and Jennings Bryant, eds. *Pornography: Research Advances and Policy Considerations*. Hillsdale, N.J.: Lawrence Erlbaum, 1989. An edited book with chapters clearly presenting controversial issues on pornography and sex offenders, child pornography and sex rings, the case against censorship, and sex education to immunize against the possible effects of pornography.

Deborah McDonald Winters

Cross-References

POSTINDUSTRIAL SOCIETIES

Type of sociology: Social structure
Field of study: Types of societies

Postindustrial society is a late twentieth century concept that highlights the declining dependence of societies on manufacturing, the rise of new service industries, and a new emphasis on the role of knowledge in production, consumption, and leisure.

Principal terms

CONVERGENCE: a process in which the structures of different industrial societies increasingly resemble one another

INFORMATION SOCIETIES: societies centered on knowledge and the production of new knowledge; synonymous with postindustrial society

LEISURE SOCIETY: any society in which work is losing its former centrality

MANAGERIAL REVOLUTION: the growth in the number and professionalization of managers who do not own the companies they control

ORGANIZED COMPLEXITY: a metaphor for large organizations and systems with numerous variables that require a certain method of management; there are three categories: "complex simplicity," "disorganized complexity," and "organized complexity"

POSTCAPITALIST SOCIETIES: societies in which owners of capital have conceded power to professional managers

Overview

The concept of postindustrial society is based on the assumption that human societies evolve, with the postindustrial being the most advanced level of development. The present concept was formulated by Daniel Bell in *The Coming of Post-Industrial Society* (1973) and Alan Touraine in *The Post-Industrial Society* (1971). Touraine's work was less popular than Bell's and placed more emphasis on the conflicts that may arise in a postindustrial society.

Although Bell is not a determinist, he predicts that a postindustrial society will emerge by the early twenty-first century. He explains that a postindustrial society results from changes within the social structure, the transformation of the economy, and the new relationship between theory and empiricism. His formulations deal with five dimensions:

1. Economic sector: the change from a goods-producing society to a service economy;

2. Occupational distribution: the preeminence of the professions and the technical class;

3. Axial principle: the centrality of theoretical knowledge as the source of innovation and of policy formulation for the society;

4. Future orientation: the control of technology and technological assessment;

5. Decision making: the creation of a new "intellectual technology."

The principal economic activity of postindustrial societies is providing services that depend on knowledge and the creation of knowledge. This does not mean that agriculture and manufacturing disappear in a postindustrial society; but as technology becomes more labor saving, displaced or future workers will shift to the service sector of the economy.

The strength of a postindustrial society is based on knowledge, the processing of information, and the production of knowledge. All knowledge is not, however, of equal value. In postindustrial societies, theoretical knowledge is most important. Thus, social resources are invested in education, research institutions, and activities that create the knowledge base for scientists, engineers, and political decision makers, because technological superiority is considered the prime basis for power and development.

With the increased efficiency and rapidity of communication, technological development, and transportation, there will also be greater population mobility. Thus, within postindustrial societies, greater sexual equality, better tolerance for different lifestyles, and mutually enhancing relationships between different subcultures ensue.

A new basis for social organization is also formed. Power is based on knowledge rather than wealth. Thus, knowledge-based professional and occupational groups achieve dominance in postindustrial societies. As a result, a type of postcapitalist society develops in which owners of capital concede power to professional managers. Owners hire managers to run their enterprises, and the managers have the power in the organizations because of their knowledge. In essence, a "managerial revolution" takes place, with a divorce between ownership and control being created. This is especially the case where ownership is diffused among numerous shareholders of a large, technologically complex organization. Control is in the hands of managers or, in the case of government, controlled by bureaucrats.

Another result is that the traditional conflict of interests between employer and employee is replaced by this new authority relationship. A new upper class develops in which a system of interlocking directorships controls large amounts of capital, forming a "managerial technostructure."

Since the advent of capitalism in the fifteenth century, economic institutions have been perceived as extremely important. They are still crucial, but now economic institutions are more dependent on technology. It is the creation of new technology that prevents economies from becoming stagnant. The influx of capital has limitations, but new technology increases speed and efficiency, which enables the economy to grow. It also decreases the need for labor, especially unskilled and semiskilled labor. Thus, more and more people move to the service sector of the economy as employment in the manufacturing and agricultural sectors decreases.

A leisure society develops in which work loses its centrality. As the postindustrial society emerges, fewer hours of paid employment are required and a greater concern for leisure results—in other words, leisure takes on the centrality formerly held by paid employment.

Postindustrial writers further hypothesize that as more and more societies enter the postindustrial phase, a process called "convergence" takes place. Explicitly developed in *Industrialism and Industrial Man* (1962), edited by Clark Kerr, the concept postulates that as different societies industrialize, they increasingly resemble one another. Based on functionalist thinking, the argument holds that as different societies enter the postindustrial phase, they face similar problems and implement comparable solutions. Consequently, as a society commits itself to the development of science and technology for industrial production, the need arises for an educated, mobile, and diversified labor force.

Applications

To demonstrate the actual workings of a postindustrial society, Daniel Bell uses the United States as a case in point. He shows that the creation of a service economy results in the majority of the work force being engaged in services such as trade, finance, transport, health, recreation, research, education, and government. The majority of the U.S. population was initially involved in agriculture or worked in the rural sector. When the country industrialized at the turn of the century, the majority moved to urban areas and worked in manufacturing and blue-collar occupations. Presently, more than half of the total employment and more than half of the Gross National Product is in the service sector. Most other economies of the world are based on the extraction of natural resources, with 70 percent of the labor force working in the agrarian sector.

In the industrial period of America's development, semiskilled workers were the largest single category in the labor force. They could be trained quickly to do simple routine operations such as machine work. In the development of the American postindustrial society, the professional and technical class has become preeminent. In this situation, scientists and engineers are the key groups. In the United States, professional employment—jobs requiring college education—has grown at twice the rate of nonprofessional employment. White-collar workers outnumber blue-collar workers, and the growth rate of the professional and technical class is twice that of the nonprofessional labor force. In addition, the number of scientists and engineers is three times that of the working population.

In a postindustrial society, theoretical knowledge is preeminent. In the industrial United States, knowledge of the organization of workers and machines to produce goods was required. Most of the major industries of the industrial period were based on the work of creative inventors and talented tinkerers, who were indifferent to science and to the fundamental laws underlying their investigations. Men such as William Kelly and Sir Henry Bessemer, who independently created the oxidation process that made possible the steel converter that led to the mass production of steel, are examples of such inventors. Neither knew anything about the microstructure of steel. Alexander Graham Bell, the inventor of the telephone, was an elocutionist who became an electrician to earn his living.

Postindustrial America, however, focuses on the means that define the characteristics of a social system so that axial principles can be understood and a conceptual scheme of society can be developed. Such knowledge has been important for all societies, but in a postindustrial society, social planning and direction are based on theoretical formulations, not empiricism. It is on this theoretical knowledge that planning and forecasting are based. Thus, in the United States, much government economic forecasting and policy is based on John Maynard Keynes' theoretical formulations. Military strategy is based on computer programs, the models of which are based on theoretical formulations. Social welfare policy is based on sociological presuppositions.

Planning and controlling technology is another dimension. In the United States, using theory, the government determines social direction and the kinds of technologies it wants to develop. The formation of those systems is encouraged or discouraged by government grants, investments, regulations, and other policy formulations.

In the industrial period of U.S. development, the industrial growth was made possible as institutions (such as banks and government levies, loans, and taxes) devoted to the creation of savings and capital formation developed. The ability to reinvest is what W. W. Rostow, in *The Stages of Economic Growth* (1960), called the "take-off" point for modernization. For an economy to avoid stagnation, however, new technology must be developed to maintain increasing production and achieve higher standards of living—investing in old systems is not enough. With the institution of planned technological change, a novel phase in economic history emerged that involved the conscious planning of technological change to reduce the uncertainty of the future of the economy.

Thus, the greatest development of postindustrial society is the rise of a new intellectual technology. This is, in essence, the management of large-scale systems with numerous interacting variables, which have to be coordinated to achieve specific goals; the metaphor for this activity is "organized complexity." The solutions to problems in this realm are stated in probabilities, and as a result, new schemes such as information theory, cybernetics, decision theory, game theory, and utility theory were developed. This was a radical change from the industrial period when problems only had one or two variables. In economics, it was supply and demand; in politics, it was balance of power. Later, systems such as the radio, automobile, and airplane, with three or four variables, came to be considered. These initial systems of around four variables are termed "complex simplicity." The next level of problems dealt with the ordering of gross numbers, such as the motion of molecules and rates of life expectancies. This level, "disorganized complexity," requires advancement in probability and statistics, with results presented in terms of chance. In the postindustrial society, "organized complexity" operates. Organized complexity deals with large-scale systems that have large numbers of interacting variables in order to achieve a specific goal.

Context

The concept of a postindustrial society is rooted in a long tradition of believing in progress. Starting with Saint Augustine's *The City of God*, Greek and Hebraic traditions fused into a philosophy of development that emphasized progress—the gradual improvement of societies. Progress has continued to be an assumption in the West ever since. Eighteenth century philosophers, such as Claude-Henri de Saint-Simon and his secretary August Comte, who coined the term "sociology," analyzed industrial society and suggested a plan for its organization. These two, among others, operated under the assumption that there are discoverable laws of social development, believing that they, as sociologists, were witnessing the elevation of human life to a higher plane. Thus, they established an assumption for sociology that the futures of societies could be predicted by means of scientific principles, since societies progressed.

It was believed that the Industrial Revolution—the term was coined by the French—would result in industrialization, which would bring significant improvement. Most scholars realized the magnitude of the social crisis that was being created, but scholars such as Saint-Simon, Comte, Herbert Spencer, and Émile Durkheim saw the disintegration that was being brought on by industrialization. Karl Marx and Max Weber were concerned that capitalism would lead to the dehumanization and mechanization of society. All these scholars, however, sought means to obtain a speedy social reintegration.

The industrial process was perceived as having the following characteristics: urbanization, population explosion, and a decreased sense of community (relationships became contractual rather than being based on community, especially blood relationships, real or assumed). Greater labor specialization developed, and industrialization was linked with a democratic and egalitarian society, with centralized planning centered in the state. Thus, religion was to decrease in importance, with a secularized, rational bureaucracy and mode of thinking coming to prominence. The nineteenth century thinkers were wrong, however, about the mode, speed, and direction of the social change taking place. The mode of change was perceived as evolutionary, not as a result of external or internal forces; the time and tempo were interpreted as revolutionary, involving the development of a new system, rather than a continuation of principles rooted in the past; and industrialization was seen to reach a terminal point that all societies would reach if they industrialized—hence the term "postindustrial."

It was World War I that shattered the idea of inevitable progress. Out of the 1914-1940 period in which doubt, dislocation, and pessimism reigned came confidence, growth, and optimism. This was a reflection of the prosperity and high production that occurred after World War II.

In the 1950's, speculation concerning the future was out of fashion, but by the late 1960's, long-range forecasting was emphasized. This change took place because governments became committed to welfare and planned for economic growth. There were two opposing views of industrialization; one group believed in the triumph of industrialization, while another saw it as problematical. There was also a renewed interest in social change, which was brought about by the Soviet Union's launching of the satellite *Sputnik*. Thus, futurology took on importance in social science.

The futurologist rejected the nineteenth century scheme of an "industrial society," perceiving the present as a transitional stage in the process of moving toward a postindustrial society. Diverse concepts, such as Amitai Etzioni's "post-modern era," Kenneth Boulding's "post-civilized society," and Daniel Bell's "post-industrial society," started from different perspectives and converged on the key ideas of "the knowledge society," power being passed to a "technostructure," the development of a "post-scarcity society," a retreat from the "Protestant ethic," an increased emphasis on leisure, and the development of a "personal service society." It was Daniel Bell's *The Coming of Post-Industrial Society* that, in 1973, brought these ideas together in the most systematic way possible. Postindustrial society is certainly plausible as a concept. Bell's classic work is well argued and verified statistically. Thus, there is no doubt that many of the changes noted by Bell are occurring. Industrial societies such as the United States are largely white-collar, service economies. This is largely because multinational corporations have their headquarters in postindustrial areas and their production plants in industrial communities. In addition, much of industrial production has been computerized and bureaucratized, and there has been increased growth in research and development in corporations, universities, and governments. The result is that a new order is developing.

Some related concepts do not show such a clear direction. The advent of the managerial revolution is not clearly forthcoming. Owners are not relinquishing their capital to managers. It must be kept in mind, however, that the dividing lines between manager, owner, and controller are not always clear.

Concerning the leisure society, studies show that more leisure was present in preindustrial communities, and concerning convergence, there are similarities among industrial and postindustrial societies. In countries of similar economic and industrial development (such as England, Japan, and the United States), however, concepts such as values in the workplace, family structure, and religious orientation are not uniform.

Recently, the writings of Ivan Illich and E. F. Schumacher have defined postindustrialism differently. Instead of emphasizing aspects that are a continuation of industrialization, as Bell has done, these writers are trying to go beyond industrialization, using advanced concepts in technology and social thinking. Thus, they look to a society in which technology and social organization are used to decrease paid work and increase leisure. An "intermediate technology" can be developed, Schumacher argues, to deliver goods and services without the cumbersome organization and impersonal atmosphere of mass industrial and postindustrial conglomerates.

Bibliography

Bell, Daniel. *The Coming of Post-Industrial Society*. New York: Basic Books, 1973. This book sets forth the current meaning of a postindustrial society.

Dahrendorf, Ralf. *Class and Class Conflict in an Industrial Society*. London: Routledge & Kegan Paul, 1967. This book develops the concept of managerial/ownership conflict, with a "managerial revolution" taking place in which managers will gain control of the production process.

Galbraith, John Kenneth. *The New Industrial State*. Boston: Houghton Mifflin, 1967. Galbraith describes how the "technostructure" will eventually be brought under the control of the intelligentsia, who are highly trained experts working in committees to pursue organizational goals.

Kumar, Krishan. *Prophecy and Progress*. London: Allen Lane, 1978. An outstanding book setting forth the development of social thought concerning industrial and postindustrial societies.

Schumacher, E. F. *Small Is Beautiful*. New York: Harper & Row, 1973. A classic book arguing that societies should change from the current large-scale industrial and profit-oriented economic systems to organizations that are smaller, emphasize ethical principles, and treat people well.

Weaver, Warren. "Science and Complexity." In *The Scientists Speak*, edited by Warren Weaver. New York: Boni & Gaer, 1947. This work sets forth a useful classification scheme concerning the development of intellectual technology.

Arthur W. Helweg

Cross-References

Capitalism, 191; Computers, Automation, and the Economy, 316; Deindustrialization in the United States, 462; Industrial and Postindustrial Economies, 940; The Industrial Revolution and Mass Production, 946; Industrial Societies, 953; Industrial Sociology, 960.

POVERTY: ANALYSIS AND OVERVIEW

Type of sociology: Social stratification
Field of study: Poverty

Poverty refers to the status of individuals, families, or households whose income or consumption falls below a determined or fixed standard of need or within a stated fraction of a social average. Sociologists have devoted extensive study to determining the prevalence, causes, and effects of poverty.

Principal terms
ABSOLUTE POVERTY: conditions under which one's consumption or income falls below a fixed or objective standard of need, based on subsistence or minimum comfort levels
POVERTY AREAS: census tracts in metropolitan counties and minor civil divisions in nonmetropolitan counties with a poverty rate of 20 percent or more
POVERTY THRESHOLDS: the dollar amounts that the Bureau of the Census uses to determine the poverty status of families and unrelated individuals; they are based on an average of a sample of families, applied to all families and unrelated individuals, and weighted accordingly by the presence or absence of children
RELATIVE POVERTY: a measure of poverty achieved by comparing one's condition to a social average—for example, one-half the average or median income of society at large
SUBJECTIVE POVERTY: a measure of poverty achieved by comparing one's consumption or income level to social attitudes (gleaned, for example, through polling data) about what constitutes a decent standard of living

Overview

In the early 1990's, poverty resurfaced—after some years during which it received relatively little attention—as both a subject of scholarly inquiry and a matter of national concern. In *The Poverty Debate: Politics and the Poor in America* (1992), sociologist C. Emory Burton notes that poverty has become a major subject of academic study. The May, 1992, riots in Los Angeles focused attention on the role poverty played as an underlying factor of the disturbances. Several major issues dominate contemporary concern among scholars and policy makers about poverty; among them are the measurement and extent of poverty, the culture of poverty, the underclass, the homeless, welfare, and workfare.

Poverty is most often viewed in one of three ways. Absolute poverty refers to conditions in which individual, family, or household consumption or income falls below a fixed or objective standard of need, such as a standard based on subsistence or minimum comfort levels. In determining the extent of poverty in the United States, the U.S. Census Bureau relies on an absolute standard. Relative poverty compares an individual's or household's condition with a social average—for example one-half the average or median income of society at large. Measures of relative poverty range from fairly simple schemes (such as arbitrarily labeling the bottom 10 or 20 percent of the income distribution as "poor") to more complex schemes, such as examining each individual's consumption of a long list of commodities and social services and then calculating a "deprivation index" based on the number of areas in which the individual's consumption falls below social norms. Finally, subjective poverty compares individual or household consumption or income level to social attitudes about what constitutes a decent standard of living. Subjective definitions are based on surveys or polling data that use households' own assessments of the minimum or "just sufficient" amounts of income or consumption needed by people like them. Both the relative and subjective definitions of poverty are problematic in that they are "moving targets," varying beyond the point where programmatic responses to ameliorate poverty can be viably designed and implemented. Since the U.S. government uses an absolute definition, the remainder of this essay deals with that conceptualization of poverty.

In 1992, 36.9 million persons, 14.5 percent of the entire civilian noninstitutional population, fell below the official poverty level, an increase from the 35.7 million poor persons, or 14.2 percent of the population in 1991. The poverty rate for children under eighteen (21.9 percent) was slightly higher than the 21.6 percent in 1991 and was the highest since 1983. It was nearly as high as it was in 1964 (23 percent), when the Johnson Administration declared its War on Poverty. Twenty-five percent of children under six fell below poverty thresholds. Nearly half of all black children under eighteen were poor.

The distribution of poverty varies along social and economic variables such as age, race, gender, education, the presence or absence of children under eighteen, and region of the country. In 1991, for example, 8.7 million (53.7 percent) of the 14.2 million poor children under eighteen lived in female-headed households with no male householder present. Nearly 4 million elderly, more than 12 percent of the population, were also poor in 1991. Of these elderly, 2.6 million lived in households as unrelated individuals, and the majority (by a 4:1 ratio) were women. Social scientists Eugene Smolensky, Sheldon Danziger, and Peter Gottschalk, in their essay "The Declining Significance of Age in the United States: Trends in the Well-Being of Children and the Elderly," in *The Vulnerable* (1988), edited by John L. Palmer, Timothy Smeeding, and Barbara Boyle Torrey, noted an inverse relationship between the poverty rates for the elderly and for children in the 1970's and 1980's. The poverty rate for all elderly persons fell substantially since 1939, but particularly since 1969, while the poverty rate for all children also fell substantially between 1939 and 1969, but rose since 1969. Beginning in 1974, the poverty rate among children exceeded that among the elderly.

Children and the elderly continue to be two of the country's most vulnerable groups with respect to poverty. In 1991, half the nation's poor were either children under eighteen years (40.2 percent) or elderly people (10.6 percent). A higher proportion of elderly than nonelderly were concentrated between 100 and 125 percent of their respective poverty thresholds. Consequently, 19.1 percent of the nation's 11.8 million "near poor" persons were elderly, compared with 10.6 percent of persons below the official poverty level.

The distribution of poverty in the United States also varies by race. In 1991, 17.7 million (9.4 percent) non-Hispanic whites fell below the official poverty level, contrasted with 10.2 million (32.7 percent) black, 6.3 million (28.7 percent) Hispanic, and 1 million (13.8 percent) Asian and Pacific Islander Americans. Despite the overall lower poverty rates for whites, the majority of poor persons in 1991 were white (66.5 percent). Blacks constituted 28.7 percent of all persons below the poverty level, a proportion that has remained fairly constant since the mid-1960's. In 1991, about 17.8 percent of the poor were persons of Hispanic origin, well above the 8.8 percent Hispanic representation in the population as a whole.

By region in 1991, the Northeast had the lowest poverty rate (12.2 percent). As has historically been the case, the poverty rate was highest in the South (16.0 percent). The South continued to have a disproportionately large share of the nation's poverty population; 38.6 percent of the poor lived in the South in 1991, compared with 33.5 percent of the U.S. population above the poverty level. The poverty rate in the West (14.3 percent) was higher than that in the Midwest (13.2 percent) in 1991. Based on a 3-year average (1989 to 1991), state poverty rates ranged from 5.8 percent in Connecticut to 23.8 percent in Mississippi. About 34.9 percent of the nation's poor in 1991 lived in areas of high poverty concentration or so-called poverty areas. Blacks living in cities, regardless of economic status, were more concentrated in poverty areas than whites or persons of Hispanic origin. About 52.9 percent of blacks living in central cities lived in poverty areas, and 64.3 percent of poor blacks living in cities were concentrated in poverty areas. Only 16.6 percent of all central city whites lived in poverty areas, while 37.9 percent of poor whites did; 43.4 percent of central city persons of Hispanic origin lived in poverty areas, while 57.7 percent of the poor did.

Applications

There has been much debate about the nature and causes of poverty in contemporary America. Political scientist Lawrence M. Mead, in *The New Politics of Poverty: The Nonworking Poor in America* (1992), for example, asserts that poverty is attributable to a lack of the work ethic—that the poor have voluntarily chosen to shun work. For the most part, Mead attributes poverty less to structural factors (such as the proliferation of low-wage jobs and the loss of high-paying manufacturing inner-city jobs) that limit opportunity and more to personal failures and cultural shortcomings that reflect a sense of internalized helplessness. The structural versus cultural polemic is most profound in the research and debate about what has been termed the "underclass." *Fortune* magazine editorial board member Myron Magnet furthers the cultural view of poverty in *The Dream and the Nightmare: The Sixties' Legacy to the Underclass* (1993). Magnet notes the self-defeating behavior of the underclass. Like Mead, Magnet saw the 1980's as boom years creating millions of jobs and offering a way out of poverty to almost any poor person with the willingness and discipline to work.

On the other side of the issue, sociologists Herbert J. Gans, William J. Wilson, and Christopher Jencks and historians Michael Katz and Mark Stern, among many others, attribute the preponderance of poverty more to structural than cultural factors. They view with alarm the moral overtones that pervade Mead's, Magnet's, and others' analyses of poverty and diatribes against the underclass. For them, erosion of the work ethic is not the relevant poverty-related issue. Instead, they link poverty to the erosion of jobs and lack of public will to fund the types of programs and policies that might more adequately deal with the issue. For example, in an article entitled "Making Jobs," in *The Nation* (September 20, 1993), Gans iterates the need for the government to start deliberately creating new jobs, despite the successful Senate filibuster against the Clinton Administration's proposed economic stimulus package. There is sufficient evidence to support challenging the "erosion of the work ethic" arguments. In 1991, according to the U.S. Bureau of the Census, 39.8 percent of poor persons fifteen years old and older worked, and 9.0 percent worked year-round, full-time. As expected, the percentages were much higher for nonpoor persons: 72.0 percent worked and 45.0 percent worked year-round, full-time in 1991. Nevertheless, despite some slight variations, the proportions of poor adults who worked and who worked year-round, full-time in 1991 were not statistically different from those in any year since 1978. There was no great diminution of labor force participation on the part of poor persons throughout the 1980's "boom."

In addition to the underclass debate, there is much contemporary discussion about the relations between poverty and the changes in the structure of the American family. Although children and the elderly are often cast as the two most vulnerable segments of American society, many scholars, public policy analysts, political figures, and others have expressed concern about increases in the numbers of out-of-wedlock childbirths and of female-headed poor households. Gertrude Schaffner Goldberg, in her chapter entitled "The United States: Feminization of Poverty Amidst Plenty," in *The Feminization of Poverty* (1990), which she coauthored with Eleanor Kremen, summarizes the factors and forces contributing to what she and others call the feminization of poverty. Goldberg notes the paradox that at the very time when women have been "emancipating themselves from unpaid domestic work," female-headed households with no husband present have become preponderant among the poor. Earlier, policy analyst Irwin Garfinkle and sociologist Sara S. McLanahan characterized female-headed family poverty as a new American dilemma in *Single Mothers and Their Children* (1986). Social science research studies such as Garfinkle and McLanahan's have linked single-headed family households with higher rates of poverty, school dropouts, and delinquency. The issue about the consequences of changes in family structure remains hotly contested terrain in academic, political, and popular literature.

Finally, no other poverty-related issue generated as much concern throughout the 1980's and early 1990's as the problem of homelessness. Two works highlight the salient issues. From the left of the political spectrum, policy analyst Joel Blau in *The*

Visible Poor: Homelessness in the United States (1992) views contemporary homelessness as a product of a transformed U.S. economy. From the right, former antipoverty planner in President Lyndon Johnson's Office of Economic Opportunity Richard White in *Rude Awakenings: What the Homeless Crisis Tells Us* (1992) argues that there are far greater numbers of mentally ill people and drug addicts among the homeless than appear in official reports. Although White views the homeless as more personally responsible for their plight that does Blau, both maintain that the changes in the American economy are part of the story. As with poverty in general, homelessness has multiple causes that defy either/or categorization of fault and that demand societal responses that address structural as well as personal factors.

Context

Throughout the twentieth century, if not most of its history, the United States has grappled with the problem of poverty. Richard K. Caputo notes that concern with identifying poor persons and groups of poor people goes back as far as the mid-nineteenth century. For the most part, those who described poverty prior to the 1960's took what might be called snapshots of the poor population rather than making detailed studies. Robert Hunter's 1904 classic *Poverty*, for example, estimated that 10 million Americans (about 12 percent of the population) were poor and that 20 percent lived in northern industrial areas, while 10 percent lived in the South. Such estimations, however, failed to distinguish the short-term from the long-term poor and therefore underestimated the poverty problem. In the 1960's, such writers as Michael Harrington conveyed the idea that most early twentieth century poverty resulted from economic weaknesses endemic to the development of industrial capitalism. By the 1960's and afterward, however, the United States' "new" poor comprised deprived minorities who were immune to the country's economic progress. Abandoned and hopeless, they lived in what has been called a "culture of poverty." Historian James T. Patterson chronicles this development in *America's Struggle Against Poverty, 1900-1985* (1986).

Modern technology and more sophisticated statistical tools have enabled researchers to conduct longitudinal studies of the poor, and these have challenged some of the snapshot views about the nature and extent of poverty. Greg J. Duncan's *Years of Poverty, Years of Plenty* (1984) reports findings from a "truly unique" social study, the Panel Study of Income Dynamics, originally funded by the Office of Economic Opportunity in 1968 and undertaken by the Survey Research Center of the University of Michigan. According to the study, by and large, many more Americans become poor during the course of a given year than had been previously assumed, but the durations of poverty for most tend to be short-term. About 2.6 percent of the population can be viewed as persistently poor—that is, as having an income below the poverty line in eight of ten consecutive years. Economist David T. Ellwood captured the diversity of the poverty population in *Poor Support: Poverty in the American Family* (1988). Ellwood distinguishes two-parent from single-parent poverty and further differentiates these from ghetto poverty. He suggests different legislative, social, and economic policies for each.

Bibliography

Burton, C. Emory. *The Poverty Debate: Politics and the Poor in America*. Westport, Conn.: Praeger, 1992. Includes chapters on the measurement and extent of poverty, the culture of poverty, the underclass, the homeless, welfare, welfare dependency, workfare, solutions to poverty, and political implications, in addition to a theory for reform. In addition, 1990 poverty data are presented in an appendix. The book contains a bibliography, as well as name and subject indexes.

Gans, Herbert J. *People, Plans, and Policies: Essays on Poverty, Racism, and Other National Urban Problems*. New York: Columbia University Press, 1991. This collection of essays devotes two of its five parts to poverty-related matters. Its focus is on how to think about national problems and contains chapters on the uses of poverty, the role of education in the escape from poverty, the black family, and the dangers of the underclass. Contains notes gathered for each chapter at the end of the book and an index.

Magnet, Myron. *The Dream and the Nightmare: The Sixties' Legacy to the Underclass*. New York: William Morrow, 1993. Magnet traces the cultural straitjacket endemic to poverty in the 1980's and 1990's to the liberal and counterculture ideas spawned in the 1960's.

Mead, Lawrence M. *The New Politics of Poverty: The Nonworking Poor in America*. New York: Basic Books, 1992. Mead is primarily concerned with the extent to which segments of the poor population have become dependent on governmental sources of income and other benefits as well as the extent to which these government programs discourage or diminish the work ethic and thereby exacerbate the problems they are meant to ameliorate. There is no bibliography, but the gathered notes are extensive. The book has an index.

Patterson, James T. *America's Struggle Against Poverty, 1900-1985*. Cambridge, Mass.: Harvard University Press, 1986. Patterson explores how and why Americans, especially authorities on poverty and welfare, have altered their fundamental assumptions about the good society during the industrial and postindustrial age. The author notes that major shifts in social philosophy occurred in 1930, 1960, and 1965. In addition to gathered notes by chapter at the end of the text and an index, Patterson describes the major archival sources and other documents used in his research.

Rodgers, Harrell R., Jr. *Poor Women, Poor Families: The Economic Plight of America's Female-Headed Households*. Rev. ed. Armonk, N.Y.: M. E. Sharpe, 1990. This book highlights the plight of America's poor single-parent female households and includes chapters on the feminization of poverty, the social welfare response to female-headed family poverty, and ideas for reforming the American welfare system. Has a reference section and an index.

Richard K. Caputo

Cross-References

Antipoverty Programs, 107; The Feminization of Poverty, 754; The Culture of Poverty, 1460; Poverty: Women and Children, 1466; Poverty and Race, 1472; The Poverty Line and Counting the Poor, 1478; Unemployment and Poverty, 2083; The Urban Underclass and the Rural Poor, 2122; Welfare and Workfare, 2172.

THE CULTURE OF POVERTY

Type of sociology: Social stratification
Field of study: Poverty

The term "culture of poverty" has been used to describe the values, principles, and lifestyles associated with people living at the lowest economic levels of society. Whether there actually is a distinctive "culture" of poverty has been debated, but the concept has at the very least proved useful in the study of how customs and traditions among the poor are handed down from parents to children.

> *Principal terms*
> CULTURE: the way of life of a people, based on their shared values and beliefs
> NONMATERIAL POVERTY: the sense of inferiority that develops among the poor, along with a sense of frustration and resentment resulting from economic inequality
> POVERTY: economic inequality based on an inability to work or by working for low wages
> SOCIAL POVERTY: poverty resulting from economic inequality; the lack of means to provide a minimally acceptable standard of living
> VOLUNTARY POVERTY: the conscious renouncing of wealth and possessions, most often in order to pursue religion, philosophy, or art

Overview

"Culture of poverty" is a term that refers to the pattern of life, the set of beliefs, and the typical behavior found among people who live in an environment dominated by economic deprivation. The word "culture" can be defined as the way in which people live their lives and includes all the habits learned by an individual from other members of the community. In its broadest sense, a culture contains the essential information one needs to live in a given environment. Since the environment found in impoverished communities is built upon deprivation, isolation, discrimination, poor education, lack of jobs, crime, drugs, alcohol abuse, and welfare, the attitudes, expectations, and behavior of residents are shaped by these negative forces.

Oscar Lewis, an American anthropologist famous for his description of the effects of poverty on human lives in *La Vida: A Puerto Rican Family in the Culture of Poverty—San Juan and New York* (1966), believed that the values children learn from their parents about how to survive in such desperate circumstances make them less able to move out of poverty. Lewis suggested that only a violent revolution overturning capitalist society would enable the poor to find dignity and equality. Working within the system would not solve any problems, because the values poor people learn include hatred for education (which rarely helps to get a person out of the slums), self-indulgence (since alcohol and drugs offer a quick way out of misery), and unwillingness to save or sacrifice for the future well-being of one's self or family (since the future offers little hope for improving one's economic circumstances). None of these values leads to educational or occupational advancement. The culture learned by the poor works against their ever getting out of poverty. For things to change, according to Lewis, the environmental conditions need to change.

Culture, then, in this context, refers to the lifestyles of the poor. "Poverty," though, is difficult to define, being relative to time and place. Incomes that define persons as poor in industrialized societies would provide a moderately decent standard of living in many nations of Africa, Asia, and Latin America. Poverty has three different meanings: social poverty, which is defined as economic inequality, or the lack of means to provide a minimally adequate standard of living; pauperism, a word that signifies an inability of individuals to take care of themselves; and voluntary poverty, which includes those who for religious and philosophical reasons give up material possessions to pursue prayer, meditation, or art. In the United States, most of the poor fall into the first two categories and include the unskilled, the uneducated, and a large number of children. As of 1993, the government defined as poor nonfarm families of four with incomes under $12,500, about half the income of an average American family of four. Farm families qualify as poor with slightly less income.

Race itself is not a cause of poverty; however, the American tradition of racial segregation and discrimination has guaranteed that large numbers of African Americans—almost two out of every five—live under the poverty line. The major causes of poverty in the United States are chronic unemployment resulting from low levels of education and lack of skills; low wages in unskilled entry-level occupations as well as in agricultural labor; old age (though the number of elderly Americans under the poverty line declined dramatically with the introduction of Medicare in 1965); catastrophes such as floods, fires, or large medical bills; and inadequate welfare payments in almost every state.

According to government figures, in 1992 about 32 million Americans, or 13 percent of the population, lived under the poverty level. That figure represented an increase of almost 4 million people since 1984, the largest proportion reported by the U.S. Bureau of the Census since the 1950's, when 22.4 percent of the nation lived in officially declared poverty. In 1988, the bureau issued a report on the American poor that showed that 10 percent of whites, 31.6 percent of blacks, and 26.8 percent of Hispanics were impoverished; 20 percent of American children lived in poverty. More than half the families labeled poor were headed by single mothers, and those numbers were growing. Many of the poor, almost 45 percent, worked full time but in jobs that required few skills, offered no opportunities for advancement, and generally had no benefits such as health insurance. For the "working poor," jobs themselves seemed to offer no opportunity for moving up the economic ladder. Working hard for forty hours a week or longer did not guarantee success.

Low-wage jobs keep people in the cycle of poverty and help to reaffirm beliefs associated with the culture of poverty. Working hard does not pay off in terms of material success; working people still live in bad housing, send their children to ineffective schools, and suffer the humiliations of inferior status. The material deprivations associated with poverty are many, but so are the nonmaterial deprivations. Poverty is seen by many as a sign of wickedness and moral degeneracy: People are poor because they are lazy and corrupt. These attitudes must be faced and absorbed into one's consciousness every day, and they only increase a sense of frustration and hopelessness. As poverty in the United States increased in the 1980's, the poor had no spokesperson or party representing their point of view. Their political interests were not represented, since one value stressed by the culture of poverty is that political participation is not important. (The lower one goes down the economic scale, the smaller the percentage of people who vote.)

Applications

Knowledge of the effects of the culture of poverty makes it possible to understand the difficulty of fighting and eliminating poverty. According to the culture of poverty thesis, ending employment discrimination, raising wages, and increasing employment opportunities through job training programs would all help to reduce poverty, but the attitudes of the poor would change only very slowly, since a whole way of life would need to be transformed. Education is the key to changing attitudes, especially by reducing the sense of despair frequently associated with poor people. Yet dropout rates approach 45 percent in high schools in slum districts, and a majority of impoverished adults are functionally illiterate; a major change in educational outcomes thus would be required before schools could be accepted as a way out of poverty. It is true that many mothers who receive welfare benefits place great value on education as a key to their children's success; however, statistics showing that children in slum school districts do not read as well or compute as well as students in middle- or upper-income districts provide little support for the hopes of these parents. The children who need education the most—to promote a feeling of control over a very hostile environment—receive the worst. Even highly motivated students seldom find success in such circumstances.

In American society, more than 71 percent of the African American poor live in large cities or surrounding suburbs, while most poor whites (almost 68 percent) are found in small towns, suburbs, and rural areas. In his book *The Truly Disadvantaged: The Inner City, the Underclass, and Public Policy* (1987), University of Chicago sociologist William J. Wilson observes that many African Americans live in neighborhoods with high concentrations of people in similarly desperate economic circumstances, with average incomes of less than $5,000 a year. Poor black people, especially, tend to live in areas surrounded by other poor blacks and thus have little opportunity to meet or learn from individuals with more secure economic futures. In the worst areas, two out of every three children live in single-parent households with incomes well below the poverty level. These are the truly disadvantaged members of American society, the people who feel most cut off from the American mainstream, and the people most influenced by the culture of poverty. They make up the underclass in the American economy.

In the environment of the slum, cultural patterns emerge that promote survival in the midst of dangerous and violent conditions. Crime rates, murder rates, and levels of drug addiction, alcoholism, mental illness, hypertension, and other measures of social disintegration, including divorce, child abuse, and spouse abuse, are far higher in inner cities than in any other parts of the United States. Survival in these circumstances requires a toughness of spirit and a distrust of others. Since slum residents usually do not get adequate city services such as garbage collection and police protection, distrust of government grows, leading to increased levels of hopelessness and helplessness. Not even the schools, historically the institutions most used by immigrant and minority groups as the path to success, typically offer the type of skills and training necessary to make it out of the ghetto. Most ghetto high schools are so bad that about as many students drop out as are graduated. The dream of college seems very distant to people without enough money to buy food.

The goals of the poor may be similar to those of the more well-to-do in terms of better jobs, improved educational opportunities, and a more pleasant future for their children, but the experience of the poor does not provide evidence that such dreams will ever come true. In many impoverished and racially segregated neighborhoods, crime, usually involving drug sales, offers a far quicker route to material success. Welfare payments, whether through Aid to Families with Dependent Children (AFDC), general assistance, or other aid programs, are another source of survival for the truly poor. Yet receiving such help, inadequate as it usually is, increases dependency and tends to reduce self-respect, as it is considered a sign of personal weakness to receive welfare. In a society that exalts the work ethic such as the United States, not to work, even if no jobs are available or one lacks the necessary training and skills required for a better job, becomes a sign of individual worthlessness and insignificance. This attitude represents one of the most devastating nonmaterial effects of being poor.

Context

The idea of a separate and distinct culture based on economic circumstances dates back at least to the early 1800's, when economists and historians talked about "working-class culture" or the "culture of the poor." In his famous history of human society *Das Kapital* (1867; *Capital: A Critique of Political Economy*, 1886), Karl Marx referred to the differing values and worldviews of capitalists and workers. Marxists were quite clear in their view that human thought and culture reflected the environmental conditions in which a person was born and reared. Socialist parties taught that only the abolition of poverty would lead to improved living conditions for the poor and that economic inequality would only be eliminated by the overthrow of capitalist ideas and values. Liberals, on the other hand, stressed economic expansion as the key to the ultimate victory over poverty and despair. With a constantly expanding economy, liberal theorists speculated, the poor would gradually be absorbed into the economic mainstream, and most poverty would disappear. Those people who could not succeed on such terms—chiefly those with physical or mental disabilities, widows, and orphans—would be taken care of by charity groups. When terrible economic depressions, especially in the 1890's and 1930's, showed that free-market capitalism had not solved all economic problems, liberal economists and many frightened conservatives pushed for social-welfare programs principally to prevent violent revolts. If the poor were given some stake in society in the form of pensions, housing, or medical care, it was thought, they would be less likely to follow revolutionary parties seeking to overthrow the whole capitalist system. The problem with "welfare" programs, however, was that they cost enormous amounts of money and required ever-higher levels of taxes to support and maintain. Though poverty was no longer believed to be a necessary part of the capitalist system and most economists believed that it could be abolished, there still was a major debate over how that could be accomplished.

The social welfare programs instituted in the 1930's, mainly Social Security payments, public-housing programs, and unemployment insurance, helped to reduce levels of poverty in the United States. Yet even in the generally prosperous 1950's, as many as 40 million people (22.5 percent of the population) were poor. It was at this point that students of poverty such as Michael Harrington in *The Other America: Poverty in the United States* (1962), Oscar Lewis in *La Vida*, and psychologist Kenneth Clark in *Dark Ghetto: Dilemmas of Social Power* (1965) began reporting on the long-term psychological and social damages caused by living in economically deprived communities. Most of these observers advocated a total change in the economic system, either through establishing a socialist economy (Harrington) or through violent revolution (Lewis). Liberal critics countered that such far-reaching changes were not necessary and that problems could be solved simply by ending job discrimination, improving educational opportunities, and promoting economic growth. The War on Poverty (1965-1967) was based on these ideas, though some recognition (especially through the Head Start program) was given to the notion that cultural attitudes would also have to be changed if the noneconomic effects of poverty were to be challenged.

Poverty in the United States did go down in the late 1960's and throughout the 1970's; by the end of the 1970's, the poverty level stood at 11.4 percent of the population (24.5 million people), the lowest level in history. Then, however, the numbers began increasing, as money for social programs was reduced by the Ronald Reagan Administration. By 1988, the number of poor people in the United States had risen to 15 percent of the population (32.5 million people). This increase resulted from the antiwelfare philosophy of the Reagan Administration, a position supported by books such as Charles Murray's *Losing Ground: American Social Policy, 1950-1980* (1984).

Murray supported the idea that a distinct culture had developed among the American poor, but he found that the attitudes and values expressed by people in poverty resulted from their acceptance of welfare rather than from discrimination, bad education, and long periods of economic deprivation. If welfare caused the attitudinal problem by making people dependent on government handouts rather than encouraging them to find jobs, Murray reasoned, then welfare had to go. Even mothers with four or more children would be better off working in low-paying, unskilled jobs than staying home taking care of their families, Murray suggested. With such attitudes finding favor with policy makers, the numbers of poor and homeless increased dramatically in the 1980's.

Bibliography

Ellwood, David T. *Poor Support: Poverty in the American Family.* New York: Basic Books, 1988. A detailed, informative review of welfare policy in the United States. Contains a brief but thoughtful analysis of the debate over the culture of poverty issue. Finds that the poor do have different attitudes and customs than do others. Has a concise bibliography and an index.

Hacker, Andrew. *Two Nations: Black and White, Separate, Hostile, Unequal.* New York: Charles Scribner's Sons, 1992. A thorough analysis of racial issues in the United States, with many statistics affirming the existence of a separate culture of poverty. A detailed bibliography and index.

Jaynes, Gerald D., and Robin M. Williams, eds. *A Common Destiny: Blacks and American Society.* Washington, D.C.: National Academy Press, 1988. Much evidence and several chapters devoted to refuting the idea of a distinct culture of poverty. Sees discrimination and racism as the only impediments to full equality. Detailed bibliography and index.

Murray, Charles. *Losing Ground: American Social Policy, 1950-1980.* New York: Basic Books, 1984. Murray sees a culture of poverty developing from American welfare programs. Calls for eliminating welfare and increasing incentives to work. The key text of antiwelfare conservatives.

Wilson, William J. *The Truly Disadvantaged: The Inner City, the Underclass, and Public Policy.* Chicago: University of Chicago Press, 1987. Shows the devastating impact of poverty and the culture of poverty on millions of Americans. Details the complex relationship between culture and economics. Lengthy bibliography and comprehensive index.

Leslie V. Tischauser

Cross-References

The Feminization of Poverty, 754; Poverty: Analysis and Overview, 1453; Poverty: Women and Children, 1466; Poverty and Race, 1472; The Poverty Line and Counting the Poor, 1478; Race Relations: The Race-Class Debate, 1566; Racial and Ethnic Stratification, 1579; The Urban Underclass and the Rural Poor, 2122; Welfare and Workfare, 2172.

POVERTY: WOMEN AND CHILDREN

Type of sociology: Social stratification
Field of study: Poverty

An increasing percentage of the poor in the United States are women and children. The increasing impoverishment of women and children can be attributed to several factors, including a growth in the number of female-headed families; the existence of a dual labor market that discriminates against women; and the unpaid domestic responsibilities of women, including child care. Millions of women and their children are without resources such as adequate shelter, food, and clothing.

Principal terms
ABSOLUTE POVERTY: the lack of sufficient resources to support a minimum of physical health and efficiency
AID TO FAMILIES WITH DEPENDENT CHILDREN (AFDC): a means-tested federal program that provides financial assistance to needy families with children
DUAL LABOR MARKET: the concept that men and women occupy separate labor markets, with women mostly working in service, sales, and clerical jobs that pay low wages
FEMINIZATION OF POVERTY: the trend under which an increasing percentage of the poor are women, many of whom are supporting children
POVERTY LINE: a figure determined by the government as the minimum income needed for food, clothing, medical care, and other necessary expenses
RELATIVE POVERTY: a cultural definition of being poor in reference to the living standard of the bulk of the population
WORKING POOR: those who lack the means for an adequate existence even though they are employed

Overview

The majority of the poor in the United States are women and children. According to the U.S. Bureau of the Census in 1989, 57.1 percent of all people below the official poverty level were female. In addition, female-headed families with children were found to be disproportionately poor, with 38.2 percent of all such white families and 56.3 percent of all such black families living in poverty. At the same time, only 18 percent of male-headed families with children were living in poverty.

Women's poverty clearly has a great impact on the economic status of children. According to Margaret DeCanio, in her book *The Encyclopedia of Marriage, Divorce, and the Family* (1989), one of the most significant socioeconomic developments in the United States during the later part of the twentieth century has been the fact that children are the age group most likely to be poor. According to the Children's Defense

Fund in 1992, child poverty rose steadily in the 1980's, and it pervades every area of the United States. The number of children living in poverty grew by more than one million in the 1980's. About 18 percent of all children were living below the poverty line in 1989. In some places, however, the rate is much higher. For example, Detroit's child poverty rate was 46.6 percent in 1989. The increase in the number of children living in poverty is particularly alarming in that many of these children will forever be trapped in poverty because of the accumulated deficits of food, housing, health care, and education.

Ruth Sidel, a scholar of women's studies, suggests in her book *Women and Children Last* (1986) that several social and economic factors have caused this increase in poverty among women and children. One factor involves changes in the traditional family structure. There are increasing numbers of single-mother families, and they often lack adequate economic resources. The increase in divorce has also been a factor. Many married women, especially those who devote themselves to full-time homemaking, are heavily dependent on their husbands' incomes. After a divorce, most women get custody of the children; child support payments from the father, however, are not enough to cover even half the cost of rearing a child. Moreover, many fathers fail to pay child support. Sidel points out the crucial nature of child support to the economic well-being of mothers and children and notes how its importance is underscored by women's low earning ability in the workplace.

Another significant factor is the dual labor market. In spite of gains by women since the 1960's, sex discrimination and occupational segregation still combine to limit women's income. According to the U.S. Department of Labor in 1991, three out of four female employees worked in one of three job categories: clerical/administrative support (28 percent), managerial/professional (27 percent), and service (18 percent). Women are concentrated in a few female-dominated professions, which tend to be the lowest paying. On average, women who are employed full-time earn approximately two-thirds of the salaries earned by men. Even when women and men are employed in the same occupation, men earn more.

Another major factor involved in the high level of poverty among women and children is cutbacks in the welfare system that helps support families below the poverty level. The cutbacks in human services since the 1980 election of President Ronald Reagan have had a major impact on the poor, especially women and children. Sidel notes that the reduction or elimination of Aid to Families with Dependent Children (AFDC) support for many families caused the percentage of working mothers living below the poverty line to double. Child nutrition programs were also cut dramatically, as was the food stamp program. In addition, the Reagan Administration eliminated many job training and employment programs.

The time-consuming unpaid domestic responsibilities of women, particularly child care, are another factor. For the most part, women bear the responsibility for child care. This fact limits their participation in the workforce, especially since good child care is costly and is often difficult to find. Day care in the United States is often viewed ambivalently or with hostility. Sidel hypothesizes that this is in part because it is perceived as a service for the poor, in particular for poor women. Day care programs receive little or no government funding, and often child care workers are exploited with very low wages.

The poverty experienced by women varies with age. Women who are sixty-five years of age and over are twice as likely to be poor as are men over sixty-five. This is the result of several factors. For many women, poverty in old age is the result of spending much of their life either as homemakers or in jobs with low wages and few, if any, benefits. Vast numbers of working women work in jobs that do not provide retirement benefits or pensions. In her book *Gender: Stereotypes and Roles* (1992), professor of women's studies Susan Basow provides some disturbing figures regarding elderly women. Twenty percent of all women over sixty years old live below the poverty level, and an additional 20 percent have incomes only slightly above the poverty level. Only 20 percent of women, as compared with 43 percent of men, receive pension benefits in addition to Social Security. Thus, older women often depend more on Social Security yet receive less in such benefits than men do.

Applications

Many of the factors involved in the increase of poverty among women and children offer support for the idea that women and children are low priorities in terms of government policy and government spending. Basow points out that in 1990 govern-ment funding for Aid to Families with Dependent Children was slightly more than 1 percent of the money spent on "bailing out" failed savings and loan institutions. The needs of women and children are often ignored and thus often public policies have a negative effect on women and their children. For example, since 1981 cuts have been made in social welfare programs including AFDC, food stamps, and Medicaid. These cuts worsened the already poor quality of life of the poor, and they affected women and their children most of all.

Stereotypes are held by many people concerning those receiving AFDC benefits. Many believe that AFDC recipients do not work or do not want to work. The problem, however, is that many single mothers can only find jobs that pay minimum wage and offer no health care benefits. There is also often a lack of affordable child care. Thus, as a practical matter, many of these women must choose welfare over employment. Welfare benefits are extremely low, yet if a recipient reports beginning to work, the benefits are reduced by nearly the amount that is earned. This leaves the woman as poor as she was before (or poorer, since she also has to find a way to care for her children while she is at work). Kathryn Edin, in her article "Surviving the Welfare System: How AFDC Recipients Make Ends Meet in Chicago" (1991), suggests some alternatives to the present system. She suggests ensuring that those who work full time can make a living wage by increasing a single mother's income through a child support assurance system and wage supplements of various kinds. She argues that women need to double their current potential earnings to make work a viable alternative to welfare. Assistance is also needed in terms of child care and health benefits in order to facilitate the transition to work from welfare.

The problem of so many women and children living in poverty has serious implications for the future of the United States. Though the United States is a country of enormous resources, many of the nation's children are growing up without adequate health care, and many suffer from malnutrition. Some are without adequate shelter; many are homeless. The lack of adequate housing, food, health care, and education, along with the enormous stress of such an existence, leads to despair and to permanent damage, both physical and psychological.

In terms of health, the Reagan Administration's cutbacks in health funding negatively affected the health care of women and children. Many families lost their Medicaid coverage because of the cuts. These budget cuts have resulted in a decrease in the number of women receiving prenatal care. Many children of the working poor or of the long-term unemployed go unprotected because they do not have health care coverage. It has been shown that the most successful and cost-effective interventions on behalf of children and families are those done early in the child's life, even before the child is born; for increasing numbers of children, such interventions are simply not possible.

The federal government's supplemental food program for women, infants, and children (WIC) has helped many female-headed families, but it is consistently threatened by budget cuts. This program provides supplemental food either in the form of vouchers or as actual food items. It is based on the assumption that inadequate nutrition and health care among low-income women and children make them vulnerable to long-term health problems and that proper foods at critical times in fetal and child development can help prevent such problems. WIC serves pregnant, postpartum, and nursing mothers and their infants and children up to age five. WIC is one of the few federal programs that serves those with incomes above the poverty line (up to 185 percent of the poverty level) as well as those below it; thus, the program is one of the few that serve the working poor. Though this program is relatively inexpensive to administer, especially given its positive preventive effects and benefits, its budget was cut in the 1980's. Many families were thus forced off the program.

Context

The problem of the disproportionate number of women and children living in poverty did not receive significant attention from sociologists until the 1980's. The problem was not widely recognized before then, nor was it realized that the severity of the problem was steadily increasing. The "feminization of poverty" has been caused by a convergence of many social and economic factors. American society provides few supports for women and children, particularly single mothers and their children. Many women have trouble making it on their own, having few marketable job skills and therefore earning low wages. An increased fragmentation of the family has occurred because of higher divorce rates and because a mobile society has created a lack of extended families living nearby. This situation has left more women on their own rearing children with little support from families or government agencies.

Female-headed families often find themselves in desperate economic circumstances. Generally women bear the responsibility for the children, which limits their participation in the workforce. Child care costs are high. Fathers frequently do not contribute adequately to the support of their children. Overall, women who have followed the traditional gender roles dictated by society find themselves in the worst situation. After a divorce, such women find that they have few job skills, and they are limited to low-paying jobs with few benefits. In old age, women are penalized again because they did not have a chance to participate fully in the labor force. The National Advisory Council on Economic Opportunity predicted in 1991 that by the year 2000 nearly the whole poverty population will be women and children living in female-headed households.

The fact that millions of women and children live in poverty is a serious and widespread problem that needs to be addressed. Women and children must receive basic services and assistance for their health and well-being. Few women are truly free from the danger of poverty. Ruth Sidel, through her interviews with women, illustrates the fact that any woman (including middle-class and upper-middle-class women), along with her children, is at risk for becoming poor if her husband should leave or if serious illness should occur. Moreover, the unavoidable process of growing older increases the risk of poverty.

The recognition of the problems faced by women and children living in poverty has led to considerable debate over how best to approach the issue. The debate touches on central and difficult policy issues, such as the degree of responsibility a society has to help its disadvantaged members. According to some experts, the United States needs a family policy that includes such items as paid parental leave, affordable prenatal care for all women, a national system of health care for all people, policies to ensure payment of child support, improvements in work opportunities, and welfare reform. Welfare reform, according to some, should include raising AFDC payments at least to the poverty line. Many other industrialized countries have already implemented such policies, realizing that the increase of women and children in poverty deeply affects the fundamental well-being of present and future generations.

Bibliography

Edin, Kathryn. "Surviving the Welfare System: How AFDC Recipients Make Ends Meet in Chicago." *Social Problems* 38 (November, 1991): 462-473. An interesting and informative study of AFDC (welfare) recipients in Chicago, based on inter-views. The study looks at the welfare system and the issue of welfare dependency. Edin suggests some interesting alternatives that would make work a more viable alternative for women on welfare.

Goldberg, Gertrude Schaffner, and Eleanor Kremen, eds. *The Feminization of Poverty: Only in America?* New York: Praeger, 1990. An informative book on the issue of women in poverty. It provides a comparison of the United States with six other industrialized countries in terms of women's poverty. A good source to assist in understanding the tragedy of the feminization of poverty.

Hewlett, Sylvia Ann. *A Lesser Life.* New York: William Morrow, 1986. This well-written book addresses issues confronting many women in American society today. Parts of the book deal with the economic hardships faced by many women. There is also an excellent chapter devoted to the effects of societal conditions and poverty on children's health and well-being.

Hoffman, Emily P. "Racial Differences in the Feminization of Poverty." *Review of Black Political Economy* 21 (Summer, 1992): 19-31. This interesting article examines the effects of race on the poverty of female-headed households from 1959 to 1989. Investigates the statistical relationship among female poverty, economic conditions, and labor market conditions.

Sidel, Ruth. *Women and Children Last: The Plight of Poor Women in Affluent America.* New York: Viking Press, 1986. A well-written and thorough analysis of the causes and consequences of the crisis of poverty among women and children. Sidel includes poignant examples of many issues, using excerpts from interviews with women. Includes a thought-provoking comparison of the policies of the United States and those of Sweden and of how these policies affect the situation of women, children, and families in each country.

Anna M. Heiberger Abell

Cross-References

Comparable Worth and Sex Segregation in the Workplace, 303; The Feminization of Poverty, 754; Gender Inequaltiy: Analysis and Overview, 820; Homelessness, 897; Poverty: Analysis and Overview, 1453; The Culture of Poverty, 1460; Sexism and Institutional Sexism, 1728; The Urban Underclass and the Rural Poor, 2122; Welfare and Workfare, 2172; Women in the Labor Force, 2185.

POVERTY AND RACE

Type of sociology: Social stratification
Field of study: Poverty

Poverty and race are directly connected to discrimination and prejudice in American society and the effect they have on the wages and salaries of African Americans. The data show that African Americans at all levels of the economic system make less money than their white counterparts do.

Principal terms
DISCRIMINATION: the denial of opportunities and rights to certain groups
GROSS NATIONAL PRODUCT (GNP): the total of all goods and services produced in a country
POVERTY: the lack of money or resources needed to obtain the necessities of life
POVERTY LINE: the minimum amount of income necessary to obtain the necessities of life

Overview

Poverty and race are linked in the United States by a long history of prejudice and discrimination against African Americans and other minority groups. The results of racial discrimination are apparent in the statistics identifying the poor in America. Almost one-third of African American families (31 percent) live under the poverty level, while only one-tenth of white families (11 percent) live in similar circumstances. The ratio has generally been the same ever since the government began collecting such numbers. Only in the 1930's, during the Great Depression, were the results different. In 1939, more than 90 percent of blacks were under the poverty line, but so were 65 percent of whites. The figures began to decline dramatically in the economic boom following World War II, but even in 1974, 30 percent of blacks remained under the poverty level, as did only 9 percent of whites, the lowest levels ever achieved by either group. During the 1980's, the percentages increased slowly for both groups; they reached their current levels by 1986 and have changed little since that year.

Poverty levels for families do not show the true difficulties of the problem because almost one-half of African American children (44.8 percent) live in households under the poverty level, and that number is growing. White children are usually better off, yet 15.9 percent, or one in seven, live in poverty. In 1989, the Census Bureau defined the poverty level as $12,675 a year for a family of four, which is hardly enough to live on in a large city such as New York or Chicago. The poverty level is about one-third of the average white family income of $36,915. Welfare payments do not even approach the poverty level for four-member families. Cash allowances for a family of four averaged just $4,644 in 1990 in the United States, with Massachusetts providing the most generous support, $7,692, and Alabama allowing the least, $1,356. Not even food stamps could make up the difference, because the monthly allowance for this program gave recipients less than 75 cents per meal. The United States provided less support for its families and children than any other society in the industrial world.

The impact of race on income and earnings reflects years of prejudice in employment and educational opportunity. African American families averaged $15,500 a year less in income than whites, $21,423 compared to $36,915. Blacks represent 12.1 percent of the population of the United States yet get only 7.8 percent of their income from wages and salaries. The influence of race on economics can best be seen when comparing wages for people with similar educational backgrounds. Black men who have not completed high school receive about 80 percent of the earnings, for similar jobs with similar skills, of whites with the same background. African American males who have completed high school are in even worse shape, getting only about 76 percent of the wages paid to white high school graduates. College does not necessarily help, since black male graduates from four-year institutions still get only about 79 percent of what male graduates command. The more education is involved, the worse the numbers get. Black males with five years or more of college get only 77 cents for every dollar paid to whites. African American male attorneys aged thirty-five to forty-five have earnings of $790 for every $1,000 earned by whites in the same age group and with similar experience and training. Race is the only difference in all these categories.

Skin color (race) also has much to do with determining who is poor and not in American society. For whites being poor is not typical. The white poor are typically addicts and alcoholics, men without steady jobs, families involved in a crisis resulting from a flood or a fire, the mentally ill, or single mothers on welfare. In some cases, such as among poor whites in the South, poverty is passed along from generation to generation, but in most cases economic deprivation can be overcome through increased educational and employment opportunity. The same solutions would not seem to work for a large number of the black urban poor (70 percent of African American households below the poverty line live in cities). The major causes of poverty for people stuck in these urban ghettos cannot be changed simply by improving schools and increasing job training programs. Only major changes in the American economy and fundamental changes in family structure and values will lead to any significant improvement in the quality of life experienced by the growing underclass in the United States.

Applications

Knowledge of the effects of racism on poverty levels can help experts to design programs and find solutions to the real economic problems afflicting the United States. According to sociologist David T. Ellwood in *Poor Support: Poverty in the American Family* (1988), the expansion in poverty in the United States results from three key factors: lagging economic growth, stagnation in the income earned by African American men, and changes in family structure leading to a gigantic increase in the number of children living in single-parent female-headed households. Because most mothers in the latter category are very young, often uneducated, and even when working holding low-wage jobs, they are typically among the poorest of the poor.

From 1939 to 1973, economic growth in the United States, measured in terms of an expanding Gross National Product (GNP), averaged 2.6 percent a year. This high rate of economic growth helped to reduce poverty for all people in America. Wages for black men improved, though they still fell far short of the white average. By 1959, however, they had improved from 60 percent to 78 percent of the latter figure. During this period, thousands of blacks left the South and found jobs in northern cities such as Detroit, Chicago, Cleveland, and Pittsburgh. By 1970, most of these northern industrial cities had African American populations of more than 30 percent, compared with less than 10 percent before 1939. The southern black population of poorly paid, often uneducated agricultural laborers fell dramatically from 77 percent of the total African American population in the United States to about 53 percent. Wages paid to blacks in northern factories, though lower than those paid to whites, still led to an increase in income for many black workers. Northern cities witnessed the growth of stable, though racially segregated, working-class communities and neighborhoods. Two-parent families were the norm. Then, beginning in 1973, the national economy began to stagnate and thousands of blue-collar workers were cut from the payrolls.

As the economy declined, with average growth in the GNP from 1973 to 1990 reaching only 1.6 percent, older factories in America's cities closed their doors in growing numbers. The job loss hurt African American males more than any other group. Since unemployment statistics were first gathered in the 1930's, blacks had always experienced about double the level of unemployment of whites. Even in the boom years of the 1960's, when white unemployment fell to 3.1 percent, that for blacks reached 6.4 percent, but beginning in 1973 the difference grew much worse. In 1990, for example, while 4.1 percent of whites remained unemployed, the African American unemployment rate had reached 11.3 percent. The number has not been out of double digits since 1973. Education did not make any difference, since the jobless rate for black college graduates remained more than twice as high as that for whites. In the 1980's, a greater proportion of black Americans were out of work than at any time since the Great Depression. The lesson seemed clear: As long as the economy stagnated, blacks would continue to experience the highest rates of unemployment and poverty of any group in American society.

Unemployment, low wages, and the loss of blue-collar jobs have affected the poor in other ways, specially in family structure and relationships. The increase in female-headed single-parent families resulted from the disappearance of jobs for black men. Black families headed by women had average incomes of $8,328 in 1990, well below the poverty level. For white families headed by mothers, the income was only slightly higher, $10,317, still under the poverty level. More than half of these women work and are self-supporting, which shows that low wages are a primary cause of poverty. People working forty hours a week or more in a minimum wage job, at $4.50 an hour, earned far less than the minimum standard of living in a year. Two-parent African American families are better off, as long as both parents work, seeing their income rise to $21,423 a year; so why do not single mothers in inner city slums get married?

The major reason, according to University of Chicago sociologist William J. Wilson, is a shortage of eligible black men. According to his analysis of the inner city, more than 500,000 black males were in prison, more than 1,000,000 had been convicted of felonies and though out of prison had great difficulty finding full-time employment because of their criminal records, unreported thousands suffered from drug and alcohol addiction, and hundreds more died every year as a result of gang wars and simple murder. Death rates for black males between the ages of fifteen and twenty-five were three times higher than those for black women. Not even half of the male residents of black neighborhoods had full-time jobs in the previous year, and one in five (20 percent) had no permanent address. None of these factors would encourage black women to find eligible mates among this population.

The number of black families headed by women increased from 17.2 percent of households in 1950 to 56.2 percent in 1990. Single parents now outnumber conventional two-parent households in black communities. White households in this category saw an equally significant increase, though the total percentage was smaller, from 5.3 percent to 17.3 percent. As previously mentioned, more than half of these women work, but mostly in unskilled, low-paying jobs that provide less than $14,000 a year. Many of these single-parent families seem to be trapped in an endless cycle of poor health, inadequate education, physical disabilities, lack of opportunity, and hopelessness. Many of the female children in these families become single mothers themselves before they reach the age of sixteen, adding to the economic burden of the household. These girls usually say they want to have a baby, regardless of how immature and poor they may be, so that they can have someone to love and someone who needs them. The children of such children are the true victims of the American system of poverty, because they get less and less from overburdened parents, schools, and social service agencies.

Context

For most of human history, poverty has been seen as a natural part of the economic system. A few people were rich and most were extremely poor, and most observers of the human condition believed that it was natural and just that this was true. God caused poverty and used it to punish the wicked and lazy. People who obeyed His will and followed His commandments might receive some material reward in this world, but it did not really matter because the true reward, paradise, was found in the next world beyond this vale of tears.

When industrialization and economic expansion seemed to make material happiness available to all, views of poverty began to change. For some, including socialists, communists, and other radicals, the problem of poverty could be ended by a fair distribution of wealth. An unequal distribution of wealth created the system in which the powerful got more and more as the poor were exploited, underpaid, and badly abused. An end to the horrors of poverty was possible in this world, but it could be achieved only by taking money from the wealthy and giving it to the poor. The idea of a welfare system to alleviate suffering developed as a compromise between the radical call for revolt and revolution and the conservative response that a free market system would gradually reduce economic inequality so that no other action would be required. Reformers argued that suffering had to be alleviated among the poor or calls for violence would continually grow louder. The first social programs aimed at reducing poverty began in Germany in the 1880's. Ideas similar to America's Social Security, Unemployment Insurance, and Worker's Compensation programs of the 1930's were passed to give the poor and the working class a stake in society. If they had a pension to look forward to or temporary income during times of unemployment, workers would be less likely to support the overthrow of capitalism. This argument carried the day, and "welfare programs" were born.

It took the crisis of the Great Depression (1929-1941) to cause the United States to adopt social welfare programs. These programs, including Aid to Families with Dependent Children (AFDC), aid to the disabled and elderly, public housing, and temporary government jobs programs during times of economic distress, continue to play a major role in fighting poverty in America. Not until the 1960's and Lyndon Johnson's call for a War on Poverty did the country add significantly to its social programs. During this crusade, social scientists played a major role in creating programs aimed at reducing high levels of economic distress in a land of great plenty. Most of the programs designed in the mid-1960's were aimed at increasing educational opportunity and improving job training programs for the 25 million Americans deemed poor. Most of these programs also accepted the principle of modest economic growth as necessary for reducing poverty levels. Few social scientists predicted the economic decline that began in 1973. The many programs created by the War on Poverty, including Head Start, aimed at improving educational readiness among children of poverty, and the Job Corps, designed to train teenagers for specific jobs, helped to reduce poverty in the United States. They were not enough, however, to overcome the huge decline in manufacturing jobs experienced by the nation in the 1970's. The programs also tended to ignore the connection between race and poverty, hoping instead that a steadily improving economic future would reduce discrimination and prejudice by opening up enough jobs for all.

In the 1980's, a debate over the merits of a welfare system broke out with the publication of Charles Murray's *Losing Ground: American Social Policy, 1950-1980* (1984). Murray argued that welfare payments encouraged laziness, irresponsibility, and self-indulgence by paying people not to work and encouraging young women to have babies out of wedlock so that they could get more money from the welfare system. These conclusions were refuted by William J. Wilson and David Ellwood, among others, who showed that unemployment resulted from a failing economy and lack of opportunity rather than laziness. When jobs were available, the unemployed showed up in record numbers to find work. The notion that women had babies to get more money from the welfare system was easily refuted by statistics showing that welfare mothers had fewer children in states paying more per child, such as Massachusetts and New York, than they did in states paying practically nothing, such as Alabama and Mississippi. Lessons for the future seem clear: Economic growth is the key to reducing poverty, but discrimination and prejudice will not disappear. Wages and salaries for African Americans continue to trail those for whites even in periods of economic growth. The third major cause of poverty, the growth of single-parent households headed by women, will decline only when more black males become employable, educated, and therefore responsible.

Bibliography

Ellwood, David T. *Poor Support: Poverty in the American Family*. New York: Basic Books, 1988. This book contains a massive amount of information on the causes and consequences of poverty in American society. Calls for a total change in the welfare system and a more humane attitude toward the victims of poverty, especially children. It has a lengthy section on the link between racism and economic inequality. Includes a lengthy bibliography and an index.

Hacker, Andrew. *Two Nations: Black and White, Separate, Hostile, Unequal*. New York: Charles Scribner's Sons, 1992. This collection of data from the Census Bureau and other sources shows the impact of racial discrimination and prejudice on economics, politics, and social relations. An excellent source of accurate, useful statistics on the growing differences between African Americans and whites. Has a useful list of references and many tables testifying to the influence of race on poverty.

Harrington, Michael. *The Other America: Poverty in the United States*. New York: Macmillan, 1971. The book that inspired the War on Poverty and one of the first to recognize the influence of race on American poverty. Contains a compelling and accurate description of the effects of poverty on American citizens, black and white, before the economy began its long post-1973 decline. Useful in demonstrating that free market capitalism helped create economic inequality in the United States and had not even come close to solving the problem.

Jaynes, Gerald D., and Robin M. Williams, Jr., eds. *A Common Destiny: Blacks and American Society*. Washington, D.C.: National Academy Press, 1989. Has several chapters by leading scholars on the history of poverty in America and efforts to end it. An extensive bibliography and detailed index are included.

Wilson, William J. *The Truly Disadvantaged: The Inner City, the Underclass, and Public Policy*. Chicago: University of Chicago Press, 1987. The latest work by the leading scholar in the field. A useful bibliography and an index are included.

Leslie V. Tischauser

Cross-References

THE POVERTY LINE AND COUNTING THE POOR

Type of sociology: Social stratification
Field of study: Poverty

A measurement of poverty has both political and technical aspects. It allows comparisons of economic well-being across families, population groups, regions, and time, and it enables assessment of the effects of policies and programs as well as identification of people and groups whose most basic economic needs remain unmet.

Principal terms

AFTER-TAX INCOME: money income that excludes federal, state, local, or Social Security (FICA) taxes and other types of deductions such as union dues or Medicare premiums

CASH TRANSFERS: cash payments, from government to individuals, including nonmeans-tested programs such as Social Security payments, unemployment compensation, and government educational assistance as well as means-tested programs such as Aid to Families with Dependent Children and Supplemental Security Income

MEANS-TESTED CASH TRANSFERS: cash payments from government to individuals that are based on the recipient's poverty status

MONEY INCOME: money income before payments of federal, state, local, or Social Security taxes and before any other types of deductions, such as union dues and Medicare premiums

NONMEANS-TESTED CASH TRANSFERS: cash payments from government to individuals, awarded regardless of the recipient's economic status

POVERTY LINE OR THRESHOLD: the dollar amount calculated by estimating the costs of food for a household (determined according to the Thrifty Food Plan of the U.S. Department of Agriculture), multiplied by three, and adjusted for family size and annually for inflation

POVERTY SPELLS: the amount of time during which an individual, family, or household lacks access to minimally adequate levels of consumption

Overview

Defining poverty is an inherently political activity. Any definition carries with it a constellation of views about the nature and extent of poverty, and these views invariably shape public and private efforts to ameliorate the problem. Advocates of governmental support for social welfare programs, such as sociologist Richard Ropers, tend to make higher estimates of poverty in the population. They view poverty as persistent, even amidst affluence, and call for continuation and expansion of a wide variety of public welfare programs. Others, however, minimize the numbers of poor in the United States. Some, such as policy analyst Charles Murray, see many opportunities for upward mobility and argue that the existing array of public programs and private efforts is sufficient to buffer people from severe or prolonged hunger, hopelessness, and despair. To date, a definition of poverty defies consensus, and its measurement remains constant. Although poverty can be conceptualized as either absolute, relative, or subjective, this essay focuses on the U.S. government's official or absolute approach to counting the poor, alternatives to this approach, and implications for public policy.

Traditionally, the U.S. Bureau of the Census presents income and poverty data based on the amount of money income received during a calendar year before any taxes and excluding capital gains. Each year, the U.S. Social Security Administration (SSA) estimates the cash income needed by individuals and families to satisfy minimum food, housing, clothing, and medical-care needs. These annual figures, adjusted for family size, are known as the poverty line. SSA updates poverty level figures according to the Consumer Price Index (CPI). These figures no longer differentiate between male and female households or between farm and nonfarm families. The poverty line is calculated by estimating the costs of food for a household (determined according to the Thrifty Food Plan of the U.S. Department of Agriculture) and multiplying this figure by three. The use of this multiple is based on the assumption that about one-third of an average household budget is, or should be, spent on food.

The official definition of poverty reflects the content of the March Current Population Survey questionnaire, carried out under the auspices of the U.S. Bureau of the Census. The March questionnaire contains no questions about taxes and, until 1980, contained no questions about the receipt of noncash benefits. Since March, 1980, the questionnaire has included items on the receipt of benefits from government programs such as food stamps, housing assistance, Medicare, and Medicaid, and from employers such as health insurance. The official definition of poverty represents an "objective" minimum, adjusted for changes in prices. This approach to conceptualizing and measuring poverty is criticized, as economist Patricia Ruggles notes in *Drawing the Line: Alternative Poverty Measures and Their Implications for Public Policy* (1990), on the grounds that what constitutes an "objective" minimum varies over a long period and across very divergent population groups. Such an approach misses shifts in consumption patterns and may therefore overstate any improvements in the lot of the poor. In addition, appropriate shares of a budget to be allocated for specific consumption needs may also change. If food costs go down, while housing costs increase, an index based on food costs alone would overstate increases in the well-being of the poor.

Complicating this and other approaches to measuring poverty and counting the poor is the concept of poverty spells—the amount of time during which an individual, family, or household lacks access to minimally adequate levels of consumption. In the short run, many people may be considered poor, while a much smaller number may experience long-term or persistent poverty. Other factors, such as what counts as income and whose income counts, further complicate counting the poor and designing programs to ameliorate poverty.

Applications

A persistent criticism of the official poverty definition is its narrowness—that is, its omission of data on taxes, realized capital gains, and the value of noncash benefits. In the early 1980's, the U.S. Census Bureau examined the effect of government noncash benefits on poverty and the effect of taxes on income distributional measures. In 1988 the Census Bureau presented calculations showing how income and poverty estimates changed when specific taxes were deducted and specific benefits were added to the income definition. An August, 1992, bureau report, *Measuring the Effect of Benefits and Taxes on Income and Poverty: 1979 to 1991*, updated estimates of the incremental effect of benefits and taxes on income and poverty for 1991 and extended the estimates back to 1979. The updated report used fifteen income definitions, four pretax and eleven after-tax. Starting with money income excluding capital gains before taxes as definition 1, the others were 2) definition 1 less government cash transfers; 3) definition 2 plus capital gains; 4) definition 3 plus health insurance supplements to wage or salary income; 5) definition 4 less Social Security payroll taxes; 6) definition 5 less federal income taxes; 7) definition 6 plus the Earned Income Tax Credit; 8) definition 7 less state income taxes; 9) definition 8 plus nonmeans-tested government cash transfers; 10) definition 9 plus the value of Medicare; 11) definition 10 plus the value of regular-price school lunches; 12) definition 11 plus means-tested government cash transfers; 13) definition 12 plus the value of Medicaid; 14) definition 13 plus the value of other means-tested government noncash transfers such as food stamps; and 15) definition 14 plus net imputed return on equity in own home. Definitions 1- 4 show poverty based on income before taxes, while definitions 5-15 are based on income after taxes.

The report contains two lengthy, detailed tables. Table one shows income distribution measures, by definition of income, from 1979 to 1991, for all households and for a variety of household structures by race, ethnic origin, and geographic area. Table two shows the percent of persons in poverty by definition of income from 1979 to 1991 for all persons and for persons categorized along lines of race, ethnic origin, age, geographic area, sex, family structure, education, and labor force status. Noting the percentages of persons in poverty by race, age, and family type helps to highlight different poverty rates obtained under varying definitions of poverty in any given year and over time. In 1991, for example, the official definition of poverty yielded a poverty rate of 14.2 percent of the population. Definitions 2 and 3 yielded the highest pretax poverty rate, 21.8 percent for all persons. Definition 6 yielded the highest poverty rate, 22.8 percent. Definition 15 produced the lowest poverty rate, 10.3 percent for all persons.

The percent of persons in poverty increased under each definition between 1979 and 1991, although decreases for each occurred between the peak poverty years of 1983 and 1989. The percentage of persons in poverty varied by race and ethnic origin under each of the different definitions of income. Whites had the lowest percentages, blacks the highest. Under definition 1, blacks were almost three times as likely as whites to be poor in 1991, a slight decline from 1979. Under after-tax income definitions 8, 11, 14, and 15, white poverty rates declined between 1979 and 1991. For blacks the poverty rates also decreased under definitions 14 and 15 but increased under definitions 8 and 11. It would thus appear that the Earned Income Tax Credit and nonmeans-tested government transfers benefit whites proportionately more than blacks. Although the poverty rate for both blacks and whites decreased under definition 14, it did so more for blacks (3.8 percent) than for whites (2.1 percent). Means-tested government programs would seem to benefit blacks more so than whites.

In addition to race, different definitions of income also affected the percentage of persons in poverty by age and family type. The rate of pretax-income poverty for children under eighteen rose 5.1 percent, from 16.0 percent in 1979 to 21.1 percent in 1991, for example, while that for persons sixty-five and over declined 2.8 percent, from 15.2 percent to 12.4 percent. After-tax poverty that included the Earned Income Tax Credit (definition 8) reduced the elderly poverty rate 5.6 percent, from 54.1 percent in 1979 to 48.5 percent in 1991, while the child poverty rate increased 4.3 percent, from 19.3 to 23.6 percent. The Earned Income Tax Credit therefore benefits households with elderly persons more so than it does those with children. The rate of pretax poverty for married-couple families rose 1.1 percent, from 6.1 percent in 1979 to 7.2 percent in 1991, while that for female-headed households with no husband present rose 4.8 percent, from 34.9 percent in 1979 to 39.7 percent in 1991.

Context

There was no official statistical poverty measure until the mid-1960's. The only comprehensive statistics available in the early 1960's, as economist Ruggles points out, were "snapshots" of the overall distribution of income; they showed little year-to-year change. Most of these studies estimated the amount of income needed for subsistence and they focused more on counting the number of poor than on measuring the depth of poverty. Modern measures account for both.

The construction of an official poverty measure by the U.S. government implied the implicit judgment that both the total welfare of all individuals in society and the well-being of those least well-off mattered. The idea that there was a minimum "decent" standard of living and that a just society must attempt to ensure that all its members have access to at least this level of economic well-being undergirded the Johnson Administration's War on Poverty, launched in 1964 when the poverty rate was 19 percent of the population.

The current official definition of poverty grew out of a series of studies undertaken by Mollie Orshansky for the Social Service Administration in the mid-1960's. Orshansky's poverty lines accounted for family size and composition, thereby making them an advance over much previous work. Her work, as economist Ruggles notes, highlighted two important points about the use of alternate poverty thresholds. First, it was possible to get essentially the same overall poverty rate at a given point in time using different methods of selecting a set of thresholds. Second, within broad guidelines of what constitutes a rough consensus about an appropriate overall poverty rate, vastly different relative poverty rates for different groups could be calculated, depending on the specific scales used. Orshansky showed, for example, that the same overall number of poor persons was essentially the same using her sliding scale of income requirement for different family sizes and compositions than the Council of Economic Advisors' single-income cutoff of $3,000. Small families with requirements of less than $3,000 were no longer counted as poor. Larger families with many children and with requirements exceeding $3,000 were included. The number of children counted as poor increased substantially, while the number of childless couples, young and old, decreased.

Although scale construction was a technical task, the choice of scale was political. The Johnson Administration adopted Orshansky's model, reflecting a preference of helping poor young people. Historically, appeals for programs to improve the quality of life for children have had more political viability than others. In addition, Johnson's decision also meant that the absolute, subsistence-level approach to estimating poverty took precedence over the income-share or relative, inequality approach. The idea of absolute poverty gave the impression that the Johnson Administration's War on Poverty could in fact be won, indicated by decreasing the numbers and percentages of children in poverty. Many antipoverty measures subsequently proposed and adopted are judged by the extent to which they lift poor children above this absolute minimum standard of economic need. Increased rates of children living in poverty invariably reflect changing demographic characteristics of the larger population, as well as economic conditions, but they also show the technical bias of the measurement process itself and the political preference to focus attention on this vulnerable segment of the population.

During the 1960's the federal government sponsored research to measure long-term poverty, and this led to determination of poverty spells. Throughout the 1970's and 1980's, researchers used the Panel Study of Income Dynamics to estimate the size of the "persistently poor" population. A 1977 Urban Institute working paper, entitled *How Big Is the American Underclass?*, by economist Frank Levy, for example, estimated that 10 million to 11 million persons were poor for at least five years between 1967 and 1973, representing 40 to 45 percent of the poor population on an annual basis. A 1986 study by sociologist Mary Jo Bane and economist David Ellwood showed that 51.5 percent of the nonelderly poverty population was in the midst of a spell of poverty lasting more than nine years.

The United States has a population known for its mobility, and sources of longitudinal data other than the Panel Study of Income Dynamics, such as the Survey of Income and Program Participation (SIPP), created by the U.S. Census Bureau in the mid-1980's, are designed to enable researchers to account for changes in families and households over time. SIPP, for example, samples households, administers questionnaires to the person paying the mortgage or rent (the reference person) and all those living with him or her, and subsequently interviews each again, plus any others who may join the household (while following those who may leave) for up to three and a half years. The highly mobile nature of the U.S. population makes counting the poor and drawing poverty lines a dynamic process.

Bibliography

Annual Statistical Supplement to the Social Security Bulletin. Washington, D.C.: U.S. Department of Health and Human Services, Social Security Administration, 1938-. This document is published every year. As an example, the 1993 supplement provides statistical tables of the distribution of absolute and relative poverty in 1991 and other selected years as well as the poverty guidelines for families of specified size between 1965 and 1993. Describes the many social welfare programs of the U.S. government.

DiNitto, Diana M. *Social Welfare: Politics and Public Policy*. 3d ed. Englewood Cliffs, N.J.: Prentice-Hall, 1991. This text highlights the relationship between social welfare programs and politics. Six of its twelve chapters deal directly with poverty, including a thorough overview of problems associated with defining poverty. Notes appear at the end of each chapter. There are name and subject indexes.

Measuring the Effect of Benefits and Taxes on Income and Poverty: 1979 to 1991. Washington, D.C.: U.S. Department of Commerce, Economics and Statistics Administration, Bureau of the Census, 1992. This report contains a wealth of information about alternative definitions of poverty, accounting for pretax and after-tax income. Information is primarily in tabular form with narrative summaries. There are ten appendices with definitions and explanations of terms, methodologies, and limitations, among other things.

Orshansky, Mollie. "Counting the Poor: Another Look at the Poverty Profile." *Social Security Bulletin* 28 (January, 1965): 3-29. This is the classic article upon which the Johnson Administration based the poverty scales it adopted and which still forms the basis of the poverty thresholds.

Ruggles, Patricia. *Drawing the Line: Alternative Poverty Measures and Their Implications for Public Policy*. Washington, D.C.: Urban Institute Press, 1990. This book provides a range of alternative approaches to measuring poverty and discusses such issues as setting the poverty threshold, adjusting for differences in family needs, time, and whose income and what kinds of income should be counted. Tables are used to illustrate the distributions of poverty populations using different poverty measures. The book has a reference section but no index.

Richard K. Caputo

Cross-References

POWER: THE PLURALISTIC MODEL

Type of sociology: Major social institutions
Field of study: Politics and the state

The pluralistic model of political power describes and normatively justifies the distribution of power and resources for a heterogeneous and diverse society such as that of the United States. Pluralist political thought defines most American political discourse.

Principal terms
ASSOCIATION: a formally organized group
COALITION: an alliance among interest groups; may include committees or institutions of the government
GROUP: an aggregation of people with a shared common characteristic or view; a group may or may not be formally organized
INTEREST GROUP: a group whose shared common characteristic or attitude leads its members to make claims on other groups in the society
POLITICAL INTEREST GROUP: an interest group that presses its claims through one or more government institutions
POTENTIAL GROUP: an interest group that, although it does not exist, would come into existence in particular circumstances (for example, if some proposal were to be made in Congress that affected its members); although nonexistent, it affects the political processes through its potential

Overview

The most common sense in which the term "pluralism" is used is as a shorthand description of interest group participation, competition, and accommodation in the political process. The pluralist sees governmental policy as the outcome of competition among groups. The process is democratic because opposing group interests are expressed and set off against each other in a system of checks and balances similar to that devised by James Madison for the American Constitution. Supporters of pluralistic democracy contend that this interplay of interests enhances individual freedom and promotes rational decision making. Critics of the pluralist model argue that many groups are not represented in the political process and are short-changed when decisions are made. The poor and ethnic or racial minorities are frequently cited as disadvantaged in the interest group process in the United States. Critics also contend that pluralism retards comprehensive planning and consistency in government.

Ever since Aristotle, who wrote that a state attempts to be "a society composed of equals and peers," social scientists have agreed that it is difficult to establish and maintain stable democratic government in a pluralistic society. Social homogeneity and political consensus are believed to be prerequisites for a stable democratic government. Democratic societies with deep social divisions, whether of class, race, or religion, are subject to instability and breakdown. The dilemma of pluralism has engaged the attention of political and social theorists more than any other problem of democratic theory during the twentieth century.

Three types of pluralism have been identified: laissez-faire, corporate, and public pluralism. Each of these models offers a different view of the openness and workings of the political system. Each is also based on very different normative assumptions about the most desirable pattern for the political process.

Laissez-faire pluralism is most clearly expressed in the works of Robert Dahl, David B. Truman, and Wallace Sayre. These writers conceive of democracy as a process involving competition among political elites and bargaining among interest groups. They believe that the political system is responsive to a variety of interests with differing policy preferences. The system is not dominated by a single ruling elite. As Dahl argued in his influential *Pluralist Democracy in the United States: Conflict and Consent* (1967):

> When one looks at American political institutions in their entirety and compares them with institutions in other democracies, what stands out as a salient feature is the extraordinary variety of opportunities these institutions provide for an organized minority to block, modify, or delay a policy which the minority opposes. Consequently it is a rarity for any coalition to carry out its policies without having to bargain, negotiate, and compromise with its opponents.

Laissez-faire pluralists also contend that the system is self-righting. If one group appears to be gaining a monopoly of political power, countervailing groups will spring up. David B. Truman argued that "potential groups" of this kind are the chief restraint on monopoly power.

While laissez-faire pluralism is chiefly supposed to be a description of the political process, it also has normative significance. The laissez-faire pluralists are the intellectual inheritors of eighteenth and nineteenth century individualism. Like James Madison, they believe that the existence of multiple centers of power will prevent despotism and enhance individual freedom.

A contrasting view of pluralism is provided by the corporate model. Corporate pluralists, especially Theodore Lowi and Grant McConnell, argue that in reality there is no open competitive political arena. They view political power as being divided among small autonomous political subsystems that operate independently of one another. Each subsystem may include one or more government agencies or congressional committees. No single subsystem can monopolize all decisions, but some effectively control certain individual policy areas. For the corporate pluralist, the self-correcting pressures posited by the laissez-faire pluralists have been overwhelmed by the power of individual interest groups or coalitions. This comes about largely because government officials and agencies have been "captured" by the very groups they are supposed to superintend. Thus, the authority of the state is used to promote the interests of private groups. There are many case studies in which government power has been shown to have been relinquished to interest groups.

Most of the social scientists who believe that the corporate model of pluralism accurately describes the political process are extremely critical, for this view implies that the national interest is often surrendered to more selfish private interests. Nevertheless, corporate pluralism has its defenders, who point out that cooperative action, especially between business and government, can have many benefits. Unlike laissez-faire pluralists, who argue that interest group competition prevents the misuse of power, some corporate pluralists believe that it is needless to worry about the use of public institutions for illicit ends because there is sufficient consensus on national goals to prevent the misuse of power. Corporate pluralists also contend that competition is a wasteful and disorderly means of reaching decisions. Programs frequently overlap one another and may have different goals. An often-cited example is the use of government funds to subsidize tobacco growers while at the same time the Public Health Service spends large sums of money to persuade people not to smoke.

Beginning in the 1970's, a reform-oriented model of pluralism was developed. This model has been called "public pluralism." It differs from its predecessors in that it begins with a prescriptive or normative model of decision making. Public pluralism recognizes that political competition does break down and that power is often vested in autonomous fiefdoms. Unlike the corporate pluralist, however, the public pluralist does not support the process. Public pluralism suggests that democratic governments can avoid the fragmentation of power on the one hand and its monopolization on the other by dealing with the weaknesses of both the laissez-faire and the corporate models of pluralism. It recognizes that many marginal groups and constituencies are in fact shut out of the political process for want of resources or incentives; it also recognizes that many agencies and their clientele groups have been able to prevent their rivals from operating in particular policy systems and therefore do not engage in open competition with others.

Public pluralism seeks to deal with the dilemma by regulating interest group activity. This goal can be achieved if the government organizes and empowers the marginal elements of society from the bottom and at the same time regulates the give and take of the interest group process from the top. In this way, the two worst defects of pluralistic government may be mitigated or eliminated. The free market or bargaining style of decision making is rejected in favor of a system that relies heavily on central management of the interest group process to ensure that the competitive nature of the political arena remains intact. The process is to be regulated or managed in three ways. First, the government may act as an advocate, defending and perhaps even organizing certain groups that have no political strength. Consumers and the poor are among those who have seemed underempowered in the United States. In stimulating such groups to participate more actively in the political process, government agencies may be able to help them oppose groups or interests that promote antithetical objectives. Second, the government must act as custodian by structuring the decision making process so as to prevent these newly formed groups from being denied access to the bargaining table. Processes that force interest groups to bargain with one another must be devised; in the same way that the government's power is used to prevent economic monopoly, it can be used to prevent political monopoly. Third, the government must manage interest group access so as to prevent "log-rolling" arrangements that attempt to shut out other interests in society.

There have been some precedents for government to play the roles of advocate, custodian, and manager of the interest group process. The establishment of the Office of Economic Opportunity during the War on Poverty in President Lyndon Johnson's administration affords examples. The OEO VISTA and Community Action programs attempted to mobilize and empower underrepresented groups and encouraged them to apply pressure on agencies of the government that were insensitive to the needs of the poor. President Bill Clinton and Hillary Rodham Clinton's struggle to reform health care in the 1990's relied in part on establishing new public constituencies and interest groups to balance the power of medical and insurance interests. Earlier in the twentieth century, the Farm Bureau, the national Chamber of Commerce, and labor unions were all provided with government organizational assistance in order to establish a political counterbalance to other powerful interest groups that already existed.

Public pluralists believe that the major interests of the public or community can be identified and that distinctions can be made between the "technical" and "political" decisions of society. Political decisions should come about through the competitive interest group and political processes idealized by laissez-faire pluralists. Technical decisions should use the kinds of cooperative processes that are characteristic of corporate pluralism.

Applications

The debate over pluralism cuts right down to the central question of democracy: How is the public good to be recognized, established, and implemented? Nothing weighed more heavily on the minds of the founders of the United States than the dangers of factionism. James Madison, perhaps the most influential of the framers of the American Constitution, held that conflict was built into human society. At the Constitutional Convention, he argued that people are diverse and have diverse interests:

> All civilized Societies would be divided into different Sects, Factions & Interests as they happened to consist of rich & poor, debtors & creditors, the landed, the manufacturing, the commercial interests, the inhabitants of this district or that district, the followers of this political leader or that political leader, the disciples of this religious Sect or that religious Sect.

Although Madison did not speak of race or ethnicity, they too can be added to the list of cleavages in American society. Madison's answer to the problem of factionism was a constitutional structure that protected the formal legal rights of minorities against majorities. Although this structure operates very well to prevent oppression by the government, it does not solve the eternal problem of allocating a society's resources—

the question of who gets what and of how groups should operate to achieve what they conceive to be in their own or the public's interest. Consequently, the application of the pluralist model of power always raises questions about the structure of politics and government. Those who believe that the system is too narrow because certain groups are excluded try to devise rules of politics that give those groups a formal voice in the process; those who believe that other claimants should have no say try to narrow the rules in order to maintain their monopoly. The establishment of the "McGovern rules" for the 1972 Democratic presidential nominating process, and their abandonment after that election, afford particularly good examples.

The McGovern rules were named for Senator George McGovern of South Dakota, who headed a commission that attempted to revise the Democratic Party's delegate selection processes after the election of 1968. Under these rules, each state's delegation to the Presidential nominating convention had to include a quota of minority and impoverished people—groups that traditionally had been disadvantaged in the electoral process. After considerable struggle in some states, delegations that met the requirements of the rules were seated at the 1972 Democratic convention. George McGovern himself received the presidential nomination, and a very liberal platform was adopted. In the ensuing election the Democrats were badly defeated. Under the McGovern rules, many of the people who participated in the convention and platform writing were far more liberal than most Democrats and, moreover, came from social groups whose voting rate is very low. The McGovern rules were quietly revised before the election of 1976 and entirely abandoned by 1980.

Similar efforts at "empowerment" were sought in the arena of higher education in the 1980's. In this policy-process struggle, which was still continuing in the mid-1990's, affirmative action and equal protection rules were used to force institutions of higher education to add more members of disadvantaged groups to their faculties. Part of the aim was to promote equality of opportunity among the professorate. The more ambitious goal was to bring about curricular revisions in which the cultural and intellectual contributions of women and ethnic and racial minorities would receive due recognition and attention.

Debate over the nature of democracy and pluralism took center stage in the discussion of both of these policy struggles. The questions raised are likely to be argued still more frequently as the United States becomes more and more diverse.

Context

The pluralistic model of political power shared with the classical political theory of the seventeenth to the nineteenth centuries a primary concern with political institutions. It began as an attack on the theories of unlimited government power that had been developed by Jean Bodin and Thomas Hobbes and refined by John Austin. At that time, the central beliefs of pluralism were in the vitality and legitimacy of self-governing associations as means of organizing social life and the idea that the political structure must respect associations such as trade unions, churches, and other voluntary bodies. In the pluralist scheme, it is such associations that perform many of the basic tasks of social life, most notably including the articulation or expression of political interests. Consequently, a basic principle of pluralism is antistatism, which is clearly reflected in the U.S. Constitution and in a great deal of nineteenth century American political discourse.

Modern theories of pluralism in the United States begin with Arthur Bentley's *The Process of Government* (1908). Bentley's work, which attempts to describe empirically and justify plural political processes, was refined and amplified by such mid-twentieth century political scientists as Robert A. Dahl and David B. Truman, whose book *The Governmental Process* (1951) did much to revive interest in pluralism. The two most influential works criticizing pluralist theory were Theodore Lowi's *The End of Liberalism* (1969) and Grant McConnell's *Private Power and American Democracy* (1966), which showed the exclusion of many groups from the political process. Attacks on the laissez-faire model brought about the development of public pluralism, whose best early expression is *American Democratic Theory: Pluralism and Its Critics* (1978), by William Alton Kelso.

Bibliography

Bentley, Arthur. *The Process of Government*. Chicago: University of Chicago Press, 1908. An early study focusing on the role of political interest groups in American politics. Until the mid-1950's, this seminal book was the most significant exposition of interest group activities in the United States (indeed, it was reprinted in 1935 and 1949); although the political issues discussed by Bentley are long forgotten, his analysis of the process is still worthwhile.

Dahl, Robert A. *Pluralist Democracy in the United States*. Chicago: Rand McNally, 1967. Dahl reviews pluralism and democratic theory from the time of the Constitutional Convention in 1787 to modern American politics. This book has been very influential because of the clarity and the scope of Dahl's analysis. Includes a good index but no bibliography. This book can be read profitably by anyone who is interested in democracy in the United States.

Kelso, William Alton. *American Democratic Theory: Pluralism and Its Critics*. Westport, Conn.: Greenwood Press, 1978. This book is prescriptive; Kelso defends the pluralistic form of democracy and proposes reforms to meet the most serious criticisms of the pluralist model. Kelso's development of the idea of "public pluralism" is in many ways analogous to the development of communitarianism in the early 1990's. This book is clearly written, and its review of the literature of pluralism is especially helpful. Very strong bibliography and index.

Lijphart, Arend. *Democracy in Plural Societies: A Comparative Exploration*. New Haven, Conn.: Yale University Press, 1977. A comparative study of pluralist thought and democratic models in developing nations as well as in the industrial democracies, excluding the United States. Useful for its cross-cultural perspective. Well written, but the analysis is sometimes difficult, making the work most suitable for specialists.

Lowi, Theodore J. *The End of Liberalism*. New York: W. W. Norton, 1969. Lowi's thesis is that laissez-faire pluralism has failed because of the exclusion of many groups from the political process and because of the emergence of "policy subsystems" that exclude many actors from participating in particular policy disputes. Well suited for college audiences and above.

McConnell, Grant. *Private Power and American Democracy*. New York: Alfred A. Knopf, 1966. This influential book was one of the first to attack the notion that interest group competition brings about democratic political processes. McConnell sees in the three-cornered relationship between congressional committees, executive branch bureaus, and business-oriented interest groups little satrapies in which policy important to business but not widely noticed by the public is decided. With its good notes and index, this book is a fine choice for those needing to sample criticism of pluralistic models of power.

Madison, James. "Federalist Ten." In *The Federalist Papers*. Garden City, N.Y.: Anchor Books, 1961. Federalist Ten was Madison's clearest and most powerful exposition of how governmental structure should be used to control the effects of factionism. The essay begins with a brilliant analysis proving that the causes of factionism cannot be controlled and goes on to show how the separation of powers offers the best possibility for dealing with the problems created by factionism. Recommended for all who are interested in democracy.

Truman, David B. *The Governmental Process*. New York: Alfred A. Knopf, 1951. Truman's book is second only to Arthur Bentley's work in terms of the discussion of interest group politics in the United States. Theoretically powerful, especially because of the development of the idea of "potential groups," this book has been widely studied. Truman's analysis is sometimes complex, but advanced undergraduates should be able to profit from reading it. Excellent annotated bibliography.

Robert Jacobs

Cross-References

THE POWER ELITE

Type of sociology: Social stratification
Fields of study: Dimensions of inequality; Politics and the state

In 1956 C. Wright Mills introduced the notion of the power elite—the interconnected leaders of political, economic, and military institutions in American society. This analysis offers insightful explanations for many realities of life in the modern world, including the formation of opinion and the structure of class relations in the contemporary United States.

Principal terms

COERCION: the removal of resistance through the exertion of power

CONTROL: power used against the relatively powerless in such a way that the exertion of power removes any possibility of choice from those affected

CO-OPTATION: the power elite's acceptance of credentials of power groups from other parts of society (for example, former military officers may be accepted on corporate boards)

INFLUENCE: power that affects others with probable but not determinable outcome, as seen in forms of persuasion and propaganda

POWER: the ability on the part of a person or group to affect human thought, action, and disposition despite resistance

POWER ELITE: a group of persons in power who control parallel social institutions and lead them as connected interests

Overview

The concept of a "power elite" in modern American society involves the idea that the leaders of a combination of economic, political, and military institutions together wield tremendous power and control over society. Each of the separate institutions within these areas of society possesses its own ruling class. Formal groups of Pentagon officials, including generals, admirals, and appointed officials, govern the military hierarchy. Likewise, boards of directors provide both leadership and control for the large corporations that dominate the economic sphere, along with institutions such as the securities markets, the Federal Reserve Board, the banking system, major pension funds, and other large sources of capital. Within politics, elected officials join with career bureaucrats and other appointees to direct the national government. Each of these institutions creates its own elite group of leaders, and each of these elite groups exercises considerable power and influence over a variety of affairs within American society.

Sociologists have identified a high degree of overlap among these distinct elite groups, and C. Wright Mills, in his influential book *The Power Elite* (1956), coined the term that has been widely used to describe them. The power elite concept points to several characteristics of the overlapping elite groups. The members of the power elite tend to share many life experiences, such as education and class notions of responsibility. Many of them know one another, even across institutional lines. For example, politicians and corporate executives not only create policies that affect one another's institutions but also socialize together, share loyalties to the same schools, join the same clubs, attend the same functions, and contribute to the same causes. Also, members of the power elite possess extensive personal resources in addition to their control over larger societal resources.

As the power elite in the United States has grown in influence, traditional institutions such as family, education, and religion have assumed lesser roles in determining values and orientations. In the case of education, advanced degrees do not confer or limit membership in the power elite. Even when certain affiliations arise between graduates of certain universities (especially Ivy League law schools), more importance may well be attached to membership in certain campus clubs reserved for elites than to factors such as academic performance and degrees earned. Likewise, regional concerns diminish in comparison with the national (and international) perspectives of the elites, who tend to be urban (or suburban) rather than rural in their perspectives.

The presence of a power elite correlates with the creation of celebrity. Some persons attain high celebrity and name recognition through their personal wealth, their corporate leadership, their political position, or their military prominence. Again, this celebrity is related not to any sort of objectively measured "success" but rather to power and influence. The corporate chief executive officer (CEO) who turns the highest profit ratios is not necessarily a member of the power elite, but the chairs of the largest corporations probably are. Similarly, politicians do not receive celebrity for high efficiency or great service, but instead for their ability to persuade and influence others with power. Celebrities become well known throughout the culture, both inside and outside their particular group of institutions. For example, many Americans do not know the names of their own senators or congressional representative, but most could name several prominent politicians from other states who have attained the celebrity accorded those members of the power elite who seek it.

The American power elite forms an entrenched class of leaders. Though celebrity attaches itself to many of them, most work behind the scenes, attaining celebrity for only brief periods of time if at all. Examples include a corporate lawyer who wields extensive power over decades but gains fame only during a cabinet appointment late in life. Even though partly enshrouded, the power elite controls most sectors of social existence. The interlocking nature of the power elite allows for interchange between different sorts of institutions, maintaining and strengthening the power of each. This co-optation of elites from one field to another furthers the connections between different sectors of power.

In theory, the United States government contains a series of checks and balances. The typical understanding of government that emphasizes checks and balances between different branches of the federal government, however, fails to recognize the interlocking nature of political, economic, and military power throughout the society.

The same economic entities that exert direct financial influence on the lives of many citizens not only participate in the military-industrial complex but also donate sizable funding to the political campaigns of congressional and presidential candidates. This reduces the effectiveness of any true balances within the political system itself. At the same time, the power elite fractures the nonpowerful classes into dispersed minority interests. This appearance of pluralism obscures the power of the elite, who often exercise their power subtly through the creation of a mythical "common interest" of the majority, against which the minority interests are doomed to fail. Such a common interest often does not reflect the wishes of any true majority but instead serves as an expression of the power of the dominant group. The mass media, controlled by the same interlocking forces of the power elite, play an increasingly significant role in the creation of such "majority" opinion. They become lenses that control public perceptions of reality and create public desires. This in turn creates "public opinion."

Applications

Since the Civil War, the United States has provided the clearest example of a power elite. As Alexis de Tocqueville had noted in 1835, early American society was highly mobile, functioning on the basis of loose affiliations rather than strict class systems. While this was true for the first century of the United States' existence as a nation, the late nineteenth century saw a variety of changes. The earliest American middle class consisted of small business owners who worked for themselves as independent proprietors. Throughout the second half of the nineteenth century, the middle class shifted. Corporations grew, and economic monopolies arose to take control of vast market segments. With the growth of corporations came the existence of numerous white-collar jobs that paid enough to maintain middle class incomes but denied mobility into the upper class. Instead, the new middle class became dependent upon corporations for its continuation. Concurrent with this change, organized labor gained in influence. The unions allowed a more significant political and economic role for groups of the lower class and lower middle class, offering a new voice for those segments of society with inadequate resources to form their own businesses. The dependent middle class and the influence of organized labor tended to cancel each other out, allowing room for the enhanced growth of the power elite at the expense of both.

In the 1930's, President Franklin Delano Roosevelt's New Deal expanded the welfare state, increasing government involvement in all economic aspects of American society. This replaced traditional laissez-faire economics with a financial situation more closely controlled by the power elite. Thus, these governmental changes combined the economic and political institutions of power. Shortly thereafter, the war economy of the World War II years produced a political and economic dependence on military production. Once the military expanded its power into the economic and political arenas, the power elite became thoroughly entrenched. Whereas President Dwight David Eisenhower decried the "military-industrial complex" that had taken over the economy and the society, C. Wright Mills emphasized the problem of the military-economic interests allying themselves with the political status quo in Washington, D.C.

A further example of the influence of the power elite can be seen in twentieth century American educational systems. The power elite combines political, economic, and military interests, making other social institutions subservient. Thus, education serves the interests of the power elite as well. Private schooling provides a place for members of the upper class to meet while they are children and adolescents, forming the basis for permanent alliances of power and for strategic marriages and other affiliations. Public education claims to increase the values of common citizenship, but too often such education emphasizes acceptance of the reality of life, increasing the power of the status quo and the present power elite. Throughout the history of the United States' public educational system, there has been no increase in the sophistication or participation of the electorate in public debate. Instead, the growth of a "conservative mood" (Mills's phrase in *The Power Elite*) has marked the acceptance of society's status quo. Such a conservative mood holds that tradition is sacred and upholds the position of the power elite. It provides ideological undergirding for the society as it stands. Education as the transmission of tradition thus enhances the values of the power elite and their influence over society.

In addition to these forms of socialization that ease the propagation of the power elite's assumed rule, the cross-pollination of the elite institutions tends to enhance the insulation of the power elite. As elite groups co-opt elites from other societal sectors, the leaders appear more and more alike, increasing the dependency on a small number of elites. Thus, corporation boards become interlocking directorates in which individuals may belong to a number of executive bodies, each doing favors for others and tending to keep the same people in power. Likewise, political leaders tend to favor graduates of certain schools; the institutions then gain influence and provide power to their graduates. For example, President John F. Kennedy had strong ties with the governmental policy programs of Harvard University. Similarly, President Bill Clinton, upon election, immediately employed large numbers of Rhodes scholars. Mutual experience becomes an important commonality forming the power elite through personal affiliation and shared loyalties to the alma mater, but this process also increases the power of elite educational institutions.

Context

C. Wright Mills's development of the concept of the power elite followed earlier notions of power systems within American society and reacted against them. Alexis de Tocqueville had provided an early statement on American power; he emphasized the affiliational elements and the possibility of social mobility. Despite the great degree of accuracy in his description of the postrevolutionary United States, de Tocqueville's analysis had grown seriously out of date as power became more entrenched in the hands of a few and as social mobility declined. During the early twentieth century, other notions of power had become prevalent. Conservative theorists often devised conspiracy theories that rooted power in devious groups of hidden actors working for personal gain. Mills, however, argued that the United States is ruled by a class or group of power elites with interlocking but not synonymous goals. At the same time, liberal theories of power emphasized the importance of common people and thus the impotence of power groups to affect public opinion. Mills asserted the naïveté of such positions and demonstrated that these views obscured and justified the true nature of power in American society.

The notion of the power elite also drew on other social concepts. Against many eighteenth century social theories, the power elite model assumes the irrationality of social actors, seeing them as influenced more by power than by thought. This incorporates essentially Freudian ideas about human behavior into a larger model of social action and organization. Likewise, the power elite model assumes that ideas about reality are socially conditioned. Because members of the power elite occupy social positions of influence, they can affect people's assumptions about reality and thus enhance their own capacity for power.

Power elite models maintain a certain popularity within sociology, and they are evolving as studies continue. These models will need to give greater attention to the processes by which power elites reorganize themselves internally and to the related processes by which the power elite brings about (and reacts to) social change. The power elite joins disparate groups from different social institutions such as politics, the economy, and the military; not all elites are equals. Not all elites experience the same opportunities for upward mobility or horizontal mobility into other social institutions. Thus, the internal organization of the elites needs further study. At the same time, some power elite models tend toward static functionalism, overemphasizing the ability of elite groups to maintain their systems of privilege. This overstatement can limit understanding of how elites not only cause change but also must react to changes in the social situation.

Studies of power have produced more recent concepts of power than Mills's, and power elite models still need full integration of these views. For example, many theorists now assert that power is interactive and relational; this view challenges the idea of a separate, autonomous power elite. The specific relationships between the elites and their constituencies need further study, with special attention paid to the means by which the populace participates in the relationships of power. Refinement of power elite models must explore further the distinction between the elites' use of power and their potential for power, since these are not equivalent phenomena. Furthermore, sociology should investigate the role of ideology in producing, maintaining, and changing the power elite. Ideological issues are especially important in understanding the role of the media in forming public opinion and in influencing the opinions and attitudes of the elites themselves.

Bibliography

Giddens, Anthony. *The Constitution of Society: Outline of the Theory of Structuration.* Berkeley: Calif.: University of California Press, 1984. One of the major theorists of the late twentieth century, Giddens connects power with the larger theory of structuration, which is the process by which social structures develop. This roots power and the existence of a power elite within a larger context of social change and development. Provides an important neofunctionalist interpretation of social structures such as the power elite.

Lenski, Gerhard E. *Power and Privilege: A Theory of Social Stratification*. New York: McGraw-Hill, 1966. In perhaps the most influential study of power of the 1960's, Lenski argues that position and private property are the only two sources of power. Shows the roots of the power elite.

Lukes, Steven, ed. *Power*. New York: New York University Press, 1986. This anthology provides easy access to many of the key writings in contemporary discussion of power and thus offers a good introduction to the issues in the current evaluation of power elite models. An excellent resource for the important background questions.

_____ . *Power: A Radical View*. London: Macmillan, 1974. The author provides an essential discussion of the connections between power and conflict, interpreting instances of power as disclosures of latent conflict. He also analyzes power as an interpretation placed upon certain events, since the attribution of power depends on the unprovable counterfactual assumption that something else would have happened had power not been exercised.

Mills, C. Wright. *The Power Elite*. New York: Oxford University Press, 1956. This is the most important study on the topic of the power elite, a phenomenon that Mills first described as such. Mills provides a strong analysis of the different segments of elites within the power elite and gives excellent descriptions of the process of the power elite's historical development in American society.

Olsen, Marvin E., and Martin N. Marger, eds. *Power in Modern Societies*. Boulder, Colo.: Westview Press, 1993. This anthology offers a strong mix of both contemporary and historic theoretical articles and case studies within American society and other worldwide examples. It provides an excellent first resource for understanding the power elite and the wider context of theoretical approaches to social power.

Prewitt, Kenneth, and Alan Stone. *The Ruling Elites: Elite Theory, Power, and American Democracy*. New York: Harper & Row, 1973. Prewitt and Stone update Mills's classic work through a number of methodological refinements, including a better integration of Marxist theory and a strong critique of democratic notions. They emphasize political and ideological dimensions, perhaps to the detriment of economic issues.

Tocqueville, Alexis de. *Democracy in America*. Translated by Henry Reeve. New York: Schocken Books, 1961. This book, first published in 1835, provides the classic study of social structure, power relationships, and the high degree of social mobility in the postrevolutionary United States. The author, a French observer of American society, offered many first-hand anecdotes to support his assertions of high mobility and voluntary associations within the culture.

Jon L. Berquist

Cross-References

Capitalism, 191; Conflict Theory, 340; Corporations and Economic Concentration, 360; Inequalities in Political Power, 972; The Military-Industrial Complex, 1207; Political Sociology, 1414; Social Stratification: Analysis and Overview, 1839; Social Stratification: Modern Theories, 1859; The State: Functionalist versus Conflict Perspectives, 1972.

PREJUDICE AND DISCRIMINATION: MERTON'S PARADIGM

Type of sociology: Racial and ethnic relations
Field of study: Theories of prejudice and discrimination

Prejudice refers to an unfavorable attitude toward certain individuals or people by virtue of their being members of a particular racial or ethnic group. In contrast, discrimination refers to an overt action, such as the denial of opportunities and equal rights to the members of that particular racial or ethnic group. Merton's paradigm shows that prejudice does not always lead to discrimination and suggests that discrimination is not always directly caused by prejudice.

Principal terms
ETHNIC GROUP: a group distinguished by its common ancestry and cultural heritage
ETHNOCENTRISM: the tendency to judge other people's behavior and values on the basis of one's own culture, which is usually considered superior
IN-GROUP: the group to which an individual belongs and feels loyalty
INSTITUTIONAL DISCRIMINATION: a denial of opportunities and equal rights to individuals or groups, resulting from the normal day-to-day functioning of a society
MINORITY GROUP: a subordinate group whose members receive unequal treatment and have unequal access to society's resources
OUT-GROUP: a group composed of people who are not members of one's in-group and are considered outsiders
SOCIAL DISTANCE SCALE: a technique for measuring the degree of one's tolerance for different people according to how close to or far from one's own group they are
STEREOTYPE: an oversimplified or exaggerated and shared negative belief concerning the characteristics of members of a group (such as an ethnic, racial, or religious group)

Overview

"Prejudice" and "discrimination" are crucial terms in the study of race and ethnic relations. In general discourse, they are often used as if they were interchangeable, but they actually denote distinct phenomena. Prejudice involves attitudes, thoughts, and beliefs about members of different groups (such as ethnic, racial, religious, or political groups). Discrimination, on the other hand, is action, either overt or subtle, that treats members of different groups differently. Prejudice may be expressed in various ways, as through negative terms, slurs, or jokes that denigrate members of ethnic or racial groups. Prejudice may also be expressed in discriminatory actions—hence the popular linkage between the terms. Discrimination may take overt forms, as in an employer's refusal to hire an Italian American or African American because the employer thinks that all people of Italian or African descent are incompetent, basing this perception on stereotypes rather than on an objective appraisal of the applicant's qualifications. Discrimination also appears in the form of institutional discrimination or racism, which is a denial by society's institutions of opportunities and equal rights to individuals or groups; this type of discrimination may be unintentional. A crucial point, and one that was long unrealized, is that individual prejudice does not necessarily express itself in discrimination; moreover, discrimination may result from causes other than prejudice.

Sociologist Robert K. Merton proposed a typology or paradigm in 1949 regarding the relationship between prejudice and discrimination. Merton's work was influential in clarifying these distinctions and in expanding the definition of discrimination to include institutional and unintentional discrimination. This paradigm appeared in an article entitled "Discrimination and the American Creed." Merton attempted to show that, although prejudice and discrimination are related, one does not necessarily cause the other. Merton identified four categories of people according to how they rate on a scale of prejudicial attitudes and discriminatory behavior.

The "unprejudiced nondiscriminators," or "all-weather liberals," are low in both prejudice and discrimination. People in this category usually believe firmly in the equality of all people, and they try to practice this belief. Yet committed as they are to equality, they often do have some shortcomings, according to Merton. For one thing, the all-weather liberals tend to be removed from reality, in the sense that they do not experience face-to-face competition from members of minority groups for limited resources.

The second category consists of "unprejudiced discriminators," whom Merton also calls "fair-weather liberals." Fair-weather liberals are low in prejudice, but they tend to discriminate against other people when it is expedient, as when it is profitable to do so. In Merton's words, this person's expediency

> may take the form of holding his silence and thus implicitly acquiescing in expressions of ethnic prejudice by others or in the practice of discrimination by others. This is the expediency of the timid: the liberal who hesitates to speak up against discrimination for fear he might lose status or be otherwise punished by his prejudiced associates.

In South Africa, for example, under the rigid racial caste system of apartheid that existed until 1994, many whites who themselves were not prejudiced remained silent about the injustices of apartheid, under which the white minority maintained privileges and absolute control over society. The fair-weather liberals did not condemn the system simply because they were benefiting from it.

The third category of Merton's paradigm involves people who do not believe in equality. These are "prejudiced nondiscriminators," whom Merton identified as "fair-weather illiberals" and called "timid bigots." They discriminate if there is no sanction against it; their discriminatory practices are situational. In the early 1930's, social scientist Richard LaPiere conducted a study in which he traveled in the United States with a Chinese couple to see how much discrimination they would encounter; prejudice against Asians was still quite strong at that time. LaPiere and his companions received warm treatment at nearly all motels, hotels, and restaurants they visited; only once were they refused service. Six months later, LaPiere sent a questionnaire to all the establishments, asking whether they would accept Chinese people as guests or customers. To his surprise, more than 90 percent of the responses revealed prejudiced attitudes and said that they would refuse service to them. This is a clear example of how prejudice does not necessarily translate into discrimination. A similar test was conducted in the 1950's with a black couple, and similar results were obtained. People seem to be able to adjust their actions and attitudes according to what sociologist W. I. Thomas called the "definition of the situation."

The final category in Merton's paradigm is the "prejudiced discriminators," also called "active bigots." These people are high in both prejudice and discrimination. They openly express their beliefs and do not hesitate to discriminate publicly. Sociologist Thomas F. Gossett presented a good example of such people, noting that in 1932 a Southern Baptist leader refused to sit at a banquet table at a meeting because a black person was present. Since court decisions and civil rights legislation in the 1950's and 1960's outlawed discrimination, active bigots in American society have found it more difficult to practice individual discrimination. Hate groups such as the Ku Klux Klan, for example, continue to espouse their prejudiced views, even on national television, but when evidence of discriminatory actions is uncovered, legal cases are filed against the perpetrators. According to the social distance scale, active bigots tend to show a high degree of intolerance for, and unwillingness to accept, members of out-groups such as racial and ethnic minorities.

Applications

The use of Merton's paradigm has enabled the development of many insights into the complexity of the problems of prejudice and discrimination. It has, for example, pointed to the possibility that many unprejudiced people are struggling with the issue of discrimination, particularly if they are surrounded by, and influenced by, prejudiced people. Particularly since the late 1950's, discrimination has been confronted in a number of arenas. With the major focus that has been applied to prejudice and discrimination, both in sociology and in intense debates over public policy, many people have become more aware of their own prejudices. Many nongovernmental institutions, including church organizations, have explored various means of confronting prejudice. Since the 1980's, the focus has expanded beyond the issues of black and white prejudice to include the diverse spectrum of racial and ethnic groups in the United States in efforts to promote understanding and reduce prejudice. Workshops on diversity and the educational emphasis on multiculturalism are representative of this trend.

The application of Merton's paradigm to discussions of how different types of people act or react with regard to discrimination has shed light on a number of behaviors. For example, it has been revealed that some people choose to minimize their social contact with members of society's out-groups even though they consider themselves to be unprejudiced nondiscriminators. Sociologist Vincent Parrillo has called this "social discrimination," which also refers to the creation of "social distance" between the individual and minority group members. This type of social discrimination is applied not only to racial and ethnic groups but also to a number of other groups, including the elderly, poor people, and people with acquired immune deficiency syndrome (AIDS). The observation of such behavior being applied to such disparate groups has made it apparent to some experts that there is probably no single approach that can deal effectively with prejudice or discrimination. A combination of approaches is necessary; among the approaches that have been used are legal methods (including affirmative action).

Legal approaches to combating discrimination are sometimes opposed by people who argue that laws cannot effectively regulate morality or control personal habits and attitudes. Although there is much truth in this argument, there is also truth in the argument that many changes which have occurred in the United States, particularly in the education system, have occurred because of legal action. The 1954 Supreme Court decision in *Brown v. Board of Education*, which ended segregation in public schools, is a prime example. Because of the policy of segregated schools, seven-year-old African American student Linda Brown had to walk about two miles to an all-black school even though there was a white school only five blocks from her house in Topeka, Kansas. When the case reached the Supreme Court, it ruled that segregated schools were inherently unequal, thus overturning the 1896 decision that "separate but equal" facilities were acceptable. This decision wrought profound changes in American education—and in American life in general—as it gave a new force to the growing Civil Rights movement. It should be noted, however, that although segregation is illegal, many schools are still unofficially segregated because of residential patterns, a condition referred to as de facto segregation (segregation "in fact" rather than sanctioned by law).

Since the 1980's, many organizations and companies have been encouraging their members or employees to take diversity workshops or undergo sensitivity training in an attempt to counter prejudicial attitudes and discriminatory behavior. Many examples can be found of ways that prejudices affect perceptions. A television news crew in Minnesota, for example, conducted a four-month study of the security personnel who monitor stores to observe shoplifters. They found that many of the security personnel, because of their own prejudices and stereotypes, targeted African Americans for observation. As a result, records from these stores showed that African Americans were overrepresented among shoplifters. When store officials were confronted with this information by the observers from the news team, some immediately dismissed the security people who were watching only African Americans. The store officials believed that the security personnel had violated company policy. Some of the store owners and officials noted that the situation indicated a need for sensitivity training. This study suggests ways that discrimination can occur and ways that it can be attacked.

Context

Sociologists and other scientists have been interested in the study of race and race relations since the 1920's. Racism and ethnocentrism have been among the central issues studied. Sociologist William Sumner is credited with coining the term "ethnocentrism" to describe the tendency for people to view their own group as the best. In-groups tend to view the race, ethnicity, and culture of out-groups as being inferior to those of the in-groups. Sociologists in the first half of the twentieth century saw a link between ethnocentrism and prejudice. For example, members of an in-group may express their dislike of an out-group by using stereotypes to rationalize their views: "I don't like black people because they are lazy," for example, or "I don't like Jews because they are stingy." Columnist Walter Lippmann described stereotypes in 1922 as "pictures in our heads" that have no scientific evidence to support them. The study of stereotypes has helped in the redirection and refinement of efforts to overcome discrimination.

Between the 1920's and the 1960's, two of the prominent subjects in studies of race relations were immigration and assimilation. Debates on these issues were highly charged. Prejudicial overtones often crept into the discussion. Prejudiced attitudes were expressed in discriminatory practices such as campaigns to restrict immigration because certain immigrants were seen as lacking the desirable characteristics of the in-group. Restrictive immigration policies targeted certain racial and ethnic groups, such as Asians, Africans, Hispanics, and people from certain parts of Europe. It was not until the mid-1960's that restrictionist sentiments in the law were reduced. The Immigration and Nationality Act of 1965 eliminated the system of quotas based on national origin, which discriminated against certain nationalities. The 1965 law did not eliminate discriminatory practices, but it did attempt to confront some of the prejudice of the past which had been codified into law.

The assumption of many people before the 1940's that prejudice was the single cause of discrimination was challenged when Merton introduced his paradigm in 1949. Since the 1950's, both social scientists and civil rights activists have made marked progress in confronting discrimination. Instead of focusing only on prejudice as the cause of discrimination, many scholars and activists have broadened their perspectives. Prejudice and discrimination have been viewed in various lights and attacked in various ways. Activist Paula Rothenberg, in her work *Race, Class, and Gender in the United States: An Integrated Study* (1992), brings to light various facets of prejudice and discrimination. She also calls attention to the use and internalization of words that subtly perpetuate prejudice, such as "culturally deprived" and "underdeveloped," which tend to be misleading as well as reflective of the attitude that only the dominant culture is acceptable and others are inferior. Awareness of how language can perpetuate prejudice and discrimination is another way of confronting the problem of racism. A broad analysis of the ways prejudice and discrimination actually exist in society, as in the case of Merton's paradigm, shifts the focus from blatant and intentional expressions of racism to all forms of discrimination—some unintentional, some incorporated into the institutions of society—in the day-to-day functioning of society.

Bibliography

Doob, Christopher Bates. *Racism: An American Cauldron*. New York: HarperCollins, 1993. This concise presentation of racism in American history predicts how racism will continue to affect the society throughout the 1990's. Useful for both college and general audiences. It gives readers insight into racism and how it influences individuals' behaviors and attitudes without their being aware of it.

Feagin, Joe R., and Clairece Booher Feagin. *Racial and Ethnic Relations*. 4th ed. Englewood Cliffs, N.J.: Prentice-Hall, 1992. This introductory text discusses important basic concepts and theories as well as various social and ethnic groups. It also provides research current at the time of publication on various topics, including prejudice and discrimination.

Gossett, Thomas F. *Race: The History of an Idea in America*. New York: Schocken Books, 1971. This text, first published in 1963, is rich in historical background on the American racist ideology and its influence in all social institutions.

McLemore, S. Dale. *Racial and Ethnic Relations in America*. 3d ed. Boston: Allyn & Bacon, 1991. This introductory book includes detailed discussion of minority groups and well-documented and footnoted summaries of research studies.

Marden, Charles F., Gladys Meyer, and Madeline H. Engel. *Minorities in American Society*. 6th ed. New York: HarperCollins, 1992. This is a good text that provides valuable information on minorities and the prejudice and discrimination they face in American society.

Marger, Martin N. *Race and Ethnic Relations: American and Global Perspectives*. 2d ed. Belmont, Calif.: Wadsworth, 1991. This introductory text takes a broad and comparative approach. Themes of prejudice and discrimination are especially well presented throughout as they apply to various social and ethnic groups.

Merton, Robert K. "Discrimination and the American Creed." In *Majority and Minority: The Dynamics of Race and Ethnicity in American Life*. Edited by Norman R. Yetman. 4th ed. Boston: Allyn & Bacon, 1985. This text contains a collection of essays on different issues pertaining to racial and ethnic relations. In this essay Merton introduces his paradigm, demonstrating that discriminatory behaviors are not always directly related to individuals' negative attitudes or prejudices.

Rothenberg, Paula S. *Race, Class, and Gender in the United States: An Integrated Study*. 2d ed. New York: St. Martin's Press, 1992. A well-written book on the consequences of racial, class, and gender prejudice and discrimination. This is one of the best integrated texts on racism, sexism, and classism. The author presents many examples of direct and indirect individual and institutional discrimination and sexism.

Schaefer, Richard T. *Racial and Ethnic Groups*. New York: HarperCollins, 1992. This introductory text is one of the best on racial and ethnic minorities. The author presents the research evidence of consequences of inequality resulting from prejudice and discrimination against minority groups. The discussion of theories and basic concepts is very good.

Rejoice D. Sithole

Cross-References

PREJUDICE AND STEREOTYPING

Type of sociology: Racial and ethnic relations
Fields of study: Basic concepts of social stratification; Theories of prejudice and discrimination

Prejudice consists of negative attitudes toward certain groups and members of groups based on classifications such as gender, race, and religion. Stereotyping is rigidly believing that individuals have certain traits simply because they belong to a particular group. Discrimination, often fueled by prejudice and stereotypical thinking, is behavior that leads to the denial of basic rights and opportunities.

Principal terms
DISCRIMINATION: the denial of basic rights and/or opportunities for economic, personal, or social advancement based on variables such as race, gender, age, and disability
HATE CRIMES: crimes of violence toward or degradation of others prompted by extreme prejudice against them, because of their race, gender, sexual orientation, or religion
IN-GROUP/OUT-GROUP DISTINCTIONS: the tendency to look favorably on actions of people like oneself and to attribute negative motives to the same actions by people outside one's group
MULTICULTURAL EDUCATION: an educational approach that strives for inclusivity and fairness regarding the contributions of all cultures and races, and both genders, to society; it sometimes challenges the dominant culture's views
PREJUDICE: a belief (a "prejudgment") about people, often entailing dislike of all members of a particular group, such as an ethnic or religious group
STEREOTYPE: an inflexible, generalized belief about the attributes of all members of a particular group

Overview

Prejudice, stereotyping, and discrimination are three closely related but distinct phenomena. Prejudice is literally a "prejudgment"—a belief about something or someone that is based on assumptions rather than on actual experiences. Strictly speaking, a prejudice may be either for or against something, but in common usage it refers to a dislike of all the members of a particular group, such as a racial, ethnic, religious, gender, or age group. Sociologist Gordon Allport defined prejudice as "an antipathy based upon a faulty and inflexible generalization." A crucial point is that a prejudice is an attitude, not a behavior.

A stereotype might simply be defined as one of the "inflexible generalizations" to which Allport referred. Stereotyping is the attributing of certain characteristics to people simply on the basis of their membership in a group. Stereotypes are oversimplified and rigid mental images; they may contain a "kernel of truth," but that kernel is overwhelmed by the false generalization that has grown around it. One of the interesting things about stereotypes is that people tend to continue to believe them even when they are presented with evidence that refutes them. People often discount their own observations, shrugging them off as "exceptions to the rule." Stereotypes therefore can be extremely persistent.

Discrimination, in contrast to prejudice, refers to behavior: the denial of basic rights and/or opportunities to members of certain groups based on such surface variables as race, age, gender, religion, or disability. An interesting finding of a number of studies of prejudice and discrimination—and one that surprised the researchers who first noted it—has been that prejudicial attitudes do not necessarily result in discriminatory behavior. Many people who state their dislike of a particular ethnic group, for example, in practice treat them with equality and civility. Moreover, discrimination can have causes other than prejudice; institutional discrimination may be unwittingly practiced by people working for institutions who are unaware that their policies and actions are discriminatory. Nevertheless, prejudice and the stereotyping that helps reinforce it can lead to discriminatory behavior as well as to the commission of hate crimes and other harmful, violent, and even fatal acts.

Prejudice and stereotyping have led to the sociological phenomena of exclusion and, in some cases, elimination of certain groups from "mainstream" society. In the United States, for example, a combination of prejudice and economic greed led to the near extinction of the American Indian population, the previous mainstream culture of the Americas, between the seventeenth and twentieth centuries. Other groups, such as women, African Americans, Hispanics, and Asians, have also felt the brunt of prejudice at various times in the history of the United States. The effects of prejudice, such as the discrimination that it can produce, are destructive both to the individuals who suffer violence or psychological harm as a result of discrimination and to the integrity of society as a whole.

A number of sociological theories have speculated about the causes of prejudice. Socialization—the process of teaching people (particularly as children) the knowledge and attitudes of a group or society—has been implicated as a cause of prejudice. Adults in society pass their prejudicial beliefs on to impressionable children. Thus, prejudicial attitudes are learned. Another theory on the cause of prejudice involves the principle of relative deprivation; relative deprivation is the gap between people's expectations and their actual condition or situation. When people see themselves as relatively deprived, they experience frustration and may look for scapegoats on which to blame their situation (a situation that is usually a result of a number of interrelated, complex causes). Historically, minority groups such as women or ethnic minorities have been "scapegoated," or blamed for someone else's economic or social misfortunes. A number of sociologists have also observed that competition increases prejudice, stereotyping, and discrimination. Muzafer Sherif, a sociologist, conducted studies showing how boys at a boys' camp could learn prejudice very quickly. The boys became biased and hostile when they were divided into groups and intergroup competition was introduced into their activities.

Social conformity is another concept that has been used to explain the cause of prejudice. Social norms—the expectations for behavior in a culture—define what kinds of behaviors or attitudes are acceptable. Thomas Pettigrew demonstrated this idea in the 1950's when he found that people from the South became less prejudiced toward African Americans when they were in the army. The army had norms that accepted blacks, so prejudice and discrimination were reduced in that social context. Robert A. Baron, a social psychologist, has written about theories that hypothesize conditions in which prejudice may occur. Baron (as well as many others) believes that periods of economic hardship and scarce resources can contribute to the occurrence and intensity of various types of prejudice. In the field of social psychology, this premise forms a part of what is known as "realistic conflict theory."

A growing body of research illustrates that class status has a profound effect on both influencing and buffering prejudicial beliefs and expectations. The interdisciplinary text *Race, Class, and Gender: An Anthology* (1992), by Margaret Andersen and Patricia H. Collins, contains a variety of articles that illustrate the intricate interplay of race, class, and gender in human experience. The text notes, for example, that racial and ethnic bias has been found to exist even among mental health professionals, a group of professionals who should, by definition, be objective and neutral in their work.

A critique of the various theories concerning the causes of prejudice suggests that there is no one single cause for the perpetuation of prejudice. Rather, sociologists believe that prejudice and stereotyping are socially determined and that multiple methods of transmission are involved. Prejudice may be said to be "multidetermined."

Applications

Research has provided a number of classic studies demonstrating the effects of prejudice. Kenneth Clark and Marie Clark, for example, conducted a study on preschool children's color preference regarding dolls. This study, published in 1947, showed that even very young African American children preferred "white" dolls to those with their own skin color. This study was among those cited in a "friend of the court" brief that was consulted by the Supreme Court in 1954 when it decided, in *Brown v. Board of Education*, that segregated schools could no longer be allowed.

In the 1970's, Jane Elliot conducted an experiment with elementary schoolchildren in which she instructed the brown-eyed children to sit in the back of the room and told them they could not use the drinking fountain. Blue-eyed children were given special privileges such as extra recess time and extra lunch helpings. The two groups of children were told not to interact with each other. Elliot belittled and berated the brown-eyed children, and their academic performance faltered. The favored blue-eyed group soon became even more belittling to the brown-eyed children than the teacher was. After several days, roles were reversed, and the negative effects of prejudice were repeated. Eventually all the children disliked one another, demonstrating the destructive effects of status inequalities.

Prejudicial attitudes regarding people with disabilities (a category including more than 36 million Americans in 1986) have been found to be an insidious form of misunderstanding. In American society, those with emotional or learning disabilities (the "invisible disabilities") often face misunderstanding and discrimination because of ignorance, perpetuation of myths, and social ostracism. People without disabilities have demonstrated lack of empathy, avoidance of social interaction, lack of eye contact, and lack of respect for those with disabilities. In reality, most people with physical disabilities have been found to have strong self-concepts and good social interaction skills and have often been more able to provide support to others than the other way around.

An aspect of stereotyping that has concerned many observers through the years and has outraged a number of groups (particularly since the Civil Rights movement of the 1960's and the women's movement of the 1970's) has been the stereotypical portrayals of minorities in the mass media. Motion pictures and television, particularly, have a tremendous effect on helping shape people's perceptions and attitudes. In the early years of film, it was tacitly assumed that the audience was primarily composed of white Americans, and members of minorities were nearly always depicted in stereotypical roles—such as a meek, timid "Chinaman" or, in the words of communication theorist Douglas Kellner, "eye-rolling, foot-shuffling, drawling" African Americans, "usually in the role of servant or clown." This pattern repeated itself half a decade later when television began. Particularly in visual media, pulling on old stereotypes was handy for writers or performers because they involve a sort of shorthand—comically depicting a hard-drinking, fighting Irishman, a shrewish housewife, or a foot-shuffling black person called up a host of associations and permitted a writer or performer to get laughs easily. A number of advocacy groups have adamantly protested such stereotyping, and blatant negative stereotypes in the media have been reduced significantly. Yet new stereotypes arise nearly as soon as old ones fade.

An interesting and surprising study on the media and ethnic images was done by S. Robert Lichter and Linda Lichter, codirectors of the Center for Media and Public Affairs in Washington, D.C., in 1988. They found that youth in the Howard Beach area of New York, even after the considerable turmoil there that had surrounded what was thought to be a racially motivated murder of a black youth by whites, felt positively about ethnic characters in the media. They also found that some (about one-third) of their sample of 1,200 high school students of various ethnic backgrounds said that there were negative stereotypical images of ethnic groups on television, but the students believed that these images were largely countered by positive role models also appearing on television.

A combination of factors, including the health care crisis of the 1990's and a fear of the disease itself led to prejudice and discriminatory actions toward victims of the acquired immune deficiency syndrome (AIDS) epidemic. The fact that the early rise of the disorder was associated with homosexual behavior and intravenous drug use also biased people against members of those populations. Even though, by 1993, a higher percentage of new AIDS cases was reported in teens, women (especially minority women), and their infected infants, the original prejudices proved difficult to correct. An advocacy group for people with AIDS called AIDS Coalition to Unleash Power (ACT-UP) was formed in 1987 to take more dramatic measures in order to call national attention to the serious epidemic of AIDS.

In the educational arena, efforts have taken the form of the development of prejudice-reduction programs, disability awareness programs, and workshops and intensive efforts directed at developing a multicultural curriculum at all levels of education. The book *Teaching a Psychology of People: Resources for Gender and Sociocultural Awareness* (1988), edited by Phyllis A. Bronstein and Kathryn Quina, discusses the refinement and inclusion of a multicultural approach to psychology. Another important text is *Issues in Diversity: Voices of the Silenced* (1990), edited by sociologist Mary Stuck.

A wide variety of social supports, both formal and informal, have been created to combat prejudice and stereotyping. Some cities have established programs that celebrate diversity, and they hold festivals and ethnic heritage events that are open and inclusive to all people. Colleges have held "Rainbow Months" in their dormitories in celebration of cultural and ethnic diversity and have presented seminars and workshops on prejudice and issues such as sexual harassment. Corporations also hold antibias workshops and have begun to set a tone that even subtle discrimination or harassment based on gender or ethnicity will not be tolerated.

Context

It is widely thought that persecuting others is not innate but rather is a learned behavior; nevertheless, the effects of prejudice and stereotyping have been observed since time began. In medieval Europe, and later in the United States, many women fell victim to religious persecution and were executed for being witches. Those scapegoated included some who were homeless, some who only had a "sharp tongue," and some who were probably mentally ill. All told, this period of religious persecution, led by religious male patriarchs of the time (representatives of the church), resulted in thousands being tortured and put to death. A key thesis underlying this massive persecution and application of prejudice was that the Roman Catholic church feared women's sexuality. This prejudice was so strong that everything from bad crops to miscarriages was blamed on certain women.

In the nineteenth and twentieth centuries, prejudice against women and various racial and ethnic groups has both persisted in large segments of the population and been opposed by groups fighting for their rights. The fight to gain legal rights and social equality for women, for example, has been ongoing. Prejudicial and stereotypical beliefs about women, including the beliefs that they were possessions of men and that their proper sphere was shaping the moral climate of the home, were quite strong. They were thought of as not being capable of pursuing higher education. Women began to fight for their rights, however, winning the right to vote in 1920.

Many of the gains women have made since the 1960's in terms of educational achievement and economic pay equity have their origins in the women's movement's fight against stereotypes and prejudice.

Social psychologist Gordon Allport wrote *The Nature of Prejudice* (1954), considered a classic book on prejudice. It elaborates Allport's approach to prejudice, an approach consistent with contemporary perspectives because of the emphasis on cognitive factors such as categorization and cognitive bias. According to Allport, there are two forms of prejudice, personal prejudice and group prejudice. Allport's model involves in-group and out-group distinctions. In an extension of Allport's theory, Thomas Pettigrew proposed the "ultimate attribution error" in an article he published in 1979. Pettigrew suggests that people tend to look favorably on the actions of people in their in-group (those whom they perceive to be like them) and attribute negative motives to the same actions by out-group members. If an in-group member observes a negative act by an out-group member, the in-group member is likely to attribute the action to genetic causes or some other concrete factor. If, on the other hand, an in-group member observes a *positive* act by an out-group member, he or she may attribute it to luck, being an exception to the rule, high motivation and effort, or the particular situational context in which the behavior occurred.

In the areas of health, mental health, and people with disabilities, several relevant advances have occurred since the early 1980's. In the late 1980's, educational information about the AIDS epidemic was sent to every household in the United States in the form of a brochure to inform the public about the ways the virus is transmitted. This concerted effort was necessary because of the number of myths and biases that people held about the disease and its transmission, including a belief that only homosexual behavior would expose someone to the disease. Social stigmatization and negative stereotypes can have far-reaching consequences. Fewer than one-third of the children in American society who have a diagnosable mental illness receive psychological or psychiatric treatment, perhaps in part because of a fear of negative stereotyping or labeling.

Bibliography

Allport, Gordon W. *The Nature of Prejudice*. Cambridge, Mass.: Addison-Wesley, 1954. A classic social psychological book on prejudice, with an emphasis on cognitive factors such as categorization and normal cognitive bias.

Andersen, Margaret, and Patricia H. Collins, comps. *Race, Class, and Gender: An Anthology*. Belmont, Calif.: Wadsworth, 1992. An interdisciplinary collection that integrates race, class, and gender into the overall framework of prejudice, oppression, and discrimination. Excellent for its first-person accounts.

Baron, Robert A. *Social Psychology: Understanding Human Interaction*. 6th ed. Boston: Allyn & Bacon, 1989. This popular undergraduate social psychology text contains an excellent chapter entitled "Prejudice and Discrimination: The Costs of Hating Without Cause." Explores social categorization, intergroup conflict, cognitive sources of bias, and stereotypes.

Freeman, Howard E., and Norman R. Kurtz, eds. *America's Troubles: A Casebook on Social Conflict.* Englewood Cliffs, N.J.: Prentice-Hall, 1969. This well-written book explores multiple issues of prejudice in American society and presents many first-person accounts that bring home to the reader the significant impact of bias on individuals, groups, and society.

Lips, Hilary M. *Sex and Gender: An Introduction.* Mountain View, Calif.: Mayfield, 1988. Lips presents a thorough review of myths, theories, and research regarding sex and gender. In addition, the author explores the behavior and experiences of males and females, comparing similarities and differences. Sex and gender are examined in social relationships, political life, and the workplace.

Stuck, Mary, ed. *Issues in Diversity: Voices of the Silenced.* Acton, Mass.: Copley, 1990. Presents a series of well-chosen articles that review historical and sociological phenomena related to the problem of oppressed groups in American society.

Thomas, Gail E. *U.S. Race Relations in the 1980's and 1990's.* New York: Hemisphere, 1990. Explores issues involving racial stratification and education, occupational mobility, economics, and cultural pluralism; special attention is paid to the neglect of the problems of the American Indian population.

Karen M. Wolford

Cross-References

Anti-Semitism, 114; The Authoritarian Personality Theory of Racism, 159; Cultural and Structural Assimilation, 405; Individual Discrimination, 547; The Frustration-Aggression Theory of Racism and Scapegoating, 773; Institutional Racism, 996; "Model" Minorities, 1233; Prejudice and Discrimination: Merton's Paradigm, 1498; Improving Race Relations, 1559; Stereotyping and the Self-fulfilling Prophecy, 1984.

PRIMARY, SECONDARY, AND TERTIARY SECTORS OF THE ECONOMY

Type of sociology: Major social institutions
Fields of study: The economy; Systems of social stratification

The sociological theory that is sometimes (inaccurately) called the dual-market theory holds that an economy is divided into three sectors: the primary sector consists of workers who are paid well and who have job security; the secondary sector consists of workers who are poorly paid, whose employment is erratic, and whose benefits are few; the tertiary sector consists of workers who are poorly paid, who have no benefits, and whose activities are hidden from the government in order to evade tax laws and other forms of regulation.

Principal terms
ADVANTAGED WORKERS: workers whose ascriptive characteristics (such as race or sex) qualify them for employment in the primary sector
DISADVANTAGED WORKERS: workers whose ascriptive characteristics disqualify them for employment in the primary sector
LABOR MARKET SEGMENTATION: the division of the employment field into discrete areas, each of which is open only to certain workers
PRIMARY SECTOR: a part of the economy that offers high wages and job security, including industries that are unionized and engaged in monopoly production
SECONDARY SECTOR: the portion of the economy in which wages are low, employment is erratic, and benefits are few, often involving nonunionized, competitive industries
TERTIARY SECTOR: the part of the economy whose operations are hidden from the government, thus allowing it to evade laws such as those mandating minimum wages

Overview

Classical economics held that the capitalist labor market evenly distributed employment opportunities depending on merit. Any two job applicants who had the same qualifications would have equal chances of getting any particular job for which they possessed the skills.

Such a model is clearly an idealization that is undercut by such facts of the "real world" as nepotism in hiring, but those economists and sociologists who see the national economy as divided into primary, secondary, and tertiary sectors—they are often called dual-market theorists, since the idea of the tertiary sector is a late addition to their originally binary conceptual network—dispute the classical paradigm on more foundational grounds. They question whether there is a single employment market into which all job seekers flow, hypothesizing that there are two or three different job markets, corresponding to different parts of the economy, to one of which a job seeker is assigned according to such characteristics as race and sex. Thus, for example, an African American male employment seeker will inevitably be shunted into the less desirable, secondary sector jobs because of his race, even if his skills should qualify him for a place in the primary sector.

The primary sector holds jobs that offer high wages, good working conditions, stability, and the possibility of advancement. Macroeconomically—that is, from the perspective of the economy as a whole—such jobs would be found in monopolized, profitable industries, such as companies that were in the U.S. automobile industry in the 1950's. During this period, three corporations dominated the market in an expanding economy, which gave them the ability to pay higher wages. They relied on skilled, seasoned workers and had locked in agreements with unions that guaranteed worker loyalty, so it made sense to invest in retaining these workers. Microeconomically, on the level of individual firms, a given company could also have sectors within its own internal labor market. Such segmentation might be seen particularly in companies that had broad seasonal variation in employment. Such firms would keep a core of better-compensated workers year round (their primary sector), but then, in the busy season, would bring in a host of temporary workers (the company's secondary sector) to augment the permanent group. Employees in the primary sector would be drawn largely from a society's dominant group (in the United States, from white males), and these advantaged workers would have character structures suited to this committed labor. They would be stable, skilled, ambitious, and dedicated.

The secondary sector would offer much harder berths. Jobs there would be temporary, poorly paid, subject to arbitrary discipline, characterized by poor conditions, and offering little prospect of moving up. Companies that were in a highly competitive situation, such as those in the textile industries in the 1980's, would fall into this category. With their profits squeezed, they could not afford the liberal pay and security offered to workers in the monopolized sector. Individual firms could also divide their workers into two categories. Bennett Harrison, in *Education, Training, and the Urban Ghetto* (1972), diagrams a representative company of this type that divides its occupational structure by race. It has one set of job tracks for whites, offering high pay, security, and an upbound ladder of promotions, and another set of tracks for African Americans, with less security, lower pay, and a job ladder that breaks off after only a few rungs. Those who take jobs in the secondary sector tend to have personalities, it is argued, that match their work. They are unreliable, rough, unambitious, and prone to seek fulfillment outside work.

The tertiary sector is one that was not included in the original schema that the dual-market theorists developed in the 1960's because this sector was not recognized in the United States until the later 1970's. This sector rests below the secondary portion of the economy and offers substandard wages, an unsafe work environment, little security, and no job improvement possibilities. It could recruit workers and operate with such abysmal conditions for two reasons. First, this "underground economy" was secretive. Work was done in small shops or was farmed out to employees' homes, and thus it could be hidden from government regulators. Therefore, this sector did not have to abide by minimum wage, child labor, or other restraining laws. Second, its labor pool consisted of immigrants who were ignorant of labor laws and who lacked other job opportunities because of limited English skills. Many were "illegals" who could not seek legitimate jobs because they had no working permits. As a result of the gradual economic downswing that occurred in the 1970's, many firms in the competitive sector subcontracted to the tertiary segment in order to cut costs. In *The New Chinatown* (1987), Peter Kwong illustrates this trend by showing how New York City's Chinatown was revitalized as the city's garment industry began relying on neighborhood businesses to manufacture clothing. Such tertiary manufacturers were not actual parts of competitive firms but temporary adjuncts that were paid for individual jobs. Those who took jobs in this sector were generally immigrants with language and legality handicaps. Often, too, these immigrants were mothers, who, no matter how harsh the conditions, could at least work at home and be with their children.

Most dual-market theorists viewed market segmentation as being historically produced. There were relatively few jobs in the economy that demanded skill and years of on-the-job training. It stands to reason that firms that had employees who held such jobs would want to retain their loyalty and would offer inducements with this in mind. A company would have less anxiety, however, about retaining the occupants of positions that demanded little training, and would not offer them strong reasons to stay at their posts.

The early factory system in the United States had utilized few skilled and many unskilled workers. As the economy matured and mass production became dominant, there was a greater division between firms that needed a large group of skilled workers and those that depended on the unskilled, and these new proportions, it was believed, eventually created dual markets for labor. Such people as African Americans who entered factory work late and women who often could not commit to full time work ended up being shut out of primary sector work, as the lines between segments hardened.

Applications

Though the view that the economy has two labor markets has many advocates, it is not an orthodox view that has been adopted by many mainstream economists or sociologists, and therefore it does not have the influence on decision making that a thoroughly legitimated view would have. The existence of an underground sector, however, has been recognized even by those who do not accept the existence of primary and secondary sectors. Clearly, there is employment that evades government regulation, and various methods have been tried to locate and regulate it.

Even if the dual-market theory were widely accepted as being responsible for minority disfranchisement from jobs, the implementation of programs to correct this imbalance would be daunting, since the problem does not depend on a particular practice, such as discrimination, but on the total arrangement of the economy, a complex social institution.

Although no attempts at a grand restructuring of society have even been contemplated by those who view the employment problem in this light, there has been what can be interpreted as one attempt to deal with market structure on a small scale by isolating various communities from general economic forces. This involves the government designation of such areas as enterprise zones, which are then released from commercial taxes and other burdens on industry in an effort to encourage businesses to relocate to depressed locales. This policy, which began being offered by various states in 1982, would have partially offset the problems of duality, since firms locating in zoned neighborhoods would be escaping the competitive pressures that might have driven them to act as members of the secondary market and offer inadequate wage and benefit packages. This program caught on in the 1980's, spreading to thirty-eight states that created six hundred enterprise zones, and then, in the wake of the 1992 Los Angeles ghetto riots, it was picked up by the U.S. federal government.

Although these programs became popular, they never had clear-cut beneficial results. For one thing, although firms did move to enterprise zones, often they did not hire local residents, because residents of the zones had no access to job training. Furthermore, it often turned out that new firms built in the zone were not created specifically for the area but were simply moved from marginally better-off areas that were not zoned. Therefore, the program could end up bringing about a new, enfeebling dual structure that incited competition between impoverished areas that had and ones that did not have enterprise zone status.

The tertiary sector has long been recognized as posing problems, especially in relation to tax collection and illegal immigration, and various levels of the U.S. government have attempted to solve these problems. If some businesses are hidden in order to avoid abiding by work-related laws, they will also be concealed from tax collectors. It was estimated in the 1980's that the underground economy contained as much as 20 percent of the United States' overall economic activity, which represents a sizable subtraction from the state's coffers. Part of the reason for the major overhaul of the tax system that occurred under President Ronald Reagan was that it was believed that lower tax rates and stiffer punishments for apprehended tax cheaters would make it less tempting for persons to move into or stay in the tertiary sector.

This quixotic plan proved to be ineffective in returning people to the tax rolls, but attempts to catch tax evaders who make money in the tertiary segment have been more successful. These ventures, such as a 1988 effort by the New York City government, involved the comparison of data from different government agencies to ferret out scofflaws through the discovery of inconsistencies. As worthwhile as such campaigns have been to revenue collectors, they are too piecemeal to have a major impact on the existence of the tertiary sector.

A report issued by Congress in 1990, "Unauthorized Migration: An Economic Development Response," pointed out that the underground economy was largely composed of illegal immigrants who were drawn to the United States by the "pull" of illicit jobs and the "push" of unemployment in their own countries. In relation to Latin

American immigrants, the study suggests that the only way to stanch the flow into the tertiary sector labor pool and therefore drain its resources is to assist in the improvement of the immigrants' native economies.

Context

The concept of the dual economy was first introduced to explain the problems of undeveloped, industrializing economies, but it quickly became part of a theory that was used to analyze disequilibrium in the industrial powers.

In 1910, J. H. Boeke, a Dutch economist, began looking at why his country's colony, Indonesia, had never acquired a full-blown capitalist economy from the seeds planted in the nineteenth century by Europeans. He theorized that "the economic laws that were found valid for capitalistic society are not applicable to societies in which capitalism lives side by side with a peasant economy still largely ruled by precapitalistic relationships."

In 1954, this conceptualization was taken up and reinterpreted in less cultural terms by the British economist W. A. Lewis. In his model, one did not have to give weight to factors such as precapitalist mentalities to explain the division; it was necessary only to imagine a society with distinct work environments. He postulated an economy with a low-wage, overpopulated (in terms of employment chances) rural sector and a higher-wage, less-populated urban sector, and he noted how such duality would establish a double labor market.

In the 1970's in the United States, in connection with the civil rights struggle, a number of urban sociologists, such as Harold Baron and Bennett Hymer (1968), who were independently studying the employment of lower-class African Americans, arrived at forms of dual-market theory. The theory was used to explain why even qualified African Americans seemed to be locked into low-wage jobs by showing how the bifurcated labor market unjustly parceled out employment opportunities.

From this beginning, the dual-market theory went on to become a vital, competing paradigm in economics and sociology that contested more mainstream conceptual networks. It was put to extended use in such works as Piore's *Birds of Passage: Migrant Labor and Industrial Societies* (1979), which views the continual influx of transitory immigrants into nineteenth century America, immigrants who would take unskilled work, as a compelling reason for the creation of a bilevel economy.

The concept of a tertiary economic sector was added to the American theory later, though more sociologists came to accept its existence than came to accept the existence of primary and secondary markets. The presence of this component of the economy had long been observed in the less prosperous economies of Europe, such as that of Italy, as well as in Third World nations. It came to be studied in the United States in the 1970's at the same time that it was becoming an influential part of the economic structure, although its exact size has baffled analysts. Paradoxically, in comparison to dual-market theory, the theory of the tertiary sector is more accepted by sociologists and economists yet less used as an integral part in grand theories of society such as the one developed by Piore.

Bibliography

Baron, Harold M., and Bennett Hymer. "The Negro Worker in the Chicago Labor Movement." In *The Negro and the American Labor Movement*, edited by Julius Jacobson. Garden City, N.Y.: Doubleday, 1968. This article, written by members of the Chicago Urban League, an African American civil rights organization, played a key role in introducing the idea of dual markets, which the authors call the white and black labor segments, into the understanding of long-term black unemployment. Aside from demonstrating the existence of this duality, the authors point out which institutions sustain it.

Fernandez-Kelly, M. Patricia, and Anna Garcia. "Hispanic Women and Homework: Women in the Informal Economy of Miami and Los Angeles." In *Homework: Historical and Contemporary Perspectives on Paid Labor at Home*, edited by Eileen Boris and Cynthia R. Daniels. Urbana: University of Illinois Press, 1989. This essay examines the underground economies of two cities. It describes the women who enter the tertiary sector of the garment trade and studies how their households are organized in terms of who does the breadwinning and how work and child care are juggled.

Gordon, David. *Theories of Poverty and Underemployment: Orthodox, Radical, and Dual Labor Market Perspectives.* Lexington, Mass.: Lexington Books, 1972. Gordon extensively and critically examines dual labor market theory. He looks at its strengths and weaknesses, and situates it in terms of what exactly it can explain, noting that its concepts have often been spread too thinly over various sociological and economic fields.

Harrison, Bennett. *Education, Training, and the Urban Ghetto.* Baltimore: The Johns Hopkins University Press, 1972. This book analytically studies inner city slums in twelve cities and points to how dual-market theory can explain their ineradicability. He goes beyond most sociological thinkers by suggesting avenues that might be followed by government agencies seeking to combat endemic unemployment and underemployment.

Lozano, Beverly. *The Invisible Work Force: Transforming American Business with Outside and Home-Based Workers.* New York: Free Press, 1989. Lozano argues that work done at home in the underground sector combines elements of self-employment and wage labor. She analyzes the growth of the United States' tertiary sector in the 1980's in relation to such matters as family structure and the move into a service economy.

Todaro, Michael P. *Economic Development in the Third World: An Introduction to Problems and Policies in a Global Perspective.* London: Longman, 1977. This textbook on the difficulties of economic development in the Third World has become somewhat dated, but Todaro here presents one of the few attempts by a dual-market theorist to integrate the existence of the tertiary sector into an overarching economic framework.

James Feast

Cross-References

PRISON AND RECIDIVISM

Type of sociology: Deviance and social control
Field of study: Controlling deviance

A prison is a building used to punish, through confinement, people convicted of serious crimes. Recidivism refers to the tendency of some criminal offenders to continue committing crimes after they have been punished. The recidivism of a high proportion of former prison inmates calls into question whether imprisonment can effectively rehabilitate offenders or deter crime.

Principal terms

CORPORAL PUNISHMENT: pain or suffering intentionally inflicted on the body of a criminal offender

DETERRENCE: a purpose of punishment according to which an offender is punished as an example to discourage other people from committing similar crimes or to discourage the offender from continuing to commit crimes

INDETERMINATE SENTENCE: a structure for setting the period a person actually stays in prison; the sentencing judge specifies a minimum and a maximum term, while a parole board sets the exact period within those limits

PRISONIZATION: assimilation into prison social life; the process whereby a newly admitted prison inmate learns and takes on the attitudes, values, and behavior of the prison subculture

REHABILITATION: a strategy of punishment, the primary purpose of which is to change whatever caused the offender to commit the offense; punishments designed to change behavior through fear alone are not included

RETRIBUTION: a principle of punishment according to which the punishment is selected solely to reflect the seriousness of the crime; the consequences of the punishment for deterrence or recidivism are not considered

TOTAL INSTITUTION: a form of social organization where the inmates are isolated from society and have every aspect of their lives controlled by staff, usually for the purpose of changing the personalities of the inmates

Overview

Through most of human history, deviants were punished through corporal means— whipping, cutting off limbs, stoning, hanging, and beheading. Deviants were generally imprisoned only until they could be punished. Even where imprisonment was widely used, corporal punishments were more common. In the mid-eighteenth century, however, imprisonment was widely substituted for corporal punishment in industrializing countries.

Few sociological theories exist regarding the origins of prisons. German sociologists Georg Rusche and Otto Kirchheimer, in 1939, explained the origins of prisons within the larger context of social change. They claimed that the crucial factor in determining the punishment a society uses is its need for human labor. Sometimes the level of technology and general social conditions produce an overabundance of people able to work at the available jobs. Under these conditions the labor of unskilled criminal offenders has little value. Harsh and physically destructive punishments are therefore used. Where a labor shortage exists, the labor of offenders is more valuable. In this case, punishments are less harsh, and they involve some type of productive labor.

Rusche and Kirchheimer found the emergence of prisons in the sixteenth century to be consistent with their theory. At that time the plague spread throughout Europe, killing a large proportion of the workforce, while growing international commerce created an increasing need for labor. Houses of correction were built all over England and Europe, beginning in the sixteenth century, to encourage unemployed people to get a job.

French social philosopher Michel Foucault in 1977 offered a different explanation for the substitution of imprisonment for corporal punishment. Beginning in the mid-eighteenth century, he said, Western societies attempted to control their citizens by focusing on their souls more than their bodies. The purpose of punishment changed from purely retributive and deterrent to corrective. Prisons were constructed in which each inmate could be closely observed and assessed. Inmates were taught self-discipline through work and highly routinized daily schedules. Similar disciplinary strategies were adopted by other social institutions—the family, school, and workplace. The underlying function of this change from punishment to discipline, according to Foucault, was to create a compliant citizenry that could be controlled without much force.

In fulfilling their corrective function, prisons have always provided prisoners with access to clergy for spiritual guidance. Basic education was introduced into prisons in 1830. The "medical model" of corrections was introduced during the Progressive era (1900-1920). Under the medical model, offenders were believed to have individual defects—physical, psychological, or social—which caused them to commit crimes. Preventing recidivism, under this model, involved first determining an offender's problem and then providing corrective treatment. Sentencing judges had broad discretion to tailor punishments to offenders' needs. Indeterminate sentences provided for release when parole boards decided that an inmate had been reformed. After release, former inmates were supervised on parole.

Many treatment programs were instituted in prisons between 1900 and the 1960's. "Treatment" was more an ideal than a reality for most prison inmates, however, as only a small percentage of inmates participated in treatment programs. A rising crime rate during the 1960's produced disenchantment with a system of punishment that seemed both ineffective and insufficiently harsh. As a consequence, the rhetoric of treatment gave way to the rhetoric of retribution and deterrence.

Under the medical model of sentencing, offenders who had committed similar offenses were sometimes sentenced to widely disparate punishments. Some disparities occurred randomly, whereas some were patterned, producing consistently harsher punishment for members of some population groups—distinguished by race, age, sex, and social class. Richard Quinney, in 1980, expressed a view shared by many other Marxist sociologists: "Prisons are institutions of control for the working class, especially the surplus population—that portion of the working class not needed for capitalist production."

A final factor diminishing the influence of the medical model was the absence of evidence that treatment was successful. No single treatment program has been found to reduce the recidivism of criminal offenders generally, though some treatment programs benefit some subgroups of offenders. The inaccurate but catchy generalization, "Nothing works," has often seemed to dominate public discussion of treatment since the mid-1970's. The reduced importance of treatment as a purpose of punishment led to the passage of laws providing for determinate prison sentences, mandatory minimum sentences, and longer sentences. The main consequence of these changes has been a dramatic increase in the number of prison inmates.

Applications

The first major sociological study of a prison was undertaken by sociologist Donald Clemmer and published as *The Prison Community* (1940). Clemmer documented the informal relationships and adaptations to prison life. He interviewed prison inmates about such important issues as informal social controls, sexual adjustment, work, and attitudes toward crime and the law. From interview responses, he was able to sketch the unique prison culture. Clemmer described the process of "prisonization" that all new inmates experience—how they learn that they must replace the values and attitudes that served them well outside prison with the informal rules of the inmate social system.

Sociologist Gresham Sykes's *The Society of Captives: A Study of a Maximum Security Prison* (1958) followed in Clemmer's tradition of observing and interviewing. Sykes focused on the difficulty of "doing time" and the challenge that prison life posed to inmates' self-respect. Prison inmates are denied access to resources—such as attractive clothes, a car, and heterosexual relations—available to them outside prison. Sykes reasoned that American males need these resources to maintain a positive self-image.

Prison inmates create a subculture with norms emphasizing toughness and self-reliance. In prisons for men, physical domination by stronger inmates of weaker ones often becomes the functional equivalent of financial success or heterosexual conquest outside prison. Inmates subscribing to this code reject the prison's rehabilitation programs as simply another attempt to manipulate them into compliance with the institution's rules.

Sociologist/anthropologist Erving Goffman, in *Asylums: Essays on the Social Situation of Mental Patients and Other Inmates* (1961), described the characteristics of "total institutions," those specialized facilities designed to control every aspect of their inmates' action and even their thoughts. Among the total institutions Goffman examined were the military, mental hospitals, monasteries, and prisons. All total institutions are characterized by a strict caste system in which every staff member has authority over every inmate. When newcomers enter these institutions, the staff tries to strip them of their individuality and autonomy to make them completely submissive to the authority of the staff. Such things as severe haircuts, uniform clothing, and demeaning forms of address are imposed on inmates. Inmates are required to abide by complex rules governing every aspect of their lives. Inmates respond to these assaults on their autonomy in a variety of ways. Some adopt the institution's ideals; some become mentally ill; many develop ingenious schemes to improve the material quality of their lives and circumvent the rigid rules of the institution. The primary psychological function of these informal adaptations, Goffman claimed, is to help inmates retain their self-respect by demonstrating that the institution does not completely control them.

Most people who enter prison are poor and unskilled. Their lives in prison are spent mostly in idleness, with little opportunity for treatment or job training. A small minority of inmates benefit directly from prison programs. Most inmates who solve their problems or develop employable skills while in prison do so despite, rather than because of, the conditions of their imprisonment. Upon leaving prison, most inmates are no better prepared to function successfully as conforming members of society than when they entered.

The period immediately following release from prison is very stressful for most releasees. A long period of isolation from conventional social life can result in attenuation through lack of use of the social skills adults typically possess. People released from prison must relearn how to function without the strict external controls imposed on them in prison. The stigma of having a prison record places an additional burden on them, as they seek a job, a place to live, and friends. These practical and psychological burdens are greatest in the period immediately following release, so recidivism is most likely to occur then.

Context

Sociological studies of prisons have been conducted only since the 1940's. Most studies have been conducted in a single prison. These case studies often provide conflicting images of important characteristics of prison structure (such as program availability and quality, or physical condition of prisons) and prison life (for example, the extent of violence, drug use, and homosexuality). Generalizations about prison life based on any one institution are suspect. Moreover, since prisons are constantly changing, even valid generalizations are valid only for short periods.

Political and social changes occurred inside and outside prisons in the 1960's and 1970's, reducing the importance of the informal norms documented by Sykes. The

Civil Rights movement of the 1960's produced a modest set of rights for inmates. In 1964, in the case of *Cooper v. Pate*, the U.S. Supreme Court abandoned its traditional "hands-off" policy and began articulating constitutional standards for prison conditions.

The limited rights granted by the courts created expectations that prison conditions would improve dramatically. The most tragic consequence of these rising expectations occurred at the Attica Correctional Facility in New York State, where, in 1971, the inmates took over the prison, demanding improvements. Many inmates mistakenly believed that, when the public saw the conditions at Attica, they would support the inmates' demands. When officials retook the prison by force, thirty-three inmates and ten guards were killed. Sociological studies of prison riots have found similar patterns of racial tensions between staff and inmates and among inmates, a perception by inmates that staff was unresponsive to their grievances, rising (and then frustrated) expectations of improved conditions, and inadequate staffing.

Prison subculture was transformed during the 1960's and 1970's. Before the 1960's, black inmates were largely powerless. The Black Power movement produced cohesive groups of black inmates whose primary loyalty was to other blacks. Prison populations divided, often violently, along racial lines. At the same time, large urban street gangs organized their imprisoned members. Gang members owed their loyalty exclusively to their gangs, even when in prison. In some large state prisons the staff lost control to racial groups and street gangs. In *Stateville: The Penitentiary in Mass Society* (1977), sociologist James B. Jacobs documented the difficulty staff members had in accommodating the expanded rights of inmates and the consequent reduction of staff authority.

During a brief period, in the mid-1960's and early 1970's, the themes of "deinstitutionalization" and "diversion" were popular in political and academic discourse about punishment. In response to criticism of correctional institutions by labeling theorists such as Erving Goffman, the strategy of punishing nonviolent offenders outside prison gained popular and scholarly support. The conventional wisdom developed within this movement argued that imprisonment did more harm than good, so it should be avoided as much as possible. This movement was quickly overwhelmed by the retributive response to rising crime rates.

Most of the studies of prisons have included only prisons for men. Women account for only 5 percent of imprisoned offenders, though, proportionately, the population of women prison inmates is growing faster than the male inmate population. Women's crimes—typically theft and drug offenses—inspire comparatively little fear, and their condition, until recently, has generated little scholarly interest. Much of the interest in women's prison has been prurient, such as curiosity about the extent of lesbianism. Serious assaults are uncommon in women's prisons, but inmates suffer greatly from separation from their children. Women's prisons are typically smaller, with less concern about security and fewer program options, than male prisons. The majority of women prison inmates are mothers, and only a few states permit the young children of inmates to live in prison with their mothers. An imprisoned single mother is likely to lose legal custody of her children.

Between 1973 and 1991, the prison population of the United States quadrupled, and the imprisonment rate more than tripled. In 1992 a total of 884,000 prisoners were held in American prisons, producing an imprisonment rate of 329 inmates per 100,000 people in the general population.

This rapid growth of the prison population has produced severe overcrowding, which has increased tensions and has made prisons more difficult to manage. In 1991, thirty-eight states were operating above their rated capacity, while the federal prison system held 46 percent more inmates than its facilities were intended to hold. Sociologists have concluded that the effects of overcrowding can only be determined when other prison conditions (such as the availability of programs) are also considered. Under conditions of overcrowding and reduced funding for treatment programs, offering meaningful programs for inmates has been difficult. Prison staff members uniformly support these programs, whether or not they believe such programs reduce recidivism. Participating in programs keeps inmates occupied and out of trouble, the dominant concerns of staff.

It might seem that filling prisons beyond their capacity with idle inmates would help deter crime. The available evidence reveals, however, that increasing the length and severity of punishments has no noticeable impact on recidivism or crime rates. More than 60 percent of people released from prisons are arrested for new felonies or serious misdemeanors within three years. More than 40 percent return to prison or jail. The most important factors in reducing recidivism are largely beyond the control of prison officials. These factors include a network of family and friends to provide emotional support and a job that provides a legitimate income and self-respect.

The high financial costs of imprisonment have made it unfeasible to continue indefinitely the rapid growth of the 1970's and 1980's. A major challenge for applied sociologists will be to determine how prisons can best function within a general punishment policy that includes other types of sanctions. More theoretically oriented sociologists will be trying to explain how competing social, political, philosophical, and economic forces determine the structure and use of prisons.

Bibliography

Allen, Harry E., and Clifford E. Simonsen. *Corrections in America: An Introduction.* 6th ed. New York: Macmillan, 1992. This is a widely used college textbook covering the entire field of corrections. It offers a balanced account of prisons in historical and organizational context and contains a glossary, lists of recommended readings, and an index.

American Friends Service Committee. *Struggle for Justice: A Report on Crime and Punishment in America.* New York: Hill & Wang, 1971. This short book, written by seventeen people from various backgrounds, contains an eloquent attack on the medical model and indeterminate sentencing.

Cullen, Francis T., and Karen E. Gilbert. *Reaffirming Rehabilitation.* Cincinnati, Ohio: Anderson, 1982. Writing in the face of widespread rejection of the medical model,

Cullen and Gilbert provide a reasonable defense of treatment as a major purpose of punishment.

Fogel, David. *". . .We Are the Living Proof . . .": The Justice Model for Corrections.* Cincinnati, Ohio: Anderson, 1975. This work introduced what is widely known as the "justice model" of corrections—a prison management scheme in which principles of due process are imported into prisons to produce safer, fair conditions of confinement.

Foucault, Michel. *Discipline and Punish: The Birth of the Prison.* Translated by Alan Sheridan. New York: Pantheon Books, 1977. This very influential, and very difficult, book by a French social philosopher places the origins of the prison in historical social context. Foucault argues that prisons were only one of several institutional forms developed to control working class people by imposing systematic classification, control over detailed aspects of life, and tightly organized work.

Garland, David. *Punishment and Modern Society: A Study in Social Theory.* Chicago: University of Chicago Press, 1990. An excellent and sophisticated critique of all the major sociological theories of punishment.

Goffman, Erving. *Asylums: Essays on the Social Situation of Mental Patients and Other Inmates.* Garden City, N.Y.: Anchor Books, 1961. This was Goffman's first major work. In it he gives a detailed account of the social processes at work within "total institutions."

Jacobs, James B. *Stateville: The Penitentiary in Mass Society.* Chicago: University of Chicago Press, 1977. The best historical account of an American prison, showing the impact of changing legal requirements, political conditions, and management styles.

Rothman, David J. *The Discovery of the Asylum: Social Order and Disorder in the New Republic.* Rev. ed. Boston: Little, Brown, 1990. This work, by a social historian, recounts the invention of institutional responses (including the penitentiary) to major social problems—crime, poverty, and mental illness—during the Jacksonian era (1820-1850).

Joseph E. Jacoby

Cross-References

PROSTITUTION

Type of sociology: Deviance and social control
Fields of study: Forms of deviance; Social implications of deviance

Prostitution refers to the practice of exchanging sexual services for financial remuneration. The practice has been reported in virtually every culture and described throughout recorded history. As a form of deviance, prostitution has been of interest to sociologists as a reflection of various social processes and phenomena.

Principal terms
DEVIANCE: a recognized violation of a social norm or rule; the term may be applied to behavior, career, and social role
INEQUALITY: disparity in status and opportunity among people and groups within a society
INSTITUTION: a stable social arrangement that serves a basic function in society
RESTRICTIVE SOCIETY: a society with explicit and rigid prohibitions; conformity to social norms is expected and enforced without tolerance
SEGREGATION: the physical or social separation of groups of people; segregation generally involves the isolation and alienation of a weaker group by a powerful one

Overview

Sociologists have studied prostitution as a form of sexual deviance and a reflection of the basic values, norms, and institutions within a society. Sociological studies of prostitution have been concerned with the function it serves in a society, the gender inequality and double standard implicit in the practice, and the social dynamics involved in becoming a prostitute. Prostitution represents a form of sexual deviance in that it is a sexual practice which is widely viewed as socially undesirable and degrading. Colloquial terms used to refer to prostitutes, such as hooker, hustler, and whore, all carry negative connotations.

An important issue is defining what constitutes prostitution. Most definitions stress the relatively indiscriminate exchange of sexual activity for economic gain. For the prostitute, the practice represents a means of deriving or supplementing an income. A person who trades sexual activity for a job promotion would not be labeled a prostitute by most observers, although this situation includes some of the same elements as prostitution. What separates prostitution from the previous example is the repeated, indiscriminate nature of the exchanges. More than an isolated deviant act, prostitution entails a deviant profession. According to Vern Bullough and Bonnie Bullough, in their book *Women and Prostitution: A Social History* (1987), prostitution is "the institutionalized marketplace for the sale of sex." As they demonstrate, this institution has been remarkably persistent over time and across cultures.

The most common form of prostitution involves women who sell sexual services to heterosexual men. The second most common group comprises male homosexual prostitutes who cater to gay men. The consistent pattern in society and throughout history is for the customers of prostitutes to be men. Male prostitutes who make themselves available to women (they are sometimes termed gigolos) are uncommon, and lesbian prostitutes are considered extremely rare.

Despite what customers or patrons may believe, the prostitute does not engage in the practice for her own sexual motives; it is purely a financial enterprise. Prostitutes do not derive pleasure from their repeated encounters with customers and, in fact, generally resent them. For the practitioner, prostitution entails the provision of a service for a fee. By definition, the transactions are void of emotional involvement. The briefer each encounter is, the more income a prostitute can generate. The term "prostitute" is derived from a Latin word meaning "to set forth" or to be exposed for sale. This is a reference to the advertising of her services by the prostitute, whether in manner of dress, verbal propositions, or location. The corresponding legal term, "solicitation," is a reference to the offer of sexual activity for a fee.

Prostitution has been called the "world's oldest profession." In reality, it is probably not any older than such social roles as medicine man and priest. Prostitution, however, remains one of the most controversial social roles. Much ambivalence has been reflected throughout history in attitudes toward the practice of selling sexual services as an occupation. Many societies have quietly tolerated the practice, while others have been more accepting of prostitution within specific boundaries. Some societies have strictly banned the practice, whereas in some parts of the world, it is regulated. Even in societies in which prostitution is a violation of existing laws, such as in the United States, it exists and even thrives in some urban areas.

Several aspects of prostitution have been evident throughout the history of the trade of sex. First, a double standard is prominent. Prostitutes are readily condemned, punished, and deplored; their customers, however, are often tolerated, exonerated, or even pitied. Prostitutes are profoundly stigmatized, while their customers ("johns" or "tricks," as they are often called in the trade) receive little attention. In the eighteenth century, convicted customers were fined, but prostitutes were publicly flogged. Her crime has consistently been viewed as worse than his. In ancient Greece, it was common for a man to visit a prostitute for sensual pleasure and to have a wife for childbearing and domestic chores; in both cases, the woman was considered a man's property, for either his sexual enjoyment or domestic comfort. In the Christian medieval period, prostitution was tolerated as a necessary evil for the gratification of man's sinful nature. Thus, throughout history different standards have been applied to prostitutes (women) and their patrons (men).

Prostitution remains the only sexual offense for which more women than men are convicted. A related observation is that prostitution is more prevalent in highly male-dominated, or patriarchal, societies, in which women have a comparatively low

status. In such societies, women typically are considered inferior, have fewer opportunities for success and independence, and are expected to cater to men's needs and
desires. Prostitution is most prevalent in patriarchal, economically depressed countries
that do not have severe sanctions for nonmarital sex; among them are Mexico, Brazil,
Ivory Coast, and Thailand. Sociologist Erich Goode observed that prostitution is most
common in restrictive societies and least common in sexually open societies. Some
have argued that in an open and tolerant society in which the genders had equal rights
and opportunity there would be no need for a clandestine sex trade.

Another consistent finding is that there are different classes of prostitutes. From
society's perspective, the lowest and most deviant form comprises "streetwalkers,"
who are the most common and visible prostitutes. Streetwalkers are virtually indiscriminate in accepting customers, have relatively low fees for services, and generally
have numerous patrons in one night. Those prostitutes who work in brothels, massage
parlors, or clubs have higher status. At the highest level are the "call girls," who often
operate through an organization such as an escort service. Call girls demand a higher
price, are more selective, and typically have a small clientele of regular customers.
Equivalent roles were found in ancient Greece, where *pornoi* (a term meaning "the
writing of prostitutes") referred to the lowest class of prostitutes, and *hetaira* (meaning
"companion") represented the higher-class courtesans. The latter held high unofficial
status, were educated and socially sophisticated, and commanded a higher price for
their services.

The social and personal dynamics of entering prostitution have been the subject of
study. Poverty and limited alternatives are common factors that may lead a person to
select prostitution as an occupation. In some Third World nations, parents have been
reported to have sold their daughters to be placed in brothels. In the United States and
Canada, a significant number of those entering the trade are adolescent runaways.
Typically, they have escaped a troubled home and found themselves with virtually no
financial resources. For a number of these females and males, prostitution is an option
for survival on the streets. Choosing the role of prostitute is usually a gradual, insidious
process rather than an abrupt entry into the trade.

Applications

The functionalist perspective stresses that, although prostitution is viewed as a
deviant and undesirable practice in most societies, it exists in virtually every part of
the world. Without a demand for paid sexual services, the trade would disappear. Yet
its persistence throughout history in most cultures reveals that the trade serves some
purpose. One view is that the practice serves to confirm and strengthen the traditional
values of marriage and monogamy. The widespread disapproval of prostitution in
society reaffirms these competing, traditional values. Society at large is united in its
disapproval of this deviant practice. As for the individuals involved, prostitution is a
means of generating an income which may be less tedious and more lucrative than
other alternatives. For a person with few marketable skills and a pressing need to
secure an income, the trade may be an appealing option. The function for customers

is the provision of sexual contacts. For lonely or unattractive males, prostitutes represent accessible partners. Males who are away from their spouses may use prostitutes as surrogates. For those males who have deviant sexual interests, prostitutes may represent cooperative participants when other females may find these deviant practices offensive. Napoleon Bonaparte was quoted as saying "prostitutes are a necessity. Without them, men would attack respectable women on the street." From this perspective, prostitution may serve multiple functions in society, whether by reaffirming conventional roles or providing outlets for men's sexual needs as well as meeting the economic needs of the prostitute.

The sociological perspective known as labeling theory simply proposes that prostitution involves any sexual transaction for hire of which society disapproves. In this view, many cases which are not generally considered instances of prostitution might otherwise be described as such if society so judged. For example, a person who "marries for money" is trading sex for financial comfort, yet that is not construed as prostitution. The relative nature of what constitutes prostitution is evident in the changing social norms toward alternatives to marriage and toward premarital and extramarital sexuality. In the Puritan society of the seventeenth century, if one divorced and remarried, one would be considered to have multiple sex partners; the situation might be considered prostitution. The labeling perspective of prostitution stresses that it is a deviant practice only because society does not condone indiscriminate sexual encounters.

Ultimately, one purpose of prostitution may be the maintenance of the gender inequality in society, an explanation favored by conflict theorists. The conflict theory focuses on the gender inequality evident in prostitution. In this view, prostitution primarily benefits men, both customers and pimps. Prostitution is based on the double standard in society, the implicit belief that women's role is to serve men's needs. Conflict theorists point out that those women who are most likely to enter the trade are economically disadvantaged, with limited education and skills, and commonly have a background of abuse. They apparently enter prostitution because they have few viable resources in society. They are powerless, and their only marketable resource is their sexuality. According to historian Barbara M. Hobson, in her book *Uneasy Virtue: The Politics of Prostitution and the American Reform Tradition* (1987), prostitution is never really accepted in any society. Prostitutes generally are held at the lowest ranks of the social ladder. Even in societies in which prostitution is legal, it is "not an expression of society's acceptance of prostitution but instead epitomizes a policy of isolation and stigma toward the prostitute." Prostitution policies and regulations in so-called tolerant societies represent variations in attempts to control or segregate prostitutes. In a fair, egalitarian society many acceptable options would be available for disadvantaged women and rarely would they select such a deviant occupation. Hobson notes:

A society that institutionalizes prostitution as a work option for the poor makes a statement about its position on inequality. One can see this in the policy toward prostitution in countries like Korea, and until recently, the Philippines. The governments have sought to legitimize prostitution as work, even elevated it to a patriotic endeavor, since sex commerce has brought in foreign tourism and reduced the national debt.

Conflict theories of prostitution emphasize this manipulation of a powerless, disadvantaged group by a powerful group, such as a government. In this view, prostitution is a reflection of the gender, racial, and economic inequality in a culture.

Feminist theories of prostitution overlap with conflict theories in placing emphasis on the gender inequality evident in prostitution. Within the feminist movement, there is disagreement over whether prostitution is degrading to women or an acceptable choice for independent women. Philosopher Rosemarie Tong noted in her book *Women, Sex, and the Law* (1984) that feminists have debated whether the prostitute is the "quintessential oppressed woman or the quintessential liberated woman." The majority of feminists have argued that women would not choose a deviant role such as prostitute if they were offered better alternatives. With the proper education, economic opportunities, and positive self-concept, women would be free to select any career, and it seems unlikely that many would choose such a socially rejected role.

Context

The study of prostitution has been of interest to sociologists for many reasons. Prostitution involves a sexual transaction of which most cultures disapprove. A sexual service is provided by an individual who advertises his or her availability to any prospective customer. Thus, prostitution involves the delivery of a service; its persistence through history attests the demand for such a service in most cultures. Yet the study of prostitution is the study of a deviant profession. What separates prostitution from most other occupations is the profound stigma associated with it. With few exceptions, prostitutes, especially streetwalkers, are held near the bottom of the social ladder. Prostitutes do not work in isolation; they belong to a deviant subculture. Generally, prostitutes work in association with other prostitutes and under the direction and protection of a pimp. The subculture has its own set of norms, and adherence to these may be essential to survival. The study of prostitution affords the opportunity of examining a deviant subculture.

Beyond the study of prostitution as a career and as a subculture, the trade of sex is of interest to sociologists as a reflection of the norms and values of a society. The inequality manifested in the practice is symptomatic of broader attitudes toward women and members of the lower socioeconomic class. Thus, the study of prostitution is also a study of prejudice and discrimination, sexism and gender inequality, and segregation.

Prostitution is a pertinent topic of study in the sociology of health and illness. Prostitutes represent a high-risk group for contracting the human immunodeficiency virus (HIV) and acquired immune deficiency syndrome (AIDS). Prostitutes engage in one of the high-risk behaviors for exposure to HIV: having sex involving fluid exchange with multiple partners. Although there has been a trend toward increased condom use among prostitutes, it is by no means consistent and universal. Further, a number of prostitutes use intravenous drugs or have sex with intravenous drug users. In a study of 1,000 prostitutes in Kenya, 85 percent tested positive for HIV. In a study in the United States, 13 percent of the prostitutes tested carried the virus. These findings have added a sense of urgency and an element of legitimacy to sociological studies of prostitution. If prostitutes represent a significant group in the spread of AIDS, the study of this form of deviance takes on new meaning. To many in society this renders a deviant profession even more deviant, since it becomes a life-threatening endeavor, both for the practitioner and for the customers. It seems likely that stigmatization of prostitutes will be increased as they are perceived to be responsible in part for the spread of a terminal illness, AIDS. Related questions include whether their customers will continue to be viewed as unfortunate victims or as sharing responsibility for the spread of the disease, and whether prostitution as an occupation will survive the epidemic. Though prostitutes represent a relatively minor source of contagion in the United States, in other countries they are one of the major agents in the transmission of HIV.

Bibliography

Bullough, Vern, and Bonnie Bullough. *Women and Prostitution: A Social History.* Buffalo, N.Y.: Prometheus Books, 1987. The authors provide a thorough historical overview of prostitution in the world from earliest recorded history to the twentieth century. Emphasis is on actual practices, social norms, laws, and roles related to prostitution.

Heyl, Barbara S. *The Madam as Entrepreneur: Career Management in House Prostitution.* New Brunswick, N.J.: Transaction, 1979. This book offers insights into another aspect of prostitution: the training that some women receive for work as a prostitute. The book provides the author's analysis of the training process as well as transcripts of actual recordings of training sessions.

Hobson, Barbara M. *Uneasy Virtue: The Politics of Prostitution and the American Reform Tradition.* New York: Basic Books, 1987. Historian Hobson offers an overview and analysis of policies and laws pertaining to prostitution in the United States. Her review begins with the period from 1820 to 1860 and continues through the 1970's. Her description of the various forms of punishment of prostitutes through history is enlightening.

Rathus, Spencer A., Jeffrey S. Nevid, and Lois Fichner-Rathus. *Human Sexuality in a World of Diversity.* Boston: Allyn & Bacon, 1993. A comprehensive presentation of the biological, psychological, and social aspects of human sexuality. One chapter is devoted to commercial sex, including prostitution.

Sheehy, Gail. *Hustling.* New York: Delacorte Press, 1973. Sheehy's impressions and analysis of prostitution are based on interviews with police officers, lawyers, prostitutes, and pimps. The author offers her own analysis of the trade of sex; she includes excerpts of interviews and the frequent use of jargon from the subculture.

Tong, Rosemarie. *Women, Sex, and the Law.* Totowa, N.J.: Rowman & Allanheld,

1984. Provides a feminist perspective on such topics as prostitution, pornography, and sexual harassment. Included are overviews of black and lesbian attitudes toward prostitution.

Richard D. McAnulty

Cross-References

THE PROTESTANT ETHIC AND CAPITALISM

Type of sociology: Major social institutions
Fields of study: The economy; Religion

Sociologist Max Weber described the "Protestant ethic" as a religious perspective which advocates hard work, sobriety, financial prudence, and deferred gratification. He concluded that this religious perspective helped the capitalist economic system to develop in Western societies such as England and the United States.

Principal terms
> ASCETICISM: a characteristic of the Protestant ethic that stresses the self-denial of worldly pleasures in favor of religious principles
> BREAKTHROUGH: Weber's term for historical periods in which circumstances push a group either toward a new way of action or toward a reaffirmation of traditional ways
> INSTITUTION: a stable social arrangement, including values, norms, statuses, and roles, that develops around a basic need of a society
> LEGITIMATION: a set of beliefs, values, and attitudes (often religious) that attempts to explain and justify existing social conditions and inequalities
> PREDESTINATION: John Calvin's Protestant doctrine which stated that all individuals are born into (and must forever remain in) one of two groups, the Elect or the Damned
> THEODICY: a religious explanation that provides believers with a meaningful interpretation of everyday events, including traumatic events such as personal suffering and death

Overview

The sociological study of religion focuses on the measurable social consequences of religious beliefs and institutions for individuals and for society as a whole. German sociologist Max Weber's interest in the sociology of religion was extremely wide ranging. He studied both Eastern and Western religions, including Judaism, Christianity, Islam, Hinduism, and Confucianism. His most widely known work in this area, however, involves his theory that the tenets of Protestantism helped enable the growth of capitalism.

In relating religious ideas to the growth of capitalism, it should be noted that although industrial capitalism in England and the United States during the nineteenth century is usually regarded as the model for laissez-faire capitalism, some features of capitalism existed much earlier in the commercial activities of the preindustrial European economy. Weber writes about the emergence of capitalism at a time when commerce was conducted by many small firms owned by individuals or families rather than by large corporate organizations.

In his writings, Weber reacted strongly against the analysis of religion in capitalist societies suggested by another influential theorist of his time, Karl Marx. Weber's unique perspective can be better understood by noting that to Marx, religion was simply an ideology, a set of beliefs and values that attempts to legitimate (explain and justify) the economic exploitation of the majority of workers by the capitalist class. Using religion as an ideological tool, the capitalist class is able to convince the majority of workers that their lack of power, prestige, and wealth in society is somehow divinely sanctioned. Marx concludes that, like a drug, religion distracts and pacifies the masses with its promises of a better life in the hereafter. In this way, the capitalists maintain their control over society and the social class system.

In his work entitled *Die Protestantische Ethik und der Geist des Kapitalismus* (1904; *The Protestant Ethic and the Spirit of Capitalism*, 1930), Max Weber disagreed with the viewpoint that religion is only an ideology, although he acknowledged that religion can certainly be used as such by those in power. Instead, Weber argued that religious ideas themselves may change society rather than merely reflecting the way in which society is already structured economically and politically. Weber referred to historical periods in which this occurs as periods of "breakthrough." To demonstrate his theory, Weber found a historical example in the rise of Protestant Christianity and its effects on economic conditions in England and the United States.

A comprehensive, wide-ranging theory such as Weber's naturally engendered criticism and debate. For example, some have argued that secular developments in the areas of finance, commerce, and industry were also important in the rise of capitalism. Others have suggested that, contrary to Weber's analysis, ideas congenial to capitalism could be found among Roman Catholics of the time as well as among Protestants. To the first criticism, Weber is careful not to deny the existence of secular economic factors that contributed to the development of capitalism. Rather, his focus is upon the religiously grounded ideas which produced the intellectual and ethical "spirit" of capitalism. Regarding the second criticism, Weber does not insist that the human desire for economic gain began with capitalism. Instead, it took on new, more rationalized and systematic forms particularly among, but not exclusively among, Calvinist Protestants.

First, Weber studied occupational statistics in Europe and found that business owners and managers as well as the highly skilled workers in business enterprises were overwhelmingly Protestant. Through such research he discovered an important connection between religious beliefs and economic activities. How was it possible for religious ideas originating in the sixteenth century Protestant Reformation to help capitalist economics develop? There was no deliberate effort or plan involved; rather, a long, slow evolution of popular religious ideas among the general public took place over many years. Specifically, the ideas of two influential Protestant reformers came together in an unplanned, unanticipated manner.

One of these reformers, Martin Luther, opposed the Roman Catholic church's insistence that only certain occupations (those directly associated with the Roman Catholic religion) could be considered legitimate in the sight of God. Luther proclaimed that honest, hard work in any occupation constituted one's "calling" by God and was therefore legitimate in the sight of God. This included secular occupations not related to any religion. According to this concept, performing hard work in one's calling was considered an inescapable moral obligation.

The Protestant reformer John Calvin proposed another radical idea: that all individuals are born into one of two groups, the Elect or the Damned. This doctrine, which was most powerful among the English and American Puritans, stated that an individual's fate in this world and in the afterlife (heaven or hell) was determined at birth. The Elect could be identified by their pious living and resultant material success while on Earth, and they were guaranteed salvation in an eternal heavenly afterlife. The Damned received none of these divinely determined benefits and could be identified by their lack of morality and their material poverty (because of which they deserved eternal damnation in the afterlife). Moreover, there was nothing an individual could do to change his or her eternal membership in one of these groups. Even doing a multitude of good works made no difference to the Calvinists. This idea became known as "predestination."

Weber notes that one significant economic effect of Calvinism in areas where it was dominant was that it reduced charity for those who begged or did not work—such individuals were seen as members of the Damned, and their poverty was assumed to be divinely ordained. For example, social welfare programs among the English Puritans were designed not so much to reduce human suffering as to discourage the allegedly slothful.

The cumulative effect of these two doctrines as they became widespread in the population in the decades and centuries following the Protestant Reformation was to create a deep sense of anxiety and uncertainty. Obviously, no one wanted to be one of the eternally damned, and how to determine one's own membership in the Elect or the Damned was unclear. According to Weber, what emerged from this psychologically distressing situation was the "Protestant ethic." Over many decades, these ideas about one's calling and predestination converged, and individuals came to believe that hard work and attaining material success in one's calling were moral obligations; moreover, having material prosperity was a sure sign that one was a member of the Elect. Put differently, material affluence and success in the secular world were viewed as divine rewards for hard work in one's calling (occupation) and as proof that one would be rewarded in the afterlife as well.

Weber also discussed the strong sense of self-denial (asceticism) and deferred gratification found in the Protestant ethic. Well illustrated by the English Puritans in the latter half of the seventeenth century, it meant that leisure, spontaneity, socializing, luxurious living, and even excessive sleep were considered sinful. Only hard, continuous physical or mental labor was considered a worthy activity in the sight of God. If one did accumulate personal wealth, it should not be flaunted or spent on frivolous personal pleasures or self-aggrandizement. As a result, wealth was typically saved and reinvested in the businesses owned by individuals, thus concentrating wealth and strengthening such businesses. When practiced on a large scale in society, this reinvestment of wealth (capital) encouraged capitalism to grow and flourish in Western societies.

Applications

Weber's conclusions have many implications for American society. For many Americans, the Protestant ethic (sometimes simply called the "work ethic") provides a strong motivation for honest, hard labor in one's chosen occupation. Weber's theory also enables one to identify the Protestant ethic at work in everyday events, as well as its use by political leaders and its impact on attitudes toward poverty and the poor.

The modern "work ethic" in American society has lost much of its originally religious meaning and become a common secular concept; this development was also predicted by Max Weber. In showing how the ideas in Protestantism contributed indirectly to the rise of modern capitalism in Western societies, he acknowledged that advanced capitalist societies would become self-sustaining and would no longer require such religious justifications. In other words, once capitalistic practices become widespread, standardized, and institutionalized in the economy, they become self-perpetuating regardless of their original source.

Even so, both mainstream and Fundamentalist Protestant churches still emphasize the virtues of hard work and tend to assume that material success is a sign of God's reward for such work. Popular television evangelists often go so far as to interpret their acquisition of material wealth publicly in this manner. In addition, the notion of finding or accepting one's calling in life is commonly expressed in religious circles and is frequently used as an explanation for everyday behavior and activities among believers.

The influence of the Protestant ethic is not confined to religious groups and individuals. It also plays a role in American politics. Sociologist Robert Bellah has described the often blurry line between church and state in the United States as a case of "civil religion." Civil religion includes religious beliefs regarding the past, present, and future of the United States as a nation. It generally expresses a nondenominational conviction that Americans are a God-fearing people and that God favors their country. In everyday life, civil religion includes religious statements found on U.S. currency, in oaths of office, at political party conventions, in courtroom procedures, and at nearly all formal public ceremonies. Civil religion has a strong Protestant ethic component. For example, religion is typically used by political administrations and political candidates as a way of legitimating American society and the capitalist economic system. Conservative political leaders who are critical of government assistance to the poor often appeal to the work ethic as a justification for cutting social services for those who are not working.

Another important effect of the Protestant ethic has been its impact on prevailing societal attitudes toward wealth and poverty. For example, once hard work and obtaining material prosperity are defined as moral obligations, those who do not or cannot succeed in the economic system are often stigmatized as being sinful as well as poor. This viewpoint is often found among those who advocate abolishing welfare and other social services for the poor. This attitude represents an ironic historical reversal, in that Christianity originated among the poor and was hostile toward the worldly pursuit of wealth and power. In those earlier times, the pursuit of wealth was morally suspect and was often regarded as a threat to the soul. In modern capitalist societies, the poor are doubly stigmatized in that they may be seen as morally inferior to the wealthy.

In analyzing the relationship between religion and economics, Weber used the concept of theodicy—a religious interpretation of life events that provides believers with an emotionally satisfying, meaningful explanation. Theodicies provide a sense of meaning or purpose for otherwise chaotic and distressing life events by placing them in a larger religious context and suggesting that, in the long run, things are as they should be. According to Weber, theodicies vary according to the socioeconomic status of the groups that subscribe to them. For example, a theodicy of dominance is often found among elites or rulers. This type of theodicy tends to explain and justify their possession of power, prestige, and wealth in society. It might, for example, claim that the present leaders have a "divine right" to govern. A theodicy of mobility is often found among middle-class members of society. It may state in some fashion that hard work and piety will lead to worldly success and great rewards in the afterlife. Finally, a theodicy of escape is common among the poor, oppressed, and outcast. In such theodicies, those with wealth and power are often viewed as sinful or corrupt, and emphasis is placed not on achieving worldly success in the present but on personal salvation and eventual rewards in the afterlife.

By using the concept of theodicy, Weber linked the individual with the larger society and with concrete, identifiable social conditions. He concluded that religion serves to legitimate both the powerful and the powerless, both the wealthy and the poor in society.

Context

Max Weber, Karl Marx, and Émile Durkheim are often regarded as the three founders of the discipline of sociology. All three theorists lived between 1818 and 1920, and all wrote extensively about the nature and effects of religion in society. Although each came to different conclusions, their theoretical perspectives continue to influence contemporary sociologists, including those who specialize in the sociology of religion.

The historical period in which Weber wrote was filled with political turmoil and conflicting theories about human behavior and the nature of society. Like other scholars, Weber studied the prevailing ideas of his time and reacted to these conflicting ideas, especially to the ideas of Karl Marx.

Of the three classical sociological perspectives on religion that emerged during this time, the theories of Durkheim and Marx were quite different from that of Max Weber. For example, as the most conservative of the three, Durkheim's theory argued that religion holds society together by morally unifying its members and increasing their sense of community. All other social institutions, including the economic system, depend on the common acceptance of religious beliefs and values. On the other hand, Marx insisted that the opposite was true regarding the economic system. He argued that religion as it existed at his time was an outgrowth of the capitalist economic system, an ideological institution that attempted to explain and justify the economic exploitation of the majority of people in society.

To these two contrasting theories, Weber added a third alternative for understanding the impact of religion in society. Weber argued that religion is not always an ideology of society's rulers and that religious ideas themselves may change society. In this way, Weber changed the course of the sociological study of religion forever. His interests included not only religion but also other sociological concerns such as the nature of authority, social stratification, and bureaucracy. In all of his writings, Weber identified a trend in modern societies that he called "rationalism." In the case of economics, this meant that economic activities are based not on custom or tradition but on deliberate, calculated efforts to achieve profits. In the case of religion, it meant that the practice of magic has been replaced by religious organizations with standardized rituals and formal doctrines.

Bibliography

Allport, Gordon. *The Individual and His Religion*. New York: Macmillan, 1970. A classic, nontechnical study of individual religiosity and its associated personality characteristics. More psychological than sociological, it includes the important distinction between intrinsic and extrinsic religion. Allport suggests that for many individuals, religion is used to further secular self-interests.

Berger, Peter. *The Sacred Canopy: Elements of a Sociological Theory of Religion*. Garden City, N.Y.: Doubleday, 1967. One of Berger's earlier, less ideological works, this short but incisive analysis of religion deals with religion as a socially constructed reality and discusses vital concepts such as theodicy, alienation, legitimation, and the secularization of the modern world. Best suited to a college audience. Includes an index and an interesting appendix listing sociological definitions of religion from different authors.

Campbell, Joseph. *The Power of Myth*. New York: Doubleday, 1988. This general, interview-style book captures the lifelong insights of philosophy professor Joseph Campbell as he discusses the importance of myths and religion in all cultures. He argues that even modern capitalist societies such as the United States need nonempirical explanations of human nature and the universe.

McGuire, Meredith. *Religion: The Social Context*. 2d ed. Belmont, Calif.: Wadsworth, 1987. An introductory college-level text, this book provides an overview of the major concepts, theories, and perspectives within the sociology of religion. Includes sections on Weber, Marx, Durkheim, and modern theorists as well as indexes and an extensive bibliography. An appendix tells how to do a literature search in the sociology of religion. A valuable resource.

Weber, Max. *The Protestant Ethic and the Spirit of Capitalism*. Translated by Talcott Parsons. New York: Charles Scribner's Sons, 1958. The definitive statement of the

Protestant ethic by Max Weber, first published in 1904. Weber provides an alternative to the Marxian view of religion and its place in modern society. Parsons assists the reader by summarizing Weber's major ideas; extensive chapter notes are included in a separate section of the book.

_____ . *The Sociology of Religion.* Reprint. Boston: Beacon Press, 1972. Best suited to the college level, this book goes beyond the Protestant ethic to include Weber's complete perspective on world religions, such as his theory on the origins of religion and concepts of supernatural beings, types of religious prophets, and the concept of theodicy and its relationship to different social classes.

Mark W. Weigand

Cross-References

Capitalism, 191; Civil Religion and Politics, 259; Industrial and Postindustrial Economies, 940; The Industrial Revolution and Mass Production, 946; Industrial Sociology, 960; Religion: Functionalist Analyses, 1603; Religion: Marxist and Conflict Theory Views, 1610; Socialization: Religion, 1894; The Sociology of Religion, 1952.

QUALITATIVE RESEARCH

Type of sociology: Sociological research
Field of study: Basic concepts

Qualitative research involves research techniques that allow investigators to study the special and unique aspects of human interaction. These techniques, while they do not allow for generalizations to other settings, allow scientists to uncover more detailed nuances of the behavior under study than is possible when using quantitative research methods such as surveys.

Principal terms
   CASE STUDY: a detailed study of a particular individual, group, or
      situation; a combination of research techniques may be used to
      describe the "case"
   DATA: information collected or observed that is relevant to the research
      question under study
   ETHICS: the rules and guidelines that guide the research and work of
      professionals; ethics in the social sciences are primarily concerned
      with protecting the rights of the human subjects being studied
   NORMS: learned rules and expectations that influence human interaction
      and individual behavior
   RESEARCH DESIGN: the plan followed by a researcher to structure data
      collection and analysis
   SAMPLE: a smaller group taken from a population for research purposes;
      the goal of sampling is to make generalized statements about the
      larger group (population)
   SOCIAL SCIENCES: the behavioral sciences, including sociology,
      anthropology, political science, psychology, and economics; these
      sciences are differentiated from the "natural" or "physical" sciences
      in that their subject of study is the group or individual behavior of
      human beings

Overview

As a research science, sociology relies on both qualitative and quantitative techniques of observation. The essence of the discipline implies a precise investigation of the environmental factors that influence how (and why) humans interact in patterned ways. Qualitative researchers employ specific techniques including participant observation, case study, content analysis, ethnography, and in-depth interviewing. Qualitative research is distinguished from "quantitative" research in that quantified (numerically based) research involves hypotheses testing, data collection, data analysis, statistics, and generalizations from samples to populations. Qualitative research, on the other hand, allows description of the unique. Case study analysis, for example, allows examination of the many complicated elements of a particular group or situation; qualitative research permits an understanding of human interaction. The lack of formal hypotheses in qualitative research does not negate the scientific contribution, significance, or value of such research.

One poignant example of qualitative research is the book *Savage Inequalities: Children in America's Schools* (1992), written by Jonathan Kozol, a former teacher in Boston and other urban and suburban school systems. The text was a series of case studies of schools in the affluent and diverse United States of the early 1990's. Kozol pinpointed and described some of the severe problems associated with the demise of urban public education in the last half of the twentieth century. He delineates race-based funding disparities, deteriorating resources, teacher and administrative apathy, white flight, and instances of political corruption in the face of increasing school failure.

According to the *Oxford American Dictionary*, a "quality" is "something that is special in a person or thing." Qualitative research is designed to unravel social events or situations in order to reveal the particular and the idiosyncratic. On the most basic level, qualitative investigation involves observation of situations that interest one personally; in this sense, most people have engaged in qualitative social research all their lives. Targets of observation in the social sciences include deviance, gangs, riots, religious movements, and the mass media. Some of the techniques sociologists utilize in their qualitative research have been borrowed from the field of anthropology. The most common form of observation is "participant observation," which forces the "objective" researcher, much like an anthropologist studying a foreign culture, to become subjectively and physically engaged in the phenomenon of scientific interest.

The level of involvement in a participant observation study varies widely. Sociologist Laud Humphreys, in a study published in 1970 as *Tearoom Trade: Impersonal Sex in Public Places*, studied casual and transient sexual encounters among male homosexuals in sites called "tearooms." He was able to learn much about the social characteristics and lifestyles of male homosexuals by becoming marginally involved in their activities. (Humphreys volunteered to serve as the lookout in the public restroom used as a tearoom.) His study was widely criticized because of its second phase: He actually identified and contacted the households of the research subjects. He was accused of being unethical, because he obtained the license plate numbers of the cars by which some of the males left the scene. By tracking the identity of the participants through the police and by surveying households, he found that most of the males lived as heterosexuals. Some were married and lived with their wives and children. In that he located the names and addresses of the men, Humphreys violated their individual rights (and the ethics of social science) by subjecting them to possible prosecution, blackmail, divorce, or embarrassment. Even though he took special precautions to protect the privacy of the men, he nevertheless placed them at risk. Another danger of participant observation is that of "going native"; the observer may become obsessed with the research context and become fully engaged in the activity, forgetting about the research goals. Passive observation is similar to participant observation except that this method constrains the researcher to remain detached (by distance, one-way mirrors, or other approaches) from the research setting, thus avoiding some of the pitfalls of participant observation, such as loss of scientific objectivity, possible physical danger, and changes in the research setting because of the presence of an outsider.

From the perspective of sociologists, qualitative research methods such as participant observation allow one to ascertain cause and effect or to describe some behavior or phenomena. The qualitative description of what transpires between and among members of society provides the details necessary to an understanding of social behavior and therefore of society. Other forms of social research (such as large statistical or survey research) tend to neglect or miss some of the details which form the "social fabric" of norms and values that help to regulate human interaction.

In a study first published in 1943, sociologist William Foote Whyte compiled a fascinating case study of an Italian slum neighborhood near New York City. He demonstrated that such working-class, urban neighborhoods maintained a social structure that influenced behavior. This study helped sociologists to recognize the fact that poor neighborhoods were not simply "disorganized" but were alienated from the mainstream in ways that helped to maintain high rates of poverty and deviance.

Content analysis is a research method that provides a vehicle for measuring "the amount of something" within various mass media productions. The method is appropriate for studies of television programming, recordings, books, letters, speeches, radio talk shows, news articles, and works of art. The "something" measured may embrace the themes presented in the work, the numbers of persons with certain characteristics, the words, expressions, stereotypes, or points of view expressed. The type of analysis performed varies from a mere enumeration (quantification) of the occurrences of a word or concept to a subjective thematic analysis and interpretation of various works.

Semistructured interviews are less specific or standardized than the types of interviews used in quantitative research; they provide sociologists with the flexibility to ask research subjects follow-up questions that they might not have anticipated prior to the interview. "Probes" may be used to induce discussion. New topics can be discussed; these might take the research project in a new and different direction. Serendipitous findings such as these sometimes create breakthroughs in knowledge not possible when the researcher's preconceived ideas are used to formulate research and interview questions.

A form of qualitative research which may involve either passive or participant observation is ethnography. According to James Spradley's *Participant Observation* (1980), "Ethnography is the work of describing a culture. The central aim of ethnography is to understand another way of life from the native point of view." This technique, which originated in anthropology, may also be used to study diverse groups within a given society.

This combination of research techniques adds another dimension to the quantitative work of sociologists. Many social problems and issues require research grounded in the cultural subtleties of human behavior and social interaction. While quantitative research maintains its importance in the discipline, qualitative methods complement statistics, experiments, and surveys in many important ways, thus providing sociologists with insights they would have missed if they had confined themselves solely to quantitative research methods.

Applications

Sociologists and other social scientists use qualitative research to look beneath the veneer of acceptable behavior in society. The complexities of human interaction are usually difficult to interpret unless one is familiar with the cultural rules and sociological contexts that constrain the persons involved. Zora Neale Hurston, an anthropologist, novelist, and writer, conducted qualitative research on African American and African Caribbean cultures (folklore and belief systems) during the 1930's and 1940's. She was one of the first researchers able to document specific folklore and religious practices of African Americans; many of these practices had "survived" the trek from Africa to North America and the Caribbean. One such study, *Tell My Horse* (1938), was an ethnographic investigation of African survivals and adaptations in Jamaica and Haiti. A similar Hurston study, *Mules and Men* (1935), was published as a collection of tales and essays on African Americans living in the southeastern United States.

Erving Goffman, an eminent sociologist, performed a content analysis study of advertisements involving men and women that was published as *Gender Advertisements* (1979). The ads indicated not only the mindset of the producers and directors of commercial advertising but also the attitudes and images the public maintains about gender groups and gender relationships. Goffman treats the ads as ritual displays of societal attitudes toward men and women. The "ideal representation" of women (and other minorities) presents them as limited, in need of support, emotional, vulnerable, and subordinate. These displays both reflect and influence societal attitudes and behaviors associated with relationships between the sexes. One common ritual found in advertising is the "mock assault." This pretend attack is said to convey not only an image of playfulness but also of the implied threat of what could happen if the male exhibiting the behavior were actually to assault the "victim." Another ritual display is the head or body "cant" (bend or tilt) that projects an image of persons (usually women) as dependent, less than serious, and nonthreatening as a result of their nonvertical posturing.

Context

The historical context of qualitative research methods stems from classical sociology and the discipline of anthropology. Émile Durkheim (1858-1917) was a French sociologist who helped to take sociological investigation from a philosophical endeavor to one grounded in science. Much of his research and writing addressed the issue of how society (social forces such as rules, laws, or traditions) controls the individual. He helped to establish a perspective in sociology that concentrated on the consequences or "functions" of social phenomena. This concentration was employed by anthropology and contributed heavily to the field of sociology. Ethnography and participant observation began as research methods in anthropology and were later adopted by sociologists such as Whyte and Humphreys.

A pioneer of the case study method in sociology was W. E. B. Du Bois. His *The Philadelphia Negro: A Social Study* (1899) was one of the first empirical or scientific studies published in sociology. Du Bois' manuscript was an advance which demonstrated the importance of the case study (including census data) as a way of unraveling and interpreting social behavior and social problems. Content analysis was used by John Naisbitt in the book *Megatrends: Ten New Directions Transforming Our Lives* (1982). After monitoring several thousand local newspapers, Naisbitt was able to describe some of the major trends in American society.

Given the vast importance of culture in today's globally interdependent and diverse world, qualitative research methods are becoming increasingly necessary. These techniques will allow human groups (within and between societies) to understand each other and to interact in less violent ways than in the past. Such techniques will also help to provide solutions to social problems that are more relevant and more effective than some of the solutions of the past.

Bibliography

Berger, Arthur Asa. *Media Analysis Techniques*. Beverly Hills, Calif.: Sage Publications, 1982. A handbook on research techniques geared to the mass media. The manual is readable and contains specific techniques on how to use each research method.

Coser, Lewis A. *Masters of Sociological Thought: Ideas in Historical and Social Context*. New York: Harcourt Brace Jovanovich, 1977. A study of classical sociologists from Auguste Comte (1798-1857) through Florian Znaniecki (1882-1958). The text provides insight and detail regarding the personal lives, intellectual influences, theories, and social contexts of each major theorist in the classical era of the discipline.

Du Bois, W. E. B. *The Philadelphia Negro: A Social Study*. Philadelphia: University of Pennsylvania Press, 1899. A case study of life among working-class African Americans based on participant observation and survey research in Philadelphia circa 1895. One of the first empirical studies completed and published in sociology.

Goffman, Erving. *Gender Advertisements*. New York: Harper & Row, 1979. A content analysis study of how gender is portrayed in advertisements. Goffman, as one of the major proponents of the sociological paradigm called "symbolic interactionism," used his insight to describe how gestures and other symbols are used to portray and interpret how women and men feel about each other.

Humphreys, Laud. *Tearoom Trade: Impersonal Sex in Public Places*. Chicago: Aldine, 1970. A case study of male homosexual encounters in a public restroom ("tearoom"). The study involved participant observation, tracking the identities of the males observed, and survey research to describe their lifestyles. The author was accused of being unethical, since he placed his unknowing research subjects in possible legal and social peril.

Hurston, Zora Neale. *Mules and Men*. Reprint. Bloomington: Indiana University Press, 1978. A collection of African American folklore and religious practices which was the initial publication of such material. The data were collected through informal interviews and participant observation. First published in 1935.

Kozol, Jonathan. *Savage Inequalities: Children in America's Schools*. New York: Harper-Perennial, 1992. A highly readable and insightful series of case studies of urban and suburban schools in American cities. Written by a former teacher, the book provides useful data on the decay of public education in America, fueled by racism, corruption, political neglect, and changes in the American economy.

Moore, Joan W. *Going Down to the Barrio: Homeboys and Homegirls in Change*. Philadelphia: Temple University Press, 1991. A sociological and ethnographic study of two Chicano street gangs in East Los Angeles. The author uses a sociological framework (exploring how class conflict and history influence contemporary gang attitudes, ideologies, and behaviors) to contextualize the behavior of two particular gangs. Even though random sampling survey techniques were part of the research design, qualitative methods were used to derive the sample. Gang cliques were located as part of a collaborative study of gangs undertaken by former gang members and social scientists.

Spradley, James P. *Participant Observation*. New York: Holt, Rinehart and Winston, 1980. A textbook on participant observation methodology, techniques, and issues. Includes several well-written articles on the different phases and problems associated with this technique of data collection.

Whyte, William Foote. *Street Corner Society: The Social Structure of an Italian Slum*. Chicago: University of Chicago Press, 1981. A sociological investigation of life in an Italian, working-class neighborhood. Whyte, an upper middle-class intellectual, moved into the community for the purpose of the study. With the assistance of his "informant" and guide Doc, Whyte was able to investigate the complicated behavior and social structure of the neighborhood.

Bruce H. Wade

Cross-References

Ethics and Politics in Social Research, 675; Ethnography, 696; Experimentation in Sociological Research, 721; Quantitative Research, 1546; Sociological Research: Description, Exploration, and Explanation, 1920; Surveys, 2030; Unobtrusive Research, 2103.

QUANTITATIVE RESEARCH

Type of sociology: Sociological research
Field of study: Basic concepts

Quantitative research attempts to categorize and summarize observations through the assignment of numbers. The numbers generated from this kind of study are frequently presented using descriptive statistics.

Principal terms
CONTENT VALIDITY: a type of experimental validity determined by whether an experiment measures a property that it is intending to measure
DESCRIPTIVE STATISTIC: a type of statistic used to summarize and describe existing data; calculations of the median and the mode represent descriptive statistics
EMPIRICISM: a method for acquiring knowledge about the world through direct observation and experience
EXTERNAL VALIDITY: a quality that enables the generalizing of results from a limited sample of subjects to a larger population
INFERENTIAL STATISTICS: statistics used to apply data obtained from a small (sample) population to a larger population
OPERATIONAL DEFINITION: a specific description of a variable that will enable it to be measured; it outlines the precise steps or operations for other researchers to use in assessing the variable
RELIABILITY: the ability of an instrument to measure a variable or construct consistently over repeated measurements
RESEARCH HYPOTHESIS: a specifically worded statement or prediction that can be verified or falsified through the collection of data; a tentative answer to a research question
SCIENTIFIC METHOD: a method for acquiring knowledge that is characterized by systematic observation, experimentation, experimental control, and the ability to repeat the study

Overview

The discipline of sociology has evolved into a well-defined body of knowledge that is composed of both factual information regarding specific areas of content and theories that attempt to organize and systematize what is currently known. In order for sociology to grow and evolve as a discipline, it must be continuously infused with new ideas. Not only is new information important for the development of sociology, but there must be a refinement of the methods and tools that are used to acquire new knowledge. One method used by social scientists that contributes to this discovery process is called quantitative research.

Quantitative research, in its most basic form, is a research strategy that attempts to assign numbers to characteristics in order to quantify specific observations that have been made. It is an epistemological approach that is closely aligned with empiricism and the scientific method. This relationship can be seen from the emphasis that quantitative research places on studying phenomena that can be directly observed. Similar to the scientific method, quantitative research strives for objectivity, systematic observation, and the analysis of quantifiable information.

Quantitative research is an approach to studying behavior that entails a series of steps. This process begins with the formulation of a statement or prediction called a research hypothesis. The research hypothesis is a special kind of statement which must meet two criteria. First, it must be verifiable. That is, once data have been collected, the data can be found to either support or falsify the research hypothesis. Second, it must be specific. It needs to clearly delineate what results would, in fact, support the hypothesis; otherwise it would not be possible to draw conclusions from the data.

Another step in conducting quantitative research concerns the emphasis placed on the measurement of variables. This step implies that a variable chosen to be studied has been adequately defined. For example, take the variable "altruism." Altruism can be defined in a number of different ways. One definition might be "concern for the welfare of others." Someone conducting quantitative research would ask the question, "How can we measure a person's concern for the welfare of others?" A specific type of behavior must be chosen that the researcher believes would adequately demonstrate an individual's concern for another person. The process of conducting quantitative research requires that altruism be operationally defined. That is, it must be defined in a way that makes it publicly observable; moreover, it must consist of a behavior or sequence of behaviors that can be both seen and recorded. The recording of an operationally defined variable most typically involves the assignment of numbers. In this case, different numbers would be assigned on the basis of differing degrees of altruistic behavior observed. Altruism could be operationally defined as the degree to which people offer assistance to a person standing on a highway next to a disabled car. A researcher could use a three-point rating system in which a score of 0 indicates that someone offered no assistance, a score of 1 indicates that someone stops and offers to call for help when arriving at his or her destination, and a score of 2 indicates that a subject offers to take the stranded person to the nearest telephone. Although this example is simplistic and by no means covers all possibilities, it demonstrates an attempt to quantify an abstract concept.

Quantitative research is characterized by the attention it gives to the topic of validity. When a researcher is conducting a study, it is important that the behaviors chosen to be observed and recorded do in fact measure the trait (or sociological attribute) that they are intending to measure. The ability of an operationally defined behavior to measure adequately what it is supposed to measure gets at the heart of content validity. Content validity is a necessary prerequisite for conducting good quantitative research. Another aspect of validity concerns the degree to which a study can obtain results from a sample of subjects and then generalize the results to a larger population. For example, if the results of a study conducted on five hundred college students from a single school can be generalized to students from nearby colleges, the study possesses external validity.

Reliability is equally important. Reliability refers to the ability of a study to measure accurately a variable over different time periods. For example, a researcher might want to study the concept "authoritarianism" using a pencil and paper test that is administered on more than one occasion. A subject might take the test and receive a score of 80 on a scale from 1 to 100. One week later, the same subject might take the test again and receive a score of 79. This test would be considered a reliable test (assuming that there had been no change in the actual level of authoritarianism in the person for that week), since it produced consistent scores over repeated testings. If, on the other hand, the second test had produced a score of 60, the discrepancy between the two scores would probably indicate that the instrument lacked reliability.

Quantitative research is also characterized by data analysis. Once the data collection is finished, the numerical information is summarized through the use of descriptive statistics. There are a number of ways to summarize data by using descriptive statistics. One such procedure involves calculating a measure of central tendency such as the arithmetic mean (average score)—one adds together all the scores and divides by the total number of scores. Another procedure would be finding the mode (the most frequently occurring score). It is also helpful to calculate a measure of variability that lets the researcher know how similar or dissimilar the scores are.

Another characteristic of quantitative research is that it uses probability theory to determine whether a research hypothesis is supported or unsupported. Basically, hypothesis testing leads to a probabilistic confirmation. To test a hypothesis, a researcher must determine how the variables expressed in the hypothesis will be measured, must make the necessary observations, must collect the data (usually in the form of numbers), and then must subject the data to quantitative analysis. Quantitative analysis attempts to summarize the vast array of numbers; it also attempts to determine whether the same results obtained in the study could also be obtained through random chance. This is accomplished through determining the probability of obtaining the results randomly. Therefore, quantitative analysis usually results in a probability statement in which the following rule applies: If the probability of obtaining the results of the study through random chance is extremely low, then the results are thought very likely to be attributable to the variables of the study. Either confirmation or falsification of the hypothesis would be presented in terms of a probabilistic statement.

Applications

A study by Robert V. Levine can be used to explore how quantitative research is implemented and how it can contribute to scientific knowledge. In his article "The Pace of Life," published in *American Scientist* (1990), Levine attempted to understand how different cultures perceive time. He suspected that attitudes toward time could impact the pace of life for a society and ultimately could lead to health problems in the form of hypertension and stress for its members. Levine was interested in testing the following research hypothesis: Cultures differ in terms of their general pace of life. This hypothesis was an outgrowth of Levine's consideration of the commonly held notion that some cultures move at different paces from that of the United States. American visitors to Japan, for example, frequently say they are overwhelmed by a faster pace of life than that in the U.S.

Levine chose to collect data from the largest city of six different countries: Japan, Taiwan, Indonesia, Italy, England, and the United States. To gauge the general pace of life of each country, he chose to study three unique objective indicators: the accuracy of outdoor clocks, the average time it took pedestrians to walk a distance of 100 feet, and the time needed for a postal clerk to complete a transaction that entailed selling stamps and returning some change. Notice that none of these measures relies on the subjective evaluations of pace of life by the person collecting the data. These indicators serve as multiple operational definitions for the construct "pace of life." In addition, the indicators are measures that can be easily assigned a number—another characteristic of quantitative research. Uninhibited walking speed and the amount of time it takes to complete a transaction at the post office both provide measures of how quickly people go about their business. The rationale behind measuring the accuracy of town clocks was somewhat different. Levine believed that the more a culture is driven by an adherence to time, the more accurate the public clocks in the culture will be. More time consciousness should translate into more accurate clocks.

These measures for pace of life fall on a scale of measurement known as a ratio scale. A ratio scale, such as time, is a scale that not only has equal intervals between different points on the scale (the amount of time between one and two seconds is the same as between nine and ten seconds) but also has an absolute zero point. Quantitative research assigns numbers to specific observations that fall on the ratio scale, interval scale (in which there are equal intervals between points, but there is no absolute zero point), or the ordinal scale (in which values can be ranked from highest to lowest). Levine preferred these particular "objective" measures to a survey approach, which might have required subjects to respond to how they "feel" about the pace of life. Thus, he was strongly concerned about the validity of the data he was collecting.

Standardized techniques were employed while collecting the data to ensure that the pace of life indicators would be measured fairly. For example, walking speed would not be measured if it was raining outside. Levine chose a covert approach to collecting data, since he did not want subjects to be aware that they were in a study. Levine thereby eliminated any bias that could be attributable to the subject's knowledge that he or she was in an experiment.

The data were collected primarily by Levine's students, who visited the countries during their summer recess from school. The data were analyzed using basic descriptive statistical procedures. Average scores for the accuracy of public clocks, the time it took people to walk 100 feet, and the completion of a postal transaction were calculated and compared across the different countries. Using probabilistic confirmation, Levine found that Japan had the fastest pace of life of all six countries; it scored the highest on all three measures. The United States came in with the second fastest pace, followed by England. Indonesia was last, having the slowest walkers and the most inaccurate clocks.

Levine extended this research by looking at associations between pace of life and both psychological and physical health. He found that the tempo of a society is significantly related to the prevalence of heart disease. In fact, the time-related variables often turn out to be better predictors of heart disease than psychological measures used to identify high-energy behaviors in individuals. He concluded that a person who chooses to live in a fast-paced city should take precautions to keep from becoming a time-urgent person. Living in a busy and stressful city, for example, can lead to unhealthy behaviors such as smoking and poor eating habits. It should be noted that, because Levine undertook a new approach in his study, a repetition of the study by other researchers would increase its credibility within the scientific community.

Context

From the beginning of humankind, people have tried to increase their understanding of the world they live in. Two approaches to acquiring knowledge that preceded the modern era were authority and rationalism. In the former, people simply accepted the words of an authority figure presumed to have inside knowledge of the topic at hand. The person could have been a priest or other societal leader. Rationalism was an approach to coming to an understanding of something through using individual reasoning skills in order to arrive at knowledge of the world. Both methods are still in evidence today in certain situations. In the scientific world, however, the scientific method has replaced such methods. This method is characterized by systematic observation, experimentation, and experimental control. Quantitative research grew out of the scientific method.

Quantitative research attempts to systematize and categorize data in order to provide as much objectivity to the data collection process as possible. The methods associated with conducting quantitative research emphasize objective data-gathering techniques and discourage casual or informal data gathering. Collecting data via informal methods can bring about a number of biases and errors. In his book *How We Know What Isn't So: The Fallibility of Human Reason in Everyday Life* (1991), Thomas Gilovich points out a number of cognitive, motivational, and social determinants that influence how people gather data and interpret the world. Informal methods can cause humans to misinterpret incomplete data. In addition, informal observers can be biased so that they see only the data they want to see. For these reasons, there has been a gradual move toward the use of more "objective" techniques, such as standardized rating scales, behavioral check lists, and structured surveys. These methods were created in order to quantify social science observations more accurately, thereby increasing the truthfulness of data. Once behaviors could be quantified, specific behaviors could be assigned numbers. They could be statistically analyzed to find real, rather than apparent, differences. This approach to data collection played a significant role in improving research practices in the social and behavioral sciences.

Bibliography

Baker, Therese L. *Doing Social Research.* New York: McGraw-Hill, 1988. Baker gives the reader a general introduction to quantitative research, observational studies, data collection methods, survey research, and sampling techniques, as well as other topics that will help the reader discern good research from poor research.

Gilovich, Thomas. *How We Know What Isn't So: The Fallibility of Human Reason in Everyday Life.* New York: Free Press, 1991. This is a marvelous book that educates the reader about how the human mind distorts information.

Judd, Charles M., Eliot R. Smith, and Louise Kidder. *Research Methods in Social Relations.* 6th ed. Fort Worth, Texas: Harcourt Brace Jovanovich College Publishers, 1991. This book provides a broad overview of quantitative statistics. Chapters of particular importance include those on measurement, scaling, and laboratory research.

Katzer, Jeffrey, Kenneth Cook, and Wayne Crouch. *Evaluating Information: A Guide for Users of Social Science Research.* 3d ed. New York: McGraw-Hill, 1991. This book is excellent for learning more about good quantitative research as opposed to bad research. Written with a general audience in mind, it attempts to teach the important questions that need to be asked about research in order to assess its quality.

Levine, Robert V. "The Pace of Life." *American Scientist* 78 (September, 1990): 450-459. Levine describes his research on cross-cultural perspectives of time. The article provides a good example of quantitative research. It describes research done internationally and within different regions of the United States.

Pagano, Robert R. *Understanding Statistics in the Behavioral Sciences.* 3d ed. St. Paul, Minn.: West, 1990. This book provides an excellent introduction to learning descriptive and inferential statistics. Only a limited mathematical background is necessary to read and comprehend most of the information in this text.

Singleton, Royce, Jr., Bruce Straits, Margaret Straits, and Ronald McAllister. *Approaches to Social Research.* New York: Oxford University Press, 1988. This well-written text discusses various aspects of quantitative research such as selecting a research setting, gathering information, scales of measurement, and differences between quantitative and qualitative research.

Bryan C. Auday

Cross-References

RACE AND RACIAL GROUPS

Type of sociology: Racial and ethnic relations
Field of study: Basic concepts

Arguments have been advanced to support both biological and social concepts of race, but most scientists believe that race is a social concept rather than a biological reality. Subjective elements in the definition and categorization of races have helped allow such problems as racism and discrimination to continue.

Principal terms

AFFIRMATIVE ACTION: a policy designed to redress past discrimination against minority groups by targeting them for recruitment into jobs and educational institutions

DISCRIMINATION: a situation in which individuals are treated differently because they belong to a particular group

ETHNIC GROUP: a group that is defined by cultural characteristics that are held in common, such as religion and language

RACISM: a belief system that views groups of people (identified by various physical characteristics) hierarchically in terms of superiority and inferiority

SPECIES: a naturally occurring population of organisms that is characterized by sexual cross-fertilization and outside which fertile offspring cannot be reproduced

SUBSPECIES: a population within a species that exhibits variations from the larger species because of geographic and social isolation

Overview

Controversy and confusion surround the term "race" for a number of reasons. One central problem is that it has multiple meanings; another is that the term itself has become emotionally loaded, leading some experts to suggest abandoning it altogether. In the nineteenth and twentieth centuries, race has been viewed both biologically and socially. That is, some have argued that there are biologically distinct races with unique, identifiable characteristics. Others, however, have argued that the idea of race is not defensible scientifically and that the "racial" characteristics of humans exist in a continuum rather than as discrete groups. The taking of one or the other of these views leads to very different implications. Most scientists today favor a view of race as essentially a social construct.

Anthropologist M. G. Smith offers the following biological definition of race in his 1989 article "Pluralism, Race, and Ethnicity in Selected African Countries": "Races are biological divisions of mankind differentiated by gross phenotypical features which are hereditary, polygenic, highly resistant to environmental influences, distinctive and of doubtful adaptive value." Some scholars prefer such biological definitions of race because they view them as being objective. In this view, races are seen as naturally occurring groupings of humans who exhibit obvious physical differences from one another. Anthropologist Ashley Montagu (one of those who dislike the use of the term "race") has stated that these differences result from isolation (geographic and social), the selection of mates with particular physical features, internal chemical changes in cells (genetic mutation), and the ability of mutants to adapt better to the environment (natural selection). Because all biological races belong to the same species, *Homo sapiens*, the racial groups that result from these forces can interbreed with one another. Thus, as biologist Theodosius Dobzhansky has stated, biological races are best regarded as subspecies, or variations on a common theme. (It should be noted, however, that many scientists classify modern humans as *Homo sapiens sapiens*, indicating that all modern humans belong to the same species and the same subspecies.)

Many scientists, however, view this conception of race as extremely problematic. First, there is the problem of deciding which criteria are to be used in distinguishing one race from another. The difficulty is that no single criterion (or even combinations of criteria) can conclusively separate humans into different races. The criteria that have most often been used to classify races are skin color, the shape and size of heads, noses and lips, hair color and type, and blood group. All of these criteria have failed as boundary markers for racial groups because exceptions can always be found. For example, skin color—the single most widely used criterion—seems at first to classify adequately the native population of Africa south of the Sahara as a distinct racial group, usually called Negroid. Populations in other parts of the world, however, have skin as dark, if not darker, than some Africans. Examples include the inhabitants of the southern part of the subcontinent of India and the Aborigines of Australia, yet neither of these groups is considered Negroid.

The African example raises another problem, that of how many races exist. A survey of the literature shows that no agreement on this number exists. For example, many people view Africans south of the Sahara simply as Negroids. Anthropologist C. G. Seligman has noted, however, that according to some definitions at least five distinct races can be found in this region. Another problem with the biological view of race is that even if it could be shown beyond any doubt that racial groups differ fundamentally with respect to their physical characteristics, there would still be the need to discover what significance, if any, such differences really have. Do these physical differences enable racial groups to cope better with their environment? Do they correlate with such factors as culture and a group's standing in society? Most authorities do not accept the idea that such correlations exist beyond the ones created by society itself.

Because of these problems, many authorities view race as a social, rather than a biological, phenomenon, and some, including Montagu, believe that the term should be dropped altogether. In his book *Racism* (1990), sociologist Robert Miles argues that, socially speaking, a race is a collectivity that is defined using biological criteria that a society views as significant. The important point is that these biological criteria are given meaning by a particular society; they have little intrinsic meaning apart from their social context. Moreover, because societies differ from one another in their views, it is possible that the same biological characteristics will be assigned different meanings in other societies. For example, sociologist F. James Davis has shown in his book *Who Is Black? One Nation's Definition* (1991) that in the United States, regardless of how an individual looks, having one sub-Saharan African ancestor is enough to define an individual as "black." That same individual, however, might be viewed as "white" in regions such as Brazil and the West Indies that have different criteria for defining whiteness and blackness.

Thus, the social view of race sees race as a relative concept. Essentially, it says that a racial group exists because a society defines it as such. Miles describes the process of racial formation within society as racialization. In this process, societies arbitrarily select seemingly important biological criteria (for example, skin color) and impute to the groups thus created additional nonbiological characteristics. For example, some races may come to be viewed as cultured, while others are viewed as uncivilized. When these additional evaluations assume a negative slant, and when the negative evaluations are used to justify the subjugation of particular races, racialization turns into racism.

Applications

A number of applications flow from the distinction between biological and social concepts of race. First, most social scientists agree that confusion surrounds the concept of race. Specifically, they argue that a wide gap exists between everyday beliefs about race and scientific fact. Ashley Montagu believes that making careful distinctions between the social and biological conceptions of race helps dispel this confusion by raising important questions in people's minds. Confronting erroneous "commonsense" beliefs about race with scientific fact challenges their ready acceptance. This counters the belief system known as racism and its active corollary, discrimination.

With respect to this, another important related concept must be taken into account: ethnicity. This concept is similar to socially defined race, and consequently the two are often confused. Ethnic groups, however, are defined using cultural rather than biological criteria. Thus, Hispanics and Jews are ethnic groups, while African Americans may be considered both a racial and an ethnic group. As Montagu points out, making these fine distinctions helps to show that much racism rests on weak foundations and may cause individuals expressing racist views to reexamine their assumptions about other groups. Furthermore, awareness of the idea that races are socially defined leads one to question the widespread assumption that races are groups with fixed characteristics and that all individuals who are seen as belonging to these races must necessarily exhibit these characteristics. Anthropologist Richard Jenkins criticizes this assumption in his article "Social Anthropological Models of Inter-ethnic Relations," noting that from the point of view of the social construction of race, races are categories that are imposed by powerful groups on the less powerful. This implies that the powerful groups gloss over differences among the individuals who are being defined in order to accentuate the differences between groups.

In practical terms, problems arise because individuals who are being racialized attempt to assert their own individuality or the uniqueness of the particular group to which they belong. This identity is often expressed in ethnic terms. Any group's sense of identity is complex and should never be oversimplified or taken for granted. Groups that are defined by society as being primarily racial might, in fact, view themselves in ethnic terms. An example is black immigrants to the United States from the Caribbean, many of whom view themselves as separate from African Americans even though the larger society views the two groups as belonging to the same race. Similarly, the term "Asian" is often used in the United States to describe people of Far Eastern descent. This racial term lumps together a number of sometimes antagonistic groups that have unique cultures. Thus, while Asians are viewed by some Americans as a single racial group, individuals who are so categorized may strongly prefer to define themselves in terms of their particular culture.

The reduction of racism and discrimination has been an active goal of many agencies. The passing of legislation to curb discrimination, for example, was the primary goal of the groups (such as the National Association for the Advancement of Colored People and the Congress on Racial Equality) involved in the Civil Rights movement of the 1960's. Many ethnic groups have founded organizations seeking to illuminate and end ethnic slurs and discrimination against them; one well-known such group is the Anti-Defamation League, founded by American Jews in 1913. These efforts remain important because the United States is an attractive destination for immigrants of all races and ethnicities, but immigration often brings conflict with native groups as well as between immigrant groups themselves. Thus, finding ways to urge groups to be tolerant of one another is extremely important, and the dissemination, throughout society, of adequate definitions of concepts such as "race" and "ethnicity" helps to achieve this goal.

Having precise definitions of these concepts is also important in the administration of affirmative action programs. These programs are predicated on the assumption that historically disadvantaged groups can be clearly identified. Any group must be identified and defined before any program can be effectively targeted at it, but this task is not always easy. The *Jane Doe v. the State of Louisiana* case of 1983, though not an affirmative action case, illustrates some of the problems involved in determining an individual's race. In that case, a Louisiana woman (Susie Phipps) who was only three thirty-seconds black was denied a passport because she checked "white" on her application form. Even though Phipps thought of herself as white (and had twice married white men), three courts held that she was legally black. This case illustrates the dilemma faced by individuals with ancestors considered to be from different races, and it underscores the importance of the concept of race as a social one.

Knowledge of this concept also facilitates smoother relationships for those individuals and organizations that deal regularly with other societies that have different conceptions of race. Cross-cultural communications can be hampered if people assume that their ideas on race are similar to those of other societies. For example,

Japanese people are viewed as Asians in the United States, but in South Africa they are categorized as "honorary whites." Similarly, in the United States, individuals such as Susie Phipps are black, but in South Africa they are accorded a separate, distinct status, "colored." A third example is that Asian Indians, though generally regarded by anthropologists as Caucasians, are often regarded as black when they migrate to Britain. Since an individual's racial status often determines how the person is treated, knowledge of how such statuses vary cross-culturally is essential for multinational corporations and political organizations such as the United Nations.

Context

Historical analysis of the concept of race shows that ideas of race are different at different periods in history. Historian Thomas Gossett, in *Race: The History of an Idea in America* (1963), notes that race thinking stretches as far back as the ancient Egyptians (1350 B.C.E.). Ancient peoples, however, while conscious of color differences, did not systematically discriminate against one another on this basis.

European world dominance following the age of exploration in the fifteenth and sixteenth centuries caused modern discussions of racial issues to be centered on Eurocentric models. European expansionism brought Europeans into closer contact with unfamiliar peoples in Africa, North and South America, Australia, and the Pacific, and this contact challenged established old assumptions about race. Theories had to be constructed to account for the evident differences between Europeans and the new peoples with whom they came into contact. From the sixteenth century to the middle of the nineteenth century, debate focused on the question of whether humankind had had a single origin and had differentiated into contrasting races or whether the various races had originated separately. The first school was known as the monogenic school of thought and the latter, the polygenic school.

This debate proved inconclusive because of the lack of firm scientific evidence. Charles Darwin's work in the middle of the nineteenth century, however, through its emphasis on natural selection (which provided a plausible mechanism for the process of evolution), seemed to lend scientific support to monogenic theories of race. The idea soon arose that the different races represent different stages on the ladder of evolution. Gossett shows that in the climate of nineteenth century European imperialism, whites widely assumed that they—especially the Nordics and the British—were the most advanced of all the races. Both biological and nonbiological ideas were adduced to support the notion of a hierarchy of races. Discussions of race began to incorporate the idea known as social Darwinism (although Darwin himself never espoused this viewpoint). Social Darwinism applied the mechanism of evolution to human social groups, arguing that human groups (particularly racial and ethnic groups) are in a conflict that results in the "survival of the fittest" and that various groups "deserve" what they get. For example, supporters viewed European culture as being far superior to all others; on the other end of the spectrum, the enslavement of Africans, they argued, "proved" the inferiority of that group.

A turning point occurred early in the twentieth century with the work of anthropologist Franz Boas, who questioned the racist assumptions of the age. It was the Nazism of the 1930's and 1940's and the genocide that it engendered, however, that decisively turned the tide away from biological notions of race. The world was horrified at the attempts of the Nazis to exterminate the "Jewish race" (as well as Gypsies and others), which caused the deaths of millions of innocent people, and world leaders vowed that it must never happen again. After World War II, scientists increasingly relied on social factors to explain human behavior. Two United Nations statements on race (on July 18, 1950, and July 15, 1952) reflected this change in underlying assumptions. These statements cast doubt on the notion of superior and inferior races and recognized the notion of socially constructed races. The hope was that revealing the complexity of the issue of race would hinder the development of destructive racist ideologies such as Nazism.

Bibliography

Cashmore, E. Ellis. *Dictionary of Race and Ethnic Relations*. 2d ed. London: Routledge, 1988. This very accessible book contains sharp and comprehensive discussions of topics relevant to the concept of race. The great strengths of the book are that it covers many fundamental concepts in depth and has a strong cross-cultural perspective. Highly recommended as a basic reference work.

Davis, F. James. *Who Is Black? One Nation's Definition*. University Park: Pennsylvania State University Press, 1991. Davis' book is required reading for those interested in how racial groups are defined. He argues that since historical and social forces shape these definitions, they change over time. Throughout, Davis compares the United States with other societies to show the uniqueness of its definition of who is black.

Dobzhansky, Theodosius. *Evolution, Genetics, and Man*. New York: John Wiley & Sons, 1963. Although this book is somewhat advanced for the nonspecialist, it contains good discussions of such fundamental issues as evolution, culture, race, and the classification of racial groups. Dobzhansky's discussion of the interaction of social and biological factors in the identification of racial groups is particularly enlightening.

Downs, James F., and Hermann K. Bleibtreu. *Human Variation*. Rev. ed. Beverly Hills, Calif.: Glencoe Press, 1972. This introductory textbook contains clear and simple discussions of complex issues relating to race. It is highly recommended.

Gossett, Thomas. *Race: The History of an Idea in America*. Dallas: SMU Press, 1975. Gossett's influential book, first published in 1963, is required reading for those interested in the history of the concept of race. It discusses in detail the various historical strands that interwove to create current American ideas on race. Although long, the book is absorbing and the writing style clear.

Miles, Robert. *Racism*. London: Routledge, 1989. Miles's book is important because of its carefully argued and detailed treatment of many issues relating to race. He treats these issues historically and, significantly, relates them to the concept of social class.

Montagu, Ashley. *Race, Science, and Humanity*. Princeton, N.J.: Van Nostrand, 1963. This small but very useful book is a collection of essays on issues relating to race. Montagu shows why the concept of race, as employed in the everyday world, is problematic. He argues for the abandonment of the term because of its embodiment of false stereotypes.

Seligman, C. G. *Races of Africa*. 4th ed. London: Oxford University Press, 1966. This small but detailed book needs to be read with a map to be truly appreciated, since it assumes familiarity with African tribes and regions. Seligman's discussion of the varieties of groups present in Africa illustrates the problems involved in classifying groups into races.

Smith, M. G. "Pluralism, Race, and Ethnicity in Selected African Countries." In *Theories of Race and Ethnic Relations*, edited by John Rex and David Mason. Cambridge: Cambridge University Press, 1986. Smith's article assumes familiarity with African political and social history. It is useful, however, because he argues strongly against the idea that race is a socially constructed concept. Instead, Smith views races as objective, genetically based phenomena.

Milton D. Vickerman

Cross-References

Affirmative Action, 21; The Authoritarian Personality Theory of Racism, 159; Individual Discrimination, 547; Ethnicity and Ethnic Groups, 689; Institutional Racism, 996; Minority and Majority Groups, 1219; Race Relations: The Race-Class Debate, 1566; The Race Relations Cycle Theory of Assimilation, 1572; Racial and Ethnic Stratification, 1579; Racism as an Ideology, 1586.

IMPROVING RACE RELATIONS

Type of sociology: Racial and ethnic relations
Fields of study: Dimensions of inequality; Maintaining inequality

Various approaches to improving race relations have been studied and tried; among them are education, increased intergroup contact, and legislation. Success has been limited, however, ultimately because the inequality of wealth and the competition for resources that underlie prejudice and discrimination have not been sufficiently addressed.

Principal terms

CLASS: a person's economic resources which determine the ability to buy what is needed for a quality existence; class is also used to refer to a stratum of people with similar economic resources

DISTRIBUTIVE JUSTICE: justice in the distribution of the "good things" in life, the most critical of which are class, status, and power

INSTITUTIONAL DISCRIMINATION: the discrimination which results when social structures (patterned, repetitive, predictable interactions) systematically confer advantages on the dominant group and disadvantages on subordinated groups

MAJORITY GROUP: a group that has enough power to impose its will on other groups and thus to take a larger share of the society's resources

MINORITY GROUP: a group that lacks sufficient power to defend its own vital (class, status, and power) interests and thus is disadvantaged with respect to important resources

POWER: the ability to exert one's will, legally, against the will of others; it determines the ability to have what one wants by calling upon the police powers of the state

RACE: a conventional way of referring to a population that has been socially defined as being biologically different from another population; race is a social reality but not a scientific reality

STATUS: reputation or social standing; one's status determines the ability to have what one wants through influence or persuasion

Overview

Two of the functions of the United States government are, in the words of the Preamble to the U.S. Constitution, to "establish justice" and to "insure domestic tranquillity." It is significant that the establishment of justice comes before domestic tranquillity. Among other prerequisites of domestic tranquillity is that the people must believe that there is what sociologists call distributive justice: fairness with respect to the distribution of scarce resources. The most vital of these resources are class, status, and power.

"Race," as nearly all scientists use the term, is a socially defined concept rather than a biologically determined reality. "Race" is therefore real only in the sense that certain groups have, for whatever reason, decided to categorize people according to certain aspects (arbitrary and even superficial aspects) of their physical appearance. Terms such as "black" and "white," then, must also be viewed as socially, rather than biologically, meaningful distinctions.

In a racist society, one race with greater legal power than other races uses its power advantage to garner even more power, as well as more than its share of class and status. Other races, now minority groups (defined as groups that lack sufficient power to protect their vital interests—especially their class, status, and power interests), become even more disadvantaged, not only with respect to power but also because of a lack of financial resources (class) and an inability to persuade (status). They find the quality of their lives greatly diminished. Further deterioration of relationships among the races occurs as the dominant race creates prejudices to justify its treatment of subordinated races, and subordinated races react with hostility to those prejudices as well as to the unfair deprivation of class, status, and power. Different subordinated races begin to fight among themselves over the reduced portion of the scarce resources which the dominant race has allocated to them.

Such a society will not enjoy "domestic tranquillity." It will be characterized by high crime rates, high rates of incarceration, disruption of educational and other institutions, and periodic riots and rebellions. Government, to perform its function of preserving (or restoring) domestic tranquillity, must find ways of improving race relations. These efforts, if they are to be successful, must begin with a respect for the rights of subordinated races. If government fails to respect and defend those rights, it loses its legitimacy in the eyes of those who, as a result of this failure, have little class, status, or power. Government seen as illegitimate cannot govern for long. It cannot expect the allegiance and cooperation of the subordinated races it abuses, and it will lose the respect of other nations who identify with those subordinated races.

The achievement of distributive justice represents the ideal in the improvement of race relations. Distributive justice could only be achieved through the cooperation of government and the dominant race. The central problem is that the dominant race would almost certainly have to relinquish some of its advantages if subordinated races are to make gains. A number of conditions would be necessary for the dominant race to cooperate in seeking distributive justice. Those in the dominant race would have to understand that American democracy is a constitutional government that protects the rights of those in subordinated races as well as the rights of those in the dominant race. (They would also have to interpret "rights" as meaning a right to a proportional share of society's resources.) Moreover, those in the dominant race would have to believe that the short-term sacrifices they would be asked to make would produce long-term benefits (including vastly improved domestic tranquillity). The sacrifices would have to be viewed essentially as demonstrations of patriotism.

Perhaps the only way such changes in the distribution of resources (the ultimate cause of prejudice and discrimination) could come about would be if the vast majority of the dominant race were to realize that it actually has more in common with sub-ordinated races than with the ruling elite, which represents a tiny portion of the dominant race.

This elite of very privileged people in the dominant race includes approximately the top 1 percent of the population. This top 1 percent owns 37 percent of the personal wealth in the United States, compared with the 31 percent of personal wealth that is owned by the bottom 90 percent of the population. This top 1 percent receives about 15 percent of all personal income, compared with the bottom 40 percent of the population, which also receives about 15 percent of personal income. During the 1980's, this top 1 percent of the population increased its real income by 100 percent, received 60 percent of all after-tax income gains, and, according to a study by the Federal Reserve and the Internal Revenue Service, increased its share of wealth by almost 20 percent. This privileged elite benefits from a low minimum wage (which was not raised for eight years during the 1980's), lower tax rates (top marginal rates were reduced from 70 percent to 28 percent), weaker labor unions, and the movement of jobs to cheaper labor markets, all of which increased profits and dividend checks but held down or reduced the number and size of paychecks in the United States.

Most of the remaining 99 percent of the American population can be defined as "workers" in that they lack sufficient investment income to meet their needs and must therefore work, either for themselves or for others (in the broadest sense, this 99 percent could be said to constitute a working class). This group has been losing ground to the privileged elite as gender and racial conflict has been increasing. Improvement in race relations would be greatly facilitated if those people in the dominant race who work were to perceive the situation as one in which they would benefit from forming political coalitions with those in the subordinate races.

Applications

Sociologists have studied various attempts to improve race relations. James W. Vander Zanden, in *American Minority Relations* (1983), provides a good review of these efforts. According to Vander Zanden, five approaches have been used: antipreju-dice propaganda, education, intergroup contact, individual and group therapy, and the legal approach. Because the first four approaches tend to assume that prejudice is the cause of discrimination, positive outcomes of these efforts have been limited. The law, which attends to the way people act, rather than to the way they think (their prejudices), has been the most fruitful approach.

Efforts directed at decreasing the prejudices (attitudes) of those in the dominant race have assumed that prejudice is the cause of inequality and that if society could eliminate white prejudice, then discrimination would end. The problem does not start with prejudice, however; prejudice itself is an ideology, a rationalization of the status quo. Prejudice rationalizes discrimination, and if society eliminates one prejudice, another will be invented to take its place as long as nothing has been done about the causes of the discrimination that necessitates prejudice.

Efforts to improve race relations have been most productive when they have focused on behavior, particularly discrimination. When discrimination was made illegal, and when the law was enforced, behavior began to change. Educational and employment and housing opportunities began to open up for subordinated races. These changes in behavior were followed by substantial reductions in traditional prejudices.

The law alone is limited, however, in what it can do. The improvement of race relations would be greatly facilitated by the willing cooperation of a majority of those in the dominant race. Social scientists have theorized about the class, status, and power incentives whites might have to help blacks gain a greater measure of distributive justice. Michael Reich, an economist at the University of California, Berkeley, provided an important part of the answer in his 1977 article "The Economics of Racism." He found that white racism adversely affects not only blacks but also most whites, who pay more for racism in the form of lower wages and poorer social services (education and health care, for example) than they would receive in the absence of racism. More specifically, Reich found that as racism increased from one metropolitan area to another, income inequality among *whites* increased, with a larger share of all white income going to the top 1 percent of whites.

Most whites are, quite obviously, in the bottom four income quintiles (a quintile represents 20 percent of the total) along with most nonwhites. This 80 percent of the population receives less than half of all personal income and owns less than 30 percent of all personal wealth. These whites could expend their resources in an effort to get a larger share of the small portion of income and wealth that is allocated to these four quintiles, or they could join nonwhites in an effort to increase the share of income and wealth that is allocated to this 80 percent of the population. Blacks and whites share the goals of being employed, being paid adequately for their labor, having some security in employment, having adequate pension benefits, and having access to quality health care and education for themselves and their children.

Research and anecdotal evidence have both indicated that contact and cooperation between groups can improve relationships between them. When people of different races cooperate on the battlefield or basketball court, for example, decreases in prejudice have been observed. It may be, therefore, that if whites were to form political coalitions with people of color to achieve their common goals, improved race relations would result.

The contact hypothesis, articulated by Gordon Allport in the 1950's, holds that intergroup bias is largely a result of ignorance and misinformation. In this concept, close contact between groups or among individuals of different groups fosters more accurate perceptions and therefore leads to a decrease in prejudice and discrimination. For such benefits to occur, however, the contact must happen under favorable conditions. Stuart Cook also researched this area; he noted that positive results among individuals do not necessarily influence the views of a group as a whole. Another problem is that positive perceptions of a member of another group may be interpreted to mean that the individual is not truly representative of the group; for contact to be positive, a person must be judged to be very typical of the group to which he or she belongs.

A famous study known as the Robbers Cave experiment explored the effects of competition versus cooperation between groups in creating and alleviating conflict and prejudice. Muzafer Sherif and his colleagues established two groups among boys at a summer camp. The two groups were generally kept separate. Contact between the groups was designed to create hostility between them. Then, researchers brought the groups together in a friendly setting. They found that the groups maintained their hostility. Only when the groups were brought together to pursue a "superordinate goal" that was not attainable without cooperation between the groups did social barriers between the groups weaken. In an application of this process to the classroom, Elliot Aronson developed a "jigsaw" model for classroom contact. Students of different races are assigned to integrated work groups and given tasks to accomplish together so that cooperation and positive group contact can be achieved. This approach has been shown to create improved interracial relations.

Context

Efforts to improve race relations started even before the abolitionist movement. These efforts have produced positive effects—slavery was ended, Jim Crow legislation was abolished, and today subordinated races enjoy more educational and occupational opportunities than they once did. Efforts were intensified after the Supreme Court, in *Brown v. Board of Education* (1954), ordered the desegregation of public schools, "with all deliberate speed." Disappointment with the results of that order, along with the heightened awareness of discrimination of black veterans who returned from World War II, gave rise to the Civil Rights movement. This movement resulted in many improvements in race relations, as large numbers of blacks were registered to vote, as various forms of segregation were ended, and as many whites joined blacks to achieve these ends.

Hopes were greater than the achievements, however, and the Civil Rights movement encountered forceful resistance from many whites. Change was slow and frustrations grew until many urban centers exploded in rioting during the late 1960's. A presidential commission, known as the Kerner Commission, was appointed in 1966 to investigate these riots. In a well-known sentence from its *Report of the National Advisory Commission on Civil Disorders* (1968), the commission concluded: "Our nation is moving toward two societies, one black, one white—separate and unequal." Once again the nation was motivated to improve race relations and affirmative action programs in employment, college admissions, and the awarding of government contracts led to the further advancement of many of those in subordinated races.

Nevertheless, subordinated races still live in segregated neighborhoods plagued by unemployment and underemployment; part-time workers there want full-time work, and full-time workers lack traditional benefits such as health insurance and retirement programs. Segregated neighborhoods suffer high crime rates, homelessness, poor health, and an inability to raise sufficient taxes to provide quality education. Each year the National Urban League publishes a report entitled *The State of Black America*. Each report, while acknowledging the progress that has been made, includes a dismal account of the extreme inequality that persists between blacks and whites in the United States with respect to every aspect of living, including health care, housing, employment, education, and family life. Theodore Cross, an authority on minority economics and law, has also documented the painfully slow improvement for blacks, even during that period of American history (1960-1980) when the greatest efforts were made.

Great disparities between whites and other races still exist, and the law is slow and cumbersome. Some whites, especially white males, have resisted affirmative action. There has been more deliberation than speed in desegregation efforts. This is attributable to perhaps the greatest failing, the failure to enlist the large-scale cooperation of whites. Little effort has been made to make the majority of whites aware that their similarities to those in the subordinated races are more important than the perceived differences.

Bibliography

Aronson, Elliot, and Alex Gonzales. "Desegregation, Jigsaw, and the Mexican American Experience." In *Eliminating Racism: Profiles in Controversy*, edited by Phyllis A. Katz and Dalmas A. Taylor. New York: Plenum Press, 1988. Examines the application of Aronson's "jigsaw" model to Mexican Americans. As this edited volume's title indicates, it also presents many other interesting and controversial views on race relations.

Cross, Theodore. *The Black Power Imperative: Racial Inequality and the Politics of Nonviolence*. New York: Faulkner, 1984. The graphics alone make this a valuable resource. Cross documents the gains made by previous efforts to improve race relations but also notes that at mid-1980's rates of improvement, it will take another 250 to 350 years to achieve parity between whites and blacks.

Reich, Michael. "The Economics of Racism." In *Problems in Political Economy*, edited by David M. Gordon. 2d ed. Lexington, Mass.: Heath, 1977. Reich, an economist, explores the underlying economic basis of racism. He studied levels of urban racist behavior and found them to be linked to levels of income inequality.

Ryan, William. *Equality*. New York: Pantheon Books, 1981. See especially chapters 6 and 7, in which Ryan notes that most whites and blacks are in the same class and that discrimination against blacks in employment depresses white wages. He argues that the way to improve race relations is to improve the quality of life of all working people, which will necessitate a shift of resources from the privileged elite.

Vander Zanden, James W. *American Minority Relations*. 4th ed. New York: Alfred A. Knopf, 1983. The greatest strength of this text is its emphasis on empirical research, including short descriptions of the ways many studies were done. Knowledge of the methodology increases confidence in the conclusions of the research. Chapter 15, "Toward Lessening Racism," is especially germane.

Donald M. Hayes

Cross-References

Conflict Theory, 340; Education: Conflict Theory Views, 579; Equal Educational Opportunity, 661; Equality of Opportunity, 668; Institutional Racism, 996; Poverty and Race, 1472; Race Relations: The Race-Class Debate, 1566; Racial and Ethnic Stratification, 1579; Racism as an Ideology, 1586; Segregation versus Integration, 1707.

RACE RELATIONS: THE RACE-CLASS DEBATE

Type of sociology: Racial and ethnic relations
Field of study: Policy issues and debates

The race-class debate refers to the scholarly argument concerning whether racial group membership or socioeconomic status is more significant in determining an individual's life chances. At its heart, this debate also concerns whether race is a fundamental organizing feature of American society or whether economic stratification is of central importance.

Principal terms
> RACE: a socially defined group for which membership is based on a combination of cultural heritage, historical circumstance, and/or the presence of distinguishable physical features such as skin color
>
> RACIAL DISCRIMINATION: behavior, practices, or policies that result in harm, intended or not, to individuals on the basis of their racial group membership
>
> SOCIAL CLASS: a category of group membership generally based on economic resources, income, occupational prestige, and educational attainment
>
> SOCIAL STRATIFICATION: a hierarchical ranking system with differences in access to social resources; individuals at the top ranks have more access, while those at the bottom lack social resources
>
> UNDERCLASS: refers to a social class at the bottom of the social strata; the poorest of the poor, among whom poverty is an ongoing feature from generation to generation

Overview

In the sociological field of race relations, great attention has been given to the ongoing subordinate status of racial minority groups. This subordinate status is manifest in many areas of social life. According to political scientist Andrew Hacker (1992) in *Two Nations: Black and White, Separate, Hostile, Unequal,* "a black woman . . . can expect to live five fewer years than [her] white counterpart. Among men, the gap is seven years." Besides lowered life expectancy, Hacker states that racial minorities are more likely than whites to experience poverty, with the result that, "among black and Hispanic single mothers, somewhat over half are on welfare, while for white women the proportion is about 34 percent." While Hacker states that the racial gap in income narrowed considerably between 1940 and 1990, there is still a significant difference between the races. White families of all types earn more income than their black counterparts. Even when blacks have the same levels of educational attainment as whites, they are likely to earn less income, though the gap between women of both races is considerably smaller than that between men.

One of the major debates to arise in the field of race relations is referred to as the "race-class debate." It centers on the issue of whether it is the treatment based on the racial group membership of minorities which explains their failure to achieve social mobility, or whether it is only poor racial minorities who face roadblocks in social mobility. Some sociologists think that racism and racial minority status are more important in determining one's life chances than is social class; racial organization, some say, is an independent and fundamental facet of American society. Others view the economic arrangement under capitalism and one's social class to be more significant than race. They view racism as an outgrowth of capitalism and the economic exploitation which, they claim, is an ongoing feature of capitalist society.

Scholars who place significance on racial organization often cite black sociologist and political activist W. E. B. Du Bois, who proclaimed in his 1903 publication, *The Souls of Black Folk*, that "the problem of the twentieth century is the problem of the colorline." This implies that racial categorization is fundamental in American society; hence, issues of poverty and social mobility, along with persistent race discrimination can be traced to the issue of a "colorline" in American society. A major race relations theory supporting such a view is internal colonialism, articulated by Robert Blauner in his *Racial Oppression in America* (1972). Internal colonist theorists view contemporary race relations as growing out of a distinct process of colonialism, which describes the manner in which people of color were incorporated into American society. In this view, the low status of racial group members results from their nations being attacked and conquered, and then from them being defined as inferior, placed in the lowest positions of the society as labor or commodities, and excluded from the means for social mobility (such as education and political participation). In contemporary society, this subordinate status is maintained by the political, economic, and social practices of a powerful white majority that continues to exclude racial minorities from positions of power and privilege and to define them as comparatively inferior.

Another sociological perspective mirroring internal colonial theory's contention that race is central to social organization in U.S. society is articulated in the 1986 book *Racial Formation in the United States*, authored by Michael Omi and Howard Winant. Omi and Winant, following the Du Bois thesis, argue that "[f]rom the very inception of the Republic to the present moment, race has been a profound determinant of one's political rights, one's location in the labor market, and indeed one's sense of 'identity.' " Their "racial formation" argues that class-based theories and colonial or nation-based theories subsume race under other social categories (class or nation). Furthermore, they argue that both mainstream (assimilationist) theories and radical (class and colonial) theories have underestimated the tremendous significance of race in U.S. society.

On the other side of the debate, class-based theories view economic forces as most significant in both determining and understanding race relations. For example, the Marxist sociologist Oliver C. Cox, in his 1970 work *Caste, Class, and Race: A Study in Social Dynamics,* argues that racism is a product of capitalism, which maintains the power of the ruling class by dividing workers from one another on the basis of race.

Furthermore, racist ideology justifies the economic exploitation of people of color. Similarly, in the 1981 publication *Racial Inequality: A Political-Economic Analysis*, sociologist Michael Reich argues that workers who allow themselves to be divided by race are victims of "false consciousness" because they would benefit more from uniting and organizing as an economic class (against capitalists). In both views, racism flows from economic exploitation, and it is economic exploitation, not racism, which is the fundamental problem.

Another class-based sociological theory is that of William J. Wilson, presented in his 1978 work, *The Declining Significance of Race*. Wilson argues that, historically, race was more significant in determining where blacks would fall in the United States' stratified society. He says that in contemporary society, however, Americans have achieved racial equality through changes brought about by civil rights legislation, which, he argues, resulted in social mobility for those blacks who are now in the middle and upper classes. According to Wilson, those blacks who remain subordinated in society are in that position primarily because of their membership in the lower class, not because of their race. Wilson, then, stresses class differences among blacks, rather than racial solidarity, as being of greater significance. He bases this conclusion on changes brought about through massive protest and the protective legislation that ensued; he believes that these changes resulted in the broader inclusion of some blacks, who were able to advance economically, and thereby to distance themselves from the ghetto. To Wilson, their poor counterparts, unable to take advantage of those gains because of their low class position, have remained stuck in the inner cities which have only continued to deteriorate.

Applications

The race-class debate has tremendous consequences for public policy, with widely divergent strategies resulting from taking either of these theoretical orientations. Generally, if the race thesis is more influential, policy makers respond by continuing to investigate the extent and manifestations of racism. They also create policies designed to minimize the social differences between racial groups and to break down barriers created by racism. If policy makers are influenced by arguments that economic deprivation, not racism, is responsible for the problems of racial minorities, then racially directed policies (such as affirmative action) lose their mandate for achieving parity between racial groups.

If racism is viewed as the critical issue, the distance between whites and people of color is the focus. Solutions revolve around protective measures to shield racial minorities from white racism. Labor experts and civil rights activists argue that when people have similar levels of educational attainment and work in similar occupations, any remaining inequality (such as Hacker documents) may be the product of race discrimination. This remains a powerful argument for both the maintenance and strengthening of civil rights legislation against race discrimination and for protective hiring practices such as affirmative action. The Civil Rights Act, Voting Rights Act, and Fair Housing Act, all enacted in the 1960's, are examples of legislation designed to promote equal opportunity and end racial discrimination. Furthermore, special educational programs in higher education, such as "remedial" courses, mentoring programs, and the like are designed to target racial minorities, who appear far more likely than their white counterparts to drop out of college.

Despite civil rights legislation, racial minority group members who believe their lives are shaped more by race than by social class may not expect the white majority-dominated government to provide relief against racial barriers. This may lead to the generation of grass roots efforts to redress grievances and to the organization of political protest among fellow racial group members, regardless of their socioeconomic status.

On the other hand, policy makers who are convinced that the major problems confronting racial minorities afflict only the poor among them may seek one or both of two routes: They may seek to abandon any and all racially designed policies such as affirmative action or school integration; and they may create policies and programs specifically targeted for poor racial minorities. For example, scholars with remarkably differing views, such as William J. Wilson and neoconservative economist Thomas Sowell, have argued that affirmative action programs benefited only middle class blacks and that group no longer faces racial discrimination. Moreover, Wilson highlights the differences between affluent and poor people of color, focusing upon African Americans, to say that class conflict has been heightened between group members and that middle-class African Americans inhabit a vastly different social universe than that of the poor, inner-city African American underclass with which he is primarily concerned. Wilson advocates government intervention for poor people of color, particularly in the devastated inner cities, to assist them in education, job training, and financial assistance. He claims that they suffer from economic dislocation caused by societal changes in the economy. Meanwhile, Sowell argues that inner-city dwellers lack the kind of "human capital," such as motivation, values, skills, and training, that employers are seeking. Sowell also finds that affirmative action policies constitute "reverse discrimination" against whites. This kind of argument formed the rationale for the well-known Bakke case (*Regents of the University of California v. Bakke*, 1978), in which the Supreme Court held that a white man, Allan Bakke, had been unfairly blocked from admission to medical school because of his race. Generally, adoption of the class-based thesis results in the advocation of policies that are color-neutral, or racially blind. Policies and programs such as the Equal Opportunity Program in higher education are generally color-blind, targeting all economically disadvantaged students for special advising, mentoring, and tutoring to overcome deficiencies in their secondary education and ensure their successful completion of college.

Context

The sociological study of race and ethnic relations has had three major variants: the assimilationist perspective, which argues that all racial and ethnic groups will ultimately be integrated into one group within the larger society; the colonialist/internal colonialist model, which characterizes American society as a dual society divided by race; and the class-based models, which propose that those problems facing racial minorities are the result of their economic exploitation as members of the lower classes. The "racial formation" thesis advanced by Omi and Winant suggests that race be considered a distinct social category in American society and that economic and cultural considerations alone cannot adequately explain the dynamics of race relations.

The race-class debate has been an ongoing feature in American sociology; however, it was heightened in the late 1970's with the publication of Wilson's *The Declining Significance of Race* and its descriptions of what he calls the African American underclass. The debate that ensued returned scholarly attention to the question of whether Du Bois was correct in his 1903 assertion that race is a fundamental problem in American society. The race thesis represents a break with traditional sociological race relations theory, which is assimilationist. It also represents a break with what Blauner refers to as the "Eurocentric" bias in both assimilationist and class-based theories. According to Blauner, this bias resulted in a tendency among scholars to give greater priority to issues of industrial society and class stratification. He claims that race is not given priority because of the assumption by assimilationist and class-based theories that race and ethnicity are social categories that lose importance in industrial capitalist society. In such a formulation, racial group identity is expected to erode in significance, both for racial minority group members and in terms of their treatment by majority group members.

Not all theorists put themselves in an either/or situation of advocating the class thesis or the race thesis. Milton Gordon was first to advocate the concept of the "ethclass," holding that both ethnicity and class are important dimensions for social organization and identity. In his 1978 book *Racial Stratification in America*, James Geschwender elaborates on Gordon's ethclass concept, arguing that both the class thesis and the colonial thesis offer valuable insight into the situation of racial minorities. Yet his concept of a colonial-class model, which combines the two, still fails to address the criticisms of Omi and Winant, who argue that race cannot be explained by class or nation models.

Generally, the race-class debate has stimulated sociological researchers to use comparative analyses of various race and class groupings in order to assess and distinguish the effects of racial minority group membership and social class. Sociologists continue to diverge, however, on whether the fates of racial minorities are bound together in the quest for racial equality or whether middle class racial minorities have more in common with their white counterparts than with the abjectly poor members of their own race. More significantly, shifts in sociological theories of race relations have had profound effects on American race policies. Perhaps the most famous example is the case of Daniel Patrick Moynihan's publication, *The Negro Family: A Case for Social Action* (1965), known as the Moynihan Report, which presented policy makers with an opportunity to "blame the victim," if they were so inclined, by claiming that blacks' cultural mores were at odds with those of others, resulting in their low socioeconomic status. Generally, when policy makers shift away from the mandates of the race thesis, civil rights legislation is weakened, as it was under the Reagan and Bush administrations. The claims of unequal treatment by racial minority group members go unheeded in favor of "race-neutral" policy. If the race-based theories are correct in assessing the persistence of racism and race distinction at all levels of the United States' stratified society, such policies bode ill for the possibility of achieving racial parity.

Bibliography

Blauner, Robert. *Racial Oppression in America*. New York: Harper & Row, 1972. Blauner criticizes trends in the sociology of race and ethnic relations for not giving racism and race relations priority in theorizing and research. He analyses racism using a colonial model, positing that American society remains divided by race and that the division is by design.

Geschwender, James. *Racial Stratification in America*. Dubuque, Iowa: Wm. C. Brown, 1978. Geschwender discusses racial stratification in the work of major sociological theorists and surveys major models in race relations, including assimilationist, colonial, and class models. After discussing the historical experience of blacks, with particular attention to slavery and labor force characteristics, he concludes by proposing a colonial-class model.

Hacker, Andrew. *Two Nations: Black and White, Separate, Hostile, Unequal*. New York: Maxwell Macmillan International, 1992. In this clearly written book, Hacker provides detailed evidence for his thesis that race remains critical to the maintenance of the United States as a dual society in which African Americans are subordinated to their white counterparts at every level of society.

Omi, Michael, and Howard Winant. *Racial Formation in the United States*. New York: Routledge & Kegan Paul, 1986. This text offers a critical assessment of the major race relations theories. The authors then propose that race be addressed as an independent force in U.S. society. They apply this thesis to an analysis of the role the state plays and to an analysis of political contention among divergent racial groups.

Wilson, William J. *The Declining Significance of Race*. Chicago: University of Chicago Press, 1978. Surveys major epochs of race relations in American society, detailing the influence of race historically and the contemporary emergence of class stratification among blacks and of an entrenched underclass.

Sharon Elise

Cross-References

THE RACE RELATIONS CYCLE THEORY
OF ASSIMILATION

Type of sociology: Racial and ethnic relations
Field of study: Theories of prejudice and discrimination

The race relations cycle theory of assimilation was developed by Robert Park to explain the process by which societies incorporate racially distinct peoples into one social entity. It consists of four stages: contact, competition, accommodation, and assimilation.

Principal terms

ACCOMMODATION: the adaptation of the individual to society and its social organization

ACCULTURATION: the process by which culturally distinct groups understand, adapt to, and influence one another

ASSIMILATION: the process by which individuals take on the language, behavior, and values of another culture, as well as the process by which outsiders are incorporated into a society

COMPETITION: the struggle for existence

MARGINAL MAN: the individual who stands between two distinct cultures or races but is not at home in either group

RACIAL PREJUDICE: a categorical disliking of a group of people on the basis of certain physical characteristics; assumes a link between physical differences and moral differences

SOCIAL DISTANCE: a mode of measuring varying degrees of intimacy, understanding, and influence between individuals and groups in society

Overview

Robert Park, a leading sociologist of the influential "Chicago school" in the 1920's, proposed a theory of race relations known as the race relations cycle. Although today it is viewed as flawed and overly simplistic, it is important in that it provided a new direction away from the pseudoscientific racialist theories prevalent at the time and toward more scientific views of race and race relations. The theory hinges on a belief that assimilation of minorities into the dominant culture is automatically desirable for both the minorities and the dominant culture and that, moreover, assimilation is an automatic process that proceeds through consistent, identifiable stages. All racial and ethnic groups will ultimately be assimilated into and indistinguishable from the larger society. According to this theory, race relations move through four stages in a progressive pattern; the movement is always toward the next stage and is never reversed. These stages are contact, competition, accommodation, and assimilation.

To begin, Park describes the first stage of race relations, contact, from the vantage point of Europeans who, as they migrated into new territories, came into contact with peoples who seemed alien in their appearance and behavior. Contact, according to Park, is established as a natural aspect of civilization, since territorial conquest is part of the process of building a civilization. Park admitted that European peoples, as they migrated into areas inhabited by other societies, disrupted the sociocultural organization of those societies. They then replaced the indigenous social institutions with their own through imposition and control. He describes the processes accompanying the formation of the new social order as unavoidable and natural occurrences that always accompany migration, expansion, and the amalgamation of peoples. As Park saw it, race relations develop as the natural product of migration and conquest. The cycle toward assimilation which accompanies race relations is a natural part of society. Society, in his view, is like a living organism that struggles to maintain balance, or equilibrium. The absorption of new groups, then, is merely part of the society's attempt to reestablish social equilibrium.

Park defined competition, the second stage, as the struggle for existence. In racial terms, this refers to the struggle of a racial group to perpetuate itself, or to continue to exist. Competition can be cooperative when it is based upon a division of labor that provides people with roles that suit them. Competition can also be conflictual, however, when different races or ethnic groups are first brought together. This conflict can be lessened through time as these differing peoples come to have greater contact with each other and become attached to the moral order of the larger society.

Park defined the third stage, accommodation, as the inevitable result of the isolation felt by immigrants or racial minorities. They respond to this isolation by desiring to play an active role in the larger society. They also become aware of the social distance which prevents their acceptance into that society. Driven to achieve higher social status according to the values of the members of the dominant society, they become self-conscious of their differences from members of the dominant society. These social distances, according to Park, may last a long time, reinforced by established social customs, forming what he termed "equilibrium" in race relations. Inevitably, however, social distance does dwindle, making possible assimilation.

To Park, assimilation is a natural aspect of what he called "civilized" society. In fact, he believed that a civilization is formed through the process of absorbing outside groups. Like other European and Euro-American sociologists, Park assumed that urbanization and modernization would break down ties based on family, race, and ethnicity. The breakdown of these ties, he believed, would free the individual to participate in modern civilization. Park assumed that the United States was a democratic and meritocratic society, one in which individuals could achieve upward mobility based on their individual achievement and in which caste and race distinctions would ultimately disappear. Park did think that assimilation, while inevitable, would take longer for people of color to achieve, particularly because prejudice against intermarriage would prevent amalgamation—a natural form of assimilation. He did not consider the difference between white ethnic groups and racial ethnic groups highly significant. He believed that, to the extent there was difference, it was attributable to the race prejudice confronting people of color because of the "racial uniform"—their physical appearance—that they could not alter. Park thought that people of color could easily assimilate new values and behaviors to take on the culture of the dominant society, but he was unsure how long it would be before race prejudice would ebb. Ultimately, he found racial prejudice to be the product of conservatism driven by the desire to maintain the racial status quo and to prevent social change or assimilation. On the other hand, he believed that racial prejudice was a natural human response to the appearance and behavior of new and unfamiliar peoples.

Another concept credited to Park is that of the "marginal man" who is caught between two cultures. According to Park, the marginal man is produced in the process of building civilization, as new peoples are incorporated into one society. The marginal man, often racially or ethnically mixed, assumes the role of the stranger because he fits into neither of the two cultures that produced him. He is a new personality type, produced by the processes of acculturation that accompany the race relations cycle. He understands both cultures or groups that produced him, but he is neither at home in nor accepted by either.

In presenting his theory of a race relations cycle, Park did not explain how and when race relations move from one stage in the cycle to another. He described each stage but remained ambiguous in explaining why some groups had proceeded more rapidly from one stage to another. Ultimately, Park's race relations cycle theory was significant in laying the groundwork for a major theoretical trend in sociology, the assimilationist theories of race relations, which assume the possibility of a harmonious "melting pot" society in which race and ethnicity are not significant to social status.

Applications

Park examined his own theory of race relations cycles by exploring and measuring racial prejudice and social distance as well as indications, such as acculturation, which would indicate movement toward assimilation. Two groups that did not seem to fit well into Park's assimilation model were—in the terminology of the time—the "Oriental" and "Negro" populations in the United States. Park held that the major obstacle to the assimilation was their "racial uniform," or obvious differences in appearance from the dominant white society. He analyzed slavery, the institution through which blacks first encountered American society, both as a particular form of accommodation and as having things in common with assimilation and absorption. Park believed that the social distance between the black and white populations was minimal during slavery, particularly in the case of "house servants," who had "more intimate ties" with their owners. This proximity, Park believed, allowed for greater ease in the transmission of values, language, religion, and civilization. Furthermore, once blacks had developed (as he believed they did) an allegiance to their master, it was easy for them to transfer that allegiance to the state following the abolition of slavery. Ultimately, then, for blacks as well as for "Orientals," the major barrier to assimilation was the prejudiced attitude whites held toward them rather than their inability or lack of desire to acculturate. Because this is a major premise in assimilationist theories, the study of attitudes has been of primary importance in sociological applications.

Park's theory of the race relations cycle that moves toward assimilation has been applied in a number of different ways, including studies of social distance; measurement of racial prejudice and changes in those attitudes over time; studies of cultural differences among those who have not been assimilated; studies of the extent to which society remains segregated; and government and educational policies that promote acculturation and assimilation.

In terms of public policy, Park's concept that society must minimize social distance and racial prejudice to achieve assimilation has been instrumental in the promotion of racial integration in education, housing, and work. In his book on segregated schools, *Savage Inequalities: Children in America's Schools* (1991), Jonathan Kozol details the social costs of segregation. He promotes the concept that only when members of different races minimize their social distance by early contact with one another, as children in schools, will American society reach accord through mutual understanding. Public and private universities across the nation have adopted programs and policies intended to end racial strife by minimizing racial prejudice through mutual exposure and appreciation. A further, controversial, policy adopted by some institutions involves punishment for the verbal expression of racial hatred ("hate speech"), though critics claim that this impinges on the constitutional protection of free speech. Numerous studies measuring social distance have polled American citizens on whether they would tolerate different racial group members in their neighborhood, in their church, in their school, and in their family. Often, results indicating that whites have minimized their social distance from people of color are taken as evidence that racial prejudice has declined and that the United States is moving toward an assimilated society. A number of sociologists, however, including Joe R. Feagin, have argued that racism is driven more by discrimination, which can be unintentional, than by prejudiced attitudes. This raises questions about the validity of a focus on racial prejudice as the underlying basis of racial conflict in society. Furthermore, Feagin indicates that studies of social distance conducted in 1990 indicated a reversal in attitudes—whites actually voiced greater racial prejudice than they had in earlier decades.

More negative, even punitive, aspects of a belief in the value of assimilation can be seen in examples in which acculturation was forced on people of color in order to minimize their differences from the dominant white society. For example, many schools for American Indian children in the nineteenth and early twentieth centuries (some run by missionaries, some by the federal government's Bureau of Indian Affairs) had as their goal the "civilizing" of the children. Children were removed from their parents and placed in boarding schools where teachers tried to eliminate any vestiges of traditional culture. This pattern of forced acculturation is a good example of how government policy toward immigrants and racial minorities traditionally has been driven by assimilationist assumptions. In other words, Park's theory of assimilation echoes the status quo in American society: Both have assumed that U.S. society is an open society in which race and ethnic divisions will be eroded, replaced by a true meritocracy. Since both government policy makers and Park assumed that accultura- tion is a necessary step toward assimilation, it is not surprising that it has been imposed. Generally, the educational system is invested with the responsibility of teaching both the English language and the values of citizenship, important tools in the acculturation process. Feagin also notes, as evidence of society's emphasis on acculturation, the development of nativist citizen groups that promote "English only" schooling. These groups insist that all children should learn the language of the land if they wish to fit in as full members of society.

Generally, assimilationist scholars have found ready partners in government policy makers. Social distance has been measured not only as representational of racial prejudice by whites against racial groups but also as reflecting differences in social custom. In the 1960's, for example, the Moynihan Report entitled *Report on the Negro Family: A Case for National Action*, heralded the "peculiar" structure of many African American families—dominated or headed by a female—as responsible for the failure of blacks to be fully assimilated into American society. This family structure, Moyni- han held, promoted values alien and oppositional to those needed for successful integration into the dominant society. Some scholars followed this report by empha- sizing that blacks who have moved into the middle class have done so by virtue of their acculturation to the dominant culture; they claimed that racial prejudice is not the true barrier to assimilation but rather that failure to acculturate is the problem. In the 1980's, such applications of Park's pioneering theory of assimilation were common among those who sought to end what they believed were "preferential" programs for assimilation such as affirmative action in hiring and in higher education admissions.

Context

Robert Park, who as secretary to Booker T. Washington developed a keen interest in race relations, is credited with developing the American sociological field of race and ethnic relations with his assimilationist theory of the race relations cycle. This theory represented a significant break with earlier racialist theories which assumed, following the beliefs of biological determinism, that people of color occupied an inferior position in society because they were genetically inferior to Europeans. During the development of American sociology, Park's work elevated the study of race relations to a major place in the discipline, inspiring many others of the "Chicago School" to focus on the nature and outcome of race relations.

Certain elements of Park's theory became cornerstones in the predominant socio- logical theory of race relations, assimilationist theory. These include an assumption that the United States is an open, meritocratic society; an assumption that discrimina- tion is caused by prejudice; the view that African Americans had lost any culture they once had upon enslavement and that they should therefore embrace acculturation; the belief in the inherent superiority of the dominant culture as more civilized; the belief that racial inequality is abnormal to what is an otherwise egalitarian society; and an assumption of the assimilative effects of urbanization and industrialization. Assimila- tionist theories, as spearheaded by the work of Park, remained predominant until the

Black Power movement and the race rebellions of the latter twentieth century signaled that racial minorities exist who neither embrace the dominant culture nor seek inclusion in the dominant society. These developments, among others, illustrated the weaknesses of assimilationist theories in both predicting and explaining the motives, desires, and likely future of racial minorities in the United States.

Generally, Park's theory of the race relations cycle is criticized for its assumption of the inevitability of assimilation. In addition, critics argue, where he found examples that might be viewed as contradictory to his theory (as in the fact that African Americans did not seem to have assimilated according to his model), he simply said that the group was struggling to overcome certain obstacles to the completion of a given stage in the cycle. Chief criticisms of Park's theory include its failure to analyze discrimination not based on prejudice and its underestimation of the extent and duration of racial animosity and racial stratification.

Bibliography

Blauner, Robert. *Racial Oppression in America*. New York: Harper & Row, 1972. Blauner begins with a criticism of predominant trends in the sociology of race relations, particularly assimilationist theories, and counters their focus on race prejudice with an analysis of racial privilege as embedded in a system of internal colonialism.

Feagin, Joe R. *Racial and Ethnic Relations*. 3d ed. Englewood Cliffs, N.J.: Prentice-Hall, 1989. This introductory text in the sociology of race relations examines sociological theories against the background of extensive case histories of both ethnic groups and racial ethnic groups. It includes analyses of events against the background of competing sociological explanations. An excellent source on each of the groups presented, with bibliographic information at the end of each chapter for those who desire more information.

Frazier, E. Franklin. *Black Bourgeoisie*. Glencoe, Ill.: Free Press, 1957. Though clearly dated, this is a classic study in the tradition of Park of the "marginal man" dilemma, in this case applied to the black middle class. Those wishing to examine further how Park's race relations cycle has been applied in sociological case studies will find this an excellent example, clearly written and detailed.

Lyman, Stanford M. *The Black American in Sociological Thought*. New York: Putnam, 1972. In this work, which is clearly written and convincingly argued, Lyman takes sociology to task, revealing some of the racial biases in the development of the sociology of race and ethnic relations, particularly of those working in the assimilationist tradition.

Omi, Michael, and Howard Winant. *Racial Formation in the United States*. New York: Routledge & Kegan Paul, 1986. The authors devote fully half of this theoretical work to an examination of the major paradigms of the sociology of race relations: the dominant ethnic model, the class model, and the nation model. Clearly written and well documented with references to original works cited, this is an excellent overview of the sociology of race relations. In the second part of the book, the authors present their own "racial formation" thesis, with documentation presented in the third and final part.

Park, Robert. *Race and Culture*. Glencoe, Ill.: Free Press, 1950. This is a collection of Park's essays in which he develops and elaborates his theory of the race relations cycle. Though somewhat wordy and not always clearly written, this is a good original source for those wishing to examine Park's works in the sociology of race and ethnic relations.

Sharon Elise

Cross-References

Assimilation: The United States, 140; Cultural and Structural Assimilation, 405; Individual Discrimination, 547; Institutional Racism, 996; Race Relations: The Race-Class Debate, 1566; Racial and Ethnic Stratification, 1579; Sexism and Institutional Sexism, 1728.

RACIAL AND ETHNIC STRATIFICATION

Type of sociology: Racial and ethnic relations
Fields of study: Basic concepts of social stratification; Theoretical perspectives on stratification

Racial and ethnic stratification refers to a persisting ranking system in which rewards, privileges, and power meted out to racial and ethnic groups are unequal and supported by social structures and institutions. This concept helps to explain how stratification can emerge as a result of the contact between racial and ethnic groups.

Principal terms
ASCRIBED STATUS: status obtained at birth, such as sex, race, or family background
DIFFERENTIAL POWER: a situation in which the majority group and minority groups have unequal access to power; it results in the dominance of the majority group and subordination of minority groups
ETHNOCENTRISM: the attitude that one's own culture is superior and should be used as the basis on which to judge other cultures
EXTERNAL EXPLANATION: the belief that the lower social positions minorities occupy primarily result from the unequal opportunity structure that restricts minorities
INTERNAL EXPLANATION: the belief that the lower social positions minorities occupy are attributable to their deficient cultures
MAJORITY GROUP: the ethnic group that enjoys the social, political, and economic advantages of a society
MOBILITY: movement in people's position in a system of social stratification
SEMICASTE STRUCTURE: class stratification within racial and ethnic groups that are also stratified

Overview

Strictly speaking, race and ethnicity are two different concepts. Race is socially defined on the basis of physical characteristics, whereas ethnicity is socially defined on the basis of cultural characteristics. Because these two concepts overlap to a certain extent, the terms are sometimes used loosely, even interchangeably. In the broadest sense, racial and ethnic stratification can be understood as the inequality between different ethnic groups in social, economic, and political areas.

It is necessary, however, to point out that stratification means more than inequality. Stratification is a hierarchical ordering of social categories supported by social institutions. In other words, stratification is characterized not by individual differences but by structured patterns. Moreover, inequality in a social stratification system is intergenerationally transmitted; that is, inequality is perpetuated from generation to generation.

As a type of social stratification, racial and ethnic stratification is a system of structured social inequality. Those who are situated at the top of the stratification system form the majority group, while those who are located at the bottom become minority groups. "Majority" and "minority," in a sociological sense, do not depend on actual numbers. Regardless of the groups' sizes, the politically, economically, and socially superior group becomes the majority group, while those that are subordinate constitute minority groups.

All social stratification systems are based on one of two stratifying criteria: ascribed status or achieved status. Ascribed status refers to the status one obtains at birth, such as skin color, sex, or belonging to a wealthy or poor family. Achieved status is the status one manages to achieve after making substantial efforts. Lawyer, physician, and teacher are all examples of achieved status. Racial and ethnic stratification is a system that ranks people according to cultural or physical characteristics of social groups. Hence, it is a type of stratification based on ascribed status. In such a stratification system, rewards and resources such as power, privilege, social status, and wealth are meted out to majority and minority groups in a systematic and disproportional way.

Under what kind of situation is racial and ethnic stratification likely to emerge? Sociologist Donald L. Noel identified three elements in his influential 1968 article "A Theory of the Origin of Ethnic Stratification": ethnocentrism, competition, and differential power. Ethnocentrism refers to an attitude that one's own culture is superior to all other cultures and should therefore be used to judge other cultures. Noel contends that ethnocentrism, competition, and differential power are essential for the emergence of ethnic stratification:

> Without ethnocentrism the groups would quickly merge and competition would not be structured along ethnic lines. Without competition there would be no motivation or rationale for instituting stratification along ethnic lines. Without differential power it would simply be impossible for one group to achieve dominance and impose subordination to its will and ideals upon the other(s).

Of the three, differential power is essential not only for the emergence of racial and ethnic stratification but also for the maintenance of a stratification system. Sociologist Marvin Olsen notes that "the twin themes that link together stratification and race relations are inequality and conflict, both of which are direct outcomes of power exertion." In a racial and ethnic stratification system, the majority group is at the top of the ethnic hierarchy. Its access to the society's resources, including power resources, is disproportionately large in comparison to that of minority groups. Hence, it is able to employ power resources to make decisions in its own favor. This is not to say, however, that all the majority group members enjoy equal power advantages. Rather, it means that the majority group, as a social category, possesses disproportionately large amounts of resources. Placed at an advantaged position, it is able to use its resources to perpetuate its advantages.

Similarly, although minority groups are situated at a disadvantaged position as a whole, it does not mean that all members of minority groups find themselves in the lower strata of the society. In fact, class stratification has emerged within minority groups in the United States. Despite the barriers they have faced as minority group members, some minority group members have managed to achieve certain degrees of social mobility. That is, they have risen on the social ladder by obtaining better social, economic, and political positions. Such a hierarchical ordering of social class within ethnic and racial categories that are also hierarchically ordered is called a semicaste structure. Sociologist William Julius Wilson suggests that class structure for African Americans, for example, has become more differentiated and that the meaning of race is declining in the economic sector of American society. Upper-class African Americans, however, are not as upper class as upper-class whites, and the lowest positions in the social class hierarchy still belong to nonwhites without exception.

Applications

Racial and ethnic stratification is a hierarchical system that ranks categories of people rather than individuals. The full significance of racial and ethnic stratification is thus best seen by comparing the majority and minority groups in social, economic, and political terms.

In a multiethnic society such as the United States, racial and ethnic lines can be drawn according to country of origin, nationality, religion, skin color, language, and so on. When sociologists examine racial and ethnic stratification, they tend to view whites, especially the so-called WASPs (white Anglo-Saxon Protestants), as the majority group and nonwhites as minority groups. Hence, African Americans, American Indians, and Asian Americans are all minority groups. Hispanics are also considered a minority group (Hispanic people may be of any race).

While the combined population of African Americans, Hispanics, American Indians, and Asians constituted around 20 percent of the American population in the 1980's, a study by Richard D. Alba and Gwen Moore in 1982 revealed that members of minorities held only 3.9 percent of elite positions in social, economic, and political institutions. WASPs alone held 43 percent of all elite positions. Business and mass media were the two fields entirely dominated by whites; in them, minorities found no representatives among the elite at all. The percentages of minorities who were members of Congress or who held elite political positions also were low—3.4 and 3.0, respectively, compared to 53.4 and 39.4 for WASPs. Obviously, whites, especially WASPs, not only were overrepresented in most sectors of the elite but also were numerically dominant.

The economic position of the majority and minority groups is one of the most important dimensions of racial and ethnic stratification. A comparison of the majority group and minority groups in this regard also displays some structured patterns. A central indicator of economic position is the median household income. In 1990, whites had a median household income of $31,231, while African Americans had a median of $18,676. Translated into a percentage, household income for African Americans was 59.7 percent of that for whites. Median household income for Hispanics also was low. In 1990 the figure was $22,330, or 71.5 percent of what whites were making. Asian Americans seemed to be an exception; their median household income was $38,450 in that year.

Since the economic position for a particular racial and ethnic group is closely related to the unemployed proportion of that group, it is necessary also to examine this percentage for whites and nonwhites. The picture remains consistent. In 1992 only 4 percent of the white population age sixteen and over was unemployed. The unemployed proportions for African Americans, Hispanics, and American Indians were all high, with 8 percent for African Americans, and 7 percent each for Hispanics and American Indians. Asian Americans provided another exception, with 3 percent unemployment.

Although education is not a central indicator of political and economic position, it is the major means by which minorities can overcome racial and ethnic barriers and achieve upward mobility. As a whole, minorities seem to have made some progress in this area. The 1992 census indicates that among those who were between the ages of twenty-five and forty-four, the percentage that had received some college education did not differ much across racial and ethnic groups. The percentage for whites was 27, compared to 26 for African Americans, 20 for Hispanics, and 30 for American Indians. When the college graduation percentage is examined, however, minorities still lagged significantly behind. Twenty-eight percent of whites in the age range of twenty-five to forty-four had been graduated from college, while only 14 percent of African Americans, 10 percent of Hispanics, and 11 percent of American Indians had done the same. The educational attainment for Asian Americans was exceptional: Forty-seven percent had been graduated from colleges or universities.

These examples reveal only a part of the picture, but the whole picture looks exactly as this part has suggested. In terms of wealth, occupational prestige, poverty rate, and living standard, a systematic and consistent pattern is constantly found. When a person from a certain ethnic group suffers from lower income, receives little education, or is unemployed, this is an individual phenomenon. When a particular racial and ethnic group suffers from such disadvantages, this becomes a social phenomenon. When a number of minority groups suffer from such disadvantages, this is definite evidence of racial and ethnic stratification.

Because Asian Americans have moved far ahead of the other minority groups and even surpassed the majority group in certain areas, some people believe that they have climbed to the top of racial and ethnic stratification. Asian Americans have been proclaimed the "model minority." Sociologist Ronald Takaki points out that the so-called model minority is only a myth. The higher median family incomes can be explained by Asian Americans' locations in large cities, where income is generally higher; their incomes, in any case, are not comparable with their higher educational achievements. Moreover, many Asian Americans are located in the labor market's secondary sector, where wages are low and promotional prospects minimal. When

Asian Americans are viewed in this light, the relationship between the majority and minority holds.

Since the Civil Rights movement of the 1960's, the practice of affirmative action and the widening of opportunities for minorities to obtain higher education have helped improve the disadvantaged position occupied by minority groups. Yet these advancements have contributed more to the establishment of class stratification within minorities than to the eradication of racial and ethnic stratification. To the extent that social, economic, and political rewards for minorities are systematically dispropor- tional to those enjoyed by the majority group, racial and ethnic stratification persists.

Context

The study of racial and ethnic stratification in the United States did not really start until the 1920's. The two important themes that run through such studies are the specific ways in which ethnic groups come into contact and the different ways in which ethnic groups fare in American society.

Sociologist Stanley Lieberson distinguished two types of contact situations: migrant superordination and indigenous superordination. Migrant superordination refers to the situation in which a powerful migrant group subdues the native population, while indigenous superordination means that migrant groups are made subordinate to a resident group.

A brief review of American history reveals that the conquest of American Indians is a good example of migrant superordination, whereas the immigration of Asian and Hispanic Americans serves as an example of indigenous superordination. The situation with African Americans is different; originally brought to the Americas as slaves, they immigrated in an entirely involuntary way. No matter the type of contact situation, a racial and ethnic stratification structure with whites as the majority group soon was established following contact.

Although initially situated at the lower stratum of the racial and ethnic stratification structure, Asian Americans have managed to move up socially and economically, if not politically, while African Americans as a whole are still occupying the bottom position in the stratification system. This raises a question as to the perpetuating and changing forces behind this racial and ethnic stratification structure.

One approach has been called the "internal explanation," which suggests that an ethnic group's achievement is primarily the result of the traits, qualities, and charac- teristics of the ethnic group. According to this approach, groups that possess cultural traits that foster success in American society—such as achievement motivation, future orientation, and reverence for scholarship—will succeed in the society, while groups lacking these traits are doomed to failure. Studies have found Asian Americans to possess these qualities. It follows that they are able to change their position in the stratification system. Characteristic of African Americans, however, according to studies, are unstable family structures, high drop-out rates at school, and a value of living for the moment. According to this approach, African Americans' low positions in the racial and ethnic hierarchy are attributable to such characteristics.

The other approach is in sharp contrast with the internal explanation. Referred to as "external explanation," this approach focuses on the opportunity structure of American society. It emphasizes the external constraints, limitations, and barriers to which minorities are subjected and ascribes the low achievement of minority groups to such structural obstacles. Moreover, the distinctive cultural traits of disadvantaged minorities are regarded as responses to the externally imposed conditions. Sociologist John U. Ogbu argues that the absence of high educational aspirations, high achievement motivation, and a future orientation on the part of African Americans is a response to the realistic perception that their opportunities in the society are extremely restricted.

The external, or structural, explanation is a view more prevalent among sociologists. If external barriers are decisive in affecting group outcomes, it follows that the breakdown of racial and ethnic stratification is dependent on change in the social structure over all else.

Bibliography

Hacker, Andrew. *Two Nations: Black and White, Separate, Hostile, Unequal.* New York: Charles Scribner's Sons, 1992. This book discusses two ethnic groups: whites and African Americans. Part 2 is especially important because it discusses the dimensions of racial and ethnic stratification: income, employment, education, political power, and so on. Besides a bibliography and subject index, the book contains a series of tables comparing whites and blacks in many regards.

Noel, Donald L. "A Theory of the Origin of Ethnic Stratification." In *Majority and Minority*, edited by Norman R. Yetman. 5th ed. Boston: Allyn & Bacon, 1991. This is a very influential article in the study of racial and ethnic stratification. Noel not only advances a theory but also applies it to the experiences of African Americans. Recommended for college audiences with an interest in ethnic stratification.

Parrillo, Vincent N. *Strangers to These Shores: Race and Ethnic Relations in the United States.* 2d ed. New York: John Wiley & Sons, 1985. This popular introductory text is divided into four major parts: the sociological framework of race and ethnicity, European Americans, racial minorities and other minorities, and an analysis of the status of minority groups. The text is highly readable and has review questions at the end of each chapter to increase reader comprehension.

Smedley, Audrey. *Race in North America: Origin and Evolution of a Worldview.* Boulder, Colo.: Westview Press, 1993. Smedley discusses the concept of race both historically and comparatively and delineates the historical and cultural context in which racial and ethnic stratification starts and persists. Contains a good index and bibliography. Written with a general audience in mind.

Vanfossen, Beth E. *The Structure of Social Inequality.* Boston: Little, Brown, 1979. Although this book is not directly about racial and ethnic stratification, it presents useful information that empirical research has been able to provide about the structure of social inequality. Includes a good bibliography as well as separate name and subject indexes.

Willie, Charles Vert. *Race, Ethnicity, and Socioeconomic Status: A Theoretical Analysis of Their Interrelationship.* Bayside, N.Y.: General Hall, 1983. This book is not as formidable as its title suggests; the majority of the book is not theoretical analysis. The author's study of social problems such as disease, mortality, delinquency, poverty, and residential stratification as well as the research on family, school, and community will enhance the reader's understanding of ethnic stratification in American society. Includes a good index but no bibliography.

Shengming Tang

Cross-References

Conflict Theory, 340; Cultural and Structural Assimilation, 405; Ethnicity and Ethnic Groups, 689; "Middleman" Minorities, 1200; Minority and Majority Groups, 1219; "Model" Minorities, 1233; Prejudice and Discrimination: Merton's Paradigm, 1498; Race Relations: The Race-Class Debate, 1566; Racism as an Ideology, 1586; Social Stratification: Analysis and Overview, 1839.

RACISM AS AN IDEOLOGY

Type of sociology: Racial and ethnic relations
Fields of study: Theoretical perspectives on stratification; Theories of prejudice and
discrimination

*Racism can be described as an ideology—a belief that helps to maintain the status
quo. More specifically, racism refers to the belief that one race is superior to other
races in significant ways and that the superior race is entitled, by virtue of its
superiority, to dominate other races and to enjoy a larger share of society's wealth
and status.*

Principal terms

CLASS: a person's economic resources, which determine the ability to
buy what is needed for a quality existence; class is also used to refer
to a stratum of people with similar economic resources

IDEOLOGY: a belief that is maintained not because empirical research
supports it but because it helps to rationalize the status quo

POWER: the ability to exert one's will, legally, against the will of others;
it determines the ability to have what one wants by calling upon the
police powers of the state

RACE: a conventional way of referring to a population that has been
socially defined as being biologically different from another
population; race is a social reality but not a biological reality

STATUS: reputation or social standing; it determines the ability to have
what one wants by influence or persuasion

Overview

Any discussion of racism must first determine its use of the term "race." Race,
according to almost all scientists, is a socially defined concept rather than a biologically determined reality. "Race" is therefore real only in the sense that certain groups
have, for whatever reason, decided to categorize people according to certain aspects
(arbitrary and even superficial aspects) of their physical appearance. Terms such as
"black" and "white," then, must also be viewed as socially, rather than biologically,
meaningful distinctions.

Sociologist Howard Schuman has defined racism as the belief that there are clearly
distinguishable human races, that these races differ not only in superficial physical
characteristics but also innately in important psychological traits, and that the differences are such that one race (almost always one's own) can be said to be superior to
another. According to this view, it follows that the advantages which the superior race
enjoys with respect to health care, housing, employment, education, income and
wealth, and status and power are attributable to its superiority rather than to discriminatory social structures. Consequently, according to this view, racial inequality is no
reason to change any of society's institutionalized ways of doing things; the social

structure can be maintained. Racism is, then, an ideology: a belief that rationalizes the status quo.

"White racism," Schuman says, "is the belief that 'white' people are inherently superior to ['black'] people in significant ways, but that the reverse is not true." Prior to the mid-twentieth century, the prevailing form of white racism was the belief that blacks were genetically inferior, especially with respect to intelligence. Since that time the view that blacks are inferior to whites has persisted, but the public has changed its mind about the cause of the inferiority. Schuman cites a helpful statistic: In 1942, 42 percent of a national sample of whites said they believed that blacks were as intelligent as whites; by 1956, 78 percent of whites agreed that blacks were as intelligent. The National Opinion Research Center (NORC) found, in 1991, that 14 percent agreed that blacks were disadvantaged in housing, income, and education because they have less inborn ability.

The remaining 86 percent, however, did not all believe that blacks and whites were biologically and psychologically equal and that the differences in housing, income, and education were attributable to discriminatory social structures. Only 40 percent said the differences were attributable "mainly to discrimination." Fifty-five percent said that the difference existed "because most blacks just don't have the motivation or will power to pull themselves up out of poverty." If racism is the belief that one race is superior in significant ways to other races, and if "free will" is considered to be a significant trait (and it is if differences in education and income are attributable to differences in free will) then such a belief is an example of racism. Schuman, analyzing similar data prior to the 1970's, concluded that "the phrase 'white racism' appears wholly appropriate."

Psychologist William Ryan (1976) concurs: The old-fashioned ideology was that blacks were genetically defective. The modern ideology is that they are environmentally defective, that the defects are caused by "the malignant nature of poverty, injustice, slum life, and racial difficulties." Ryan notes that "the stigma, the defect, the fatal difference—though derived in the past from environmental forces—is still located *within* the victim, inside his skin." Ryan is explicit about the ideological function of this belief:

> With such an elegant formulation, the humanitarian can have it both ways. He can, all at the same time, concentrate his charitable interest on the defects of the victim, condemn the vague social and environmental stresses that produced the defect (some time ago), and ignore the continuing effect of victimizing social forces (right now). It is a brilliant ideology for justifying a perverse form of social action designed to change, not society, as one might expect, but rather society's victim.

Are people willing to "ignore victimizing social forces"? A 1991 NORC survey found that only 22 percent agreed with the statement, "Blacks have been discriminated against for so long that the government has a special obligation to help improve their living standards."

The ideology of racism has injured not only those in "non-white races," but those in certain white ethnic groups as well. The historian John Higham (*Strangers in the Land: Patterns of American Nativism 1860-1925*, 1955) traced the history of "race thinking" about European immigrants to the United States:

> Several generations of intellectuals took part in transforming the vague and somewhat benign racial concepts of romantic nationalism into doctrines that were precise, malicious, and plausibly applicable to European immigration. The task was far from simple; at every point the race-thinkers confronted the liberal and cosmopolitan barriers of Christianity and American democracy.

Applications

The most direct attack on the ideology of racism has been challenges to the very concept of race. If there are not in fact different "races" of people, then obviously all arguments about the superiority and inferiority of various races are false. Science has challenged the concept of race. The sociologist James W. Vander Zanden (1983) has traced the progress of science's views from the "fixed type school" to the "breeding population school" and ultimately to the "no-race school." The fixed type school held the view that "races are relatively fixed and immutable hereditary groupings that reach back into antiquity." The breeding population school held the view that races start with a common genetic heritage and that geographic and social isolation (breeding barriers), mutation, natural selection, and genetic drift gave rise to "more or less stable, differentiated gene pools among humankind"—populations that differ with respect to the frequency of certain genetic traits. The "no-race school" denies that races, as discrete biological entities, are real.

Vander Zanden holds that there are two primary premises of the no-race school. First, "racial differences are continuous." This means that skin color, hair form, head shape, and so on are continuous variables. In other words, if all the people of the earth were lined up according to, say, degree of skin pigmentation, there would be no natural breaking point between darkly pigmented, medium pigmented, and lightly pigmented people. Each degree of pigmentation would shade off almost imperceptibly into the next degree of pigmentation. When a continuous variable such as skin color is used to classify people into races, therefore, very subjective and inconsistent judgments are made. Second, in Vander Zanden's words, "trait distributions tend to be discordant." This means that one skin color, for example, is associated not with one hair form and head shape but with the whole range of human hair forms and head shapes. The anthropologist Ashley Montagu provides an exhaustive critique of the concept of race in his influential books *Statement on Race* (1951) and *Man's Most Dangerous Myth: The Fallacy of Race* (1965).

Race nevertheless remains a social reality. People are socially defined as belonging to different races, and they are treated differently based upon these social definitions. The differences in treatment produce differences in outcomes for the different races, and these different outcomes are then used as evidence to support the ideology of racism. Consequently, the ideology of racism can also be challenged by examining the way any social institution functions. If the institutions of education, health care, religion, the family, the polity, or the economy treats all races equally, then differences among races with respect to that institution might be attributable to racial differences. If those institutions treat people in different races unequally, then these differences in treatment may be sufficient to explain any differences among groups, and any racial explanation would more likely be an expression of the ideology of racism.

The institution of education provides a good illustration of this point. The educational structure includes many examples of institutionalized racism, and an analysis of this structural racism provides a scientific explanation for the differences in educational achievement (between whites and blacks, for example), in contrast to the ideology of racism, which merely asserts inadequacies of those in certain races as the cause of differences in academic achievement.

Many studies of the educational structure have concluded that it generates differences in achievement by race and class. Books on these studies include James Jones and Kenneth Clark's *Youth in the Ghetto* (1964) and Virginia C. Shipman's *Schools Can and Do Make a Difference: Findings from the ETS Longitudinal Study of Young Children and Their First School Experiences* (1981). This research has found that many teachers have low expectations of minority and poor students and that these students "despond" to these low expectations just as other children respond to high expectations (Robert Rosenthal and Lenore Jacobson's often-cited *Pygmalion in the Classroom*, 1968, presents such findings). Research shows that poor and minority students are placed in slow tracks early in their school experiences and are then left in those tracks. Published research by Ray Rist (1970), Eigel Petersen (1978), John I. Goodlad (1981), and many others reports such findings.

Research of the educational structure finds great differences in the amount of money spent on a child's education from one community to another and from one state to another. According to a 1985 press report, Harold Howe, cochairman of a study done by the National Coalition of Advocates for Students, concluded that the top 100 school districts in Texas spent $5,500 per student, compared with $1,800 per student in the bottom 100 districts. Educational research also reveals great differences in the curriculum provided to students. One school in the Goodlad sample, a predominantly minority school, had more vocational education teachers than it had English, math, science, and social studies teachers combined. According to a 1989 press report, the San Elizario Independent School District, near El Paso, Texas, offered no foreign language classes, no prekindergarten, no chemistry, no physics, no calculus, no college preparatory or honors program, virtually no extracurricular activities such as band, debate, or football, and no elementary school libraries. Intelligence quotient (IQ) tests have long been used to track children in school, but research on IQ tests has revealed cultural biases which make the tests destructively discriminatory.

In like manner, one could examine victim-blaming myths about racial differences in incomes, rates of employment, rates of illegitimacy, morbidity and mortality rates, and other differences, in each case showing that the causes of the differences have to do with the relevant social structures rather than the victimized races.

Context

The ideology that one race is superior to others, particularly with respect to intelligence, has existed for thousands of years. The sociologists Brewton Berry and Henry L. Tischler quote a letter from Cicero, the Roman statesman and orator, to Atticus (ca. 100 B.C.E.): "Do not obtain your slaves from Britain because they are so stupid and so utterly incapable of being taught that they are not fit to form a part of the household of Athens." Almost two thousand years later, Count de Gobineau returned the insult, complaining about the Italians, as well as the Irish and "cross-bred Germans and French" who were immigrating to the United States. They were, in de Gobineau's opinion, "the human flotsam of all ages . . . decadent ethnic varieties."

Just as de Gobineau was not deterred by Cicero's low opinion of northwestern Europeans, so are many of the descendants of those Italians, Irish, Germans, French (and others) not deterred by de Gobineau's opinion from thinking that they constitute a superior race. Consequently, one of these descendants, psychologist R. Meade Bache, in an 1895 study entitled "Reaction Time with Reference to Race," reached the conclusion that whites were intellectually superior to blacks and American Indians, even though whites had the slowest reaction times of the three groups. Bache interpreted the results to mean that whites "were slower because they belonged to a more deliberate and reflective race."

Bache was the first of a long line of so-called scientists who managed to confirm the superiority of their own race. After him came the famous psychologist Robert Yerkes, who developed intelligence tests for World War I recruits and concluded that the tests proved the intellectual inferiority of blacks. Then Carl Brigham used the Yerkes data to prove that more recent European immigrants were genetically intellectually inferior to earlier European immigrants. This ideology of racism has continued to the present day, when many are still convinced that whites are intellectually superior to other races because they average higher scores on IQ tests.

The sociologist Donald L. Noel ("A Theory of the Origin of Ethnic Stratification," *Social Problems*, Fall, 1968) attributes racist attitudes toward blacks to (class) competition for labor in the South, resulting in slavery and, in the North, to some class competition, but a greater amount of status competition. Blacks originally arrived in the United States as indentured servants in 1619. Between 1619 and 1660, laws were written to restrict the rights of blacks (with respect to interracial sex and the possession of firearms, for example) and to extend the period of servitude. Once servitude was extended to life, laws were passed that extended lifetime servitude to the children of slaves. During this process, beliefs (prejudices) were developed to rationalize the wrong being done. These beliefs at first focused not on color but on religion and class. As Noel says,

> The priority of religious over color prejudice is amply demonstrated by analysis of the early laws and court decisions pertaining to Negro-white sexual relations. These sources explicitly reveal greater concern with Christian-non-Christian than with white-Negro unions.

Even class, according to Noel, was more important than race: "The laws against Negro-white marriage seem to have been rooted much more in economic considerations than they were in any concern for white racial purity."

During the last four centuries, prejudices toward blacks have changed, but such prejudices still exist. As scientific research slowly convinces many people that a particular prejudice is factually incorrect, informed people begin to laugh and scorn when it is expressed, and others become ashamed to express it. Yet as that particular prejudice falls into disuse, another is invented, often by respected and influential people, to take its place. This occurs because continuing discrimination requires prejudice to rationalize it. In the future, if racial discrimination continues, so will racism as an ideology.

Bibliography

Gould, Stephen Jay. *The Mismeasure of Man*. New York: W. W. Norton, 1981. Gould challenges the concept of intelligence as a single entity which can be quantified by one number (as an IQ score) which can then be used to rank order according to worthiness—invariably to find that oppressed groups are innately inferior and least worthy.

Ryan, William. *Blaming the Victim*. Rev. ed. New York: Vintage Books, 1976. This is an excellent rebuttal of racism as an ideology. Some of the statistics are dated, but the arguments are still valid and germane today.

Schuman, Howard. "Sociological Racism: Free Will and Determinism in Public Beliefs About Race." *Trans-Action* 7 (December, 1969): 44-48. Schuman provides an interesting array of statistics and conclusions on the concepts of race and racism, including a useful definition of the ideology of racism based on his work.

Vander Zanden, James W. *American Minority Relations*. 4th ed. New York: Alfred A. Knopf, 1983. The greatest strength of this text is its emphasis on empirical research, including short descriptions of how many studies were done. Knowledge of the methodology increases confidence in the conclusions of the research. Chapter two includes a discussion of the concept of race.

Yetman, Norman R., ed. *Majority and Minority: The Dynamics of Race and Ethnicity in American Life*. 5th ed. Boston: Allyn & Bacon, 1991. Includes twenty-nine articles, most of them research reports, pertaining to the dynamics of relationships among dominant and subordinated races and ethnic groups. Editorial comments by Yetman, introducing each of the four parts of the collection, provide the theory that unites the contributions into a coherent whole.

Donald M. Hayes

Cross-References

RAPE

Type of sociology: Sex and gender

Rape, or sexual assault, refers to forced sexual relations. The number of victims is extraordinarily high, but only a minority report the crime. Most rapists attack an acquaintance; female victims are at greatest risk in their teens and early twenties, and most rapists fall into that age range as well.

Principal terms

ACQUAINTANCE RAPE: rape committed by someone who is known to the rape victim

DATE RAPE: a type of acquaintance rape committed in a courtship situation

RAPE: sexual intercourse as a result of force or threats of force rather than consent; the legal definition varies from state to state

RAPE TRAUMA SYNDROME: a two-phase reaction to rape that is characterized by disruption of the victim's lifestyle and reorganization of the victim's life

SEXUAL ASSAULT: any type of sexual activity that involves the use or threat of force

STRANGER RAPE: the rape of a person by an unknown assailant

Overview

Rape can be defined in many ways, and the legal definitions vary from state to state. The law in most states specifies that rape is sexual intercourse with an unconsenting woman by a nonspouse that involves actual or threatened force. Current terminology puts rape, involving penile-vaginal intercourse, in the category of sexual assault. Sexual assault includes a variety of criminal acts, such as forced oral-genital contact, forced touching of the rapist's penis, forced kissing of the victim, masturbation by the rapist, and the placing of semen on the victim's body.

Forcible sexual assault is thought to include components of power, anger, and sexuality, in varying proportions. Although sexual motivation can play a role, contemporary social scientists are of the opinion that in most situations, sex itself is rarely of primary importance. Instead, the sexual act is a means to make someone submit or to express one's hostility.

The number of reported rapes has grown alarmingly, probably both because of an increase in the incidence of rapes and because of a greater willingness of victims to go to the police. The vast majority of rapes, however, are believed to go unreported. Thus, statistics concerning reported sexual assault crimes underestimate the prevalence of rape. According to the Federal Bureau of Investigation (FBI) records kept by the United States Department of Justice in 1990, there were 102,555 forcible rapes reported. In other words, a woman was reported to have been raped every five minutes, on average. Precise statistics concerning the frequency of rape are difficult to document, but a review of the best available evidence suggests that between 15 and 25 percent of women in the United States have been raped or will be raped at some point during their lifetimes. The prevalence of reported rapes in the United States tends to be much greater than in other industrialized countries.

There are various types of rape. Rapes typically reported to the police are stranger rapes. Stranger rape refers to the fact that the assailant was not previously known to the victim. People who rape strangers often select victims who seem vulnerable, such as women who live alone or are walking alone. Women are more likely to be raped by men they know, however, including classmates and fellow office workers. These so-called acquaintance rapes are much less likely than stranger rapes to be reported. One reason is that victims may not think of sexual assaults by acquaintances as rapes. Acquaintance rape that occurs in a dating situation is called date rape. In several studies of college women, about 15 percent of the women have reported that they were victims of a completed or attempted rape by a date. Men who commit date rape may believe that acceptance of a date indicates willingness to engage in intercourse or that women should engage in intercourse in exchange for gifts, flowers, or dinner. Some date rapists believe that a woman who resists their advances is merely "saying no" so that she can engage in sexual activity without appearing promiscuous. Date rapists may not even see themselves as guilty of committing a crime.

Another type of sexual assault is gang rape. Exercise of power appears to be the major motive for gang rape. One study showed that sexual assaults involving a group of assailants tend to be more vicious than those by individuals. Gang rape victims tend to be more suicidal afterwards and are less likely to have known the offenders beforehand than victims of individual rapists are.

Until the 1980's, most states had legal protections that prevented husbands from being prosecuted for the rape of a spouse, even if the rape was violent. Legal changes in several states, however, have now made it possible for husbands to be convicted on rape charges. One factor in spousal rape is that a husband may believe that it is his wife's duty to satisfy his sexual needs even when she is uninterested. Marital rape goes largely unreported and unrecognized by victims as rape. Motives for marital rape vary. Some men use sex to dominate; others use it to degrade the spouse. This type of rape often occurs within the context of marital violence, such as in relationships characterized by verbal and physical abuse of the wife.

The rape of a man may not be recognized as rape in states that abide by legal definitions that require forced vaginal penetration. The prevalence of male rape is unknown because most are never reported. Some experts estimate that perhaps one in ten rape victims is a man. Most men who rape other men are heterosexual. Motives include domination, retaliation, and infliction of pain and degradation, as opposed to sexual motives. Most male rapes occur in prison settings. Outside of prison, male victims are more often attacked by multiple assailants, are held captive longer, and are often reluctant to go to authorities. Victimization does not fit the male image of capacity for self-defense. Although most male rape victims are raped by other men, some have been assaulted and threatened by women; nevertheless, rape of any kind by women is rare. When it does occur, it often involves assisting men who are attacking another woman. In some cases, a woman may be used to lure a victim to a reasonably safe place for the rape.

Applications

Women of all ages, races, and social classes are potential rape victims. Young women, however, are at greater risk than older women. Women between the ages of sixteen and twenty-four are at the highest risk. Although many more reported rapes involve victims from lower socioeconomic classes, it may be that more affluent victims do not report attacks to avoid dealing with the police and media. Findings that are based on representative samples show that a female's risk of being assaulted is not related to her social class.

As mentioned, the large majority of rapes that occur outside prison walls are carried out by men against female victims. Many people who survive a rapist's attack suffer long-lasting emotional effects, labeled "rape trauma syndrome" by professionals. There are two phases of rape trauma syndrome. The first, or acute, phase starts immediately following the rape and may last for hours, days, or weeks. Immediately after the attack, the woman tends to react in either an expressive or controlled way. In the controlled reaction, she appears subdued, but she may experience the expressive reaction at a later date. In the expressive reaction, she cries or is otherwise noticeably upset. A wide variety of physical symptoms, such as nausea, headaches, and sleep disorders may be noticed. A variety of psychological symptoms, such as guilt, self-blame, anger, fear, and nervousness, are also seen. During the second phase, "long-term reorganization," which may last for several years, fear and nervousness often continue. The woman may fear retaliation from the rapist, may move, and may have negative feelings about sexual intercourse with a partner to the point of abstaining from sex for several months or desiring sex less frequently than before the attack. Rape survivors often find that supportive counseling can help with the trauma caused by the rape. Most survivors find that they need to talk about the assault and their emotional responses to it in order to gain control over their feelings and to begin the psychological healing process. Most cities in the United States now have rape advocacy programs and rape crisis centers that provide assistance for victims ranging from acting in the role of facilitator between the police and the victim to providing support while at the hospital to providing counseling services on a sliding fee scale.

There are a number of myths about rape that are widely believed, such as, "Only bad girls get raped," "A healthy woman can resist being raped if she really wants to," and "Women 'cry rape' if a partner breaks up with them or if they feel guilty after having sex." Another myth is that rapists are not responsible for their actions but are driven to commit rape by uncontrollable sexual urges aroused by provocative women. Yet another is that women secretly want to be raped. Many women do report experiencing rape fantasies within the safety of their own minds, but this does not mean that they wish to have the fantasy enacted in reality.

Rape myths create a social climate that legitimizes rape and increases the potential for rape. Research has shown that college men show greater acceptance of rape myths than do college women. College men who endorse rape myths are more likely to see themselves as likely to commit rape. Such myths are related to other social attitudes. Some scientists think that American society breeds rapists by socializing males into dominant roles. In societies in which rape is most prevalent around the world today, research shows that several cultural factors are influential, including the nature of relations between the sexes, the status of women, and the attitudes that boys learn while growing up. Societies with a high incidence of rape tend to encourage men and boys to be aggressive and to view physical force as a natural expression of their nature. Men in these societies also frequently demean the judgments of women and distance themselves from child rearing and household duties. In comparison, in societies where there is almost no rape, men and women tend to share power and authority, and all children are reared to value nurturance and to avoid violence. In addition to the different socialization processes that frequently distinguish rapists from nonrapists, other characteristics have been linked to men who rape. Studies on rapists who have been caught and sent to prison for rape have shown that the men tend to have problems with social skills. They have had difficulty establishing meaningful relationships in their lives, and they tend to feel inadequate. Other research suggests that rapists may have a tendency to have fairly conservative attitudes toward a variety of sexual topics. Alcohol use may also contribute, given that rapists have often been drinking right before assaulting their victims.

Context

Susan Brownmiller, in a book called *Against Our Will: Men, Women, and Rape* (1975), was one of the earliest authors to examine rape systematically. She says that in the 1960's, criminologists passed the task of studying rape to sociologists. Brownmiller points out that rape has been a part of almost all cultures in which women have been viewed as property rather than individuals. By 1000 B.C.E., most societies had become patriarchal, and the subordination of women had begun. In both the ancient Babylonian and Hebrew cultures, rape was not seen as a crime against a person but as a violation of property rights. A girl belonged to her father until she was married, and then she became the property of her husband. Brownmiller argues that many present-day attitudes, issues, and laws regarding rape stem from the historical status of women and rape. Traces of the past can certainly be seen in present society and its views and laws concerning rape. For example, it is not a crime for a man to rape his wife in most states, because the law implicitly assumes that the wife is the property of the husband. Historical records also show that a societal tendency to blame the victim is partially responsible for sexual assault.

In modern society, few rapists are convicted. The legal system in the United States gives the benefit of the doubt to the accused, believing that it is better to free a guilty person than to imprison an innocent one, contributing to the failure to convict many rapists. Most states have strict rape laws, yet few rapes actually result in the conviction of the rapist.

The feminist movement of the 1970's was responsible for making people more aware of sexual assault, and it led to a considerable amount of research being conducted. Many experts contend that American society breeds rapists by socializing men into socially and sexually dominant gender roles. Men are also reinforced for stereotypically aggressive behavior from early childhood. Research supports the connection between stereotypical masculine identification and tendencies to condone rape. Women, too, can be socialized from early childhood into assuming the role of the submissive and passive victim.

Rape could conceivably be eliminated, but only if there were major changes in cultural attitudes and in the socialization process. Educational intervention on a smaller scale might serve to reduce the number of rapes. One study showed that college males who were more knowledgeable about the trauma caused by rape were more likely to say that they would not commit a rape in the future.

Bibliography

Bart, Pauline, and Patricia O'Brien. *Stopping Rape: Successful Survival Strategies.* New York: Pergamon Press, 1985. The book is an excellent and especially informative overview of various strategies that can be used by anyone to reduce the risk of becoming a victim of sexual assault.

Brownmiller, Susan. *Against Our Will: Men, Women, and Rape.* New York: Simon & Schuster, 1975. This classic account of many different perspectives of rape made the public aware of rape as a crime of violence and helped shatter the myths about rape and the rape victim. The book is comprehensive. The year it was published, it was chosen by *The New York Times Book Review* as one of the outstanding books of the year. It is available in paperback.

Groth, A. Nicholas. *Men Who Rape.* New York: Plenum Press, 1979. The author is the director of a sex offender program in Connecticut. The book provides detailed insights into the personalities and motivations of some of the men who have been arrested for sexual assault.

Higgins, Lynn A., and Brenda R. Silver, eds. *Rape and Representation.* New York: Columbia University Press, 1991. The editors have chosen fourteen essays by literary scholars that discuss how culture creates and reinforces the attitudes and behaviors that perpetuate sexual violence. The essays examine various societies and historical periods through their art and literature.

Russell, Diana. *Rape in Marriage.* New York: Macmillan, 1982. This book summarizes the results of a comprehensive study of marital rape. The author provides an excellent analysis of the prevalence of the rape of wives and draws connections to the battering of women and to alcoholism. She describes the underlying cultural attitudes that contribute to this crime.

Deborah McDonald Winters

Cross-References

RELIGION: BELIEFS, SYMBOLS, AND RITUALS

Type of sociology: Major social institutions
Field of study: Religion

Beliefs, symbols, and rituals are major components of all religions, and many social scientists have suggested that they are the primary "building blocks" of religious institutions. Beliefs are strongly held ideas; symbols are ideas and images that stand for or relate to other ideas and images; rituals are more or less fixed sequences of behavior that assume special importance when performed within a religious context. Social scientists contend that beliefs, symbols, and rituals are necessary for the creation and maintenance of religious institutions the world over.

Principal terms
ANTISTRUCTURE: a situation, which can be created by ritual, in which a society's normal hierarchical structures are inverted
MULTIVALENT: possessing a number of different values or meanings
SYMBOLIC REALISM: the concept that religious symbols are "real" from the perspective of believers
SYMBOLS: images, animals, or objects that stand for something other than themselves; religious symbols invoke a transcendent meaning
WORLDVIEW: the way a group perceives and conceptualizes the world

Overview

Throughout history, there have been numerous interpretations of the importance of beliefs, rituals, and symbols within religious institutions. Some contemporary social scientists contend that these are key components of all religious systems. Yet while rituals and symbols are cultural universals, notions of the importance of belief tend to be culture-specific. Many religions—such as Hinduism—do not emphasize belief as a major concern of religious life. It has even been suggested that the close association between belief and religion may be a particular manifestation of Western Protestant Christianity.

Every religion has an essential cognitive component that serves to organize individual perceptions of the world and acts as a basis for action. Actions and beliefs are very much intertwined. In other words, religious activities are best understood with reference to belief, and belief is often best understood in terms of ritual activities. Within the Christian tradition, belief is understood to be a highly subjective experience, centering on the individual. From the Christian perspective, beliefs are not philosophical abstractions but are instrumental in decision-making, interpreting events, and planning for future activities.

Like belief, symbols occupy a central place in all religious institutions. Members of religious groups frequently utilize images, ideas, and signs that are thought to "point to" the sacred and to suggest some of its qualities. Such pointers may take the form of words, physical objects, sounds, smells, tastes, textures, or actions. Symbols are by definition multivalent; in other words, they represent and evoke a number of significant aspects of the cultures of which they are a part. Whatever their form, the power of religious symbols rests in their unique ability to point to something beyond themselves and to represent and create meaning in the lives and experiences of a religious community. Ritual is the enactment and reenactment of religious meaning. Among some religious groups, ritual may be more central than belief. Social scientists have demonstrated that religious ritual can be a highly effective way of transforming perceptions of space and time.

Historically, the concept of belief has been closely tied to the concept of conviction; belief implies that a set of ideas has greater than normal value and that it in some way corresponds to the true nature of reality. In common usage, the term "belief" signifies the acceptance as true of a proposition for which empirical evidence is lacking. Belief entails an "emotion of conviction" that cannot be reduced to something more fundamental than itself. In the eighteenth century, Scots philosopher David Hume stated that the difference between fiction and belief is largely a matter of "feeling."

While belief can be an act of will which involves mental effort—a "leap of faith"—on the part of the believer, such is not always the case. Some religious and quasi-religious beliefs are said to have primarily socal origins; for example, superstitions may be held by individuals simply because they are members of particular groups. Thus, many beliefs have their roots in the community, the church, or the school.

Christian theologians draw an important distinction between religious beliefs and all other forms of belief. According to theologians, religious belief differs from everyday belief because religious belief introduces the element of the supernatural (one problem with this concept, however, is that it is often difficult to distinguish between what is considered natural and what is considered supernatural). Unlike everyday belief, theologians argue, religious belief is based on faith. It has an origin outside the individual believer and is thought to be based on revelation rather than personal experience.

Applications

Religious symbols, as they point beyond themselves and beyond the everyday world, can direct attention toward the sacred. Religious symbols may be either natural or manufactured. Rivers, mountains, and the sun, for example, have served symbolic functions in many religious traditions alongside such human-made items as wine, bread, and crosses. Every religion has central and peripheral symbols, and social scientists have attempted to differentiate between them. Placement of an item sometimes gives clues as to its importance within a particular faith. Other times, significance is not as readily discerned. Symbols can be both public and private. Public symbols may be understood by many members of a religious community, while private symbols focus on the internal consciousness and experiences of a particular individual.

While symbols may provide valuable hints about a religion's notion of the sacred, they also complicate the understanding of religious systems because symbols by their nature are necessarily ambiguous. Because a symbol is never the idea, image, or object it represents, it is always open to interpretation. In a number of religious traditions—notably orthodox Judaism and Islam—it is asserted that no symbol can adequately represent what is being worshiped. In Judaism and Islam, visual symbols referring to the ultimate power in the universe are not encouraged (hence injunctions such as those against "graven images"). These traditions do not want adherents to confuse the symbol with what is being symbolized. The refusal to allow such symbolic representation is in itself a crucial symbol. Finally, it should be noted that no object, image, or feeling is inherently sacred; it becomes sacred as a religious community's interpretation makes it so.

Rituals, like symbols, can say much about the world. In *The Rites of Passage*, Arnold van Gennep (1908) suggested that initiation rites represent a particular type of transformation in which the initiate leaves childhood behind, goes through an intermediate stage (which van Gennep calls the "liminal" or "threshold" stage), and later reemerges in the world of adulthood. Another common example of a ritual of passage is a religious pilgrimage. Pilgrims enact (both literally and symbolically) a transition from one situation and self to another situation and self.

Sociologists and anthropologists have devoted considerable attention to the "liminal" stage in ritual, emphasizing that this stage is governed by rules which are often the opposite of ordinary life. Authority, for example, is frequently inverted, and special license is allowed to participants: kings are mocked; women rule men; children rule adults. Max Gluckman, in *Rituals of Rebellion in South-east Africa* (1954), contends that such rituals of inversion ultimately confirm and support the social structure. One learns the rules of society by seeing those rules violated.

As noted, various religions place different emphases on ritual forms. Protestants in general do not stress ritual as much as Roman Catholics do, for example, but even groups that claim to deemphasize ritual (Revivalists and Quakers, for example) manifest it to a limited degree. Folklorist Richard Bauman points out that Quakers ritualize being antiritual.

The above discussion suggests that it is not necessarily the content of an act which makes it religious; rather, the meanings attached to the act make it religious. The dynamic potential of religious ritual has been noted for all traditions, and ritual words, songs, and actions frequently evoke heightened experiences of awe, mystery, wonder, and delight. As sociologist Émile Durkheim suggested, ritual has important consequences for both the individual and the group. It is primarily through ritual that group members come to identify with the group and its goals. At the same time, ritual allows groups to remember their shared traditions and to revitalize their collective consciousness. Sociologists of religion have established a high correlation between attendance at religious rituals and acceptance of belief systems. Rituals, symbols, and belief tend to be mutually supportive.

Rituals sometimes express disagreements and disorganization as well as agreement and social cohesion. They can subvert traditions and facilitate social change. In *Ritual Theory, Ritual Practice* (1992), Catherine Bell cogently notes that the earliest studies of ritual emphasized ritual's capacity to give expression to, and to symbolize, the central features of a society. A number of studies have supported the idea that ritual plays a part in reinforcing cultural worldviews, identities, values, attitudes, and beliefs. At the same time, it is recognized that ritual does not only mirror these ideas but also helps to shape them. The ethnographic studies of Victor Turner and Max Gluckman document ways in which ritual challenges society. Turner, especially, helped illuminate ritual's capacity to bring into existence radically new and unforeseen images, ideas, values, and social arrangements. Ritual's primary role, Turner suggested, is to introduce egalitarian and communitarian social arrangements to the everyday world and to replace hierarchical social structures with what he calls "anti-structure." Ritual, he postulates, makes possible a time and place in which participants can be "liberated" from rigid social classifications and burdensome social duties.

Contemporary theorists see ritual more broadly as repetitive performative acts. While earlier studies emphasized predictability and routinization as key components of ritual, more recent studies have expanded the concept of ritual to include all human communication and all interactions with the enviroment. Jonathan Z. Smith, for example, has put forth a theoretical framework that combines ritual performances and ritual transformations. He argues convincingly that ritual is "a means of performing the way things ought to be in conscious tension to the way things are." Ritual thus is able simultaneously to create, support, and challenge the social system.

Context

A major figure in the study of religious symbolism and ritual was Émile Durkheim. Among Durkheim's influential works in this area was *Les Formes élémentaires de la vie religieuse: Le Système totémique en Australie* (1912; *The Elementary Forms of the Religious Life: A Study in Religious Sociology*, 1915). Unlike his predecessors, Durkheim sought to uncover the social implications of symbolic forms, and he addressed the effects of religious symbols on the society that uses them. He suggested that social structure plays a major role in the formation of ritual and symbolic forms. Anthropologist Victor Turner expanded many of Durkheim's ideas. In *The Forest of Symbols* (1967), Turner argued forcefully that religious symbols can be understood only when one places them in context. He postulated that symbols play a cathartic role by releasing pent-up and potentially dangerous feelings and emotions.

French anthropologist Claude Lévi-Strauss suggested—in opposition to the ideas of Durkheim and Turner—that the social contexts of symbols are sometimes less significant than what they reveal about mental processes and "human nature." To Lévi-Strauss, symbols were more basic than any potential meaning they might bear.

Clifford Geertz suggested a slightly different reason that symbols seem so critical for religious institutions. He contended that religious meaning can only be stored in symbols—such as a cross, a crescent, or a feather—and that "such religious symbols, dramatized in rituals or related in myths, are thought to in some way sum up what is known about the way the world is."

Bibliography

Alexander, Bobby C. *Victor Turner Revisited: Ritual as Social Change*. Atlanta, Ga.: Scholars Press, 1991. Alexander argues that Victor Turner's theory of antistructure explains more satisfactorily than functionalist theory why ritual is such a compelling form of social protest.

Bell, Catherine. *Ritual Theory, Ritual Practice*. New York: Oxford University Press, 1992. Offers a theoretical discussion of ritual; Bell presents revisions of classical theories and theorists (van Gennep, Durkheim, Geertz, and Turner).

Bellah, Robert N. *Beyond Belief: Essays on Religion in a Post-Traditional World*. New York: Harper & Row, 1970. A collection of essays that include Bellah's ideas concerning the evolution of religious beliefs and his theory of "symbolic realism."

Durkheim, Émile. *The Elementary Forms of the Religious Life*. 2d ed. Translated by Joseph Ward Swain. London: Allen & Unwin, 1976. A classic study that relates religious rituals and symbols to social structure.

Geertz, Clifford. *The Interpretation of Cultures*. New York: Basic Books, 1973. Geertz's work has been influential in the field; this book is a seminal collection of essays dealing with symbols in religious and everyday life.

Gennep, Arnold van. *The Rites of Passage*. Translated by Monika B. Vizedom and Gabrielle L. Caffee. Chicago: University of Chicago Press, 1960. Gennep outlines three stages in rites of initiation (separation, a liminal period, and reintegration).

Gluckman, Max. *Rituals of Rebellion in South-east Africa*. Manchester, England: Manchester University Press, 1954. Discusses how classical functional theory postulates that violation of norms does not challenge but supports social structure.

Morinis, Alan, ed. *Sacred Journeys: The Anthropology of Pilgrimage*. New York: Greenwood Press, 1992. A good collection of essays that examine pilgrimages as symbolic rites of passage.

Rappaport, Roy A. *Ecology, Meaning, and Religion*. Richmond, Calif.: North Atlantic Books, 1979. Rappaport presents a cogent argument for the ecological significance of rituals and belief.

Smith, Jonathan Z. *Imagining Religion: From Babylon to Jonestown*. Chicago: University of Chicago Press, 1982. Contends that ritual is both transformative and performative.

Turner, Victor W. *The Forest of Symbols*. Ithaca, N.Y.: Cornell University Press, 1967. An important collection of essays stressing the key symbols in Ndembu ritual.

Stephen D. Glazier

Cross-References

Christianity, 231; Churches, Denominations, and Sects, 246; Confucianism and Taoism, 347; Cults, 399; Islam and Islamic Fundamentalism, 1022; Judaism, 1029; Millenarian Religious Movements, 1213; The Nation of Islam, 1275; Religious Miracles and Visions, 1623; The Sociology of Religion, 1952; Types of Supernaturalism, 2024.

RELIGION: FUNCTIONALIST ANALYSES

Type of sociology: Major social institutions
Field of study: Religion

Functional analyses of religion examine the role of religion according to the "functions" it performs in a society. An understanding of the basic functions of religion helps to explain the historical trends and current makeup of the American religious landscape.

Principal terms
ANOMIE: a state in which the norms of society are weakened to the point that they no longer affect the behavior of individuals
FUNCTIONAL ANALYSIS: a method of studying social institutions and patterns and how they contribute to stability in society by examining their functions
LIBERAL MAINLINE RELIGIOUS GROUPS: often referred to as "liberal Protestant," the three major religious groups defined as liberal mainline are the Episcopalian church, Presbyterian church, and United Church of Christ (Congregationalist church)
RELIGION: a system of beliefs and practices regarding sacred things that unites people into a religious group, community, or congregation
SECTARIAN RELIGIOUS GROUP: a religious group that is usually conservative in theology and that maintains strong tension between its values and those of the rest of society; examples of sectarian religious groups are conservative Baptists, the Church of Christ, and the Assemblies of God

Overview

Interest in examining the role of religion in society is as old as sociology itself. Many of the early social theorists, such as Karl Marx, Max Weber, and Émile Durkheim, were interested enough in the role of religion in society to write major works on the subject. One reason for this interest is that virtually all societies, no matter how simple or complex, have some form of religion.

Historically, many sociologists have assumed that religion was a dying institution because of the rationality brought on by scientific advances and industrialization. Many studies, however, have found this not to be the case. In reality, American society has not been turning away from religion. According to sociologist Jeffrey Hadden, church membership, attendance, individual devotional life, and financial contributions were all remarkably stable between 1950 and 1990. It appears that this pattern is not simply a short-lived modern trend. Religion has most likely increased in its importance since the American Revolution. In their book *The Churching of America, 1776-1990: Winners and Losers in Our Religious Economy* (1992), sociologists Roger Finke and

Rodney Stark found that in 1776 roughly 17 percent of people in the colonies were church members. This figure had risen to approximately 56 percent of the United States population by the late 1980's and early 1990's.

Why does religion remain so strong in American society? Functional analysis addresses this question by examining what religion accomplishes that makes it an indispensable part of the society. Functional analysis views society as a system of interrelated parts. Like the human body, each part serves a function that benefits the whole system. Each of the various parts of society must fulfill its function if the entire social system is to run smoothly. If one part ceases performing its function, it must be replaced with something else that provides the same function if society is to continue normally. This perspective can be used to analyze the persistence of religion in society by examining its functions. While there are numerous levels at which religion may be functional (such as global, societal, and individual), this discussion will focus on the functions that religious groups perform in the lives of individuals who participate in religion.

There have been many functions attributed to religion, but the two most lasting and important are the provision of meaning and the creation of a sense of belonging for members of society. Religion provides meaning in the lives of individuals by promoting sacred explanations for worldly events. In his book *Why Conservative Churches Are Growing* (1986), sociologist Dean Kelley calls the provision of meaning the "indispensable function of religion." He asserts that meaning is the one function over which religion has a true monopoly. No other social institutions attempt to explain worldly events through sacred means, so people are drawn to religion to obtain this commodity. Religion continues to exist because human beings have an insatiable appetite for "explaining the meaning of life in ultimate terms," and they cannot obtain it elsewhere in society.

In his book *The Sacred Canopy: Elements of a Sociological Theory of Religion* (1969), sociologist Peter L. Berger discusses the important role of religion in creating and maintaining a sacred world that provides ultimate explanations for events and meaning for those who live in that world. Berger states that every human society engages in a similar activity, called "world-building." Unlike animals, which are programmed with natural instincts, human beings are "underspecialized." Stated simply, humans have few instincts to define their world for them. Neither do they have a program regarding how to relate to others with whom they share the world. In order for human beings to survive, human societies must create their own culture, including norms, values, and beliefs to help them make sense of their world. According to Berger, religion contributes in a crucial way in providing the beliefs that create meaning for people.

The belief system that provides meaning also serves as a remarkable social control mechanism. According to Berger, religion in a society is necessary to create and maintain sacred legitimation of the norms and values of that society. If religion ceases to provide sacred meaning associated with society's norms, those norms tend to lose their power to control people's behavior. Berger asserts that sacred meanings are most powerful when they are followed without being questioned. These sacred meaning systems become humankind's protection from anomie. Anomie refers to a state in which the norms of a society have little meaning and are not rooted in any transcendent values. When this occurs, people have no sense of moral guidance. In Berger's estimation, this is society's "hell on earth." Without the sense of ultimate (sacred) meaning provided by religion, the existing social order would eventually break down. Avoiding this state of anomie is the prime importance of the "meaning" function of religion. Religion helps society to avoid anomie by maintaining belief in a system of sacred rewards and punishments (such as the belief in heaven and hell), which goes beyond that offered in the secular realm.

An additional and related function of religion is to provide a sense of belonging. People feel the greatest sense of belonging among those with similar values, beliefs, and social characteristics as themselves. They also tend to make friendship and marriage choices based on similarity of values, beliefs, and social characteristics. In fast-paced industrial society, it is often difficult for individuals to find opportunities for personal relationships with others who hold similar beliefs and live similar lifestyles. People often turn to religion for the sense of "fellowship" they feel when interacting with others holding beliefs like their own. In a study of Pentecostals published in 1980, sociologist Douglas McGaw found that belonging was as important as meaning for many people who were members of Pentecostal churches. Religious groups accomplish this function by binding people together in social relationship within an integrated community with similar beliefs and lifestyles. Obviously, people cannot interact with "society" as a whole, but they can develop social relationships with members of the social institutions to which they belong. The important role of religious groups in providing friendship opportunities is clear when one notes that church members often draw most of their closest friends from within their congregation. Religious groups give people the opportunity to engage in religious practice and to interact socially with people they would choose as close friends. These relationships not only provide social support but also reinforce the religious beliefs that people already hold. According to Berger, religious meaning systems remain plausible as long as people are engaged in this type of social interaction with others who share their beliefs. When these beliefs are not reinforced through regular social interaction, the meaning they provide is eroded.

Applications

Functional analysis can be used to explain the development of the religious landscape in the United States. Using the functions of meaning and belonging, one can gain insight into why some religious groups are increasing while others are declining. Many sectarian religious groups have been increasing their share of the religious "market," while liberal groups have declined.

Among liberal Protestant denominations, the Episcopal church, Presbyterian church, and United Church of Christ all declined in membership between 1965 and the early 1990's. In that same time period, sectarian religious groups such as the

Southern Baptist Convention, Assemblies of God, Church of Jesus Christ of Latter-day Saints, Seventh-day Adventists, and Church of the Nazarene increased the size of their memberships.

Although liberal denominations began their numerical decline in the 1960's, Finke and Stark found that the liberal decline actually began as early as 1776. In 1776, the Episcopalians had 15.7 percent of the religious marketplace, while the Presbyterians and Congregationalists (now the United Church of Christ) had 19.0 percent and 20.4 percent respectively. By 1850, the share of adherents (church members) held by the Episcopalian church had declined to 3.5 percent. The Presbyterian share declined to 11.6 percent and the Congregationalist share declined to 4.0 percent of all church members. During this time period, the Baptists increased from 16.9 percent of all religious adherents to 20.5 percent, while the Methodists increased from 2.5 percent to 34.2 percent.

Why have many sectarian religious groups prospered while liberal groups continue to decline? Some insight can be gained through an examination of which groups are more successful at providing a sense of meaning and belonging. Sectarian religious groups provide meaning and belonging for their members in very distinct ways. First, they claim to possess ultimate truth. At times, these beliefs appear to others as dogmatic and intolerant, but this unwavering commitment to one set of beliefs and rejection of all others prevents relativism from becoming a threat to established beliefs. When relativism and diverse beliefs are allowed to exist within a social group, no particular set of beliefs can be totally accepted as truth without alienating other members of the group. Because sectarian religious groups tend to maintain very homogeneous belief systems, those beliefs are not severely questioned and they provide a strong sense of meaning.

In contrast, liberal mainline denominations tend to value ecumenism, maintaining working relationships with many other denominations of various faiths. While this teamwork approach to religion has many advantages, it also tends to foster a relativist view toward other faiths outside the belief system of the group.

Growing religious groups also tend to maintain a morality that is distinct from other churches and the surrounding culture. This anti-ecumenical approach is called "boundary maintenance" and emphasizes differences between group members and outsiders. Among sectarian religious groups, this distinctive morality is stressed as an all-encompassing worldview that extends into all other spheres of life. Members of these groups have the advantage of a set of beliefs and values that give religious significance to all of life's events.

The importance of belonging is also easy to see by examining the American religious scene. Members of growing denominations (usually conservative) tend to view their church as a large family, while members of liberal mainline denominations are more likely to view their congregation as a loose association of individuals. Churches that are drawing many new members also tend to have members who draw more of their closest friends from church than members of declining denominations. In a study published in 1989, sociologist Daniel V. A. Olson found that conservative churches tend to be very successful in providing a strong sense of belonging (often referred to as "fellowship"). Members of conservative religious groups place considerable emphasis on friendship with fellow church members. Olson states:

> Persons with many church friends appear bound by their friendship ties; they are less likely to leave when dissatisfied with other areas of church life. . . . Such ties renew the relevance of attenders' beliefs and become social plausibility structures that counter the privatizing effects of life in a pluralistic society.

In a pluralistic society such as the United States, people are forced to interact with others holding a variety of beliefs and values. This may create a sense of normlessness, because one's own beliefs are called into question by the various beliefs of others with whom one interacts. In this type of society, religious groups function as subcultures to re-create a social world in which others support one's own beliefs. This makes each individual's religious worldview more plausible because it is supported by the consensus within the group. Communal ties reinforce the sacred worldview constructed by the group, maintaining a sense of social solidarity even in a highly differentiated and pluralistic society.

The Roman Catholic experience is also a good example of the importance of a distinctive, non-accommodating morality. Prior to the Second Vatican Council (1962-1965), the Catholic church was unwilling to recognize any other religious group or lifestyle as legitimate. Since Vatican II, Catholics have been allowed to marry non-Catholics, individual confession has been replaced by non-obligatory counseling (resembling that of many Protestant denominations), and Catholics have been allowed to eat meat on Fridays. Soon after this accommodation, the Roman Catholic church experienced its first numerical decline in the twentieth century.

Thus, the strength of religious groups lies in their ability to provide the two crucial functions of religion. These two functions, meaning and belonging, are related. Because of this, it is difficult for a religious group to provide one and ignore the other. Strong religious beliefs are constructed and maintained through regular social interaction among people with strong emotional ties. On the other hand, those strong social ties are much more likely to exist among people with similar beliefs.

Context

Religion is among the oldest concerns in sociology. The classical sociological theorists (such as Karl Marx, Émile Durkheim, and Max Weber) devoted great attention to explaining the relationship between religion and the rest of society. In the broadest sense, all the classical attempts to explain religion incorporated functionalist elements in them even though they were not functionalist theories. Karl Marx, when he called religion the "opiate of the masses," implied that religion functioned to help maintain the status quo by directing the attention of oppressed people away from the inequalities of the present life and toward the promises of the afterlife. In his book *Die Protestantische Ethik und der Geist des Kapitalismus* (1904; *The Protestant Ethic and the Spirit of Capitalism*, 1930), German theorist Max Weber discussed how religion functioned to create sacred legitimation of a capitalist lifestyle. Despite these superficial similarities, however, it was from French sociologist Durkheim that the functionalist perspective originated. In his book *Les Formes élémentaires de la vie religieuse: Le Système totémique en Australie* (1912; *The Elementary Forms of the Religious Life: A Study in Religious Sociology*, 1915), Durkheim discussed how religion creates a sacred reality that helps people to organize and find meaning even in the mundane experiences of everyday life.

Religion remained of primary interest to sociologists until the end of World War I and the death of Max Weber in 1920. Interest in the sociological importance of religion was more or less dormant from that time until after World War II. The 1950's saw a renewed interest in religion among the American population. The percentage of the American population who attended church on an average Sunday rose from about 39 percent in 1950 to approximately 50 percent in 1955. Along with the renewed interest in religion on the part of the population came renewed academic interest in trying to explain the phenomenon.

During the 1940's and 1950's, Talcott Parsons was proposing the sociological perspective called "functionalism," which studied social institutions based on the "functions" they perform for society. Since that time, other approaches to the study of religion have become popular, but the basic functions of religion have remained an important topic of discussion in the sociology of religion. Sociologists have continued to make great contributions in explaining the role of religion in society through the use of functional analysis.

Bibliography

Berger, Peter L. *The Sacred Canopy: Elements of a Sociological Theory of Religion.* Garden City, N.Y.: Doubleday, 1967. A classic work in the sociology of religion. Berger proposes that religion creates and maintains a social world that allows people to survive in their environment. Although written in the language of an intellectual, it is easily understood.

Finke, Roger, and Rodney Stark. *The Churching of America, 1776-1990: Winners and Losers in Our Religious Economy.* New Brunswick, N.J.: Rutgers University Press, 1992. This is a major contribution in the discussion of the social history of American religion. Finke and Stark challenge conventional wisdom and examine data that explain how many sectarian religious groups prospered while mainline groups declined. Very well written and easily understood, this book is an irreplaceable resource.

Hatch, Nathan O. *The Democratization of American Christianity.* New Haven, Conn.: Yale University Press, 1989. Hatch presents a beautifully written historical analysis explaining how sectarian religion came from a marginal status to dominance on the American religious landscape.

Kelley, Dean. *Why Conservative Churches Are Growing.* Macon, Ga.: Mercer University Press, 1986. Although this book was originally published in 1972, it remains a valuable resource in explaining the growth of sectarian religion in the United States.

Although the data are somewhat dated, the patterns persist and have been supported by subsequent research.

Roberts, Keith. *Religion in Sociological Perspective*. 2d ed. Belmont, Calif.: Wadsworth, 1990. Perhaps the best overview of the sociology of religion available. Roberts includes a detailed discussion of the various theoretical approaches to religion including functional, conflict, and social psychological theories.

Roof, Wade Clark, and William McKinney. *American Mainline Religion: Its Changing Shape and Future*. New Brunswick, N.J.: Rutgers University Press, 1987. A fine work focusing on the trends associated with liberal mainline religion. This book is an explanation of the social factors that have affected the liberal mainline in the past and will probably have a profound influence on its future.

David P. Caddell

Cross-References

Churches, Denominations, and Sects, 246; Cultural Norms and Sanctions, 411; Functionalism, 786; Legitimation of Inequality: Religion, 1068; Religion: Marxist and Conflict Theory Views, 1610; Secularization in Western Society, 1700; Socialization: Religion, 1894; The Sociology of Religion, 1952; Values and Value Systems, 2143.

RELIGION: MARXIST AND CONFLICT THEORY VIEWS

Type of sociology: Major social institutions
Field of study: Religion

Karl Marx's description of religion as the "opiate of the masses" pointed to religion's possible use as a weapon in battles within societies, by means of which one class induces docility in another.

Principal terms

CONFLICT THEORY: a framework for sociological interpretations that assumes competition among human individuals and groups for limited resources

CRITICAL THEORY: a framework for understanding culture that began in 1930's Germany and integrates conflict theory, Marxism, and other strains of social thought

FALSE CONSCIOUSNESS: in Marxist theory, a notion believed to be true by one sector of the populace that is misleading in ways that are beneficial to a more powerful group

IDEOLOGY: a collection of human thoughts about the assumed nature of reality, as shared by a group and used as a basis for thinking about the world

MARXIST THEORY: a framework for sociological interpretations that is based upon Karl Marx's assertion that the mode of production determines social organization

PRODUCTION: in Marxist theory, the creation of material goods and resources that occurs when human labor interacts with the environment

RELIGION: a system of human thoughts and beliefs about the assumed nature of reality which involves some supernatural or transcendent nonhuman deity or principle

REPRODUCTION: in Marxist theory, society's ongoing attempt to continue itself through new members who hold old values, orientations, and behaviors

Overview

Though sociologists have not produced a commonly accepted definition of religion, there have been many attempts to do so. Common to most definitions is the recognition that religion remains a powerful motivating factor for human behavior. In the supposedly "secularized" societies of the modern Western world, it may be fashionable to downplay religion's importance, but its ability to influence action is readily apparent.

Karl Marx developed a thoroughgoing theory of society's organization and interaction. Marx held that the primary determining factor in human social existence was the means of production—that is, the way that capital is used to harness labor and turn the environment into produced resources. One's position within this society-wide process of production determined one's class, and one's class shaped one's consciousness. This shaping process included the broad spectrum of notions called "ideology"— all those basic assumptions about reality on the basis of which humans see alternatives, evaluate options, and make decisions. From the dictum that "class creates consciousness" comes the conclusion that the economic reality shapes the ways in which people think about things and the very basis of what is held to be real.

Within different ideologies lie different assumptions, and these assumptions move people to act in different ways. Marx tied these actions to the groups who would benefit from them the most, noticing the inevitable connections between ideology and interest. For example, a national ideology that included the idea of the king's divine right to rule served the king's interest. By making it more difficult to question publicly the king's judgment, the society would shift more of its resources toward the king, and the presence of surplus capital would support the continuation of the ideology of the king's blessed nature. Marxist theory identifies some set of interests with every class and every ideology.

Religion, then, is a special case of ideology, according to Marxist theory. Since religion roots the rationale for social organization in the divine, where it holds sway all classes tend to accept the status quo. In the specific case of European religion in Marx's time, Marx interpreted the dominant forms of Christianity as supporting a hierarchicalized worldview that supported the elite group that possessed the society's capital. The wealthy benefited from a religion that emphasized hard work in this world (the so-called "Protestant work ethic") in exchange for benefits in the afterlife, since that religion enabled the wealthy to gain more from the labor of the working poor. The ideology served the interests of the wealthy. This was perhaps Marx's chief contribution to the society of religion: He held that the sociologist must analyze religion by determining who materially benefits from it and noticing the ways in which religion functions as an ideology to protect the interests of those who receive that benefit.

Religion's ideological function was, however, even deeper than that. Ideologies can alter the perceptions of reality by changing the ways in which people categorize their experience. Not only did Western European religion reinforce the presumed "right" of the materially powerful to keep their power and encourage the working class to remain in their oppression, but it also limited the population's ability to conceive of nonhierarchical ways of organizing society. The religion so strongly answered the question "Who should be rich and powerful?" that the people never thought to ask, "Should wealth and power exist at all?" In this context, Marx referred metaphorically to religion as the opiate of the people. In that day, an opiate was a mild analgesic or palliative; Marx was saying that the religion kept the people from feeling their own pain and thus from perceiving their own reality. Religion was thus a false consciousness; it was a way of perceiving reality that removed people from the material base of their reality and subjugated them to the desires of an oppressive upper class.

Many of the conflict theories of religion share the same orientations as Marxist theory; at times, the terms are used interchangeably. In general, however, conflict theories are less interested in the material basis for the ideology than in the contests of power between different ideological groups. Whereas Marxist (and other material-ist) theories of religion remain rooted in concrete economic concerns, conflict theory makes it possible to analyze other struggles within cultures around the issue of religion. For example, wealth is not the only form of power. In recent political campaigns for the presidency of the United States of America, power has been the key issue, even though the president does not directly receive money in proportion to the power of the office. Still, conflict theorists would correctly note the use of religious themes and images in presidential campaigns, in attempts to establish support for a particular candidate. Religion is a powerful motivating force, and it can certainly swing votes. When candidates use religious images to produce a popular ideology that is in the candidate's own interest, conflict theory can be used to analyze the use of the power that is embodied in those religious symbols.

Marxist theory tends to look for the economic bases of power, but conflict theory asserts the importance of power in and of itself. Similarly, whereas Marxist theory locates interests (and thus the origins of corresponding ideologies, including religion) in classes (defined in the economic terms of the mode of production), conflict theory opens up new possibilities. Interest groups can define themselves in many different ways. Most of the larger American Protestant denominations, for example, have experienced deep conflict, at times leading to divisions into competing churches. Each faction forms its own "interest group," and the intensity of the political fighting may be completely disproportionate to the amount of capital that is involved. At the same time, the sociologist should not be blind to the examination of who benefits materially as well as in terms of power and influence.

Applications

During the 1950's and 1960's, the United States (especially in its southeastern regions) experienced great upheaval in racial relations. As it had in the conflicts over slavery three-fourths of a century earlier, Protestant Christianity occupied vocal and active positions on both sides of the issue. Marxist and conflict approaches can help to illuminate the role of religion in this time of social movement around the issue of civil rights.

The Marxist theoretical perspective offers a strategy that begins with the question of material benefit. To the extent that the continued prosperity of European Americans was dependent upon the continued existence of an African American underclass, the elites' interest resided in the suppression of the civil rights movement. The presence of "second-class citizens" meant that European Americans would have higher rates of employment and lower rates of poverty than they would have had if such misfortune were shared equally throughout the community. Thus, many European American churches proclaimed that African Americans were not deserving of God-given (and constitutionally guaranteed) rights. The continued exclusion of persons of color from the buildings of the church (and thus symbolically from the presence of God) paralleled the exclusion of those same persons from full economic participation. Certainly, the long-persuasive teaching of the dominant churches that African Americans needed European Americans to guide them in the way of Christian faith served to anesthetize many people from the pain of segregated life; religion operated then (as it often has) as a system for the denial of oppression. It allowed both rich and poor to declare themselves the same before God, joint recipients of a heaven set aside for them. This encouraged both sides to remain within the status quo.

Some historians of the period have noticed that the European American churches that were most willing to accept African Americans were those of "mainline" Protestantism, whose adherents constituted one of the wealthy segments of the society. Since these people had less to lose than the more marginal members of their class did, they may have seen integration as less of a potential loss. Perhaps they even thought of racial integration as a means of reaching new markets. Regardless of conscious motivation, the African Americans with the most material advantage to gain were the first to make religious arguments for equality, followed much later by those European Americans who were least likely to suffer material loss. The middle-class embraced integration and its theological warrants only afterward, in most cases.

Marxist analysis of religion becomes more problematic in other situations, such as those that exist throughout much of contemporary Central America. In many Central American countries, the church (usually the Roman Catholic church) has been involved in both sides of the civil unrest. Often, the church owns sizable amounts of land and other capital; therefore, some of the official religious rhetoric encourages workers to strive in this life for the rewards of the next, thereby benefiting the totalitarian leaders of the Central American government. Many local priests, however, have embraced the doctrines of liberation theology, a religious system that affirms the right of the poor to overthrow their oppressors and begin a new life for themselves.

The competing ideologies match well with the conflicting interests in many cases, but the role of the priests is distinctive. Many priests have taken vows of poverty in exchange for guaranteed employment within the church, and thus they have no direct opportunity for material gain. (The presence of the central church's large resources, however, should make one hesitant to rule out economic motives and results.) Conflict theory, however, allows a more thorough analysis of the priests' participation. Through their immersion in the culture of the indigenous populations, the local priests have taken on many of the values of their parishioners. They identify themselves with the interest groups of the locals, rather than with the hierarchy of their own institution. This shift in loyalty is represented both in ideology and in interest. In other words they have not only cast their cultural lot with the oppressed but also have adopted the theological positions that reflect that social position in life. Such notions may include ideas of God's valuation of the poor and love for the oppressed, or God's vengeance against those who hoard resources. The theology may also provide norms for a new way of life, such as equality and respect. These theological resources are in no way to be minimalized, and they may produce long-term economic benefits for the priests as well, but the more immediate concern is the conflict between different ideological groups. Even within the upper echelons of ecclesial bureaucracy and in the rarefied air of academic theology, careers are made and lost over the battles between conflicting religious ideologies.

Context

Émile Durkheim understood religion as the personification and deification of society's understanding of itself, providing a way for society to justify and enforce its own values and norms. Karl Marx's interpretation of religion is not much different, except that Marx perceives society as being fragmented into classes. Religion, then, is not the reification of society for itself, but the justification of one class's way of life as opposed to another class's interests. If the elites have sufficient power, they may be able to construct ideologies that the lower classes will accept and use as reasons to maintain the situation of domination.

Conflict theory has allowed the sociology of religion (as well as the sociology of ideology) to include nonmaterial factors more readily in its analysis. Power becomes a resource with value in and of itself, rather than merely as a corollary of capital and wealth. Religions are contentious by nature; that is, it is the nature of a religion to contend its truth, and thus to seek its defense and its expansion in the context of other systems of belief.

The so-called "Frankfurt School" has developed a form of "critical theory" that builds upon many of these insights about culture and ideology, especially in the work of scholars such as Hans-Georg Gadamer, Jürgen Habermas, Max Horkheimer, Herbert Marcuse, and others. By constructing theories about the interest-ideology connection in the light of postmodernist understandings of language and society, this group has pushed the frontiers of Marxist sociology of religion. This new field has not yet, however, produced much interaction with the traditional descriptive study of the sociology of religion, and that integration needs to take place in order to complete the development of critical theory.

There is a need for theories that more directly connect values and the material aspects of religion. In many cases, the self-interest and class-consciousness of religious belief is apparent, but there are also many other cases in which religion promotes the abandonment of self-interest. These cases are still poorly understood in sociological terms, and in most cases they receive treatment only as individual psychological deviations from the sociological expectation.

In a related area, sociologists need to examine the interplay between materialist perspectives (which stress external observation) and subjective interpretations of religion (which emphasize the actor's self-perception). How do believers feel when they undertake acts that have material ramifications? What do they think they are doing?

Finally, sociologists of religion are becoming increasingly interested (and should become even more so) in conflicts within religious groups. What are the processes for choosing leadership within a group with a shared belief system? Furthermore, to what extent is any belief system "shared" by a group? Many opportunities for study exist, including clergy-parishioner relationships and the presence of power issues in them, the infighting among clerics of one or more denominations, and the degree of diversity that is allowed within a single church. In the same way that Marx expanded the field of sociology by examining competing interests within one society, the sociology of religion should examine the interaction of religious beliefs on the microsociological level in order to understand its importance for the larger scale of religious activity.

Bibliography

Brown, Michael E. *The Production of Society: A Marxian Foundation for Social Theory*. Totowa, N.J.: Rowman & Littlefield, 1986. This book attempts to integrate Marxist theory into several other theoretical movements, from psychoanalysis to postmodernism. Though there is no particular discussion of Marxist views of religion, there is a stimulating chapter on ideology and culture that shows the connections that neo-Marxist studies make between all forms of ideology and the means of production.

Elster, Jon. *An Introduction to Karl Marx*. Cambridge, England: Cambridge University Press, 1986. This book provides an excellent short introduction to the thought of Karl Marx. Religion is discussed under the topic of ideology, and one might wish for more detail on Marx's sociology of religion, but the book does give a solid overview of Marx's original concepts, emphasizing the thought of Marx rather than that of his later interpreters.

Kellner, Douglas. *Critical Theory, Marxism, and Modernity*. Baltimore: The Johns Hopkins University Press, 1989. Kellner provides a thorough retracing of the historical steps between early twentieth century European Marxist and materialist thought and the rise of the so-called "Frankfurt School" of critical theory. Though it provides very little material on religion, the book offers clues to the future of at least some neo-Marxist interpretations of religion.

Kinloch, Graham C. *Sociological Theory: Its Development and Major Paradigms*. New York: McGraw-Hill, 1977. The ideas of Karl Marx and other conflict sociologists are presented here in brief form for easy comparison with other sociological perspectives. Kinloch's typological arrangement of sociological methods betrays a functionalist predisposition, but there is still much good information here to help place Marx's sociology of religion within the larger context of sociological theories.

McGuire, Meredith B. *Religion: The Social Context*. 3d ed. Belmont, Calif.: Wadsworth, 1992. McGuire offers an excellent introductory text for the entire field of religion's social dimensions. Of particular relevance here is the chapter on religion's role in both cohesion and conflict, which offers a very balanced view with a strong emphasis on conflict among civil religions.

McLellan, David. *Marxism and Religion: A Description and Assessment of the Marxist Critique of Christianity*. New York: Harper & Row, 1987. This book is quite helpful for disentangling Marx's sociology from the many forms of Marxism present today and throughout the past century. The clear historical presentation demonstrates the ways in which Marxist thought has changed in its evaluation of religion's protection of bourgeois power, and it also indicates some of the major responses to the Marxist critique.

Wuthnow, Robert. *Meaning and Moral Order: Explorations in Cultural Analysis.* Berkeley: University of California Press, 1987. Rather than examine religion separately, Wuthnow integrates it into an investigatin of how humans produce meaning. Though the core of the book does not reflect particular Marxist strands, there are good chapters on the connections of religion and state order, as well as the role of technological change in affecting ideology.

Jon L. Berquist

Cross-References

RELIGION VERSUS MAGIC

Type of sociology: Major social institutions
Field of study: Religion

The distinction between religion and magic refers mainly to the ways social institutions and individuals think about their beliefs and actions with regard to supernatural beings or forces. Some sociologists, anthropologists, and folklorists have suggested that magic is essentially mechanical and that religion is based on the assumption that the course of nature and human life is controlled by beings superior to humans. Other social scientists have stated that religion is largely a group activity, while magic is largely an individual activity.

Principal terms

LAW OF CONTAGION: the principle of contagious magic, whereby things that were once in contact will continue to influence each other

LAW OF SYMPATHY: the principle of sympathetic magic, whereby things that look alike are believed to influence each other

MANA: a Melanesian word that stands for an impersonal, powerful force in the universe; it may be tapped in magical rites in order to influence natural or social events

RELIGION: a system of beliefs and practices regarding sacred things that unites people into a group or community

SORCERER: a practitioner of magic who consciously performs magical rites

SYMBOL: something that represents something else, particularly a material object that stands for something invisible or intangible

Overview

Religious beliefs and belief in the powers of magic have certain elements in common, but sociologists and anthropologists have evolved a number of schemes for classifying and distinguishing between them. Both involve a belief in forces, powers, or entities that exist beyond the empirical world—in the realm of the supernatural—and that are therefore not subject to disproof. One difference that has been drawn between religion and magic is that religion is primarily oriented toward supernatural beings. These entities are prayed to, worshiped, or revered in various ways. Magic, on the other hand, is generally concerned with controlling and using impersonal super-natural forces; it is practical, seeking to use the supernatural for immediate and concrete ends. Others have distinguished between the two by classifying religion as a group, and magic as an individual, activity. Early studies of magic were sometimes predicated on the idea that magic represents a primitive form of religion. Anthropologists and sociologists who subscribed to this view saw magic as a part of the development of a group of people who had yet to develop a true religious system; a transition from magic to religion was seen as a part of the evolution of a society. This view was soon discarded as being too simplistic. One problem with such a definition is that the boundaries between religion and magic are not as rigid as might at first be assumed. For example, religious symbolism and ritual are seen by some as employing many of the elements of magic. Throughout history, there have been numerous definitions of magic, a situation which has led to considerable confusion in the literature. In many early societies, magical beliefs and practices were intimately associated with religious rites and were usually considered to be within the domain of religion. On the other hand, in industrialized societies, religion and magic are seen as being quite separate in thought and action. Magic, for most people in industrialized societies, is perceived as mere superstition. In countries of the developed world, many people think of magic as little more than a form of entertainment suitable for nightclubs and television. Nevertheless, quasi-magical attitudes persist in the industrialized world.

The term "magic" has carried different connotations at different times and for different people. In popular discourse, it has long had unfavorable connotations. (The Latin word *magia*, in the strictest sense, originally referred to the occult practices of the Persian Magi, or priests of Zoroaster.) Magic, to the Western mind, implies mysterious witchcraft and sorcery. Modern social scientists use the term without intending such connotations, but early social scientists were strongly influenced by their own cultural biases and often denigrated a belief in magic. In his influential work *Primitive Cultures* (1871), British social anthropologist Edward B. Tylor saw magic as the "confusion of objective and subjective connections" and suggested that magic is simply gross superstitions. Unlike religion, Tylor contended, magic is futile, the "misapplied association of ideas born of fallacies to which the human mind is naturally prone."

Scots folklorist James G. Frazer, in his classic twelve-volume compilation *The Golden Bough* (1890), postulated that there was a fundamental opposition between magic and religion. Magic, he contended, operated at a much lower intellectual level. Throughout the world, he said, magic universally preceded religion. According to Frazer, magic differs from religion to the extent that it conceives the universe to be operating mechanistically; that is, the magical practitioner sees events as occurring in fixed, invariable sequences, without the intervention of superhuman agencies. He was the first to suggest that the question as to whether a particular action or belief is religious depends largely on the degree to which participants feel that they have control over the situation. If there remains a high degree of uncertainty about the results, then these activities can be seen as religious. If there is a perception of relative certainty, the activities can be seen as magical.

Frazer suggested that magic shares a common attitude with science because science, like magic, assumes that there are natural laws in the universe that magic, like science, seeks to discover. Religion, in contrast, is seen as opposed to both magic and science because its basic assumption is that the course of nature and all human life is controlled by beings who are thought to be superior and to lack accountability to humans. Frazer divided magic into two general types: sympathetic magic, which is based on the law of similarity and assumes that "like influences like," and contagious magic, which is based on the law of contiguity or contact and assumes that if two objects were once related (such as clothing or other personal possessions) then they will continue to influence each other.

Frazer's typology laid the basis for Bronislaw Malinowski's multivolume *Coral Gardens and Their Magic*, and E. E. Evans-Pritchard's *Witches, Oracles, and Magic Among the Azande* (1937). Both ethnographers argued that magicians strive to keep magical acts and practical acts separate. For Malinowski, who agreed with Frazer's earlier formulations, words were thought to be the essence and foundation of all magic. Malinowski emphasized the idea that magical utterances differ from regular speech by what he termed a "coefficient of weirdness."

Nineteenth century theorists such as E. B. Hartland and Robert R. Marett suggested that religion and magic are both rooted in a common belief in an impersonal power in the universe. Marett's ideas were borrowed from early anthropological descriptions of *mana* in the South Seas. Others asserted that religion and magic are essentially two different ways of dealing with the miraculous or supernatural, religion being primarily social, and magic being primarily antisocial. Henri Hubert and Marcel Mauss argued in the early twentieth century that the major difference between religion and magic is that the former is an individual act, whereas the latter is part of an organized cult and is usually a group activity. According to this concept, because magic is solitary activity, it tends to be viewed with suspicion. The magician thus becomes an outcast of society and magic is gradually differentiated from religion because of its outcast status.

Applications

Robert R. Marett, an anthropologist who studied religion in the early twentieth century, believed that magic ritual had its origin in habit. Magic, he asserted, had its base in an attempt to justify habitual behaviors—whether in the realm of clothing, manufacture, or the uttering of words in a specific order or manner. This desire to justify behavior causes humans to translate the value of habit into a notion that there is power in certain ways of doing things; that is, they work independently of human actors to bring about desired results. Such acts, Marett emphasized, might also provide emotional support and comfort for practitioners. Magic, unlike religion, can be seen as practical and unreflexive. It is a way for humans to take an active stance in a universe over which they believe that they otherwise have only limited control. Religion, from this perspective, can be seen as being a passive form of magic. In magic, the power difference between the practitioner and his or her ability to achieve a desired result is seen as being much less than the power differences involved in religious rites and beliefs.

Anthropologists such as Stanley J. Tambiah have emphasized that magic, science, and religion may be seen as having very different goals. For these scholars, the central question is whether practitioners of magic actually believe that their magic "works." Many practitioners, some scholars contend, fully realize that they are performing rituals which are more aesthetic than practical in their consequences. In other words, many magic practitioners may realize that their magic is more expressive than instrumental. Much anthropological research and debate followed the publication of Malinowski's *Coral Gardens and Their Magic*, which focused on the metaphorical and metonymical aspects of magical utterances in an attempt to understand magic in terms of a group's conceptions of social control and causality. From this perspective, religion is seen as noncausal, whereas magic is seen as relating to a group's ideas concerning universal or natural laws.

Research has found that a belief in magic—at least if it can be defined broadly enough to include superstition, or "quasi-magic"—persists in the industrialized world. In a study done in England in 1970, researchers found that 22 percent of their sample believed in lucky numbers, 18 percent believed in lucky charms, 15 percent avoided walking under ladders, 50 percent threw spilled salt over their shoulders, and 75 percent touched wood for protection (as in "knocking on wood"). George Gmelch, in his article "Baseball Magic," in *Trans-Action* 8, no. 8 (1971) found that many players followed quasi-magical patterns such as rising at a specific time, eating only certain foods before a game, taking the same route to the stadium each day, and so on. These players believed that if they did not follow these rituals their game would be "jinxed." Interestingly, researchers have found that people who characterize themselves as "religious" are more likely to subscribe to quasi-magical beliefs than those who characterize themselves as nonreligious.

Context

Religion, magic, and superstition have been studied in their various forms by sociologists, anthropologists, and psychologists since these disciplines began. Belief in supernatural forces and/or beings seems universal among humans, even when belief is suppressed by political leaders; the power and tenacity of belief have intrigued social scientists and led them to put forward many theories and observations concerning religion since the nineteenth century.

Auguste Comte, often credited as the founder of sociology, believed that religion was evolving and would eventually lead to the pursuit of an enlightened morality with a rational basis. He went so far as to attempt to form a "church of positivism." Comte's work in the area of religion is most important for the influence it had on other early sociologists, such as Émile Durkheim and Max Weber. Durkheim defined religion as a system of beliefs and practices shared by a community of followers. He considered how religion helps to maintain the social structure and promote social harmony. He argued that religion is crucial to both preindustrial and modern societies. Religion, he noted, performs a number of functions in society. His work *Les Formes élémentaires de la vie religieuse: Le Système totémique en Australie* (1912; *The Elementary Forms of the Religious Life: A Study in Religious Sociology*, 1915) explored how religion provides a society with necessary forces for cohesion. Durkheim also stated that religion promotes the ascetic aspect of human behavior, encouraging self-discipline and self-sacrifice.

Max Weber examined the link between religion and social change, arguing that systems of religious belief can foster widespread societal and economic changes. His tremendously influential work in this area was *Die Protestantische Ethik und der Geist des Kapitalismus* (1904; *The Protestant Ethic and the Spirit of Capitalism*, 1930). Weber presented a view that opposed Karl Marx's earlier formulation that material and economic conditions are at the root of social phenomena and that these conditions influence such things as religion. Weber argued that ideas and beliefs can affect society's infrastructure (material base). Specifically, he suggested that the system of ideas and beliefs that came about because of the Protestant Reformation created the conditions in which capitalism could develop and flourish.

One of the most influential works in the sociology of religion in the second half of the twentieth century was Peter L. Berger's *The Sacred Canopy: Elements of a Sociological Theory of Religion* (1967). Berger attempted to use classical sociological theory to construct a framework that would allow effective study of religion. He stressed that sociologists must remain "disinterested" in that they must carefully avoid becoming entangled in questions about theological validity or truth. Berger emphasized the concept that, since all social orders are arbitrary and reality is, to a certain degree, socially constructed, religion provides an important set of symbols that, when collectively shared, can provide support for the status quo.

Bibliography

Evans-Pritchard, E. E. *Witchcraft, Oracles, and Magic Among the Azande.* Oxford: Clarendon Press, 1937. Evans-Pritchard discovered that among the Azande there was constant discussion of witchcraft, which was believed to be an unconscious act, but little talk of magical practitioners or sorcerers. His study provides a clear statement of the difference between magic and witchcraft and a cogent discussion of the relationship between magical and religious worldviews.

Frazer, James G. *The Golden Bough.* 3d ed. London: Macmillan, 1980. This extensive compilation contains an in-depth discussion of the major types of magic. Frazer was one of the first to focus on the centrality and significance of words in the performance of magic.

Malinowski, Bronislaw. *Coral Gardens and Their Magic.* 2 vols. New York: American Book Company, 1935. This study looks at magic as practiced by Trobriand islanders, paying particular attention to magical spells and incantations.

Marett, Robert R. *The Threshold of Religion.* 2d ed. London: Methuen, 1914. Argues that the belief in mana or "animatism" is the elementary form of religion and that it exists at an earlier stage of social development.

Tambiah, Stanley J. *Magic, Science, Religion, and the Scope of Rationality.* Cambridge, England: Cambridge University Press, 1990. Argues that magicians not only distinguish between the methods of magic and practical work but also perceive them as having radically different goals. Tambiah suggests that magic may "simulate" work but is never confused with work.

Stephen D. Glazier

Cross-References

RELIGIOUS MIRACLES AND VISIONS

Type of sociology: Major social institutions
Field of study: Religion

Miracles and visions have important places in most of the world's religions; they signify the interest and intervention of a deity in the affairs of humans and thus provide hope as well as a unifying force to religious groups.

Principal terms

DEITY: a divine entity; a non-embodied agent of great power
DENOMINATION: a religious group that is often considered a subgroup of a religion; Anglicans, Baptists, and Catholics may be considered members of Christian denominations
RELIGION: an organized system of faith and worship; Christianity, Islam, and Judaism are among the world's major religions
SHRINE: a place where veneration is given to a saint or deity; a place hallowed by its association with a deity
VISION: something seen by a means other than ordinary sight, as in a trance or a dream, that has spiritual meaning

Overview

In one form or another, miracles play important roles in most of the world's major religions. Yet it is difficult to provide a precise definition of what constitutes a miraculous occurrence; this is so partly because different religions and philosophies have differing views of how the "natural," or nonmiraculous world operates. Miracles might be defined generally as extraordinary events that demonstrate "divine intervention in human affairs." A miracle is considered inexplicable by the standards of normal daily life. Beyond that, however, a miracle also carries meaning in that it points to the existence of a divine power.

A distinction is sometimes drawn between miracles, which most often involve effects on (or by) the physical environment, and visions and other interior phenomena that are experienced by a means other than the normal perceptions of the senses. In a broader sense, however, visions may be seen as a type of miraculous event, and this is how they are considered here.

It has been debated for centuries by theologians, philosophers, and scientists whether miracles are "real." Because an acceptance of the reality of a miracle is predicated on faith—and by definition, therefore, cannot be proved or disproved scientifically—it is outside the domain of the social sciences to decide whether miracles occur in fact or whether they are subjective phenomena important to adherents to a particular religious belief.

When sociologists of religion look at miracles, they are generally concerned with studying the sociological or historical context of the reported event and with examining the effects the miracle has on a large or small group of people. Certain miracles, for example, have been said by some sociologists to have provided spiritual sustenance to a people facing adversity.

A number of types of miracles have been described. One of the most common is the vision. Other miraculous events include omens (as of the birth or death of a great leader), accounts of feats such as walking on water, and weather-related or environment-related miracles. In many religions, acts of divination and shamanism may also be included as aspects of the miraculous.

A miracle often provides immediate results, such as making possible an escape from danger (as when the parting of the Red Sea allowed the Israelites to elude their Egyptian pursuers), healing a sick person, feeding hungry people, or reviving someone from the dead. Beyond that, however, it reveals the existence of a god that is willing to intervene in human affairs and therefore may unite a group in service to the power that, directly or indirectly, made the miracle occur. A miracle may also help authenticate or validate an individual's claim to religious or political authority. Belief in a miracle is usually localized within the group to which the miracle has occurred or the vision has appeared, and it may be challenged by outside parties.

Richard Swinburne gives four kinds of evidence by which miracles may be classified and evaluated. The first is personal memory of first-hand experience. The second kind of evidence is the memory of others, whether spoken or written. The weight given to this evidence is usually dependent upon how individuals or groups view the character and credibility of the individual(s) who have witnessed the miracle. Most visions that have altered history have been experienced by people of good character (Muhammad and Black Elk are two examples). The third type of data is physical evidence, such as a handprint, footprint, or other impression, as on a cloth. These items usually engender much debates as to their validity and are sometimes subjected to scientific examination. Most miracles do not involve physical evidence. The fourth type of evidence is defined in terms of contemporary understanding of the physical nature of things—what events are probable or improbable. A miracle may be defined, in physical, nonreligious terms, as a suspension of a natural law.

A miracle is often used by the group that experiences it as an authentication of religious validity. Religious (and sometimes political) leaders may be signified by the miraculous events that surround them. Christians point to the miracles brought about by Jesus as evidence of His divinity. Some religious leaders eschew the importance of miracles. Gautama Buddha once met a holy man who claimed to be capable of walking on water. Buddha replied that he regretted the wasted effort of the holy man because, for only a penny, the ferryman could take him across the river.

There is no such thing as an "objective miracle"; the term is an oxymoron, or a contradiction in terms. To believers, a miracle is a confirmation of their deity's interest in humankind. The miracle is an interaction between a god and a subject or subjects, showing the deity's concern for the needs of humans; it typically provides a religious group with spiritual renewal or strength.

Applications

Many well-known accounts of miracles involve controlling the environment. In the Old Testament, for example, Joshua turns back the sun so that the Israelites can triumph in battle. A miraculous weather-related event that received various attributions occurred in ancient Germany, where a Roman legion known as the Thundering Legion was delivered from thirst. The legion, which had run out of water, was marching through Germany; a sudden shower provided the men with drinking water. A number of gods received credit for the event. Followers of Isis claimed that rain was sent in answer to the prayers of an Egyptian priest accompanying the army. State Romans attributed the event to Jupiter Pluvius, provider of rain. The early Christian historian Tertullian gave credit to the Christian god as a result of the prayers of devout Christians in the army. In Nevada in 1889, Paiute Indian Jack Wilson (Wovoka) received a great vision for his people; after this vision, he was known to have "weather power"; among other things, he caused ice to fall from the sky in July, caused water to appear in an empty container during a drought, and ended the drought of 1889.

Another type of miracle that has been reported a number of times in history is walking on water. One example concerns Alexander the Great, for whom the Euphrates became solid so that he could cross. The most well-known example is the Christian miracle of Jesus walking on the Sea of Galilee. In 1928, a professor of Sanskrit named William Brown suggested that the Christian account of walking on the water may have been influenced by earlier East Indian stories of similar events. He gives examples of followers of Buddha walking across water to be taught by him. In this case, it was lesser persons, not Buddha himself, who walked on water.

Other accounts of miracles involve omens at the birth or death of great or divine individuals. In Christianity there is the virgin birth of Jesus, heralded by angels and signified by a star in the heavens. Although Buddha never claimed to be divine, stories of his birth and death include such supernatural events as heavenly music and flowers descending from heaven.

The vision is one of the most familiar and important types of miracles. A vision, almost always a sign to an individual, may be a sign or message intended for the individual alone or for a community or society. The Old Testament contains many visions given to prophets, including Isaiah and Ezekiel. In the New Testament, two examples are the visit to the Virgin Mary by the messenger Gabriel with the announcement of the coming birth of Jesus and the vision of Saul (Paul) of Tarsus of the resurrected Jesus. The religion of Islam essentially began with Muhammad's visions in which were revealed the Koran, the word of Allah to His people.

Accounts of miracles and visions by no means belong exclusively to the domain of ancient history. In 1531, on Tepeyac Hill, Mexico City, Juan Diego saw a vision of the Virgin Mary. A shrine was later built on the site. In 1820, in New York State, fourteen-year-old Joseph Smith had a vision of God the Father and Jesus the Son that led to the formation of the Church of Jesus Christ of the Latter-day Saints (the Mormon church). In 1858, in Lourdes, France, fourteen-year-old Marie-Bernarde Soubirous had a series of visions of the Virgin Mary. A shrine built on the site remains one of the most popular Catholic pilgrimage sites. In 1873, the Oglala Sioux Indian child Black Elk received a vision for his people that gave them new hope for survival. In 1889, Paiute Jack Wilson had a vision urging him to teach the doctrine which became known as the Ghost Dance to his people. In 1917, in Vila Nova de Ourem, Portugal, three young peasant children saw a vision of the Virgin Mary.

Similarities have been noted concerning the situations of many people who have received visions. Marie-Bernarde Soubirous was reportedly in ill health when she received her vision, as were Black Elk and Jack Wilson. Another similarity that has been noted is that visions often occur at times of social disruption or hopelessness. When Juan Diego saw his vision, for example, the Indians of Mexico City were destitute and lacking spiritual (as well as temporal) hope; his vision has been described as providing them with sustenance. The visions of Black Elk and Jack Wilson had similar effects on people devoid of hope at a time when European Americans were expanding rapidly into their territories with strongly deleterious effects on their social structures and on their very survival.

Context

Discussion as to the existence of miracles has been occurring for centuries. Much of the debate has taken place either within or regarding the Roman Catholic church, since the Catholic church both has been a major religious power in the world and has maintained records of inquiries concerning miracles. Circa 200 C.E., the early Christian writer Tertullian noted with regret the loss of spiritual gifts (including miracles) from the church. In the thirteenth century, Thomas Aquinas stated that a miracle had to be an event that the natural world could not produce. In the eighteenth century, Pope Benedict opined that angels and even humans could work miracles if they were endowed with incorporeal power from an agent able to bestow such power. Philosopher David Hume, writing in the 1700's, defined a miracle as an event which violates a law of nature; this was the beginning in English philosophy of strong arguments against the existence of miracles.

To the believer there is no question that miracles exist. Many Christian denominations, including Pentecostalism, believe that miracles and visions are an important part of the religious observance. Miracles form an important part of the Jewish tradition as well. Islam was founded on a series of visions; two modern Christian denominations were founded on visions; the Church of Jesus Christ of the Latter-day Saints and the Seventh-day Adventists. Visions continue to have a meaningful place in Catholic faith.

Among American Indians, visions have played an important role both for nations and for individuals. Revelations were sought both by holy men and by ordinary individuals. The ritual of the vision quest was a significant part of the life of many people, both young and old; it was most widely practiced by Plains and Eastern Woodlands people. The vision quest served as a part of the rite of passage from childhood to adulthood. Boys (and sometimes girls) sought supernatural power from a spiritual guide, often manifested in the form of an animal. This event may not have been completely understood by the young person, but as he or she grew older, the meaning became more clear. In some Indian ceremonies, peyote was (and still is) used in rituals to obtain visions; peyote use is part of the rituals of the pantribal Native American Church, thought to have originated about 1885.

Miracles and visions have played a part in religion for thousands of years. They are important in the religions of Asia and Europe as well as the religions of Africa and the Americas. For centuries it has been debated by theologians and philosophers whether it is the miracle that gives religion its power or whether miracles presuppose faith: Does the miracle precede faith or does faith precede the miracle? However one views this conundrum, there is no doubt that miracles and visions will continue to be strong forces in the world's religions.

Bibliography

Black Elk. *Black Elk Speaks*. New York: Pocket Books, 1959. The story of Black Elk, warrior and medicine man of the Oglala Sioux, includes his famous vision at about age nine, which was to be a guide for his people. See also *The Sacred Pipe* (1953), as related by Black Elk and edited by Joseph Epes Brown.

Brown, William Norman. *The Indian and Christian Miracles of Walking on Water*. Chicago: Open Court Press, 1928. This text discusses the religious significance of the act of crossing water magically, including walking and flying. Brown suggests that the Christian water-walking traditions are rooted in the earlier East Indian stories carried to the Middle Eastern area by Buddhists.

Burns, R. M. *The Great Debate on Miracles: From Joseph Glanvill to David Hume*. Lewisburg, Pa.: Bucknell University Press, 1981. This comprehensive writing on the centuries-old debate on miracles contains a good summary of the subject. A comprehensive bibliography lists primary and secondary sources from as early as the 1600's, including works by Francis Bacon, Immanuel Kant, John Locke, and Zachary Pearce.

Campbell, Joseph. *The Flight of the Wild Gander*. South Bend, Ind.: Regency/Gateway, 1979. While Campbell rarely deals directly with miracles and visions, he addresses the topic indirectly in his discussions of the role of symbol and myth. Here he considers the role of vision among mythic events of several groups, including the people of Black Elk.

Eliade, Mircea. *Man and the Sacred*. New York: Harper & Row, 1974. This book is one example from the prolific pen of religious historian Mircea Eliade. His works are a good source of information on the history and anthropology of religions from around the world. He discusses the importance of symbolism, ritual, and myth in religion, including the aspects of miracles and visions.

Kehoe, Alice Beck. *The Ghost Dance: Ethnohistory and Revitalization*. New York: Holt, Rhinehart and Winston, 1989. This is a study of the Ghost Dance and other messianic movements around the end of the 1800's and beginning of the 1900's. The first part discusses the Ghost Dance and related events and persons, while the second part is a survey of analyses of such messianic movements.

Lessa, William A., and Evon Z. Vogt, eds. *Reader in Comparative Religion*. New York:

Harper & Row, 1979. Contains fifty-six essays spanning one hundred years of research on religion. This text gives an overview of anthropological findings about religions throughout the world. Many of the essays are classics in this field, and the list of references cited is impressive. An excellent and interesting background text for persons interested in the meaning of religion to all cultures.

Lewis, C. S. *Miracles: A Preliminary Study*. New York: Macmillan, 1947. Author and philosopher Lewis' contribution to the debate and study of miracles is an interesting piece; it reflects the time of its writing.

Swinburne, Richard. *The Concept of Miracle*. New York: St. Martin's Press, 1970. This monograph discusses two important philosophical questions: What precisely is meant by a miracle, and what conditions are necessary for an individual to have a rational belief in miracles? Additionally, he discusses David Hume's objections to belief in miracles.

_____ , ed. *Miracles*. New York: Macmillan, 1989. A collection of essays discussing the idea of miracles. Contains Thomas Aquinas' work "Miracles" and David Hume's "Of Miracles," along with more recent commentaries on the subject. An excellent reference.

Susan Ellis-Lopez

Cross-References

Christianity, 231; Cults, 399; Millenarian Religious Movements, 1213; Religion: Beliefs, Symbols, and Rituals, 1598; Religion versus Magic, 1617; The Sociology of Religion, 1952; Types of Supernaturalism, 2024.

REMARRIAGE AND "RECONSTITUTED" FAMILIES

Type of sociology: Major social institutions
Field of study: The family

"Reconstituted" families result when a couple marries and at least one of the two has a previous marriage involving children. The increasing frequency of these families has focused attention on the stresses these families experience and their unique problems in functioning effectively.

Principal terms

DYSFUNCTIONAL FAMILIES: families that fail to perform important social or psychological functions such as the nurturance and socialization of children

EXPANDED FAMILY: a family system that results when children develop strong ties to two households, those of their two biological parents as well as their stepparents

EXTENDED KIN NETWORK: all persons sharing kinship relationships, including biological relatives, in-laws, and stepfamily members and their biological relatives

FAMILY BOUNDARIES: the subjective limitation to membership in one's "immediate family," traditionally constrained by household residence but more ambiguously defined in reconstituted families

FAMILY SYSTEMS THEORY: a concept that conceptualizes the family as a network of interacting and reciprocal relationships

FAMILY THERAPY: therapy that treats families as systems rather than treating individual family members

NONCUSTODIAL PARENT: a parent who does not reside in the same house as his or her children; he or she is usually legally restricted in decision-making but retains "parental rights," typically involving visitation with children

NUCLEAR FAMILY: a two-generation family consisting of parents and children in one household

ROLE AMBIGUITY: unclear expectations concerning the normative performance of a social role

STEPFAMILY: a family in which a remarriage creates nonbiological kin relationships involving adults and children; for example, stepparents, stepchildren, and stepsiblings

Overview

The nature of the family changed dramatically during the late twentieth century. Many sociologists have investigated the consequences of sharp increases in the divorce rate. One consequence is the single-parent family; another is remarriage and the "reconstituted" family that results. With nearly half of all marriages ending in divorce, and with more than three-fourths of divorced people remarrying, there has been a sharp increase in the number of these families. In fact, more than 40 percent of all new marriages involve a remarriage.

Reconstituted families are not new; it is only the increase in their number which has brought them attention. A reconstituted family consists of a marriage between two people, at least one of whom has been previously married (which may have ended through widowhood or divorce) and at least one of whom already has children. The term "reconstituted" suggests that a family which has not been complete is made so by this marriage. As with the similar term "blended family," this concept is seriously questioned by those who have studied or lived in these families. Remarriage does not "fix" a "broken" family; rather, a clearly different kind of family is created. This fact has enormous consequences for performing the basic social functions of the family: the socialization and nurturance of children.

The common usage of the term "stepfamily" acknowledges in some ways more clearly what is different about these families. Parent-child relationships are fundamentally altered by the existence within a family household of people who are not biologically related. Even that term ignores, however, the complex nature of the changed relationships; relationships among biological relatives living in different households are also altered by the remarriage, as are relationships among biological relatives within the same household.

The types of reconstituted families possible vary greatly, depending on previous marital statuses and the numbers and ages of children. Ronald G. Stover and Christine A. Hope list eight kinds of reconstituted families without even taking into account the presence of children. Moreover, additional children may be born into the new family. Finally, the term "reconstituted" may obscure the changed household structures of remarried families in which one parent has a noncustodial relationship (involving visitation) with children from a prior marriage.

Family systems theory provides a coherent framework for comprehending this complexity. All family members are viewed as part of an interacting system in a network of reciprocal relationships. Any family can be understood as a functioning system. All family systems make adjustments, as when children grow up and leave the household. The adjustments in a reconstituted family are similar in kind but of greater number and complexity. Postdivorce families have already made one such major adjustment in creating two households and establishing custody and visitation arrangements. Remarriage requires an additional major adjustment.

One significant difference between reconstituted families and traditional families is what have been termed family "boundaries." Not all biological family members reside in the same home; thus, the boundaries of the house are not the boundaries of the family. Whether through joint custody or through the strength of parent-child ties, another parent continues to have influence on the socialization of children. Since no two households are identical in lifestyle or values, children often have difficulties discerning these values. Alternatively, children can manipulate parents because they may have a real or perceived option to live elsewhere, thus undermining the authority role of the parent. This absence of boundaries occurs in any postdivorce family, but it creates particularly severe role ambiguity for the stepparent. The most complex and ambiguous reconstituted families are those involving children from more than one prior marriage. Stepsiblings may be living in the same house or may be visiting and living in multiple households. The addition of new stepsiblings with a marriage alters major sibling relationships in the family system. For example, an only child, or the only child of a given gender, may no longer be so. The oldest child may no longer be oldest; the youngest no longer youngest. This situation creates further conflicts with which parents and stepparents must contend.

The stepparent role is not clearly defined in American society, either in terms of socialization or nurturance. In fact, legally, stepparents may even find themselves unable to authorize emergency medical procedures. The issue that most stepparents and stepchildren cite as the area of greatest contention, however, is discipline, which lies at the core of the family's socialization function. The disputes thus generated, along with the system adjustments noted above, are believed to help explain the higher divorce rate found in remarriages.

Applications

The higher divorce rate of remarriages is indicative of greater stress, but it does not indicate that they must fail. As Stover and Hope note, there are three possible outcomes. First, a child may respond as a member of no family, alienated from both parental households. Second, a child may respond as if the stepfamily is in fact a new nuclear family. This corresponds most closely to the concept of a "reconstituted" family. Finally, a child may come to belong to an expanded family, with an enlarged extended kin network (adding new grandparents, aunts, uncles, and cousins). In this case, the child may even be at an advantage.

Most experts on stepfamilies cite unrealistic expectations as an important source of difficulty. Stepparents may view themselves as rescuing a child from a bad family situation. The child understandably may continue to feel loyalty to both biological parents and may find the remarriage threatening rather than positive. The stepparent cannot replace a biological parent (living or dead) but in fact occupies a different role with many of the same functions. Time and communication are critical to easing this role transition. The loyalty to the biological parent should not be undermined; this may mean the stepparent avoiding the label "Mom" or "Dad." It is also recommended that a stepparent take on discipline slowly, starting from existing household rules. Realistic anticipation of possible concerns and open communication and cooperation among all "parents" are essential for success.

The opposite situation may also occur; that is, stepparents may not desire a nurturing or socializing role. They may choose to defer these roles to the children's "real" parent(s). The overall picture, however, is often one of differences in role expectations among one or both of the biological parents and the children themselves. Moreover, the reality of living with minor children requires that some component of these roles be adopted. Again, a realistic anticipation of these issues can offset many problems.

Any changes in the existing family system should proceed slowly, if possible, and with open communication in any case. Moving to a new location or changing visitation arrangements are among the sorts of changes to be made with care. With stepsiblings, arrangements related to sharing bedroom space are frequent areas of friction. To children, bedrooms are their haven for privacy as well as their only area of control in the house. Threats to these intangibles are aggravated by issues such as accommodating a younger stepsibling's bedtime or intermittently accommodating a visiting stepsibling or half-sibling. The role of parents, besides arbitrating, is in respecting the reality of their children's or stepchildren's worldview.

Noncustodial parents and stepparents must also contend with many of these same issues. They are generally less likely than the custodial family to have foreseen all of the ramifications of their remarriage, as the children live outside of their home. That "outsider" status can, in fact, impair adjustment. Prolonged or frequent visitation disrupts an ongoing system; nurturing and socialization may be viewed as threatening to the children or to their custodial parents; and the children are frequently aware of their outsider status, especially if other children reside in the home they are visiting. Since the children have the perceived option of leaving/not coming back, and the parents have the option of sending home/cutting off visits (or instilling the fear of such reactions), creating a new functioning system is fraught with difficulty.

Another major contributor to overall adjustment is the ages of the children involved. The age group that appears to have the greatest difficulty is adolescence. Adolescents frequently view their family as "complete" and are more resistant to change in what is, in effect, a functioning system. Furthermore, they are the age group with which biological parents in intact marriages also report the greatest problems. Socialization issues are more urgent for parents with children approaching adulthood, while discipline is more problematic from the perspective of teenagers attempting to assert their growing independence. Finally, teenagers have a legally recognized role in determining their own custody, which can undermine parental authority.

By the time family problems become obvious, open communication and cooperation may not have existed for some time; families often need help. The mental health practice most influenced by the systems perspective has been the growing field of family therapy. Adherents to this perspective refuse to label an individual client in therapy. The strongest advocates of this view include Augustus Y. Napier and Carl A. Whitaker, family therapists and authors of *The Family Crucible* (1978). They refuse to treat individuals or even to treat families unless all family members come to therapy. Most family therapists regard that expectation as unrealistic, especially in the case of reconstituted families. Family therapy assumes a systems approach wherein all relationships in the system are examined.

Family therapy focuses on improving communication among family members and providing insight into others' perspectives. Often the therapist's role is that of a mediator. Techniques such as role-playing can be beneficial; for example, teens and parents may be asked to dramatize a typical family conflict, reversing roles while doing so. The goal for therapy with reconstituted families is to improve the likelihood that they will function either as new nuclear families or, better, as expanded families.

Context

Two of the major functions of the family are the socialization and nurturance of children. When families fail to perform these functions, they may be regarded as "dysfunctional." Stepfamilies are over-represented among families that are clearly dysfunctional.

Incidents of physical and sexual abuse are higher in stepfamilies, for example, as are incidents of neglect. Psychologists have reported that murder of children in stepfamilies is much more common; stepchildren under the age of two were found to be sixty to seventy times more likely to be killed than children living with their biological parents. Certainly, most reconstituted families do not approach these extremes, but social critics are concerned that these data reflect a generally poorer functioning by reconstituted families.

Researchers disagree on the overall impact of remarriage on children's mental health. Few differences between stepchildren and other children have been found in self-confidence or self-esteem. On the other hand, there is a greater incidence of behavior problems (such as fighting and drug use) among stepchildren. They also leave home at an earlier age. As with all children from divorced parents, there is an increased likelihood that they will themselves divorce. Whether these data reflect "dysfunction," however, is much more ambiguous than is the case with data on abuse or murder. Moreover, aggregate data reflect general stresses and do not reveal the potential strengths of successful reconstituted families. Nevertheless, the implications for the future are obvious if increasing numbers of children are growing up in homes that are either dysfunctional or functioning poorly.

Social critic and historian Christopher Lasch, in his book *Haven in a Heartless World: The Family Besieged* (1977), expresses the concern that famlies are losing their functions not only to government agencies but also to a general trend of professionalization. The use of family therapy, for example, even when it is sought voluntarily, reflects the surrender of authority from the family to professional "experts." The role of courts in deciding custody and visitation is viewed in this light by some observers as an unconscionable intrusion into family life. Yet the alternatives, in face of the high divorce and remarriage rates, are unclear.

Sociologists of the family note that definitions of the family have been significantly altered in the late twentieth century. These changes reflect a growth of freedom and personal choice. Sociologists' concern, by and large, is not with undoing change but with responding appropriately to it. The aim is to strengthen new family arrangements so that they can effectively perform their necessary functions.

Bibliography

Crosbie-Burnett, Margaret, Ada Skyles, and Jane Baker-Haven. "Exploring Stepfamilies from a Feminist Perspective." In *Feminism, Children, and the New Families,* edited by Sanford M. Dornbusch and Myra H. Strober. New York: Guilford Press, 1988. The authors present a feminist analysis of remarriage. They criticize traditional conceptualizations of the family but do so without a strong ideological current. In addition to a good summary of the general issues facing stepfamilies, there is an enlightening discussion of the legal and policy concerns created by stepfamilies, concluding with specific policy recommendations.

Kaplan, Leslie S. *Coping with Stepfamilies.* Rev. ed. New York: Rosen, 1991. Kaplan provides a discussion of a range of issues, shedding light on the perspectives of all family members. Making much use of actual cases, the author creates a sense of hope while dealing realistically with the stresses. Aimed at a general audience, particularly at readers coping with stepfamily concerns.

Napier, Augustus Y., and Carl A. Whitaker. *The Family Crucible.* New York: Harper & Row, 1978. A case study of one family in therapy with the authors. Although the book describes an intact family, it is useful for understanding the general practices of family therapy, and it includes discussion of remarriage issues. The "Forum" chapter at the end presents a general discussion of issues aimed at practitioners.

Silverzweig, Mary Zenorini. *The Other Mother.* New York: Harper & Row, 1982. An autobiographical account of a noncustodial stepmother's personal experience. The author discusses the stresses involved while maintaining an optimistic tone.

Stover, Ronald G., and Christine A. Hope. *Marriage, Family, and Intimate Relations.* Fort Worth, Tex.: Harcourt Brace College Publishers, 1993. A general text on the family for college-level sociology and psychology classes. Several chapters are relevant and include material on social change and divorce. The chapter on remarriage and stepfamilies provides an excellent discussion of stepfamily concerns.

Victor, Ira, and Win Ann Winkler. *Fathers and Custody.* New York: Hawthorn Books, 1977. The authors focus on the concerns of fathers who seek or have custody, dealing with remarriage issues in that context. It is important to be aware of the many possible forms of nontraditional families and the concerns raised by each. The authors include useful (although somewhat dated) appendices on support groups and legal referral.

Nancy E. Macdonald

Cross-References

Causes of Divorce, 554; Effects of Divorce, 560; The Family: Functionalist versus Conflict Theory Views, 739; The Family: Nontraditional Families, 746; Nuclear and Extended Families, 1303; Parenthood and Child-Rearing Practices, 1336; Socialization: The Family, 1880.

RESIDENCE PATTERNS

Type of sociology: Major social institutions
Field of study: The family

Residence patterns are used by sociologists to describe who lives with whom. The question of how households are defined is linked to other elements of kinship and social structure.

Principal terms

AVUNCULOCAL RESIDENCE PATTERN: a postmarital residence preference for living with the groom's mother's brother

DESCENT GROUP: a corporate kin unit based on common ancestry, typically traced through either the mother's or the father's line

MATRILOCAL RESIDENCE PATTERN: a postmarital residence preference for living with the bride's family

NEOLOCAL RESIDENCE PATTERN: a postmarital residence preference for setting up an independent household

NOMENCLATURAL SYSTEM: the terms by which kin are known (for example, "cousin" versus "mother's brother's son")

PATRILOCAL RESIDENCE PATTERN: a postmarital residence preference for living with the groom's family

Overview

Although it is tempting to look at family structure and kinship organizations as part of human nature, in fact there is great variability from one society to another as to how such relations are defined. Because many smaller-scale societies base their entire social structure on kin relations, kinship studies have been called "the ABCs" of ethnography (the study of cultures). Kinship is divided into several key areas. The study of descent focuses on how corporate groups (people who have rights and obligations in common) are defined. The study of nomenclatural systems—the terms that people employ when referring to kin—complements the focus on descent. Residence patterns—the rules or preferences for who lives with whom—is the third focus of kinship studies.

In contemporary North America, the neolocal residence pattern is most common. "Neolocality" means that, after marriage, the bride and groom typically establish an independent household rather than live with other relatives. Neolocality is dependent upon a certain level of economic independence and is linked to a kin system based on nuclear families rather than on larger descent groups. The North American nomenclatural pattern, which provides specific terms for close family members but not for more distant relatives, likewise fits into the generally truncated kin system of modern society. A high level of geographic mobility contributes to all these features of North American kin relations.

In societies in which larger extended families rather than nuclear families form the building blocks of society, neolocal residence is not common. Patrilocal residence, in which the newly married couple goes to live with the groom's family, is common in societies with patrilineal inheritance patterns such as traditional China. (This type of residence pattern is sometimes called "virilocal" in anthropological scholarship.) In China, clans, or large groups of relations linked through males, were important units of the social structure. Women who married into a patrilineal clan were uprooted from their native homes and brought to live as strangers in the patrilocal household. Margery Wolf's classic study *Women and the Family in Rural Taiwan* (1972) poignantly described the situation of Chinese women in such patrilineal, patrilocal households.

Matrilocal households, created when newly married couples live with the bride's family, are less common. (In traditional anthropological scholarship, this pattern is sometimes called "uxorilocal.") The Hopi in the American Southwest have traditionally preferred a matrilocal residence pattern. When combined with matrilineality (descent and inheritance traced through females), this gives women a relatively high status in society. It is important to note, however, that neither matrilineality nor matrilocality implies that a society is matriarchal (that is, that primary power is held by women).

Not all matrilineal societies are matrilocal. A characteristic pattern that undermines the authority women might have in a matrilineal system is called avunculocality. In this system, a newly married couple lives with the groom's mother's brother. Although descent may be traced through women, therefore, the actual authority figure in the household is not the mother but the mother's brother. Bronislaw Malinowski conducted a classic study of this kind of system and the impact it had on the psychodynamics of the family among the Trobriand Islanders, publishing his findings as *The Sexual Life of Savages in North-Western Melanesia* (1929).

In addition to these residence patterns, anthropologists and sociologists have observed various combinations. In a duolocal system, the groom may remain with his kin while the bride remains with hers. In an ambilocal or bilocal system, the new couple may choose to live with either the groom's or the bride's kin, as circumstances and personal preferences dictate. Residence patterns are rarely hard-and-fast rules; more often, such patterns are generally accepted ideals. In much of the world, traditional residence patterns are being disrupted as economic, social, and demographic changes make the classic norms more difficult to maintain.

Applications

Detailed examination of individual societies can illustrate the range of variation in the way that marriage, family, and household can be defined. The Nayar of southern India, for example, provide one of the most interesting cases for sociologists and anthropologists to study, as the Nayar define marriage, family, and household very differently from the way these concepts are understood in the West. Among the traditional Nayar, households were composed of groups of people related through women but headed by a senior male. These groups, called *taravads*, were linked to other *taravads* in the region, from which girls would formally take husbands in special ceremonies held every dozen or so years. The "husbands" acquired in this way, however, played little further role in the girls' lives. Rather, after such a formal "marriage" ceremony, the Nayar girls were free to establish romantic and sexual liaisons with Brahmin men, who came from a higher class in the Indian caste system. These relationships, called *sambandham*, could be short- or long-term in nature but did not result in common residence. When a child was conceived out of one of these relationships, fatherhood was sometimes acknowledged by the father's payment of the midwife's fee, but the child was actually reared by the mother and her own male relatives in the *taravad*. In the Nayar system, therefore, it was actually the brother-sister bond that was central in household life, with sexual relationships conducted outside this residential unit.

While the Nayar were matrilineal, tracing kin ties through females, their neighbors in southern India, the Toda, were patrilineal, tracing relationships through males. Among the traditional Toda, polyandrous marriages in which one woman was married to several men were common. Girls would be betrothed to a group of men, typically brothers, at an age as early as two or three. The men could also become engaged to other women at the same time, resulting in a group marriage in which several women could be wives simultaneously to several men. Since paternity in this situation would be impossible to ascertain, one of the men would be ritually designated as the "father" of a particular child or of the children born of a particular woman during a certain time period.

In Iran, the traditional Muslim family is patrilineal, patrilocal, and often polygynous, with one husband taking several wives. Arrangements for marriages are made by parents, with negotiations often beginning at birth. After marriage, women go to live with their husbands and with any other wives their husbands may already have. Within the household, there is typically a division between the private, interior area called *andaruni* and the public, external area called *biruni*. While both men and women occupy the interior reserved area, only men are allowed into the exterior area in which outsiders are received. This wall of privacy surrounding the world of women is carried over into the traditional dress of the women, which features a veil to keep out the prying eyes of strangers. This strict separation of male and female spheres within the patrilocal household creates a child-rearing environment in which co-wives and "aunts" may be as central to a young child's development as his or her father.

Among the Kwaio of Melanesia, territory is traditionally divided up into dozens of defined regions believed to have been founded by known ancestors. All descendents of a founding ancestor have the right to live on that ancestor's territory, whether the descendents are related to the founder through male or female lines. This flexible system presents a problem: How does an individual with the right to live in multiple territories decide in which to live? In fact, most of the territorial groups center around the patrilineal descendents of the founding ancestors, with wives coming to live on their husbands' territories. Yet individuals can choose to do otherwise, or can shift from one territory to another during their lifetimes. As long as they appropriately perform their duties to the residential groups, those related through other kinds of bonds are included as fully functioning members of the territorial unit. The Kwaio system, then, is one marked by great individual variation despite the generally patrilateral bias of the culture.

In her book *Brave New Families* (1990), Judith Stacey emphasizes how unique the "traditional" American family pattern is. Although the image of the nuclear family based on romantic love between a man and a woman—with the man then becoming the breadwinner and the woman the stay-at-home mother—is portrayed in American popular culture as timeless, in fact it was a product of specific historical circumstances. The only time when this type of family structure really predominated was during the 1940's and 1950's, when economic expansion and declining birthrates conspired to create the conditions conducive to it. Before that, Stacey points out, men rarely had access to the "family wage" required for this kind of structure; afterward, economic factors pushed more and more women into the workforce. The system of industrial capitalism first played a role in exacerbating the separation of public and private spheres (community and family life), then pushed women into the private sphere at the same time as it encouraged male-female ties based on "love." Such conditions eventually resulted in feminist challenges to the situation that may prove to be the undoing of the "traditional" American family.

Nonfamily residence units have also played a role in many societies. The *kibbutz* communities of Israel are a well-known example of a conscious attempt to move beyond kinship in the definition of who lives with whom. In many aboriginal societies, "men's houses"—lodges in which men live, conduct secret rituals, and train boys into adult male roles—are an important part of the social landscape. Household groups formed through adoption, inclusion of servants in the definition of the residential unit, or voluntary coresidence on the part of unrelated adults are other variations on the theme of residence patterns.

Context

Kinship studies have been an important part of sociological and anthropological thought since the inception of these disciplines in the eighteenth and nineteenth centuries. One intriguing aspect of this area is its clear link to biology: people mate and bear offspring as do all other mammals, yet humans, uniquely, find a variety of ways in which to do these things. Thus, the basic questions for early social scientists— what makes humans different, and what justifies a separate academic area to study them?—found its key testing arena in kin studies.

The incest taboo was the focal point of much early thought on human kinship patterns. The taboo seemed to be a human universal, yet the group of tabooed relatives varied so widely from society to society as to make it inaccessible to biological analysis. If one's mother's sister's offspring was a tabooed relative in a given society, but one's mother's brother's offspring was not, how could such a restriction be explained by a recourse to biology? The genetic relatedness of the two prospective mates would be the same, but in many societies they were classified differently. This sort of phenomenon, uncovered by ethnographers in one region after another, gave challenge to the simple notion that relatives did not mate because of the genetic consequences. Social thinkers came to realize that, as sociologist Émile Durkheim put it, social facts were "things" that needed to be exlained on their own level, as social facts, and not reduced to matters of biology. (Subsequent scholarship has discovered that the reasons why a parallel cousin might be tabooed as a marriage partner and a cross cousin preferred have to do with the descent organization of the society: The former could be a member of the same descent group and hence tabooed as an insider, while the latter, as a member of a different descent group could be preferred as potentially creating a valuable alliance between groups.)

Kinship studies as a theoretical area went through many of the same phases as did other areas of focus within the social sciences. Almost every great sociologist and anthropologist dealt with kinship on some level. Lewis Henry Morgan, the "founder" of American anthropology, produced a major work on kinship patterns, *Systems of Consanguinity and Affinity of the Human Family* (1870), which was probably the first truly cross-cultural analysis of variation in family structure. Morgan made the development of the human family a key part of his evolutionary framework; his ideas were picked up most influentially by Friedrich Engels, whose *Der Ursprung der Familie, des Privateigentums und des Staats* (1884; *The Origin of the Family, Private Property, and the State*, 1902) became central to the Marxist analysis of the family. Functionalists such as A. R. Radcliffe Brown and Meyer Fortes were fascinated by the integration of kinship patterns within the overall structure of society, while anthropologists such as Margaret Mead found the impact of varying family situations on child rearing to be of great importance in understanding the maintenance of cultural traditions. The French anthropologist Claude Lévi-Strauss, who founded the school of thought called structuralism, wrote a major interpretation of kinship as symbolic structure called *Structures élémentaires de la parenté* (1949; *Elementary Structures of Kinship*, 1969).

In the latter part of the century, sociobiology, a new field attempting to reincorporate the study of human behavior into the overall study of animal behavior, posed a challenge to social sciences that emphasized the distinctiveness of human beings. Kinship, with its clear link to biological instincts and constraints, came under particular scrutiny; anthropologists with their disciplinary ties to comparative primate studies became most directly engaged with the sociobiology controversy. After a flurry of vehement exchanges in the 1970's and 1980's, sociobiology as an approach has continued to attract a vocal minority of social scientists; the field's greatest difficulty has continued to lie in the explanation of social diversity, exemplified in the area of kinship as in every other area of human activity.

Feminist analyses of kinship and those coming from gay and lesbian studies have also provided a challenge to much traditional thinking about family life. It is clear that the study of marriage, descent, and residence patterns will continue to play a central role as the social science disciplines struggle to keep up with the rapid changes going on in society itself.

Bibliography

Collier, Jane Fishburne, and Sylvia Junko Yanagisako, eds. *Gender and Kinship: Essays Toward a Unified Analysis*. Stanford, Calif.: Stanford University Press, 1987. This series of essays represents an attempt at rethinking kinship analysis from a feminist perspective. A useful complement to other sources.

Ember, Melvin, and Carol R. Ember. *Marriage, Family, and Kinship: Comparative Studies of Social Organization*. New Haven, Conn.: Human Relations Area Files, 1983. A collection of studies attempting to test various theories of kinship on a cross-cultural basis. Useful as a follow-up to the other introductory essays reviewed here.

Frayser, S. G. *Varieties of Sexual Experience: An Anthropological Perspective on Human Sexuality*. New Haven, Conn.: Human Relations Area Files, 1985. A challenging attempt to explore the diversity of sexual customs using a comparative approach. There is important discussion of the links between sexuality and marriage, family life, child rearing, and social structure.

Keesing, Roger M. *Kin Groups and Social Structure*. New York: Holt, Rinehart and Winston, 1975. A classic text on kinship, written in jargon-free prose. Contains many useful diagrams that help explain the complexities of kin organization. A good introduction to the field.

Pasternak, Burton. *Introduction to Kinship and Social Organization*. Englewood Cliffs, N.J.: Prentice-Hall, 1976. One of the standard sources on kinship; contains easily understood diagrams and case studies. A good comprehensive introduction to kinship analysis.

Schneider, David M. *American Kinship: A Cultural Account*. 2d ed. Chicago: University of Chicago Press, 1980. An important interpretation of U.S. kinship patterns, focusing on symbolic elements.

Schusky, E. L. *Variation in Kinship*. New York: Holt, Rinehart and Winston, 1974. A solid introduction to kinship, descent, and residence.

Cynthia Keppley Mahmood

Cross-References

REVOLUTIONS

Type of sociology: Collective behavior and social movements

Revolutions are complex phenomena that have inspired both speculation and serious scholarship. The French Revolution of 1789, the writings of Karl Marx, and the Russian Revolution of 1917 led theorists to think in terms of broad, often international movements, but more recent studies have emphasized the varieties of revolutionary experience and the importance of local, regional, and national factors.

Principal terms
ALIENATION: a feeling of distance or isolation among people in which human relationships are distorted or destroyed
BUREAUCRACY: a structured organization with many functions and levels of authority, usually run by a central administration
NATION-STATE: the central government of a particular country
OLD REGIME: the social, economic, and political structures that collapse as a result of the outbreak of a revolution
STATE: not simply the government of a province (or state), but government in general, usually including a centralized bureaucracy
THEORY: in the social sciences, an organized body of ideas and information that attempts to explain some aspect of human behavior

Overview

In the political sense of the word, a revolution can be defined as an uprising of people who overthrow their existing social, political, and economic institutions in the hope of creating a better society. These revolutions vary in magnitude. Some originate from local issues and may be confined to a particular community, but the best-known and most-studied were quite extensive in that they involved outbreaks of civil violence and widespread disruptions in the normal operations of commerce, agriculture, and manufacturing. Only a few revolutions of this size have occurred in modern history. While scholars often disagree about the makeup of this list, there seems to be fairly broad agreement on five that should be included: the French Revolution of 1789, the Russian Revolution of 1917, the Mexican Revolution of 1910, the Cuban Revolution of 1959, and the Chinese Revolution of 1949.

There are other types of upheavals sometimes called revolutions. Such events generally involve the overthrow of a government, but they usually have a much more limited impact on society in general than the five events listed previously. Such a limited movement concerns short-term political change—for example the removal of a discredited head of state—and can be more appropriately termed a rebellion or a coup d'etat.

The five revolutions listed have generated much serious study and considerable debate among sociologists and historians. Some students of revolution have devised theories to explain at least two major aspects of revolution: their causes, or the conditions that led to the mobilization of people to overthrow the established order, and their consequences, or the changes that revolutionary leaders or groups carried out once they gained power.

Karl Marx was widely considered to be the leading theorist of revolution for more than a century, from the upheavals in Europe in the mid-nineteenth century to the worldwide Cold War (between the 1940's and the 1980's). Born on May 5, 1818, in Trier, Germany (then Prussia), Marx studied philosophy at leading German universities and became a close observer of the condition of the working class, especially in England, where he lived from 1849 until his death in 1883. His voluminous writings have been the subject of various interpretations and many disputes among his followers. Generalizations about Marx's theory of revolution, therefore, are difficult but also necessary in order to gain some appreciation of his contribution to this controversial subject. He saw revolution as the inevitable result of class conflict, or the struggle between workers and their employers (the capitalists). Marx argued that material interests were the driving forces in society and the primary cause of revolutions. Factory owners sought greater profits and pushed their workers beyond the limits of human endurance. In this hostile environment, workers experienced a sense of alienation from their employers and from the economic and political institutions that reinforced this system. This conflict, according to Marx, would provide the spark for a massive revolution that would, in time, destroy the capitalist system.

Marx's view of the benevolent results of revolution were quite different from his grim portrayal of the exploitation and social conflict that caused revolution. After the overthrow of the old regime, a new economic and social system was to emerge under the tutelage of the revolutionary state. This new system would be built on harmonious human relationships that would eventually make the existence of government unnecessary. Thus, the state would "wither away," leaving a society free of the material inequities that had led to the class struggle. Alienation would disappear, and human interaction, while still subject to discord, would no longer be determined by material interests.

Marx's vision of postrevolutionary society proved to be unrealistic, but his analysis of the causes of revolution provided a theoretical formulation that gained widespread credibility with Vladimir Ilich Lenin's triumph as leader of the Marx-inspired Bolshevik Revolution in Russia in 1917. Lenin's astute use of Marxist rhetoric along with political and military maneuvering established a Communist government—the Soviet Union—that lasted until 1989.

The Marxist theory of revolution, however, did not gain universal acceptance. For example, two pioneering European theorists in sociology presented alternatives to the Marxist perspective. One was Émile Durkheim, a French sociologist whose writing in the late nineteenth century argued that revolutions are the primary causes of unrest and disorder rather than their results. For Durkheim, revolution exacerbated existing problems and brought disruptive, harmful behavior. After the storm of revolution had passed, the reconstruction of key social institutions would require many years of concerted effort.

The second theorist, Max Weber, was a German sociologist who emphasized another side of the consequences of revolution: the rise of the centralized state. In theory the state was supposed to create Marx's version of the ideal society, but, in reality, it became a calculated grasp for power by revolutionary leaders who used governmental authority to cement their control. In brief, Weber's theory held that revolutions tend to overthrow the old, abusive system only to replace it with new forms of expansive bureaucratic control that also contain the potential for abuse.

Applications

Marx established the framework for much of the early theoretical discussion of revolution. Even critics such as Durkheim and Weber referred to some of his key ideas, such as alienation and class conflict, in the development of their theories. Later sociologists, however, devised new theoretical assumptions and then applied these assumptions to the growing accumulation of historical research and new sources of information on contemporary events. The application of their theories to the historical revolutions and more recent eruptions of social unrest have supplied this field of study with a healthy diversity of opinion on a topic of lasting importance.

Immanuel Wallerstein has developed an extensive revision of Marx's views of the causes of revolution. Trained as a sociologist at Columbia University, Wallerstein's interests expanded from his dissertation on the end of colonial rule in Ghana and the Ivory Coast to a conceptual framework that encompasses the consequences of the spread of capitalism across the globe. His "modern world system" theory generalizes that large capitalist enterprises cross national boundaries to create networks of commerce that have transformed the world into a single economic unit. Although these capitalist enterprises are based in what Wallerstein calls the core regions of Western Europe and the United States, their penetration into other parts of the world creates situations that may lead to revolution.

Wallerstein divides the world outside this core into two large regions: the periphery and the semiperiphery, both of which are linked to the world system by arrangements that shift wealth to the core nations while bringing inequities, unrest, and, in some cases, revolution to the less developed areas. In the periphery, which is composed of the least developed nations, the impoverished masses feel the brunt of the arrival of capitalist enterprises under conditions of domination and exploitation by local elites allied with corporations from the core nations. Thus capitalism can turn peripheral areas into breeding grounds for revolution.

In the semiperiphery (made up of nations with some significant industrialization, such as Brazil and South Africa), revolutionary situations arise during economic crises or perhaps as the result of the efforts of national leaders to challenge the dominance of international corporations based in the core nations. In the periphery, as in the semiperiphery, Wallerstein sees the causes of revolution in the spread of capitalism.

Whereas Wallerstein emphasizes that the causes of revolution are economic in nature, Theda Skocpol has turned her attention to the place of government in the revolutionary process. Skocpol, who studied sociology at Harvard University under Barrington Moore, tends to follow her mentor's historical approach. In her book *States and Social Revolutions: A Comparative Analysis of France, Russia, and China* (1979), Skocpol compares the revolutions in those three countries and concludes that bureaucracies and politics played decisive roles in all three cases. External military threats combined with internal peasant or worker unrest and administrative corruption to cause the collapse of the old regime.

One of Skocpol's major points in the analysis of revolutions is her concentration on the rise of a strong central government as a consequence of revolution. In her view, revolutionary leaders use the government in order to defend a nation against its external enemies and to bring about a significant redistribution of property and power at home. These difficult tasks—one directed at threats from the outside world and the other intended to rectify domestic injustices—result in the growth of the size of the nation-state, which gains the potential to go beyond these responsibilities as it becomes a large and powerful institution with the capacity for coercion as well as compassion in its many functions.

A third theoretical position has emerged in the writing of a group of scholars who look at revolutions from a perspective quite different from those of Wallerstein and Skocpol. Instead of international economics and nation-states, this third theoretical school, often called the moral economy school, emphasizes that revolutions sometimes originate among peasants and artisans in societies caught in the transition from traditional, small-scale, village agriculture to modern, large-scale, commercial enterprises. Among the leading students in the multidisciplinary moral economy school are anthropologist Eric Wolfe, sociologist Craig Calhoun, social historian Michael Adas, and political scientist James C. Scott.

They use the term "moral economy" to describe the attitudes and values of those peasants and artisans who initiate revolutionary (or protest) movements in order to preserve their communities based on traditional property and market arrangements from the arrival of modern commercial enterprises that absorb local resources and labor or to struggle against the intrusion of the modern nation-state with its power of taxation and its potential for the deployment of police coercion. These communities devise a wide variety of responses to such intrusions that range from overt violence that may become part of a major revolution to subtle, often hidden rhetoric that belittles, lampoons, and, to the local people, discredits the newly arrived modern institutions.

Moral economy theory provides a valuable perspective on the revolutionary process. Instead of emphasizing massive worker-peasant uprisings that seize centers of power (as in the French and Russian revolutions), this theoretical approach focuses on small provincial movements that may collapse under the weight of state coercion. These revolutionary movements seem to have become increasingly evident as the industrialized portion of the world's economy has expanded its reach into Asia, the Middle East, Africa, and Latin America.

Context

Until Lenin led the Communists to power in Russia in 1917, few sociologists studied revolution. Lenin's claim that his updating of Marx's theory provided a formula for revolution in which a vanguard group could direct workers' frustrations to overthrow virtually any government sent a shock wave around the world. This perception of revolution inspired by, and perhaps engineered by, Communist followers of Lenin led sociologists to intensify their examinations of the imbalances and inequities that could contribute to such movements.

For about half a century, many sociologists (and other academics) regarded Marxist-Leninism as a kind of theoretical model for the study of the causes and consequences of revolutions. Yet the seizure of power by Chinese Communists in 1949 and Fidel Castro's revolution in Cuba a decade later indicated that the Marxist-Leninist formula's reliance on industrial workers had to be modified to allow for the participation of peasants and rural guerrillas. By the 1960's and 1970's, serious students of social change began to make comparative studies that included the historical revolutions and contemporary movements that seemed to have the characteristics of revolution. The Mexican Revolution, previously regarded as an aberration or as a failed revolution, became the subject of sociological and historical inquiry as a movement built on a unique confluence of sporadic surges of peasant and worker activism modulated by the nation-state. In general, theories of revolution in the last few decades of the Cold War turned increasingly to regional or local movements that had their roots in peasant and artisan communities.

Sociologist Paul Hollander launched a new attack on the mystiques associated with the Russian, Chinese, and Cuban revolutions in his 1981 book, *Political Pilgrims*. Hollander charged that many academics from nations such as the United States, Great Britain, and France were predisposed to look favorably on these revolutions to a large extent because of their alienation from the industrial societies in which they lived. These prejudgments heightened their willingness to write sympathetic portraits of revolutionary regimes that challenged the material and ideological aspects of capitalism. Once in the revolutionary nation, these same academics enjoyed special treatment, including guided tours of selected sites arranged by the revolutionary governments. Hollander's book questioned the conclusions reached by numerous traveler-commentators, including C. Wright Mills's account of his 1960 trip to Cuba.

The waning of Communism in the Soviet Union and Cuba in the last years of the Cold War and the increasingly authoritarian nature of the Communist government in China contributed to a general shift away from Marxist and neo-Marxist theory and ushered in more eclectic approaches toward the study of revolution. At the same time, the world became more tightly interconnected through the spread of modern communications and transportation. The flood of information from areas outside the United States and Europe provided sociologists with many examples of revolutionary movements both of large and, more often, small magnitudes that drew from a variety of causative factors and proclaimed revolutionary visions that looked to the past as well as the future. Wallerstein, Skocpol, and especially the moral economy school of

theorists became increasingly aware of the multiplicity and complexity of revolutionary movements in a world that was rapidly becoming more deeply interconnected.

Bibliography

Adas, Michael. *Prophets of Rebellion: Millenarian Protest Movements Against the European Colonial Order*. Chapel Hill: University of North Carolina Press, 1979. A detailed but readable analysis of prophetic religious movements that arose in Java, New Zealand, India, East Africa, and Burma as social protests against and ill-fated violent confrontations with European colonial authorities.

Billington, James H. *Fire in the Minds of Men: Origins of the Revolutionary Faith*. New York: Basic Books, 1980. Historical study that traces the ideas, religiosity, personal idiosyncrasies, and clandestine practices of revolutionaries from the French Revolution to the early twentieth century.

Calhoun, Craig. *The Question of Class Struggle: Social Foundations of Popular Radicalism During the Industrial Revolution*. Chicago: University of Chicago Press, 1982. A sophisticated study in the moral economics school which emphasizes the traditional roots of English textile workers' radical protests in the early 1800's.

Goldstone, Jack A. *Revolution and Rebellion in the Early Modern World*. Berkeley: University of California Press, 1991. Impressive synthesis that covers revolutions in Britain, France, the Ottoman Empire, and China from 1500 to 1850. Goldstone emphasizes population pressure as a crucial causative factor in the breakdown of the old regimes. The last two chapters deal with the consequences of revolution and the applications of Goldstone's theories to more recent revolutionary movements.

Kimmel, Michael. *Revolution: A Sociological Interpretation*. Philadelphia: Temple University Press, 1990. A very useful, balanced survey of the analyses of revolutions made by major theorists beginning with Marx and including Durkheim, Weber, Wallerstein, and Skocpol as well as Barrington Moore, Charles Tilly, and the moral economy school.

Marx, Karl. "The Communist Manifesto." In *Capital: The Communist Manifesto and Other Writings*. Edited by Max Eastman. New York: Modern Library, 1959. A succinct summary of the Marxist view of revolution. Marx's writings are also available in many other editions.

Scott, James C. *The Moral Economy of the Peasant*. New Haven, Conn.: Yale University Press, 1976. The first of many studies by a pioneer in the moral economy school. Drawing from specialized research on the peasantry in Vietnam, Scott develops insightful generalizations with broad application.

Skocpol, Theda. *States and Social Revolutions: A Comparative Analysis of France, Russia, and China*. Cambridge, England: Cambridge University Press, 1979. A well-organized study of a complex subject: the comparative history of three of the major revolutions in world history. Although some scholars have criticized her findings, Skocpol's book remains one of the most influential in the field.

Wallerstein, Immanuel. *The Modern World System*. Vols. 1 and 2. New York: Academic Press, 1974 and 1980. Vol. 3. San Diego: Academic Press, 1989. The first three volumes in a projected four-volume synthesis of ideas on the evolution of capitalism from the Middle Ages to modern times. Volume 3 reaches the mid-nineteenth century and includes Wallerstein's evaluation of the French Revolution.

Wolf, Eric. *Peasant Wars of the Twentieth Century.* New York: Harper & Row, 1969. An anthropologist's clearly written analysis of six revolutions (Mexican, Russian, Chinese, Vietnamese, Algerian, and Cuban) with an emphasis on the increasing importance of peasant participation in such movements.

John A. Britton

Cross-References

RITES OF PASSAGE AND AGING

Type of sociology: Aging and ageism

Rites of passage as a term refers to ceremonies that mark a person's passage from one age group to another or from one social status to another. Though it may also include rites that mark seasonal and annual changes, it refers mostly to ceremonies that accompany birth, coming-of-age (initiation), marriage, senility, and death.

Principal terms

CIRCUMCISION: the practice of ritually or medically cutting off the foreskin of the penis

CLITORIDECTOMY: the practice of ritually cutting off a portion of the clitoris

INITIATE: a person who has been or is being admitted to a group, society, or status through formal or secret ceremonies

LIBATION: the offering of food or drink to ancestors by living family members

LIVING-DEAD: an ancestor; in some cultures the dead are regarded as still living in another sphere where they take active interest in their earthly lineage

MARGINAL RITES: ceremonies that mark the period in which a person/ group is detached from one status but not yet admitted to the next; a period of transition from one status or age to another

POLYGYNY: the marital practice under which a man can have two or more wives; also called polygamy

RITES OF AGGREGATION: ceremonies that mark the actual entry of an individual into a new status; the person becomes a new member; (s)he is incorporated into the new "family"

RITES OF SEPARATION: ceremonies that mark physical separation of a person from group/society

RITUAL: prescribed formal behavior, oftentimes symbolic, fixed and solemn, which follows a cultural tradition

Overview

Every human being ages daily. Because of the inevitability of this process, key aspects of a person's movement from birth to death are ceremonially recognized in varying degrees in all cultures. In some societies, emphasis may be on the different social statuses one achieves; in others, the ritualistic observance of seasonal and annual changes may dominate. Such observances remind people of the passage of time and the changes they go through as they grow and age. In all cultures, this passage of time in human beings is marked by birth, maturity or initiation, marriage, old age, and death. The ceremonies performed to mark these various progressions of one's age and life are referred to as rites of passage.

As a term, "rites of passage" is the English translation of the French *rites de passage*, introduced into the social sciences in 1909 by the French anthropologist Arnold van Gennep. In his book *Les Rites de passage*, Gennep stated that the principle of "regeneration" governs life and the universe—that life energy becomes gradually spent and needs renewal at intervals. This revitalization is most noticeably expressed in the rites of death and rebirth which are found not only among humans but also in seasonal and annual changes. In some sense, all life is change or transition. The changes a human goes through between birth and death are often challenging, upsetting, and dangerous to social and individual life. It is during those important and turbulent changes that rites of passage show their unique relevance and importance: They help to "cushion the disturbance," to ease the pains and difficulties that occur in the society's or the individual's transition from one status to another.

Gennep's unique contribution to understanding the rites of passage is his analysis of the ceremonies that accompany these "life crises." Such ceremonies or rites are characterized by three consecutive, easily distinguishable phases: *séparation* (separation), *marge* (transition), and *agrégation* (incorporation). During the stage of separation (also called the preliminal or before-the-threshold period), the individual or group on whom the ceremony focuses is symbolically separated from the previous status in life or office. It is the first step in the movement from what he or she now is to what will be. The transition stage (liminal or at-the-threshold period) is the transitional moment in which the individual or group ritually loses the former self or status but has not yet assumed the new one. It is the indescribable middle passage, the state in which the person or group is suspended between past and future statuses. The final stage is that of incorporation (the postliminal or after-the-threshold period), in which the individual or group officially assumes the new status and receives reincorporation into society.

Gennep points out that these three sequences in a rite of passage are not necessarily present in every case, nor are they developed to the same extent. For example, rites of separation play a dominant role in burial ceremonies; marginal rites assume prominence in initiation; while rites of aggregation are ever-present in marriage. The three categories do, however, constitute a universal pattern.

Rites of passage often function within a religious framework and are therefore regarded as religious events. That religious attachment helped to imbue them with sacred authority and reverence. It is said that these rites, when performed in the true spirit and manner, are capable of bringing blessings upon a marriage, protect pregnancies and childbirth, give initiates some mystical power, and send the dead to a peaceful hereafter to meet the saints or ancestors who have gone before them. Contemporary sociological inquiries, citing examples from industrialized and technologically advanced cultures, note that rites of passage may be secular rather than religious. They point to the essentially secular natures of initiation into fraternities, sororities, and honorary societies, and the fact that baby showers and marriages can be entirely secular affairs. Human beings, it is contended, devote social, not religious, attention to events thought to be socially important.

Max Gluckman, arguing from a functionalist perspective, sees some rites of passage as "rituals of rebellion" that give voice and acceptability to the inferior and the oppressed. Victor Turner, focusing on the liminal nature of rites of initiation, sees such rites as agents of levelling. Subjected to the same process as everyone else, the initiate is united with fellow initiates. Others, such as Albert Anthony, Richard Kluckhohn, and J. W. M. Whiting, have proposed that such ceremonies as male initiation be seen as rituals of socialization and control by which a male-dominated society tries to break mother-son emotional attachments in order to bring a young man into strong male gender bonding.

The observations of Gennep and psychologist Erik Erikson still hold true—transitions from a given social position to another are existentially factual, and human life consists of a series of successive stages with similar ends and beginnings: birth, maturity, marriage, parenthood, social advancement, and death. Ceremonies for each of these stages exist whose purpose is to help the group or individual move smoothly from one stage to another.

Applications

Rites of passage and aging are found in all human societies. In the United States and most Western societies, rites of passage and aging are mostly experienced in terms of lifelong patterns of development from childhood to adolescence, early adulthood, middle adulthood, and late adulthood. Erikson and Daniel Levinson point out that this life cycle is marked by relationships with shifting importance: peer bonding, friendship, ethnicity ties, religion, occupation, marriage, family, and leisure. Though all aspects of the process of growth and aging are important, old age (Erikson's eighth and last stage of human development) commands special attention because it is the culmination of earlier stages of human transition. It is marked by various forms of peer group socialization rites, mostly occurring in senior citizens' centers, nursing homes, and retirement facilities, where elderly people share meals, dance, date, tell stories, play games, and participate in leisure activities. Through these rites, the loneliness that accompanies the passage of old age is minimized.

Many African societies provide good examples of rites of passage. In the rites of initiation among most African societies, especially among those that practice circumcision and clitoridectomy, one observes Gennep's categories of separation, transition, and incorporation. The youth to be initiated are camped outside the village for some period. This marks the stage of separation. They are taught the art of communal living, morality, responsibility, and some secret knowledge. This is the transitional period. When they re-emerge from isolation to join the society, they have new identities; some societies even give them new names. This is the phase of reincorporation, which is usually marked with festivities.

Among the Akamba people of Kenya, the first stage of initiation rites involves circumcising the boys by male specialists; female specialists perform clitoridectomy on the girls. It is a group act performed the same day in a designated place. The activity symbolizes separation from childhood. Anyone who does not go through this first stage of initiation rites, even when he or she attains maturity and age, is communally despised. It is believed that ritually cutting the skin from one's sexual organ liberates the individual from the state of sexual inactivity and ignorance. One enters a state of activity and knowledge, of sexual reproduction necessary to keep the lineage and society going.

An uninitiated person is not expected to be sexually active; neither is she or he supposed to marry and procreate. The shedding of the blood into the earth during the excision mystically binds the initiate to the living-dead who symbolically dwell on earth and can be reached through libation. The pain the initiates experience prepares them for the problems they will encounter in their lifetime. They are encouraged to endure and overcome such pain. The initiates are then given presents—an introduction to owning property. There is general merriment and dancing to emphasize communal solidarity.

The second stage of initiation is mostly educational, meant to help the initiates as they approach full maturity. The ceremony lasts for about a week, during which the initiates are sequestered in huts built outside the village and away from public interaction. Accompanied by watchful older people, the youths are taught all they need to know concerning adulthood, a process referred to as "brooding over the initiates." Among other things, they learn moral and corporate responsibilities and are reminded of their religious obligations. They have full access to the wisdom of the elders and the secrets of their society. When they emerge from their seclusion, they are capable of protecting themselves, their dependents, and their society. A new generation capable of carrying on the life of the community thus comes into being, and the community is assured of its immortality.

Another example of the application of rites of passage is marriage. In Africa, marriage is a requirement of the corporate society, and it is understood to go along with procreation; marriage without procreation is thought to be incomplete. Humanity, through procreative marriage, tries to recapture the lost gift of immortality, since husband and wife reproduce themselves through their children and by so doing perpetuate their family lineage and humanity. John S. Mbiti sees marriage in the African society as a "rhythm of life" that involves everyone. Under normal situations, failure to engage in procreative matrimony is a rejection of the society. Because of the importance attached to procreation, Mbiti in *African Religions and Philosophy* (1988) says that in some African societies, marriage is not fully recognized or consummated until the wife bears a child:

> First pregnancy becomes . . . the final seal of marriage, the sign of complete integration of the woman into her husband's family and kinship circle. Unhappy is the woman who fails to get children for, whatever other qualities she might possess, her failure to bear children is worse than committing genocide: she has become the dead end of human life, not only for the genealogical line but for herself. When she dies there will be nobody of her own immediate blood to "remember" her, to keep her in the state of personal immortality: she will simply be "forgotten." The fault may not be her own, but this does not "excuse" her in the eyes of society.

To reduce the pressure that marriage puts on barren people, polygyny is allowed, but it is the performance of the rites of marriage that helps to soften the hard side of that institution. Such rites involve the various methods of choosing a partner, the use of intermediaries and matchmakers, disapproval of marriage of close relatives, courtship, exchange of gifts between families, marriage covenants, symbolic fight for the bride by the groom, and the paying of a bride price. The rites of marriage in Africa help prevent divorce, make the wife comfortable in her new home, and elevate the value attached to the woman. The involvement of both families at every stage of the rites reminds the couple that a successful marriage involves two families and that there are people to help them. The groom is reminded that his bride is not a bought or stolen "property"; his wife is being given to him under mutual agreement between the families. It is also a reminder to the marriage partners that they cannot simply terminate their marriage on their own: People other than themselves are involved.

Context

When Gennep wrote *Les Rites de passage*, there was much intellectual growth and excitement occurring in the social sciences. Sociologists and anthropologists were engaged in the first scientific explorations and classifications of the world's cultures. Lewis H. Morgan and Herbert Spencer were applying Charles Darwin's theory of evolution to the development of civilizations (much of their work has since been disputed and has fallen out of favor), and Auguste Comte had theorized a set of sociological principles to be tested through objective studies of societies.

The older civilizations of Africa, Australia, the Americas, and Asia were studied and compared, although much of the materials used were anecdotal (rather than scientific) accounts furnished by travelers, colonialists, and missionaries. Gennep's studies of religious beliefs, rituals, and ceremonies were influential. Creating his own classifications, he insisted that the ceremonies and rites of a people must be studied in their entirety and in their social setting. He was thereby among those directing social science toward empirical observation rather than "metaphysical speculation." This movement coincided with the beginning of the influence of major French sociologists—Gennep's contemporaries Émile Durkheim, Marcel Mauss, and Henri Hubert—on functional anthropology.

Rites of passage are seen today as important human endeavors. In some societies (notably modern industrial societies) they may include both secular and religious rites; graduation ceremonies and New Year's Eve celebrations are both examples of essentially secular rituals. Nevertheless, religious rites of passage are always present, whether represented by ceremonies of religious transformation, blessings of marriage vows, or the elaborate funeral rites found in African cultures in which the dead are separated from the living and go through the stage of losing their corporeality in order to be incorporated into the community of the ancestors.

Rites of passage will always provide psychological satisfaction as they help to bridge and soften critical stages of human life process. By readily making available a predictable, societal context for group or individual experience, such rites therapeutically relieve the anxieties that changes in age, status, or experience bring. They are clear signals of communal support and an affirmation of the common culture. They express moral and social values sanctioned in the ceremonies and foster a sense of unity. On an aesthetic level, rites of passage provide entertainment by use of songs, music, dance, art, and drama.

Erikson points out as an example the importance of the rites of aging in the United States. Old age is the period in which one achieves not only a sense of integrity and wisdom but also fulfillment of one's social and historical existence. Though elderly people may despair over the loss of youthful vigor and may anguish over things unaccomplished, their wisdom about the facts of life and death and their faith in some form of continuity after death helps calm this anguish. Old age is the voice of experience and wisdom; every human society needs this wisdom and integrity to gain correct balance, vision, and perspective.

Bibliography

Erikson, Erik H. *Childhood and Society*. 2d ed. New York: W. W. Norton, 1963. An outstanding and influential research work on the Sioux and Yurok American Indians. Should be read with Erikson's *The Life Cycle Completed* (1982), which elaborates on the author's analysis of the ego, society, and history.

Fine, Irene. *Midlife and Its Rite of Passage Ceremony*. San Diego, Calif.: Woman's Institute for Continuing Jewish Education, 1983. Focus is on the ritual that some Jewish women in the United States enact during their midlife. The passage is celebrated with songs, folk stories, poetry, and study of the Torah. Easy to read.

Fried, Martha Nemes, and Morton H. Fried. *Transitions: Four Rituals in Eight Cultures*. New York: W. W. Norton, 1980. Focuses on birth, puberty/adolescence, marriage, and death rituals as critical transitions. Gives extensive accounts of the lives of peoples of diverse cultures.

Gennep, Arnold van. *The Rites of Passage*. Translated by Monika B. Vizedom and Gabrielle L. Caffee. Chicago: University of Chicago Press, 1960. This 198-page English translation of the book written by the man who brought the rites of passage into prominence in 1909 is important reading. The translation is good, and the introduction by Solon Kimball is also quite interesting.

Kett, Joseph F. *Rites of Passage*. New York: Basic Books, 1977. Taking a historical perspective from 1790 to the 1970's, the book studies the process of aging in the United States and the critical transitions that occur. There is a special focus on "youth" with its broad age range.

Leemon, Thomas A. *The Rites of Passage in a Student Culture*. New York: Teachers College Press, 1972. An eyewitness account of the process of recruitment, training, and induction into a fraternity in an American college. Employs Gennep's categories of separation, transition, and incorporation.

Levinson, Daniel J., et al. *The Seasons of a Man's Life*. New York: Alfred A. Knopf, 1978. Discusses the life cycle with examples drawn from contemporary Americans. Fascinating reading that sheds light on the life cycle as it is viewed in American society. Has useful notes and an index.

Mbiti, John S. *African Religions and Philosophy*. London: Heinemann, 1988. Discusses African rites of passage along with traditional religions and thought. A very useful book; includes a map of Africa showing the countries and peoples.

Turner, Victor. *The Forest of Symbols*. Ithaca, N.Y.: Cornell University Press, 1967. Rituals performed by the Ndembu peope of Zambia are the focus of this book. Chapter 4 stands out for Turner's discussion of the liminal phase in rites of passage. Has a useful index for those who prefer selective reading.

I. Peter Ukpokodu

Cross-References

Age Grading and Age Stratification, 27; Age Inequality: Functionalist versus Conflict Theory Views, 34; Ageism and the Ideology of Ageism, 41; Aging and Retirement, 47; The Aging Process, 53; The Elderly and Institutional Care, 621; The Elderly and the Family, 627; Social Gerontology, 1799; Social Security and Issues of the Elderly, 1832.

ROLE CONFLICT AND ROLE STRAIN

Type of sociology: Social structure
Field of study: Components of social structure

Role conflict is theorized to develop when an individual experiences competition within or among his or her social positions and their corresponding expectations. Role strain is the general stress experienced when the demands of one or more roles are inappropriate, unfair, or unrealistic. Stress and conflict within social groups and personal relationships may be explained in terms of role conflict or role strain.

Principal terms
BURNOUT: emotional exhaustion, depersonalization, and a reduced sense of accomplishment caused by role strain of human services work
DEPERSONALIZATION: a loss of emotional commitment to work and people as a result of role strain
INTERROLE CONFLICT: conflict between the demands of two or more roles occupied by one person
INTRAROLE CONFLICT: stress caused by different views of a role
NORM: an accepted and expected guideline for social behavior
PERSON-ROLE CONFLICT: a mismatch between an individual's abilities and the demands of a role
ROLE: a set of norms attached to a particular social position
ROLE CONFLICT: stress created when roles are ambiguous, unrealistic, or inappropriate
ROLE REVERSAL: a stress reduction strategy in which parties assume each other's perspectives to establish understanding
ROLE STRAIN: stress created by role conflict, role change, mismanagement, or misunderstanding

Overview

A role is a set of norms (obligations or expectations) attached to an individual's social position, occupation, or relationship status. People are motivated to adhere to norms and perform roles in order to win approval, avoid social penalties, and develop self-esteem. Role conflict is the psychological stress created when persons do not fit their roles (person-role conflict), when relevant others disagree with the individual about his or her role (intrarole conflict), or when several different roles make mutually exclusive demands on an individual (interrole conflict).

Role strain is a collective term including different kinds of role conflict as well as the general stress experienced when roles are changed, misunderstood, or mismanaged. For example, because roles are composed of norms, and norms undergo social change, people may find that during the time they are filling a given role, social expectations of the role have altered. For example, a man whose boyhood models of masculinity emphasized strength and independence will experience role strain in adulthood, when he discovers that such macho ideals are outmoded and no longer optimally valued in the workplace or the family.

In addition to role conflict, sources of role strain include overload and misallocation. Overload occurs when one person has too many roles to perform adequately or when demands placed on a group exceed the group's resources. The problem of overload is particularly difficult in understaffed environments, where there are more roles than there are people to fill them. Misallocation occurs when people disagree about who should perform which roles in a relationship. For example, the chairperson of a problem-solving group may believe that it is her duty to dictate group values, whereas members may think she should refrain from unduly influencing group deliberations. Their disagreements about how responsibilities have been allocated will be a source of role strain for all in the group. Misallocation can also plague personal relationships, as when husbands and wives disagree on the division of household labor and decision-making power.

Research on marital satisfaction frequently implicates role misallocation as a source of distress. Particularly challenging are the changes and innovations associated with nontraditional household arrangements. For example, if one spouse carries a disproportionate share of household chore assignments, yet both work outside the home, this inequality (unfairness) will contribute to marital role strain. Some critics argue that a return to traditional household roles—husband as breadwinner, wife as homemaker—would simplify labor and reduce stress for all concerned. While this may be true in a limited sense, it is unrealistic; multiple roles are inevitable now that women as well as men seek the benefits of education and careers. Additionally, economic conditions make it advantageous, and often necessary, for both spouses to work.

Do multiple roles—each partner performing roles related to work as well as the home—necessarily create relationship distress? In *Intimate Relationships* (1992), social psychologist Sharon S. Brehm describes the contrasting predictions of two hypotheses about multiple roles. According to the scarcity hypothesis, more social roles invariably lead to more stress, since an individual's limited resources are spread to meet more demands. According to the enhancement hypothesis, however, defining oneself through more roles means less stress, since disappointments in one role can be compensated for by success in others. According to Brehm, research evidence favors the enhancement hypothesis: "Having multiple roles is usually associated with increased well-being." Whether multiple roles increase or reduce stress may depend on such factors as the quality of one's job, one's commitment to working, and the social support provided by partners and other members of one's social network.

Two sources of role strain with clear applications to work performance are depersonalization and burnout. Depersonalization occurs when an individual's work requires him or her to occupy an emotionally detached or dehumanizing role. By consistently withholding involvement and intimacy from other people, people in depersonalization roles learn to "blame the victim": to hold needy persons responsible for their own plight. Professional caregivers may lose their ability to care, and educators may lose the desire to teach. When detachment is combined with overload, human service workers are at risk for burnout, described by Christina Maslach as "a syndrome of emotional exhaustion, depersonalization, and reduced personal accomplishment" (*Burnout: The Cost of Caring*, 1982). Victims of burnout experience "compassion fatigue," an inability to connect emotionally with their clients. They begin to intellectualize or trivialize others' suffering and seek to escape or minimize their contact with those who seek their help. Finally, burnout victims find that their work is no longer satisfying. They feel helpless, inadequate, and joyless. They may also develop physical and behavioral symptoms of stress, such as sleeplessness, psychosomatic illness, depression, anger, and inflexible thinking. Research has identified several strategies to solve the problems of role strain, conflict, and burnout.

Applications

If a group member's talents do not fit an assigned role, he or she experiences person-role conflict. For example, most work groups involve two sets of duties: task-oriented roles and relations-oriented roles. A task-oriented person who is assigned to perform a relations-oriented role, such as improving group morale, may find such activity uncomfortable and difficult. Many person-role conflicts stem from individuals' uncertainty about what is expected of them or how they should achieve it. Thus some role conflicts are based in role ambiguity. Person-role conflict may also result from temporary stresses. For example, an individual with serious personal problems may be unable to act as the good listener his friends have come to expect, so that at least temporarily he experiences person-role conflict in his relationships with others.

Perhaps the most common form of role conflict is interrole conflict, the stress experienced when one person attempts to fulfill two or more competing roles. For example, an employee who is also a student may find that, as an employee, he is expected to work additional hours on occasion, but as a student, he should not let changes in his work schedule disrupt his class attendance. In order to perform one role well, he must disappoint expectations in the other. Interrole conflict can also cause problems in personal relationships. For example, a woman trying to care for her ailing mother may be unable to spend enough time with her own children because of the interrole conflict between her duties as daughter and mother.

A subtler but no less stressful problem is created by intrarole conflict, experienced when one's role is perceived differently by different groups or individuals. For example, a newly elected employee representative will experience role conflict on learning that her coworkers expect her to represent their interests to management, while her supervisors expect her to represent management's point of view to her fellow employees. In order to meet one group's expectations, she must disappoint the other group, and vice versa. The individual is caught between different, even contradictory, interpretations of the same role.

Intrarole conflict can challenge personal relationships as well. For example, if a man thinks that he can fulfill the role of "good husband" merely by financially supporting his family, his self-perception is challenged when his wife argues that, in her view, a "good husband" must also meet the family members' social and emotional needs.

General role strain, in addition to specific forms of role conflict, includes changes in role expectations as a result of time or experience. Some roles, such as jobs, are rigidly defined and resist change over time. Other roles, however, especially those in the interpersonal domain, are sensitive to subtle social changes, personal experience, and interpersonal redefinition. For example, as a result of financial pressures and personal frustrations, a married couple may reexamine their assumptions that the husband should be the breadwinner for the family. The family may decide that it will be best for all members if the wife earns the income by working outside the home while the husband works in the home, caring for the house and children. Their decision is not unique, but their arrangement is not normative—it is not typical of other households like theirs—so they lack external models or guidelines for their new roles. The wife may find that she has difficulty redefining herself as a "good wife" if she is not doing most of the cooking and cleaning; her husband may have difficulty feeling like a "good husband" now that he no longer brings home a paycheck. Even if the arrangement works well for the family, it will probably strain their self-concepts and their sense of community acceptance. Role strain in this example is pervasive: Prior to rearranging household duties, both spouses experienced role strain because their work was unsatisfying; after establishing the new arrangement, both are still under stress—this time because of their lack of standards or experience.

Because people who work in human services professions must meet many demands in relationships with their clients, researchers have closely examined the causes and consequences of job-related role strain. This work has led to the development of stress-reduction recommendations for coping with role conflict and burnout.

One strategy recommended for alleviating role conflict is the technique of role reversal. Because roles often come in pairs—teacher and student, parent and child, employer and employee, physician and patient—each party to a conflict can benefit from briefly adopting the other's perspective. Role reversal may be effective either as a mental exercise (imagining each other's perceptions) or as a spoken dialogue in which each person attempts to articulate the other's position to the other's satisfaction. Role reversal may be effective because it reestablishes empathy and cooperation after polarizing circumstances.

Because burnout is a complex and gradual process, it is difficult to remedy. Social psychologist Christina Maslach has recommended several strategies for coping with burnout. Among her suggestions are to set realistic goals, perform the same tasks in different ways, take intermittent breaks or rest periods, resist the tendency to take things personally, concentrate on successes rather than failures, pay attention to one's own needs and feelings, and get adequate rest and relaxation. She advises engaging in "decompression" exercises to resolve work-related problems before going home and developing satisfying nonwork interests and activities. If all else fails, she concludes, change to a job with less risk of role strain.

Context

A role organizes several norms—guidelines and standards that govern one's behaviors, especially in social situations. Norms are seldom transmitted formally, in the form of rules, doctrines, or obvious standards. Instead, people tend to infer norms and roles on the basis of personal experience and social observation. For example, the role of student at one institution may involve many precise customs, including expectations for attendance, class participation, interacting with instructors, and following dress codes, whereas at another school the minimum standards for accepted student behavior might be less clear and more flexible. Through a process of social comparison—observing others' actions—an individual learns how to behave acceptably in a particular social context.

Most people conform to norms and roles in order to reap the benefits of social acceptance and approval and to escape being judged as deviant or a failure. The severity of sanctions varies for different kinds of roles. For example, in most cultures the penalties are harsher for being a "bad mother" than for being a "bad student," or even a "bad father." During childhood socialization, individuals learn to base their self-concept to some extent on role adherence. For this reason a person who fails to fulfill role expectations may suffer not only social punishments such as disapproval and ostracism but also self-punishments such as personal embarrassment, self-recrimination, and reduced self-esteem.

Originally, role theorists characterized roles in terms of group structure and function. Within any problem-solving or social group, different individuals take on different activities and perform different functions, such as providing leadership, conflict resolution, or moral support. One form of role conflict, person-role conflict, develops when an individual's personality or abilities are mismatched with his or her role. In the context of group function, interrole conflict can also develop when an individual who belongs to two or more different groups finds that a role in one group competes with that of another. Intrarole conflict involves several different perceptions of a single group role. Eventually, the concept of role was expanded to include the context of larger "groups" such as institutions, culture, and gender. The concepts of role strain and role conflict in this broader sense have also been expanded.

As studies of roles within social groups have been extended to include dyads (two-person groups such as married couples) as well as families and friendship networks, the concept of role conflict has been applied to interpersonal relationships as well as to groups and institutions. Because roles vary with culture, it is obvious that much, if not all, of a role's specifics are acquired through learning. The flexibility of a role may depend on whether it is achieved or ascribed. The components of achieved roles, roles adopted through personal effort or training, may be learned through schooling or experience. For example, the role of supervisor is achieved: An employee who begins in a lower-status position can advance through effort and education. In contrast, the components of an ascribed role are determined by one's relationships to other persons. For example, a man who fathers a child acquires the ascribed role of father, regardless of whether he has earned or prepared for that role. He cannot be dismissed as one could from an achieved role. Yet the expectations and standards for an ascribed role may be more ambiguous and susceptible to social change.

Because roles and role expectations are learned, through both formal education and socialization, role strain in general and role conflict in particular can be mediated by new information and experience. By learning about common sources of role strain, people can anticipate stressors, recognize the symptoms of inequity or burnout, and take action to reduce the damage. Ultimately roles are useful in assembling and transmitting the norms of one's culture and aspirations. Despite social change and role ambiguity, people can learn to meet the challenges of changing expectations and social structure, to meet their own and their society's goals.

Bibliography

Baron, Robert A., and Jerald Greenberg. *Behavior in Organizations: Understanding and Managing the Human Side of Work*. 3d ed. Boston: Allyn & Bacon, 1990. This management text explores the ways in which workers are assigned to roles in group contexts and the various agendas that groups must learn to address.

Brehm, Sharon S. "Conflict and Dissolution." In *Intimate Relationships*. 2d ed. New York: McGraw-Hill, 1992. This chapter in Brehm's excellent text on personal relationships puts the concept of role strain in the context of other sources and causes of relationship breakdown. Ideal for a college audience. Comprehensive and well-written.

Cherniss, Cary. *Staff Burnout: Job Stress in the Human Services*. Beverly Hills, Calif.: Sage Publications, 1980. An academic presentation appropriate for college readers, this short book examines the risk of burnout in human services. Topics examined include how organizational design contributes to burnout, the impact of supervisors and social support, and strategies for prevention.

Hochschild, Arlie. *The Second Shift*. New York: Viking, 1989. Hochschild interviewed couples about their job arrangements, household labor, child care, and leisure in this study of how working people spend their time.

Maslach, Christina. *Burnout: The Cost of Caring*. Englewood Cliffs, N.J.: Prentice-Hall, 1982. This relatively short book by the acknowledged expert in the field of burnout is full of case studies, practical suggestions, and sound advice. Appropriate for college-level readers and human service professionals who wish better to understand and address their own needs and experiences.

Ann L. Weber

Cross-References

ROMANTIC LOVE

Type of sociology: Major social institutions
Field of study: The family

Romantic love refers to an affectional relationship between partners of choice, based on interpersonal and sexual attraction, emotional attachment, and passion. Cultures that value romantic love in mate selection may differ from other cultures in terms of relationship expectations, marital satisfaction, and the dynamics of relationship breakdown.

Principal terms
ATTACHMENT: a need for access to a significant other
ATTITUDE: an evaluation or opinion of a person or thing that affects one's thoughts, feelings, and behaviors
COURTLY LOVE: a pattern of ritualistic attraction, popularized in twelfth century Europe, involving romantic themes, physical attraction, and desire to be joined with the beloved
LIMERENCE: the experience of falling or being in love, involving uncertainty, arousal, and preoccupation with the other person
ROMANCE: an unrealistic or fantastic story, especially one about lovers
ROMANTIC LOVE: a form of affectional relationship based on interpersonal attraction, emotional attachment, and passion
TWO-FACTOR THEORY OF EMOTION: a theory that emotional experience has two components—physiological arousal and a cognitive label based on expectations or experience

Overview

Social scientists are relative latecomers to the study of love, intimacy, and personal relationships. Social psychologist Zick Rubin, in *Liking and Loving: An Invitation to Social Psychology* (1973), uses the metaphor of a party to describe the situation, noting that the party "had been going on for some time," with poets, playwrights, journalists, and a philosopher all in attendance before "finally, in the wee hours of the morning, the social psychologist arrived."

Today the multidisciplinary field of close relationships involves experts as diverse as counselors, sociologists, psychologists, and anthropologists, all concentrating on an exhaustive list of underresearched topics including friendship, social support, jealousy, relationship conflict, and divorce. Arguably the most popular topic with professionals and nonprofessionals alike is romantic love. Romantic love is one form of affectional bond between partners of choice; it is based on interpersonal attraction, emotional attachment, and passion. Historical evidence suggests that romantic love developed relatively late in Western civilization as a prerequisite for commitment and marriage. Earlier in history, and elsewhere in the world today, marriages have primarily been arranged on the basis of family background and economics rather than love.

Although the confluence of many events and concepts produced the medieval cult of romantic love, modern society, media, and literature often portray it as a unified and universal emotion. Social scientific research has failed to confirm that romantic or any other type of love is a form of instinctive affect (inborn emotion). Even the fondness of most parents for their children is learned through experience and socialization; the attachment of young children to caretakers is based primarily on need. These experiences affect and are affected by concepts of romantic love, but they are not synonymous with it.

Researchers have collected correlational data about real-life experiences as experimental data from laboratory studies in an effort to understand the nature of romantic love. One theory, proposed by sociologist Elaine Hatfield and psychologist Ellen Berscheid, argues that love is similar to other emotions as explained by the two-factor theory of emotion: Once arousal is triggered by any cause, the misconstrusion that the source of arousal is an attractive other may be sufficient to prompt associations of passionate love. In this sense, "love" is any emotional experience that one labels as such, which explains the enormous variability in the dynamics and endurance of love from one person to the next.

Another theory, proposed by social psychologist Rubin, views love not as an emotion but as an attitude whose components are attachment (need to be with the beloved), intimacy (close communication) and caring (promoting the other's welfare). In a similarly component-oriented view of love, Yale psychologist Robert Sternberg proposes that love is composed of three distinct and somewhat independent components—intimacy, passion, and commitment—and that different combinations of all or part of these three components are involved. Canadian psychologist John Alan Lee has proposed that there are six distinct styles of love, corresponding to a spectrum of emotions originally identified by the ancient Greeks: eros (erotic or romantic love); ludus (playful, game-playing love); storge (lasting friendship); mania (insecure, possessive attachment); pragma (practical, selective attraction); and agape (altruistic or selfless love). Finally, Hatfield and Berscheid's work has culminated in their conclusion that, in mate selection, people distinguish between two general experiences of love: passionate love, an aroused experience marked by intense emotional highs and lows; and companionate love, a more slowly developing, lasting attachment based on security and trust.

The "American ideal" of romantic love reveres individualism. Freedom to choose one's partner (on any basis, lasting or transitory) includes freedom to leave a relationship no longer considered satisfying. As Nathaniel Branden remarks about the United States in *The Psychology of Romantic Love* (1981), "Critics like to point out that the country in which romantic love found its best home is also the country with the highest divorce rate in the world." This seeming paradox—that romantic attraction is intensely arousing but is an inadequate basis for commitment in a relationship—has prompted research into the exact nature of romantic love. Modern sociological research has examined the assumptions and tensions of romantic myths, such as the idealistic expectation that "love conquers all" and the fear that becoming romantically committed can leave one vulnerable to the pains of unrequited love, exploitation, or abandonment. Social psychological research has focused on the components of romantic (and other types of) love rather than its social context. In these theories, love is characterized as an attitude, a complex of behavioral reactions, or a pattern of thoughts and feelings made of different components. Some theories distinguish love from friendship, while others consider friendship one of several forms of love.

In most typologies of love today, romantic love emerges as but one color in a broad spectrum of relationship experiences. Most theorists agree that romantic love is characterized by intensity, physical focus, volatility, and an emphasis on sexual expression. Researchers have also found that passion need not be short-lived or doomed, especially when friendship and intimacy are as well developed in a relationship as passion. Although the intense arousal of early romance may fade, it can be revitalized and relied upon indefinitely by partners who are committed, cooperative, and creative.

Applications

Early in the history of the concept, "romantic" became synonymous with "unrealistic." In the late 1950's, sociologist C. W. Hobart, contrasting romantic with realistic attitudes about love and relationships, found that among survey respondents, men were more romantic—less realistic in their thinking—than women. In contrast, when romance is defined as emotional and physical feelings of arousal stimulated by thoughts of another person, women rate themselves as more romantic than men. Gender differences continue to be a popular focus of research on romantic love.

In their studies of romantic love in the early 1970's, Hatfield and Berscheid sought an understanding of why so many modern marriages end in divorce. Most spouses claim that their primary reason for marrying is "love," yet the current divorce rate—estimated to be approximately one-half of all new first marriages—seems to indict love as an inadequate basis for marriage. Hatfield and Berscheid's conclusions that love is an idiosyncratic, personal labeling process seem to indicate that even if most couples agree on the importance of love, few would agree about the precise nature of love itself.

If love is a labeling process, then an individual's determination of what should be labeled as love is shaped by learning, including family socialization, education, and media influences. One application of this perspective may be found in the examination of individuals' earliest behavioral models and standards. Ethel S. Person, in her book *Dreams of Love and Fateful Encounters: The Power of Romantic Passion* (1988), presents a psychodynamic argument that most people's romantic ideals are based on unconscious childhood images of their parents. Social science writer Maggie Scarf (*Intimate Partners: Patterns in Love and Marriage*, 1987) similarly argues that lifelong patterns of mate selection and relationship repeat early family struggles of separation and individuation. Because every individual develops through a unique family environment, each person will acquire distinctive ideas and ideals about love, despite the cultural consensus portrayed in social behavior and media representations.

If, as some psychologists assert, love is a multimodal attitude rather than an emotion, then love is largely acquired through direct and observational learning and can be modified through similar strategies. This characterization of love as a "learned response" is implicit in Debora Phillips and Robert Judd's *How to Fall out of Love* (1978), which recommends a behavior modification program for "unlearning" the obsessive thinking and unstable emotional patterns of a disappointing romantic experience.

Much love research has focused on the experience of disappointed or victimized lovers. Social scientist Dorothy Tennov found it helpful to distinguish between more stable forms of romantic love and the sometimes-ecstatic, sometimes-devastating experience of falling or being "in love" by coining the term "limerence" to describe the latter state (*Love and Limerence: The Experience of Being in Love*, New York: Stein and Day, 1979). Tennov and other researchers have observed that disappointment in romantic love is often associated with measurable psychological and physical symptoms, which might be attributable to body chemistry changes induced by the perception of relationship loss. A better understanding of how people define, seek, and experience romantic love can support more effective medical and psychotherapeutic treatments of such loss-related disorders as depression.

Romantic love research has been more optimistically applied in studying relationship maintenance. Romantic love is a much promoted and greatly desired experience, considered by most people in Western culture to be essential to relationship commitment and marriage. Research examining the nature of romantic expectations suggests that, in order to resolve conflicts and survive difficulties, couples may wish to develop practices associated with relationship longevity. Effective strategies and qualities include shared history, time, and interests; effective communication; commitment to the relationship; empathy and perspective-taking; humor and playfulness; and each individual's cultivation of friendships and interests outside the relationship.

Context

Romance originally developed as a tradition in Western literature and folk culture. Prior to their full development in twelfth century Europe, romantic stories and songs were more likely to celebrate stories of the heroic quest. The earliest analogues to medieval ballads of passionate love were ancient Greek narrative works, usually presenting a theme of lovers who are separated and reunited only after a series of adventures. The ancient Roman poet Ovid characterized love as an obsessive affliction.

In twelfth century England, the word "romance" had come to connote an entertaiment unconnected with reality, particularly a story about the passions and pains of love. Inspired by heroic tales of the Crusades, troubadours brought their romantic songs to the French and English courts. Their ballads often incorporated local myths, usually modifying the message by downplaying the gory detail and favoring the love story. The ideal of romantic love, as celebrated in courtly songs, gossip, and parodies, was to experience a consuming passion for devotion itself—not necessarily marriage or sexual consummation with one's beloved. It is important to understand that romantic love, as celebrated by the ruling classes in medieval Europe, was not viewed as a reasonable or acceptable basis for mate selection and marriage. The basis for pair-bonding had always been primarily economic. Overly individualistic concerns could undermine group or societal interests, and so possible appropriate partners were considered interchangeably attractive. The best that prospective spouses could hope for was that their guardians would arrange a match with a partner who proved to be compatible.

In the eighteenth century, during the era of the Enlightenment, attitudes expanded to accept the view that passionate love could be consistent with reason and intellect. Nevertheless, the late-eighteenth century European revival of Romanticism in literature (as in Sir Walter Scott's *Ivanhoe*) harkened to the earlier sense of romance as unrealistic, fantastic, or doomed. With the Industrial Revolution and the rise of capitalism in the West in the nineteenth century, notions of individuality and personal freedom came to include the freedom to choose marriage partners. By the twentieth century, the idea was becoming widespread in the Western world. Denis de Rougement, author of *Love in the Western World* (1940), wrote that the freedom of mate selection, particularly as practiced in the New World, was a "pathological experiment" because marriage was then based on "romance, which is a passing fancy."

In the United States, romantic love is widely seen as the only truly valid reason for marriage. American culture extols and idealizes romance in its television programs, motion pictures, and popular songs. Yet it has been pointed out that romantic love usually does not last beyond the first year or so of marriage because, in many ways, romantic love is not suited to the demands and day-to-day realities of married life. Romance must evolve into other forms of love and caring for a marriage to thrive.

Bibliography

Baumeister, Roy F., and Sara R. Wotman. *Breaking Hearts: The Two Sides of Unrequited Love*. New York: Guilford Press, 1992. The authors summarize their findings after numerous interviews and surveys of survivors of unrequited love, both the would-be lovers and the unwilling targets of their attentions. A fascinating, informative, and well-written volume.

Branden, Nathaniel. *The Psychology of Romantic Love*. New York: Bantam Books, 1981. This extremely reader-friendly review of some of the psychological dynamics and personal benefits of romantic love begins with a fascinating history of the subject, from the literature of courtly love to the challenges of modern marriage and divorce.

Hatfield, Elaine, and Richard L. Rapson. *Love, Sex, and Intimacy: Their Psychology, Biology, and History*. New York: HarperCollins, 1993. A lively review of what is revealed by research into all aspects of the human experience of love by a social psychologist and her husband, a historian.

Hatfield, Elaine, and G. William Walster. *A New Look at Love*. Reading, Mass.: Addison-Wesley, 1978. One of the first and most reader-friendly text treatments of

social scientific research and theory focusing on "the most elusive of all emotions."
Sternberg, Robert J. *The Triangle of Love: Intimacy, Passion, Commitment.* New York:
Basic Books, 1988. Yale psychologist Sternberg outlines his "triarchic theory" that
all forms of love are built of three related but distinct components, which explains
the variability and complexity of experiences commonly described simply as
"love."

Ann L. Weber

Cross-References

Arranged Marriages, 134; Causes of Divorce, 554; Exchange in Social Interaction, 715; Extramarital Sex, 727; The Family: Functionalist versus Conflict Theory Views, 739; Types of Marriage, 1120; Nuclear and Extended Families, 1303; Remarriage and "Reconstituted" Families, 1629.

RUMORS AND URBAN LEGENDS

Type of sociology: Collective behavior and social movements
Field of study: Cultural variation and change

Rumors and urban legends are studied by both folklorists and sociologists. Either perspective offers interesting and productive viewpoints from which to analyze their content, structure, performance, and dissemination as cultural and social phenomena.

Principal terms

COMMUNAL RE-CREATION: the process via which a group absorbs and assimilates new material into its oral tradition

DISSEMINATION: the process by which rumors and legends spread

FOLKLORE: the oral transmissions that endure and become part of a cultural tradition

LEGENDS: narratives presented as truth that relate to relatively recent times rather than to the distant past

RUMORS: oral transmissions similar to legends but lacking formalized structure and plot development

Overview

Urban legends—or urban belief tales, as they are sometimes called—are narrative accounts of allegedly true, but completely fallacious, events. They are usually passed on from storyteller to listener as factual accounts, and their source is often attested to be some reliable, close acquaintance, usually a friend or relative who either witnessed the event or heard of it directly from the people involved. Sometimes the news media is credited as the source, further adding support to claims of authenticity. The story frequently has an ironic or supernatural twist at the end.

Most of the preceding characteristics apply to rumors as well. Rumors are very similar to urban legends in content. Their structure, however, is not quite as formalized as that of legends. While an urban legend is a complete story with a fully developed plot, transmitted in narrative form, a rumor's plot is generally less developed. The supernatural or ironic ending is not necessarily present in a rumor. Another difference lies in their respective abilities to endure through time. Although urban legends undergo many surface changes in their life spans, the core of their meaning—the central motif or the plot of the narrative—remains relatively unchanged through time, and they continue to circulate for many years. In contrast, rumors are more short-lived and generally circulate for only a few weeks before they dissipate.

For example, in the story of "the vanishing hitchhiker," a hitchhiker on a lonely road gets a ride from a considerate driver. The driver later discovers that the hitchhiker is really a ghost. Specific details and elaborations in the story vary. Sometimes the ghost is met at a party or nightclub. Sometimes the ghost leaves behind an item—a purse or a scarf, perhaps—that reveals her or his identity. Sometimes the driver visits the house where the ghost asked to be taken and recognizes the hitchhiker from a family portrait. Elements of the "disappearing ghost" story have been found in narratives dating as far back as the late nineteenth century. Details in the story have changed over the years: Early stories mention horse-driven vehicles, for example, while later versions incorporate automobiles. Over the years, the story has taken on many other different elements as well. The central theme of the story, however, a nonmalevolent, disappearing ghost, persists in all variants.

Another difference between rumors and urban legends is that, while rumors are localized, a particular urban legend may be found, in several different forms, over a much larger geographic area. The vanishing hitchhiker narrative, for example, can be found throughout several countries, including the United States, Britain, and Canada.

Generally speaking, the time and space considerations that qualify rumors and urban legends are viewed differently by folklorists and sociologists. For folklorists, persistence through time and space is an essential quality of an urban legend. Such oral narratives must prove their ability to endure and become part of a culture's tradition in order to be considered a legend. Once the endurance of a narrative has been proved, the next step in its analysis is to examine its components. Folklorists isolate the stable, underlying motifs—the constants that persist with time and which may be rooted in earlier legends. The stable elements are usually the basic plot elements. They also take note of the variants—how each of these stories with a common, central meaning or motif varies through time or geography. Like all legends, urban legends develop two kinds of variations. First, they adapt to local particularities and modern conditions. In other words, they accommodate themselves so that they remain applicable and appropriate. They also accumulate additional elements as they circulate; new characters, objects, or plot twists are added, as are the performer's or storyteller's comments and explanations. Listeners adopt these new elements and incorporate them when they retell the legend. This phenomenon is referred to as communal re-creation; it describes the process by which a community or folk group absorbs and assimilates new material into its oral culture. As a result, although such narratives are in general somewhat stereotyped and formalized, the details are always fluid and changing.

Sociologists, on the other hand, see rumors and urban legends as unique examples of group behavior, as aspects of a much larger system of interpretation. Either can be studied as collective behavior. In addition, a legend, because of its universality and proven ability to last from generation to generation, opens itself to analysis from a larger, more global standpoint. This enables sociologists or folklorists to hypothesize about an entire culture or society. By virtue of its brief lifespan and its limited geographic distribution, a rumor reveals things about only a specific section of the population. As sociologist Dan E. Miller states in " 'Snakes in the Greens' and Rumor in the Innercity" (1992), "In this sense urban legends are associated with social movements as rumors are associated with collective behavior."

Applications

Analyzing the content of rumors and urban legends can reveal a culture or a social group's fears and value systems. All cultural data has meaning and relates to other aspects of society and tradition. The themes and elements found in rumors and legends, together with information about the storytellers, the listeners, and the cultural influences and institutions that shape their ideologies, may divulge much about the culture that produces the stories and its worldview.

For a rumor or legend to survive, its content must be relevant to the people who disseminate it. In his study of commercial rumors, Fredrick Koenig offers an especially appropriate analogy. He compares a rumor to a spark and the people who hear it to either cement or dry grass. A rumor may or may not "catch fire." Whether or not an alleged truth becomes a rumor depends entirely on its relevance to the social group in which it circulates. The geographical region it covers will therefore be directly proportional to the universality of its relevance. A conspiracy rumor (for example, that a particular business donates a portion of its profits to the Church of Satan) will circulate in a smaller population sample than a contamination rumor (that there is horse meat in hamburgers). Health and cleanliness are more universal concerns than the Satanic church and its financial situation. The former appeals to a more widespread population; the latter would be of more concern to certain Christian groups.

Legends, because they are complete, developed narratives, may demonstrate relevance and meaning on two levels: They may contain primary and secondary messages. Rumors, on the other hand, do not usually contain enough detailed information to be analyzed beyond the level of their primary message. Primary messages are generally straightforward cautions or statements; they are the obvious themes or morals of the narrative. One of the most common primary messages centers on contamination: rats fried along with chicken in a fast-food restaurant; mice in soda cans; snakes nestled in rugs, coat linings, or supermarket produce; or sewer-dwelling albino alligators. Each theme places a fearsome object in an undesirable context. Such stories demonstrate that members of industrial urban societies are generally concerned with issues of hygiene and safety. The fact that the stories continue to spread reveals much about a society's values and expectations about such matters. The fact that they are believed may show that the members of that society do not completely trust standard health and safety regulations.

Secondary messages are less obvious. They are suggested metaphorically or symbolically rather than directly stated, and they may provide deeper criticisms of social behavior. An example of secondary messages can be demonstrated through analysis of a variant of the "lovers' lane murderer" horror classic. Two teenagers out on a date park in an isolated area and discover (usually through a radio broadcast) that a homicidal maniac has escaped. The killer has a steel hook for a hand, which he uses to murder his victims. They leave immediately. The boy brings the girl to her house, and they discover a hook hanging from the car door. In some versions, the boy angrily speeds away when the girl insists upon leaving. In this case, the secondary message would imply certain social expectations of men and women with regard to dating. Whether a social group or culture questions the reasoning behind his response—or whether the storyteller adds or omits this data—can reveal cultural or social assumptions on men's and women's behavior.

Other elements may also provide information on a society's expectations, or beliefs. Even the seemingly nonessential components of a rumor or legend can be used to draw conclusions about the societies in which they circulate. For example, many of these stories refer to an automobile, which may or may not be an essential plot element. Regardless of whether the automobile is central to the plot, such an element would not appear in the rumors or legends of a society that did not rely so heavily on this type of transportation. In addition to the revelations they offer about a group or a society's values, rumors and urban legends provide a means of understanding the relationships between storytellers and listeners. More than a simple exchange of information takes place when people share these narratives. Rumors and legends are never random in their dissemination. Examination of the social networks and motives behind these exchanges may provide understanding of the functions they serve for the group in which they circulate.

In a more specific sense, rumors and legends can be interpreted within the context of conversations and social interactions. For example, sociologists and folklorists might consider the context in which these exchanges occur, examining who tells the rumor or legend and to whom, and for what purpose (for example, entertainment, warning, or social commentary). One example is the "razor blade in the apple" warning, which is very situation-specific. Generally speaking, it is given at a certain time of the year (Halloween) and almost always by an adult to a child. From this perspective, it may be noteworthy that the text is repeated only in highly specific circumstances.

Context

Legends and rumors can be amusing diversions, embellishments within the framework of a conversation. On this level, they may serve as conversation starters or conversation directors. In this case, participants share a common concern and react to it similarly, thereby establishing the tone and direction of the conversation. An account of slashers who hide in the back seats of cars and wait for their victims to drive off, for example, may serve as a prelude to a general discussion of crime or a more directed criticism of security. The story of the robber who tried to smuggle a frozen chicken out of the supermarket by hiding it under his hat and fainted in the checkout line when his brain froze could do the same. On the other hand, such a story may function as nothing more than a humorous anecdote or an interesting bit of information. A rumor of a baby-sitter on drugs who roasted the baby instead of the turkey can serve as a cautionary tale and may precede a longer discussion or warning of similar dangers. In each case, the rumor or legend is a conversation tool, used by the speaker to manipulate the conversation along a specific path.

Aside from the conversational value it possesses, a legend or rumor must fill some social or cultural need if it is to be retained and repeated. In the first place, rumors and legends preserve and validate the identity of the groups that circulate them. They may accomplish this by providing the group with a common enemy, thus reinforcing internal stability. Furthermore, through their implied warnings or criticisms, rumors and legends delineate and reinforce a group's standard, accepted ideologies. They thereby function as didactic narratives—carriers and preservers of the group's opinions and convictions. In addition to strengthening the group as a unit, rumors and legends may reinforce the members' interpersonal relationships by confirming or reiterating common beliefs. In all these cases, rumors and legends may be said to unify members of a group, society, or culture.

Legends in general have always functioned as attempts to explain exceptional, uncommon occurrences. To some extent this is true for modern urban legends as well. Their ironic or supernatural endings remind people that anything is possible, even in the industrial, mechanized world. Fate, justice, and luck happen as they will, in spite of human effort, science, or logic. Certainly, rumors and legends that focus on humiliating, frightening, or gruesome events appeal to listeners' morbid curiosities and sensationalistic predispositions. More important, however, they present both teller and listener with the opportunity to confront and understand issues with which they are not entirely comfortable.

Bibliography

Brunvand, Jan Harold. *The Baby Train and Other Lusty Urban Legends*. New York: W. W. Norton, 1993. Brunvand has published a series of widely read books on urban legends, and his work has been influential in the field. This book includes a useful type index of urban legends.

_____ . *The Vanishing Hitchhiker*. New York: W. W. Norton, 1981. This is the first of Brunvand's collections and analyses of urban legends. Brunvand groups these narratives into seven chapters, categorizing them according to subject matter: "The Classic Automobile Legends"; " 'The Hook' and Other Teenage Horrors"; "Dreadful Contaminations"; "Purloined Corpses and Fear of the Dead"; "Dalliance, Nudity, and Nightmares"; "Business Ripoffs: Two Favorite Media Legends"; and "Urban Legends in the Making." Throughout the text, Brunvand draws conclusions on the meanings behind the stories. His preface, chapter 1 ("New Legends for Old"), and the afterword also provide information helpful in understanding urban legends.

Fine, Gary Alan. "The City as a Folklore Generator: Legends in the Metropolis." *Urban Resources* 4 (Spring, 1987): 3-6, 61. Fine's article examines four popular urban legends in an attempt to show how each of them demonstrates social and cultural characteristics particular to urban life. Fine also considers reasons behind their development.

Koenig, Fredrick. *Rumor in the Marketplace: The Social Psychology of Commercial Hearsay*. Dover, Mass.: Auburn House, 1985. Koenig focuses particularly on the rumors that attack businesses and corporations or their products. Koenig examines how these rumors affect the businesses they target and investigates the reasons for their development. He also examines their dissemination, including the patterns or networks of oral communication.

Miller, Dan E. " 'Snakes in the Greens' and Rumor in the Innercity." *The Social Sci-*

ence Journal 29, no. 4 (1992): 381-393. Miller traces the development of a rumor as it moves through different communities and social groups. He examines the process of rumor transmission—the social networks that operate in such a process. He also investigates the function of the rumor in each particular situation and the attitudes of teller and listener.

Sanoff, Alvin P. "How a Tale Becomes 'An Urban Legend.'" *U.S. News & World Report* 101 (September 22, 1986): 82. A very short but helpful discussion, this article offers examples and explanations of urban legends. It uses as its source Jan Harold Brunvand's 1986 work *The Mexican Pet: More "New" Urban Legends and Some Old Favorites*.

Wolkomir, Richard. "If Those Cobras Don't Get You, the Alligators Will." *Smithsonian* 23 (November, 1992): 166-173. The article cites several examples of the most common urban legends and discusses the possible reasons for their development. Wolkomir bases his article on Jan Harold Brunvand's series of urban legend books and includes information on Brunvand's life and studies.

William Nelles
Stephanie Pierrotti

Cross-References

Collective Behavior, 291; Crowds and Crowd Dynamics, 393; Fads, Fashions, and Crazes, 733; Mass Hysteria, 1134; Mobs, Riots, and Panics, 1226; Social Movements, 1826.

RURAL SOCIETIES

Type of sociology: Urban and rural life

Rural society refers to groups of people who live in sparsely populated and sometimes isolated areas of the world. Rural sociology, the study of rural society, developed in the United States in the 1880's in response to the needs of rural peoples.

Principal terms
DEPOPULATION: decrease in rural population because of mechanization in agricultural production and specialization in industry
ETHNICITY: in rural societies, group differences and social boundaries recognized by members of a group
ETHNOS: a group of people sharing a relatively stable language and culture within a historically established space and recognizing, through self-awareness, their difference from similar groups
REPOPULATION: the migration of urban retired people into rural areas, where they buy homes, thereby creating an aging, middle-class population
RURAL: general reference to areas of low population density and small settlements; sometimes defined by other economic, geographic, political, and social criteria
RURAL SOCIOLOGY: the systematic study of rural society and the knowledge obtained from that study; currently, an international discipline

Overview

Rural society, in its most general sense, refers to sparsely settled, usually agricultural, communities. Within such communities, the inhabitants are often isolated from other rural societies and from urban societies by a combination of custom, geography, history, culture, and climate.

According to sociologists T. Lynn Smith and Paul E. Zopf, Jr., in *Principles of Inductive Rural Sociology* (1970), the study of rural societies, as a part of rural sociology, was introduced into U.S. universities in the 1880's and 1890's by researchers such as George E. Vincent and Charles R. Henderson at the University of Chicago and Frank H. Giddings at Columbia University. During this time, sociologist Edward Alsworth Ross observed what he called "folk depletion"—depopulation of rural areas because of industrialization. Consequently, Ross and others developed a humanitarian interest in improving the quality of rural life. By the turn of the century, courses in rural social problems were offered at the University of Chicago, the University of Michigan, Michigan State College, and the University of North Dakota.

On August 10, 1908, as a result of the interest stimulated in the problems of rural society, President Theodore Roosevelt formed the Commission on Country Life. In part as a result of the activity of this commission, in 1916, when George E. Vincent was president of the American Sociological Society, the selected theme for the eleventh annual convention was "The Sociology of Rural Life." During this same decade, the first textbook of rural sociology was published—John M. Gillette's *Constructive Rural Sociology* (1913).

During the years leading up to World War II, interest in rural societies mushroomed. In the United States, the government funded research on rural societies and developed agricultural experimentation stations and agricultural colleges. By the onset of World War II, research had become international, mainly through clergy, anthropologists, and sociologists, but the main international movement began after World War II.

Between 1945 and 1970, rural sociology moved into more than one hundred countries, and many sociologists researched rural society in several countries. Most of the work presented much information, but the information lacked sufficient organization to be accessible. Though pre-World War II sociologists, such as Dwight Sanderson, in his *Rural Sociology and Rural Social Organization* (1942), had tried to organize rural sociology, much more needed to be done, especially as the discipline became international. Until 1970, with the publication of *Principles of Inductive Rural Sociology*, by T. Lynn Smith and Paul E. Zopf, Jr., little was done to meet this need.

Smith and Zopf, expanding upon the work of earlier sociologists, enumerated nine significant sociological areas of difference between rural and urban societies: occupation, size of community, population density, environment (physical, biological, and sociocultural), degree of social differentiation, degree of social stratification, degree of social mobility, social interaction, and social solidarity. They concluded that, in rural societies, lesser degrees of social differentiation and social stratification exist than exist in urban areas and that social mobility and social interaction were also restricted. They determined that social solidarity, or community cohesion, among rural inhabitants was based on similarities but that among urban inhabitants it was based on contractual relationships.

Part of Smith and Zopf's attempt to organize rural sociology involved comparative sociology. In looking at types of settlements, for example, they drew models from Senegal, Africa; Peru; Germany; Mormon villages; Nahalal, Israel; and farming communities in Iowa and Louisiana. From there, they compared advantages and disadvantages of the various types of settlements, acknowledging that not all types of settlements have been identified.

Guy M. Robinson, in *Conflict and Change in the Countryside: Rural Society, Economy, and Planning in the Developed World* (1990), gives a post-1945 view of twenty-three "developed" rural societies that debunks pastoral myths of an unchanging, rustic environment. He approaches his analysis by using the metaphors of change and conflict and explores the forces shaping rural societies at the end of the twentieth century. Acknowledging different criteria for determining rural populations (for example, in Switzerland, communities of 10,000 or fewer people are considered rural, and in Norway, communities of 200 or fewer are considered rural), Robinson focuses the rural population by determining, first, the percentage that is economically active in agriculture. Using this criterion, rural population ranges from 25.9 percent in Greece to 2.2 percent in Belgium and Luxembourg. According to Robinson's figures, the United States has 3.1 percent of its population economically active in agriculture but 26.3 percent living in rural societies.

As Robinson and others point out, however, the line between rural and urban cannot easily be drawn. While one can look generally to definitions that include low population density and small settlements, both "low" and "small" are defined differently from context to context. Even once a line is drawn, for purposes of research, say, for example, at villages of 200 or fewer, the village of 287 may be more "rural" in its economic, political, and social patterns than a village of 123 people. Other definitions involve distance between houses or even self-identification of the population as rural. Still other definitions involve relying on numbers of people entering or leaving areas.

Study of rural "society," as opposed to rural "societies," in itself poses a problem of definition. For example, among rural peoples are loggers, farmers, fishers, miners, and diversified groups. Rural society is also broken into other groups by race, gender, age, education, and religion. Within such groups, such as religious and educational constructs, other rural societies emerge. Rural societies have many subgroups based on social, political, cultural, and economic conflicts. For example, U.S. farmers may belong to the Grange, Farmers' Union, Farm Bureau, or National Farm Organization. Sometimes towns of two thousand people have as many as ten churches, each with its own social organizations and events. Smith and Zopf observe that sometimes competition arises among churches, and, at other times, churches and schools compete as community centers. Finally, some rural societies are separated by combinations of differences in politics and culture, as are the Indian tribes on reservations in the United States.

Rural sociologists have the challenge of exploring these differences in rural societies and helping people adjust to changes that occur when rural and urban society merge in rural areas.

Applications

In the study of rural societies in the late twentieth century, rural sociologists are integrating earlier approaches with international case studies. Typical of such applications are Lucy E. Creevey's collection of sociological essays *Women Farmers in Africa: Rural Development in Mali and the Sahel* (1986), Tadashi Fukutake's *Japanese Rural Society* (1967), Ranjana Kumari, Renuka Singh, and Anju Dubey's *Growing Up in Rural India: Problems and Needs of Adolescent Girls* (1990), and Tamara Dragadze's *Rural Families in Soviet Georgia: A Case Study in Ratcha Province* (1988).

Lucy Creevey's work with women farmers in Africa, like the work done earlier in the twentieth century, springs from several individuals who presented papers at a workshop for rural women. This research, motivated by humanitarian impulses, sought to identify specific problems faced by this faction of a rural society and to solve those problems. Creevey, in her introduction, speaks of the "pervasive bias . . . against the technology and needs of rural women," but, as she herself recognizes, the workshop is not linked to a system that would illuminate a course of action. She notes that the researchers have no "unified set of recommendations" and "no common view of how to confront the problems" they identified. In a study of Japanese rural society, Fukutake takes a political and sociological approach to exploring the exploitation of Japanese farmers. Fukutake's farm research, like Creevey's, is locked into the specific political context of the country. The information in the studies interlocks, but readers are left to make the comparisons. Researching such studies, Smith and Zopf's 1970 call for further systems and organization of information still holds.

Another typical late twentieth century application of rural sociology to rural society is Kumari, Singh, and Dubey's 1990 study *Growing Up in Rural India: Problems and Needs of Adolescent Girls*. Kumari, Singh, and Dubey explore Indian society from the perspectives of age and gender, including discussions of educational discrimination, early marriage and pregnancy, maternal and infant mortality, divorce, health care, and role responsibilities. These discussions are given a sociological context by establishing a sociodemographic profile of the villages in which the girls live—Delhi, Bharatpur, and Haunpur—and by sketching a profile of religious attitudes and influences. For example, some girls still quite strongly felt the restrictions of impurity during menstruation, attitudes that originated in early religion and were reiterated in Hindu laws. These same religious traditions dictated the early marriages of Indian girls. The father who did not find a marriage partner for his sexually mature daughter was considered guilty, by religious tenets, of the "sin of embryo murder." Consequently, in this rural society, marriages of girls eight to twelve years old occurred, and marriages of girls fifteen to sixteen years old were fairly common. The study revealed, not surprisingly, a fairly low educational level, with much illiteracy. Kumari, Singh, and Dubey conclude their work with a call to action, suggesting a program that could improve the quality of life for rural girls in India.

Tamara Dragadze, in applying principles of rural sociology to her study *Rural Families in Soviet Georgia: A Case Study in Ratcha Province*, explores how a rural society held its character despite the influence of the larger Soviet economic, political, and ideological system in which it was embedded, prior to the disintegration of the Soviet Union. For the study, which extended over several years, Dragadze went to Ratcha Province in northwestern Georgia to observe a rural society, including three villages—Likheti, Abari, and Uravi.

The people of the area identified themselves by province as well as by village. They considered those who lived within Ratcha Province as desirable mates for marriage, generally believing that Ratchuelians are honest, straightforward, and polite and that their land is more "picturesque" than land elsewhere. (Dragadze observes that outsiders joked that the Ratchuelians were "slow-witted.") The people of Ratcha Province, like Georgians in general, were attached to their area. At the time of Dragadze's study, 96.5 percent of all Georgians lived in Georgia.

Dragadze approaches rural society in Ratcha Province as an ethnic area, where people have their own ethnos and call themselves Ratchuelians. In exploring this rural society, Dragadze begins at the local level, moves to the provincial level, and then proceeds to the Soviet context. In the context of rural societies, she shows similarities between the Abari settlement and several Mediterranean peasant societies, particularly resemblances in familial structure.

Dragadze, in her ethnographic account of rural society in Soviet Georgia, demonstrates a "persistence of traditional values and structures despite expectations of radical change under Soviet rule." Still, she identifies changes over decades and realizes that political and economic changes will continue to influence these rural societies. Sociologists and anthropologists of rural society will have the task of studying further changes that result from later restructuring of Soviet societies after the dissolution of the Soviet Union.

Context

Rural sociology, the study of rural society, began in the last two decades of the nineteenth century, primarily in the United States. In the years before World War II, rural sociologists used mostly geographical and historical approaches to gather data from farming areas in the United States.

Modern study of rural society is international and includes case studies, as well as comparative sociology. Particularly in the study of rural society in the United States, sociologists are setting new goals. Sociologists D. A. Dillman and D. J. Hobbs, for example, in *Rural Society in the United States: Issues for the 1980s* (1982), aspired to describe rural society, to approach issues of rural society from an environmental perspective, to explore the effects of rural change, and to find methods of resolving conflicts in rural society. They, like other rural sociologists, have become concerned with assisting rural societies in solving problems.

The study of rural society is not, however, the exclusive domain of rural sociologists. Psychologists, anthropologists, political scientists, economists, and historians are also among those who study rural society. (For an introductory discussion of the psychology of rural society in the United States, see *Rural Psychology*, 1983, edited by Alan W. Childs and Gary B. Melton.)

In the context of modern rural sociology, sociologists are exploring diverse perspectives within specific societies, such as the study of adolescent girls in India and the studies of women farmers in Africa, mentioned earlier. Another such study is Rachel Ann Rosenfeld's *Farm Women: Work, Farm, and Family in the United States* (1985), in which Rosenfeld, a professor of sociology, researches farm and ranch women in the United States, both those women who own farms and ranches and those who work with their spouses. Rosenfeld overlays the study of rural society with a feminist perspective, bringing new sociological information to the surface.

In the late twentieth century, keeping current becomes increasingly important as rural societies meet more rapid and dramatic changes. As Guy M. Robinson contends, the urban middle-class shift to rural areas has brought "new forms of impoverishment for some rural dwellers," and, in many cases, the shift has meant a "destruction of the isolation and peace that for many was the chief quality of the rural areas." Smith and Zopf contend that migration in rural society needs to be studied carefully not only for farm productivity but also for the effects on cities in areas of housing, school, health care, and employment. They conclude that, despite a "complicated network of social problems" in rural societies, "life in the urban centers, although often harsh and frustrating, on the whole presents migrants with more in the way of material comforts than were to be had in the rural countryside." They observe that in every country in the world there is a disparity in rural education and that this disparity impedes an increasingly necessary social mobility.

At the end of the twentieth century, rural sociologists are working on organizing and developing systems for comprehending the changes that are taking place in many rural societies. They are studying the blendings of cultures, both assimilation and acculturation, and looking at the general and specific effects of social mobility. As rural and urban societies enmesh, sociologists have noted a decline in the extended family system, a decrease in the strength of traditional behavioral norms, an increased division of labor, a decrease in political power for rural inhabitants, a move for equal quality of life, a decrease in the ability of rural parents to acculturate children to rural society, and an increase in the power of outside influences.

Bibliography

Childs, Alan W., and Gary B. Melton, eds. *Rural Psychology*. New York: Plenum Press, 1983. This exploration of rural psychology, 442 pages with an index, is written by specialists on various topics. The more illuminating discussions examine rural social institutions, aging in rural society, linguistic development in rural subcultures, and religious fundamentalism in rural society.

Creevey, Lucy E., ed. *Women Farmers in Africa: Rural Development in Mali and the Sahel*. Syracuse, N.Y.: Syracuse University Press, 1986. Creevey's book, 212 pages with photographs and an index, examines women in rural African societies and analyzes their roles within these societies. Creevey focuses both on farm productivity and on developing programs to assist these women.

Dragadze, Tamara. *Rural Families in Soviet Georgia: A Case Study in Ratcha Province*. New York: Routledge & Kegan Paul, 1988. Dragadze's case study, 226 pages with graphics and an index, introduces the Georgian villager in the Soviet context. Within the rural society, she focuses on domestic units, marriage, and the morality of age, gender, and kin distinctions.

Fukutake, Tadashi. *Japanese Rural Society*. Translated by R. P. Dore. New York: Oxford University Press, 1967. Fukutake's book, 230 pages with photographs and an index, begins with a historical overview of rural society in Japan and moves toward family structures and kinship relations in rural areas. Particularly interesting are his views on the social characteristics and political attitudes of rural Japanese societies.

Kumari, Ranjana, Renuka Singh, and Anju Dubey. *Growing Up in Rural India: Problems and Needs of Adolescent Girls*. New Delhi, India: Radiant, 1990. This book, 124 pages with graphics and an index, reports the authors' research on adolescent girls in rural Indian society. Particularly useful in understanding rural sociology are the sections on early marriage, health work roles, and the aspirations of the girls.

Robinson, Guy M. *Conflict and Change in the Countryside: Rural Society, Economy, and Planning in the Developed World.* New York: Belhaven Press, 1990. Robinson's book, 482 pages with extensive graphics and an index, begins with a 129-page discussion of rural society in twenty-three "developed" countries. His approach adds much to rural sociology in that he explores both the depopulation of rural areas and the urbanization of rural communities.

Rosenfeld, Rachel Ann. *Farm Women: Work, Farm, and Family in the United States.* Chapel Hill: University of North Carolina Press, 1985. Rosenfeld focuses on the position of women in rural society. The book, 354 pages with graphics and an index, includes discussions of women's roles in farm work, off-farm employment, and farm and household decision making. Rosenfeld devotes a full chapter to the self-perceptions of farm women. Includes a list of tables and figures and two sets of surveys.

Smith, T. Lynn, and Paul E. Zopf, Jr. *Principles of Inductive Rural Sociology.* Philadelphia: F. A. Davis, 1970. A revision of Smith's 1940 work, this book, 558 pages with illustrations and both an author and a source index, explores rural society from the perspectives of social ecology, competition and conflict, cooperation, organization, and structure. The authors, whose focus is international, also include a lengthy section on "Social Processes in Rural Society."

Carol Franks

Cross-References

Agrarian Economic Systems, 60; The Agricultural Revolution, 67; Hunting and Gathering Economic Systems, 909; The Industrial Revolution and Mass Production, 946; Industrial Societies, 953; The Urban Underclass and the Rural Poor, 2122; Urbanization, 2129.

SAMPLES AND SAMPLING TECHNIQUES

Type of sociology: Sociological research
Field of study: Basic concepts

A sample is a portion of a population. Based on scientific sampling techniques, a sample is an accurate representation of the larger population, and study findings in the sample can be extended to the population.

Principal terms

BIAS: the deviation of the expected value of a statistical estimate from the true value for some measured quantity

ELEMENT: the basic unit of a population, such as an individual, household, segment, or social organization, for which information is sought

MUTUALLY EXCLUSIVE: a situation in which, if outcomes 1 and 2 are mutually exclusive, and 1 occurs, then 2 logically cannot occur

POPULATION: the entire collection of elements of a specific type defined over a given space and time

SAMPLE: a portion of all the elements in a population that is used to obtain information about the entire population

SAMPLE SIZE: the number of population elements contained in a sample

SAMPLING: the process of selecting a sample from an existing population

SAMPLING FRAME: the actual list of sampling units from which the sample, or some stage of the sample, is selected

SAMPLING UNIT: an element or a set of elements considered for selection in some stage of sampling

TARGET POPULATION AND SAMPLE POPULATION: the former is the population about which information is desired, while the latter is the population to be sampled

Overview

Sampling is the process of selecting a representative group from a larger population for the purpose of providing statistical information on the nature of the larger population. Sampling is employed in almost every area of research in social science and business.

Sampling has several advantages over collecting information on every member of a population, a process called a census or complete enumeration. First, a sample can provide useful information at a much lower cost than a complete enumeration. Second, data can be collected and summarized much more quickly with a sample; therefore, data from a sample are usually more up to date than data obtained from a complete enumeration. Third, sampling can allow resources to be directed to hire personnel better qualified, give intensive training to interviewers, improve supervision of both the field work and data management processes. Consequently, the sample may provide more accurate data than complete enumeration. Finally, by virtue of its flexibility and adaptability, sampling has greater scope regarding the variety of information accessible.

Moreover, sampling is the only option in some situations. Because investigation of product quality, such as the strength of construction materials, often requires the destruction of the product itself, only a sample can be tested. Measuring air pollution is an extreme example of a situation in which complete enumeration is unattainable, because of the target population's infinite size.

Approaches to sampling, or selecting elements from a population, fall into two broad categories: nonprobability (nonrandom) sampling and probability (random) sampling. With nonprobability sampling, the chance of being selected is unknown. Methods for nonprobability sampling include convenience sampling, judgment sampling, and quota sampling. All nonprobability samples are potentially biased by nonrepresentative selection. With probability or random sampling, each element has a known chance of being selected from the population. Probability sampling avoids selection bias and permits effective statistical generalization from sample to population. In this article, probability sampling methods are emphasized.

In probability sampling, a sample is selected from a sampling frame, or list of sampling units. Basic probability sampling techniques include simple random, systematic, stratified, and cluster sampling. Simple random sampling is the most basic probability sampling method. In this method, each element of the population has an equal chance of being selected, much as a coin has equal probability of landing on heads or tails. Systematic sampling selects elements at even intervals, such as every fifth house on a street, often beginning with a randomly selected element. Stratified sampling divides a population into mutually exclusive groups, or strata, each of which is relatively homogeneous, and then a simple random sample is selected from each stratum. Finally, the separate simple random samples are combined. Cluster sampling divides a population into clusters, such as dividing a city into neighborhoods. A smaller number of clusters is then selected at random, with all members of a selected cluster included in the sample.

An important variation of clustering is called two-stage sampling. In many situations, particularly when the target population is very large, such as the population of a nation, a list of clusters is the only available sampling frame. Even if the list of every element of a population were available, it would be very expensive to conduct a single-stage random sample. In order to concentrate location of selected population elements, and thereby reduce the travel expenses of conducting interviews, a multistage sampling plan is often preferred. Clusters are selected in the initial stage of sampling, followed by random selection of elements from within each selected cluster. The clusters selected at the initial stage are commonly termed primary sampling units (PSUs).

If multiple stages of sampling are required, sampling frames are needed at different stages. Elements of the target population are randomly selected at the final stage of the multistage sampling from the list of sampling units selected in the prior stage.

Multistage sampling is often employed in population research. Census tracts, residential blocks, segments, and dwellings are defined as clusters at different stages. When dwellings are finally drawn from the selected segments, households are selected from each sampled dwelling. Finally, individuals are selected from the sampled households.

No matter how good a sample is, it always carries some error; this fact must be explicitly considered for effective sampling design. Error is usually composed of three parts: nonsampling bias, sampling bias, and sampling error. Nonsampling bias is error that can arise when the target population is not properly defined, questions are poorly constructed or poorly presented, respondents do not respond or furnish inaccurate information, and mistakes occur in recording information. Sampling bias occurs when sampling frame is inaccurate or when nonprobability sampling is applied. Nonsampling and sampling bias cannot be reduced by simply increasing sample size. It can be reduced or eliminated only if the above problems are carefully handled.

Sampling error results from the sampling process itself. Different samples, drawn from the same population at the same time using the same procedures, should produce similar, though not identical, results. The average value of many such samples is considered to be an unbiased estimate of the population value. The variability among these samples is called sampling error. With probability sampling, sampling error can be estimated from a single sample itself.

Sampling error or sampling variability does not cause bias or systematic differences between the population and the sample. If the sampling error is large, however, the precision of the sample is said to be low. Sampling error or sample precision is affected by sampling techniques used and sample size. Usually clustering increases, and stratification reduces, sampling error. When sample size is sufficiently large, sampling error is very low with probability sampling.

Applications

In most cases, sampling is the most affordable method for collecting demographic and socioeconomic data. Since 1940, sampling has been used by the U.S. Bureau of the Census along with the census itself to obtain additional information about occupation, income, education, reproduction, migration, and so on, as well as to speed publication of results. In addition, a great majority of Bureau of the Census activities have been devoted to a series of sample surveys, providing up-to-date demographic and economic data between decennial census surveys. As statistician William G. Cochran said of the 1960 and 1970 censuses, "except for certain basic information required from every person for constitutional or legal reasons, the whole census was shifted to a sample basis."

Another familiar application of sampling is the opinion poll. Polls, undertaken to determine the opinions and attitudes of the public on issues of interest, are usually carried out on only a small fraction of the total population, yet they can provide accurate information about people's opinions. For example, in the final weekend of the 1992 presidential campaign, five polls with different sample sizes, conducted by different agents, had striking agreement. They showed that Bill Clinton's support was about 44 percent, George Bush's was about 36 percent, and Ross Perot's was about 16 percent. The poll predictions were very close to actual election results. The predictions were all based on small samples relative to the voting population, ranging from the *Washington Post* sample of 722 to *The New York Times*/CBS sample of 2,248 likely voters.

At one time, polls relied on the notion that the larger the sample size, the more representative the sample. This is not true. A classic example is the *Literary Digest* opinion poll that was taken before the 1936 presidential election. About 10 million sample ballots were mailed to *Literary Digest* subscribers, people selected from telephone directories, and automobile owners. About 2.3 million ballots were returned, showing Alfred Landon to be the winner over Franklin Roosevelt by 57 percent to 43 percent. Yet Roosevelt won the election by the huge margin of 62.5 percent to 36.5 percent. The large error was attributable to nonresponse and selection bias: Only about 23 percent of the ballots were returned, and the people selected by the magazine were likely to have higher-than-average incomes.

The World Fertility Survey (WFS), the largest social survey in history, is a good example of applying the multistage probability area sampling method for data collection. The world population has experienced tremendous growth since World War II. The WFS was designed to document the pace and regional distribution of population growth. A "world census" is clearly impossible. Instead, the International Statistics Institute (ISI), the United States Agency for International Development (USAID), and the United Nations Fund for Population Activities (UNFPA) sponsored the worldwide survey during the period between 1974 and 1982. A total of 330,000 women between the ages of fifteen and forty-nine were interviewed in sixty-two countries, countries that made up 40 percent of the world's population. Three-stage area probability sampling was applied. Large-area, primary sampling units (PSUs), were identified, and some were then randomly selected. Each selected PSU was divided into subareas, called second stage units (SSUs), and some SSUs were randomly selected from each PSU. Ultimate area units (UAU) were then randomly selected within each of the selected SSUs. Finally, a systematic sample of households was selected from each selected UAU, and all eligible women in the selected households were interviewed.

Sampling is used extensively and has far-ranging applications in many areas of contemporary society. Sampling has been adopted by manufacturing and business for quality control of goods and services. When the quantity of goods produced is large, a complete investigation is costly and, in fact, unnecessary. When an investigation requires the destruction of products, such as testing the life of electric bulbs, one can only investigate a sample. Small samples of products are frequently drawn, and appropriate quality measures are plotted on a chart. If the values shown on the chart are not randomly scattered around the expected average value, it is a warning that some part of the manufacturing process may be defective.

Sampling is the only means of estimating population size in the study of wildlife populations. A frequently used method is to select a random sample of a wildlife population of interest with a size of n_1. Each animal is tagged and released. Sometime later another sample is taken from the same population with a size of n_2, The estimated wildlife population size is approximately n_1/p, where p is the proportion of animals with a tag in the second sample.

Context

Sampling has a relatively short history. At the beginning of the twentieth century, the demand for social and economic data in Europe increased. This social need stimulated the development and application of sampling techniques. After vigorous debate among statisticians on the validity of sampling, the International Statistical Institute (ISI) accepted the principles of sampling techniques in 1903. Since then, a range of sampling techniques for survey samples has been developed.

The contemporary development of survey sampling is largely attributed to American researchers. The Statistical Research Division of the Bureau of the Census made substantial contributions to the development of sampling methods for use by the bureau in the late 1930's and 1940's. Commercial polling firms, such as those organized by George Gallup, Elmo Roper, and Louis Harris also generated significant support for the development and use of sample survey methods, particularly in the areas of marketing and opinion polling. In addition, the U.S. Department of Agriculture played an important role in the development of sampling methods. To meet the need of predicting crop yields, the U.S. Department of Agriculture developed a comprehensive probability sampling procedure to sample land areas. This sampling method was successfully extended to social surveys by social scientists in the 1940's. This method has evolved in both theory and practice, and since the 1940's it has become the most highly regarded population sampling method.

Methods of sampling have become increasingly useful, sophisticated, and extensively applied. Besides area probability sampling, the most notable advance probably has been the development of telephone sampling techniques. Since the 1970's, more than 90 percent of American households have used telephones. As a result, telephone sampling methods have undergone a rapid development in response to the sharp increase in the costs of conducting face-to-face household surveys. Telephone samples based on new sampling techniques are much more representative than ever before. Besides the advantages of cost-effectiveness and fast data collection, telephone sampling permits supervisors to monitor the process of ongoing interviews, thereby increasing data quality.

With improvements in sampling techniques and successful applications, increased use of sampling has become an international trend. Most data now used in government statistics, business, social, and policy sciences are collected from samples. In return, the achievements of sampling stimulated the growth of empirical research in those fields in the late twentieth century. The role of sampling will become even more important with the advent of widespread computerization.

Bibliography

Cochran, William G. *Sampling Techniques*. 3d ed. New York: John Wiley & Sons,

1977. This is a widely recommended textbook that provides a comprehensive account of sampling theory. Familiarity with advanced algebra and probability is recommended.

Fowler, Floyd J. *Survey Research Methods*. Rev. ed. Beverly Hills, Calif.: Sage Publications, 1988. Describes the standards and practical procedures for drawing a representative sample. Fowler melds the three components (sampling, questionnaire design, and interviewing methodologies) of survey together and shows how each of the components affects the quality of a sample.

Henry, Gary T. *Practical Sampling*. Newbury Park, Calif.: Sage Publications, 1990. This book is oriented toward the researcher who needs to apply sampling as a research tool. It addresses fundamental concepts of sampling and includes detailed examples of practical alternatives of sampling.

Hess, Irene. *Sampling for Social Research Surveys: 1947-1980*. Ann Arbor: University of Michigan Press, 1985. This monograph is a rich source of practical survey sampling for social research. It provides extensive information for sampling design based on the sampling experience of the Survey Research Center (SRC) of the University of Michigan.

Kalton, Graham. *Introduction to Survey Sampling*. Beverly Hills, Calif.: Sage Publications, 1983. A valuable text for those with limited knowledge of mathematics and statistics. It provides readers with a broad overview of survey sampling and a firm understanding of the major components of survey sampling design; also discusses practical considerations.

Kish, Leslie. *Survey Sampling*. New York: John Wiley & Sons, 1965. This is probably the best specialized textbook on sampling methods and application. It has been nicknamed the "green bible" of survey sampling because of its color and utility. Indeed, many solutions can be found in this book concerning difficulties with sampling design.

Lavrakas, Paul J. *Telephone Survey Methods: Sampling, Selection, and Supervision*. Beverly Hills, Calif.: Sage Publications, 1987. This book is designed to assist persons who do not consider themselves experts in planning and executing telephone surveys. It discusses how to conduct a telephone survey and how to control and monitor the data collection process.

Jichuan Wang
James H. Fisher
Jiajian Chen

Cross-References

SCHOOL DESEGREGATION

Type of sociology: Major social institutions
Field of study: Education

School desegregation, mandated by the Supreme Court's 1954 Brown v. *Board of Education decision, involved first the dismantling of legally required separate schools for whites and blacks and later "affirmative action" to produce genuine integration. Expected results, such as higher black achievement and greater opportunity, were only partially achieved. Unexpected consequences such as white flight and resegregation occurred.*

Principal terms
AFFIRMATIVE ACTION: policies going beyond allowing free choice among schools; under affirmative action policies, a school district must initiate programs that guarantee multiracial, integrated schools
DE FACTO SEGREGATION: separation of races created as a by-product of economic and social factors rather than by direct governmental actions
DE JURE SEGREGATION: separation of the races mandated by laws making it illegal for blacks to use white facilities
DESEGREGATION: the abolishing of a system of required separation of the races; under desegregation, blacks can associate with whites and can choose to go to previously white schools
INTEGRATION: the free and easy mutual associations between races to the degree that the racial distinctiveness of an institution is lost

Overview

School desegregation refers, in the narrowest sense, to the policy of dismantling the legally enforceable system of separate schools for black and white Americans that prevailed in some seventeen Southern and border states from the late nineteenth to the mid-twentieth century. The Fourteenth Amendment to the Constitution of the United States, ratified in 1868, proclaimed in no uncertain terms the "equal protection of the law" for all citizens of the United States. In 1896 the Supreme Court held in the case of *Plessy v. Ferguson* that separate public facilities for African Americans were legal as long as they were "equal." Since that time black plaintiffs had sometimes won cases arguing that inadequate schools for blacks were unequal in public funding or physical facilities with the corresponding schools for whites. In the landmark *Brown v. Board of Education* decision in 1954, however, the doctrine of "separate but equal" was itself challenged. The African American plaintiffs argued, and the Supreme Court of the United States agreed, that such a legally mandated, separate school system for blacks was inherently unequal and hence denied African American citizens the equal protection of the law.

The logic of this decision assumed a crucial importance. Written by Chief Justice Earl Warren and unanimously endorsed by the nine justices, it established the framework for a chain of later decisions. The court maintained, first, that education had become essential to the exercise of citizenship and that hence people's education was entitled to such equal protection. Second, it maintained that intangible factors must be considered in the assessment of equality. A lack of opportunity to interact in discussions and exchange views with those of the majority culture might itself handicap a minority. Among these intangible factors, the court borrowed heavily from a brief submitted by social scientists as "friends of the court." Segregation, this brief maintained, was construed by both whites and blacks to imply black inferiority. This feeling of inferiority had depressed the motivation of black children to learn and hence depressed their educational progress. Implied by the decision was a third strand of the social science argument: that stereotyping by whites in their views of blacks (and hence, prejudice) was promoted by racial segregation.

For a decade following this decision, the courts were lenient, white resistance was high, and only small-scale token desegregation occurred in most Southern states. While it was held that school districts should proceed to desegregate "with all deliberate speed," the truly operative principle here was "freedom of choice." No black child who wished to attend a previously white school could be refused, but no one would be expected to beat the bushes to encourage such a child to apply. Blacks were inhibited by custom and by social and economic pressures, and only a small number chose to go to traditionally white schools. Many whites opposed any desegregation whatsoever. An influx of black students, they argued, would "ruin" the public schools by flooding them with students who were functioning at a level behind that of their white age-mates. Various strategies were employed to avoid large-scale integration. New private academies for whites were constructed, and states provided tuition grants to assist students to attend such academies; in a few locations public schools were closed. In 1964, a decade after the *Brown v. Board of Education* decision, fewer than 2 percent of all Southern black students were attending integrated schools.

In 1964, during the presidency of Lyndon Johnson, an era of federal activism began. The passage of the Civil Rights Act of 1964 provided, in Title VI, the mandatory suspension of federal aid to a school district that could be shown to be practicing racial discrimination. In 1966 this antidiscrimination clause was invoked, and federal funds were withdrawn from some of the more resistant school districts. In 1966, the influential Coleman Report was released. This large-scale study suggested that African American children progressed faster academically when they attended an integrated school. In 1968, the Supreme Court, in the influential *Green v. County School Board of New Kent County* decision, reinterpreted the *Brown v. Board of Education* mandate to require whatever "affirmative action" was necessary to achieve an integrated, unitary school system. In later cases (*Swann v. Charlotte-Mecklenburg Board of Education*, 1971, and other cases) the court elaborated that such affirmative action could require the transportation of students between schools, the reassignment of teachers, and a consideration of the white-black student ratio in evaluating the success of such affirmative action. Unlike "freedom of choice," the activist approach obtained results. By 1975, 44 percent of the black students in Southern states were in schools with a white majority.

Yet the times were changing, and the late 1970's to the early 1990's were a period of consolidation. Patterns of social separation became more complex and ambiguous. Many cases of racial segregation that attracted the attention of the courts were in such Northern cities as Boston and Detroit. Racial separation was imposed not by the law (de jure segregation), but by economic and social factors such as housing patterns (de facto segregation). Much of the middle class, including most whites, either moved to suburban communities or placed their children in private schools. Court orders to desegregate seemed only to encourage "white flight" and resegregation. Public opinion also became more complex. While the public continued to support racial integration, it became strongly opposed to "busing" to achieve this integration. Some of what had once been a solid black constituency for integration now championed the alternative of black separation and empowerment. Political leadership and finally the Supreme Court grew more conservative. In a series of legal challenges, the courts held that remedies such as busing between school districts could not be prescribed unless each of these school districts was guilty of deliberate segregation. Prosecutions by the Justice Department for violations of Title VI of the Civil Rights Act slowed to a trickle. While blacks continued to become part of an increasing variety of society's institutions, legal and political pressures to desegregate diminished greatly.

Applications

The effect of school desegregation, applied to individual school districts, was influenced by a number of factors, some of them fortuitous ones that could hardly have been foreseen in 1954. A comparison of two such districts, those of Washington, D.C., and Prince Edward County, Virginia, makes this point evident. Although in the mid-1950's, Prince Edward County was small and rural and Washington was large and urban, both had a roughly equal percentage of white and black school-age children, both were operating a system of separate black schools, and both were ordered by the courts in 1955 to desegregate.

The Washington system conscientiously complied with the court order by desegregating the system, employing geographic boundaries alone in assigning students to schools. Superintendent Carl Hansen emphasized educational basics, regular achievement testing, grouping students according to ability, and the color-blind selection of teachers based on competence alone. He accepted steadily rising average achievement test scores as self-evident proof of the effectiveness of his program. Since the Washington, D.C., schools were also becoming more heavily black as some whites left for nearby suburbs, this was at the time considered a sort of triumph which dramatically contradicted segregationist predictions of black inability to learn at the pace of whites. Much attention was focused on Washington as a "showcase of successful integration."

Prince Edward County, in contrast, became a symbol of segregation's last stand. In

1959, after preliminary legal skirmishes, the county was ordered to take "immediate action to desegregate." As an alternative, the county's governing body, with the overwhelming support of the white citizenry, lowered the tax rate drastically and abolished the public school system entirely. Citizens were encouraged to apply the tax money saved to the funding of private schools. The white citizens complied; they constructed a handsome academy outside the county seat. For five years, some black children were educated by leaving the county, other sporadically by volunteers, and many not at all. In 1964, by court order, the public schools were reopened to accommodate fourteen hundred black students and seven whites. Since white students continued to attend the private academy, segregation mostly had been preserved.

The subsequent trend in the Washington, D.C., showcase school system was toward the resegregation of poor blacks because not only whites but also middle-class blacks were leaving the city public schools for private education or the suburbs. The unraveling was precipitated by policies based on the observation of Julius Hobson, a radical black engineer, that the upper ability groups within the fairly rigid tracking system contained disproportionate percentages of both the remaining whites in the district and blacks from the more prosperous families. Hobson argued, and the federal district court agreed in 1966, that the poorer blacks were being deprived of equal opportunity by being relegated to the lower, less-challenging tracks based on tests that had been developed for whites and hence were inappropriate for black children. After the exit of ability grouping, standardized tests, and Superintendent Hansen, various plans were tried under a plethora of superintendents, but neither the plans nor the superintendents endured more than a year or so. In 1978 the federal court rescinded most of the Hobson restrictions. A new black superintendent emphasized the basics tempered with more attention to black studies and more flexible ability groupings. Revived standardized testing revealed that scores had dropped precipitously while the Hobson ruling had been in effect. Large numbers of middle-class blacks and remaining whites left the public school system. In the 1980's, it was estimated that 97 percent of the public school population of Washington was minority.

The Prince Edward public schools, in contrast, moved from segregation to integration. One ally of integration was the fact that many white citizens of the county were less affluent than white (and some black) Washingtonians and hence had fewer options to consider. From 1964, a steady trickle of white children whose families believed they could not afford the academy returned to the public schools. Another strong influence was Superintendent of Schools James Anderson, who tempered an emphasis on the basics, standardized testing, and flexible ability grouping with sensitivity to black concerns. The smallness of the community afforded cooperative interracial participation in such activities as scouting and sports. Still another factor supporting integration was a loose coalition of faculty members of the two local colleges, black public school teachers, ministers, and some members of the local business community, who began publicly to support the ideal of academic excellence in a multiethnic environment. During the 1980's, the trickle of returning white students had become a flood. About this same time, the public school supporters became powerful enough to elect a majority of the county's governing board, which resulted in more generous funding of public education. As a final irony, in the mid-1980's, the private academy initiated an affirmative action program to attract black students.

Context

The jurists who decided *Brown v. Board of Education* were informed by social science findings that were both critical of the present and optimistic about the future. Sociologist Gunnar Myrdal, in his influential book *An American Dilemma: The Negro Problem and Modern Democracy* (1944), interpreted the incompatibility between the American ideal of equality of opportunity and the continuing presence of a legally sanctioned, race-based caste system as a chronic source of embarrassment to the national psyche. The research that was presented to the court in *Brown v. Board of Education* suggested that the isolation of one group from another in a competing environment could breed mutual antagonisms and unflattering stereotypes. Once formed, such stereotypes become self-fulfilling prophecies influencing both the responses of others and one's perception of oneself. A famous study by psychologist Kenneth Clark showing that black children select white dolls as prettier was submitted as evidence that black children often adopt a negative, prejudiced view of themselves. This thesis—that segregation breeds prejudice, which in turn breeds mutual hostility, self-hate, and failure—was explicitly cited in Chief Justice Warren's opinion. It could be inferred that Warren also agreed that closer contact between blacks and whites would result in more equal opportunity by reducing prejudices, raising black self-esteem, and increasing academic success by African Americans.

Studies of the short-term effects of desegregation in schools have concentrated on changes in academic performance, changes in black and white attitudes toward each other, and changes in black self-esteem. More often than not, black academic achievement tends to be modestly improved after desegregation, and white academic achievement is not adversely affected. Attitudes of whites about blacks sometimes become more positive, sometimes become more negative, and sometimes change not at all. A crucial factor in increased positive attitudes is the existence of relationships that are both equal-status and cooperative in the pursuit of common goals. Black self-esteem has shown little change. At least 65 percent of black children still prefer white dolls, just as in Clark's pre-1954 studies.

An examination of the broader, long-term social and economic effects of desegregation also suggests a mixed picture. The resegregation of cities offers to inner-city black children opportunities that are dramatically unequal. Fear of changes in the quality of education following desegregation has in urban areas exacerbated white flight and the flight of middle-class blacks from urban areas. Indeed, many minority children of the inner city seem trapped in areas of crime, drugs, and violence in schools that are underfunded, underheated, undertaught, and overcrowded; the students have few middle-class black role models. These children seem to have little more opportunity than segregated black children did in 1954. For them, the net effect of the many social changes has been, at best, to break even.

There are, however, winners. Many graduates of the more successfully desegregated schools report cross-racial friendships of a quality that would have been rare before 1954. The highest-ranking black graduates of Southern high schools are admitted to highly selective colleges with a regularity that would once have been astounding. The bottom line is that the *Brown v. Board of Education* decision was historically inevitable. That a constitutional democracy such as the United States would have approached the twenty-first century with a legally mandated caste system is almost unthinkable.

Bibliography

Allport, Gordon W. *The Nature of Prejudice*. Abridged ed. Garden City, N.Y.: Doubleday, 1958. Allport discusses the origin of prejudice and the effects of prejudice in creating self-fulfilling prophecies. Describes much of the theory and research included in the social science brief in the *Brown v. Board of Education* decision.

Gerard, Harold B. "School Desegregation: The Social Science Role." *American Psychologist* 38 (August, 1983): 869-877. Reconsiders predictions made by psychologists in *Brown v. Board of Education*, arguing that they were too optimistic. View contrasts with that of Walter G. Stephan (see entry below).

Hochschild, Jennifer L. *The New American Dilemma: Liberal Democracy and School Desegregation*. New Haven, Conn.: Yale University Press, 1984. Reconsiders Gunnar Myrdal's definition of the "American dilemma." Argues that desegregation is resisted because racism is as firmly rooted in the United States as is the ideal of equality.

Kozol, Jonathan. *Savage Inequalities*. New York: Crown, 1991. An impassioned account of children of the black and Hispanic underclass in some large U.S. cities and of the underfunded, overcrowded schools they attend. Argues that these inner-city schools are "savagely unequal."

Metcalf, George R. *From Little Rock to Boston: The History of School Desegregation*. Westport, Conn.: Greenwood Press, 1983. A detailed history of the Supreme Court and the federal government's efforts to desegregate schools. Particularly rich in describing the many conflicting pressures at work in the administration and the legislating of policy.

Myrdal, Gunnar. *An American Dilemma: The Negro Problem and Modern Democracy*. New York: Harper Brothers, 1944. Highlights the incompatibility between such core American ideals as equal opportunity and the treatment and segregation of black Americans. Myrdal's work was a major influence on opinion and the Supreme Court in 1954.

Stephan, Walter G. "School Desegregation: An Evaluation of Predictions Made in *Brown v. Board of Education*." *Psychological Bulletin* 85 (March, 1978): 217-238. Reviews research on the main points made in the brief submitted by the mixed support for the validity of these points.

Wolters, Raymond. *The Burden of Brown: Thirty Years of School Desegregation*. Knoxville: University of Tennessee Press, 1984. Detailed account of how five communities responded to the necessity of desegregating schools between 1954 and

1984. Enriched by first-hand accounts from participants with many different viewpoints.

Ziegler, Benjamin, ed. *Desegregation and the Supreme Court*. Boston: D. C. Heath, 1958. Contains the text of the *Brown v. Board of Education* decision and other related decisions. Comments by legal scholars.

Thomas E. DeWolfe

Cross-References

SCHOOL SOCIALIZATION

Type of sociology: Socialization and social interaction
Fields of study: Agents of socialization; Education

School socialization refers to the formal and informal ways that schools systematically communicate and reinforce knowledge, values, beliefs, myths, and expectations about school, society, and adult life. Because of their strong influence on children's development, schools are perceived by some as places that are essential to maintaining society. Because of this same influence, however, others view schools as places that perpetuate societal oppression.

Principal terms

CLASS: the group to which one belongs that indicates one's position in the societal hierarchy; determined by such factors as ethnicity or race, economic resources, education, and occupation

EQUAL OPPORTUNITY: a situation in which all members of society have an equal chance of achieving power, social status, and economic resources

GENDER: a term referring to sex-appropriate beliefs and behavior patterns that are culturally determined; differentiated from "sex," a term for one's biological designation as male or female

LABELING: the process of assigning a role, usually a negative or stigmatized one, with its attached behavioral expectations

SOCIALIZATION: the processes that communicate society's knowledge, values, norms, roles, and expectations

STEREOTYPE: an exaggerated belief about the behavior or attributes of a group for the purpose of justifying conduct toward people belonging to the group

STRATIFICATION: the unequal distribution of power, privilege, and economic resources and opportunities within a social system

Overview

Socialization is the process through which individuals learn the knowledge, beliefs, values, norms, and roles of their society. The process of socialization continues through the life cycle from infancy to old age as people learn, then relearn, the ways of their society and of the particular subgroups to which they belong. People are socialized according to class, for example, and according to expectations relating to their gender. The term "agents of socialization" refers to the societal institutions and forces that are important in this process. The first agent of socialization an individual encounters is the family. The next agent is the school, and school socialization plays a major role in the lives of nearly all children and adolescents (as well as young adults in college) in the United States.

Since the formalization of education in the nineteenth century, schools have traditionally been viewed as institutions whose primary responsibility is to teach general knowledge, democratic values, and societal customs—thereby preparing individuals to assume essential roles within the workforce and within society as a whole. According to this view, education is a positive and democratic institution that helps sustain the economic and political workings of society. Schools make deliberate efforts to socialize children and prepare them for adulthood. Most children will grow up to fill a number of social roles—spouse, parent, employee, citizen—and the continuation of any society depends on the continuation of effective socialization of its young people.

On the other hand, the socialization that occurs at school also contains components that began to be strongly criticized in the last third of the twentieth century. Many studies have explored school socialization relating to students' social class and gender, for example. Children from different classes and of different races are socialized into having different expectations about what to expect later in life. Such socialization, it is argued, helps perpetuate social stratification and the reproduction of class differences. Gender socialization occurs in many subtle ways; studies have shown that many teachers act differently toward boys and girls in their classes; teachers' preconceptions lead them to have different expectations of boys and girls.

The Civil Rights movement brought about changes in the American institution of education that focused attention on certain aspects of school socialization. The related issues of whether schools could continue to act as socializing agents to maintain the status quo and how they might provide equality of educational opportunity to all children were raised and debated. In 1964, the federal government commissioned a study, directed by educational researcher James Coleman, to ascertain the impact of school desegregation. The group's report, published in 1966, contained two findings that were particularly important regarding minority groups. First, minority children began school with a serious educational deficit that was the result of their home and community environments. Second, children from these groups finished school with an even more serious deficiency than they had when they began. Coleman concluded that this deficiency had to be at least partly a result of what happened to students during their schooling.

These findings led sociologists and educators to explore classroom interaction for the first time. In his 1968 book *Life in Classrooms*, educator Philip Jackson suggested that, in addition to the obvious academic curriculum operating in schools, a "hidden curriculum" was at work. This other curriculum involved the social expectations that each classroom teacher holds regarding how he or she expects students to behave. "As a matter of fact," stated Jackson, "the relationship of the hidden curriculum to student difficulties is even more striking than is its relationship to success." Students were more likely to be successful in school if they conformed to teachers' expectations than if they simply did well academically. Jackson speculated that the use of these two curricula in school resulted in differentiating opportunity for various groups of students.

In their 1976 publication *Schooling in Capitalist America*, sociologists Samuel Bowles and Herbert Gintis supported Jackson's position, arguing that this differentiation was a product of the social relations in school and the organization of the curriculum. They alleged that school administrators, support staff, and parents, as well as teachers, held different expectations for students from different social classes. They further asserted that these separations tended to reproduce social classes, and that these separations tended to reproduce the class structure found in society. In order words, school acts as an agent of socialization into a particular social class.

Subsequent work identified a number of mechanisms that seemed to determine who was more likely to be successful within the hidden, as well as the official, curriculum of schools and what subsequent opportunities might be available to these populations. These mechanisms included the use of intelligence tests, ability grouping, tracking, and career counseling. With teacher expectation proposed as perhaps the most influential factor in school socialization, these multiple processes combined to differentiate opportunity for various groups of students. Research began to confirm the validity of these suppositions. Studies indicated that teacher expectations were operative from each student's initial experiences at school. Several sources of information about a student's cultural and family background, religion, parental income, family status, medical history, and behavior were available to teachers and helped to shape these expectations.

By the late 1970's and early 1980's, sociologists were able to collect data from the first groups of minorities who were eligible to be graduated from integrated schools. Information released by the Bureau of Labor Statistics reported that in 1983, only 59.1 percent of blacks and 50.3 percent of Hispanics eighteen to nineteen years old had been graduated from the nation's high schools. The lack of educational attainment among these minority youths led to an unparalleled research focus on the socializing processes of schools. In a 1986 study, sociologists Glenna Colclough and E. M. Beck analyzed data collected from high school seniors over a period of seven years. They examined the allocation of students into public and private schools, the socioeconomic composition of the school community, and the use of curriculum tracking as three principal means through which individuals' social class positions are reproduced. Their findings indicated that these factors significantly influenced whether students were identified as suitable for either academic or manual careers. They also found that more than 60 percent of those studied did not change their class positions during the seven years of the study.

Applications

As these discrepancies in schooling emerged, it became clear that the processes supporting this institutionalized discrimination were complex. Researchers turned their efforts to identifying and explaining the processes through which school socialization—most notably class and gender socialization—operated.

The renowned study *Pygmalion in the Classroom: Teacher Expectations and Pupils' Intellectual Development* (1968) provided impetus for this research. By controlling certain information, researchers Robert Rosenthal and Lenore Jackson led teachers to believe that particular students were more intellectually capable than others. They found that there was a direct correlation between gains in the students' IQ scores and teachers' perceptions of the students' classroom behavior—that it was the teachers' expectations, not the students' actual abilities, that tended to determine academic performance.

The self-fulfilling prophecy, a theorem proposed by sociologist W. I. Thomas and discussed by Robert K. Merton in his classic work *Social Theory and Social Structure* (1949), illustrates the processes involved in relationships between expectations and behavior. Thomas' theorem states that if people define situations as real, they are real in their consequences. Merton described the first part of the theorem as an unceasing reminder that people respond not only to the objective features of a situation but also to the *meaning* the situation has for them. The perceived meaning of a situation, or expectation, is expressed through interactions which, in turn, shape the subsequent behavior in the direction of the original perception. Merton carefully pointed out that the original definition of the situation is false. As a result, the new behaviors that are evoked cause the originally false conceptions to become true.

The operation of this theorem in schools was explored in sociologist Ray Rist's classic study "Student Social Class and Teacher Expectations: The Self-Fulfilling Prophecy in Ghetto Education" (1970). Rist found that early and permanent grouping, again based on socioeconomic and racial background, set the stage for a year of communicated expectations. The teacher consistently supported, coached, and taught her "fast" learners, while restricting most of her interactions with the "slow" students to disciplining, even ridiculing them. Prevented from learning and suffering from poor self-esteem, those perceived as slow learners actually manifested that behavior by the end of the year. As Rist tracked these students through their next two years of schooling, it became apparent that moving out of a fast or slow track was highly unlikely.

The validity of the concept of the self-fulfilling prophecy became a point of controversy among educators and sociologists, many of whom argued that performance differences in school were caused by genetic or cultural factors. The research of Rist and others proposed that labeling theory would help end the controversy because it provided a viable framework for analyzing the social processes that influence success or failure in schools. Several specific classroom processes were identified as integral to understanding the self-fulfilling prophecy within the context of labeling theory. Briefly, the teacher expects specific behavior and academic achievement from particular students. Subsequent teacher treatment tells each student what behavior and achievement is expected. If this treatment is consistent over time, the students' behavior and achievement will conform more and more closely with that teacher's original expectations. Although many variables affect the culmination of the self-fulfilling prophecy, the vulnerability of children remains unquestioned.

As evidence of the influence of school socialization based on students' combined race and gender statuses accumulated, attention turned to exploration of how specific groups were affected. In her article "Race-Gender Status, Classroom Interaction, and Children's Socialization in Elementary School" (in *Gender Influences in Classroom Interaction*, edited by Louise Cherry Wilkinson and Cora B. Marrett, 1985), Linda Grant conducted a longitudinal study to explore the classroom processes that contribute to divergent outcomes.

Researchers have also attempted to codify teacher-student interactions on the basis of sex. One study in 1985 found that at all grade levels, in all settings, and in all subject areas, boys dominated classroom communications. Boys were eight times more likely than girls to call out answers. Teachers tended to accept boys' answers more readily than girls' and to reprimand girls if they called out. Further, teachers were less informative to girls regarding the quality of their answers. Researchers found that girls were less likely to take mathematics and science courses and were more likely to attribute failure to internal factors, such as ability, than to external factors.

Context

The theoretical work of sociologists Karl Marx and Max Weber provided the interpretive foundation for looking at schools as reproductive agencies that engage in class socialization. Through analysis of economic systems, political power structures, and their relation to education, social scientists explored issues of institutional domination and subordination. As interest in the relationship between schooling and society increased, sociologists looked both at what occurred outside schools (input factors) and at what occurred inside schools (interactions).

Marx conducted his analyses of domination and subordination from economic perspectives, and he presented the relationship between social class and economic power in explicit terms. Discussing ownership and the power of production, Marx attempted to demonstrate how these factors influenced the stratification of classes within society. Although Marx did not discuss education as existing apart from the societal superstructure, later Marxist theorists contended that there is a clear and important relationship between schools and other societal institutions. They believed that changes in one structure effect changes in all structures, and they were especially interested in studying how schools seem to legitimize class-based perceptions of stratification. For those who believed that school socialization is instrumental in influencing class structure, understanding how schools act as agents of socialization for either reproduction or transformation became the focus of analysis.

Marx's method of dialectic analysis became a mainstay of many sociologists who specialize in studying schools. Dialectic analysis allows the challenge of all assumptions that underlie any theory or conceptual framework, and it has provided a forum through which sociologists can raise questions about school socialization and issues of merit, rewards, drop-out rates, definitions of intelligence, and reform.

Conversely, Max Weber viewed education as central to affecting societal structures and values. Like Marx, Weber conducted economic analysis to understand institutional domination; however, Weber also discussed how politics and government, representing organized power and authority, utilize educational systems to sustain inequity among societal groups. He proposed that each society creates educational systems that are directly related to sustaining the systems of power and authority at work within that society. Schools, he contended, are used to prepare and educate the leaders of that society. Therefore, Weber and other sociologists of his time were interested in studying school populations, curricula, and the distribution of knowledge among various societal groups.

Weber's analyses of authority types fostered within different societies led to one of his most important contributions to understanding schooling. Weber found that leadership can best be taught within societies that are based on meritocracy, in which individuals hold positions of power based on their achievements as opposed to relying on charisma or birthright to gain access to power. Because societies based on meritocracy can recruit qualified individuals from any social class to fill positions of wealth and power, schools can be used to provide qualified candidates for these positions. Weber, therefore, saw schools as vehicles of social mobility.

As sociologists came to understand the nature of social classes, attention was turned to understanding the significance of the impact of schools on socially constructed identity and social mobility. In the middle of the twentieth century, symbolic interactionism emerged as a sociological field of study that paid particular interest to the interactions that occur among participants in schools.

Bibliography

Bennett, Kathleen P., and Margaret D. LeCompte. *How Schools Work: A Sociological Analysis of Education*. New York: Longman, 1990. Although a theoretical work for the lay reader, this book provides a sound introduction to the sociology of schooling. Most pertinent regarding school socialization are chapters 5 through 8, which discuss social class, the stratification of knowledge, ethnic minorities, and gender in relation to schooling.

Blau, Peter M., and Otis Dudley Duncan. *The American Occupational Structure*. New York: John Wiley & Sons, 1967. This classic may appear unwieldy, but it offers an important analysis of the American occupational hierarchy. The authors discuss race, kinship, careers, marriage, and geographic locality in terms of social mobility. Chapter topics of particular interest discuss the process of stratification and equality of opportunity.

Jackson, Philip. *Life in Classrooms*. New York: Holt, Rinehart and Winston, 1968. This work represents one of the first examinations that takes into consideration students' and teachers' views of school. Twenty-five years after its publication, Jackson's work is still insightful, and his combination of research and narrative testimonial brings new perspectives to life in schools.

Klein, Susan S., ed. *Sex Equity and Sexuality in Education*. Albany: State University of New York Press, 1992. This collection of articles represents the thinking of the late twentieth century regarding sex equity and sexuality issues. Both the lay and professional reader will find treatment of theory and issues regarding education highly relevant and informing.

McLaren, Peter. *Life in Schools: An Introduction to Critical Pedagogy in the Foundations of Education*. New York: Longman, 1989. In a frank introduction, McLaren chronicles various crises in education and then takes the reader on a journey into the ghetto classrooms where he first taught. The remaining text presents critical theory in a clear and readable way as McLaren attempts to bring theoretical understanding to real life in schools.

Pignatelli, Frank, and Susanna W. Pflaum, eds. *Celebrating Diverse Voices*. Newbury Park, Calif.: Corwin Press, 1993. This well-edited volume will be particularly enjoyed by those who have an interest in exploring how educators and schools might resolve some of the problems of inequity. Twelve essays span several disciplines; school restructuring, alternative education, parental involvement, school research, staff development, and community are discussed.

Rist, Ray. "Student Social Class and Teacher Expectations: The Self-Fulfilling Prophecy in Ghetto Education." *Harvard Educational Review* 40, no. 3 (1970): 411-451. Although this article is an exemplary research model, its greatest strength lies in its many explicit examples of how one teacher's day-to-day treatment of perceived "fast" learners differed from that of her "slow" learners. In a clear analysis, Rist demonstrates how class-based and race-based expectations were manifested in actual outcomes among the different learners.

Spring, Joel. *The Sorting Machine Revisited: National Educational Policy Since 1945*. New York: Longman, 1989. A readable and informative book that provides a critical analysis and interpretation of how American educational policy is used as a vehicle for selecting and channeling human resources to meet needs of the labor market. Provides an excellent overview connecting major social events with school policy.

Denise Kaye Davis

Cross-References

Education: Conflict Theory Views, 579; Education: Manifest and Latent Functions, 593; Educational Inequality: The Coleman Report, 607; Equal Educational Opportunity, 661; Gender Socialization, 833; Social Stratification: Analysis and Overview, 1839; Social Stratification: Marxist Perspectives, 1852; The Sociology of Education, 1939.

SECULARIZATION IN WESTERN SOCIETY

Type of sociology: Major social institutions
Field of study: Religion

Secularization is the process by which cultural and social institutions become independent of religious domination and relatively autonomous in relation to each other. Simultaneously, individuals gain more freedom in choosing their religions and meaning systems but also experience higher levels of doubt in relation to their chosen beliefs.

Principal terms

ANOMIE: a situation characterized by perceptions of meaninglessness and a lack of moral order, resulting in personal frustration and social disorganization

BUREAUCRACIES: impersonal forms of administration that govern by means of rationally constructed rules that are applied uniformly to all

DISENCHANTMENT: a human mode of perception in which the world loses its spiritual significance and is viewed in terms of material utility

INSTITUTIONAL DIFFERENTIATION: a process in which social functions are delegated to specialized institutions, each performing a particular activity and filling a social role (for example, political or educational)

LEGITIMATION: a process in which accepted structures of knowledge and beliefs explain and justify the social order and its policies to its members

PLURALISM: a situation characterized by the existence of a variety of religions and worldviews, none of which is fully dominant

PRIVATIZATION: the loss of public significance of certain institutions and their relegation to the realm of individual preference and meaning (for example, religion, family, and the arts)

RATIONALIZATION: the organization and evaluation of human activity according to measurable, logical criteria related to immediate, empirical ends and with a stress on efficiency

Overview

In the past, people lived in societies and cultures dominated by religion. Religious stories, rituals, and rules prescribed every activity and provided legitimation for the social order. Political leaders were viewed as deities or else as descended from or appointed by them. Laws, such as those contained in the Ten Commandments, were understood as having come directly from the divine. Economic activity was governed by religious ritual, and rites were performed to facilitate hunting, planting, and harvesting. The whole of life had religious significance, and people were careful not to offend the spiritual world.

Modern societies are radically different. They are distinguished by high levels of institutional differentiation, with distinct functions and rules pertaining to each institution. Economic institutions are governed by rules of efficiency and probability. Education has standards of excellence that are expected to be unrelated to religious or political ideology. Consequently, institutions are no longer legitimated by reference to religious authority but by how well they perform their appointed roles. Nevertheless, while all modern secular societies have separate standards, another characteristic of such societies is that all the individual standards are related to the process of rationalization. These standards are set through the use of human reason as it attempts to discover universal, empirical standards of evaluation. The physical sciences (biology, chemistry, physics) attempt to find laws that explain physical processes. Psychology searches for laws with which to explain the human mind and personality. Similarly, the other social sciences, political science, sociology, and economics, search for laws that explain social life, societal interaction, and change. Even in the realm of morality, the work of the German philosopher Immanuel Kant (1724-1804) initiated an ongoing process to find universal, rational moral laws that can be used to regulate the behaviors of all people in all societies. The final goal of the rationalization of all spheres of life is to bring all spheres of existence under human control, thus freeing people from fear of the random and the arbitrary.

Additionally, secularization focuses on the changed relationship between believers and their religious beliefs. In traditional cultures, persons are immersed in uniformity of religious belief and practice. Religion permeates all of existence, which makes it seem real and objective. Doubt is not a serious possibility in such settings. In the modern world, however, the public world is divorced from the religious. The performance of economic, political, and public tasks is not informed by religious belief. Modern societies are also marked by religious pluralism as well as open, avowed atheism. The individual is thus forced consciously to choose to continue or affirm a religious tradition. The very act of being forced to choose makes religious beliefs seem less certain and more arbitrary; therefore, doubt becomes an inescapable part of religious belief. Religion is reduced to the realm of individual meaning and thus becomes privatized.

Secularization appears to be a product of Western (Christian) civilization but has spread globally in the twentieth century with the spread of Western colonialism. Although it became highly visible in the nineteenth century with the rise of industrial capitalism, secularization is, in fact, a long historical process. The disenchantment of the world begins with the Jewish concept of monotheism and its doctrine of creation, in which God creates the world and stands apart from it. The world becomes a material creation and is no longer populated by gods and spirits. Similarly, Greek culture, in the work of its philosophers, especially Plato and Aristotle, begins the process of rationalization, using the human mind to analyze all phenomena and all human experience. While Christianity accelerated the process by synthesizing elements from both traditions, it was not until the sixteenth century Renaissance and Protestant Reformation that the logical implications of these earlier claims began to be developed. This period marks the beginnings of modern science, philosophy, and the social sciences. It also marks the beginnings, as Max Weber demonstrates in his famous work *Die Protestantische Ethik und der Geist des Kapitalismus* (1904; *The Protestant Ethic and the Spirit of Capitalism*, 1930), of modern capitalism.

While the economic sector became the primary force in driving the process of secularization, that process was further encouraged by several centuries of religious warfare and a growing awareness of religious pluralism. In response to both, an attempt was made to find beliefs and a morality that transcended particular religious claims. Modern societies are thus marked by patterns of religious tolerance, and people are expected to commit themselves to forms of government and law based on rational rather than religious principles. In sum, secularization freed human inquiry and activity from the constraints of religion and tradition, giving birth to concepts of individual freedom and liberty; the development of modern science; a new political system, democracy; and an explosive, wealth-generating economic system, capitalism. In exchange, religious belief was reduced to a matter of personal preference, leading to increased levels of doubt and anxiety regarding the issue of the ultimate meaning, if any, of human existence.

Applications

The concept of secularization has been used as a broad analytical tool to study and suggest policy in a wide range of areas related to societal and cultural change. Political scientists and economists who are concerned about development and modernization have used it to analyze various Third World countries to discover impediments to development. They focus on elements of tradition, religion, and superstition that they believe prevent societies from adopting rationalized modes of economic production, and political and legal systems based on merit, equality, and constitutional rather than on religious or informal law. Special emphasis is given to transforming education and relegating religious influence to the private realm.

Many sociologists, following the lead of French sociologist Émile Durkheim, have focused on the issue of political legitimation and political instability in modern societies. These scholars focus on the ability of modern pluralistic societies to generate a set of morals and beliefs that will be accepted by the vast majority of the populace. Similarly, they are concerned about the ability of secular societies to elicit the loyalty required if people are to accept the sacrifices of taxation, legal restrictions, and military service that are necessary for the smooth functioning of government. In response, theorists such as sociologist Robert Bellah have argued that modern societies generate a universally shared, cohesive "civil religion" that functions as traditional religions once did. A civil religion has symbols such as flags and national heroes, rites and celebrations in the form of national holidays, and a set of shared beliefs and values that are often identified in the nation's founding documents. Such functional religion can be found in self-proclaimed secular states such as The People's Republic of China and the former Soviet Union as well as in nations such as the United States and the European nations, which are supportive of religion but practice separation of church and state. Theorists attempt to identify the components of the civil religions of various nation states as a way of gaining greater cross-cultural understanding and therefore improving international communication.

Other theorists are more pessimistic about the possibilities of finding a source of political legitimation once religion is banished to the realm of the personal. The sociologist Peter Berger is part of a group that uses the concept of secularization to explain current social instability and the rise of social problems. According to these scholars, as people lose their sense of shared commitments and values, society becomes increasingly conflictive. People refuse to make sacrifices for the common good, and society becomes more litigious. These observations have been used by religious fundamentalists to attack secular society and to support the claim that the loss of religious values is causing social collapse. Although religious fundamentalists have called for a return to traditional religion and the dominance of society by a single religious tradition, social scientists have been less certain about how to counteract the disintegrative effects of secularization in pluralist societies.

Yet another approach is to explain the change in the individual's relationship to religion and the change in religious structures. While traditional religions have lost much of their social power, their structures have also changed. Like other modern organizations, they have become bureaucratically structured and governed by technically trained specialists. This has led to a separation between the clergy and laity by virtue of which the religious concerns and policies of the two groups are often at odds. This has led to both a decline in membership in some traditional religious bodies and the emergence of popularly based religious movements, both conservative and liberal (as found in certain forms of liberation theologies). Similarly, since individuals are free to choose a religion and shape it to their personal wants and needs, modern religious institutions have become less concerned about preserving the essentials of their traditions and more concerned about packaging a message that will attract adherents. In the process, religious traditions have been minimizing uncomfortable moral requirements and emphasizing and creating alleged benefits of the religion to its subscribers. So, for example, the popularized Christianity of televangelism promises healing of physical and emotional traumas, economic enrichment, and eternal salvation, but seldom encourages listeners to love their enemies or sell all they have and give it to the poor, which are moral tenets of the Christian faith.

Finally, the theory has been used to analyze the fundamental discontent that seems to be inherent in modern cultures. Economic prosperity was expected to bring happiness and contentment. The end of religious ideology was expected to usher in an age of unprecedented peace. Neither has come to pass. Sociologists such as Andrew Greeley and Thomas O'Dea question whether people can be content without some sense of ultimate meaning and purpose. Yet secularized societies provide no such meaning and purpose; they focus only on immediate political, societal, and economic tasks. In such societies, people live with an inescapably high degree of anxiety and anomie. A related question is whether people are innately religious or religion is a holdover from the childish, superstitious past. Bellah and others see religion as being part of human consciousness and therefore hold that the reemergence of religious fundamentalisms and the emergence of new religious movements, including forms of feminist and ecological spirituality, provide evidence of religion's natural persistence. Bellah's theory of religious evolution argues that social instability is a transitional phase in a process in which religion is being transformed into symbols and structures that are more suited to the modern era.

Context

The emerging independence of culture and society from religious control was evident as early as the sixteenth century in the Church's struggle against Copernicus to suppress modern science and in the struggles of the European monarchs to free themselves from papal influence. The full significance of the shift was first clearly articulated by Auguste Comte, the nineteenth century French philosopher. He described the shift as freeing the human mind from bondage to a superstitious, pre-rational past. He mirrored the optimism of the early rationalists, who saw the change as ushering in a new age of prosperity, peace, achievement, and happiness.

Responding to the conditions generated by the early industrial revolution, a group of late nineteenth and early twentieth century sociologists, including Max Weber and Émile Durkheim, began to articulate more clearly the nature of the changes that were occurring. They highlighted the appearance of institutional differentiation and specialization, the emergence of forms of bureaucratic rationalization, and the focus on efficiency that are defining characteristics of modern societies. While still guardedly optimistic, all began to notice the negative underside of modern culture, with its dehumanizing bureaucracies, destruction of natural communities, suppression of emotion, and amoral character. In *The Protestant Ethic and the Spirit of Capitalism*, Weber worried that the society of the future may feel like an "iron cage" to its inhabitants.

The concept of secularization, however, did not receive full definition and elaboration until the 1960's. In response to growing societal unrest and rapid social change, especially in the area of public morality, a group of sociologists began to focus on the interaction of religion, society, and culture. Of particular interest were the individual's need for a system of ultimate meaning and society's need for a final source of legitimation for its laws and policies. According to Peter Berger, both are secure only if they reside in a sacred, unquestioned realm, a "sacred canopy." It is this very canopy that secularization is dismantling. Consequently, persons are being left without meaning and societies are becoming unstable, lacking legitimation. Other theorists, such as Bellah, argued that secularization created instability as new systems of meaning emerged to replace the old, but also held a new order was emerging. Still others, such as Thomas O'Dea, view secularization as an ambiguous process that frees individuals and societies from captivity to traditions and therefore offers new freedoms and creativity. Inevitably, the same process threatens social stability and human meaning. Debate surrounding the theory of secularization continues to center on the evaluation of modern social systems, their promises, and their limitations.

The recent global revival of religion in all its forms, including fundamentalism, liberation theology, and new religions, raises questions about both the extent and the reversibility of secularization. Is this religious revival simply the "last gasp" of religion before it is swallowed by a totally secular future? Alternatively, have the discontents generated by modern societies become so great that religion, in some form, will return to a position of cultural and social preeminence?

Bibliography

Bellah, Robert N. *Beyond Belief: Essays on Religion in a Post-Traditional World.* New York: Harper & Row, 1970. An important collection of essays that includes essays on civil religion and religious evolution. It provides cross-cultural examples on the influence of religion in modern societies.

Berger, Peter L. *The Sacred Canopy: Elements of a Sociological Theory of Religion.* Garden City, N.Y.: Doubleday, 1967. The book traces the process of secularization in Western culture. The primary analytical focus is on the problem of legitimacy and the shift in religious institutions and beliefs.

Durkheim, Émile. *The Elementary Forms of the Religious Life.* Translated by Joseph Ward Swain. New York: Free Press, 1965. This classic text, first published in 1915, presented religion as primarily a set of social symbols and rites. As such, religion is seen as the basis of social cohesion. This work is the foundation for contemporary theories of civil religion.

Greeley, Andrew. *Unsecular Man: The Persistence of Religion.* New York: Schocken Books, 1972. The author presents evidence of the persistently religious nature of human beings. He argues that both people and society are much less secular than theorists indicate.

Hammond, Phillip E., ed. *The Sacred in a Secular Age.* Berkeley: University of California Press, 1985. A collection of essays that explore the changing nature of religion and its influence in modern societies. It represents some of the ongoing debate surrounding the secularization thesis.

Luckmann, Thomas. *The Invisible Religion: The Problem of Religion in Modern Society.* New York: Macmillan, 1967. The classic study in the privatization of religion in modern culture. Luckmann traces the decline of traditional religious institutions as individuals construct their own individualized systems of meaning.

McGuire, Meredith B. *Religion: The Social Context.* 3d ed. Belmont, Calif.: Wadsworth, 1992. A general textbook on the sociology of religion that provides an overview of the social function of religion. Chapters 7 and 8 provide a useful summary of the secularization debate and a good discussion of religion and social change.

Martin, David. *A General Theory of Secularization.* New York: Harper & Row, 1978. This book traces the secularization of Western culture but argues that it may take a variety of forms. The author then traces some of these patterns by reference to Western societies.

O'Dea, Thomas F. *The Sociology of Religion.* 2d ed. Englewood Cliffs, N.J.: Prentice-

Hall, 1983. A very short, readable introduction to the sociology of religion. It focuses particularly on the role of religion in modern society and the social and religious effects of secularization.

Weber, Max. *The Protestant Ethic and the Spirit of Capitalism.* Translated by Talcott Parsons. New York: Scribner's, 1958. First published in 1904, this influential work traces the contributions of Protestantism to the development of modern capitalism. Weber highlights the components of modern societies, including rationalization and institutional differentiation.

Charles L. Kammer III

Cross-References

Bureaucracies, 172; Churches, Denominations, and Sects, 246; Civil Religion and Politics, 259; Religion: Functionalist Analyses, 1603; Religion: Marxist and Conflict Theory Views, 1610; The Separation of Church and State, 1714; Socialization: Religion, 1894; The Sociology of Religion, 1952; Values and Value Systems, 2143.

SEGREGATION VERSUS INTEGRATION

Type of sociology: Racial and ethnic relations
Field of study: Patterns and consequences of contact

Segregation refers to the separation of groups of people, either by law or because of custom or economic disparities. Integration means that all people and groups in a society are considered equal under the law and are allowed to move freely and live without unequal restrictions. Integration is the ideal in American society, but, for a number of reasons, segregation is still the reality.

Principal terms
  DE FACTO SEGREGATION: separation of racial or ethnic groups that results from attitudes, habits, and housing patterns; separation "in fact"
  DE JURE SEGREGATION: separation of racial or ethnic groups based on law; this type of segregation has been illegal in the United States since 1954
  DISCRIMINATION: the denial of opportunities and rights on the basis of characteristics such as race, ethnicity, or religion
  INTEGRATION: the condition that exists when all people in a society live together freely and experience equality under the law
  PREJUDICE: arbitrary beliefs or feelings about an individual belonging to a certain group or toward the group as a whole

Overview

Segregation refers to the geographic separation of ethnic, religious, or racial groups by law or custom. Examples of segregation may be found throughout history, as groups considered inferior or subordinate have been forced to live in specific areas of a city or town. Jews in Europe were forced into separate communities, called ghettos, in the Middle Ages by Christians who believed the Jews were "unclean" and racially inferior. The caste systems in India and Southeast Asia forced persons born into "inferior" castes to live in separate areas of a community. Some people, considered so unclean that merely breathing the same air they breathed would contaminate a higher caste member's body, were forced to live outside the walls surrounding many Indian villages. These "untouchables" suffered miserably, but their status was defined by Hindu religious beliefs, and they could do little to improve their living standards. Though the caste system has been outlawed by the Indian government and all citizens are considered equal in the eyes of the law, beliefs die hard, and Indians considered lower caste are still victims of discrimination and segregation. Other examples of segregation include the apartheid system that existed in South Africa and the Jim Crow system that existed in the southern part of the United States. South Africa officially repudiated its system of separate racial communities in 1992, and, since 1964, discrimination based on race has been illegal in the United States. Yet segregation is still found in both countries. Though legal (or "de jure") segregation has largely disappeared, "de facto" segregation resulting from attitudes and customs, can be found almost everywhere in those two countries.

In 1954 the United States Supreme Court outlawed racial segregation in public schools in the famous case *Brown v. Board of Education.* Separating children by race, the Court found, created a feeling of inferiority among African American students. Segregation made them feel unwanted by the white majority, and this feeling prevented them from getting an equal educational opportunity. The Court ordered school districts to desegregate "with all deliberate speed." White reaction, however, which turned violent in many southern communities, prevented rapid compliance with the Court's ruling. By 1966 only 15 percent of southern school districts were desegregated. In an effort to push integration forward, the Office of Civil Rights in the Department of Health, Education, and Welfare began to withhold federal money from segregated districts. These financial sanctions encouraged fuller compliance with the *Brown* ruling so that by 1973 almost half of the districts in the South had desegregated. In the North and West, on the other hand, where the government did not threaten to withhold money, almost 70 percent of school districts remained highly segregated.

In 1990 racially integrated schools (defined as those with some black students but with white students in the majority) remained a distant goal. More than 63 percent of African American children attended segregated schools. Housing patterns and neighborhood segregation were the primary reasons for this racial division. Segregation in the American school system has also resulted directly from the attitudes and actions of white parents who refused to send their children to schools attended by blacks.

Many white Americans, according to studies of public opinion, hold beliefs that help prevent integration. Generally, whites say that they believe in equality for all, but when it comes to action that would make that principle possible, they reject any changes. For example, many white Americans fear that once a few black people move into a neighborhood, more will quickly follow, and the racial change will greatly lower the value of their property. They also fear that crime rates will increase—even if many, or most, of the newcomers are middle class—and that educational quality will decline. White residents flee, and neighborhoods quickly become resegregated. Unlike most whites, a majority of African Americans (more than 70 percent) support and say they would choose to live in mixed communities. The ideal neighborhood, according to polls of African Americans, would be 55 percent white and 45 percent black. Whites polled, on the other hand, have said they would probably move if the black population reached more than 20 percent.

Many white Americans do not believe that racism and racial discrimination are major problems. These whites believe that integration and affirmative action programs have all but ended inequality and that blacks exaggerate the negative effects of inequality on their educational and employment opportunities. Only 26 percent of white Americans in a national poll thought that African Americans faced any "significant" discrimination in their daily lives. More than twice as many blacks (53 percent) responded that they faced significant amounts of prejudice and discrimination in their day-to-day affairs. Many white Americans believe that African Americans deserve the rejection they receive in American society, believing that it is "their" fault they are economically and socially unequal. If "they" simply worked a little harder, drank less, made a greater effort to find better jobs, and took firmer control of their own lives, this argument goes, they would be accepted as equal by whites. Other surveys of white attitudes, however, show that this belief is not borne out in reality. Many whites want little or no contact with blacks and will, in fact, go to great expense and move considerable distances to maintain racial isolation and separation. This type of de facto segregation is the norm in American society, and it is very difficult to change.

Applications

Segregation in the United States can only be ended through a change in white attitudes so that integration of neighborhoods and schools may be accomplished. Few whites seem willing to change, however, and most assume that black people, no matter what their accomplishments or talents, are associated with crime and neighborhood deterioration. Such perceptions are based on stereotypes, which are notoriously difficult to eradicate. Education has some affect in reducing notions of white supremacy and separation, as people of any race with higher levels of schooling are more tolerant of contact with others. Yet African Americans at every level of income, education, and status generally live in separate communities. One measure of separation is called the "segregation index," in which 100 represents a totally segregated community and 0 measures a totally integrated community—one in which people are randomly distributed regardless of race. Sociologist Gary Orfield has shown that residential segregation in the United States has grown since 1980. The average index for communities is 78, a number that varies only by relatively minor amounts depending on education and income. In communities with high levels of educational achievement (meaning two or more years of college on the average), the index in northern cities and suburbs is 71. In many white areas of cities and suburbs where the average level of education is a high school diploma or less, the index is in the 90's, which indicates almost total segregation. In contrast to black/white relations, the index for Asian Americans and Hispanic Americans drops to 50 or less depending on educational achievement.

Such high levels of segregation mean that many whites have few contacts with African Americans anywhere outside their work environment. Even at work, because of past discrimination and segregation in the workforce, blacks are frequently in more demeaning and less prestigious occupations. In Detroit, Chicago, and Cleveland, separation of the races is almost complete; this is also true for a majority of those cities' suburbs. Few white Americans see this result of their attitudes as desirable, with 97 percent saying they are opposed to discrimination in employment, 90 percent rejecting segregation in education, and 85 percent supporting open housing. These opinions, however, support only the *ideal* of equality; when programs that would significantly change traditional patterns of white privilege are suggested, such as school busing or affirmative action programs, they are overwhelmingly rejected by white opinion.

In 1971 the Supreme Court in *Swann v. Charlotte-Mecklenburg Board of Education* called for busing to break down traditional patterns of school segregation. The result was an angry series of demonstrations, riots, and protests led by white parents and political leaders protesting "forced busing." Even though in most cases it was shown that housing segregation was the chief cause of school segregation, therefore making it necessary to move students by public transportation out of their segregated communities if integration was to be accomplished, most white parents refused to support the idea. The courts and government officials backed away from this solution to the problem of de facto segregation. This occurred despite the fact that after many years of busing in cities such as Hartford, Connecticut, and Richmond, Virginia, both black and white parents said that they were satisfied with the results and no longer objected to being bused away from their neighborhood school.

Sociologists have demonstrated that integrated learning can have positive effects on educational outcomes. The original *Brown v. Board of Education* decision held out the hope that freeing African Americans from segregated institutions would enable black students to improve academically and to see themselves as fully equal to whites. Indeed, in integrated school settings, blacks and whites do make more friends with members of the other race, and black students who are graduated from integrated high schools are much more likely to go to college, work in higher status jobs, and live in integrated neighborhoods. Black students in integrated schools also score higher on reading tests and are far less likely to be involved with the police—a point of key importance, since it shows the connection between criminal activity and lack of education. Desegregation has been demonstrated to produce better black-white relations.

Such evidence makes developments in school and residential desegregation in the 1980's even more troubling, because the levels of racial separation throughout American society have actually increased. In 1990 white enrollment in public schools in Washington, D.C., stood at 4 percent; in Atlanta it was 8 percent, in Newark 9 percent, and in Detroit 12 percent. Chicago remained the most residentially segregated city, with a segregation index of 91, but many other northern cities were in the 80's. Census tracks in southern cities indicated less neighborhood segregation, but schools, as in Atlanta, showed little integration. Most whites attended either all-white private schools or went to public schools in virtually all-white suburbs. The only possible solution to the problem of school segregation would be a combining of city and suburban school districts, but only a very few white parents would support such a policy. Isolation and racial polarization will be likely to continue in American schools and neighborhoods.

Context

Before the Civil War (1861-1865), slavery was the principal system of maintaining white supremacy in the United States. The slave system rigidly segregated African Americans into an inferior status; under the laws of most slave states, slaves were not even considered human beings. With the abolition of slavery in the aftermath of the bloodiest war in American history, Southern whites constructed a system of legal segregation to maintain white supremacy and keep blacks in an inferior economic and social status. That system of legal segregation, in which it was a violation of state law for black and white Americans to attend school or church together, or to eat together, lasted until the 1960's. Officially the Civil Rights Act of 1964 barred discrimination in education, employment, or housing based on race, religion, ethnicity, or gender. Still, the attitudes of white superiority remained dominant in the minds of most whites, and actual integration in schools, employment, and housing, occurred very slowly, if at all. In Illinois, for example, African Americans composed 18.7 percent of the student population, and 83.2 percent of them attended totally segregated schools. In Mississippi, African Americans totaled 55.5 percent of school enrollments, with 80.3 percent going to segregated classrooms. Such numbers reflect the continuing segregation of American society.

Even within integrated schools some observers find an internal system of student segregation. Black students make up about 16 percent of all public school students in the United States but 40 percent of all pupils considered to be retarded, to have a disability, or to be deficient. This has led to segregation by "tracking," in which students are separated by scores on standardized tests and according to their "potential." Black students are found in overwhelming numbers in the lowest track. African American children enter school with great disadvantages in socioeconomic backgrounds and cultural opportunities; those two factors, especially the first (which refers to family income), are directly related to doing well in school and on achievement tests. Unless economic opportunities for black families greatly improve, it is likely that the large gap in educational outcomes will not be significantly reduced. Disparities in family income account for most of the differences among white students on these same tests, so it should not be surprising that, given the large income gap between white and black families, with median wealth for black families ($6,837) being less than 25 percent of white family wealth ($32,667 in 1984), African Americans would do less well in schools.

Some American communities have successfully achieved integration, but usually it requires some restrictions and positive actions on the part of local leaders. "Managed integration" is a requirement: The number of black residents cannot be allowed to become more than 16 to 20 percent of any neighborhood, or whites will begin to move. Citizens interested in integration must take charge of their own communities and not allow real estate interests to take advantage of racial fears through "blockbusting" tactics. Oak Park, Illinois, has shown that a carefully controlled housing market can promote racial integration. It has been shown in this Chicago suburb that white citizens will not run from the community as long as black residents make up less than half of the population. White anxieties about crime are significantly reduced in these circumstances.

In other areas and communities, desegregation of public schools could be accomplished only by an extensive busing program that would take students out of their neighborhoods and bring them to integrated school facilities. Other ideas, such as freedom of choice plans (whereby students can voluntarily attend any school in the district), and so-called "magnet schools," offering special programs for selected students, have done little to reduce segregation. Integration is worthwhile as a goal for American society because it has at least three positive consequences for all citizens: First, it improves black performance in schools; second, it improves race relations by allowing students from different backgrounds an opportunity to know and understand one another; and third, it reduces social isolation between all Americans. Isolation drives people further apart and allows people to believe that they are much different from or much better than others. Seeing people on a day-to-day basis conducting normal human activities such as work, play, and learning, shows that much of what people do, regardless of race, is quite ordinary and that most Americans share similar desires and ways of doing things. Such truths can only be learned if people begin to live together as equals. To produce this result, white Americans' attitudes are in need of great change.

Bibliography

Clark, Kenneth B. *Dark Ghetto: Dilemmas of Social Power*. New York: Harper & Row, 1965. Clark, a black psychologist, surveys the effects of segregation on African American society. Written before the explosion of racial violence in the mid-1960's, the book provides deep insights into black rage and the potential for violence. A beautifully written study that captures the tragic spirit of black American society. Calls for dramatic changes in white attitudes, the true source of race problems in the United States, according to Clark.

Davis, Allison, and John Dollard. *Children of Bondage: The Personality Development of Negro Youth in the Urban South*. New York: Harper & Row, 1964. Originally written for the American Council of Education in 1940, this book by two leading students of race relations captures the terrible consequences of segregation for black students in the Jim Crow South. Presents life histories of people terrorized and victimized by a society devoted to white supremacy. A classic work that makes a lasting contribution to the field of sociology.

Franklin, John Hope. *The Color Line: Legacy for the Twenty-first Century*. Columbia: University of Missouri Press, 1993. A series of lectures delivered by an eminent African American historian looking into the past and the future of race relations in the United States. Finds that, despite limited improvements, white Americans are still a decidedly racist community.

Hacker, Andrew. *Two Nations: Black and White, Separate, Hostile, Unequal*. New York: Charles Scribner's Sons, 1992. Provides direct statistical evidence from polls bearing witness to the deteriorating state of race relations in the United States. Well-written (and opinionated) analysis of the crisis by a leading white political scientist. Highly recommended.

Myrdal, Gunnar. *An American Dilemma: The Negro Problem and Modern Democracy*. 20th anniversary ed. New York: Harper & Row, 1962. A classic study in two volumes of race relations in the United States. Originally completed and published by Swedish sociologist Myrdal in 1944. Myrdal remained hopeful, because Americans appeared dedicated to an ideal of racial equality. Simply believing in that concept, he concluded, would help Americans eventually achieve that goal, though Myrdal offered no prediction as to when the ideal would actually be realized. Often considered one of the great sociological studies of all time, this work is well worth reading or consulting.

Leslie V. Tischauser

Cross-References

Affirmative Action, 21; Apartheid, 127; Busing and Integration, 179; The Civil Rights Movement, 265; Individual Discrimination, 547; Institutional Racism, 996; Microsociology, 1192; Racial and Ethnic Stratification, 1579; Racism as an Ideology, 1586; School Desegregation, 1686.

THE SEPARATION OF CHURCH AND STATE

Type of sociology: Major social institutions
Fields of study: Politics and the state; Religion

Separation of church and state means that the government may not establish a particular church or religious faith, legislate on behalf of religion itself or a specific institutional expression of religious faith, or interfere with an individual's free exercise of religion. By staying clear of religious activities, the government ensures that all citizens possess full religious liberty.

Principal terms
> CIVIL RELIGION: a set of religio-political beliefs that unifies a people, gives sacred meaning to the ongoing political life of the community, and provides common goals and values for society's existence
> DISSENTERS: those who practice a religion different from that which has been established
> ESTABLISHMENT OF RELIGION: a situation in which a specific religious faith is recognized by the ruler or legislative body as the official faith of the nation and accordingly is given special privileges
> NEUTRALITY: a situation in which the state shows no preference for or bias against any specific expression of religion
> NEW CHRISTIAN RIGHT: a strongly conservative political movement that arose among Protestant fundamentalists in the late 1970's, promoting a sweeping socio-moral agenda centering on so-called traditional values
> SECULAR ORIENTATION: an orientation toward matters in this world; the opposite of a spiritual, religious, or otherworldly orientation
> TOLERATION: a situation in which adherents of the majority faith within a region permit adherents of a dissenting or minority religion to practice their faith there

Overview

From the dawn of history, religion and public authority have been inseparably linked. Whether it involved tribal gods, the gods of a city, a national deity such as Yahweh for the nation of Israel, or a ruler possessing divinity, such as an Egyptian pharoah or a Roman or Japanese emperor, religion was an integral part of life in every state. The cults and priests were supported from the public treasury, and the entire populace was expected to participate in religious rites. Many of these religions were really civil religions that provided a kind of social glue for the political community. Even Christianity, which began as a dissenting faith in the Roman Empire, eventually became established. It then expected the secular authorities to preserve doctrinal orthodoxy, and heresy in religion came to be regarded as treason against the state.

The Protestant Reformation ended the religious unity that characterized medieval Europe, but except for the Anabaptists (who rejected any tie between church and state), the Reformers insisted on religious conformity. Many rulers in sixteenth and seventeenth century Europe, both Protestants and Catholics, persecuted dissenters and forced them to leave their territories. Others, however, decided that national unity was more important than religious unity and tolerated some significant expressions of dissent. Expressions of the latter view include the Edict of Nantes of Henry IV in France (1598), which granted civil and religious rights to the Huguenot (Calvinist Protestant) minority, and the Act of Toleration (1689) in England, which allowed freedom of worship to Protestant dissenters, although the Test Act of 1673 denied them the right to hold public office. The eighteenth century Enlightenment did much to undermine religious establishments, since most of its leading figures were indifferent to the existing churches. The French writer Voltaire in particular condemned the official churches and championed religious liberty.

In the American colonies, the idea of religious freedom took root. Although most colonies had religious establishments, they were not particularly severe ones. Dissenters were usually tolerated or they moved to the frontier away from colonial control. Some groups even came to America to find religious freedom, and the colonies of Rhode Island and Pennsylvania from the beginning rejected the idea of an official church and permitted the religious practices of nearly all sects. The Enlightenment affected many American leaders, including Benjamin Franklin, George Washington, Thomas Jefferson, and James Madison, who were strong proponents of religious liberty. Two highly significant statements of this view were Madison's *Memorial and Remonstrance* (1785), in which he opposed a Virginia measure to support teachers of religion, and Jefferson's *Bill for Establishing Religious Freedom* in Virginia (1786).

Although vestiges of the colonial establishments remained in some states, religious liberty was enshrined in the federal Constitution. Article Six stated, "No religious test shall ever be required as a qualification to any office or public trust under the United States," and the First Amendment affirmed: "Congress shall make no law respecting an establishment of religion or prohibiting the free exercise thereof." After he had become president, Thomas Jefferson explained to a group of Baptists in 1802 that "religion is a matter which lies solely between man and his God, that he owes account to none other for his faith or his worship, that the legislative powers of government reach actions only, and not opinions," and that thus the First Amendment built "a wall of separation between church and state." In other words, the First Amendment would prevent domination of the various churches by the state and protect the state from domination by any church.

Most states adopted bills of rights containing guarantees for religious liberty, while the remaining state religious establishments were eliminated by 1833. The Fourteenth Amendment, adopted in 1868, seemed to make the federal Bill of Rights applicable to the states, but only in the twentieth century did the Supreme Court rule that this was actually the case. Still, the idea of church-state separation was popular in the United States. It was based on the premise of "benevolent neutrality" (the government was favorably disposed toward, not hostile to, religion) and the assumption that evangelical Protestants (for all practical purposes a de facto establishment) could secure legislation at all levels reflecting their views and at the same time shape the civil religion. In fact, Protestants used the separation doctrine against dissenters such as Mormons and Roman Catholics to prevent them from gaining special privileges.

The emergence of religious pluralism in the twentieth century, however, subjected the idea of separation of church and state to increasing strain. For example, Catholics demanded public assistance for their schools (called by critics "parochiaid"), Jehovah's Witnesses refused to accept limitations on the right to propagate their faith or to engage in the civil religion exercise of saluting the flag, and Jews and atheists objected to Christian religious observances in public school classrooms. Some people who were fearful of Catholic assertiveness formed Protestants and Other Americans United for Separation of Church and State (now simply Americans United) in 1946 to counter efforts to "breach" the wall of separation. Others who were apprehensive about the growth of secularism and the threat of atheistic communism reaffirmed the civil religion in the 1950's, through such measures as adding "under God" to the Pledge of Allegiance, adopting "In God We Trust" as the national motto, and instituting a National Day of Prayer.

Applications

Much of the controversy over separation of church and state focused on Supreme Court rulings. In a Jehovah's Witnesses' case in 1940, the court "incorporated" the Free Exercise Clause of the First Amendment into the Fourteenth Amendment (applied it to the states), and in a parochial school busing case in 1947, it did likewise with the Establishment Clause. This laid the groundwork for the Court's most controversial actions, the school prayer and Bible reading decisions of 1962 and 1963. The Court ruled that both an innocuous "nondenominational" prayer and the reading of the Bible at the beginning of the school day constituted an official establishment of religion and therefore were not permissible.

In these cases and in a subsequent case in 1970 involving tax exemptions for properties used for religious worship, the justices developed a series of tests with which to evaluate government involvement in the religious realm. Summarized in a 1971 case (*Lemon v. Kurtzman*), they are commonly known as the "*Lemon* test": (1) "secular purpose"—whether the law in question is designed to advance or inhibit religion; (2) "primary effect"—the primary effect of the law must be neither to foster nor to oppose religion; and (3) "excessive entanglement"—it must not require a high level of governmental involvement to ensure that the effect of a program is not helping or hindering religion. Although the three tests operate independently, a measure must meet all of them to be ruled constitutional.

What followed was a bitter controversy between adherents of the "accommodationist" or "no preference" and the "separationist" or "no aid" approaches to church-state matters, although views about the proper relationship between religion and civil authority actually are more varied than these opposites suggest. The New Christian

Right and its allies in the Roman Catholic church and some Orthodox Jewish circles, together with the Ronald Reagan and George Bush administrations, insisted that the nation was founded on Christian or "Judeo-Christian" values, that the "original intent" of the First Amendment was merely to preclude the formation of a national church, and that a cooperative relationship between government and religious institutions was proper so long as aid was given fairly and without favoritism to any specific group. Separationists contended that the amendment banned both a single church and "multiple establishments" in which the government would fund many religions on an equal basis. Nondiscriminatory, even-handed aid was not allowable because religion and government must be independent. As Supreme Court Justice Hugo Black put it, "a union of government and religion tends to destroy government and degrade religion."

The New Christian Right argued strongly for the "restoration" of school prayer through a constitutional amendment that would overturn Supreme Court rulings prohibiting officially sanctioned prayers and devotional Bible reading, even though prior to 1962 these practices had already been discontinued in many states and localities. This restoration was expanded by logical implication to include such things as moments of silence for prayer and meditation, organized prayers by high school football teams, the posting of the Ten Commandments in classrooms, and expressly Christian baccalaureate services and invocations at high school graduations. One of the most popular clichés of the Christian Right campaign was "Where were we when God was expelled from the classroom?" Although legislation permitting "voluntary prayer" never cleared Congress, the high court in 1990 did uphold the Equal Access Act, which allowed student prayer and Bible clubs to meet at public schools during noninstructional times under certain conditions.

Another way in which the Religious Right sought to influence the public schools was by pressuring them to teach "creationism," a religious doctrine that is contrary to the view of evolution held by most scientists, but the courts have rejected this attempt. The Christian Right also accused the schools of teaching the "religion of secular humanism" or promoting "new age religion," and called for the censorship of textbooks that present ideas or values that they reject.

A highly significant school issue is that of state aid to sectarian schools. An attempt in the 1870's to secure a national constitutional amendment prohibiting the expenditure of public funds for private institutions failed, but nearly half of the states adopted language in their constitutions barring such tax aid. Throughout the twentieth century, Catholic leaders have demanded assistance, and they have found formidable allies among the New Christian Right and even the Republican Party itself.

Thus, in the 1980's and 1990's, the Congress and state legislatures were bombarded with schemes for "vouchers," tuition tax credits, and other types of aid that would benefit sectarian or parochial schools. Often this was done by means of popular initiatives or referendums. Conservatives insisted that parents should have the right of "school choice," even though these institutions accepted or rejected whomever they wished. They also argued that "competition" with private schools would force public schools to improve. Since these measures regularly fell afoul of the *Lemon* test when brought before the courts, advocates of subsidies to religious schools called for the appointment of justices who would overturn this rule.

Controversies arising from the "free exercise" of religion have not been as politically charged as the establishment ones, but the issues could be just as knotty. They include such things as Mormon polygamy, aggressive proselytism by Jehovah's Witnesses, forced medical treatment for those who believe in faith healing, conscientious objection to war, Seventh-day Adventists' refusal to work on the sabbath, Sunday closing laws, the Amish rejection of compulsory public school attendance, and animal sacrifice by adherents of the Afro-Cuban faith called Santería. In 1963, the Supreme Court began applying a "compelling state interest" test to such matters, which meant that government may not restrict one's religious rights unless it can first demonstrate that a compelling state interest justifies such infringement and that a "less restrictive alternative means" to achieve the state's secular objectives does not exist. When the Court in 1990 threw out the compelling state interest test in a case from Oregon regarding the use of peyote in a Native American religious rite and ruled that laws that might infringe on religious belief need only be "neutral and generally applicable," Congress passed the Religious Freedom Restoration Act in 1993, which reaffirmed the principle.

There are other issues of church-state separation that continue to be debated and litigated. One involves the use of religious symbols on public property, such as crosses, nativity scenes, and Menorahs in a town square or on a courthouse lawn. Another involves state-funded legislative and military chaplains. A third involves ceremonial proclamations, such as the Year of the Bible and the National Day of Prayer. An important issue is the tax-exemption enjoyed by church property and the question of whether it is endangered by political activity by clerics and church members. The establishment of diplomatic relations with the Vatican in 1984 also has important church-state ramifications. Some even see the abortion issue as having church-state overtones because of the theological debate over when life begins and its impact on legislation.

Context

Separation of church and state is a particularly American institution. The United States pioneered the practice of having no established church and permitting all religious groups to worship freely. To be sure, this occurred in a Christian context, but the language of the First Amendment left the door open for the inclusion of other religions as the nation became increasingly pluralistic.

European countries gradually followed the American example. France severed all ties with Roman Catholicism in 1905, and the 1919 constitution of the German Republic declared that there was no state church, although it did go far to accommodate the major faiths, particularly in the realm of education, and this continued to be so after the Nazi dictatorship. Soviet Russia ended the connection with the Orthodox church, and its post-World War II satellites did likewise, but since the revolutions of

1989, some of them have turned back to the old ways. Britain is moving toward ending its religious establishment, as its dominions did theirs long ago.

Roman Catholic countries have been much more reluctant to permit separation, but anticlerical movements such as the one in Mexico have been effective. The Catholic church has lost much of its political power in Italy and Spain, and Protestants are now allowed religious freedom. The Jewish establishment in Israel, however, has restricted the freedom of the Protestant and Orthodox minorities, while Muslim countries possess some of the most rigid religious establishments in the modern world. With the rise of fundamentalist movements in all the major world religions, the freedom of dissenters is in serious jeopardy. In many parts of the globe, the future of church-state separation is in doubt.

Bibliography

Ivers, Gregg. *Redefining the First Freedom: The Supreme Court and the Consolidation of State Power.* New Brunswick, N.J.: Transaction, 1993. A superb study of church-state law developed by the Supreme Court in the 1980's which explains the erosion in religious freedom that has occurred.

Levy, Leonard W. *The Establishment Clause: Religion and the First Amendment.* New York: Macmillan, 1987. A brilliant historical analysis that shows conclusively that the First Amendment was designed to separate religion and government and that it did not allow nonpreferential aid to religion.

Miller, Robert T., and Ronald B. Flowers. *Toward Benevolent Neutrality: Church, State, and the Supreme Court.* 4th ed. Waco, Tex.: Markham Press Fund, 1992. An indispensable reference work that contains the texts of key decisions on church-state matters. Also provided are informative interpretive essays on the scope and effects of the rulings.

Noonan, John T., Jr. *The Believer and the Powers That Are: Cases, History, and Other Data Bearing on the Relation of Religion and Government.* New York: Macmillan, 1987. A distinguished professor of law has brought together here an impressive collection of documents on the role of religion and government in Western society and the development of separation in America, and he provides insightful commentary on these materials.

Pfeffer, Leo. *Church, State, and Freedom.* Rev. ed. Boston: Beacon Press, 1967. This is the classic work on the historical origins and development of religious liberty in America. It is especially useful for its documentation.

Pierard, Richard V., and Robert D. Linder. *Civil Religion and the Presidency.* Grand Rapids, Mich.: Zondervan Academie Books, 1988. A historical discussion of American civil religion that centers on the presidency and reveals the relationship between civil religion and the current attacks on church-state separation.

Robbins, Thomas, and Roland Robertson, eds. *Church-State Relations: Tensions and Transitions.* New Brunswick, N.J.: Transaction, 1987. An important collection of essays written mainly by sociologists who apply the insight of sociology of religion to church-state issues in the United States and other countries. The comparative dimension is the book's greatest strength.

Swomley, John M. *Religious Liberty and the Secular State: The Constitutional Context.* Buffalo, N.Y.: Prometheus Books, 1987. A noted social ethicist provides a brief but stirring defense of the secular democratic state as the best guarantor of religious freedom for its citizens.

White, Ronald C., Jr., and Albright G. Zimmerman. *An Unsettled Arena: Religion and the Bill of Rights.* Grand Rapids, Mich.: Wm. B. Eerdmans, 1990. Essays by a number of leading scholars that deal with the conflicts surrounding the religion clauses of the First Amendment and their application to the contemporary scene.

Richard V. Pierard

Cross-References

Democracy and Democratic Governments, 483; The Nation-State, 1282; Political Influence by Religious Groups, 1394; The Protestant Ethic and Capitalism, 1533; Religion: Functionalist Analyses, 1603; Religion: Marxist and Conflict Theory Views, 1610; Secularization in Western Society, 1700.

SEX VERSUS GENDER

Type of sociology: Sex and gender
Field of study: Components of social structure

Sex and gender are concepts that differentiate the biological from the psychological and sociocultural attributes of human beings, respectively. This distinction helps to make clear the differences between men and women in society and to indicate why these differences exist.

Principal terms
GENDER SOCIALIZATION: differential child-rearing practices based on gender
GENDER STEREOTYPES: socially accepted ideas about the roles and behaviors of men and women
GENDER STRATIFICATION: a system in which groups are ranked hierarchically by gender
LABELING: a social process by means of which people are given specific characteristics that they come to accept
SEX/GENDER SYSTEM: a system in which social institutions, implicitly and explicitly, support gender stratification
SOCIOBIOLOGISTS: scientists who seek to explain human social behavior by means of biological factors and observations of nonhuman behavior

Overview

Sex and gender are concepts that are used to differentiate the biological characteristics of human beings from those that are socially learned. Sex refers to a person's biological makeup and establishes whether a person is a male or a female, while gender refers to the psychological, cultural, and social attributes that are associated with being male and female in a specific society—that is, masculinity and femininity. Both concepts are oppositional in that characteristics that are considered masculine are usually defined in contrast to those that are considered feminine. For example, in many societies, men are thought to be strong and rational, while women are considered weak and emotional. As a result, a person can belong to only one sex and gender. Most societies, with the exception of some Native American groups, consider a crossover between the categories undesirable and inappropriate, and advocate sex- and gender-specific behaviors. The latter are also known as gender stereotypes.

Until the 1960's, most scholars used the concepts of sex and gender interchangeably. Among the first to differentiate between the two concepts was the psychologist Robert Stoller. In his book *Sex and Gender* (1968), Stoller stated that the assignment of a particular sex to an individual was based on biological characteristics such as chromosomes, external genitalia, gonads, hormonal states, and secondary sex characteristics. Although this assignment is fairly clear-cut in most individuals, there are many cases in which individuals have biological characteristics that are both male and female. By contrast, Stoller argued, the term "gender" has psychological and cultural connotations and can be independent of (biological) sex. Most individuals, however, develop a gender identity that is consistent with their sex; that is, males develop masculine identities and females develop feminine identities, though there might be mixtures of both gender identities in some people. Although the distinction between sex and gender is very important in its consequences for research and life, most social scientists recognize that these concepts are not independent of each other. For example, notions of sex influence gender expectations, and vice versa.

Before this distinction became prominent in social scientific thought and literature, sociologists considered most gender differences between men and women—such as their social and cultural roles and psychological traits—to be universal, exclusive to each sex, and based on biological differences. For example, the division of labor by sex in societies, whereby men work outside the home and women work in the home as caregivers, was regarded as true in all societies and was believed to reflect the biological role of women in bearing children. Anthropologist Margaret Mead, in her classic study *Sex and Temperament in Three Primitive Societies* (1935), challenged this view by showing that in three South Pacific societies men engaged in activities, such as child care and nurturing, that in Western societies were provided exclusively by women. Gender differences not only vary across cultures, but within a culture they differ over time; in other words, what is considered gender-appropriate behavior in the United States today is different from what was acceptable in the 1950's.

With the sex and gender distinction, social scientists began to explain gender differences as socially learned through different socialization of girls and boys in society (gender socialization) and socially constructed through the sex/gender system in which social institutions, directly and indirectly, reproduce gender stratification (unequal access to social rewards and opportunities based on gender, favoring men). There is a consensus among social scientists that gender differences are a product of societal and environmental forces (nurture). Yet some scholars, notably the sociobiologists, argue that these differences are a product of biological differences (nature). Very few scholars, however, hold an extreme position on the nature-nurture continuum. Most recognize that gender differences are a product of interaction between nature and nurture.

Among the most important consequences of supporting one or the other side of the nature versus nurture debate are the implications for social change. If gender differences are constructed and learned in society, then they can be constructed and changed to eliminate gender stratification. If, however, gender differences are based in biology, then they appear to be inevitable and immutable.

Applications

The sex versus gender conceptualization raises three important questions for daily life: What are the differences between the genders? Why do these differences exist?

(Are they biological or are they learned?) What are the consequences of these differences for men and women in society? The first and third questions have great consequences for the social roles and the social opportunities available to the two sexes while the second question is very important in terms of social change and the creation of new roles and opportunities for the sexes.

Eleanor Maccoby and Carol Jacklin's *The Psychology of Sex Differences* (1974) is one of the most frequently cited reviews of the literature on sex differences. These psychologists found that of the nineteen areas that the various studies had examined, there were only four areas in which sex differences, however small, were well established: aggression, spatial ability, verbal ability, and quantitative ability.

Differences in aggression are documented widely in real life and to a lesser degree in socio-psychological studies. Unfortunately, definitions of aggression are variable from study to study. In the United States as well as in other societies, men are found to commit physical and verbal aggression more frequently than women. Maccoby and Jacklin found that 46 to 61 percent of the studies reported greater aggression by males. This aggression started between the ages of two and three and continued through the college years, after which no data were collected. Psychologist Janet Hyde, in her article "How Large Are Gender Differences in Aggression? A Developmental Meta-Analysis" (1984), used meta-analysis—in which one studies the size of the group differences in comparison to the variability of the entire population—to review the studies dealing with aggression. She found that gender differences accounted for only 5 percent of the variance in aggression, with within-gender differences considerably larger than between-gender differences. She also found that older studies based on direct observation or peer reports rather than self-reports or reports by parents and teachers tended to find greater gender differences than did more recent ones, reflecting a bias in those who conducted the studies. Besides bias, another major problem with these studies is that most include only preschoolers, school children, and college students, with few adults. Thus, one can conclude from a review of the various studies on aggression that there are small differences in aggression between males and females.

What accounts for these differences in aggression between men and women? In her book *Myth of Gender* (1992), biologist Anne Fausto-Sterling examines the biological explanations provided by various scientists. These include the presence of the Y chromosome in men, the prenatal influence of the male hormone on the developing brain of the fetus, and the level of male hormones, especially testosterone, circulating in the male individual. She concludes that most of these explanations are based on inconclusive studies that are poorly designed, are based on questionable definitions of aggression, and are unclear about whether a particular testosterone concentration causes aggression or vice versa. Yet, based on these explanations, sociobiologists argue that aggression and male domination are inevitable and that women will be limited by biology in the social roles they can perform.

Unlike the sociobiologists, sociologists provide explanations such as different socialization of boys and girls, different social expectations about aggression, and the availability of more male models of aggression as reasons for differences in aggression. In her book *Sex and Gender* (1993), psychologist Hilary Lips cites various studies that support these sociological explanations. She reports that when girls and boys are similarly rewarded for aggressive behavior, both are equally aggressive, though in most cases males are rewarded for aggressive behaviors while females are rewarded for inhibiting aggressive behaviors. She concludes that while biological differences might render men more predisposed to aggression, they do not lead to gender differences in aggression unless society encourages and rewards such behaviors. She cites cross-cultural studies that show that different societies differ in their encouragement of such behaviors and that gender differences reflect such norms. For example, in societies in which aggression and violence of all kinds are considered undesirable, there are no gender differences in aggressive behaviors.

Gender differences were also noted in cognitive skills, leading to the popular notion that "boys are smarter than girls" generally, and particularly so in math and science. Early in the twentieth century, Francis Galton, the famous geneticist, concluded that women were inferior to men in all their capacities. A few years later, James Cattell and Edward Thorndike, professors at Columbia University, argued that men were genetically more variable than women and therefore were likely to have a greater range of intelligence. Therefore, men were more likely than women to be geniuses, at one extreme, or idiots, on the other. Given this biological difference between the sexes, they argued that women should be confined to occupations such as nursing, social work, and teaching, which require "average intelligence." Leta Hollingworth, a female psychologist, was the first to question this greater-variability proposition and show that social factors influenced the underrepresentation of women at both ends of the intelligence distribution.

Today, most studies find few significant differences between men and women in general-intelligence tests. Maccoby and Jacklin argued in 1974 that, based on their review of relevant studies, one could conclude that females do better than males on verbal tasks, while males excel on visual-spatial and quantitative tasks. Hyde's 1984 review, however, found that gender accounted for only 1 percent of the difference in these skills. Furthermore, Lips reported that a 1988 study that compared children's performances between 1947 and 1983 showed that differences between males and females in verbal and other cognitive skills have declined over the years. Despite the declining evidence for differences in these skills, researchers continue to emphasize them and look for explanations based on nature.

Those who offer biological explanations indicate the presence of an X chromosome-linked intelligence gene, the presence of a larger frontal lobe in males, or (the most frequently cited reason) sex-differentiated lateralization of the human brain. Human brains are differentiated into right and left hemispheres, with each controlling certain abilities and functions. Scientists have linked this functional differentiation with sex differentiation and have argued that men's and women's brains are developed differently, which could account for differences in cognitive abilities. Yet most scientists agree that the male and female brains are more similar than different and hence do not offer evidence for different skills.

Scholars on the other side of the debate argue that these differences could be explained by social factors, such as the implicit and explicit labeling of quantitative/mechanical skills as masculine and verbal skills as feminine. This labeling results in the differential training and experience of boys and girls, such as engaging in different kinds of play activities that develop "gendered" skills; boys' emphasis on math, science, and technical courses; and the reinforcement of gendered roles and activities by parents and teachers. Differential training and experience also affect the confidence and motivation of girls to engage in "traditionally male" activities.

The preceding examples indicate that, despite little scientific support for the existence of differences between men and women in terms of cognitive skills and personality traits, many scientists continue to emphasize differences between the sexes rather than similarities, and to offer either biological or sociological explanations rather than both for these perceived phenomena. This has grave consequences, especially for women in the economic and political arenas. Economically, women suffer in several ways: First, most of what women do, such as raising families and doing housework, is not considered "work" and is therefore not remunerated. Hence, most women are not economically independent. Second, when women are remunerated for work outside the home, they are paid much less than men. According to the U.S. Bureau of Labor statistics, in 1992, on average, women earned only 75 cents for every dollar made by men. Third, women are segregated in "pink collar" occupations such as elementary school teaching, nursing, social work, and secretarial work that are typically low-paying. Finally, because women who work outside the home are seen as deviating from expected behavior, they face many hurdles in the workplace, including sexual harassment.

Politically, women have very little power. In the United States, it was only in 1920 that women won the right to vote. Although the 1992 election year was nicknamed the "year of the woman," women's representation in the House of Representatives increased in 1992 from 23 to 47, only 11 percent of the total, while in the Senate their number tripled from 2 to 6, only 6 percent of the total. It was in response to the exclusion of women from social and political life that many women launched a renewed challenge for gender equality in the late 1960's. From equal pay, equal educational, and equal occupational opportunities to redefining appropriate masculine and feminine behaviors, the women's movement of the 1960's fought for and won many changes for both men and women.

Context

Before the late 1960's, discussions of sex and gender were absent from most areas of sociology. In those areas where they were discussed, such as family and marriage, the terms "sex" and "gender" were used interchangeably, and most sociologists took sex and gender differences for granted without trying to explain them. Sociologists such as Talcott Parsons, who studied the division of labor by sex in family and society, understood the different roles played by men and women as complementary to each other and helpful in keeping society in equilibrium. Except for family sociologists, sociologists did not pay much attention to the role of gender in society.

This situation changed in the late 1960's with the emergence of the second wave of the women's movement in the United States. The feminists involved in the movement were educated, middle-class women in colleges and in government and nongovernment bureaucracies who argued that women's low status in society was a product of gender stratification, not of innate biological differences. Based on their analysis, they demanded changes in ideas about gender and gender roles as well as in the real status of women in education, occupation, and other areas.

In response to the demands of the feminist activists, Women's Studies courses were instituted in universities and colleges in the early 1970's that reflected the new thinking on gender differences. Since then, gender has become an important concept in sociological research and teaching, providing a greater understanding not only of gender stratification and ways of changing it but also of the ways in which gender interacts with race, class, and other social forces in shaping individuals and society.

Bibliography

Fausto-Sterling, Anne. *Myths of Gender: Biological Theories About Women and Men.* 2d ed. New York: Basic Books, 1992. This book is a very good critical review of biological theories about gender differences in such areas as intelligence and aggression and about science in general.

Hyde, Janet. "How Large Are Gender Differences in Aggression? A Developmental Meta-Analysis." *Developmental Psychology* 20 (July, 1984): 722-736. In this article, Hyde describes the new method of meta-analysis and reviews many studies that look at gender differences in aggression. Although somewhat technical, it provides a good critique of aggression studies.

Lips, Hilary. *Sex and Gender: An Introduction.* 2d ed. Mountain View, Calif.: Mayfield, 1993. This book is a good introduction to myths, theories, and research issues in sex and gender; similarities and differences between female-male behavior; and sex and gender in social and political relations. Includes an extensive bibliography.

Maccoby, Eleanor, and Carol Jacklin. *The Psychology of Sex Differences.* Stanford, Calif.: Stanford University Press, 1974. This was the first book to bring together all the research on differences between men and women and to provide a biological explanation for these differences. Although dated, it is frequently cited because of its pioneering efforts.

Mead, Margaret. *Sex and Temperament in Three Primitive Societies.* New York: William Morrow, 1935. This classic book provided the first cross-cultural challenge to the notion of universal gender roles. Mead documented how, in the three societies that she studied, men performed roles that were considered strictly female roles in the West, and vice-versa.

Stoller, Robert. *Sex and Gender: On the Development of Masculinity and Femininity.* New York: Science House, 1968. Stoller makes a case for the sex versus gender distinction by examining the identities of eighty-five patients with and without biological sexual abnormalities and their treatments. This book documents the complexity in assigning a sex to such persons and the strong role that society plays in the development of their gender identities.

Manisha Desai

Cross-References

SEXISM AND INSTITUTIONAL SEXISM

Type of sociology: Sex and gender

Sexism refers to both the ideology of male supremacy and the range of practices by which men are privileged, resulting in their collective dominance over women and in women's subordination. Institutional sexism refers to male dominance which is embedded in the daily operations and policies of social institutions, often in a hidden manner. Both unintentional and intentional discrimination on the basis of sex lie at the heart of institutional sexism.

Principal terms

GENDER: the social creation of differentiated roles and behaviors deemed appropriate to individuals on the basis of their sex

IDEOLOGY OF MALE SUPREMACY: the system of beliefs that supports male dominance and female subordination as the "natural" order of society; often referred to as patriarchal ideology

OCCUPATIONAL SEX SEGREGATION: the concentration of women in particular positions in the labor force, usually low-paid, low-skilled jobs such as clerical and service work

SEX DISCRIMINATION: behavior, practices, or policies that, whether intended or not, result in harm to individuals on the basis of their sex, such as denying opportunities and rights to women or giving preferential treatment and privilege to men

SOCIAL INSTITUTIONS: arrangements and interactions that order familial relations, religious beliefs and practices, governance, economic relations, education, and culture in society

SOCIAL STRATIFICATION: a hierarchical ranking system; under sex stratification, men as a group are ranked higher than women

Overview

Sexism refers to both individual and collective behavior by men that perpetuates male dominance and female subordination. Sexism is viewed as a product of androcentric, or male-centered, society in which the masculine is viewed as more valuable than the feminine. Such societies are also said to be patriarchal; patriarchy refers generally to any social arrangement in which male dominance is imbedded in social institutions and customs. While sexism was first associated primarily with male attitudes of their own superiority, it has become a more complex concept, referring both to patriarchal ideology and to the range of practices which support male dominance over women. The term "institutionalized sexism" was coined to refer to the often-hidden manner in which sexism is embedded in social institutions, operating with and without the express intent of harming women. Generally, institutional sexism refers to institutional discrimination against women.

According to Joe Feagin and Clairece Feagin in their book *Discrimination American Style: Institutional Racism and Sexism* (1987), institutionalized discrimination takes two forms. One form, referred to as "direct institutionalized discrimination," is intended to result in negative consequences for the subordinate group. The other form, "indirect institutionalized discrimination," refers to patterns of behavior or policies and practices that, while viewed as neutral, still result in unintended negative consequences. Generally, discrimination, in their view, does not rely upon prejudice to sustain it. Sometimes indirect institutional discrimination is brought about when prior intended discrimination has shaped organizational or community composition, practices, and policies. For example, Feagin and Feagin claim that seniority rules safeguard the positions of white males who, because of previous direct discrimination, came to dominate organizations. They are then able to establish rules which, though they seem neutral (such as weight and height requirements for positions involving work in public safety), prevent women from attaining membership in those institutions. This phenomenon is referred to as "past-in-present-discrimination" by Feagin and Feagin. Yet another aspect of indirect institutional discrimination is called "side-effect discrimination," referring to cases in which discrimination in one area leads to indirect discrimination in another. For example, if women experience direct discrimination in education that prevents them from gaining access to similar training as men, they then go on to experience discrimination in the economy because they cannot compete on equal footing with men for jobs.

The concept of institutional sexism developed on the heels of analyses of race relations and race discrimination in society in the 1960's. Just as the term "sexism" was not developed until after the term "racism," analyses of the differential treatment of women in society were patterned after those of the treatment of racial minorities. As women became active participants in equal rights campaigns, chiefly the Civil Rights movement of the 1950's and 1960's, they began to see their problems as synonymous to those experienced by people of color facing racism. Women began to view themselves as a minority group because of their experience of social inequality in all aspects of society. Women such as Helen Hacker, in her 1951 essay "Women as a Minority," used Louis Wirth's definition of a minority group to claim minority status for women. According to Wirth, minority group status refers not to the numerical representation of a group but to its subordinated position in society. Hacker and others argue that, just as racial groups face racism in society, so do women face sexism. Following the racial equality movement's shift in focus from individual prejudice to institutional racism, women's rights advocates and scholars turned their attention to an examination of institutional sexism.

American society is a gender-stratified society in virtually every aspect. Gender stratification refers to gender inequality in access to social resources such as wealth, power, and prestige. A gender wage gap in which full-time male workers earn at least 30 percent more, on the average, than full-time female workers demonstrates the economic inequality between women and men. According to studies by the National Academy of Sciences (NAS), the wage gap cannot be fully explained by men's greater preparedness for the labor market, since men and women have the same median level of education. In 1981, NAS found that only 25 to 50 percent of the wage gap can be explained by male/female differences in education and work experience. This means that discrimination must account for a significant proportion of the wage gap between men and women. One problem facing women is that they remain highly segregated in occupations. These feminized occupations, such as clerical and service work, afford little upward mobility, low pay, and low prestige to the women who work in them. Women are represented only in token numbers among elected officials, so they have little direct impact on major social policy. While the perpetuation of violent crime is associated with men, women are most likely to be the victims of sexual violence, with at least one in three women likely to experience a sexual assault in her lifetime. Furthermore, because of sexism in the criminal justice system, men who commit violent crimes against women are seldom prosecuted and even less often convicted and sentenced to prison terms. Women experience institutional sexism in their intimate relationships with men, in schooling, at work, and in their relations with religious, health, legal, and political institutions. Men continue to dominate these social institutions.

Sociological concern with institutionalized sexism is primarily associated with those sociologists who claim that patterns of gender stratification cannot be explained by sex role socialization alone or by any "natural" arrangement for the sexes. Rather, they claim that women's subordinated position in society can only be explained by the presence of a particular form of discrimination against women, institutional sexism. In such an analysis, the sexist beliefs of men do not solely determine women's subordinate status in society. Rather, the mechanisms which promote the subordinate status of women are critical, as are assessments of the effects of institutionalized sexism.

Applications

The analysis of institutional sexism has led to the documentation of the various mechanisms by which discrimination against women operates as well as to a range of solutions for dismantling them. Major concern has been devoted to economic aspects, including sexual harassment, differential career ladders and the "glass ceiling," and differential application of standards or even different rules for hiring and promotions. Solutions proposed have included specific civil rights legislation, lawsuits to enforce such legislation, proposals for "comparable worth," and the ill-fated Equal Rights Amendment, which was to have banned sex discrimination.

One mechanism perpetuating institutional sexism in the economy is the recruitment of women into a limited number of occupations consisting of low-paid, low-status jobs such as clerical work. This is referred to as occupational sex segregation: Women are "segregated" into a few occupations. In part, this is accomplished through gender role socialization, in which both men and women are taught to view certain occupations as more appropriate to one gender than another. It can also occur through the preferential recruitment of men. For example, women graduate students complain that "word of mouth" recruitment for positions often gives advantages to male students, who receive such information at traditionally male locales such as the locker room, the basketball court, and the poker party. Women are similarly affected in bids for promotion by what some have called "the old boy network."

According to economist Robert Cherry in his book *Discrimination: Its Economic Impact on Blacks, Women, and Jews* (1989), the institutional sexism women face may be, in fact, intentional, because male workers benefit—with access to better jobs and more likely promotions—from institutional sexism, as do employers in lower-paying areas of the economy, the secondary sector. If this is true, Cherry suggests, then aggressive efforts toward pay equity are warranted, including affirmative action and comparable worth programs. Affirmative action legislation was developed to combat institutional sexism and racism in hiring practices. Affirmative action legislation ensures only that both racial minority candidates and women candidates have access to information about positions and to the interview process. It forces all institutions who have government contracts to post positions forty-five days in advance of the application due date and to interview members from the "protected groups"—white women and men and women of color. There is no requirement to hire members of the protected groups.

Comparable worth programs are designed to combat institutional sexism by increasing economic equality between women and men. According to Joan Acker in her book *Doing Comparable Worth: Gender, Class, and Pay Equity* (1989), this involves raising the wages in occupations which have been feminized, or filled predominantly by women. The assumption behind such programs is that when jobs are feminized they are undervalued because of institutional sexism. Although the practice of paying men and women different wages for doing the same work was outlawed by the Equal Pay Act of 1963, a wage gap between men and women has persisted because women usually work in female-dominated jobs that pay less than male-dominated jobs. According to Acker, actually "doing comparable worth" is difficult because of several factors: There is tremendous resistance; it is difficult to calculate the actual "worth" of a job; and it is therefore hard to determine when pay equity has been achieved. Acker also claims that most attempts to redress institutional sexism are thwarted because when one source of institutional sexism is uncovered and undermined, new sources emerge.

While many scholars and policy makers acknowledge the existence of institutional sexism, little has actually been accomplished in applying this knowledge to social change. This is attributable in part to the weakening of the original civil rights legislation that occurred under presidents Ronald Reagan and George Bush. Areas in which attempts to combat discrimination have been most successful include the more middle-class occupations, such as law, and public sector employment, where civil rights legislation has been followed more extensively.

Context
Women have a lengthy history of fighting for equity in American society, though

much attention has been focused on the late twentieth century women's liberation movement. In fact, a large-scale "woman movement" developed in the nineteenth century in which women, largely from the abolitionist movement, sought to reexamine relations between men and women in society. Initially concerned with a range of issues including property rights, guardianship rights, and the right to divorce, this movement ultimately culminated in the suffrage movement. A large majority of women activists believed that, by getting the vote, they would be able to change other social arrangements which concerned them. In addition to active championship for women's rights, women have a lengthy history of involvement in the labor movement and trade unionism. Overall, their involvement in the struggles for the abolition of slavery and for better working conditions and their involvement later in the Civil Rights movement led women to reanalyze their own conditions as comparable to those who faced racism. These analyses were not addressed in any significant way by sociologists until the 1960's, when women in sociology, influenced by the women's liberation movement, began to call for "a sociology for women."

The field some refer to as the "sociology of gender" and others call "sociology for women" developed out of the sociology of race and ethnic relations. This is clear in Helen Hacker's essay "Women as a Minority," in which she extends Robert Park's race relations cycle theory and his concepts of the "marginal man" and "social distance" in order to develop an analysis of the position of women as compared with that of men in society. Hacker's work is also influenced by assimilationist scholar Gunnar Myrdal, who drew parallels between the status of women and blacks in the United States.

Many sociologists have focused on sex differences (actual biological differences between men and women) and gender roles (roles that are taught to males and females by socializing agents, including the family, schools, and the media). Studies of institutional sexism, however, grew out of the works of Myrdal, Wirth, and Hacker, who focus on the minority group status of women, and the barriers to their equal participation in society. One of the major problems with extending analyses of racial minorities to that of women involves the question of group identification. As Wirth defines minority group status, it includes both discrimination and a realization on the part of minority group members that they are being disadvantaged because of their minority status. While racial minorities exhibit a collective realization of discrimination, women have been far less likely to voice similar understandings of their experiences in society, particularly in intimate social organizations and relations such as the family.

Studies of institutional sexism have provoked criticisms of sociology itself, generating feminist analyses of how sociological work is organized and focused. In "Some Implications of a Sociology for Women" (1977), Dorothy Smith argues that the discipline has been organized and directed by men in a very status quo manner, leading to the exclusion of women from decision making and from serious consideration.

While examinations of women's minority group status led to calls for equity in a wide range of social organizations and institutions, including sociology itself, some have seen the focus on minority status and institutional sexism as limited. Scholars who view sexism as embedded in the very structure of society say that women cannot achieve equality solely through changes in gender role socialization or through changes in legislation. They see institutional sexism not as a surprising element in an otherwise equal society but as a built-in element of the larger social structure that permeates all social relations and social organizations. This has led to a series of works that embrace the study of institutional sexism along with studies on how to restructure gender relations in society. Generally, feminist sociologists concerned with women's equality consider discrimination to be the basis for women's unequal position in society and believe that equity in the labor force will effect changes in other social institutions, such as the family, as well.

Bibliography

Andersen, Margaret. *Thinking About Women: Sociological Perspectives on Sex and Gender.* 3d ed. New York: Macmillan, 1993. An introductory text to the sociological study of women in American society. It presents a variety of sociological perspectives on sex and gender differences, documenting these in a variety of social relationships and institutions. Included are discussions of work, family, health care, the legal system, and religion. Thorough attention is given, as well, to race and class differences among women. Periodically revised to reflect changes in society or in the sociological study of gender.

Cherry, Robert. *Discrimination: Its Economic Impact on Blacks, Women, and Jews.* Lexington, Mass.: Lexington Books, 1989. An excellent socioeconomic analysis, this book details scholarly explanations of discrimination, applying them to blacks, women, and Jews. The book, according to the author, is written with the nonspecialist in mind; it is understandable but detailed. Tables depicting racial, ethnic, and gender differences in income, education, occupation, and poverty are included, along with a detailed index and reference listings at the end of each chapter.

Feagin, Clairece Booher, and Joe R. Feagin. *Discrimination American Style: Institutional Racism and Sexism.* Englewood Cliffs, N.J.: Prentice-Hall, 1978. The authors compare and contrast institutional racism and sexism in the context of both sociological theory and documented discrimination in a variety of social settings. Excellent detail is included on the types of mechanisms used to discriminate and the effects these have on women and racial minorities.

Glazer, Nona, and Helen Youngelson Waehrer, eds. *Woman in a Man-Made World: A Socioeconomic Handbook.* 2d ed. Chicago, Ill.: Rand McNally, 1977. A classic collection of clearly written articles documenting male dominance both in the study of gender/sex differences and in society. Includes discussions by Hacker on women's minority group status and by Dorothy Smith on building a "sociology for women." Also included are articles on the competing sociological theories of gender stratification including sex differences, gender role socialization, minority group theory, and class/caste theory.

Sapiro, Virginia. *Women in American Society: An Introduction to Women's Studies.*

Palo Alto, Calif.: Mayfield, 1986. This is an introductory text which places the study of gender and institutional sexism in the intellectual context of women's studies. Topics presented include competing explanations of gender differences, as well as male dominance in education, health, religion, media, governance, language, relationships and work. Includes tables, index, and bibliography.

Sharon Elise

Cross-References

Individual Discrimination, 547; The Feminization of Poverty, 754; Gender and Religion, 813; Gender Inequality: Analysis and Overview, 820; Gender Inequalty: Biological Determinist Views, 826; Gender Socialization, 833; Health Care and Gender, 858; Women in the Labor Force, 2185; Women in the Medical Profession, 2191.

THEORIES OF SEXUAL ORIENTATION

Type of sociology: Sex and gender

Various theories have attempted to explain how a person's sexual orientation (heterosexual, homosexual, or bisexual) is formed. Theories have looked to the environment (learning and experience), to neurophysiology, and to genetics to discover explanatory mechanisms. Understanding how sexual orientation is formed is critical to the study of human sexuality, to the development of social policy, and to a general understanding of human physiology and genetics.

Principal terms

BIOLOGICAL THEORY: a theory that accounts for sexual orientation in terms of the genetics, anatomy, and biochemistry of the body

BISEXUALITY: a type of sexual orientation in which the sexual behaviors and feelings of a male or female are directed toward both males and females

HETEROSEXUALITY: a type of sexual orientation in which sexual behavior and feelings of a male or female are directed toward a person of the opposite sex

HOMOSEXUALITY: a type of sexual orientation in which sexual behavior and feelings of a male (gay) or female (lesbian) are directed toward a person of the same sex

LEARNING THEORY: a theory of sexual orientation that accounts for it in terms of the rewards and punishments one receives

MULTIFACTORIAL: the belief that sexual orientation is not exclusively the result of environment or biological factors but is caused by an interaction of the two

PSYCHOANALYTIC THEORY: a theory of sexual orientation that stresses how the child is brought up and the dynamics between the father and the mother

SEXUAL ORIENTATION: the direction of one's sexual feelings and behavior; the term is preferred to "sexual preference," which implies that a conscious choice has been made

Overview

Sexual orientation is defined as the direction or orientation of one's sexual feelings and behavior. The term "sexual orientation" generally replaced "sexual preference" in the 1980's because evidence generally suggests that sexuality is not a preference. It is not something that is chosen or is changeable.

There are three types of sexual orientation or direction. Heterosexuality refers to sexual behavior and feelings between two persons of the opposite sex—that is, between male and female. Homosexuality refers to sexual behavior and feelings between two persons of the same sex. Homosexual males are commonly referred to as gays, and female homosexuals are commonly referred to as lesbians. Bisexuality refers to sexual behaviors and feelings of a male or female that are directed toward both males and females. The percentage of the population that is homosexual has often been estimated at 10 percent, but studies have produced various other figures, particularly when a distinction is drawn between homosexuality and bisexuality. Some data suggest that about 1 to 2 percent of the population is strictly homosexual. According to David L. Rosenhan and Martin E. P. Seligman, bisexuality is significantly more common, occurring in about 15 percent of men and 10 percent of women. The majority of bisexuals have sex with partners of their own sex only a small portion of the time. Thus, about 73 or 74 percent of the population is heterosexual.

Sexual behavior in general and sexual orientation in particular form a central part of people's core personality and give meaning and direction and richness to their lives. A considerable number of studies have thus been devoted to trying to understand how sexual orientation is formed. These studies fall into three theoretical orientations: psychoanalytic, learning, and biological theories.

Psychoanalytic theory is based on the work of Sigmund Freud. According to Freud and his followers, sexual orientation is determined by the parent with which the child learns to identify. Heterosexuality results from identification with the same-sex parent, and homosexuality results from inappropriate identification with the parent of the opposite sex during development. Psychoanalytical studies have found that homosexuals frequently have overprotective, dominant mothers and passive, ineffective fathers. Psychoanalytic theory is no longer in favor because many defects have been found in the theory. For example, many individuals simply do not fit into the pattern of family dynamics required by Freudian theory. There are so many exceptions that the theory lacks predictive power. Furthermore, psychoanalysis has consistently failed to show that homosexuality is malleable and can be reversed by therapy. Homosexuals do not convert to heterosexuality as a result of therapy.

According to learning theory, sexual orientation is learned, much as any human behavior is learned, through the application of rewards and punishments to encourage the acquisition of desired behavior (heterosexuality) and discourage acquisition of undesired behavior (homosexuality). If, however, young people have unpleasant experiences with the opposite sex but rewarding and pleasant experiences with someone of the same sex, they could learn to become homosexual.

Learning theory also founders as a suitable explanation, however; there is no compelling evidence to suggest that sexual orientation is learned in the manner described in the previous example. Also, it has been shown that children reared by a homosexual parent are statistically not likely to become homosexual. This contradicts the belief that homosexuality can be learned from others. Again, learning theory implies that homosexuality is malleable and can be reversed, when evidence suggests otherwise.

The failure of psychiatry and learning theory to explain sexual orientation created a vacuum that biological theories have moved to fill. There is compelling evidence that sexual orientation is strongly influenced by genetics. A 1993 study reported the results of a study that found a gay-gay concordance rate of 11 percent for adoptive brothers, 22 percent for fraternal or dizygotic twins, and 52 percent for identical or monozygotic twins. That is, gays who are more closely related show a higher likelihood of both becoming gay if one of the pair does. Similar findings have been reported with lesbians. The finding suggests that homosexuality is highly attributable to genetics—by some measures, 70 percent attributable. The fact that not all identical twins are concordant for homosexuality, however, suggests that environment is also involved.

Of considerable interest is how genetics expresses itself. A particularly intriguing line of inquiry involves the search for differences in brain structure. A 1990 study reported that a cluster of cells in the human brain called the suprachiasmatic nucleus was dimorphic according to sexual orientation; the nucleus was nearly twice as large in homosexual males as it was in heterosexual males. A 1992 study found that a group of cells in the hypothalamus was also dimorphic according to sexual orientation, being more than twice as large in heterosexual males compared with homosexual males.

Other research has examined the role of biochemical factors. One possibility is that different levels of prenatal hormones may affect brain function prior to birth, which in turn may produce different sexual orientations. In a condition known as congenital adrenal hyperplasia (CAH), the fetus' adrenal gland cannot produce a hormone called cortisol. John Money reported that 37 percent of CAH women identified themselves as lesbian (only about 1 to 2 percent of the total female population is lesbian). Researcher Richard Pillard has speculated that a certain hormone, the Mullerian inhibiting hormone, may have brain-organizing effects. Its failure to operate properly may create "psychosexual androgyny." Thus, gay males are masculine males with certain female cognitive and emotional sensibilities, and lesbian women are women with certain male cognitive and emotional sensibilities.

The search for the specific biological mechanism(s) determining sexual orientation is controversial, tentative, and often muddled. Failures to replicate results and to account for alternative explanations abound. What does seem clear is that sexual orientation has significant biological determinants. Homosexuality is not malleable or reversible. Homosexuals have long maintained that sexual orientation is not a personal choice or lifestyle; it is neither chosen nor changeable, and homosexuals report that they knew at an early age that they were "different" from heterosexuals. Sexual orientation probably represents a complex interaction between environment, genetics, and physiology that is only vaguely understood.

Applications

Research on the basis of sexual orientation has several implications for science and for society. For science, there are possible indirect benefits. There are some poorly understood diseases, for example, that are believed to be neurological disorders that affect males and females quite differently. Examples include autism, dyslexia, and

schizophrenia. Research on the riddle of sexual orientation could also help to understand and possibly provide a cure for such diseases. Research about sexual orientation
also suggests that traditional ways of regarding sexual orientation may be inadequate.
At the beginning of this article, three types of sexual orientation were described—
heterosexual, homosexual, and bisexual. The fact that the heritability factor for
homosexuality is less than 100 percent, however, suggests that sexual orientation is
"multifactorial"; it is influenced by several variables, such as genetics and environment. (Eye color is "unifactorial," since it is wholly genetically determined. Height is
multifactorial; its heritability factor is about 90 percent, but not 100 percent, because
it can be affected by other factors such as nutrition.) A multifactorial model of sexual
orientation suggests that it exists on a continuum rather than being an either/or
proposition. Most people are heterosexual, and homosexuality and bisexuality could
anchor the end points of the continuum. Between heterosexuality and homosexuality
and between heterosexuality and bisexuality there could exist subtle shadings and
gradations of sexual orientation that represent normal variations of the three orientations.

A third significant implication of research on sexual orientation is its impact on the
formulation of social policy, the development of attitudes about sexual orientation,
and the fundamental issues of human rights, freedom, and tolerance. To some people,
the evidence that sexual orientation is very strongly influenced by biological determinants is cause for alarm. Throughout history, heterosexuality has been the accepted
and approved sexual orientation. Homosexuality has been variously considered a sin,
a crime, and a mental illness. Once homosexuality was labeled a mental illness, the
mental health profession attempted to treat and cure it. This treatment was undertaken
in a context in which homosexuality was viewed as an abhorrence to be cured by any
means. In extreme cases, hysterectomies and estrogen injections were forced upon
lesbians, even though there was absolutely no evidence that these treatments affected
sexual orientation. Gays were subjected to transorbital lobotomies, electroshock
therapy, castration, and aversion therapy, even though, once again, none of these
treatments was shown to have any effect on sexual orientation. Even less invasive
techniques such as psychoanalysis or psychotherapy were ultimately shown to be
worthless in changing sexual orientation.

The search for biological determinants is disturbing to some individuals who are
aware of the indignities homosexuals have suffered. Although society may have
become more tolerant of homosexuality, there is still significant opposition to it and
disapproval of it by individuals, government, and religion. Should biology ever
progress to the point of sufficiently understanding the genetic-physiological basis of
homosexuality, some people fear that such knowledge will be used once again to
"cure" homosexuality by those who abhor it—the idea of surgical or chemical attempts
to change the nervous system represents one such issue. Although the potential for
abuse exists and requires vigilance, it could be argued that this is true for much
biomedical knowledge.

Scientific investigation of what causes sexual orientation began around 1900 and is divided into two eras. The first era was a psychological investigation, initiated by Sigmund Freud and his fellow psychoanalysts. Learning theory weighed in later in the twentieth century with its own psychological investigation. The second era was initiated by the failure of these psychological theories to explain sexual orientation satisfactorily. Neurobiological research began in the 1950's and has subsequently expanded into a significant number of promising lines of investigation.

Most of this work is inconclusive and fraught with methodological and interpretative problems, no doubt because of the relative newness of such research. It is reasonable to expect that with time the neurobiological approach will significantly increase understanding of sexual orientation. The situation is not unlike that of psychology's and psychiatry's attempts to understand abnormal behavior. Environmental theories such as psychoanalysis and learning theory have increasingly given way to neurobiological theories in the explanations of a number of abnormalities, such as schizophrenia, mood disorders, addictions, and anxiety disorders. Neurobiological research will continue to occupy a prominent role in the study of sexual orientation.

Context

One's sexual orientation forms a core part of one's personality. Understanding how personality develops includes understanding how sexual orientation develops. Such knowledge is important both from the point of view of basic research and in terms of the implications of such findings for the formulation of social, political, and religious policy. Neurobiologists recognize that sexual orientation is not exclusively a product of biology and that it represents a yet to be understood interaction of environment and biology.

Psychological and neurological theories of sexual orientation focus on individual behavior. The implication of these theories for sociology will relate to the study of their impact in influencing social, political, and religious policy. Three facts about sexual orientation now seem unarguable: that biological factors play a critical role in determining sexual orientation; that sexual orientation is not a personal choice nor a lifestyle (it is neither changeable nor chosen); and that sexual orientation is independent of mental health. Sexual studies have convincingly demonstrated that homosexuals and bisexuals are no different from heterosexuals in their levels of mental health and adjustment. In 1973 the American Psychiatric Association dropped homosexuality from its official *Diagnostic and Statistical Manual of Mental Disorders*, officially ending homosexuality's status as a mental disorder or illness.

Given these three facts, it is appropriate to ask how the widespread homophobia and resulting discrimination that persist among much of the population and in governmental and religious institutions can be justified. Many people have answered that homophobia and discrimination cannot be justified and that society must end these attitudes and practices. It is at this point that sexual orientation becomes a concern of sociology. Sociology can help provide understanding of how culture reconciles and justifies patterns of thought and action that contradict scientific knowledge. Perhaps sociology can also suggest solutions to this impasse.

Bibliography

Diamant, Louis, ed. *Male and Female Homosexuality: Psychological Approaches.* Washington: Hemisphere, 1987. This volume presents a comprehensive organization of topics pertinent to understanding homosexuality. The first eight chapters discuss the major theories of sexual orientation. The rest of the book discusses homosexuality and its relationship to mental disorders and to the homosexual's role in society.

Friedman, Richard C. *Male Homosexuality: A Contemporary Psychoanalytic Perspective.* New Haven, Conn.: Yale University Press, 1988. Friedman's book reviews the literature on biological factors concerning the role of sex hormones and genetic factors, on gender identity during childhood, and on Freud's theory of homosexuality. Friedman also presents in-depth analysis of homosexuality according to modern psychoanalytic theory and ends the book by synthesizing the various approaches and developing a holistic analysis of homosexuality.

Geer, James H., and William T. O'Donohue, eds. *Theories of Human Sexuality.* New York: Plenum Press, 1987. This multidisciplinary inquiry into the origins of human sexuality presents fourteen different approaches to sexual orientation. Besides the psychoanalytic, learning, and biological theories, the book discusses human sexuality from such perspectives as evolution, theology, phenomenology, and sexual scripts.

Green, Richard. *The "Sissy Boy Syndrome" and the Development of Homosexuality.* New Haven, Conn.: Yale University Press, 1987. Green presents a detailed analysis of homosexuality within the context of the family and peer groups. Homosexuality is studied longitudinally (that is, the same people are followed through time). A number of interviews with homosexuals are presented, and interesting questions are discussed, such as when the earliest homoerotic feelings arose.

McWhirter, David P., Stephanie A. Sanders, and June Machover Reinisch, eds. *Homosexuality/Heterosexuality: Concepts of Sexual Orientation.* New York: Oxford University Press, 1990. Researchers from a wide range of disciplines address central issues in human sexuality. The twenty-two papers are divided into seven different perspectives: historical/religious, biological, evolutionary, cultural/sociological, identity development, relational, and conceptual/theoretical. The papers are based on presentations at a symposium sponsored by the Kinsey Institute.

Money, John. *Gay, Straight, and In-Between: The Sexology of Erotic Orientation.* New York: Oxford University Press, 1988. Money discusses sexual orientation primarily from a biological viewpoint. Money introduces a new concept, "love maps," which he defines as a developmental representation in the mind and brain that depicts the various aspects of one's conception of an ideal relationship with one's sexual partner. The book contains an excellent glossary.

Socarides, Charles W., and Vamik D. Volkan, eds. *The Homosexualities: Reality, Fantasy, and the Arts.* Madison, Conn.: International Universities Press, 1990. This book examines homosexuality from a psychoanalytic perspective. The contributors discuss recent psychoanalytic findings about child development, object relations, and female psychology. Also discussed in detail is the Oedipal conflict: its role in homosexuality, the nature of the conflict, unconscious fantasies, identifications, and the existence of traumas and developmental defects.

Laurence Miller

Cross-References

Deviance: Biological and Psychological Explanations, 532; The Gay Liberation Movement, 799; Discrimination Against Gays, 806; The Medical Profession and the Medicalization of Society, 1159; The Medicalization of Deviance, 1178; The Institution of Medicine, 1185; Sex versus Gender, 1721; Sociobiology and the Nature-Nurture Debate, 1913.

SEXUALLY TRANSMITTED DISEASES

Type of sociology: Major social institutions
Field of study: Medicine

Sexually transmitted diseases, often referred to as venereal diseases, are similar to a variety of other bacterial and viral infections; it is only their mode of transmission which distinguishes them. Sexually transmitted diseases have been known throughout recorded time, and their existence has had a significant effect on the course of human events.

Principal terms

ACQUIRED IMMUNE DEFICIENCY SYNDROME (AIDS): a fatal disease caused by the human immunodeficiency virus (HIV); HIV is transmitted primarily through sexual contact or the sharing of needles by intravenous drug users

CHLAMYDIA: a sexually transmitted disease caused by a bacterium; primary symptoms include genital discharge, painful urination, and, in women, bleeding between menstrual periods

GENITAL HERPES: a sexually transmitted disease caused by a virus; primary symptoms include blisters in the genital area

GONORRHEA: a sexually transmitted disease caused by a bacterium; primary symptoms include genital discharge

PELVIC INFLAMMATORY DISEASE: a complication of any of several diseases, including chlamydia and gonorrhea; symptoms include inflammation and abscesses in a woman's ovaries and pelvis

SAFE SEX: practices which include sexual abstinence or delaying the onset of sexual intercourse, limiting the number of sexual partners, and using condoms in conjunction with a spermicidal gel

SYPHILIS: a sexually transmitted disease caused by a bacterium; initial symptoms include an open sore (chancre), followed about six weeks later by a rash, hair loss, and swollen glands

TRICHOMONIASIS: a sexually transmitted disease caused by a parasite; primary symptoms are generally limited to females and include genital discharge and itching and redness of the genitals

VENEREAL WARTS: a sexually transmitted disease caused by a virus; primary symptoms include cauliflower-shaped warts

Overview

Communicable diseases that are passed on through sexual activity are usually referred to as sexually transmitted diseases (STDs) or as venereal diseases (VD). The only factor that distinguishes them from the plethora of other infectious diseases to which humans are susceptible is their means of transmission. Rational discussion of sexually transmitted diseases, let alone efforts to control their spread, has long been inhibited by their very association with sexual acts; the subject of sexuality has traditionally not been considered appropriate for general conversation in Western culture. This attitude began to change in the mid-twentieth century; even now, however, attitudes range widely. Although the subject of STDs for some people represents simply an embarrassing possibility that may be difficult to broach with a sexual partner, for others it is a topic that cannot be discussed because of its association with immoral or unacceptable conduct.

Throughout history, attitudes toward sexuality—and therefore attitudes toward how to deal with STDs—have been deeply intertwined with religious beliefs, cultural norms, and social conventions. For example, between the sixth and fourth centuries B.C.E., sexually transmitted diseases were endemic in ancient Greece. Classical Greek culture fostered the transmission of sexually transmitted diseases in a number of ways—the culture accepted, even celebrated, sexuality, prostitution, and pederasty—while mitigating effects were provided by an acceptance of masturbation and the practice of nonpenetrating sexual activities.

Many centuries later, after the fall of Rome, the Christian church came to dominate Western attitudes toward sexuality. To the church, sex for purposes other than procreation was degenerate, and intercourse outside marriage was immoral; homosexuality, sodomy, zoophilia, masturbation, and fellatio were abominations and sins against nature. Prostitution, although officially abhorred, tended to be tacitly viewed as a necessary evil. In the sixteenth century, the prevalence of syphilis reached epidemic proportions; patronage of brothels eventually declined. The syphilis epidemic had profound effects on sexual attitudes and behaviors. It was not until the nineteenth century that prostitution again flourished as it had in the fifteenth century. The relationship between prostitution and the transmission of STDs has been amply demonstrated; generally, when restrictive laws have driven prostitution underground, infection rates have risen.

In the earliest years of the twentieth century, the most common methods for addressing the spread of sexually transmitted diseases in the United States were punitive in nature. While these methods met with some success, they broke down with the advent of World War I. It has been estimated that nearly half of all U.S. military personnel contracted gonorrhea between 1914 and 1916; closing brothels and imposing sanctions against infected servicemen were the primary methods of control. When the military turned to a more positive approach based on what could be called a "public health" model, infection rates from all forms of sexually transmitted diseases combined dropped to one man in seventeen. It is speculated that if the public-health approach had been strengthened further and all negative sanctions for becoming infected had been dropped, infection rates would have shown even greater rates of decline.

Sexually transmitted diseases remain far more common than most persons realize. In 1990, in the United States, there were more than 11,900,000 new cases of sexually transmitted disease. Given that some of these disease processes cannot be cured (among these are acquired immune deficiency syndrome, or AIDS, genital herpes, and venereal warts), the number of infected persons climbs each year.

Some of the most common sexually transmitted diseases in the United States, with estimated numbers of cases as of 1990, are as follows: chlamydia (3,000,000 cases), trichomoniasis (3,000,000 cases), gonorrhea (1,800,000 cases), venereal warts (1,000,000 cases), genital herpes (500,000 cases), syphilis (90,000 cases), AIDS (the number of new infections by years is unknown, but it is estimated that, as of 1993, 1.5 million persons in the United States were infected with the human immunodeficiency virus, HIV, and, as of 1992, 202,000 people were suffering from AIDS), and other sexually transmitted diseases (2,500,000). The symptoms and complications associated with sexually transmitted diseases are profound, and some are potentially lethal. Sterility, rash, hair loss, swollen glands, chronic back pain, urinary problems, arthritis, pelvic inflammatory disease, blindness in babies born to infected mothers, cervical cancer, heart disease, dementia, and death by secondary infection are complications associated with some of the most common sexually transmitted diseases.

Applications

Beginning in the 1920's, the idea grew that sexually transmitted diseases would be conquered by medical science. Since the discovery of penicillin by the British bacteriologist Alexander Fleming in 1928, a variety of antibiotics have become available. By the 1950's effective antibiotic preparations were available for the treatment of syphilis and gonorrhea. Remedies for a number of other sexually transmitted diseases followed. Despite the availability of effective treatments, however, the 1970's saw a dramatic increase in the rate of new infections. It was clear that factors transcending the availability of treatment would have to be considered if the spread of sexually transmitted diseases were to be arrested.

The 1970's brought another truth into acknowledgment: Not all sexually transmitted diseases can be successfully treated. No cure was developed for genital herpes, venereal warts, or late-stage pelvic inflammatory disease. While there was considerable talk about safe sex—particularly as it related to the spread of genital herpes and later, in the 1980's, to infection with HIV—there was little change in the sexual behaviors of a large number of the people who constitute the at-risk population. This conclusion may be inferred from the number of new cases of syphilis reported to the Centers for Disease Control during the 1980's. In 1989, nearly 45,000 cases of syphilis were reported. This figure represented a forty-year high in regard to new cases. Clearly, a significant portion of the population was not practicing safe sex.

There is no doubt that either sexual abstinence or a lifelong pattern of having sex with only one partner would be the most effective method for ending the spread of sexually transmitted diseases. While for many people this represents the ideal alternative, for most people it is not the norm. When the number of persons engaging in all forms of nonmarital and extramarital sex are combined, one finds that the vast majority of both men and women will have had more than one sexual partner.

For persons who are not abstinent, the most effective protection against the heterosexual transmission of sexually transmitted diseases is the use of a condom combined with a spermicidal gel. Gabriele Fallopius, a sixteenth century Italian anatomist, claimed to have invented the condom. The term "condom" came into use when animal intestines replaced linen in the manufacture of the sheaths in the eighteenth century. Following the vulcanization of rubber by Charles Goodyear in 1839, condoms made of the new material were cheaper to manufacture and more effective; however, starting in the late 1800's social events restricted access to condoms. Anthony Comstock, a nineteenth century moral crusader, successfully argued that birth control devices and information were obscene and that therefore they should not be allowed passage through the U.S. mail. Following Comstock's efforts, laws restricting access to condoms and other forms of birth control were passed by a number of states. Laws outlawing the sale of condoms remained in force as late as 1965, when the Supreme Court struck down a Connecticut law which prevented the sale of contraceptives.

As the continued presence of syphilis, gonorrhea, chlamydia, and a number of other curable sexually transmitted diseases attests, halting the spread of STDs is no easy task. A more profound knowledge must be garnered of the personal and sociocultural factors which make it easier to have sex with another person than to discuss issues related to possible infection rationally and meaningfully. The religious and social mores which restrict access to knowledge, and therefore increase the probability that people will act in ignorance, need to be analyzed and examined. Furthermore, cultural traditions which promote or ignore behaviors that place individuals at increased risk for exposure to sexually transmitted diseases must be studied and changed.

The 1980's brought a new threat in regard to sexually transmitted diseases, that of AIDS. For the first time in fifty years, an untreatable, lethal sexually transmitted disease was spreading through the population. AIDS was unknown prior to 1981, yet as of 1993, more than twelve million people worldwide were infected by the virus which causes AIDS. (A person infected with HIV does not necessarily have AIDS; AIDS is the final stage of the HIV infection.) In the early 1980's, in the United States, AIDS was largely confined to the homosexual community. Some people viewed the disease as a just punishment sent by God; others simply ignored it because it did not affect them. These attitudes did little to stop the spread of AIDS, and they adversely affected public support for prevention efforts. As the epidemiology of the disease was traced, however, and as modes of transmission became more clearly understood, most people began to realize that AIDS represented a threat to the entire population, not only a few restricted subgroups such as male homosexuals, intravenous (IV) drug users, or recipients of transfusions involving infected blood.

While many writers purported that the advent of AIDS materially changed the sexual practices of persons in the general population, as of the early 1990's there was little or no evidence to support the assertions that sexual abstinence and "safe sex" were being practiced on anything approaching the scale which would be needed to have a material effect on the spread of HIV infection. While certain groups, such as health care providers, must take special precautions in regard to exposure to blood and body fluids, for most people risk is associated with unprotected sexual activities or sharing the needles used to inject drugs. The limitation of the number of sexual partners, the use of a condom combined with a spermicidal gel, avoiding anal intercourse, and not sharing needles remain the most effective methods for stopping the spread of HIV.

Context

Prior to the 1980's, sociologists were seldom involved in the study of sexually transmitted diseases. It was rare to find an introductory sociology text, social problems text, or medical sociology text which devoted more than a few pages to the discussion of sexually transmitted diseases. As of the early 1990's, neither the preceding books nor marriage and family texts were likely to include an extended section on sexually transmitted diseases anywhere other than in an appendix. Furthermore, the material which was included was seldom more than an enumeration of statistics related to incidence and prevalence, combined with descriptions of the physical symptoms of the most common sexually transmitted diseases; this information was typically followed by a few paragraphs on prevention.

The first broad social surveys of sexual behavior were completed by persons from outside the field of sociology. Alfred Kinsey, a biologist, can be credited with completing the first comprehensive survey of sexual attitudes and behaviors of persons residing in the United States. In 1948 Kinsey published the book *Sexual Behavior in the Human Male*; this was followed in 1953 by *Sexual Behavior in the Human Female*. While Kinsey's sampling techniques have been repeatedly criticized, the interviewing techniques through which data were collected remain highly regarded. Whatever the validity and generalizability of Kinsey's initial data, his work made obvious the need for a database concerning sexual behavior and set a high standard for the many studies to follow.

Perhaps the greatest contribution of sociologists to the study of sexually transmitted diseases has been their involvement, along with public health officials and other social scientists, in epidemiological research that has tracked the rate and distribution of sexually transmitted diseases. The value of the techniques and methods of epidemiology are preeminently demonstrated through the process which led to the identification of the distribution and behaviors associated with the transmission of AIDS. Had it not been for the insights of epidemiologists, recognition and preventive efforts in regard to AIDS would have been delayed for years.

Bibliography

Brandt, Allan M. *No Magic Bullet: A Social History of Venereal Disease in the United States Since 1880*. New York: Oxford University Press, 1985. This book is dated in that it provides only minimal coverage of AIDS and is devoid of references to chlamydia. Still, the author does an excellent job of tracing the history of venereal diseases. Of equal value is the author's recognition and discussion of sexually transmitted diseases as shaped by biological, medical, social, and cultural influences.

Feldman, Douglas A., ed. *Culture and AIDS*. New York: Praeger, 1990. This book provides a focus on social and cultural processes as they relate to AIDS. In the process of discussing stigmas, cultural taboos, information on groups at risk, and an analysis of homophobia, this text brings the discussion of AIDS into the framework of social theory.

McKinney, Kathleen, and Susan Sprecher, eds. *Human Sexuality: The Societal and Personal Context*. Norwood, N.J.: Ablex, 1989. Of particular interest is the chapter "AIDS: Social Causes, Patterns, 'Cures,' and Problems," by Rick Zimmerman. Here the social aspects of AIDS are discussed in regard to epidemiology, prevention, and public policy.

Paalman, Maria, ed. *Promoting Safer Sex: Prevention of Sexual Transmission of AIDS and other STDs*. Amsterdam, The Netherlands: Swets & Zeitlinger, 1990. This book has a number of chapters of value in regard to an understanding of AIDS and other sexually transmitted diseases. Two chapters of interest in regard to the sociological perspective are those by Chuck Frutchey, "The Role of Community Based Organizations in AIDS and STD Prevention," and Allan Brandt, "AIDS in Historical Perspective: Four Lessons from the History of Sexually Transmitted Diseases."

Rathus, Spencer A., Jeffrey S. Nevid, and Lois Fichner-Rathus. *Human Sexuality in a World of Diversity*. Boston: Allyn & Bacon, 1993. In addition to a general discussion of issues related to human sexuality, this text provides two chapters devoted exclusively to sexually transmitted diseases. While neither chapter provides much in regard to sociological perspective, both provide needed information concerning epidemiology, symptoms, and prevention.

Reinisch, June M., and Ruth Beasley. *The Kinsey Institute New Report on Sex: What You Must Know to Be Sexually Literate*. Edited and compiled by Debra Kent. New York: St. Martin's Press, 1990. This book summarizes the results of a survey commissioned by the Kinsey Institute. The authors conclude that Americans are not sexually literate. An attempt is made to offer factual information concerning areas of ignorance and interest.

Walker, Robert S. *AIDS—Today, Tomorrow: An Introduction to the HIV Epidemic in America*. Atlantic Highlands, N.J.: Humanities Press International, 1991. Walker's book provides an analysis of the history and impact of the AIDS epidemic. He shows how an appreciation of social issues, sociology, and social anthropology can enable our understanding of AIDS.

Bruce E. Bailey

Cross-References

SIGNIFICANT AND GENERALIZED OTHERS

Type of sociology: Socialization and social interaction
Field of study: Interactionist approach to social interaction

The American philosopher George Herbert Mead developed the theory of significant and generalized others as an integral element of his theory of self. According to Mead, it is only through interaction with significant others and the development of a generalized other that people are able to develop a sense of who they are.

Principal terms
LOOKING-GLASS SELF: the sense of personal identity that is the image reflected by the "mirror" of other people; it includes both identity and self-esteem
NORM: a rule or expectation about appropriate behavior for a particular person in a particular situation
PEER GROUP: people who are the same age and are roughly equal in authority
REFERENCE GROUP: a group or category that people use to evaluate themselves and their behavior
ROLE-PLAYING: acting out the script that is usually clarified in role-definition
ROLE-TAKING: seeing the world from the perspective of other individuals and groups, and directing one's own actions accordingly
ROLES: behaviors that are expected of a person who occupies a social position; counterparts to social norms
SELF: a person's representation of himself or herself as an object in the world of experience
SOCIALIZATION: the process by which people learn the culture of a society and become full participants in that society
SYMBOLIC INTERACTIONISM: a theoretical perspective according to which mind and self are not innate parts of the human body but are created by communicating with other people

Overview

The philosopher George Herbert Mead is widely acknowledged as the founder of the largest and most influential field in modern American sociology: symbolic interactionism. Symbolic interactionism is a theoretical perspective that, among other things, holds that people create their own meanings and reality through communication with one another. One of the most important elements of symbolic interactionism is the concept of self. In referring to the human being as having a self, Mead meant that an individual acts socially toward himself or herself just as he or she acts toward others. People may blame, praise, or encourage themselves; they may become disgusted with themselves and seek to reward or punish themselves. Thus, individuals may become the objects of their own actions.

The self is absent at birth. It develops only in the process of social experience through taking the role of the other, through using the attitudes and evaluations of others as a basis for attitudes and evaluations about oneself. The self is reflexive; it has the ability to be subject and object to itself at the same time. Symbolic interactionists believe that the self is formed in the same way that other subjects are—through the definitions made by other people. Mead placed these definitions into two categories: those made by significant others and those made by generalized others.

Significant others are those who have had or still have an important influence on a person's thoughts about self and the world. For a child, the most obvious significant others are parents, but they can also be other relatives, television heroes, and friends. As a person grows older, the potential number of significant others increases greatly, and can include such individuals as Socrates, Jesus, a parent, a spouse, a child, a boss, the president of the United States, a minister, a movie star, or a rock musician. A significant other does not have to be physically present and can be living or dead. Although significant others are directly responsible for the internalization of norms in an individual, the character of one's emotional ties with them may differ. It is possible to love, like, or respect some significant others and to dislike or hate other significant others. There is no limit to the number of significant others one has, but they usually change according to one's stage in life. For example, as people grow older, their peers may become more important as significant others than their parents or other family members.

While significant other refers to a specific person, Mead viewed the generalized other as consisting of the general expectations and standards of the community in which the individual lives. These expectations and standards may include specific customs and normative patterns or highly abstract ideals and values in terms of which people define their overall orientations and life goals. The generalized other appears as the attitude of the community in direct or indirect manifestation, as an instrument of the social control of the self, and as the abstract formulation of the ethos of a community or society. A generalized other is a set of rules which develops in interactions and which individuals use to control themselves in interactions. Although Mead does not always make it clear whether the individual has one generalized other or several, other sociologists who have elaborated on his theory say that what begins as one generalized other increasingly becomes several. Because most people interact with many different groups, they most likely will develop more than one generalized other.

Mead used the term "generalized other" to describe the shared culture of a group— its religious systems, philosophies, legal systems and ideologies, mythology, literature, and art. The development of a generalized other by a person is the internalization of society as the individual has come to know it, and once a person has developed a generalized other, he or she can act in an organized, consistent manner and can view himself or herself from a consistent standpoint. The individual can transcend the local and present expectations and definitions with which he or she comes into contact.

According to Mead, it is in the form of the generalized other that the community exercises control over the conduct of its individual members. In abstract thought, the individual takes the attitude of the generalized other toward himself or herself, without reference to its expression in any particular other individual. In concrete thought, the individual takes that attitude as it is expressed in the attitudes toward his or her behavior of the other people with whom he or she is involved in a given social situation.

Although Mead was careful to point out that the generalized other does not necessarily correspond to any particular individual but is a composite, he nevertheless conceived of the relationship as an interactional one: The person takes the attitude of the generalized other toward itself, interprets it, understands it, and then incorporates it into his or her own self-conceptions.

Applications

The concepts of significant and generalized others are essential in the development of self, which is an important part of socialization. Mead described self-development as consisting of three stages: the preparatory stage; the play stage, in which the role of significant other is crucial; and the game stage, in which the role of the generalized other is necessary.

The preparatory stage is one of meaningless imitation by the infant, such as "reading" the paper, "feeding" the doll, or "cooking" the dinner. The child does certain things that others around him do without any understanding of what he or she is doing. Mead did not specifically name this stage, but he described it and said that it was necessary because the imitation implies that the child is incipiently taking on the roles of those around him or her and is on the verge of actual role-taking.

The play stage occurs once the child has begun to acquire a vocabulary by means of which people and objects can be designated. The child plays at various roles made evident by others, including their use of language. The child plays at being mother, police officer, grocery clerk, or teacher. What is of central importance in such playacting is that it places the child in a position from which it is able to act back toward itself in these roles. At this point, the individual becomes a social object to himself or herself. During the play stage, the child assumes the perspective of his or her significant others as a boy, for example, learns how the significant others label him: John, good boy, handsome, smart, bad, slow, funny, and so on.

Mead called this second stage the play stage because the child assumes the perspective of only one significant other at a time. The child segregates the significant others, and the view of self is a segmented one. Play refers to the fact that group rules are unnecessary because the child takes the role of one significant other—mother, father, Superman—and acts in the world as if he or she were that individual. Therefore, play is an individual affair, subject to the rules of single persons. It is in this stage that the child first begins to form a self by taking on the roles of others. This is indicated by the use of the third person instead of the first person in referring to himself or herself; for example, "Mary is a bad girl" or "Mary can run fast." Because the child takes the role of only one significant other at a time, however, he or she has no unitary standpoint from which to view himself or herself; therefore, he or she has no unified self-conception.

The third stage of self-development is the game stage. According to Mead, this stage completes the development of self by creating a self that incorporates all of one's significant others into one generalized other. Mead called this stage the game stage because he believed that the organized game epitomized what must be done in taking the role of the generalized other. Using the example of baseball, he said that playing catcher, unlike playing mother or Superman, requires the child to take the perspective of the team as a whole toward himself or herself as a particular player. To view oneself as a catcher, one must have a composite, simultaneous idea of a baseball team, the various positions that are involved, the object of the game, and the relationship of the catcher's position to the activity as a whole. Beyond this, the participants in a baseball game are also oriented toward the general rules that define the game of baseball, and they control their own actions in terms of these impersonal rules. In this situation (playing baseball), the child must take the roles of groups of individuals instead of a specific role. The child is able to do this by abstracting a composite role out of the concrete roles of specific people. By doing this, the child builds up a generalized other, a generalized role or standpoint from which he or she views himself or herself and his or her behavior. According to Mead, it is this generalized other in the child's experience which provides him or her with a self.

The concepts of significant and generalized others are also important in understanding how people develop self-esteem. What people think and feel about themselves, like all else about the self, results from interaction; self-judgment is a result, to a high degree, of judgment by others. A person's very first important self-judgments come from significant others. As people develop their senses of self and progress past the game stage, the judgments of their community as embodied in their generalized other become increasingly important. The relationship between self-esteem and significant and generalized others is not, however, as simple as it appears. It is not the judgments of others per se that are important; it is how a person defines his or her views that matters. A person selects from whatever others think; he or she ignores, exaggerates, or alters whatever fits his or her self-image. As people get older, they sometimes select their significant others in order to enhance their self-judgments. This is usually not possible when a person is younger (in the play stage) and the self is developing. When that situation exists, a person is usually dependent upon significant others—usually parents, other family members, and teachers—to guide his or her self-judgments. If the information that the child receives from these significant others is negative, the child's self-esteem also will be negative. The negative feelings about self that emerge from such encounters affect subsequent actions. Low self-esteem leads to anxiety and may make it difficult for the person to be an accurate role-taker or to feel well-disposed toward others, which in turn will result in negative judgments being given, and so on. Significant others have a very large impact on a child's actual and potential interactions with others.

Context

The existence of significant and generalized others is what makes it possible for people to develop a sense of self that enables them to view themselves as social objects. This ability to create a sense of self is one of the central tenets of symbolic interactionism; therefore, significant and generalized others are essential to the theoretical perspective of symbolic interactionism. It was in the early part of the twentieth century that the concept of symbolic interaction emerged as one of the most important developments in American sociology, but its roots can be found as far back as the eighteenth century. For example, the concepts of the generalized other and role-taking, which is essential to the idea of the significant other, were heavily influenced by a school of philosophers called the Scottish moralists. These philosophers—David Hume, John Millar, Thomas Reid, Adam Ferguson, and Adam Smith—introduced the concepts of sympathy and the impartial spectator, which laid the groundwork for Mead's theory of significant and generalized others.

The concepts of significant others and generalized others are important because they explain how individuals receive the information they need to form the self. Since, according to Mead, the self is not present at birth, but develops in a three-stage process, people must use the judgments of others to form their own selves. It would be impossible to explain symbolic interactionism without the existence of significant and generalized others.

In addition to being an integral part of symbolic interactionism, the concepts of significant and generalized others have led to the development of several other important concepts in sociology, such as role theory, reference-group theory, and self theory. Mead's concept of the self as developed by significant and generalized others explains how the development or socialization of the human being both enmeshes the individual in society (through the use of the generalized other as a regulatory tool) and frees him or her from society (by allowing the self to choose different significant and generalized others). These ideas are important not only for symbolic interactionism but also for other areas of sociology, such as child and adult socialization, culture, deviance, and social control.

In the 1980's and 1990's, there was growing concern among parents, teachers, and politicians regarding the influence exerted by some television characters and rock musicians on young people who considered them to be significant others. An even greater concern was the increasingly large number of adolescents who were joining gangs. Gang members exchange the more traditional generalized other of society as a whole for the generalized other of the gang. These concerns illustrate the continuing importance of significant and generalized others in modern society.

Bibliography

Aboulafia, Mitchell, ed. *Philosophy, Social Theory, and the Thought of George Herbert Mead*. Albany: State University of New York Press, 1991. This book provides a thorough analysis of Mead's theories and their development. Contains a useful bibliography of secondary literature on Mead and a detailed index.

Hewitt, John. *Self and Society: A Symbolic Interactionist Social Psychology*. 5th ed. Boston: Allyn & Bacon, 1991. Hewitt defines and discusses Mead's conceptualization of the significant and generalized others in great detail. His discussion of the generalized other in a complex situation is an especially interesting extension of Mead's original theory. Contains an index but no bibliography.

Manis, Jerome, and Bernard Meltzer, comps. *Symbolic Interaction: A Reader in Social Psychology*. 3d ed. Boston: Allyn & Bacon, 1978. This book gives the reader an excellent introduction to Mead's theory of significant and generalized others; it is also very readable and interesting. Provides an index but no bibliography.

Mead, George Herbert. *Mind, Self, and Society from the Standpoint of a Social Behaviorist*. Edited by Charles W. Morris. Chicago: University of Chicago Press, 1934. This book, which was published after Mead's death, is a compilation of his students' notes on his lectures. It presents Mead's theories in a clear and readable form. A chronologically arranged bibliography of all of Mead's writings is included, as is an index.

_____. *The Social Psychology of George Herbert Mead*. Edited by Anselm Strauss. Chicago: University of Chicago Press, 1956. Strauss discusses the role of self, the generalized other, significant others, and society in great detail. His book is very readable and is suitable for a college audience. Provides a limited index but has no bibliography.

Meltzer, Bernard. *The Social Psychology of George Herbert Mead*. Kalamazoo: Western Michigan University Center for Sociological Research, 1964. Meltzer gives a concise yet thorough discussion of the roles of the significant and generalized others in the genesis and formation of the self in this very short (31 pages) publication. Contains no index or bibliography.

Meltzer, Bernard, John Petras, and Larry Reynolds. *Symbolic Interactionism: Genesis, Varieties, and Criticism*. London: Routledge & Kegan Paul, 1975. The authors give a good explanation of Mead's theory of the development of self, and they put his theory in context with the theories of those who influenced him. Contains both a bibliography and an index.

Stone, Gregory, and Harvey Farberman. *Social Psychology Through Symbolic Interaction*. 2d ed. New York: John Wiley & Sons, 1981. This book is particularly useful because it goes into detail in discussing the role of "play" and "game" in the development of self, and the roles played by significant and generalized others. Provides both a name index and a subject index.

Karen Anding Fontenot

Cross-References

Dramaturgy, 566; Exchange in Social Interaction, 715; Internal Colonialism, 1015; The Looking-Glass Self, 1099; School Socialization, 1693; Socialization: The Family, 1880; Symbolic Interaction, 2036.

SLAVERY

Type of sociology: Social stratification
Field of study: Systems of social stratification

Slavery refers to a condition in which individuals are held as property and exploited for their labor; absolute control is exercised over their lives. Though slavery now exists in very few places in the world, legacies of the institution survive, especially in American racism.

Principal terms

CHATTEL: a slave; the term emphasized the fact that the slave is
   property that may be used, moved, or sold at will by an owner
EMANCIPATION: the freeing of slaves by law
MANUMISSION: the granting of freedom individually to slaves before
   formal emancipation
MAROON: an escaped West Indian slave or a descendent of such slaves
SLAVE MODE OF PRODUCTION: an economic system in which slaves
   were the principal work force and slavery was central to and
   integrated into the overall economic structure
SOCIAL STRATIFICATION: differentiation of people into vertically
   arranged categories or classes

Overview

Slavery encompasses various forms of dependent labor based on the ownership and domination of one individual by another. Slaves are deprived of all legal rights normally accorded citizens and are juristically considered the property of their owners. Slaves are distinguishable from other dependent laborers such as indentured servants, debt bondsmen, serfs, and peons by their total powerlessness; slaves lack the intervention of the state, kinship groups, or religious institutions. As an institution, slavery was once universal, existing in one form or other in practically all societies. Because slavery as an institution has been abolished throughout almost all of the world, it may be spoken of as a thing of the past. It should be remembered, however, that slavery in some form still exists in a few limited areas and that the social and economic legacy of slavery continues in larger areas, including the United States.

Slavery was traditionally characterized by a number of elements. Since owners exercised proprietary rights over slaves, slaves were treated as commodities (chattel) that could be sold and bought. Slaves were typically alien to the society that enslaved them. They were outsiders who were characterized by kinlessness, having been uprooted from their natal societies and dehumanized into objects. Slavery was a form of exploitation, whether for economic, political, or social purposes. Slavery was often initiated by and sustained through violence such as warfare, kidnapping, raiding, or banditry. Indeed, throughout history, violent methods have accounted for more enslavement than any other method of acquisition such as sale. Slavery could also emanate from judicial punishment for offenses such as murder, adultery, theft and sorcery.

Slavery was principally, though not always, tied to labor. Slaves performed a variety of economic tasks including agricultural and mining, often doing work that was the most menial, hazardous, or laborious. Slavery, however, often existed alongside other forms of labor. The sexual and reproductive capacities of slaves were controlled by their masters. Women were commonly treated as sexual objects, while males in some instances could be castrated. Marriages could not be contracted without the master's consent. Even slaves' offspring were legally considered to belong to their masters rather than to their biological parents.

The legal status of a slave was usually hereditary, though over time the status became modified in some societies. Offspring of slave parentage were thus born into slavery. Generally, slave populations did not tend to sustain their numbers and were replenished. Several reasons accounted for this: the severely harsh conditions of servitude; their relatively short life span; the demographic imbalance between males and females, with males often outnumbering females; and manumission. Slave possession was regarded as a conspicuous example of wealth and high status. While a combination of many of these factors prevailed in all slave societies, not all the conditions may have been present, or present to the same degree, in every slave-owning society.

Theoretically a distinction can be drawn between societies in which slavery was a marginal or incidental aspect of the economy and those in which slavery was a central feature. In the latter case, a slave mode of production can be said to have existed; methods of enslavement, slave production, and slave regeneration were integrated into the very socioeconomic structure of society.

Though the exact origins of slavery are speculative, archaeological evidence suggests that slavery existed among ancient Europeans and Asians going back several millennia B.C.E. Slave laws dating back to 2000 B.C.E. have been found among the Sumerians of ancient Mesopotamia, and the Hammurabic Code of Babylon in the eighteenth century B.C.E. contained sections dealing with slaves. Similarly, the presence of slavery has been noted in ancient Egypt from the beginning of its recorded history. Yet despite its antiquity, slavery in the context of chattel or property and as an institution central to the economic structure did not evolve until the Greek era.

By the second century B.C.E., the Greeks had developed an economic system in which slave labor was a principal mode of production. Slaves were engaged in agriculture, mining and craft industries, and civil service tasks. Slavery became an important institution that supported the elevated social status of rich merchants and the urban aristocracy. Hellenistic society became stratified, with slaves occupying the lowest stratum. It is estimated that by 300 B.C.E. the population of Athens had a population that was probably at least 25 percent slave-based. The frequent wars against Persians and other peoples generated a regular source of slaves.

Under the Roman Empire, slavery reached its highest point of development in the classical period. The use of slave labor freed the Romans from agricultural production, thereby enabling them to undertake prolonged wars, which in turn brought increasing numbers of slaves. In addition to external warfare, with its plundering and kidnapping, internal methods of enslavement, including criminal convictions, developed. Besides working on agricultural plantations, slaves were engaged in public works such as canal construction and in mining. It is estimated that about 30 percent of the population of the Roman Empire was of servile origins.

Slavery was also practiced in practically all the old states of South and Southeast Asia, including China, Japan, India, Burma, Thailand, Indonesia, Malaysia, and the Philippines, again largely for the use of the upper class. The institution also existed in Mongolia and Korea, where slavery assumed a significance closely paralleling that of Greece and Rome. In China, slavery is known to have existed as far back as the Shang Dynasty (from the eighteenth to the twelfth century B.C.E.). As elsewhere, slaves were acquired through wars and raiding. In addition, self-sale and the sale of children and women, often for reasons of financial insolvency, became important sources of slaves in China. Most slaves worked in the domestic sphere, although some were engaged in agriculture, mining, and craft industries.

In India, the Sanskrit Laws of Manu provide evidence of the establishment of slavery by the first century B.C.E., with most slaves performing agricultural and domestic tasks. Slavery existed in one form or another in Indian society through the periods of Muslim domination in the twelfth and thirteenth centuries until the British abolished it in the nineteenth century. Vestiges of the institution persisted well into the second half of the twentieth century.

Continental Europe similarly had slave institutions in a number of areas: the Germanic lands, the Scandinavian territories during the period of the Vikings, England (where the Doomsday Book of 1086 included an entry on the number of slaves), Gaul (France), Poland, Lithuania, and Russia, among others. In the Iberian peninsula (Spain and Portugal) during the Middle Ages, the crusades between Muslim (Moorish) and Christian forces created an environment in which both sides regularly enslaved prisoners of war.

Slavery was closely integrated into the Muslim societies of the Middle East and Africa right from the birth of Islam in the seventh century. Islamic conquests and holy wars regularly generated enslaved victims. Yet Islam did not dehumanize slaves. On the contrary, Muslim slaves were recruited into administrative bureaucracies, military establishments, and commercial systems in addition to performing the more familiar household roles. Slaves could even advance into elite political and military positions such as prime ministers, governors, and ruling dynasties. Though most Muslim slaves were engaged in nonagricultural tasks, some examples of plantation-type production occurred in areas such as Zanzibar, Pemba, and coastal Kenya in the nineteenth century.

Like practically all ancient societies, the peoples of sub-Saharan Africa knew slavery. Methods of slave acquisition included prisoners of war and victims of judicial processes and debt pawnage. Yet the institution of slavery in Africa was strikingly different from that of the Americas to which it later became linked. African slavery was mostly a social institution rather than an economic one, and slave trading remained incidental to economic organization. Most African slaves were acquired for lineage incorporation, and thus women and girls were preferred (in contrast to a preference for men in American slavery). Through integration into families, servile origins disappeared over generations. Overall, slaves had legal rights and avenues for upward mobility, and in many societies they did not constitute a separate class.

Applications

The institution of slavery perhaps found its most widespread application after Europeans began to colonize the New World and other parts of the globe. The effects of slavery as it existed for four centuries in the Americas are still being felt in the societies of both North and South America.

The creation of modern-day slave regimes was the direct consequence of the European entry into the Western Hemisphere that was initiated by Christopher Columbus in 1492. The tasks of creating towns, opening mines, and establishing sugar plantations were labor-intensive undertakings. With the indigenous populations decimated within decades through Spanish conquest, enslavement, and European-imported communicable diseases, the Spanish colonizers turned to the importation of African slaves as a source of cheap labor. Thus began the massive system of enslaving Africans and transporting them across the Atlantic (the transatlantic slave trade) to work on plantations in the Caribbean, South America, and ultimately the American South. The Americas rapidly became the nuclei of global economic complexes centered on monocultures (single-crop economies)—usually based on sugar, but sometimes based on other tropical staples such as cotton and tobacco that utilized and exploited African labor. European merchants took merchandise such as guns and cloth to Africa, where they acquired slaves, who were then transported across the Atlantic to the Americas. It is estimated that between 1600 and the end of the slave trade in the second half of the nineteenth century some ten to twelve million African slaves were landed in the Americas. Perhaps an equivalent number of Africans may have lost their lives in the operations connected with capture and shipment across the Atlantic.

The history of slavery in the North American colonies is usually dated from 1619, when twenty Africans were landed in Jamestown, Virginia, from the West Indies. In the next fifty years, the importation of African slaves into the American colonies steadily grew; by the time of the American Revolution, some 500,000 African slaves were working for Southern planters, principally in cotton production.

It was in the plantation systems of the Caribbean, South America, and the United States that slavery developed into its most rigid and regimented form. Various legal systems, known generally as slave codes, were promulgated to define the position of slaves and to regulate their treatment. Although in principle these codes incorporated so-called protective elements guaranteeing certain minimal rights, in practice the absence of institutional intervention on behalf of slaves meant that abuses could not be punished. Inhumane systems evolved in which slaves were denied basic legal rights, forbidden to congregate or possess arms, and deprived of their indigenous names and the right to maintain family institutions. The system has been characterized as one of "social death." Therefore, comparative descriptions of slave systems based on relative mildness or harshness are often superficial.

New World slavery lasted for three and a half centuries; it was profitable despite the inherent high mortality in the system. Far from recognizing the immorality of the institution, the Christian states of western Europe that created slave regimes in the Americas argued for centuries that slavery was a natural condition. Before the emancipation laws of the nineteenth century, only small numbers of slaves were liberated through manumission in one of several ways: self-purchase by slaves themselves, being the offspring of slave and free parentage, and being rewarded for faithful service. Emancipation came about through the combined impact of a number of developments: first, slave revolts in the Caribbean and Latin America; second, the campaign in England of humanitarians such as Thomas Clarkson and William Wilberforce and of organizations such as the Quakers; third, the growth of laissez-faire economic policies that made slave systems based on monopolies and protectionism counterproductive; and fourth, the intellectual influence of philosophers, such as Montesquieu and Jean-Jacques Rousseau.

Britain took the lead in abolishing slave trading in 1807 and emancipating slaves in 1834. Emancipation subsequently came to other colonies: the French colonies in 1848, the Dutch colonies in 1863; the Spanish territories between 1873 and 1886, and Brazil, the last to abolish slavery, in 1888. In the United States it took a costly and divisive civil war between a pro-abolitionist North and a pro-slavery South before Abraham Lincoln's Emancipation Proclamation Act of January 1, 1863, laid the groundwork for ending slavery. Isolated vestiges of slavery are known to have survived well into the late twentieth century in parts of Asia and Africa, despite United Nations declarations against slavery and the slave trade in 1948 and 1956.

Context

Debates among historians, economists, sociologists, anthropologists, psychologists, and specialists of other disciplines regarding the impact, ideology, legacy, and implications of slavery will perhaps never end. While there are many divergent views and perspectives on the issues, some common conclusions may be drawn. Slavery, throughout history, was exploitative and was almost always instituted to support an aristocratic class and lifestyle to the detriment of the slaves themselves. That the prosperity of Athens and the Roman civilization was largely built upon the sweat and toil of slaves, or that slave labor contributed immensely to the economic development of the American South, does not exonerate the inhumanities of the system. Moreover, whereas the Caribbean plantation system and the African slave trade provided the basis for Western capital formation, industrial growth, and mercantilist ascendancy, they conversely laid the foundation for the underdevelopment of Africa and the Caribbean region.

The historiography of slavery that has developed since the 1960's has moved from questions of whether slavery can be investigated as a purely economic system devoid of moral considerations to analyses of the internal workings of slave cultures and slaves' survival mechanisms. Constructions of slave personalities, which have shifted from images of docility to those centered on resistance, have also been explored. Thus, historical and sociological scholarship has given attention to constructions of slave identities that were shaped by continuous resistance, whether of the group type such as revolts and mutinies or of the individual and daily variety such as feigning illnesses, damaging crops and tools, and poisoning overseers and animals. The most celebrated revolt was certainly that led by Toussaint L'Ouverture, which succeeded in emancipating slaves in Haiti and creating that nation in 1804 as the first independent black republic in the Americas. Another form of resistance was the creation of Maroon communities by escaped slaves who established self-supporting, alternate structures, some of which have survived to the present day.

The nature of slavery's legacy on the institution of the black family is another debate in the sociological literature. On the one hand, scholars of the pathological school argue that the dislocations planters wrought on the slave family were so devastating that they contributed to a dysfunctioning condition, which has contemporary relevance for the analyses of the African American family. On the other hand, the adaptive/vitality school contends that the adaptations that have resulted in the black family since slavery are evidence of strength and vitality rather than weaknesses.

Prejudice based on race and color is ultimately a legacy of New World slavery, for nowhere else was race manipulated as a factor of enslavement as thoroughly as it was in the Americas. Whereas, for example, Greek slavery was based on the enslavement of whites by whites, and African slavery integrated other Africans into new lineages, in American slavery race was the primary factor in the enslavement of Africans by whites. More positively, the African diasporan presence, although it occurred because of slavery, has resulted in the retention, adaptation, and re-creation of a wide range of African cultural traits and practices and provided a vital dimension to the multicultural character of the American experience.

Bibliography

Finley, Moses I. *Ancient Slavery and Modern Ideology*. New York: Viking, 1980. A volume of four essays by Finley, a leading scholar, on slavery in antiquity. Enables one to draw comparisons between ancient slavery and the forms that developed after the fifteenth century.

Fogel, Robert. *Without Consent or Contract: The Rise and Fall of American Slavery*. New York: W. W. Norton, 1989. Fogel's book is a monumental overview of slavery in the United States from the beginnings of the slave trade through the abolition of slavery.

Goodheart, Lawrence, Richard D. Brown, and Stephen Rabe, eds. *Slavery in American Society*. 3d ed. Lexington, Mass.: Heath, 1993. A useful collection of essays dealing with a number of themes, including the definition and emergence of slavery; slave life and culture, family, and gender; and slavery and society. The essays are by notable scholars, including Orlando Patterson, Eugene Genovese, and David Brion Davis. Includes an extensive bibliography.

Klein, Herbert S. *African Slavery in Latin America and the Caribbean.* New York: Oxford University Press, 1986. Klein focuses on slavery as it developed in Latin America and the Caribbean. He compares slavery in the two regions and provides information on how it was both like and unlike slavery in North America.

Lovejoy, Paul. *Transformations in Slavery: A History of Slavery in Africa.* New York: Cambridge University Press, 1983. Lovejoy presents an excellent analysis of the development of indigenous African slavery and its relationship with the international system of slavery.

Smith, John D. *Black Slavery in the Americas: An Interdisciplinary Bibliography, 1865-1980.* 2 vols. Westport, Conn.: Greenwood Press, 1982. Smith's two-volume bibliography contains more than 21,000 entries. Coverage is thorough and interdisciplinary, and the work is extensively cross-referenced.

Joseph K. Adjaye

Cross-References

SMALL-TOWN SOCIETIES

Type of sociology: Urban and rural life

From 1930 to 1970, paralleling the rise of industrialization, rural inhabitants left small towns to seek conveniences and employment in the city. This rural-urban migration continued until the 1970's, when disillusionment with urban life spurred city dwellers to relocate to small towns across America. By the early 1990's, more people were leaving cities than were entering, inspiring a renewed sociological interest in small-town communities.

Principal terms

COMMUNITY: a geographical nucleus that provides a variety of services to families from several neighborhoods

FORMAL ORGANIZATION: a structured group of members and administrators who associate for a common purpose

INFORMAL ORGANIZATIONS: groups that develop around communication channels and friendships

METROPOLITAN: relating to a major city or a large urbanized area, including suburbs and adjacent towns

NEIGHBORHOOD: a geographical nucleus around which several families organize for mutual aid, religious worship, and education

SERVICE CENTER: an area that provides marketing, educational, and recreational services for a rural community

Overview

Originally, the United States was a rural society; agriculture was the primary means of survival. As rural populations increased, trade centers evolved where farmers could market their goods and purchase supplies. These trade centers began to offer more services, so that communities evolved to satisfy the educational, economical, spiritual, and recreational needs of local dwellers. These centers were often separated by the distance that a team of horses could travel in one day. Because the populations being served were small and shared similar needs, a strong sense of community developed; concern for the well-being of local residents was the common bond in these rural centers.

These rural communities were, however, greatly affected by the Industrial Revolution during the mid-nineteenth century. Rural dwellers left their farms to work in factories, and populations located near industries. This wave of rural-urban migration caused many towns to become ghost towns; some survived but struggled economically for decades. Cities, however, boomed. Populations often outgrew city boundaries and spread into suburbs, "bedroom communities" that surround cities.

At the workplace, specialization developed to accommodate various types of industry. As specialization increased, social classes emerged. The lure of the city began to diminish as the gap between the haves and the have-nots widened. Congestion created tension in the city, and violence became an expression of that tension. In time, many urban dwellers longed to return to small towns.

Urban-rural migration grew strong in the 1970's as urbanites sought locations that would provide them with a strong sense of community. In their book *Country Bound!* (1992), Marilyn and Tom Ross refer to this out-migration from urban centers as a rural renaissance. They claim that trendiness, materialism, and unemployment motivated city dwellers to seek the wholesome values and community bonds associated with rural life. Those fleeing the city imagined that a slower pace of life would replace the regimentation and fast pace of the city. They envisioned family and community replacing the indifference, rudeness, and selfishness found in urban environments.

In rural counties, communities offer strong social bonds. A small population centered around a geographical core brings people together frequently. These repeated associations create trust and openness. A cooperation and intimacy exists in the small town precisely because of the small population. Sociologists suggest that the optimum size for a neighborhood is 500 people, while the optimum community has 5,000 occupants. These numbers seem ideal for fostering the intimate relationships associated with small towns.

Although neighborhoods within the urban environment tend to be based on income status, economic stratification is not pronounced in small towns. Great distances do not separate the rich from the poor, the old from the young, the mayor from the mail carrier. The small town does, however, have various social groups. Some of these are formal organizations, while others are informal.

Formal organizations bring people together for a common purpose. These groups, which have a formal structure of members and leaders, meet at scheduled times and designated places. Such organizations might include churches, school support groups, political parties, civic clubs, youth organizations, and social clubs. Members of any organization are likely to belong to several groups, so that association with particular members is frequent.

The importance of informal relationships in small towns cannot be overlooked. These associations are formed by extended family, gossip groups, and "cracker-barrel" groups, the regulars who gather around the general store. These groups do not have the structured, ritualistic procedures of formal organizations, but their communication power is enormous. Through this "grapevine" of interpersonal relationships, culture, social values, and public opinion are transmitted. The real issues of everyday life are discussed thoroughly through these casual channels before groups meet formally to determine a course of action.

The formal and informal organizations within the small town give the town its identity. The decisions and actions that affect the town are made by the inhabitants, not by distant politicians. A close bond exists between the people who plan procedures and those who carry out the operations of the town. This is the "community sense" that many urbanites seek as they migrate to small towns.

Applications

Beginning with the 1970's, a large number of urbanites packed up their city belongings and headed for small towns and rural environments. Sociologists have identified various groups of urban-rural migrants. One group consists of people longing to set up family farms. This group might also be construed to include craftsmen and creative artists who want to free themselves from the chaos of the city in order to perform their work. Another group consists of those who can operate home-based businesses from any location. Given a choice of environments, they decide on small towns. Some employees of large companies can relocate to small towns without giving up their professions, thanks to telecommunication. Companies such as Pacific Bell, New York Life, and Citibank allow telecommuting. Sociologists have also noticed that retirees are choosing small towns, which are less congested and less violent than metropolitan areas. In fact, many small towns, especially those located in the Sunbelt states of California, Arizona, New Mexico, and Florida, are luring seniors who pay taxes but do not use expensive social services such as schools. Another group seeking safe haven in small towns is composed of parents who want to raise their children in healthy, nonviolent communities. These families seek a simpler lifestyle that makes it possible to spend more time together and less time on freeways. The basic humanistic values of small towns provide a more nurturing environment for children than that of the crime-ridden, congested cities.

The combination of formal and informal organizations builds strong interpersonal bonds in the small town. Close geographic proximity brings small-town dwellers into frequent face-to-face contact. Also, the number of possible partners of interaction is limited because of the small population. These factors contribute to the personal nature of small towns.

Person-to-person contacts make for a humanistic environment that focuses more on intimacy than on material acquisitions and exciting entertainment. In small towns, relationships tend to be deeper and more permanent than those in cities because people have more time for human interaction. Frequent, unhurried communication allows emotions, attitudes, and moral judgments to be expressed. The deeper communication that occurs in small towns eliminates the loneliness that is often experienced by urban dwellers who are surrounded by people on the surface level only.

Rather than adapting the standardized facade that is needed to handle the variety of contacts in the city, rural dwellers can be less mechanical and more human. Because there are fewer contacts in a small town than in an urban environment, however, the population in a small town becomes increasingly homogeneous. The more defined the homogeneity, the less able individuals are to deviate from that standard. Small-town dwellers are products of a homogeneous set of manners, activities, and attitudes. These residents are molded by traditional values and are judged by their adaptation to and application of those values. Adherence to the unwritten as well as the written small-town standards often seems restrictive to urban migrants.

The urban environment offers anonymity because city dwellers can get lost in the crowd. Some urbanites find a "freedom" in being unknown. In addition, the heterogeneous nature of the city provides few restrictions. In small towns, however, limited boundaries and few contacts mean that everyone knows everyone. A trade-off is required when moving from the city to the small town. Urbanites must adapt to the homogeneous nature of the small town; in exchange, they will be rewarded with genuine relationships because time and communication are more plentiful.

Living in small towns offers further advantages. Community development around a nucleus brings housing, shopping, schools, and workplaces within walking or biking distance. This eliminates dependence on automobiles, which reduces auto-associated costs for the individual and road-building and road-maintenance costs for the community. In addition, the natural environment is healthier without auto-induced pollution. Small-town dwellers who use muscle power in place of automobiles are physically healthier than those who sit passively in cars. Also, people who walk and bike are free of the stress that urbanites experience in city traffic. Although the pace of life is slow in small towns, walking increases opportunities for social interaction with neighbors.

Additional benefits result when residential and commercial buildings are close together. The compact nucleus of a small town is less expensive to maintain than is the sprawl of suburbs. The costs of land, roads, utilities, water, and sewer lines are lower. Also, because mills and industry have been replaced by offices and electronic plants, pollution has decreased. As a result, zoning that segregates housing, commerce, and industry is no longer needed. People can live close to where they work, shop, and receive services, so that a sense of community develops.

Within that tight communal web, residents continually come into direct contact with the providers of services. In the city, a customer walks into a supermarket and selects a piece of meat from a group of plastic-wrapped, prelabeled choices. That customer rarely sees the butcher or the meat-wrapper. In the small town, however, a customer speaks frequently with the butcher, who probably wraps his own meat in his own shop. Small-town residents will undoubtedly know their baker by name and may even know the farmer who grows their produce. Because no distance separates the producer from the product, the producer takes great pride in his workmanship and in his customer service. This pride in delivering a fine product is often lost in the city, where merchandise is handled by a stream of individuals before it reaches the customer. Small-town residents receive personal attention with their daily purchases. Producer, product, and consumer are closely related in the small town.

When ex-urbanites speak about their returns to small towns, they often refer to a sense of "coming home." They feel a strong identity in a population that shares common values and experiences. They feel secure in an environment that does not require superficial facades but that allows genuine communication.

Context

During the 1930's and 1940's, sociologists such as Pitirim A. Sorokin, Carle C. Zimmerman, and Charles J. Galpin (1965) studied rural life and traced its development from the single farm to the neighborhood to the service and market center to the community and, finally, to the emergence of the small town. Many of these sociologists studied farmers and how their need to market their goods led to the development of societies. Cooperatives were formed, along with political groups that were concerned about rural representation on the national level. Small towns contained an intricate pattern of structured groups as well as communication channels. Sociologists investigated the formal and informal organizations found in small towns, which were the bonding elements for the desired "community spirit."

As factories drew rural dwellers away from the farms and into industrial centers, however, the sociologists had two phenomena to study: the decrease in small-town populations and the growth of urban centers. Sociologist Richard Lingeman (1980) gives a comprehensive view of life in small towns and discusses the effects on small towns as populations deserted, migrating to mining and factory communities. As urban centers expanded, sociologists studied urban ecology, urban growth patterns, urban housing, and urban subcultures. As suburbs increased, sociologists studied the effects of decentralization on life in the inner city. As cities expanded into the "green belts" surrounding the city limits, sociologists examined life in the suburbs. Andres Duany and Elizabeth Plater-Zyberk have described a suburb as "an agglomeration of houses, shops, and offices connected to one another by cars, not by the fabric of human life." They claim that the lack of community bonding in the suburbs motivates suburbanites to return to small towns.

To accommodate the rapidly increasing number of urban escapees to small towns, many popular books are now giving advice about how to make the transition. Books such as Charles Long's *Life After the City* (1989) and Frank Ruegg and Paul Bianchina's *You Can't Plant Tomatoes in Central Park* (1992) educate the urban dropout about relocating in small towns. Norman Crampton's *The 100 Best Small Towns in America* (1993) gives detailed descriptions of the geography, businesses, schools, and recreation opportunities of many towns across the country. Marilyn and Tom Ross have written *Country Bound!* (1992), a book that discusses the ways in which individuals can develop small-town businesses. The popularity of these books reflects the increasing migration of urban dwellers to small towns. Sociologists are examining the demographic shifts in population based on culture, race, age, and occupation.

As urbanites shift from big-city expansiveness to small-town compactness, they will need to make many adjustments. They cannot live as anonymous or passive isolationists; instead, they must become involved in the community. In the city, many urbanites leave civic matters for others to handle, but in the small town each individual must take an active part. A small town reflects the collective attitudes and participation of its residents. The commitment on the part of each individual maintains the "community spirit" that many urbanites seek as they move to the small town.

Bibliography

Eberle, Nancy. *Return to Main Street.* New York: W. W. Norton, 1982. A personal account of the author's shift from urban to small-town life. Although many issues are discussed, the emphasis is on relationshps, the binding center of small-town communities.

Finsterbusch, Kurt, and Janet Schwartz, eds. *Sources: Notable Selections in Sociology.* Guilford, Conn.: Dushkin, 1993. This annual anthology covers many sociological issues, including groups and roles in transition, institutions in crisis and change, and the impact of technology and changing social values on the future.

Lingeman, Richard. *Small Town America.* New York: Putnam, 1980. This collection of narratives covers settlement in America from 1620 through 1980. Pioneer towns, mining camps, and prairie junctions are discussed. The impact of factories on town development is covered, and there is a chapter on town and community. An excellent bibliography is included.

Ross, Marilyn, and Tom Ross. *Country Bound!* Bueno Vista, Colo.: Communication Creativity, 1992. This book is devoted to helping people make the transition from urban to small-town living. Personal considerations are discussed, as are business options. A discussion of small-town social life and community is also included. Thirty pages of resources are offered, along with an excellent bibliography.

Sorokin, Pitirim A., Carle C. Zimmerman, and Charles J. Galpin. *A Systematic Source Book in Rural Sociology.* New York: Russell & Russell, 1965. This is an old book, but it is an excellent source for studying rural sociology from ancient societies through the nineteenth century. Two excellent discussions that are relevant to modern rural studies focus on the fundamental differences between rural and urban worlds and the formal and informal social organizations of small towns.

Taylor, Carl C. *Rural Life in the United States.* New York: Alfred A. Knopf, 1949. This excellent source for rural studies includes an examination of the evolution of American rural societies and the ways in which those societies organized and developed. A thorough discussion on the differences between neighborhoods and communities is included, as is an analysis of formal social groups and informal associations. An excellent, although dated, bibliography is included.

Linda J. Meyers

Cross-References

Industrial Societies, 953; New Towns and Planned Communities, 1296; Rural Societies, 1673; Suburbanization and Decentralization, 2010; Urban Planning: Major Issues, 2109; Urbanization, 2129.

SMOKING AND CANCER

Type of sociology: Major social institutions
Field of study: Medicine

Tobacco smoking and exposure to tobacco smoke cause lung cancer and many other diseases. This fact has given rise to efforts to eradicate smoking, which have been hampered by propaganda disseminated by tobacco companies. Smoking, the anti-smoking movement, and the actions of the tobacco companies represent important medical and sociological phenomena.

Principal terms
ADDICTION: a habit based on a physical and/or psychological dependence
EPIDEMIOLOGY: the study of epidemic diseases and related widespread medical phenomena
NICOTINE: a naturally occurring poisonous drug found in tobacco that gives tobacco its euphoric and addictive properties
PASSIVE SMOKING: the inhalation of smoke from tobacco used by others; passive smoking is believed to cause cancer and other diseases
PROPAGANDA: the systematic dissemination of the viewpoint of a special interest group
WITHDRAWAL: the physical and emotional changes caused by stopping the use of an addictive drug

Overview

The practice of smoking tobacco came to Europe after European explorers in the fifteenth century observed pipe smoking among the North and South American Indians. Such observations reportedly began with the voyages of Christopher Columbus in the 1490's. It was not until the late 1500's, however, that the habit of tobacco smoking took root in the Old World. It then quickly became both widely practiced and a subject of great social contention.

This contention has waxed and waned for approximately four centuries, reaching a peak in the modern worldwide controversy regarding the intrinsic suitability of the smoking of tobacco and its connection to cancer and other diseases. The views of antismoking organizations (such as the American Cancer Society) and cigarette companies on these issues, as well as the related actions of governments, have very important medical and social ramifications.

The study of the phenomenon of tobacco smoking has uncovered considerable archaeological evidence that it has existed for at least ten centuries. The use of tobacco smoking at first had religious significance and served as a signal of both peace and welcome to strangers. In the way that it was practiced by North and South American

Indians, in infrequent shamanistic and semireligious rites, tobacco smoking induced mind-expanding and mellowing psychedelic experiences.

In contrast, in modern Europe, the United States, and elsewhere—because consumers overindulge—the smoking of pipes, of cigars, and of cigarettes elicits only very mild feelings of well-being. Moreover, the use of tobacco in any smoked form is potentially dangerous, because of the poisonous nicotine that is present in the inhaled smoke. The toxicity of nicotine is demonstrated by the fact that soaking a cigar in a glass of water for a few days will produce a nicotine solution that will kill anyone who drinks it.

Smokers do not die of acute nicotine poisoning because the process of burning tobacco destroys most of its nicotine, leaving just enough of the drug to produce mild stimulatory effects. In addition, as if the poisonous nature of the nicotine were not bad enough, other chemicals in tobacco smoke (for example, those that come from radioactive radon) are strongly linked to lung cancer. These toxic substances are also associated with heart disease, emphysema, and other serious diseases. The preceding information makes one wonder why people smoke. The first answer to this question is that tobacco is highly addictive. The second is that peer group pressure and propaganda disseminated by tobacco advertisements also encourage people to smoke.

The process of breaking an addiction to tobacco smoking requires that an individual spend three to four weeks without smoking. During this period, smokers are likely to crave cigarettes, to become nervous and irritable, and to have some trouble sleeping. Although it would seem that smoking deaddiction would therefore be simple, it is not. Three main reasons have been proposed to explain why many smokers cannot (or do not) stop smoking. First, most smokers are not convinced that they are really engaged in a dangerous and addictive habit. Second, the sociological phenomena of peer group pressure and tobacco company propaganda combine to make many smokers wish to continue to smoke. Third, many smokers do not possess the self control that is needed to face the challenge of quitting smoking.

There is no doubt, however, that cigarette smoking is a very dangerous addiction. It has now been definitively shown that the risk of lung cancer is twenty to thirty times higher in heavy smokers than it is in nonsmokers. In addition, cancer and the other diseases associated with the smoking of cigarettes are believed to kill more than 300,000 people yearly. The identification of cigarettes with "smoking" is a result of the fact that cigarettes are the form in which most people inhale tobacco smoke. Other forms of tobacco smoke intake (for example, pipes and cigars) cause many of the same problems and a few of their own.

Nonsmokers should be aware that being in the same room where tobacco is being smoked by others is a very risky business. The risk arises from exposure to so-called passive smoking, which increases the chances of a person's developing lung cancer and other tobacco smoke-related diseases, without smoking. The term "passive smoking" is meant to indicate that nonsmokers can inhale dangerous amounts of nicotine and other toxic chemicals from exhaled tobacco smoke, as it spreads through a room. The result of the continuing social controversy regarding active and passive cigarette smoking seems likely to produce future stigmatization of the habit that could lead to its being practiced mostly in the privacy of people's homes.

Applications

There is no evidence of any kind that frequent tobacco smoking has any truly positive value for humans. The only benefits of the addiction are that it relieves tension to some extent and that having a cigarette in one's mouth "keeps food out," thus helping a smoker to keep his or her weight down. Despite these facts, the widespread occurrence of smoking has led to the belief by many (including a large number of physicians) that the tobacco smoking habit—though it should not be practiced— satisfies some basic human need.

Strangely, few smokers can explain why they started to smoke, except to say that they wished to satisfy their curiosity or were influenced by peer pressure. At best, studies seem to indicate that many smokers are restless, tense people who are calmed down by the very mild euphoria that is produced by routine tobacco smoking; this may be the sole "basic need" for using tobacco. Yet one wonders if such a calming effect is worth the increased risk of lung cancer and the overall increased risk of early death.

The realization that smoking is very dangerous on the part of the general adult population has led to a marked decline in smoking since the 1960's, as evidenced by the fact that almost 50 percent of the population smoked in the early 1960's, while only 24 to 26 percent smoked in the early 1990's. In the 1980's and 1990's, the most frequent smokers were people in lower socioeconomic groups. A huge number of teenagers now smoke, and most teenage smokers began to smoke before they reached age thirteen.

It appears that teenage smoking is a sociological and psychological phenomenon that is driven by peer pressure, rebellion against authority, and media advertising aimed at the young. For this reason, Congress, in 1971, banned all television and radio commercials by cigarette companies. Yet cigarettes continue to be the among the most heavily advertised products in the United States, even if such advertising is now limited to passive forms such as billboards and magazines. It has now been suggested by the American Cancer Society and other health groups, however, that all cigarette advertising should be banned. The tobacco companies, understandably, vigorously oppose this idea.

Another social issue is related to the ambivalence of national, state, and local governments toward cigarette bans. In spite of the fact that the federal government has required statements concerning the dangers of smoking to be included on cigarette packages—and in advertisements—and has financed many reports that conclude that cigarettes are extremely dangerous, no outright ban on smoking has yet been instituted.

A number of social and economic issues have probably contributed to this lack of direct action. For example, a cigarette ban might lead to the development of black markets similar to those that sell other illegal drugs, and the cigarettes that would be disseminated to the public by those markets could be even more dangerous. Illegal cigarette providers might use low-quality tobacco or might add even more addictive substances to the contraband cigarettes. Furthermore, such a ban on cigarettes could stimulate cigarette smoking in the same way that Prohibition stimulated the use of alcoholic beverages. In addition, there is the socioeconomic impetus of the tremendous amount of revenue generated by cigarette sales that is brought in by local, state, and federal governments (cigarette taxes earn about $5 billion per year in federal taxes). Finally, the banning of tobacco would damage a socioeconomic group that is already in great financial difficulty: American tobacco farmers.

There are a number of reasons why tobacco farmers resist the suggestion that they grow crops other than tobacco. First, most farmers are overextended and are fighting to survive financially even when they are engaged in the area of agriculture that they know best. Second, tobacco is one of the most lucrative cash crops that is available to the farmer; it earns about six times as much as cotton and about twenty-five times as much as wheat. Finally, American tobacco is grown in only six states: North Carolina, South Carolina, Georgia, Kentucky, Tennessee, and Virginia. The cessation of tobacco production in those states, whose economies depend heavily on it, could have severe social and economic consequences.

One area in which it seems likely that public health will be served by legislation is that of passive smoking. It is now clear that simply dividing restaurants, workplaces, and other sites where people congregate into smoking and nonsmoking sections is not adequate to serve the needs of people who are allergic to the components of tobacco smoke. In addition, the increased health risk to the general public that is caused by passive smoking cannot be addressed in this way. Therefore, steps are being taken at several levels to produce smokeless environments for the public. Airlines are now smoke free, and many restaurants enforce no-smoking rules. In addition, numerous businesses of varying sizes are developing smokeless environments. Furthermore, laws limiting smoking in public places have been passed in several states and in many individual cities, and the movement to expand such laws is growing rapidly.

Context

It has already been mentioned that a major aspect of the importance of smoking to the American Indian societies in which it originated was the social acceptance of strangers and potential enemies. It is also believed by many sociologists and psychologists that the smoking of tobacco in modern society has a somewhat similar purpose in that the offer of a cigarette to others is a gesture that indicates friendliness. Furthermore, this gesture reportedly leads to a release of tension in the person who receives the cigarette. Other related social aspects of tobacco smoking include feelings of oneness (or togetherness) that are reported to exist among groups of people who smoke together.

In addition, it is commonly thought that much of the reason that smoking is so widespread is that the advertising of tobacco companies makes many smokers believe that they are—momentarily—like the heroes and others whom they wish to emulate. Thus, it would appear that a major role of sociologists and educators in diminishing or stopping smoking might be the development of an educational strategy that defuses the mind-set that smoking together is a friendly action and that doing it is a useful success surrogate.

Such efforts will have to draw the attention of both potential and actual smokers to the fact that the tobacco habit is not only unhealthy but also can never make them into the people whose success they wish to emulate. A social message that might be a good substitute is that hard work and other positive attributes will be much more likely than smoking to get people where they wish to go. Another crucial issue is the need for parental support and guidance for incipient smokers. This is important because most smoking begins when people are teenagers—few people begin smoking after age twenty-one—and those youngsters who are at odds with their parents are most likely to become smokers.

Finally, although nonsmokers must be protected from deleterious effects of passive smoking, such protection must be afforded in a way that also protects the rights of those who wish to smoke in spite of smoking's ill effects. Simply legislating that all smoking must stop is unlikely to be an adequate solution and may even produce a social backlash that would increase the number of smokers.

Consequently, an adequate and widely disseminated information base regarding the dangers of smoking, sound methodology that defuses the idea that smoking is a good social action, and legislation that sensibly satisfies smokers and nonsmokers will probably be the best means of solving the problems that are related to smoking.

Bibliography

Douville, Judith A. *Active and Passive Smoking Hazards in the Workplace.* New York: Van Nostrand Reinhold, 1990. This useful book is designed to help executives and other officials cope with the hazards of workplace smoking. It covers smoking hazards, smoking decisions and policy making, programs for smoking cessation, and workplace smoking policy implementation and outcomes. A modern, broad-based endeavor, it also contains a wide-ranging and useful reference list.

Gahagan, Dolly D., and Frederick G. Gahagan. *Switch Down and Quit: What the Cigarette Companies Don't Want You to Know About Smoking.* Berkeley, Calif.: Ten Speed Press, 1987. This interesting book is predominantly concerned with smoking cessation, but it also contains useful information on social aspects of cigarette production, tobacco manufacture, and government taxation. It also contains much information on the many health hazards of smoking.

Gano, Lila. *Smoking.* San Diego, Calif.: Lucent Books, 1989. This informative book describes many important aspects of smoking and associated problems. It discusses the history of smoking, media involvement, smoking and antismoking groups, diseases caused by smoking, and legislative aspects. An excellent glossary and a list of agencies to contact for more information are included.

Murray, L. Jarrett, A. V. Swan, and R. Rumun. *Smoking Among Young Adults.* Aldershot, England: Avebury, 1988. This careful report describes a study of smoking in Britain that examined the smoking habits of young adults. It came up with information on the basis for smoking, the places where it occurs, its effects on health, and a social model of smoking. Also included are a set of valuable references on many aspects of the sociology and psychology of smoking.

Royal College of Physicians of London. *Smoking and Health*. New York: Pitman, 1962. This book is quite interesting in that it covers many of the same bases as the newer references. This points out that the problems of smoking, the poisonous nature of tobacco, and ways to fight smoking have been discussed for many years. Many useful older references are included in a copious reference list.

Troyer, Ronald J., and Gerald E. Markle. *Cigarettes: The Battle over Smoking*. New Brunswick, N.J.: Rutgers University Press, 1983. This text covers cigarette smoking from the point of view of the sociologist but also deals with medical issues and other topics. It is extremely readable and contains both much data and many useful references.

U.S. Department of Health and Human Services. *Smoking and Health in the Americas*. DHHS Publication CDC 92-8419. Atlanta, Ga.: U.S. Department of Health and Human Services, 1992. This informative, multiauthor compendium addresses several issues related to tobacco, including its history, smoking prevalence and mortality, economic aspects, legislation, and control programs.

Sanford S. Singer

Cross-References

Drug Use and Addiction, 572; The Environment and Health, 647; Health and Society, 852; Social Epidemiology, 1793; Socialization: The Family, 1880.

SOCIAL CHANGE: EVOLUTIONARY
AND CYCLICAL THEORIES

Type of sociology: Social change
Fields of study: Cultural variation and change; Theories of social change

Social change is the process or series of processes that modify social structures, such as nations, over a long period of time. Some sociologists believe that social change occurs in a linear and evolutionary fashion and that society is progressing, or changing for the better. Others suggest that change is cyclical; in imitation of nature, societies are born, grow, and die.

Principal terms

ANOMIE: a sense of rootlessness fostered by the absence of social norms
CULTURE: the beliefs, values, knowledge, and symbols held in common by a group of people that enliven all aspects of social existence; said by Spengler to be the basic unit of social change
CYCLICAL SOCIAL CHANGE: a model of social change that emphasizes the repetitive, cyclic changes that societies undergo
EVOLUTIONARY SOCIAL CHANGE: a model of social change that emphasizes the linear, progressive changes that societies undergo
SOCIAL GROUP: any collection of people who share a common purpose which provides them with a sense of belonging

Overview

Social life is characterized by permanence, continuity, repetitiveness, and change. Social change can be discussed on at least two levels: the processes of change which (paradoxically) sustain the social structure and those processes which modify the social structure. Many things that are experienced as permanent features of social living (such as the sustained existence of a nation) may in fact require ongoing change and may be called linear, or *evolutionary*. Other features of social living can be considered to be in decline, in progress, or repeating *cyclically*; these features depend on processes of change which modify the social structure rather than maintain it.

Some evolutionary theories of social change claimed that human beings are subject to natural laws of change which are predetermined, inevitable, and capable of being known through scientific methods. These laws, which were initially fashioned after the findings of Charles Darwin and came to be known as Social Darwinism during the nineteenth century, had among their chief proponents Herbert Spencer. Social Darwinists suggested that in human societies, as in nature, change is developmental and progressive. The success of particular social groups at the expense of others was seen to parallel Darwin's theory of natural selection, according to which the "fittest" species survive. In this model, some societies could be described as underdeveloped and primitive, whereas others, the developed societies, were viewed as having a natural right to thrive and dominate other societies.

Auguste Comte (1798-1857) proposed a different theory of evolutionary social change, dividing it into three stages of thought: the religious stage, dominated by belief in supernatural powers, dogmatic religion, and theocratic government; the metaphysical or philosophical stage, dominated by abstract, deductive thinking; and the scientific, or positivist, stage, dominated by empirical research and inductive thinking. Societies in the supernatural or religious stage are, in this view, more primitive than societies in the positivist stage. Comte's evolutionary theory concludes (as did all evolutionary theories of that time) that European society was the most progressive and developed.

Other evolutionary theories were presented: that human societies evolve from simple, homogeneous, nonspecialized cultures into complex, heterogeneous, specialized cultures (Herbert Spencer); from "barbarian" to "civilized" (Lewis Henry Morgan); from animistic to polytheistic to monotheistic (Edward Tylor); and from communities bound together by tradition and affection to those characterized by nonemotional objectivity (Ferdinand Tönnies). All these theories reached the same conclusion—that the Western world is the end product of natural social evolution— and all have had a profound effect on the way scholars and the general public have viewed their societies. For example, many historians still speak of the ancient, medieval, and modern worlds in a way that assumes that the ancient world was less developed than the modern.

Some evolutionary theorists distrusted this inherent assumption that the West is at the apex of development. Karl Marx (1818-1883), for example, claimed that "progress" could sometimes mask a growth in people's alienation. As societies develop, Marx theorized, people can lose control over what they have produced through their own activities. The result is a highly developed society which continues to divide rather than unite its members and which, in particular, increases the distance between what people do (production) and the fruits of what they do (product). Marx proposed an alternative evolutionary view which incorporated a cyclic view as well: He believed that society would evolve—through a series of cycles of revolution, equilibrium, and new revolution—to a point at which all people would live together in peace based on equality of ownership in the means of production.

Unlike the more optimistic Comte and Spencer (and even Marx), Émile Durkheim (1858-1917) claimed that the increased specialization and individualism of modern life would result in growth, but not necessarily growth for the better. Instead, he foresaw an increasing breakdown in organic solidarity as societies became more complex, more industrialized, more specialized, and more fragmented, with their members more cut off from one another. The members of such a society, he argued, would be characterized by increasing anomie—rootlessness and detachment from society—as common moral values were abandoned and social contracts deteriorated. Such a development would not lead to a better life but to the ultimate abandonment of all that is good in Western culture. Durkheim's theory is an example of theories of linear development that result from negative rather than positive change.

Evolutionary thought was a child of modernity. As such, it reflected the characteristics of modernity: rationality, reductionism, analysis, optimism, and antitradition- alism. As the science and technology which acted as the tools of modernity were found wanting in their ability to sustain a high level of human happiness, other models of social change developed. One of these was the cyclical model, which dominated thought at the beginning of the twentieth century.

Oswald Spengler (1880-1936) and Arnold Toynbee (1889-1975) are the two most famous advocates of the cyclical interpretation of social change. Spengler began with a unit of social change which he called culture. A culture is a group of people united by a unique spirit of life which enlivens their art, religion, philosophy, politics, sports, technologies, and economies—all the elements that form a society. Cultures undergo change in imitation of the seasons of the year and the aging of nature. During its spring, a culture is agricultural, rural, and feudal; such a culture is mirrored in its heroes and the myths that describe them. During its summer, a culture begins to establish towns that, as yet, are not separate from their rural roots. At this stage, the culture is led by an aristocracy which controls the society. Autumn brings the fruition of the seeds planted during the spring and nurtured during the summer. The culture's particular spirit is expressed in its growing cities, increased commerce, and centralized monar- chies; religion is challenged by philosophy and science. At the same time, autumn brings the beginning of a disintegration that is concluded during the winter. Winter is marked by imperialism, political tyranny, constant warfare, the appearance of large cities, workers without geographic roots, esoteric art, and rule by the wealthy. The culture has lost its spirit and has hardened into a bureaucracy that supports the wealthy; the workers have lost their spirit and purpose for living.

Toynbee criticized Spengler for not being scientific and proposed twenty-one "civilizations" within which he discerned certain rhythms or cycles. Central to these rhythms was the fact that a civilization grows when it responds creatively to the challenges of its minorities and declines when the leadership cannot respond. Neither growth nor disintegration is determined. A phase of experienced disintegration is frequently succeeded by a pulse of power and control—but not for long, because usually, when leadership does creatively respond to the challenges, a short time later a deeper relapse usually occurs. One knows when a civilization is declining because creativity lessens and standardization increases.

Applications

Experience of contemporary life suggests that societies have regular patterns of development, from life cycles to business cycles. A variation of the cyclical pattern, which might be described as a three-stage S pattern, also seems to exist: An example of this S pattern may be seen in the relationship of population change to birth and mortality. In preindustrial societies, both the birthrate and the mortality rate are high; as a consequence, the population grows slowly. When mortality decreases, the popu- lation grows much more quickly. In the third stage, both the birth rate and the mortality rate have become low, and the population growth approaches zero.

At the same time, social change is experienced in a linear mode when, for example, old, no-longer-practical ideas and processes are replaced with new, more effective ones or when, as a result of new technologies, disease-caused suffering is reduced, hunger is satisfied, or weather-related destruction is avoided.

Day-to-day experience, then, supports both a linear (evolutionary) and cyclical view of social change, and each process influences and complicates the other. For example, tracing population growth and its effects on social change is not as easy as it may at first seem. On one hand, some theories hold that population growth was a stimulus for change in Europe during the eleventh through thirteenth centuries; on the other hand, other theories hold that population growth today is at the root of social stagnation. These contrary claims for the consequences of population growth suggest the problem of applying evolutionary and cyclical theories: They are not as scientific as their authors claim.

Every culture has stories of the beginning and end of the world. Certainly more colorful than scientific theories, they are also quite significant. They attempt to describe, based on human experience, the development of the world as a whole, from beginning to end. By definition, science cannot provide such a model, since it is restricted to the natural world—space and time. If the story of social change is to be told scientifically by sociologists, it must be presented in small, historical samplings. These theories can provide probable explanations for what has happened and what may be happening now. Predicting long-range change, however, is a very tenuous exercise.

Context

All scientific theories are developed within a social context, and this context is particularly noteworthy when one is considering theories involving human life and society. The early evolutionary theories of social change were put forward in the nineteenth century, when European industrialization and technological invention were creating profound and rapid changes in society. Many European thinkers, in keeping with the currents of the age and enamored with "progress," saw these changes as positive and ongoing. Karl Marx, on the other hand, dissented, seeing the miseries created by capitalist exploitation and arguing that society evolved through economic conflict between classes. The cyclical theories of the early twentieth century developed in a different context. The senseless carnage of World War I (1914-1918), which ravaged Europe—considered by most European thinkers to be the most developed and highly evolved part of the world—created a deep sense of pessimism and doubt. Within this context, Spengler's *The Decline of the West* (1918), with its view of inevitable cultural decline, resonated throughout the philosophical and sociological communities.

Every individual and society must have a sense of past, present, and future in order to have a sense of identity: We must know not only who we were but who we will be. Theories of social change provide a sense of identity and usefulness in everyday life because they give us a way of knowing what change, history, and the future are all about. In the midst of serious individual or social suffering, they offer an explanation:

What we are going through is part of making life better (evolutionary theory); what we are going through is part of the disintegration that must occur before integration occurs (cyclical theory). The individual or society convinced that these are reflections of the real world certainly can cope with the present and maintain hope for a different future.

If these theories are accepted as true, then one is faced with a number of important questions. How does one act in the face of change? Are the changes in ecology, technology, and social values natural and thus to be endured, even embraced? Is it wise to wait before making decisions that would slow or reverse these changes? Is the acknowledgment of change itself a Western ethnocentric norm, used to impose its modern value system on other cultures?

How any change, including social change, is interpreted is always conditioned by a cultural point of view. It is easy to understand development in terms of one's own cultural values. Technology is so highly valued in North American society, for example, that it is easy to project the end of development or the apex of the cycle to be a highly developed technological society that serves the basic needs of every individual in the society. Some societies, however, would not consider such development as an ideal to be striven for. Therefore, central considerations of social change theories are always biased, because one's view of change is always biased.

A constant danger in sociology, particularly in the sociology of change, is to translate what is into what should be—facts into necessities. Sociologists often take on an activist role in that they see problems in society and reflexively think about, and make recommendations and predictions about, what might be done to improve things. Such recommendations, by necessity, are always grounded in a theoretical view of social change, and this fact raises questions about their viability. If one grants that a particular theory of social change has been demonstrated, all that one is actually acknowledging is that it describes how humans have reacted to change in the past, not how they will act in the future. Attempts to predict the future scientifically are, at best, representative of inductive rather than deductive reasoning—they assume that, because things have happened a certain way before, they will continue to happen that way. Arguably, claims regarding what will happen in the future place one outside the realm of the sociology of change altogether and into the realm of religion, with its claims to know the beginning and end of the world. Moreover, the generalizations and abstractions necessary to develop a hypothesis to explain social change lead to doubts regarding whether it is possible to provide a scientific explanation for entire cultures or the whole world.

Bibliography

Kerr, Clark. *The Future of Industrial Societies: Convergence or Continuing Diversity?* Cambridge, Mass.: Harvard University Press, 1983. Industrialization and the social change it brings are part of any modern society. This book discusses whether it must be part of every future society. North America, for example, is considered to be a postindustrial society.

Kollar, Nathan. "Visions of the End of the World: Past and Present." *Death Education* 7, no. 1 (Spring, 1983): 9-24. A detailed analysis of the stories present in various world cultures which describe the changes associated with society before and after the end of the world.

Lasch, Christopher. *The True and Only Heaven: Progress and Its Critics*. New York: W. W. Norton, 1991. A review and critical analysis of the thesis of evolutionary progress. Lash argues that progress cannot be an interpretative model for change.

Lenski, Gerhard, and Jean Lenski. *Human Societies: An Introduction to Macrosociology*. 4th ed. New York: McGraw-Hill, 1982. A textbook that places sociological knowledge in the context of social change.

Nisbet, Robert A. *Social Change and History: Aspects of the Western Theory of Development*. New York: Oxford University Press, 1969. A classic and influential work that reviews the Western view of development.

North, Douglas C. *Structure and Change in Economic History*. New York: W. W. Norton, 1981. A significant area within which social change occurs is economics. North places theories of social change in their economic context.

Nathan R. Kollar

Cross-References

SOCIAL CHANGE: FUNCTIONALISM VERSUS HISTORICAL MATERIALISM

Type of sociology: Social change
Fields of study: Sociological perspectives and principles; Sources of social change; Theories of social change

No society stays the same for very long, and sociologists have explained societal change in many different ways. This article focuses on the functionalist perspective (that each social institution fulfills a function relative to other social entities) and the materialist perspective (that the production and ownership of goods determines social relationships) concerning social change.

Principal terms

EVOLUTIONISM: an explanation for social change that emphasizes a society's gradual progress over time, moving through a series of distinct and predictable phases

FUNCTIONALISM: a sociological theory that explains social institutions and events in terms of the effects that they produce throughout the rest of society

HISTORICAL MATERIALISM: a sociological theory that explains social features through an analysis of the economics involved in the material production of goods and the reproduction of social institutions

MARXISM: a general term for the several schools of sociological methodology deriving from Karl Marx, which share notions of social class and material production as important social determinants

MEANS OF PRODUCTION: in Marxist and materialist sociology, actual physical processes by which individuals and groups transform the environment into products for human use and consumption

SOCIAL CLASS: a group with a shared experience of the means of production; often used in relation to other social classes to analyze the relative distribution of resources and power

TECHNOLOGY: ways of effecting changes in the environment by using human-invented processes and tools to produce goods and services for human use and consumption

Overview

Just as societies vary around the globe, societies change over time. Though this fact has never escaped the notice of those who study people and civilizations, sociologists have never been able to agree on an explanation for why change happens in the way that it does. Even though there may well be random events that shape societies, most scholars have believed that there were patterns to social change and that these patterns could be identified in order to understand the nature of social change, to recognize the causes of particular events in society, and perhaps even to anticipate or predict changes likely to happen in a society's future. Among the many sociological models for the explanation of social change, two conflicting options have risen to the forefront: the functionalist and the historical materialist approaches.

The functionalist approach to sociology (also called "structural-functionalism") sets a research agenda that begins with observation. Once a researcher sees what is happening in a society, he or she describes it. A good sociologist notices each aspect of society, from the individual actor with stated reasons and internalized intentions to the huge multinational conglomerate corporation, including institutions and belief systems as varied as churches, schools, prisons, restaurants, and governments. Structural-functionalist sociologists then examine and analyze the results of social activity, asserting that the actual function of that social activity is its outcome. For example, if a sociologist saw that high school graduates were less likely to be convicted of crime than non-high school graduates, then this would identify one function of high-school education as the prevention of crime (or the protection from successful prosecution for crimes committed). (A proper functionalist analysis would consider many more factors than these in its search for explanations.) Thus, the meaning of any activity is in its result, or function.

Functionalism as a whole tends to see the world as a mostly stable place. Some scholars have likened the functionalist perception to a large machine, with each cog and gear in its rightful place, doing whatever its particular function is. There is movement through the system, but the parts stay in their places. Many sociologists have criticized functionalism for its seeming inability to explain change. While it may be true that functionalism's inherent bias is toward stability, certainly it can explain change as well. If it is true, to return to the example above, that high school graduation reduces the likelihood of imprisonment, it is likely that more persons will seek high school graduation. Thus, over time, the society as a whole raises its educational level, creating long-term social change. Education also has many other functions, and therefore the increased activity of these other functions creates other social changes, and one is left with the notion of a very flexible, constantly changing social world.

Historical materialist sociology has a very different basis. Its deepest assumption is that human social existence is constrained by the physical realities of anatomy and ecology. Humans need air, land, food, water, and stimulus. The drive to gain control over these material parts of life organizes society around these material causes. Even though these resources exist in large amounts, they are limited. Human social organization arises to create and mediate different levels of access to these resources, and ideologies follow to justify the social divisions. With a historical materialist research strategy, therefore, one does not look for the effects of a social action; instead, one looks at its material connections to discover how any social activity shifts the costs of living in the world. For example, in the United States, rates of birth steadily declined throughout most of the twentieth century. Even though some commentators argue that this is because of a decline in the valuation of the family, a materialist would analyze the high cost of rearing a child (currently more than $100,000) and the rather low long-term economic benefits of parenthood (since government-run welfare systems have at least partly taken over the care of the elderly) and would conclude that the high costs and low returns of child-bearing have decreased the birth rates, and that this change in the economics of material conditions then caused the changes of values within American society.

Many sociologists have argued that functionalism actually does provide helpful explanations of change, whereas numerous Marxist and historical materialist scholars assert that functionalism is unable to deal with anything but static models of societies. In recent years, a growing number of "neofunctionalist" theories have addressed functionalism's inherent weaknesses concerning issues of change, conflict, and power, but historical materialism still enjoys more of a connection to conflict theories and analyses of power in both social and economic manifestations. Some scholars would suggest that functionalism best interprets gradual institutional change, whereas historical materialism best reflects times of sudden, disorienting social change. Certainly, both methods have adherents, and both serve well to produce interpretations of social change, even when their interpretations markedly diverge.

Applications

In ancient Israel, a major instance of social change occurred roughly between 1200 and 1000 B.C.E. (The biblical books of Joshua and Judges comment on this historical period.) At the beginning of this period, the people were organized in a very loose fashion around extended kinship groupings, but at the end of the two-hundred-year period, they had developed a full monarchy with a very different pattern of social organization. Both functionalism and materialism can interpret the causes of these changes, but these two approaches yield different results.

From a functionalist perspective, Israel's original leadership structures underwent a slow, gradual growth from tribal to monarchic organization. Perhaps each of the tribes did well in providing some of the appropriate functions, such as the provision of family stability. An agricultural populace, however, would require increased stability in the face of unpredictable yields caused by weather. The need (protection from the vagaries of the climate) was better met by a different institution (a larger-scale bureaucracy that would distribute food throughout a wider area); thus, the monarchy's function was what brought it into power in the first place.

A materialist sociologist would interpret this social change quite differently, because the materialist's first questions would deal with the material basis for life. At the early part of Israel's development from tribalism into monarchy, the technology of metal production was increasing in that region. Iron tools made the agricultural tasks more productive, creating more surplus. This meant that some persons would not have to farm the ground for their living, if they could encourage others to give them the extra food. At the same time, iron spearheads made weapons more fearsome, allowing more control over others' surplus. The change in material technology resulted in a change in social organization, as power groups came to control increasingly large segments of the land; these groups traded "protection" for food in an early governmental system.

England's period of Industrial Revolution provides another case of social change for which functionalist and materialist strategies provide competing explanations. Social change occurred simultaneously in several different societal sectors; family dynamics changed as the roles of children shifted, and many in the society abandoned geographical loyalties in favor of urbanization. Lifestyles for many people were changed almost beyond recognition in this process. Functionalism might examine, for example, the family's earlier role as a center of economic protection. Each family member functioned as insurance for the others, because the large web of the extended family made it possible to care for a needy family member. If safety was a key function of family, other institutions became more important in fulfilling this function over time. Since one's economic safety depended upon employment, it was important to have marketable skills. Thus, over time, it became increasingly clear that education functioned as safety, and thus dependence upon the family was decreased, especially if proximity to the rest of the family impeded one's own search for economic security.

In sharp contrast, materialism might see the English family of workers within the context of its class connections. In other words, the chief characteristic of this group was not "family" (a term referring to social organization) but "workers" (a term referring to their mode of production). With this shift in interpretive emphasis, the English workers become a social class, set at odds with the social class of the factory owners. It was in the owners' best economic interest to produce as many workers as possible, so they employed ever younger members of the family, concerned not for values of family solidarity but instead only for material profit. At the same time, it was in the workers' best interest to work as hard as possible in order to get paid, but they ran into the limits of their physical exertion. The two classes inevitably conflicted, with the owners demanding more work (for less pay) and the workers demanding more money for an increased standard of living.

The historical materialist and functionalist interpretations are not necessarily mutually exclusive. They do create strikingly different impressions, however, by focusing on the very different elements within the entire situation. Both of these approaches can be illuminating, but either by itself can stunt the growth of fully adequate explanations for social change.

In general, functionalist explanations tend to depict social change as slow and gradual, whereas historical materialist explanations envision sharp conflict. Both approaches have been sharply criticized, and rightly so. Functionalism's tendency to produce stable portrayals of situations means that it is very difficult for this perspective to explain, for example, severe social changes such as revolutions. Historical materialism, however, attempts to link most social causation to the economic order, and some materialist interpretations are guilty of reducing human behavior to a meaningless search for food and shelter. Perhaps both interpretations are necessary to achieve a fuller understanding of social change.

Context

Both of these explanations for social change, functionalism and historical materialism, are firmly grounded in even older traditions of sociological research. Some of the earliest theories of social change were evolutionistic or developmental models. These models still attract loyal adherents, especially in modified forms among anthropologists. Evolutionary theories proposed a set of discrete "stages" in a culture's development, usually progressing from scarcely organized hunter-gatherer societies to tribal federations, then to monarchies and empires, and then into the industrialized "modern" world. Sociologists who favored such theories proposed schemes of successive categories that would explain all cultures. This notion still lies behind terms such as "primitive" culture; the very nomenclature assumes that the culture would eventually grow to become an "advanced" society.

Both functionalism and historical materialism objected to such a sociological depiction of history and its changes. Any close observation of history reveals that developmental explanations are highly problematic; though one can construct some sort of "typical" pattern, the variations are immense. No linear theory of development can explain the variation at hand. Karl Marx and other early historical materialists of the nineteenth century attempted to correct this evolutionistic bias, and they added the political critique that the present form of society was not some ultimate utopia toward which all history had moved. Instead, Marx focused on the conflict between competing groups of class interests in the early industrial capitalist society. Marx's political and historical insights proved to be somewhat accurate; today, no government attempts pure capitalism, but all modify it with some sort of governmental controls and a safety net for a wide number of people. Even though Marx's theory effectively explained change as a product of class conflict, however, it still assumed some progression toward a final end, a perfect state.

Structural-functionalism grew as a mostly American (and British) academic movement of the twentieth century. In times of optimism about cooperation, sociologists produced a theory that allowed for more diversity and for more harmony than Marx's theories did. Functionalism assumes a final stage to a much lesser degree than do earlier theories, but it tends toward stasis and views societies as having much less conflict than is normally the case.

In recent years, there have been numerous attempts to synthesize these approaches. There is a general recognition that materialist strategies need to take into account the realities of mental images of the world and of ideological systems; in addition, most functionalists strive to explain change and power more effectively than before. There is an increasing range of hybrids, and many sociologists work within the muddled theoretical area between these poles. At this point, no clear methodological statement has arisen to replace the prominence of structural-functionalism and historical materialism. Clearly, such a solution will not only need to solve the previously identified problems of the main theories, but will also need to be very clear about the interrelationship of microsociological and macrosociological factors, since personal choice and the global economy are both increasingly important factors in daily life.

Bibliography

Alexander, Jeffrey C., ed. *Neofunctionalism*. Key Issues in Sociological Theory 1. Beverly Hills, Calif.: Sage Publications, 1985. This book provides a helpful introduction to structural-functionalism's internal realization of its problems and to several of the newer methodological steps taken to enhance this theory's usefulness in the light of materialist criticisms. There is some specific material about social change.

Blumer, Herbert. *Industrialization as an Agent of Social Change: A Critical Analysis*. Edited by David R. Maines and Thomas J. Morrione. New York: Aldine de Gruyter, 1990. This extended analysis of industrialization was first written in the middle of this century in the context of labor negotiations, but has been revised thoroughly on the basis of Blumer's continuing theoretical work, especially regarding symbolic interactionism. The book details an interactionist view of the changes resulting from industrialization, which is closer to functionalism than to materialism but incorporates some aspects of both.

Doob, Christopher Bates. *The Open Covenant: Social Change in Contemporary Society*. New York: Praeger, 1987. Doob examines the decline of exclusion in the capitalist United States, especially during the nineteenth century, and interprets it as an opening of America's original perception of a convenantal society to include new groups of previously marginalized peoples. The method is mostly functionalist, with a strong emphasis on how ideas and notions function within social institutions over time. Economics receives correspondingly little attention.

Girling, John. *Capital and Power: Political Economy and Social Transformation*. London: Croom Helm, 1987. Girling begins with a Marxist/materialist view of history and modifies it using concepts of political institutions. Thus, he forms an interesting mix of methodologies that focuses mostly on capital and the production of surplus but also is sensitive to noneconomic societal forces. This provides a Marxist attempt to bridge (part of) the gap between the approaches to social change.

Gottwald, Norman K. *The Tribes of Yahweh: A Sociology of the Religion of Liberated Israel, 1250-1050 B.C.E.* Maryknoll, N.Y.: Orbis Books, 1979. This mammoth, difficult book asserts a powerful thesis about social change in earlier Israel. Gottwald's examination of social change focuses on the technological innovations that produced shifts in social organization and in the ideological features of Israelite culture. This controversial book provides an excellent example of materialism's explanatory power, even for ancient societies.

Harris, Marvin. *Cultural Materialism: The Struggle for a Science of Culture*. New York: Vintage, 1979. Harris provides some of the classic statements of recent materialism, especially from the anthropological viewpoint. Though this book does not deal specifically with social change, it provides a broad overview of the strategy of cultural materialism, along with a defense of its assumptions against the criticisms of other perspectives. It is also an entertaining book, full of anecdotes showing the benefits of materialistic explanations.

Lauer, Robert H. *Perspectives on Social Change*. Boston: Allyn & Bacon, 1973. Lauer offers an extensive overview of different theories about social change. The book perhaps leans toward functionalist interpretations of change, providing solid material on the evolutionary and developmental models for change. While treating conflict and materialism as "mechanisms" for change, Lauer does provide a good analysis of the role of technological innovation.

Thompson, Michael, Richard Ellis, and Aaron Wildavsky. *Cultural Theory*. Boulder, Colo.: Westview Press, 1990. This book offers a strongly theoretical approach to sociological and anthropological issues that allows for a vivid overview of both functionalist and materialist positions within their theoretical contexts. The book is critical of Marxist claims to have transcended functional explanations. The book's chief weakness, therefore, is its tendency to see functionalism everywhere and to obscure the real differences in perspective.

Vago, Steven. *Social Change*. 2d ed. Englewood Cliffs, N.J.: Prentice-Hall, 1989. This book contributes an excellent overview of the theoretical issues regarding social change, with a very even-handed presentation of the different theories and perspectives, including functionalist and materialist views. Vago considers change at both the macrosociological and microsociological levels. This is perhaps the best book-length starting point for a study of theories about social change.

Jon L. Berquist

Cross-References

Conflict Theory, 340; Culture and Technology, 443; The Environment and Social Change, 654; Functionalism, 786; Marxism, 1127; Revolutions, 1641; Social Change: Evolutionary and Cyclical Theories, 1773; Social Change: Sources of Change, 1786; Social Movements, 1826; Technology and Social Change, 2043.

SOCIAL CHANGE: SOURCES OF CHANGE

Type of sociology: Social change
Fields of study: Sources of social change; Theories of social change

The two major approaches to viewing social change are the evolutionary perspective and the revolutionary perspective; in other words, change can be viewed as gradual or as sudden and disruptive. Technological, environmental, and demographic factors have all been identified as sources of social change.

Principal terms
ADAPTATION: the way in which social systems of any kind respond to their environment
ALIENATION: an individual's feelings of estrangement from a situation, group, or culture
CONFLICT: the overt struggle between individuals or groups within a society or between nation-states
CULTURE: the socially shared symbolic system composed of values, meanings, beliefs, and knowledge
DEMOGRAPHY: the study of the size, structure, and change of human populations
ENVIRONMENT: the surroundings or context within which humans, animals, or objects exist or act
EVOLUTIONARY: a view of change that emphasizes continuities or analogies between biological evolution and sociocultural evolution
INTEGRATION: the extent to which the activities or functions of different institutions or subsystems within a society complement rather than contradict one another
MODERN: a pattern of social organization and social life that is linked to industrialization
REVOLUTIONARY: a form of social movement that arises from strong dissatisfaction with the existing society and seeks radical change
SOCIAL PROCESSES: the ways in which social systems or units influence and respond to one another when a society changes
TECHNOLOGICAL DEVELOPMENT: the application of scientific or other forms of knowledge to the solution of practical problems
WORLD SYSTEMS: the relationship between the developed and less developed countries in the context of economic, geographical, historical, and political factors

Overview

The attempt to understand or determine sources of social change has coalesced into two broad theoretical perspectives: evolutionary and revolutionary. The evolutionary approach focuses on long-term and large-scale change. Influenced by Charles Darwin's model of biological evolution, proponents of social evolution assume a commonality of social processes, or "social laws" of human behavior; they assume also that societies progress. Thus, social theorists such as Lewis Henry Morgan and Edward Burnett Tylor, following the model of biologists studying evolution, sought to determine stages of social and cultural progression and to observe the regularities that all societies follow in that developmental process. Later, because of the apparent conflicts between the works of Leslie White and Julian Steward, Marshall D. Sahlins and Elman R. Service in *Evolution and Culture* (1960), distinguished between two types of evolution: "general evolution," which dealt with humankind as a whole and was the focus of White, and "specific evolution" or "multilinear evolution," which deals with the specific ecological adaptation and the development of different levels of sociopolitical complexity in specific societies. (This was the focus of Steward's work.) Specific or multilinear evolution tends to deal with the revolutionary perspective of social change.

Building on the works of Auguste Comte, Herbert Spencer, and Émile Durkheim, functionalist analysis of social change perceives change as an adaptation of a social system to its environment by the process of mental differentiation and increasing social complexity. Proponents of modernization theory also accept these tenets, as they assume a uniform and linear progression by which all societies advance to modernity.

The revolutionary framework is less ambitious in that its goal is to hypothesize about the general causes of social change within a society. Instead of looking for historical development and a general evolutionary law, it connects social change with specific causative factors: adaptation, conflict, environment, demography, idealism, integration, conflict, and technology. The revolutionary perspective has the advantage that detailed social histories can be compared and general conclusions and uniformities can be determined.

Environmental and demographic factors, along with technological changes, have been and continue to be the most important and general causes of social change. Among the three, technology is often considered the most important. The technological revolution enabled humankind to shift from hunting and gathering to sedentary agriculture and later to develop civilizations. Technological revolution enabled societies to industrialize, urbanize, specialize, bureaucratize, and take on other characteristics that are considered central aspects of a modern society. The development of industrial technology is also crucial in Karl Marx's analysis of how alienation became a prominent part of the human condition in Western societies. According to general evolutionists, the development of technology enabled humankind to extract energy from the environment more efficiently, thus facilitating sociocultural evolution.

Environmental factors include the sum of outside influences on society. These may include the social reaction to ecological aspects of the physical environment and social response to an action of a state on the other side of the world. This global perspective is prevalent in world-system theory, under which all such aspects are considered part of a society's environment, whether the influence is direct or indirect. The point, however, is that the society must adapt to the influences impinging on it.

Culture consists of socially shared mental concepts that define relationships between and among people. These ideas change through three processes: innovation, the creation of new ideas; discoveries, the gaining of empirical knowledge; and diffusion, borrowing from others. Diffusion is the most prominent source of change. As the culture changes, the society responds because it is from the culture that rules, goals, and acceptable means are defined to guide social behavior. If the response is not proper, the units are malintegrated and must adjust to one another until integration is achieved.

Migration, a changing birthrate, wars, and disease are all factors that influence the demographic composition of a group. This composition is continually changing, and societies continually respond. Sometimes these changes can lead to internal conflict, in which groups within the society fight with one another. Conflict results in change, but the conflict does not have to be destructive. As Lewis Coser shows in *The Functions of Social Conflict* (1956), dissension within a society can have integrative and adaptive functions. As the causative agents of social change are examined, it must be kept in mind that there is generally no single cause of change; almost all aspects of social life, at one time or another, singly or in combination, can produce change.

Applications

The applications of evolutionary and revolutionary schemata to social change are many and varied. In the evolutionary framework, some concepts deal with the development of institutions such as the family, while others deal with whole civilizations or even with humankind in general. The formulations of Lewis Henry Morgan can be used to illustrate this idea. Concerning social institutions, Morgan set forth five successive family forms: "consanguine," based on group marriage; "punaluan," group marriage in which brothers cannot marry sisters; "syndyasmian" (or pairing), a transition between group marriage and monogamy; "patriarchical," in which supreme authority rests in the male head of the family; and "monogamian," which features female equality and monogamy. An example dealing with humankind as a whole is Morgan's postulation that history has three major "ethical periods": savagery, barbarism, and civilization. In both frameworks, according to Morgan and others, civilizations and institutions follow similar linear paths of progression. The concept of linear stages of evolution was highly criticized and fell into disrepute until Leslie White redefined general evolution in terms of efficient energy use rather than levels of complexity. Under this definition, Western civilizations may be viewed as being on a higher level of evolution because they capture more energy from the environment.

Within the revolutionary framework, an example of the ramifications of environmental change can be seen in the Fang people of Central Africa. After being colonized, they had to respond to the policies and practices of French society and government that originated thousands of miles away. Being Christianized and colonized by the French, the Fang had to face three challenges to their worldview: The "far away," represented by the colonizers, challenged "the near" and familiar; the traditional protective powers of "the below" were challenged by the missionaries' message of divinity "from above," and the pluralism of colonial life was challenged by the stratification and double standard of the colonized being treated differently from the colonizers. They responded to the far away challenging the near by using *ebago*, a drug which enabled the Fang to go out to the far and convert it to the near. Concerning the Christian God above and their own deities below, they incorporated both of them into the Bwiti religious pantheon, establishing a creative tension between the two. To deal with the double standard of colonial life, they promoted rituals that developed a "one-heartedness" among themselves.

The adaptation of the Fang included a cultural—more specifically a religious— change that enabled them to cope with social dislocation and exploitation. Some old metaphors (such as the forest and the body social, or kinship system) were reanimated. Additionally, new metaphors (such as red and white uniforms, a path of birth and death, and the world as a globe or ball) were created. The old and new fitted together. The Fang have closed themselves off from the wider society, and Bwiti, their religion, is a kind of escape from the pressures of the outside world.

Max Weber, in *Economy and Society* (1922), concluded that it was only in Western Europe that there was a singular drive toward orderly, predictable, and rational explanations of social life and the natural universe. The ecological and political setting of Europe in the Middle Ages favored the development of independent towns run by merchants and artisans, who were generally considered more rational and calculating than peasants. Kings used economic strength and administrative expertise to over- power feudal lords and control the church, which also provided administrative talent. By the fourteenth century, towns, nobles, and the church had compromised to support strong states.

Thus, it was no accident that with Protestantism flourishing where weak royal power and strong towns existed, Protestantism became associated with economic and scien- tific progress. Nor is it surprising that the Industrial Revolution first appeared in the late eighteenth century in Northwestern Europe, where all the right historical circum- stances (the commercial and scientific progress of the seventeenth century) were present.

Context

In essence, the field of sociology is a result of the study of social change because it emerged as a discipline when theorists attempted to understand the dramatic social, economic, and political upheavals associated with the Industrial Revolution of the eighteenth and nineteenth centuries. Émile Durkheim, Karl Marx, and Max Weber were the key figures in developing the foundation of the revolutionary perspective on social change. Durkheim, following in the positivist tradition of Claude-Henri de Rouvroy (Compte de Saint-Simon), argued that social phenomena exist in the objec- tive realm and are external to individuals. In other words, societies operate according to their own principles, which are different from the sum of the behavior of individual members. Thus, for Durkheim, social phenomena are not explained in terms of the motivation of individuals; rather, individuals are seen as molded and constrained by society. One goal of this perspective is to understand social systems in terms of their function—that is, their contribution to the maintenance of the whole society. This approach gave rise to the school of functionalism. Modern functionalism, deeply indebted to the work of Talcott Parsons, views society as a social system of interrelated and interdependent parts. This system seeks equilibrium or balance. Therefore, when this stability is disturbed or society is malintegrated, change occurs. In other words, to Durkheim and the functionalist school, change results from a causative agent that causes malintegration; social institutions then seek integration to adapt or assimilate to the new circumstances. The precepts of functionalism and Durkheim's thinking are prevalent in modernization theory.

Karl Marx, on the other hand, saw technology and the economy as the major causative factors, a perspective known as conflict theory. Marx argued that in industrial and capitalistic societies, social classes develop from a group's relationships to the means of production. As one class exploits another, tensions arise. The reconciliation of these tensions results in something new—social change. Marx's ideas provided a basis for world-system theory. Marx also developed the concept of alienation, according to which, because of industrialization, workers are estranged from their products; because of other results of industrialization, they also become estranged from their world, their fellow creatures, and themselves. Basically, Marx postulated a "materialist" explanation for social change; that is, economic and technological systems are the primary determinants of social and cultural systems as well the prime source of social change (ideological and social relationships do have an impact, but to a much lesser degree). This materialistic perspective, along with his analysis of capitalism, arguably made Marx the most influential figure in twentieth century political, economic, and social thought.

Max Weber argued that orientations to certain religious, political, and social values created ideas and structures that inhibited progress in some cases and facilitated it in others. In the case of western Europe, he postulated in *The Protestant Ethic and the Spirit of Capitalism* (1922), that the Calvinists and their concept of predestination helped facilitate the rise of capitalism. Weber did not negate economic or technological factors, but he believed that beliefs and values were not being given sufficient emphasis in explaining social change.

These three major figures studied social change by focusing on industrial and capitalist societies; other theorists, ranging from Auguste Comte to Edward Tylor, focused on the evolutionary framework, within which society was analyzed on grandiose terms, with history and development interpreted in terms of progressive stages. Many of the problems of evolutionary theory were addressed in the works of its adherents. Karl Popper, however, in *The Poverty of Historicism* (1957), examined change from a philosophical perspective and argued that social development is inherently unpredictable because it is affected by the growth of knowledge, which is unpredictable. Thus, processes can be described but not in terms of a universal law. Ernest Gellner added to the criticism of evolutionary approaches by noting that the ordering of stages is superfluous if the mechanism, sources, or causes of change are not identified or are insufficient; simply placing something in a sequence does not explain it.

Charles Tilly, in *As Sociology Meets History* (1981), has shown that a society can be partially understood through the study of its origins. He classifies two major types of change that have occurred during the last four centuries and are continuing today: the increasing power of the state and the proletarianization of labor. Studying these changes helps clarify changes in family organization, political structure, types of protest, work habits, and many other areas. Barrington Moore, in *Social Origins of Dictatorship and Democracy* (1966), explains why the modernization process can produce different outcomes—democracy, fascism, and communism. His proposition is that development under a state-noble alliance results in fascism. When the state's power is curbed by a noble-bourgeois alliance, democracy results. Failed state-noble alliances, which allow successful peasant revolutions, result in communism. Theda Skocpol, Moore's student, in *States and Social Revolutions* (1979), shows that the failure of states to keep up with foreign competitors and intrusions has been the cause of most revolutions.

A number of key issues remain for future research to explore. Will poor parts of the world be able to achieve rapid economic growth, or will the world social system have to be altered to spread modernity more equitably? As states strengthen, will scientific and technological progress decrease? Third, will the proletarianization of labor and the strengthening of the state result in a drastic reduction of freedom for individuals? Finally, will ecological changes brought on by technology create problems for future generations?

Bibliography

Chirot, Daniel. "Social Change." In *The Social Science Encyclopedia*, edited by Adam Kuper and Jessica Kuper. London: Routledge & Kegan Paul, 1985. This is an excellent review and analytical article concerning social change and the relevance and place of various causative factors concerning social change.

Durkheim, Émile. *The Rules of the Sociological Method*. Edited by George Catlin. Translated by Sarah A. Solovay and John H. Mueller. 8th ed. New York: Free Press, 1938. This work, first published in 1895, sets forth the foundation of functionalism. It is not Durkheim's most popular work, but it presents his basic premises concerning the means for understanding social behavior.

Fernandez, James W. *Bwiti: An Ethnography of the Religious Imagination in Africa*. Princeton, N.J.: Princeton University Press, 1982. A good ethnography of social change in which revolutionary change is examined. In this case, the response is to environmental and political changes resulting from colonialism.

Marx, Karl. *The Communist Manifesto*. Edited by Friedrich Engels. Translated by Samuel Moore. New York: New York Labor News, 1948. A short but representative work presenting Marx's analysis of capitalism and the Industrial Revolution; first published in 1848.

Steward, Julian H. *Theory of Culture Change: The Methodology of Multilinear Evo-*

lution. Urbana: University of Illinois Press, 1955. A classic account setting forth the specific or multilinear evolutionary perspective on social change.

Weber, Max. *The Methodology of the Social Sciences.* Translated and edited by Edward A. Shils and Henry A. Finch. New York: Free Press, 1949. Sets forth Weber's concepts of understanding social behavior; first published in 1903.

White, Leslie. *The Evolution of Culture.* New York: McGraw-Hill, 1959. A classic account setting forth the general evolutionary perspective on social change.

Arthur W. Helweg

Cross-References

Demographic Factors and Social Change, 492; The Environment and Social Change, 654; Marxism, 1127; Modernization and World-System Theories, 1241; Revolutions, 1641; Social Change: Evolutionary and Cyclical Theories, 1773; Social Change: Functionalism versus Historical Materialism, 1779; Social Movements, 1826; Technology and Social Change, 2043.

SOCIAL EPIDEMIOLOGY

Type of sociology: Major social institutions
Field of study: Medicine

Social epidemiology is the study of the distribution of disease, impairment, or social behaviors across different social groups or populations. Epidemiologists seek to describe and explain differences in health and social phenomena by linking their incidence and prevalence to demographic and environmental factors.

Principal terms

CRUDE RATE: the measure of the occurrence of a disease or behavior per unit of population

ETIOLOGY: the ordering of causal events

HYPOTHESIS: a prediction about a relationship between variables

INCIDENCE: the number of new cases of a disease or behavior reported during a specified time period, usually one year

PREVALENCE: the total number of cases of a disease or behavior at a particular point in time

RISK: the probability that an event will or will not occur

SPECIFIC RATE: the measure of the occurrence of a disease or behavior for particular subgroups of the population, such as by age or sex

STANDARDIZED RATE: the application of known rates of a disease or behavior for each known population to the structure of a fictitious population for purposes of comparison

Overview

Epidemiology is essentially concerned with the study of the spread of disease. Social epidemiologists study the relationships between disease, impairment, or behaviors and social groups or populations. The epidemiological method, originally developed to understand and stop the spread of epidemic infectious diseases, has also been applied to such social behaviors as the use of seatbelts, the use of motorcycle helmets, and alcohol and drug use.

The field of epidemiology can be divided into two main categories: descriptive epidemiology and analytic epidemiology. Descriptive epidemiology, as the name implies, attempts to detail fully who is affected by the disease or who engaged in the behavior under study, where cases of the disease or behavior occur, and when cases of the disease or behavior occur. By fully understanding the "who," "where," and "when" of the disease or behavior, the epidemiologist can formulate hypotheses concerning the causes and correlates of the phenomenon.

In order to describe the occurrence of a disease or behavior completely, social epidemiologists rely heavily on the use of rates. A rate is a measure of some disease, event, or behavior relative to a particular unit of population. The use of rates is important for epidemiologists because they are often attempting to compare the incidence of a phenomenon across social or population groups. Using rates allows for better comparison across dissimilar groups. There are three general types of rates used by social epidemiologists: crude rates, specific rates, and standardized rates.

Crude rates are calculated simply as the number of events divided by the total population and multiplied by some large number, such as 1,000. The interpretation of the rate would then be the number of events per 1,000 population. The main advantages of crude rates are their ease of calculation, their general use as summary measures, and their utility for international comparisons when differences in the types of more detailed information vary or are missing. Unfortunately, crude rates can be affected by large differences in the demographic composition of the groups of populations under study.

Specific rates are calculated for subgroups of the population. For example, the epidemiologist may be interested in the age-specific rates of drug use in a population. This rate would be calculated by dividing the number of drug users in an age group by the total number of people in that age group, then multiplying by a large number. The main advantage of specific rates is their utility for public health and research purposes and for focusing on relevant groups. The chief disadvantage is that the calculations can become extremely cumbersome if too many subgroups are examined.

Standardized rates are used when the groups under study have very different age structures. In such a case, the known rates of the disease or behavior for each population are applied to the structure of a fictitious population. This allows the epidemiologist to take differences in population composition into account in order to make unbiased comparisons. The disadvantages of standardized rates are that, because a fictitious population is used, the rates themselves are not real and their magnitudes depend on what fictitious population is selected.

Once the distribution of the disease or behavior has been completely described, the epidemiologist develops hypotheses as to the causes of the differences. This is the focus of analytic epidemiology, which emphasizes the construction of an etiological chain of events leading from a particular social group engaging in particular identifiable behaviors, through the contraction of the disease or the development of the behavior. Typically, hypotheses concerning causation are best tested through experimental research. Often, however, it is not possible to develop an experimental design without seriously breaching professional ethics. For example, it would be extremely unethical for an epidemiologist to expose an individual to a serious or fatal disease such as acquired immune deficiency syndrome (AIDS) to study its effects. In many cases, prospective or retrospective observational studies are employed.

Integral to analytic epidemiology is the estimation of risk. Risk refers to the probability that some event or behavior will or will not occur. Once the who, where, and whens of the disease or behavior have been described in terms of social group characteristics, the epidemiologist attempts to measure the risk of those groups contracting the disease or engaging in the behavior compared to other social groups. This is often referred to as relative risk. It is sometimes assumed by epidemiologists that the higher the relative risk for a group with a particular characteristic, the greater the likelihood that the characteristic is causally related to the disease or behavior.

The development and advancement of modern social epidemiology has been attributed to the development of survey research techniques. Medical sociologist Minako Maykovich, in his text *Medical Sociology* (1980), notes that social epidemiologists helped advance the development of health surveys and sampling techniques to assist in the collection of nonmedical epidemiological data. By using a survey approach, social epidemiologists are able to collect a wide range of information on a large number of people. This information is used to identify the social and demographic correlates of social behavior and to help identify its etiology.

Applications

When the first case of AIDS was reported in 1981, epidemiologists began working to uncover answers concerning the who, where, and when of the disease. As more cases were reported, epidemiologists attempted to discover patterns in the spread of the disease across social groups. Within a few years, they determined that homosexuals and intravenous drug users were at highest risk of contracting AIDS. Further investigation of the disease indicated that it is transmitted by the transfer of bodily fluids, such as blood or semen, from an infected individual to an uninfected individual. Epidemiologists at the Centers for Disease Control (CDC) estimated that nearly three-quarters of all AIDS victims were identified as homosexual or bisexual men. The development of an etiological chain from this group, coupled with the knowledge of how the disease is transmitted, resulted in recommendations that condoms be worn when engaging in any sexual activity with a partner not known to be AIDS-free. The use of condoms suppresses the transmission of semen from one sexual partner to the other, which in effect breaks the etiological chain. Subsequent public health interventions, including educational programs and public service announcements, have been directed at this behavior modification.

Another application of social epidemiology is in the area of substance abuse. Researchers have been using an epidemiological approach to the study of substance abuse for some time. Beginning with descriptive studies, however, it was clear that different drugs had different etiological chains and that, in all likelihood, no single cause of drug use could be found. Many national studies of the social and demographic characteristics of drug users have been conducted to ascertain the who, where, and when of the behavior. It has proved extremely difficult to determine the underlying reasons why some people engage in certain behaviors while others do not.

A national study of drug use conducted for the National Institute on Drug Abuse (NIDA) by researchers Robert Flewelling, J. Valley Rachal, and Mary Ellen Marsden and published in the monograph *Socioeconomic and Demographic Correlates of Drug and Alcohol Use* (1992) measured the degree of association between social, economic, and demographic factors and substance abuse. Although nearly all forms of drug use occur across all social groups, some groups are at higher risk of use than others. For example, with regard to cocaine use, risk is highest among people earning less than

$9,000 per year, among those who have never been married, among Hispanics, among males, and in the eighteen-to-twenty-four age group. Thus, epidemiologists have described the "who" of cocaine use. The report also describes the "where." Cocaine use is highest in areas in the western United States, in large metropolitan areas, and in areas where less than 50 percent of the residents own their own houses. What is difficult to determine, however, is the "why" of cocaine use. Without understanding why people choose to use cocaine, it is not possible to develop a legitimate etiological chain. Subsequently, it is impossible to provide definitive recommendations for helping to stop the use of the drug.

Context

The history of epidemiology can be traced back to the ancient Egyptians and Greeks. Epidemiology, as it is known today, however, began in the late eighteenth century with the work of Percivall Pott. Pott investigated scrotal cancer in England in 1775. By using deductive reasoning, he was able to determine cancer rates among one subgroup of the population: Scrotal cancer rates were extremely high among white, lower-class, urban males.

Pott began his investigation by trying to make the causal connection between a particular social group and the disease. Pott believed that the cause of scrotal cancer was related to cleaning chimneys. The advent and widespread use of space heaters fueled by coal had created a new occupation, that of the chimney sweep. Because the coal did not burn completely and efficiently, residual soot accumulated in the chimneys, resulting in a fire hazard. Therefore, regular cleaning of chimneys became a necessity. It was a dirty and distasteful job that most people did not want to perform. The occupation of chimney sweep was relegated to the lower social classes who could ill afford to turn any job away.

Pott made his first connection between the social group and an occupation. Next, he linked the occupation with a particular behavior, namely working with the soot. That behavior was then linked to a vehicle (the soot) that transmitted the unknown agent, or direct cause of the disease, to the chimney sweep. The chimney sweep, in turn, was affected by a tissue change resulting in scrotal cancer.

Pott made a major contribution to the field of epidemiology by establishing the etiological chain as a research strategy. It remains a fundamental approach today. A second major contribution made by Pott was the notion that the etiological chain, once established, could be broken at any of its links. Doing so reduces the rate of the disease. In this case, Pott prescribed regular baths for chimney sweeps to remove the harmful soot, thus reducing the rates of scrotal cancer.

Eighty years later, in 1855, John Snow used Pott's strategy to uncover the source of a cholera outbreak in London. The cholera outbreak resulted in more than eight thousand deaths. Snow plotted the location of all the victims of the disease on a map and conducted detailed interviews with their surviving family members in an attempt to determine their behavioral patterns. By working backward from the disease itself, Snow slowly developed the etiological chain of events. Ultimately, he determined that all the victims had received the water from the same source, the Broad Street pump. From this information, he hypothesized that cholera must be a waterborne disease, a fact unknown at the time. To stem the epidemic, Snow ordered the closing of the Broad Street pump. Snow's research reaffirmed and advanced Pott's earlier work in two ways. First, Snow confirmed that the etiological chain was a legitimate strategy for investigating epidemic disease. He advanced the method by demonstrating that the chain could be developed by working back from the disease to the beginning of the chain. Second, Snow verified that breaking the etiological chain at any of its links will curb the spread of the disease.

Today, epidemiologists often do not specify the exact etiological chain of events in their research. It is, however, an implied component in all forms of epidemiological investigation. In cases involving disease, the construction of an etiological chain permits the epidemiologist to make informed recommendations regarding what measures need to be taken to reduce the incidence of the disease. One problem with this process, however, is that often diseases can be caused by more than one fact. This is known as multiple causation. When it occurs, the breaking of the etiological chain at some points may only slow the disease spread by eliminating one factor while other factors continue to cause the disease unchecked. Epidemiologists continue to use sophisticated statistical methods to uncover the causes and effects of social behavior and disease. Their work helps provide the solutions to a host of health and social problems.

Bibliography

Alderson, Michael. *An Introduction to Epidemiology*. London: Macmillan, 1976. Although this is a standard introductory text, it can be difficult reading. It tends to be heavy on the methodology side and light on general explanation. Provides examples with the introduction of statistical practice.

Cockerham, William C. *Medical Sociology*. 5th ed. Englewood Cliffs, N.J.: Prentice-Hall, 1992. A good introductory text overviewing the field of medical sociology. What differentiates this book from other generic medical sociology texts is its public health approach. The chapters on epidemiology and the demography of health are particularly pertinent. This book has an extensive bibliography and is completely indexed.

Dever, G. E. Alan. *Community Health Analysis: Global Awareness at the Local Level*. 2d ed. Gaithersburg, Md.: Aspen, 1991. A reasonably sophisticated introduction to many of the basic measures and methods used by epidemiologists for practical application. Includes a complete and easy-to-use index.

Flewelling, Robert L., J. Valley Rachal, and Mary Ellen Marsden. *Socioeconomic and Demographic Correlates of Drug and Alcohol Use: Findings from the 1988 and 1990 National Household Surveys on Drug Abuse*. Rockville, Md.: National Institute on Drug Abuse, 1992. This is a technical government report with many statistics and many tables. It is not indexed, but it does have a list of tables and a reasonably short executive summary.

Maykovich, Minako K. *Medical Sociology*. Sherman Oaks, Calif.: Alfred, 1980. An introductory text on medical sociology. Its unique feature is the application of general theoretical orientations to research in health care. The book is somewhat dated, but it provides an excellent analysis of the historical development of medical sociology and the role played by social epidemiology in that development.

Morton, Richard F., J. Richard Hebel, and Robert J. McCarter. *A Study Guide to Epidemiology and Biostatistics*. 3d ed. Rockville, Md.: Aspen, 1990. This short book provides an introduction to the epidemiologic logic and method with a special emphasis on measurement. There is no bibliography, but the book is well indexed and contains a good introductory glossary of terms. Its unique feature is the inclusion of 125 multiple-choice questions located at the end of chapters.

Shilts, Randy. *And the Band Played On*. New York: St. Martin's Press, 1987. This work provides an interesting look at the epidemiology of AIDS from a journalist's perspective. The author attempts to include an analysis of the politics of an epidemic disease as well as attempting to humanize the victims of AIDS. There is an extremely thorough index.

Wolinsky, Fredric D. *The Sociology of Health: Principles, Practitioners, and Issues*. 2d ed. Belmont, Calif.: Wadsworth, 1988. This book provides an excellent overview of the field of medical sociology. It is recommended for those with little or no background in the field. The first chapter provides a simple summary of social epidemiology. It is easy to read, well indexed, and has a complete bibliography.

Ralph Bell

Cross-References

Acquired Immune Deficiency Syndrome, 8; Alcoholism, 74; Drug Use and Addiction, 572; Endemic and Epidemic Diseases, 640; Health and Society, 852; Inequalities in Health, 966; Medical Sociology, 1166; Quantitative Research, 1546; Samples and Sampling Techniques, 1680; Smoking and Cancer, 1767.

SOCIAL GERONTOLOGY

Type of sociology: Aging and ageism
Field of study: Policy issues and debates

Social gerontology is the study of the historical, cultural, biological, physiological, psychological, and social contexts of aging. Social gerontologists explore the impact of the process of aging on both older persons as a social group and society's social structure.

Principal terms
ACTIVITIES OF DAILY LIVING (ADLs): a measure of functional health which summarizes the abilities of a person to perform specific common tasks, such as dressing, managing money, shopping, and doing light housework
COHORT: a group of people born approximately during the same time period and thus exposed to particular historical and sociocultural events, attitudes, and behaviors
EXTENDED FAMILY: relatives other than a mother, father, and siblings who constitute the nuclear family; for example, grandparents
INFORMAL AND FORMAL SUPPORT SYSTEMS: informal support systems are exchanges of goods and services between family, friends, and neighbors; formal support is aid received through a government, proprietary, or nonprofit agency that is reimbursed for such aid
LIFE-COURSE PERSPECTIVE STUDIES: studies that focus on the historical periods and social conditions through which specific cohorts have lived

Overview

Social gerontology (the term was coined in 1954 by sociologist Clark Tibbitts) is the study of the impact of the process of aging on society—social structure and cultural attitudes—and vice versa. By looking at the historical, cultural, biological, physiological, psychological, and social contexts of aging, social gerontologists study a wide range of topics including the ways in which aging affects and is affected by the family, the community, the health care system, the economy, and public policies.

According to the 1990 National Center for Health Statistics, there are 30 million persons aged sixty-five or older in the United States—13 percent of the population. As the "graying" of America continues, this figure is expected to rise to 59 million by the year 2025—20 percent of the population—the fastest growing age group being those persons eighty-five or older. Predictions estimate that there will be between 11 and 18 million persons aged eighty-five or older by 2050.

These changes are in large part a result of the decline in mortality rates caused by the improved treatment of acute disease and improved maternal, infant, and early childhood care. Another factor is the proliferation of healthier lifestyles—-better nutrition, more exercise, and reduced alcohol consumption and cigarette smoking—throughout adulthood. Although life expectancy has increased to 74.9 years in 1990 for persons born in 1989 (78.8 for women; 71.9 for men) and is anticipated to extend to 81.2 years by 2080, biological, physiological, and psychological decline continue to plague many older persons.

The aging population is not a heterogeneous group. Differences depend upon ethnic and minority group identification, educational and economic status, and geographical location. Nonwhites will make up 32 percent of all elderly people by 2050. Substantial increases in the African American, Hispanic, and Asian elderly populations are expected. The proportion of Native American elderly people has grown faster than that of any other minority group. As many social scientists, social workers, health care professionals, and policy analysts have noted, the implications are that greater diversity in health and social policies will be required in the future.

Older populations also differ in the amount of education they have received and consequentially how much income they have to live on. According to a study conducted in 1988 by the American Association of Retired Persons (AARP) of those sixty-five or older, the median level of education for European Americans was 12.2 years, compared with 8.4 for African Americans and 7.5 for Hispanic Americans. Access to education reflects access to employment opportunities. Approximately 12 percent of all elderly people live below the poverty line. Poverty rates among older women, ethnic minorities, single persons, and persons over eighty-five who have been subjected to mandatory retirement policies are much higher.

Geographical distribution also plays an important role in the process of aging. Some states have a much higher proportion of elderly persons than others do. Florida, Arkansas, Iowa, Missouri, Pennsylvania, Rhode Island, and South Dakota rank among the highest. Alaska and Utah have the lowest percentages of elderly people. In-migration of retired persons is responsible for higher percentages in some states, and out-migration of younger persons in search of employment opportunities (such as in the state of Maine) is a contributing factor in others. Whether the percentage of elderly people is dependent upon in- or out-migration is significant. In the case of in-migration, elderly people who are presumably "better off" can increase the financial stability of a community. Out-migration of young and middle-aged persons, however, is an indicator of a failing economy, and in such cases the elderly people who are left behind are, more often than not, poor.

Variation of elderly populations within states is also significant. Studies indicate differences between urban and rural locations. Although a large number of elderly people live in urban centers and urban ghettos, approximately one out of every four elderly people in the United States lives in rural America. According to the 1980 and 1990 census, the proportion of the elderly population and size of place are inversely related. In other words, the smaller the place, the larger the percentage of elderly people.

Because there is a global "graying" taking place—according to the United Nations

Secretariat, one out of every seven persons will be sixty-nine or older by 2025—an increase in cross-cultural studies focusing on the impact of demographic change on societies has begun. Shifting from descriptions of individual and small-scale aging within particular societies, sociologists and anthropologists have begun to concentrate on the national and global impact of different rates of population aging in the industrial and developing countries. It is anticipated that by the year 2025, 72 percent of the world's elderly population will reside in developing countries.

The increase in the proportion of elderly people, both globally and in the United States, raises fundamental moral, civic, and social issues regarding the distribution of society's resources, the definition of quality of life, and stereotypes of the elderly. Older people in industrial societies are living longer and healthier lives, surviving twenty to thirty years after retirement. They are also gaining political power. The AARP is one of the largest and most effective lobbying groups in the United States. Thus far, the AARP has been able to protect federal entitlements for the elderly from severe budget cuts. As sociologist Robert Binstock noted (1990), this has led some people to believe that the elderly are benefiting at the expense of younger generations. It is clear that demographic aging will have profound effects on society's cultural beliefs and values, major social institutions, and social structure.

Applications

Given the wide range of issues studied by social gerontologists, it will be impossible to cover all aspects of the field in this brief article. The following examples of shifts in informal support and attitudes concerning elderly subpopulations will, however, indicate the types of research questions that social gerontologists ask. In addition, the examples will demonstrate the interdependence of macro (national and international) and micro (regional and local) policies and sociocultural environments.

Many social scientists have been concerned with informal and formal support systems for the elderly. As people's functional capabilities decline, their need for help in activities of daily living (ADLs) increases. Many older persons in the past relied on family members for assistance. In recent years, however, several significant economic and demographic changes have occurred which have a direct bearing on intergenerational relationships and social structure.

Dual-income families have become a necessity for most people, causing changes in family patterns. The once "typical" American middle-class family in which the father worked outside the home to support the wife and children now makes up only 3.7 percent of the nation's families. According to the 1990 Bureau of Labor Statistics report, 96 percent of fathers and more than 60 percent of mothers work outside the home.

In the past, wives or unmarried daughters assumed the role of unpaid caregiver for young children, ill family members, and aging parents. Given the economic and social structure of the latter half of the twentieth century, however, this is no longer a viable alternative. This does not mean that family members are unwilling to care for other members. Many adults, mainly women, carry the double load of being a full-time employee and an active member of an informal support system, contributing financially and socially to the maintenance of the nuclear family as well as the extended family.

In an effort to alleviate some of the burden placed on primary caregivers, new policies have been introduced at the local, state, and federal levels. Some policies focus on the family, while others target the elderly in particular. The Family Medical Leave Act, introduced in several states and enacted on the federal level by the Clinton Administration in 1993, ensures some wage earners jobs and medical benefits in the event of a family member's illness. This enables employed adults to fulfill caregiver roles under limited conditions. Policies such as the Medicaid Waiver Act (which allows for reimbursed home health care) and the Long-Term Care Act (nursing home insurance) seek to give the elderly greater access to community services.

Although the above policies address issues of aging and caregiving, stereotypes of idyllic rural and ethnic aging remain. The romantic assumption that rural life in general is "better" than urban life and that the rural elderly are more firmly ensconced in family and community structures than their urban counterparts can lead to a reduction in formal supports. Policies that rely upon assumptions based on rural myths, in an attempt to reduce public spending, can place the elderly in a vulnerable, dependent position, forcing them to rely upon the availability and goodwill of families, friends, and neighbors. Unfortunately, given the depressed local economies of rural America, families, friends, and neighbors are increasingly seeking employment in urban areas, leaving the elderly dependent on limited formal services.

Similarly, the popular images of ethnic and minority cultures are inaccurate. Because these groups are thought of as static and homogeneous, their social cohesion and solidarity are taken for granted rather than documented. Ethnic and minority elderly people are portrayed as uniquely advantaged by their kinship ties. Studies done by John Weeks and Jose Cuellar in San Diego on Chicanos and by Ernesto Gomez, Kyriakos Markides, and Harry Martin in San Antonio on Mexican Americans indicate, however, that kin support is declining. At the same time, the elderly among these groups are showing higher levels of mental stress than those of the elderly in other groups and a lower rate of participation in community services. Whereas older studies glorified the status of the aged in Asian American and Pacific Island American families, researcher John Weeks discovered that many elderly women felt isolated and lonely within the family arena. In the case of African Americans, much has been written about the strength of kinship ties as a survival strategy. Effective in acute medical situations, these same ties strain, attenuate, and rupture when it comes to long-term care.

Using a life-course perspective, social scientists stress the importance of recognizing the different immigration histories of older persons. For example, the older Chinese Americans who immigrated in the early 1920's were primarily single men looking for employment, but the Japanese Americans who immigrated between 1907 and 1924 did so as families. According to anthropologist Jay Sokolovsky, invoking the Asian stereotype of filial devotion can lead to policies based on the assumption that informal supports exist, although they do not. Similarly, the recognition of generational differences within ethnic groups has increased. For example, the three generations of Japanese Americans—the Issei, Nisei, and Sansei (1907 to 1924, pre-World War II, and post-World War II, respectively)—coincide with specific immigration and civic laws in conjunction with the rise and fall of anti-Japanese sentiments. The experience of aging and the degree of "Americanization" for each generation is therefore very different.

Context

Growth in the aging population and the emergence of retirement policies in industrial societies were primarily responsible for causing sociologists to focus on the sociocultural factors of aging instead of biological and physiological change. The Social Security Act of 1935 provided the impetus for studies that focused on personal and social adjustments in later life, leading to the examination of the social roles played by the elderly in society. During the 1940's and 1950's, several institutions were funded by the Rockefeller Foundation and the National Institutes of Mental Health to conduct life-span studies. With the establishment of the Gerontological Society of America in 1945, the study of aging in social context grew. As knowledge about aging increased and cross-cultural studies advanced, campaigns against ageism (the term, coined by psychiatrist Robert Butler, means discrimination against persons because of age) proliferated in the 1960's, along with theories of successful aging, particularly disengagement theory and activity theory.

Introduced by sociologists Elaine Cumming and William Henry in their book *Growing Old* (1961), disengagement theory postulates that older people willfully withdraw from society as their energy levels decline and their expectation of death increases. It holds that disengagement is not only beneficial for the elderly as an adaptation strategy but also benefits society on the whole because it leaves room for the next generation to assume positions of power. This theory assumes that disengagement is inevitable, functional, and universal. It fails to account for variability and diversity.

In contrast, activity theory, developed by sociologist Robert Havighurst as a result of his Kansas City study, states that older persons who remain socially active are more satisfied and better adjusted than those who do not. This perspective is consistent with American values of work and productivity and has resulted in numerous programs targeting the elderly: recreation events, travel tours, adult education, group meals, and senior centers. Similar to disengagement theory, it too fails to account for differences among older people. This theory does not address what happens to people when they can no longer participate at expected levels.

Disenchantment with the limitations of both of these theories has led to introduction and testing of other perspectives. Age stratification theory builds on basic sociological constructs of role, status, norms, and socialization in an effort to compare one age stratum to another. The interrelationships of individuals with their physical and social environments are the focus of the interactionist perspective. Symbolic interactionists, such as Jaber Gubrium, argue that the way in which older people interact with their environment and with other people can affect their aging experiences significantly. For example, an older person in a nursing home may become confused and be mistakenly labeled as senile. The way in which this person is treated by others, based on the definition of senility, will affect his or her experience of the aging process.

Social exchange theory, which is rooted in behavioral psychology and utilitarian economics, looks at inequalities in access to power and resources between different age strata. According to this theory, as a result of past mandatory retirement laws, older persons are deprived of the resources they need to participate in meaningful exchanges. This theory is limited by its emphasis on monetary resources for exchange, since most older people, despite their dwindling incomes, remain active in exchanging services.

Taking a macro approach, political economy theorists examine the relationship of the social construction of aging and public policies. In her book *The Aging Enterprise* (1980), Carroll Estes demonstrates how Medicare and the introduction of the Older Americans Act in 1965 contribute to the definition of old age as a social problem in need of special services. More recent studies by Estes and Elizabeth Binney have shown how the federal funding of academic research contributes to the preservation of aging as a separate problem instead of addressing social and economic inequalities.

As the national and global society continues to "gray," contributions in the field of social gerontology will remain imperative. Studies of aging challenge commonly held beliefs and values about the aging process as well as fundamental sociological definitions and theories. For example, looking at aging as a continuum throughout the life-cycle instead of a particular stage of development, as proposed by the Department of Health and Human Services assistant secretary for aging Fernando Torres-Gil, calls for a reexamination of social roles, status, inequality, and social institutions in relationship to all ages.

Bibliography

Benet, Sula. *Abkhasians*. New York: Holt, Rinehart and Winston, 1974. This classic case study documents the social roles and status of older Abkhasians. Abkhasia, located between the Black Sea and the Caucasus Mountains, attracted the attention of physicians, sociologists, and demographers from the mid-1930's on because of its inhabitants' legendary longevity.

Binstock, Robert H., and Linda George, eds. *Handbook of Aging and the Social Sciences*. 3d ed. San Diego: Academic Press, 1990. Filled with articles by leading social gerontologists, this is an excellent reference text. Anyone interested in sampling the range of this field should examine this book.

Cattell, Albert, and Maria G. Cattell. *Old Age in Global Perspective*. New York: Macmillan, 1993. This collection of essays focuses on global, national, and local cultural, social, and historical contexts.

Jacobs, Jerry. *Fun City*. New York: Holt, Rinehart and Winston, 1974. This easy-to-read case study documents the daily routines of senior citizens living in a retirement community. The study questions the validity of establishing separate communities for the elderly, particularly ones that only affluent elderly people can afford.

Meyerhoff, Barbara. *Number Our Days*. New York: E. P. Dutton, 1978. Looking at a Jewish community in California, Meyerhoff documents the ways in which older persons use ritual to make their lives meaningful. An award-winning film based on the book is also available.

Stoller, Eleanor Palo, and Rose Campbell Gibson. *Worlds of Difference*. Newbury Park, Calif.: Pine Forge Press, 1994. Using a life-course perspective, the editors weave together essays and poems written by academic and nonacademic people of all colors to give the reader an understanding of diversity in the aging experience.

Joann Kovacich

Cross-References

Age Grading and Age Stratification, 27; Aging and Retirement, 47; Demographic Factors and Social Change, 492; The Elderly and Institutional Care, 621; The Elderly and the Family, 627; The Graying of America, 846; Social Security and Issues of the Elderly, 1832.

SOCIAL GROUPS

Type of sociology: Social structure
Field of study: Key social structures

Social groups are ubiquitous, and they have profound effects on human behavior and interaction. Sociologists often categorize certain types of groups as primary, complex (or secondary), and reference groups. Primary groups, small groups such as family and friendship groups, generally have the strongest influence on people's lives.

Principal terms
COMMUNITY: a subgroup of a society that contains all or most of the features of a society
COMPLEX GROUP (secondary group): a large group that typically exists to achieve a single goal; its members have more distant and indirect relationships than those among members of primary groups
PRIMARY GROUP: a small social group whose members interact frequently with one another on a face-to-face basis, have intimate knowledge of one another, and share emotional ties
REFERENCE GROUP: a set of individuals or a social group that provides a standard of comparison for an individual who is evaluating his or her own accomplishments or opinions
SOCIAL GROUP: a set of individuals who interact with one another in patterned ways, share elements of a culture, and identify with one another
SOCIAL INSTITUTION: a set of beliefs and practices that emerge in response to a need or interest of those in a society; examples include the family, education, the economy, and religion
SOCIETY: a social group whose members reside within a fixed geographical area and that contains all of the major social institutions

Overview

Sociology has several related definitions, one of which is that it is the study of social groups. A social group is a set of individuals who interact with one another in patterned ways, who share a culture that contains beliefs about the group and rules of conduct that shape behavior, and who identify with one another.

The identification of individuals with the group and with one another results in two statuses: member and nonmember. Identification creates a wall or boundary separating members from nonmembers. Identification may result from sharing a surname or living in the same household (as in the case of the family), feeling a special bond with someone else (as in the case of a clique) or from satisfying explicit conditions of membership (as in the case of a club or an organization).

Saying that interaction is organized or patterned means that members have ways of interacting with one another that are different from the interactions that they have with nonmembers. For example, the group may have designated certain times when members are to meet. At those meetings, individuals may occupy statuses, in addition to that of member, such as president, vice president, department head, treasurer, and so on.

When members meet as a group, their behavior follows certain routines; there are various group customs by which members abide. Further, what happens at one time is similar to what happens at another time. For example, two members' way of interacting in a meeting, when all or large numbers of members are present, is similar, though not necessarily identical, to the ways they interact when only the two of them meet. Finally, group members share a culture that contains beliefs about the group and explicit or implicit rules of conduct (or role expectations) that prescribe and proscribe how members should act. This culture sustains the customs and patterned behaviors in which members engage.

Examples of various groups are families, cliques, schools, factories, businesses, sports teams, clubs, fraternities, hospitals, churches, legislative bodies, professional associations, neighborhoods, and communities. Each of these shows the three features that distinguish groups from nongroups.

In the classification of groups, one major distinction is between primary groups and complex (or secondary) groups. The differences lie in size (or number of members), reason for existence, and, because of these first two, nature of interaction. Primary groups are small, consisting of a few members who interact with one another on a face-to-face basis. Examples are the family and friendship groups. These groups exist primarily to meet the psychic needs of members and, in the case of the family, to meet the important function of replenishing members of the larger society and socializing the young to the customs and beliefs of the larger society. Because there are few members, each can gain intimate knowledge about the others. Because primary groups exist to meet psychic needs, their members typically have emotional ties to one another.

Another type of group is known as either a secondary group or complex group. Secondary group is the older term; it is still used, but many sociologists now prefer the designation complex group. This type of group is large. Its many members cannot all have direct face-to-face contact with one another; hence their relations are typically distant and indirect. Further, such groups exist to meet specified goals—often a single goal: to produce and sell a product, to educate students, to enforce laws, to care for the sick, and so on. Because there are many members, the rules of conduct must become codified in constitutions, by-laws, or operating procedures. This is in contrast to the primary group, in which the rules of conduct are "carried around in peoples' heads." The ties among members of a complex group are instrumental (they exist to carry out the group's goals) rather than expressive (existing to provide emotional gratification). In the complex group there may be an elaborate division of labor and a highly articulated hierarchy, with the hierarchy dictating relations of authority and communication.

Other kinds of social groups are the community and society. A society is a social group whose members reside physically or symbolically within some geographic area and among whom are found all of the major social institutions. Social institutions are those practices and sustaining beliefs that emerge to meet a need or interest of the members of society. The major social institutions are family, economy, government, religion, and education. Some writers would also include the military, entertainment, and recreation, as these also reflect interests of most members of society. Though some communities and societies are large, these are distinguished from complex groups not by size but by the activities that occur in the groups. Some complex groups are larger (have more members) than some communities, such as small rural towns.

Another type of group, the reference group, is not, strictly speaking, a social group, but it is of interest to sociologists studying social groups. One of the things that a person in a modern, other-directed society frequently does is to ask himself or herself questions such as "How am I doing?" or "How should I think about x or y?" In attempting to answer questions such as these, the individual seeks standards of comparison. These standards frequently are the views of other people. Individuals compare their situations with those of others, who then constitute a reference group. A reference group may be a loose collection of individuals or a social group (one's family or work group). It might also be the set of all individuals of one's own age or members of a group (such as a certain profession) whom one does not know but uses as a model.

Applications

Perhaps the most frequent and useful application of the concept of the social group is in studies of the effects that group membership has on individual behavior. One example of this is found in studies of social control. Social control refers to the mechanisms that are used by group members to convince or force one another to conform to the rules of conduct of the group.

To explain delinquent behavior, for example, sociologist Travis Hirschi developed a control theory that contains four interrelated elements: attachment of the individual to the group, which means that the individual is sensitive and responsive to the opinions of group members; commitment, by which Hirschi means the rational decision not to deviate because deviant behavior would exact a cost to the individual; involvement, or the participation of the individual in conventional activities, which makes it more difficult to deviate; and belief—the individual's belief in the rightness of the rules. Hirschi provided evidence from a large-scale study (a survey of more than four thousand youths matched with police records) to support his theory.

Bernard Berelson and Gary A. Steiner, in 1964, examined a large number of studies and essays, from which they compiled a set of propositions on behavior. They listed seventeen major propositions and a number of corollaries on relations in small groups. For example, the effects of the group on individual behavior are greater if members interact frequently (rather than infrequently), if group members all tend to be social equals (rather than relating in a hierarchical fashion), and if members like one another (as opposed to being indifferent or being divided into cliques). In addition, they listed eleven propositions and a number of corollaries on organizations (complex groups), which also contain some propositions about the effects of group membership. For example, the stronger a member's commitment to group values, the more likely he or she is to move up in the hierarchy. Additionally, the more decentralized the organization is, the stronger its members' identification with the organization will be.

Over the years there have been a number of other studies of social groups and their effects. In a study of 652 voters, reported in *Public Opinion Quarterly* in 1991, Paul Allen Beck arrayed evidence on the influence of group membership on people's political knowledge and thinking. While television and the print media had some effect, an individual's family and work friends had substantially greater effects. Further, individuals talked most frequently with those who shared their beliefs.

An example from political science occurs in one explanation of the so-called paradox of voting. This paradox holds that the benefits of voting are very low (it is quite unlikely that one's single vote will change the course of the election and therefore influence policies to be more favorable to oneself); the costs, when compared with the benefits, are relatively high—one must take the time to vote (perhaps leaving work early) and travel to a designated location. Therefore, if people are seen as attempting to maximize expected utility, they should refrain from voting; yet people vote anyway. One explanation for this behavior has been supplied by incorporating the influence of social groups into a model of voting behavior. Voters are seen as being influenced to vote by the groups to which they belong; the utility of voting then has to do with one's standing and membership in groups and with the effect the election may have on the groups.

Another body of thinking and research relevant to groups was initiated by Mark Granovetter's article "The Strength of Weak Ties," in the *American Journal of Sociology* 78 (May, 1973); he noted the effects of "weak ties" between individuals. In the "Overview" section, it was noted that one defining characteristic of a group is that group members have ties with one another. Granovetter noted that the ties between pairs of individuals can have varying strengths (they are quantitative rather than simply being present or absent), which depends on the frequency of interaction between individuals, the "services" they provide one another, the amount of personal information that is transmitted, and the feelings they have for one another. He argued that if such ties are weak, they can nevertheless have effects on diverse social phenomena, such as the diffusion of innovations. Research by others has sustained some of Granovetter's conclusions.

One of the many issues in the study of social groups concerns the stability of groups: What factors determine which groups survive? Much work has discussed this problem. Illustrating work at one extreme, Kathleen Carley's paper "A Theory of Group Stability," in the *American Sociology Review* 56 (June, 1991), developed a theoretical model of competing organizations in a society; the central elements in her theory were the number of groups, the size of the population of the society, and a culture consisting of facts to be known. Carley used a technique known as Monte Carlo simulations—in which a computer runs a number of probabilities randomly—to evaluate how these elements affect group stability.

An illustration at the other extreme is found in Martin Jankowski's participant-observation study of gangs, reported in his 1991 book *Islands in the Street*. He found that gang persistence is a complex phenomenon that depends on the internal structure of the gang, the gang's changing environment, and the tenuous relation between the gang and its environment.

Context

The notion of social groups has existed since sociological writing began, though the concept was not explicitly analyzed for many years. Herbert Spencer's early *Principles of Sociology* (1876) makes no reference to social groups as such. Though he discussed several types of organizations (ecclesiastical, ceremonial, and industrial), his main concern was to describe society as a whole. Franklin Giddings, influenced by Spencer as well as a number of others, used the notion of the group, but he did not explicitly define or analyze social groups; he primarily makes references to groups in explicating Spencer's sociological ideas. Albion Small, in his text *General Sociology* (1905), also invoked the notion of the group, but as the unit in which individual interests become organized and expressed. Many would probably trace the explicit and focused entry of the notion of the social group into sociological thinking with Charles Horton Cooley's book *Social Organization* (1909). Here Cooley introduced and defined the notion of the primary group and distinguished it from the secondary group (this latter term having subsequently lost favor in sociological thinking). This distinction parallels the one made by Ferdinand Tönnies in *Gemeinschaft und Gesell-schaft* (1887; *Community and Society*, 1957).

Robert K. Merton's *Social Theory and Social Structure* (1949) provided a clear definition of the social group; his book also provided one of the best discussions of reference groups in the sociological literature. Apart from this, discussions of social groups have tended to focus on theorists or theoretical orientations. This suggests that the social group is one of those ideas that has become so incorporated into sociological thinking that it is taken for granted; explicit analyses of the concept itself are no longer thought necessary.

Bibliography

Berelson, Bernard, and Gary A. Steiner. *Human Behavior*. New York: Harcourt, Brace & World, 1964. The authors compiled findings from studies and essays and presented a number of propositions, some of which are supported by more evidence than others. The propositions, stated in a fairly clear fashion, are classified into sections dealing with major sociological areas of concern (culture, institutions) as well as a few of psychological concern, such as perceiving and motivation.

Hirschi, Travis. *Causes of Delinquency*. Berkeley: University of California Press, 1969. Using a unique conception of social control, this is a classic and widely read analysis of the causes of delinquency. Beautifully written and free of jargon, it impresses one as having been written by a humane sociologist.

Homans, George C. *The Human Group*. New York: Harcourt, Brace, 1950. Homans used research from a number of well-known studies to write this classic and influential theoretical essay on small groups.

Kephart, William M., and William W. Zellner. *Extraordinary Groups: An Examination of Unconventional Life-Styles*. 4th ed. New York: St. Martin's Press, 1991. This is an informative and readable book that discusses eight "unconventional" groups, such as the Old Order Amish, Hasidim, and Mormons.

Nisbet, Robert A. *The Social Bond*. New York: Alfred A. Knopf, 1970. Written for the general reader, this book uses the notion of the social bond as its organizing idea. Nisbet's conception of the social bond is somewhat expansive, containing such core notions as authority, roles, and norms.

Dean Harper

Cross-References

Bureaucracies, 172; The Family: Functionalist versus Conflict Theory Views, 739; Interactionism, 1009; Organizations: Formal and Informal, 1316; Socialization: The Family, 1880; Socialization: The Mass Media, 1887; Socialization: Religion, 1894; Socialization and Reference Groups in Race Relations, 1900; Workplace Socialization, 2202.

SOCIAL MOBILITY: ANALYSIS AND OVERVIEW

Type of sociology: Social stratification
Field of study: Social mobility

Social mobility refers to movement (or lack of movement) by individuals or groups from one social role or social status to another. Mobility is an important element of social interaction and an indicator of the strength of stratification and the potential for social change in society.

Principal terms

HORIZONTAL SOCIAL MOBILITY: movement across social ranks of approximately the same status

INTERGENERATIONAL MOBILITY: changes in social status from one generation to the next

INTRAGENERATIONAL MOBILITY: the vertical mobility an individual experiences in his or her own lifetime

STATUS ATTAINMENT: an individual's arrival at a socially defined position in a specific group, usually based on a socioeconomic category

STRUCTURAL MOBILITY: mobility that occurs because of changes in the economic or social system rather than through personal achievement

VERTICAL SOCIAL MOBILITY: movement upward or downward in the social hierarchy

Overview

Social mobility refers to the movement of people from one status category to another in society. Essentially, then, the study of mobility is the study of social behavior from the perspectives of both the composition and organization of social groups, and it generally emphasizes some sort of disruption. Social mobility is a complex field of study which may involve consideration of causes, rates, processes, functions, and dysfunctions. Many social scientists consider the study of mobility significant because it is suggestive of the quality of life in a social group and of the extent to which social democracy is present in society.

Social mobility is often defined as the movement of people through the social structure, but this rather vague definition can be subject to a variety of interpretations. For example, some sociologists believe that changes such as salary increases, owning a home after years of renting, improvement in living conditions, or even steady employment are evidence of upward movement through the social structure. Others, however, search for more significant shifts in class standing—for example, movement from lower to middle class or from lower-middle to upper-middle class. Such differences of approach are important because the researcher's definition of the basic concept of mobility will affect the methods of measurement the researcher uses, which will in turn produce results and conclusions that may vary dramatically from those based on different concepts.

Despite such possible differences, the study of social mobility involves two basic elements, which at first seem simple. One is "position"—that is, the present level of the individual or group under investigation. The second component, "motion," also appears uncomplicated. Most simply, "motion" is the direction and distance the subject travels. Yet it may be very difficult to be certain of the exact position a person or group occupies in society and even harder to monitor movement, or lack of it, through a complicated social structure.

In addition, sociologists are interested in the mechanisms by which understandings of status are communicated and the ways in which individuals accomplish social mobility. Social groups vary in terms of the ease with which people can move from one social status to another. Although no society is completely open or closed to mobility, social structures may be described in terms of relative openness or closedness. Studies have shown that, in general, industrialized, technologically advanced societies tend to be open, and preindustrial, agricultural societies closed, to mobility. An open society tends to permit movement through any levels of status achieved through one's own efforts; in a more closed system, status and position are assigned according to standards (such as parentage, sex, and age) which are beyond the individual's control.

To complicate matters further, social scientists often equate position with inequality or social stratification. In every society, individuals and groups perform many different functions, which generate many different sorts of rewards, such as power, wealth, and prestige. This situation leads to a hierarchical ranking of individuals, groups, and activities according to the power, wealth, or prestige they accumulate or signify. Again, from the researcher's point of view, it is difficult to measure prestige or power empirically. In addition, such rankings often involve different sorts of rewards, and it is not clear how one type of reward, such as wealth, may be translated into an exact amount of another, such as power. Also, individuals may occupy several roles or positions simultaneously, such as lawyer, politician, and teacher. Each position has its own rewards, and the rewards of all social roles must be accounted for in order to measure an individual's social position accurately.

Changes in social position are generally referred to as either "vertical" or "horizontal." Vertical mobility indicates individual or group movement either upward or downward in the social hierarchy, although downward mobility is rarely investigated. It would seem a matter of common sense that the conditions determining downward mobility are merely the opposites of those for upward movement. In actuality, however, the variables affecting downward mobility can be quite complex and are not simply the flip sides of upward movement.

Upward mobility may be affected or prevented by factors such as urbanization, industrialization, geographic mobility, mass communication, form of government, and traditional social mores. Upward mobility may take two basic forms: "contest" and "sponsored." Contest mobility refers to upward mobility that is the result of competition based on some sort of supposedly objective standards of merit, such as high test scores. In contrast, sponsored mobility is dependent on special, subjective relationships, as in the case of an individual whose upward mobility is the result of having a mentor in an organization or group.

Horizontal mobility involves movement from one social rank to another social position of equivalent status. In addition, changes in social position involving non-hierarchical social categories, such as religion, political affiliation, or age are often considered kinds of nonvertical mobility. Because of the number and complexity of potential variables, coupled with complications arising from issues of definition and measurement, understanding the patterns and significance of social mobility is a challenging task.

Applications
Most studies of mobility have focused on men's intragenerational mobility or on intergenerational mobility, comparing sons with fathers. An important work by Peter M. Blau and Otis Dudley Duncan, *The American Occupational Structure* (1967), developed a formal model for investigating the ways in which a father's occupational status does and does not influence the status and mobility of his sons. While recognizing that life is a complicated, ongoing process, Blau and Duncan attempted to discover and trace a sequence of life events and social variables with measurable traits which could be correlated with later outcomes. That sequence is known as the process of status attainment. Of central interest to Blau and Duncan were the specific ways in which fathers influenced their sons. Using simple correlations, they found that a father's education and occupation each had about an equal influence on sons' occupations; that sons' education (both dependent and independent of family background) had the most significant impact on eventual occupation; and that family background could play a role in occupational choice even after formal education was completed. A later repetition of Blau and Duncan's work by David Featherman and Robert Hauser, published as *Opportunity and Change* (1978), reported reasonably parallel findings. Featherman and Hauser did note significant differences, however, when race was added as a status attainment variable.

In part because of the American and Western European dominance of data gathering and research after World War II, there is extensive analysis of the mobility patterns of white males. Until relatively recently, there has been little information about, or interest in, the mobility experiences of women or people of color. Certainly the lack of available data may be traced to the fact that members of subcultural groups often focus their energies and attention on forms of achievement other than occupation, the traditional focus of mobility studies. In addition, disadvantaged and minority members of society are often the victims of acts of discrimination, both historical and contemporary, which act as barriers to their occupational and social mobility.

Researchers such as Reynolds Farley, interested in understanding the mobility patterns of minority groups, began to investigate changes over time and comparisons among different groups in the same society. In his *Blacks and Whites: Narrowing the*

Gap? (1984), Farley defined inequality as differences in income, occupational prestige, and education. From this set of elements, he was able to illustrate a complex set of relationships. Focusing on the period between 1960 and 1980, he found that income disparities between blacks and whites had narrowed, that the two groups were moving toward equality of access in education, and that occupational differences had also declined, although occupational parity had by no means been achieved.

Mobility and status attainment researchers most often absorb sexual difference as a variable in whatever model they employ, applying the same methods and measurement categories to men and women. As a result, despite the different experiences men and women have in the labor market, their occupational and marital mobility patterns are, for the most part, the same. These findings should not be taken as evidence of gender mobility equality, however, because variables such as pay, educational status, and marriage can affect women's social mobility differently from the ways they affect men. For example, a review of data available for the period from 1962 to 1973 led Robert Hauser and David Featherman to conclude, in an article entitled "The Measurement of Occupation in Social Surveys" (1977), that while women's social "origins" may be the same as men's, the social "destinations" available to, or chosen by, women are often very different.

Discussion of mobility among different groups in society raises the issue of differences in attitudes toward social mobility in any social group. It has long been a central part of American ideology that everyone in society has a common definition of success and mobility and has the ability to rise in social status. The stories of Horatio Alger, a popular novelist of the nineteenth century, embody this American Dream: a poor boy, through "pluck and luck," becomes rich and successful beyond his wildest imaginings. Various studies, however, make clear that there are differing attitudes toward social mobility as well as various experiences of both upward and downward mobility within the geographical boundaries of the United States. A number of studies have found that social mobility indeed exists in the United States, but not to the extent that "rags-to-riches" stories would have one believe. Upward mobility usually involves movement of one or two steps up the social ladder. Therefore, moving from poverty to wealth, although it cannot be called impossible, is an extremely rare event in any society, including American society. Variables such as social class, race and ethnicity, aspiration level, the role of family, and the effects of downward mobility are all beginning to receive increased attention from scholars, including Judah Matras in his book *Social Inequality, Stratification, and Social Mobility* (1984). It may be that the assumption that mobility is a central social value whose increase, by any means, is to be universally desired, must be examined more critically. Questions of both the assets and liabilities of social mobility in the context of the larger social order and in terms of individual lives are increasingly at the center of research on mobility and status attainment.

Context

While most of the research and writing in the field of social mobility has occurred since World War II, even ancient social philosophers such as Plato and Aristotle considered social mobility an important element of efficiency and stability in the formation and maintenance of the state. In his *Republic* (c. 380 B.C.E.), Plato categorized individuals as being made of gold, silver, or bronze thread, and he argued that while a heredity of social status should be expected, the gold children of bronze parents needed to be recognized and advanced to their rightful places in society. Similarly, the bronze children of gold parents needed to be detected and not given access to power. (Prophecy foretold the destruction of the state if led by men of bronze.) In his work *Politics* (384-322 B.C.E.), Aristotle discussed the establishment of the social class system and the logic of the rule of the middle class, seen as a "mean" that could counterbalance the ambitions of the upper and lower classes.

The first modern treatment of social mobility was Pitirim Sorokin's classic *Social Mobility* (1927). His central argument was that there are inevitable, permanent, and global points of occupational, and therefore social, inequality. Like Karl Marx, Sorokin held that a belief in vertical mobility has a stabilizing effect in that it provides motivations to the lower orders which keep them from disrupting the prevailing system. High rates of social mobility act as a safety valve, releasing the pressures of a discontented lower class. While Sorokin argued that social mobility was inevitable, however, he was unwilling to suggest any sort of enduring linear progression or digression in its spread or intensity.

Right after World War II, mobility studies tended to focus on specific societies, communities, and populations. In large measure, this interest was generated by concern for "openness," a term used in this context to describe the fluidity of movement among social strata and seen as a measure of social inequality. A society was described as open, fair, or just depending on the rates of both intergenerational and intragenerational mobility. The International Sociological Association encouraged and supported comparative research on this topic in the early postwar period. Despite problems with many of these studies, especially in terms of incompatible data categories and structural variables, cross-cultural studies continue to make up a large percentage of work in the field.

The most significant works in the area of social mobility studies since Sorokin's theoretical breakthrough have perhaps been in the collection and analysis of data. Beginning in the late 1940's, for example, social mobility studies focused on social inequalities rather than on social stability. A major theme of this branch of research became the consequences of mobility for individuals and societies. For example, in *Political Man: The Social Bases of Politics* (1960), Seymour Lipset emphasized the destabilizing effects of too much mobility. His analysis was based on a view of social stratification, which acknowledged its multidimensional nature. For Lipset, society is a complex system of multiple, often mutually exclusive hierarchies based on status, class, and authority. An individual might be mobile on one dimension but not on another. For example, a person might attain a high occupational position yet encounter prejudice because of ethnicity or social origin. Similarly, although an upper-class family might suffer a reversal of its financial standing, it might still retain a high social position. Lipset concluded that these sorts of inconsistencies were dysfunctional and could provoke frustrations which might lead to interest in radical political and social changes.

Few social scientists have systematically investigated nonvertical social mobility; as a matter of fact, most research has focused on vertical, intergenerational occupational changes. Although a few studies have included consideration of the possible influences of differences in stratification structures and economic systems, few, if any, have investigated differences other than those considered occupational or economic.

Scholars of social mobility must address issues of exactly what is being measured and what precisely is being described in discussions of mobility. The important connections between mobility, social inequality, and individual attitudes and values present sociologists with a special challenge to include both quantitative and qualitative data in their analyses of social mobility's importance and meanings. Just as modern social mobility studies emphasize the idea that class structures and social categories are never static, so the study of mobility must be prepared to meet the challenges of a dynamic and diverse area of research.

Bibliography

Blau, Peter M., and Otis Dudley Duncan. *The American Occupational Structure*. New York: John Wiley & Sons, 1967. One of the most comprehensive works on intergenerational mobility; it makes a substantial contribution in terms of methodological issues.

Farley, Reynolds. *Blacks and Whites: Narrowing the Gap?* Cambridge, Mass.: Harvard University Press, 1984. Examines the differences and similarities in social mobility between African American and European American men during the period from 1960 to 1980.

Featherman, David, and Robert Hauser. "The Measurement of Occupation in Social Surveys." In *The Process of Stratification: Trends and Analyses*. New York: Academic Press, 1977. This article discusses sexual difference as a variable in stratification and mobility. The volume includes several excellent articles on the subject of mobility in relation to social stratification.

_____. *Opportunity and Change*. New York: Academic Press, 1978. A well-written and well-researched examination of mobility, stratification, and occupational issues among various racial, ethnic, and socioeconomic groups in the United States.

Lipset, Seymour. *Political Man: The Social Bases of Politics*. Garden City, N.Y.: Doubleday, 1960. A theoretical and empirical analysis of the relationship between social and political behaviors and structures.

Lipset, Seymour, and Reinhard Bendix. *Social Mobility in Industrial Society*. Berkeley: University of California Press, 1959. Despite its age, this volume continues to be an important source of theory and empirical information on social mobility in different societies.

Matras, Judah. *Social Inequality, Stratification, and Mobility*. 2d ed. Englewood Cliffs,

N.J.: Prentice-Hall, 1984. A basic summary of research and theory in the fields noted in the title.

Sorokin, Pitirim. *Social Mobility.* New York: Harper & Brothers, 1927. By all accounts, the first systematic study (and a still-classic work) in the field of social mobility theories and research.

Jackie R. Donath

Cross-References

Caste Systems, 198; Embourgeoisement and Proletarianization, 633; Equality of Opportunity, 668; The Culture of Poverty, 1460; Social Mobility: Intergenerational versus Intragenerational Mobility, 1819; Social Stratification: Analysis and Overview, 1839; Social Stratification: Functionalist Perspectives, 1845; Social Stratification: Marxist Perspectives, 1852.

SOCIAL MOBILITY: INTERGENERATIONAL VERSUS INTRAGENERATIONAL MOBILITY

Type of sociology: Social stratification
Fields of study: Dimensions of inequality; Social mobility

Being old and being young are not the same thing—the roles that are possible change as one ages. There is also larger-scale change over time, as anyone knows who has heard stories of "the old days" when both the standard of living and the dominant values were different. Intergenerational and intragenerational social mobility describe the ways in which individuals and groups experience these gradual changes.

Principal terms

AGE COHORT: a group of people sharing approximately the same age and thus sharing a large number of experiences at roughly the same development stage

AGEISM: any ideology that justifies and rationalizes discrimination on the basis of age; this term can refer to attitudes and structures that bias in favor of or against older or younger age cohorts

CASTE SYSTEMS: systems of social stratification that separate people into permanent categories, such as race or place of origin

CLASS SYSTEMS: systems of social stratification that separate people into categories that are stable over the long term but are still changeable, such as income level, educational level, or language spoken

IDEOLOGY: systems of thought and action that persuade people to assume certain limited views of reality, especially including biases for and against certain groups, often on the basis of that group's assumed "nature"

INTERGENERATIONAL MOBILITY: the social mobility of a family over time, such as the ability of a future generation to join a class different from that of present or previous generations

INTRAGENERATIONAL MOBILITY: the social mobility of an individual through that person's lifetime, as measured against the social movement of the individual's age cohort

SOCIAL MOBILITY: the ability and tendency of persons to change status in society, usually involving movement into another social class, whether upward or downward

SOCIAL STRATIFICATION: systems by which societies create classes and status levels of an enduring nature; though social mobility is usually possible, social stratification provides the structure against which one moves and is thus a construct of the forces that resist mobility

Overview

Societies contain many factors that define their dynamic equilibrium. Social stratification and social mobility are two such forces, working against each other to differing degrees that represent the various life possibilities open to individuals. Social stratification refers to the social structures that keep individuals "in their place"; that is, within their socially defined roles. Modern industrial (and postindustrial) societies are highly stratified, with rules and structures separating many groups from one another on the basis of factors such as race, ethnicity, gender, sexual orientation, income, language, wealth, power, prestige, and educational level, among many others. Such high stratification creates social locations for individuals, who tend to live their entire lives within their socially defined spaces. Social mobility, however, refers to the opposite reality. No matter how highly stratified and fragmented a society becomes, it is still possible, at least in some cases, to move between these rigidly defined social categories. When a society divides on the basis of a permanent category, such as race, then there is a caste system, a stratification pattern in which mobility is not possible because the factor responsible for social location is not changeable. (Note, however, that society can change its definition of such factors, and thus allow for mobility even in caste systems. One must remember that even race and gender are social constructs.)

If other factors enter into the formula for stratification, however, there may well be the possibility for change within one's ascribed status. For example, education and income may be changeable variables, so one can cross into new social categories by increasing one's education or income. These changeable situations represent class systems, in which mobility is possible to one degree or another. In most social realities, numerous factors are part of the social stratification. If at least some of the factors are not permanently assigned at birth, then the stratification forms a class system, and therefore at least some social mobility is possible.

Stratification assigns different roles to different statuses. In other words, persons at different social locations (statuses) perform different social tasks (roles). Status reflects many different variables, such as wealth, power, and prestige. Gender, race, and age can also be social factors in the construction of individual status. These relate to specific social roles, in both informal and formal ways. For example, the social role of president in the United States is formally limited to persons older than thirty-five years of age by the Constitution. Thus, those persons lacking such status because they are "too young" cannot attain that role. At the same time, almost all recent presidents have been millionaires, and certainly members of the upper class. Though this is an informal criterion, there is a strong correlation between the status associated with that wealth and the ability to assume the social role of president. In more everyday ways, the same pattern repeats itself throughout society. Some roles are strongly correlated with status in general or with specific factors of status.

Modern complex societies, however, possess a high degree of social mobility. When one examines the larger picture of historical change in the United States, it becomes clear that whole groups have made radical shifts in their social situations. Consider, for example, the roles and statuses of African Americans as they have changed over the last two centuries. Whereas once almost all African Americans were slaves, at the bottom of the socioeconomic ladder, there are now a number of high-prestige and high-status roles that are filled by African Americans, including seats in Congress and on the Supreme Court. These roles would have been unthinkable even fifty years ago, and therefore there has been great social mobility over time. This type of mobility is called intergenerational mobility; as one generation replaces another, the newer generation has more options available to it as a result of social change, and so the newer generation achieves greater social status, eclipsing the accomplishments of its ancestors. Many modern corporate executives are descendants of working-class parents and grandparents, for example.

Another type of social mobility is intragenerational mobility. As a person ages, she or he takes on new roles and statuses, usually increasingly as time goes on. The individual acquires more education, more income, more wealth, and more prestige over time. For this reason, most older adults in the United States have a greater accumulation of wealth than they did as children and as young adults. Many of the cultural stereotypes about the aging process assume this sort of intragenerational mobility: a child lives with relatives, a late teenager or college student lives with friends, a newly married couple lives in a small apartment and then later buys a small house, and perhaps at retirement the family will own a sizable house or even a vacation cottage. Not all individuals in the same age group experience social mobility in the same way. Some of the age cohort will attain much greater status than others very quickly. Such persons, those who are "most likely to succeed," end up with much higher status than those of their early friends, some of whom may actually lose status as they age and slip into poverty.

Even though such social mobility is highly uneven, societies possess a wide range of ideologies that support and rationalize these changes. For intergenerational mobility, these ideologies contrast "today's young folks" with the "way things were in my day." Families pass down stories about when the family did not have "luxury items" such as refrigerators and automobiles; these stories stress that the family has increased its status and its standard of living over the passing generations. In intragenerational mobility, the ideologies often reflect the tendency to move into roles held by one's elders, who are then characterized as "too old," or to protect one's status from encroachment by younger persons who are advancing quickly. These ideologies produce notions of ageism, depicting older persons as decrepit, incompetent, and uninterested, while simultaneously fostering the portrayals of younger persons as sloppy, lazy, or self-centered. Such stereotypes and ideologies rationalize an individual's status.

Applications

Often, citizens of the United States refer to the "American Dream" while thinking of the intertwined effects of intragenerational mobility ("I deserve to acquire more as I grow older") and intergenerational mobility ("I deserve to have more than my parents did"). The strong form of this ideal is the rags-to-riches story, in which a poor person attains great wealth and prestige over the course of one successful lifetime. Though this pattern does occur in actual society, it is the exception rather than the rule. Most of U.S. history has been characterized by a slow progression of upward social mobility throughout the generations. Not only do certain families acquire their wealth slowly over generations but also the overall standard of living throughout the country has increased throughout the last two centuries. As the small upper classes have been unable to produce enough new elites to fill the slots created by an expanding economy, persons from the middle class have been enabled to join the upper class through jobs with higher pay and greater prestige. At the same time, the regular entry of immigrants into the economy has created a new lower class in almost every generation, allowing more and more lower-class persons to step up to the middle class.

This pattern, however, may be at the point of reversing itself in recent decades. Increasingly, today's young persons may receive a lesser education than their parents did, and opportunities for home ownership and other indications of status have been made less available by sharp increases in the cost of living from the 1970's onward. Consistent and universal intergenerational mobility requires an expanding economy, but such an economy has not existed in the late twentieth century. Political slogans have ranged from "the age of malaise" to the need for "austerity" and the necessity for greater individual "contribution."

Upward mobility has never been a simple linear process. Mobility reflects the economic fortunes of the larger society and therefore is uneven at best, but there is also a strongly cyclical nature to mobility, especially at the family level. For example, consider the Kennedy family. This family of Massachusetts nobility had increased its wealth and power in slow intergenerational fashion, but the middle third of the twentieth century showed a very sharp increase in its power, when it produced a president, senators, and cabinet members. Through the 1970's and later, however, the power of the family underwent a slow decline. Though the Kennedys are still very powerful, they no longer have the status that they did in the 1960's. As a new generation experiences the intragenerational factors of age and education, its members are rising into positions of power, and it remains to be seen if their eventual rise will culminate at a higher or lower level than that of the generation of John, Robert, and Edward Kennedy.

Most of the studies of intergenerational mobility have reflected functionalist assumptions, emphasizing slow change as a result of larger social factors, but there are also conflict models that interpret the changing status of generations in the United States. Such conflict perspectives notice that different age cohorts have conflicting interests. For example, retired persons in the United States receive an array of governmental benefits, including Social Security's guaranteed income and subsidized medical care. These benefits are funded by tax money, the bulk of which is paid by middle-aged employees from the middle and upper classes. Senior citizens' interests include higher taxation and higher benefits; taxpayers desire low tax rates and receive no immediate advantage from the benefit programs. (Almost all citizens in the United States receive government benefits from one source or another, either directly or indirectly, but Social Security taxes mostly distribute money collected from middle-aged adults to senior citizens.)

This conflict between age cohorts has also appeared in "generation gaps." Such conflicts are fueled by ideologies about what different age groups can and cannot do. Society defines many jobs (and thus the accompanying statuses) as age-limited; some people are simply "too old" or "too young" to be able to perform certain tasks. These ideologies limit social mobility, but they also perpetuate slow upward intergenerational mobility by urging older Americans to leave their jobs (and thus their income and prestige), creating spaces for younger persons, while at the same time teenagers and other young persons take minimum-wage jobs with promise for advancement. The ideologies of age stratification encourage both young and old to accept the roles that the dominant members of the society assign to them.

Context

Theories of stratification and mobility arose as attempts to explain society's peculiar mix of stability and change. Marx produced the first thorough theory of stratification to explain why some people held control over others. Stratification theory concentrated on the influences of various social institutions in creating classes and assigning people to rigid class systems. Thus, early Marxist theory underemphasized any notions of social mobility, including intergenerational and intragenerational mobility.

Functionalist theories from those of Max Weber onward tended to rely on notions of social mobility as a corrective to the idea of social stratification. Though the society as a whole did create class boundaries, functionalists typically understood the boundaries to be necessary parts of the social structure, and they were not troublesome because they were rather permeable boundaries. Most individuals could move themselves to a new social class, whether by themselves or through the work of a family over time.

More recent works, including so-called "evolutionary" theories of stratification, emphasize a balance between the conflict and functionalist perspectives. They recognize the possibility of social mobility as distinct from the likelihood of such change for any individual. Instead, the fates of most individuals—even their changes in social status—are the results of larger social forces that cause the relationships between the classes to evolve.

It is likely that sociological theory will continue to investigate the problematic and inconsistent relationship between stratification and mobility. Certain topics will expand in their attractiveness to sociologists. As the United States becomes more ethnically and culturally pluralistic, the interrelationships of mobility in different ethnic groups are certain to receive more attention. The aging of the baby-boomer generation has created more interest in middle-life transitions in status, and soon more attention will be paid to the status of the elderly vis-à-vis other age cohorts. Recent years have seen the first treatments of the next major generational category, variously called the baby busters, the thirteenth generation, and generation X. The clash of values between this generation and its predecessors will be the subject of much sociological investigation. Also, the increasing attention given to ideology in society will probably extend into ideologies of stratification, expanding the study of how such stereotypes originate and serve to create the social differences of continuing stratification.

Whereas sociologists of the 1950's through the 1970's emphasized the presence of a slow upward intergenerational mobility, more recent sociological studies have concentrated on the much more chaotic situation of the 1980's and 1990's. Without a widely expanding economic base, many Americans are experiencing downward mobility. For this reason, studies of mobility will require greater attention to the causes of differential mobility, as some groups increase in status and others decline. Also of significance will be the various interrelationships between intergenerational and intragenerational social mobility. If one's whole family is losing status but one finds ways to increase personal status, what are the causes and effects, at the levels of the individual, the family, and the greater society? The more complex realities will require that such questions about mixed situations be addressed.

Bibliography

Bennett, Linda L. M., and Stephen Earl Bennett. *Living with Leviathan: Americans Coming to Terms with Big Government*. Lawrence: University Press of Kansas, 1990. In an engaging style, these sociologists discuss how different age cohorts react to the realities of American big government. This approach provides essential data for a conflict analysis of the age cohorts' power struggles as mediated by the governmental structures that aid each group differentially.

Bernardi, Bernardo. *Age Class Systems: Social Institutions and Politics Based on Age*. New York: Cambridge University Press, 1985. This interesting volume contrasts the formation of age groups in a wide variety of societies throughout the world. Bernardi's theoretical assumptions are thoroughly functionalist, and he provides solid treatments of political and power considerations regarding age groupings. The book is very helpful for seeing how other societies manage the aging process.

Eisenstadt, Samuel N. *From Generation to Generation: Age Groups and Social Structure*. Glencoe, Ill.: Free Press, 1956. Eisenstadt portrays the connections between age groups and the larger questions of social structure. He examines a number of societies worldwide and gives conclusions that attempt to explain all of them, whereas a narrower focus would have been more helpful. This book's chief problem is that it is now quite dated, but it is still somewhat useful.

La Fontaine, J. S., ed. *Sex and Age as Principles of Social Differentiation*. New York: Academic Press, 1978. This volume collects eight articles by social anthropologists that attempt to integrate the social constructions of sex and age. The book provides some good insights into how the aging process differs between genders and illustrates how these processes operate in different societies.

Pampel, Fred C., and John B. Williamson. *Age, Class, Politics, and the Welfare State*. New York: Cambridge University Press, 1989. The authors offer a careful study of the role of age cohorts (especially senior citizens) in the development of the welfare state. By paying close attention to the actual patterns of income distribution and redistribution in welfare systems of taxation and benefits, they suggest a much more nuanced understanding of the social effects of such political organization on the social mobility of the aged.

Stewart, Frank Henderson. *Fundamentals of Age-Group Systems.* New York: Academic Press, 1977. Stewart proposes a rigorous theory of age-group systems. There is a strong individualistic emphasis that sometimes obscures how the age-groups function within society as a whole. Of primary interest is the book's careful working of transitions between age-groups, which this article refers to as intragenerational social mobility.

Taylor, Robert M., Jr., and Ralph J. Crandall, eds. *Generations and Change: Genealogical Perspectives in Social History.* Macon, Ga.: Mercer, 1986. In sixteen chapters, numerous contributors examine the use of genealogy in the study of history. Several of the articles concentrate on intergenerational social mobility in a variety of social settings, often covering a century or two of time. The close attention to specific historical detail offers great insights, but more use of the sociological theory of social mobility would have enhanced the volume's usefulness.

Jon L. Berquist

Cross-References

Caste Systems, 198; Embourgeoisement and Proletarianization, 633; Gender Inequality: Analysis and Overview, 820; Industrial Societies, 953; School Socialization, 1693; Social Mobility: Analysis and Overview, 1812; Social Stratification: Analysis and Overview, 1839; Social Stratification: Functionalist Perspectives, 1845; Social Stratification: Marxist Perspectives, 1852; Social Stratification: Modern Theories, 1859; Social Stratification: Weberian Perspectives, 1866.

SOCIAL MOVEMENTS

Type of sociology: Collective behavior and social movements

A social movement is an organized attempt by a number of people united by a shared belief to effect or resist changes in the existing social order by non-institutionalized means. The ultimate objective of a social movement is what its members see as the betterment of society.

Principal terms

COLLECTIVE BEHAVIOR: behavior exhibited by large groups of human beings in concert

INSTITUTIONALIZED BEHAVIOR: behavior widely accepted as binding by all or most members of a society

INTEREST GROUP: an identifiable subculture whose members share similar views of social organization

SOCIAL INSTITUTION: a way of meeting a real or perceived human need; major institutions include education, the family, religion, and the state

SOCIAL PROBLEM: a real or perceived defect in the social organization of a given society

Overview

Social movements have been responsible, directly or indirectly, for much of the social change that has characterized the modern era of history. Modern societies undergo constant dialectic change as different social classes, generations, ethnic groups, and regional groups develop new (or revive old) views of what society should be and attempt to implement changes according to those views. Competing social groups, opposing ideas of social perfection, and irreconcilable interest groups permeate modern society and give birth to social movements. A social movement is usually large in membership, with goals that its members perceive will reshape their country or world, or will at least bring about improvement for a substantial portion of humanity. The members of a social movement usually believe that only non-institutionalized (sometimes even illegal) means can bring about the ends they desire, and are prepared to use them.

Since sociologists began to study social movements as distinct phenomena, they have evolved two basic paradigms to facilitate their study by dividing social movements into distinct types. All contemporary studies of social movements incorporate some combination or permutation of these two paradigms. the first attempt to differentiate between the multitude of social movements and divide them into types appeared in a textbook by Ralph Turner and Lewis Killian, *Collective Behavior* (1957). Turner and Killian divided all social movements into three categories: value oriented, power oriented, and participation oriented.

Value-oriented movements include those in which the members commit themselves to a principle they steadfastly refuse to compromise in order to gain their ends. Examples include the international pacifist movement before World War I, and utopian religious communities. Members of the pacifist movement eschewed violence as a means to their end and even when violence was employed against them. A number of utopian religious movements have faded into oblivion at least partly because their members strictly adhered to doctrine forbidding sexual intercourse, thus making it impossible for the membership to perpetuate itself.

Power-oriented movements include those which have as their primary goal the acquisition of power, status, or recognition for the members of the movement. The dogma of this type of movement includes the premise that only through becoming economically or politically empowered can they eliminate what they perceive as the evils of their society. Convinced of the righteousness of their cause, they are willing to use any means or compromise any principle to achieve power, which frequently becomes an end in itself. An example of this sort of social movement is the Nazi movement in Germany during the 1930's.

Participation-oriented movements subordinate the acquisition of power or implementation of reform to the personal satisfaction gained from participation in the movement. Turner and Killian subdivided this type into three groups. Passive reform movements identify and denounce imperfections in society but do not actively work to eliminate them. Examples include several antislavery movements in the United States before 1830. Personal status movements advocate a redefinition of the prevailing status system by which their own status will be enhanced. Limited personal movements appeal to members through the movement's own exclusivity (secret societies, for example).

David Aberle formulated a second and more sophisticated typology of social movements in *The Peyote Religion Among the Navaho* (1966). He divided all social movements into what he called transformative, reformative, redemptive, and alternative movements. Aberle's classification attempts to type social movements by the locus and amount of changes sought by its adherents. He defined "locus" as being either changes in individuals or changes in the social structure, and "amount" as being whether the movement seeks minor changes or total restructuring of the individual or society.

Transformative movements, in Aberle's typology, aim for total change of the individual or society. The desired change is all-embracing, usually violent, often cataclysmic, and always imminent. They include the many millennial religious movements that have appeared throughout history. Also part of this group of social movements are Bolshevism and anarchism. The locus of the transformative movement always encompasses all of society, and the amount of change advocated or prophesied is always total. Redemptive movements are also total in scope but aim at changing individuals rather than changing social institutions. Most of the world's great religious movements fall into this category, but so also do several secular movements. Notable among the secular movements is the eugenics movement of the late nineteenth and early twentieth centuries. Reformative movements are usually geared toward eliminating a flaw or flaws in the existing social system but leaving the basic structure relatively intact. Contemporary examples in the United States include the Civil Rights movement of the 1950's and 1960's and the Progressive movement of the early twentieth century. The members of both movements were more or less satisfied with existing institutions except those which they identified as evil. Alternative movements, the fourth and last type in Aberle's system, are those which strive to alter partially the behavior of individuals. The members of these groups hold that human beings are basically good but can become better through altering certain characteristics or habits; society will thus become better as well. Examples of this category include the temperance movement, the antismoking movement, and, arguably, the pro-life and pro-choice movements.

Applications

Many contemporary social scientists argue that social movements result from social change. The movements in turn cause more social changes, which in turn give birth to more social movements. In this view, contemporary pluralistic societies are locked into a continuous cycle of rapid change that makes social planning difficult and the danger of violent social upheavals more likely. The other extreme, a static, totalitarian society in which change is suppressed, holds little attraction for most people. The study of social movements holds out the possibility that societies will learn to mitigate the actions of social movements by identifying and dealing with their causes. If the Old Regime in prerevolutionary France had recognized the nature of the widespread and related social movements in that country before 1789, for example, and been flexible enough to deal with their causes, it could have avoided the worst excesses of the Terror.

Many sociologists believe that social movements have a definable life cycle: genesis, social unrest, enthusiastic mobilization, maintenance, and termination. The American abolitionist movement illustrates the cycle. The genesis of the movement dates back to the 1690's and the first voices raised by the Quaker community to condemn slavery as an evil institution. Slowly, during the eighteenth century, leaders of other religious groups and a number of intellectuals in the United States and abroad began to denounce slavery and seek ways to end it. By the early nineteenth century the "social unrest" period had begun. Abolition became a political issue, pushed by several abolitionist organizations. In the 1830's "enthusiastic mobilization" began, with sizable groups demanding an end to slavery. The leader of the largest of these groups (the American Anti-Slavery Society) was William L. Garrison, who also called for the extension of full citizenship rights to the slaves once they had been freed. The "maintenance" period of the abolitionist movement came during the period between 1840 and 1860, when the various factions of abolitionism attempted to perpetuate themselves and keep their cause before the public eye. "Termination" came after the Civil War with the passage of the Thirteenth, Fourteenth, and Fifteenth amendments to the United States Constitution during the 1860's.

Although establishing cause and effect in history remains problematic, most historians would probably agree that the abolitionist movement contributed to the outbreak of the Civil War. The war caused terrible suffering and arguably created many more problems than it solved. One possibility for applying studies of social movements is that movements could perhaps be identified when they are still in the "genesis" or "social unrest" periods. Society could then attempt to identify and understand the social problems (real or perceived) that gave birth to the movements. If these identifications can be made, and if society can develop the flexibility to address the problems, then the violent and destructive upheavals that sometimes result from social movements might be avoided. To give one historical example, if, after World War I, the German Weimar government and the victorious countries in the war had been able to identify and address the dire social problems in Germany that made the National Socialist movement so attractive, Adolf Hitler might not have come to power in 1933, and the world could have been spared the catastrophic events of 1939-1945. Similarly, if the czarist regime in Russia had been willing and able to identify and address the underlying causes that made Bolshevism possible and popular in the early twentieth century, the horrors of the later Stalinist era would not have occurred, and the decades-long trauma of the Cold War would have been averted.

There are seemingly numberless social movements in the world. Many of them are small and apparently of little consequence, with virtually no chance of affecting society seriously. Nevertheless, careful study of these groups and the circumstances that gave them birth may allow sociologists to identify—and society to correct— currently barely perceptible problems that might evolve into large problems in the future. Study of the larger contemporary social movements—the environmental movement, the international human rights movement, the feminist movement—will almost certainly provide meaningful results, especially if society develops the flexibility to deal with the problems from which those movements developed. As human societies around the globe become increasingly interdependent and integrated, the understanding of social movements becomes more critical. Movements with the potential to seriously disrupt society could cause upheavals that would dwarf those of the world wars of the twentieth century.

Context

Sociologists did not begin the systematic study of social movements as distinct phenomena until after World War II. Prior to that time, only historians had written about social movements. Some of those historians employed sociological terminology in their accounts, but most were untrained in sociological concepts. The great political mass movements of the early twentieth century interested some sociologists enough that they began investigating them during the 1920's and 1930's, but the work was done almost exclusively in a political context.

In the United States during the 1950's, in the midst of the "enthusiastic organization" stage of the Civil Rights movement, a number of sociologists began studying and writing about social movements as distinct phenomena rather than as an aspect of "collective behavior." Books such as Wendell King's *Social Movements in the United States* (1956) and Turner and Killian's *Collective Behavior* alerted sociologists that the field might be of great importance. In the 1960's, when the Civil Rights movement and its close relative, the antiwar movement, convulsed American society almost to the breaking point, sociologists produced new studies on social movements in bewildering profusion. That explosion of scholarship continued into the 1970's, tapering off only in the 1980's. It seemed that only when the turbulent decade of the 1960's demonstrated the potential power of social movements did sociologists begin to take it seriously (or perhaps more accurately, it was only when they were threatened by social revolution that politicians began appropriating research funds to study the groups they perceived as threatening).

The profusion of scholarship during the 1960's and 1970's produced much valuable work defining and categorizing social movements and noting their dynamics, psychology, and rhetoric. Little insight was forthcoming, however, on addressing the underlying social problems that cause these movements. The greatest problem in addressing the causes of social movements is the profusion of seemingly irreconcilable subcultures and interest groups in modern society. To eliminate the social problem perceived by one social movement may do significant damage to another group or even to society as a whole. For example, to eradicate tobacco use in the United States (as the antismoking movement advocates) would directly remove more than a million jobs from the United States economy, reduce U.S. imports by more than $5 billion per year, drain at least $13 billion from federal and state tax revenues, and eliminate a further $20 billion from the U.S. economy. It would also be very likely to spark a new social movement: angry tobacco addicts.

Bibliography

Denisoff, R. Serge. *Great Day Coming*. Urbana: University of Illinois Press, 1971. Shows the importance of folk music to various social movements of the 1950's and 1960's. Not only reveals aspects of the dynamics of the movements but also, through the lyrics of the songs themselves, shows many of the underlying social problems that gave birth to them. Good index and extensive bibliography.

Garner, Roberta Ash. *Social Movements in America*. 2d ed. Chicago: Rand McNally, 1977. A brief history of American social movements and an in-depth investigation of contemporary movements. Written as an introductory text for college students. Good index and excellent bibliography.

Jameson, J. Franklin. *The American Revolution Considered as a Social Movement*. Princeton, N.J.: Princeton University Press, 1926. One of the earliest American efforts to define and evaluate social movements. Jameson, a noted historian, concluded that the American Revolution was indeed a social movement, thus suggesting that social movements should be studied in their own right. No index, very brief bibliography.

McLaughlin, Barry, ed. *Studies in Social Movements*. New York: Free Press, 1969. Includes articles concerning a number of the social movements of the 1950's and 1960's. The articles are primarily concerned with the nature and dynamics of particular social movements than with their causes.

Oberschall, Anthony. *Social Conflict and Social Movements.* Englewood Cliffs, N.J.: Prentice-Hall, 1973. Examines social movements from the perspective of conflict theory. Concerned primarily with the origins and causes of social movements rather than with their dynamics. Good index and bibliography.

Stewart, Charles, Craig Smith, and Robert E. Denton, Jr. *Persuasion and Social Movements.* Prospect Heights, Ill.: Waveland Press, 1984. Explores the importance of charismatic leadership in the dynamics of social movements. Also contains a good discussion of the origins, nature, and life cycle of social movements. Readers will need a working knowledge of sociological terminology to follow all the book's arguments. Good bibliography and index.

Toch, Hans. *The Social Psychology of Social Movements.* Indianapolis, Ind.: Bobbs-Merrill, 1965. As the title implies, Toch is concerned mostly with the social psychological dimension of social movements. The book makes some interesting points, but it is rather heavily laden with psychological argot.

Turner, Ralph, and Lewis Killian. *Collective Behavior.* Englewood Cliffs, N.J.: Prentice-Hall, 1957. One of the first studies to recognize the importance of social movements and to advocate the specialized study of the subject. A seminal attempt to differentiate between various types of social movements and to identify their causes and purposes. Good index.

Walker, Daniel. *Rights in Conflict: The Walker Report to the National Commission on the Causes and Prevention of Violence.* New York: Bantam Books, 1968. Highlights the most perplexing problem confronting efforts to prevent social upheaval by addressing the problems that give birth to social movements: differing, irreconcilable visions of what society should be. Good index, short bibliography.

Wilson, John. *Introduction to Social Movements.* New York: Basic Books, 1973. Written as an introductory college text on the subject, this book offers perhaps the best brief analysis of the subject. Relatively free of jargon, the book will be accessible to most lay readers. Excellent index and bibliography.

Paul Madden

Cross-References

Antiwar Movements, 121; The Civil Rights Movement, 265; Collective Behavior, 291; Deprivation Theory of Social Movements, 512; The Free Speech Movement, 767; The Gay Liberation Movement, 799; Revolutions, 1641; The Structural-Strain Theory of Social Movements, 1997; The Women's Movement, 2196.

SOCIAL SECURITY AND ISSUES OF THE ELDERLY

Type of sociology: Aging and ageism
Field of study: Policy issues and debates

Social Security is the mainstay of federal domestic policy programs designed to provide support to the large and growing elderly population in the United States. Sociologists are especially concerned with how well this program works to eliminate poverty among the elderly, what inequities are perpetuated or created by the program in its present form, and how it might be improved.

Principal terms

COST-OF-LIVING ADJUSTMENT: the raising of Social Security benefits to take inflation into account in order to stabilize the purchasing power of Social Security recipients

DEPRESSION: a period of long-term low levels of economic activity; the Great Depression of the 1930's lasted almost a decade and resulted in one-fourth of the work force being unemployed at one point

FUNCTIONALISM: a theoretical framework in sociology based on the assumption that society is a complex system whose parts work together to promote stability

POLITICAL ECONOMY OF AGING: a conflict-oriented theory that focuses on the ways in which the political, economic, and social structures of advanced capitalism affect the treatment of the elderly

REGRESSIVE TAX: a tax that has a single rate (such as the sales or Social Security tax), rather than "brackets" (such as the federal income tax); regressive taxes take a larger share of poor people's income than they do of wealthier people's

RETIREMENT TEST: the formula used to determine whether to reduce a recipient's Social Security benefits; the amount of income from wages and salaries is the determining factor

SOCIAL DEMOGRAPHY: the scientific study of human populations, with an emphasis on the age, sex, racial/ethnic, and socioeconomic structure of society, and how it changes, stressing the importance of the social determinants and consequences of fertility, mortality, and migration

SOCIAL GERONTOLOGY: the area within sociology that focuses on the study of aging and the elderly, with special emphasis on the social determinants and consequences of aging for the individual and society

Overview

There is hardly a substantive area in sociology that is not explicitly concerned with poverty per se and/or poverty as a direct or indirect cause of a long list of social problems of interest within the discipline. The analysis of issues that are related to impoverishment among the elderly in the United States necessarily involves an examination of Social Security. The Social Security Act of 1935 included Old Age Insurance (OAI), which has come to be commonly referred to as Social Security. This program, which was originally enacted because the Great Depression had plunged many elderly citizens into abject poverty, is the federal government's mechanism for providing basic retirement income to the elderly. This program has been controversial since its inception. In fact, by 1935, twenty-seven other countries had already established public systems of insurance against old-age dependency, and the United States was one of the last modern industrialized nations to do so, in spite of strong political opposition to the program. Although Social Security has never lacked critics, there is no doubt that it has had a tremendous impact on reducing poverty among the elderly and is the sole source of retirement income for a majority of elderly Americans.

In his 1992 book *The Economics of Aging*, James H. Schulz asserts that Social Security was designed both to assist the elderly financially and to encourage them to leave or remain out of the labor force in order to reduce competition for jobs in the face of the high unemployment rates of the Depression. Schulz points out the basic principles on which the program was based. Among these is compulsory participation, a system in which all workers, with few exceptions, are required to pay into the Social Security fund through monthly payroll deductions and thus are eligible to receive retirement benefits. Another important principle is that the program has never been need-based, in that only workers who make contributions to the system are eligible for benefits, and the amount of benefits is based on salary earned while working. Additionally, Social Security was never intended to be the sole source of income for the elderly; they are expected to provide for retirement through private pension plans or investments. Schulz also points out that perhaps the most important of these principles is the requirement of a retirement test for Social Security recipients. This means that there are severe restrictions on the amount of money they can earn through employment, although there are no limits on income from pensions and investments. This provision is designed to get and keep the elderly out of the paid labor force.

In recent years, several important questions have been raised regarding Social Security. One such question relates to whether the program accomplishes its originally stated goals. The two main objectives of Social Security were to enable workers to transfer funds from their active labor force years to their retirement years through contributions to the system, and to redistribute retirement income among the elderly in order to create a minimum income to protect the poorest. It has long been asserted that these two functions are somewhat contradictory. That is, the payments-based-on-contributions feature impairs the antipoverty function, because it essentially means that if one was poor before retirement one will be poor when one is elderly. In addition, the retirement income redistribution function impedes the efficient transfer of money into a retirement fund, because wealthier workers receive a smaller percentage of their former earnings as benefits.

Another set of compelling issues involves the concentrations of poverty found within the elderly population. Sociologists are concerned with the structural inequities that led to the creation of Social Security, but they are also disturbed by the inequities that seem to have been perpetuated or created by the system itself. The term "triple jeopardy" has been used to refer to the fact that women, the oldest old, and members of racial minority groups experience rates of poverty that are higher than those experienced by other elderly Americans. Therefore, if one is a very old minority woman in America, one is probably among the poorest of the poor.

Professional housewives suffer high rates of poverty in old age because a lifetime of financial dependency means that when they become widowed they typically experience a dramatic reduction of Social Security benefits and the simultaneous elimination of private pension benefits. Many women who have been employed in the paid labor force receive Social Security benefits lower than those of their male counterparts because childrearing and elder-care responsibilities can cause peripheral labor force participation, and women, on average, earn less than men do. Women are also much less likely than men to be covered by a private pension. A divorced woman has very limited rights regarding her former husband's Social Security or private pension benefits.

The oldest old are at increased risk of poverty for a number of reasons. As Sally Bould, Beverly Sanborn, and Laura Reif state in their 1989 book *Eighty-five Plus: The Oldest Old*, the very old elderly have serious problems finding employment to supplement their retirement income because of increasing health problems and age discrimination. The higher institutionalization rate of the oldest old can also very quickly lead to impoverishment, because most nursing home costs are paid out-of-pocket until these individuals have "spent their way down" to poverty, at which point Medicaid will take over.

Many elderly minority group individuals in America have experienced socioeconomic marginality throughout their lives because of institutional discrimination. For example, Latinos and African Americans have much lower than average educational attainment, which restricts many of them to low-paying jobs as laborers and domestics, positions that typically provide neither health benefits nor pensions. Because much of this work is seasonal or is done in private homes or small businesses not covered by Social Security regulations, many minority individuals have never paid into the Social Security fund. As a result, elderly minority group individuals are highly overrepresented in the ranks of the impoverished in America.

Applications

Because of the problems and inequities built into the original Social Security legislation as well as those that have resulted from social and economic changes that have occurred since 1935, there have been numerous revisions of and additions to this government program. A landmark year for Social Security reform was 1972. Some of the most important provisions of the 1972 Social Security amendments involved significant increases in benefit levels, the initiation of cost-of-living adjustments (beginning in 1975, benefits were automatically increased by the same percentage as that of the increase in the consumer price index), and increases in both the base of taxable earnings and the tax rate for employees and employers, in order to pay for the increased benefits.

Possibly the most important of the 1972 changes was the creation of Supplemental Security Income (SSI). This program, which took effect in 1974, was established to replace Old Age Assistance (OAA), the program that had been designed to aid those who were not covered adequately by Social Security. OAA was administered through local welfare offices, and the existence and extent of this coverage was left up to the discretion of individual states. SSI is managed by the Social Security Administration, but the funding comes from general U.S. Treasury funds. The program is designed to provide a minimum annual income for Social Security recipients.

In 1983, another set of important changes in Social Security was enacted by Congress. Many of these changes were designed to address the solvency of the system, which had operated at a deficit from 1975 to 1983. They included accelerating Social Security tax rate increases, gradually raising the eligibility age for full benefits in the future, substantially increasing tax rates for the self-employed, levying an income tax on higher-income Social Security beneficiaries, expanding coverage to include newly hired federal employees, and creating sharper decreases in starting benefits for early retirees.

In fact, one of the most important societal ramifications of Social Security-related issues has been the intensifying debate over the advisability of attempting to continue to ensure the system's solvency at current benefit levels. The constant increase since World War II in the proportion of the U.S. population that is elderly has led to serious concerns about the future of Social Security.

Many Americans labor under the misconception that each worker's contribution goes into a fund that is invested for him or her until retirement. The truth is that the current working-age population's Social Security taxes are paid to the current retirement-age population. In 1945, forty-two workers paid into the Social Security fund for every retiree, while currently there are only about three workers per Social Security recipient, and the "baby boom" generation has not yet reached retirement age. Average retirees receive back their and their employers' entire contributions to the fund less than five years into retirement. There are those who claim, however, that while the shifting age structure will mean a higher proportion of elderly people in the future, there will also be a reduction in the proportion of children. This could mean that the overall dependency burden will not increase significantly, but the nature of that burden will shift from the very young to the elderly.

Recognition of these facts has led to an ongoing and heated debate between those who support the concept of Social Security as it was originally conceived, and see the only legitimate policy goal as being the expansion and fine-tuning of the original system, and those who have serious reservations about the effects of recent changes in the system, and its economic feasibility. Morton C. Bernstein and Joan Brodshaug Bernstein strongly advocate the former position in their 1988 book *Social Security: The System That Works*. They maintain that the system does, indeed, work now and will work in the future, in part because of the 1972 amendments and the subsequent changes.

The latter position in this debate is taken by those who advocate a major structural overhaul of Social Security, which in their view is a system that is inefficient and unfair. These reformers claim that the same 1972 amendments that are applauded by the system supporters served to increase the costs of an already inefficient system and have exacerbated the inequities originally built into the system. This latter charge stems from the view that the retirement test exempts the wealthiest Americans' income from private pensions, interest, and investments, while reducing the benefits of the nonaffluent, who must work to supplement their Social Security income. Proponents of this view believe that raising the payroll tax in order to finance higher benefits would be morally insupportable, given the regressive nature of that tax. Henry J. Aaron, Barry P. Bosworth, and Gary Burtless contend in their 1989 book *Can America Afford to Grow Old?* that the survival of old-age insurance in America depends on major reforms, including much more creative methods of financing.

Context

The interest in Social Security per se is of relatively recent origin in sociology, since it has only been in existence since 1935. Interest in elderly support systems, however, of which Social Security is the cornerstone in the United States, has been of paramount importance in the fields of social demography, social gerontology, and the sociology of aging.

Contemporary economic and demographic realities have served to speed the development of these areas. The dramatic aging of populations in the industrialized world has produced a compelling need to consider issues of dependency and intergenerational obligation. This situation has led to the multidisciplinary nature of the sociology of aging. In order to address effectively the sets of complex issues within this area, sociologists, in their teaching and research, must incorporate the relevant aspects of economics, biology, and psychology. Those who specialize in the sociology of aging must now have more than a nodding acquaintance with several areas of expertise within sociology, such as social demography, social stratification, minority-group relations, gender studies, political sociology, and the family. Furthermore, an entire list of sociological theories relating to the elderly must be taken into account, including disengagement theory, activity theory, continuity theory, age stratification theory, and modernization theory, as well as the application of broad theoretical perspectives, such as symbolic interactionism, functionalism, and conflict theory.

This response to the need for sociology to come to terms with issues relating to the well-being of a quickly growing elderly population has been a major accomplishment. The oft-stated need to evaluate critically and synthesize a number of substantive areas and theories into a broader area of expertise has seldom been put into practice, and this effort has been very fruitful for sociology as a whole.

Furthermore, the continuing debate between supporters of the functionalist and conflict-oriented theoretical perspectives regarding the modern welfare state under industrial capitalism has found an interesting focus in the issue of elderly support systems such as Social Security. In his 1989 book *Old Age and the Welfare State*, John Myles describes what are, in his view, some of the important differences in the functionalist and political economic views on elderly support programs. Regarding the functionalist perspective, Myles says,

> The distinguishing feature of all such theories is the negligible role played by the political process per se in explaining welfare-state policies. Rather, the state is conceived of as responding in a predictable fashion to the functional imperatives generated by the underlying structure of the larger society.

Simply stated, Myles claims that functionalists believe that industrialization produces new types of social support problems, and the result has been the creation of the same set of social-welfare provisions, including old age insurance, in all industrialized nations. He goes on to point out that the political economic position is that differences in the quality of elderly support provisions between different societies and among different groups within a given society are really a function of political power differentials. In other words, the relative political powerlessness of the poor in America would explain the noncomprehensive nature of U.S. elderly support systems, the reluctance of Congress to do anything about gender-, race-, age,- and class-based inequities in Social Security, and the fact that the United States was the last of the industrialized giants in the world to institute old age insurance—which it did with a considerable degree of vacillation.

Bibliography

Aaron, Henry J., Barry P. Bosworth, and Gary T. Burtless. *Can America Afford to Grow Old? Paying for Social Security*. Washington, D.C.: Brookings Institution, 1989. Represents the position taken by many economists in the debate over Social Security reform. The authors strongly recommend the implementation of more creative means of financing the system in order to ensure its future economic viability. Suitable for advanced high school and college students. Contains an index. References are found in footnotes.

Bernstein, Merton C., and Joan Brodshaug Bernstein. *Social Security: The System That Works*. New York: Basic Books, 1988. The position of those who are opposed to major structural changes in Social Security is well-represented in this book. The entire history of the program is given in detail, including the problems that have arisen and the amendments that have been designed to address them. Appropriate for high school or college students. Includes a guide to Social Security terms and an index. References are contained in a chapter-by-chapter notes section.

Bould, Sally, Beverly Sanborn, and Laura Reif. *Eighty-five Plus: The Oldest Old*. Belmont, Calif.: Wadsworth, 1989. These three sociologists have produced a well-written book on the fastest growing segment of the U.S. population: those Americans over eighty-five years of age. This comprehensive treatment of the topic analyzes in depth the problems of this age group relating to the economics of aging and elderly support systems. Suitable for high school and college students. Contains an index and a references section.

Myles, John. *Old Age in the Welfare State: The Political Economy of Public Pensions.* Rev. ed. Lawrence: University Press of Kansas, 1989. Myles is a recognized authority on the application of the political economic perspective to aging issues. This revised edition incorporates research conducted since the 1984 edition was published. Hypotheses relating to the book's main thesis are developed and tested. For college and graduate students. Includes an index, a bibliography, and notes sections at the end of each chapter.

Schulz, James H. *The Economics of Aging.* 5th ed. New York: Auburn House, 1992. Earlier editions of this book have been the most-cited sources in all manner of publications dealing with the economic implications of the aging population. This expanded edition has become the bible of the economics of aging. It is a very comprehensive examination of not only Social Security but also every other aspect of U.S. policy relating to elderly support. Suitable for advanced high school, college, and graduate students. Contains a notes section, a glossary, a references section, and an index.

Jack Carter

Cross-References

Age Inequality: Functionalist versus Conflict Theory Views, 34; Ageism and the Ideology of Ageism, 41; Aging and Retirement, 47; The Aging Process, 53; The Elderly and Institutional Care, 621; The Elderly and the Family, 627; The Graying of America, 846; Social Gerontology, 1799.

SOCIAL STRATIFICATION: ANALYSIS AND OVERVIEW

Type of sociology: Social stratification
Fields of study: Basic concepts of social stratification; Components of social structure

Social stratification refers to a phenomenon that exists in all complex societies: the hierarchical ranking of groups of people according to such criteria as relative economic wealth, political power, and social honor.

Principal terms
BOURGEOISIE: the term used by Karl Marx to define those who control a society's means of production
CLASS: a group of people of similar social rank; largely defined in economic terms, but also often considering such factors as political power and lifestyle
INTERGENERATIONAL SOCIAL MOBILITY: social movement from one class to another that takes place over the course of generations
INTRAGENERATIONAL SOCIAL MOBILITY: social movement from one class to another that occurs within an individual's lifetime
POWER: the ability of individuals or groups to attain desired objectives or to force others to do as they wish
PRESTIGE: reputation or social honor; generally used to define status
PROLETARIAT: the term used by Karl Marx to define workers, those who survive by selling their labor to the bourgeoisie
PROPERTY: income, wealth, and other material resources
SOCIAL MOBILITY: the movement of groups and individuals within and between social levels in a stratified society
STATUS: any defined or acknowledged position within a group or society

Overview

Social stratification is as old as human civilization. When humans moved from fishing or hunting and gathering societies to sedentary agricultural societies with a surplus economy, a variety of occupations developed that were essential to the proper functioning of that society. Inevitably, these occupations began to be ranked hierarchically, usually based on the amount of preparation and training needed or the importance of that occupation to a particular society.

So prevalent was social stratification in all societies that over the centuries its existence was seldom questioned. It was generally accepted as part of the "natural" order. Religion was used to support stratification, for example, with the head of state often being considered divinely sanctioned. In the eighteenth century, however, the American and French Revolutions, with their emphasis on human rights and their call for equality, changed the accepted way of thinking. Efforts were made both to understand the reasons for social inequality and to seek means of lessening its negative effects.

Since the second half of the nineteenth century, four broad sociological theories have been used to explain and interpret social stratification: the natural superiority theory, the functionalist theory, the Marxist class conflict theory, and the Weberian multiple-hierarchies theory.

The natural superiority theory, also known as Social Darwinism, was a popular and widely accepted theory of social stratification in the late nineteenth and early twentieth centuries. Promoted by Herbert Spencer in England and William Graham Sumner in the United States, Social Darwinism saw social organization as an environment. Certain individuals or groups had the requisite skills or attributes to compete and to rise in that environment; they would become the leaders and the economically fortunate. Others, not so endowed, would fail. The not-so-subtle implication of this idea was that the rich deserved to keep their great fortunes intact. The poor also deserved their lot, because it was the result of sloth, ignorance, or some other flaw; they deserved no pity. The Social Darwinists believed that their theory was part of the law of nature. Spencer coined the widely quoted phrase "survival of the fittest."

Some of the ideas of the Social Darwinists were contained in the functionalist theory of social stratification, promoted by Kingsley Davis and William E. Moore in the 1940's. Essentially, the functionalist theory maintains that a variety of skills are needed for the effective functioning of a modern industrialized society. Some of these skills require greater ability and longer, more costly training than others. It is argued that people would only undergo the training necessary for these more demanding occupations if they knew that they would be amply rewarded in money and respect. Social stratification, then, can be seen as an organizing force in society—a kind of ladder with closely adjacent rungs that individuals may climb or descend according to their ability.

If any one individual could be called the founder of the study of social classes, it would be Karl Marx, who saw the conflict between social classes as the driving force in history. For Marx, writing in the mid-nineteenth century, there were only two classes: the bourgeoisie, controlling wealth and the means of production, and the proletariat. The proletariat work for the bourgeoisie and are increasingly exploited and increasingly thrust into poverty; ultimately, according to Marx, they will take political action. Although often challenged and, arguably, partially discredited, Marx's work was that of a careful and brilliant scholar. In an increasingly polarized Western society, many of Marx's theories are being re-examined. Among his lasting contributions are the idea of social mobility and the concept of "class consciousness"—a subjective feeling without which, Marx maintained, individuals are powerless.

Even though the functionalist approach, with its basic idea that talent, persistence, and hard work ultimately will be rewarded, was popular (especially in the United States), its limitations soon become apparent. Rising in the stratification system of a complex, industrialized society requires more than those character traits. Many sociologists were drawn to the theories of the German sociologist Max Weber. Weber's approach was multi-hierarchical and dynamic. He viewed social stratification as resulting from the interaction of three factors: class, status, and power. To Weber, social class is largely based on property. Social status, on the other hand, is mainly determined by occupation and how that occupation is socially evaluated. Power—the capacity to get others to act in accordance with one's wishes even when they prefer not to do so—was also considered by Weber. Other factors, such as being the right sex, attending elite schools, having wealthy, supportive parents, and belonging to the right religious and ethnic groups are also contributory factors to social stratification.

Weber's theory became the basis for the "objective method" of determining social stratification—that is, establishing a number of criteria for each of several strata. The subjective method is the other form of determining social stratification. In the subjective method, the composition of each stratum is determined either by the way individuals view themselves or by the way others view them. The limitation of this method is that individuals seldom view themselves objectively; moreover, people's evaluations of others would be valid only for a relatively small, stable community.

Any system of social stratification must be viewed in the context of whether it exists in an open or closed society. An open society is one in which individuals can move freely from one social stratum to another. A closed society is one in which there is no movement and children inherit the social status of their parents. The term "caste system" is usually applied to this kind of society. In practice, the completely open or closed society no longer exists. Societies only tend toward being one or the other, with a general (if often slow) movement toward open societies.

Applications

Functionalist theory has provided a widely cited and widely applied view of social stratification at least partly because of the work of functionalist theorists who have made it relatively easy to identify the status of individuals by their occupations. In 1946 the National Opinion Research Center asked a representative sample of American people to rank ninety different occupations. The ranking system, which was established according to prestige, training, and income ranged from the highest occupation, a U.S. Supreme Court Justice, to the lowest, a bootblack. Numbers one to thirty-six could be considered professions with considerable requisite training.

Although many sociologists have argued that the work of Karl Marx has been discredited, his ideas have been tremendously influential in sociological studies of class and stratification. Moreover, his ideas increasingly seem to be coming back to life. Marx envisioned the increased polarity of society into the "haves" and the "have-nots," with a group consciousness developing for each. Eventually, Marx held, the proletarians whose income has fallen below the subsistence level will rise in revolt. Sociologists are uncomfortably aware that in the United States and other industrialized countries there is an increased concentration of wealth in the hands of a few and increased poverty among the masses. In 1980, less than 2 percent of the population of the United States controlled 44 percent of the country's wealth and 62 percent of its corporate shares. With computer networking that enables wealthy individuals to work with others on a global basis and with the ability to transfer vast amounts of money electronically in a matter of seconds, the spread between the rich and the poor seems destined to grow. In 1972 Richard Parker wrote *The Myth of the Middle Class*. Twenty years later, Greg J. Duncan, Timothy M. Smeeding, and Willard Rogers echoed the ideas of these writers in an article entitled "The Incredible Shrinking Middle Class," which appeared in the May, 1992, *American Demographics*. A number of economists and sociologists reinterpreted and adapted Marxist theory in the late twentieth century.

A composite portrait of the U.S. class structure on the Weberian model was constructed by Dennis Gilbert and Joseph A. Kahl in *The American Class Structure: A New Synthesis* (1987). They list six social classes, ranging from the capitalist class (people with a very high income, prestige university degree, and an executive or professional occupation), which makes up 1 percent of the population, to the working poor and underclass (those with some high school or grade school education who are in service work or are laborers, unemployed, or surplus labor), which makes up 25 percent of the population.

An aspect of the Weberian multiple-hierarchies theory that interests many sociologists is the use of power in social stratification. In 1956 C. Wright Mills argued that the heads of government, the military, and business made up a "power elite." Later other sociologists concluded that less than one half of one percent of the population makes up this "governing class." Power can be obtained through contributions to politicians and political parties or through control of the media; most often, however, it is family related. The family, in this view, may be seen as the greatest force in maintaining social stratification.

A belief in social mobility—the idea that through hard work and perseverance anyone can rise on the social scale—is a central part of the American ideology. Yet a number of studies have shown that social mobility is about the same for all industrialized countries. If and when movement does occur, it usually involves, at most, a few vertical steps; more often movement is horizontal—to another position on the same social stratum. The "rags-to-riches" story, although it does happen occasionally, is more myth than reality.

Possibly the greatest practical application of a concept based on studies of social stratification involves what are called "life chances." High social position translates into better schooling, housing, and medical facilities, which means that upper-class persons live longer, are in better health, and live in healthier surroundings than lower-class persons. Lower-class people live in poorer housing and are more likely to commit crimes and to be imprisoned; they are also more likely to be the victims of crime. One's position in the stratification system, then, can determine not only health or sickness but also life or death.

Context

Auguste Comte, often called the founder of sociology, was strongly influenced by the nineteenth century faith in science. Comte believed that the laws of the social sciences were as unchangeable as the laws of the physical sciences. This belief was shared by Karl Marx and Herbert Spencer. Marx believed that revolutions would inevitably result from class conflict. Comte and Spencer advocated a laissez-faire or "hands-off" attitude which would result in the formation of class and status in every society. The study of "social classes" became part of the academic discipline of sociology. The term "social stratification" did not come into general use until the 1940's.

The first social scientists to explore the system of ranking in modern communities in any depth were W. Lloyd Warner and Paul S. Lunt, in their *Yankee City* series (1942). Using a stable New England community as their model, they divided the social classes into six parts, two each for upper, middle, and lower. The upper two classes constituted 3 percent of the city's total population; the lower classes, 58 percent. Studies by Dennis Gilbert and Joseph A. Kahl in 1987 and by Daniel W. Rossides in 1990 found virtually identical percentages existing in similar class categorizations.

World War I and its aftermath—with its destruction of the traditional class structure in many European countries and the economic dislocation of millions—destroyed the concept of sociology as an exact science. Sociologists began to rely on empiricism based on experience or educated guesswork. They established ideals, or working models, rather than attempting to study human social phenomena exactly as a "hard science" would. After World War I, Fascist regimes rose in Europe. Marx had noted that the bourgeoisie would use their control of the police and of governments to keep themselves in power. Indeed, such actions seemed to account for the rise of Fascism in nations such as Germany, Italy, and Spain. What probably spared the United States from a similar upheaval during the Great Depression of the 1930's, when millions were unemployed and there was widespread malnutrition, even starvation, was the deeply ingrained American belief that theirs was an open society and that with perseverance and hard work, any person could rise and succeed in it.

World War II and its aftermath continued the dislocation of World War I. Now the dislocation was global, with the fall of the great colonial empires; India, for example (traditionally the most "closed" of societies), emerged as an independent state. The polarization between the wealthy and poor, however, continued and generally became even more pronounced. Riots by members of subgroups of the lower classes became more common. Some observers argued that these were a prelude to the revolutions that Marx had predicted. The old assumption that revolutions such as those that occurred in Russia, China, and Cuba only happen in agricultural, underdeveloped societies was challenged.

Today, industrialized countries are committed in varying degrees to lessening the most severe economic inequities among their citizens. This commitment manifests itself in two ways: "negatively," through taxation, transfer payments, and subsidies; and "positively," through providing greater opportunities for advancement by education and the outlawing of discrimination. Nevertheless, stratification will continue to exist, because while those in power—whether known as the upper class, the power elite, or another name—may make concessions to other groups, they will not willingly relinquish their power or control of society. If social stratification or structured inequality cannot be eliminated, however, at least some of the worst abuses can be corrected.

Bibliography

Barber, Bernard. *Social Stratification: A Comparative Analysis of Structure and Process.* New York: Harcourt, Brace and World, 1957. A rather lengthy and detailed work, this book is for someone who wants to learn more about social stratification in detail. The author is considered to be one of the leading authorities on stratification and is the major contributor on social stratification to *The International Encyclopedia on the Social Sciences.* Barber deals with social stratification not only in European countries but in Asian and Latin American countries as well.

Bottomore, T. B. *Classes in Modern Society.* New York: Pantheon Books, 1966. This is among the best short introductory works on social stratification. Written in a concise, straightforward manner, it discusses its historical development, its application to industrial societies, and its impact on politics and culture. Although British, Bottomore is knowledgeable about American social stratification and has included a "Postscript to the American Edition" as a separate chapter. Excellent bibliography.

Bryjak, George J., and Michael P. Soroka. *Sociology: Cultural Diversity in a Changing World.* 2d ed. Boston: Allyn & Bacon, 1992. This work is a clear and comprehensible introductory sociology text with a good chapter on social stratification. A list of readings follows each of the chapters. The chapter on social stratification, for example, gives readings relating to Mexico and Japan. Chapters end with well-written summaries. Profusely illustrated with numerous charts and graphs, the book also contains a glossary. Extensive bibliography.

Dahrendorf, Ralf. *Class and Class Conflict in Industrial Society.* Stanford, Calif.: Stanford University Press, 1959. As its title implies, this work treats social stratification within the context of a modern industrial society. Carefully researched and translated from the German, this work would be valuable to the reader interested in pursuing the study of social stratification in depth. The detailed bibliography is divided not only into subject areas but also by time periods.

Krauss, Irving. *Stratification, Class, and Conflict.* New York: Free Press, 1976. This work is noted for its breadth, dealing as it does with virtually all aspects of social stratification, including its historical development, its importance to group life, its relation to life chances such as good health and longevity, its effect on class behavior, and the unique aspects of American social stratification. Discusses the potential for class conflict using as examples the French Revolution, the Civil War draft riots in the United States, and the rise of the Populist movement. A major drawback is that the book lacks a bibliography.

Nis Petersen

Cross-References

SURVEY
OF
SOCIAL
SCIENCE

ALPHABETICAL LIST

CATEGORY LIST